ENCOUNTERS IN PLANNING THOUGHT

Encounters in Planning Thought builds on the intellectual legacy of spatial planning through essays by leading scholars from around the world, including John Friedmann, Peter Marcuse, Patsy Healey, Andreas Faludi, Judith Innes, Rachelle Alterman and many more. Each author provides a fascinating and inspiring unravelling of his or her own intellectual journey in the context of events, political and economic forces, and prevailing ideas and practices, as well as their own personal lives.

This is crucial reading for those interested in spatial planning, including those studying the theory and history of spatial planning. *Encounters in Planning Thought* sets out a comprehensive, intellectual, institutional and practical agenda for the discipline of spatial planning as it heads towards its next half-century. Together, the essays form a solid base on which to understand the most salient elements to be taken forward by current and future generations of spatial planners.

Beatrix Haselsberger is Senior Researcher at the Department of Spatial Planning at the Vienna University of Technology, Austria. She is also Visiting Professor at the Dipartimento di Ingegneria Civile, Ambientale e Architettura at the University of Cagliari, Italy. Her current research focuses on the nature of borders (physical and invisible) and their impacts on space and people, cross-border interaction and cooperation, as well as planning cultures, their diversity and origin. With her research she seeks to bridge the gap between planning theory and practice. Beatrix is active in the Association of European Schools of Planning and the Regional Studies Association, where she has been a member of the executive committees, as well as on the editorial boards of a wide range of journals. Together with her partner, an ecologist, she will open a spatial research and planning consultancy in Austria, in the near future.

"Good planning theory, which advises 'What do I do when . . . ?,' is based in understanding 'Who have I been?' and 'What have I done?' The essays in this book recognize this foundational link. These scholars write usefully about planning because they know themselves as human beings. They recognize their theorizing as ways of making sense of their experience. Anyone interested in understanding planning as a self-conscious human activity should read this rich collection."

Howell Baum, University of Maryland, USA

"These wonderfully rich life-histories of sixteen of the most influential spatial planning theorists demonstrate a key message of the book: place and history shape thought and world-view. As planning theorists from the global South and East begin to make their voices heard this book will provide an invaluable launch-pad."

Vanessa Watson, University of Cape Town, South Africa

ENCOUNTERS IN PLANNING THOUGHT

16 Autobiographical Essays from Key Thinkers in Spatial Planning

Edited by Beatrix Haselsberger

First published 2017
by Routledge
711 Third Avenue, New York, NY 10017

and by Routledge
2 Park Square, Milton Park, Abingdon, Oxon, OX14 4RN

Routledge is an imprint of the Taylor & Francis Group, an informa business

© 2017 Taylor & Francis

The right of Beatrix Haselsberger to be identified as the author of the editorial material, and of the authors for their individual chapters, has been asserted in accordance with sections 77 and 78 of the Copyright, Designs and Patents Act 1988.

All rights reserved. No part of this book may be reprinted or reproduced or utilised in any form or by any electronic, mechanical, or other means, now known or hereafter invented, including photocopying and recording, or in any information storage or retrieval system, without permission in writing from the publishers.

Trademark notice: Product or corporate names may be trademarks or registered trademarks, and are used only for identification and explanation without intent to infringe.

Library of Congress Cataloging in Publication Data
Names: Haselsberger, Beatrix, editor.
Title: Encounters in planning thought : 16 autobiographical essays from key
    thinkers in spatial planning / edited by Beatrix Haselsberger.
Description: New York : Routledge, 2016.
Identifiers: LCCN 2016027198 | ISBN 9781138640863 (hardback) |
    ISBN 9781138640870 (pbk.) | ISBN 9781315630908 (ebook)
Subjects: LCSH: City planners—Biography.
Classification: LCC HT166 .E499 2016 | DDC 711/.4092/2 [B]—dc23
LC record available at https://lccn.loc.gov/2016027198

ISBN: 978-1-138-64086-3 (hbk)
ISBN: 978-1-138-64087-0 (pbk)
ISBN: 978-1-315-63090-8 (ebk)

Typeset in Bembo
by Apex CoVantage, LLC

Wholeheartedly dedicated to
all those for whom spatial planners plan.

CONTENTS

List of Figures	*x*
List of Contributors	*xi*
Front Cover Image: A Short Description by Beatrix Haselsberger	*xiv*
Acknowledgements by Beatrix Haselsberger	*xvi*

PART 1
Introduction
1

1	Encounters in Planning Thought: An Introduction *Beatrix Haselsberger*	3
2	Autobiography as a Method of Inquiry *Laura Saija*	8

PART 2
16 Autobiographical Essays from Key Thinkers in Spatial Planning
13

3	Planning as a Vocation: The Journey So Far *John Friedmann*	15
4	From Utopian and Realistic to Transformative Planning *Peter Marcuse*	35
5	Visions of Contemporary Planning: Stories and Journeys in Britain and America *Peter Hall*	51

viii Contents

6 An Ancient Future   71
   Luigi Mazza

7 Understanding and Improving Planning Processes
   and Planning Institutions: A Moving Target   88
   Andreas Faludi

8 Finding My Way: A Life of Inquiry into Planning,
   Urban Development Processes and Place Governance   107
   Patsy Healey

9 Educating Planners: The Dream of a Better Future   126
   Gerhard Schimak

10 From Informing Policy to Collaborating Rationally   145
    Judith E. Innes

11 A Renegade Economist Preaches Good Land-Use Planning   165
    Barrie Needham

12 Strategic Planning as a Catalyst for Transformative Practices   184
    Louis Albrechts

13 Places Matter: Creativity, Culture and Planning   202
    Klaus R. Kunzmann

14 Challenging Institutions That Reproduce Planning Thought
    and Practice   222
    Cliff Hague

15 A Science of Cities: Prologue to a Science of Planning   242
    Michael Batty

16 Planners' Beacon, Compass and Scale: Linking Planning
    Theory, Implementation Analysis and Planning Law   260
    Rachelle Alterman

17 On the Evolution of a Critical Pragmatism   280
    John Forester

18 Pragmatism and Plan-Making   297
    Charles Hoch

Contents **ix**

PART 3
Epilogue **315**

19 Back to the Future: A Personal Portrayal in the Interface
of Past Planning and Planning Futures 317
Beatrix Haselsberger

Index *325*

FIGURES

6.1	Primary road network prepared for the Plan for Alessandria, 1968	79
10.1	DIAD Diagram: Bringing together diverse and interdependent interests can result in authentic dialogue (DIAD), which in turn can produce desirable and collaboratively rational outcomes	159
13.1	The European Grape	215
13.2	The founding fathers of AESOP on the terrace of Schloss Cappenberg near Dortmund, Germany	217
15.1	Quarry Bank High School, Liverpool, 1957	246
15.2	Manchester University's Town and Country Planning Class of '62 in a pub in Canterbury, Kent, April 1966	249

CONTRIBUTORS

Louis Albrechts is Professor Emeritus of Strategic Spatial Planning at the Department of Architecture, Urbanism and Planning at the University of Leuven, Belgium. His current research focuses on the practice and nature of strategic spatial planning, diversity and creativity in planning, planning as a process of co-production, and bridging the gap between planning and implementation.

Rachelle Alterman of the Technion–Israel Institute of Technology holds degrees in planning and in law from Canadian and Israeli universities. Her academic work has forged global links between planning theory and planning law, culminating in the establishment of the International Academic Association on Planning, Law and Property Rights.

Michael Batty is Bartlett Professor of Planning at University College London, UK, where he is chair of the Centre for Advanced Spatial Analysis (CASA). His most recent book is *The New Science of Cities* (MIT Press, 2013). He received the Lauréat Prix International de Géographie Vautrin Lud in 2013 and the Founders Medal of the Royal Geographical Society in 2015 for his work on simulating cities.

Andreas Faludi is Professor Emeritus for Spatial Policy Systems in Europe, Delft University of Technology, the Netherlands. He attended school and university in Vienna where he earned his PhD (1967). He has taught planning history and planning theory in the UK (1967–1973) and the Netherlands (1974–1994) and, whilst still based in the Netherlands, his current work focuses on European spatial planning (1995–present).

John Forester earned his BS, MS, MRP and PhD at the University of California, Berkeley, USA. As Professor of City and Regional Planning at Cornell University, USA, he studies the politics and ethics of planning practices with special attention to issues of power, conflict and improvisation. His best-known books include *Planning in the Face of Power* (University of California Press,

xii Contributors

1989), *Making Equity Planning Work* (with Norman Krumholz, Temple University Press, 1990) and *Planning in the Face of Conflict* (American Planning Association, 2013).

John Friedmann is Professor Emeritus in the School of Public Affairs at UCLA, USA and Honorary Professor in the School of Community and Regional Planning at the University of British Columbia, Canada. His current research is on urbanization processes with special reference to China. Recent books include *The Prospect of Cities* (2002), *China's Urban Transition* (2005) and *Insurgencies: Essays in Planning Theory* (2011).

Cliff Hague taught on planning and housing programmes at Heriot-Watt University in Edinburgh from 1969 to 2004 and then became a freelance consultant/researcher, working mainly on European and international projects. He is a past president of the Royal Town Planning Institute and of the Commonwealth Association of Planners.

Sir Peter Hall was Bartlett Professor of Planning and Regeneration at UCL, UK, from 1991 to 2014. He wrote some 50 books and over 2,000 articles and related commentaries. He was active in both academia, where he was revered, and in policy and planning practice where he influenced the heart of government. His most influential books were *The Containment of Urban England, Cities of Tomorrow* and *Cities in Civilization,* for which he was awarded the Balzac Prize amongst his many other honours. He was knighted in 1998.

Beatrix Haselsberger is Senior Researcher at the Department of Spatial Planning at the Vienna University of Technology, Austria. She is also Visiting Professor at the Dipartimento di Ingegneria Civile, Ambientale e Architettura at the University of Cagliari, Italy. Her current research focuses on the nature of borders (physical and invisible) and their impacts on space and people, cross-border interaction and cooperation as well as planning cultures, its diversity and origin. With her research she seeks to bridge the gap between planning theory and practice.

Patsy Healey is Professor Emeritus in the School of Architecture, Planning and Landscape at Newcastle University, UK. She is a specialist in planning theory and the practice of planning and urban regeneration policies.

Charles Hoch has taught urban planning at the University of Illinois at Chicago, USA, since 1981. He is currently studying how professional planners and others make spatial plans and the kind of work plans do. Hoch has taught lecture and workshop courses on the history, theory, organization and practice of urban planning.

Judith E. Innes is Professor Emerita in the Department of City and Regional Planning, University of California Berkeley, USA, where she has taught planning theory, research methods and collaborative process. She has studied collaborative planning in water, transportation and sustainability. Her most recent book is *Planning with Complexity: Introduction to Collaborative Rationality for Public Policy* (Routledge, 2010).

Klaus R. Kunzmann graduated from the School of Architecture of the Technische Universität München, Germany, in 1967. He received a PhD from the TU Wien, Austria, and an honorary

PhD from the University of Newcastle-upon-Tyne, UK. From 1974 to 2006 he was Professor at the School of Planning, TU Dortmund, Germany. He is an Honorary Professor at the Bartlett School of Planning at University College London, UK and a Visiting Professor at the Dong Nam University in Nanjing, China. As a Visiting Professor he has taught at universities in Europe, the US and East Asia. His research interests are around the role of knowledge, culture and creative industries in strategic urban development. Married to a Chinese citizen, he frequently travels to, teaches in and works in China.

Peter Marcuse, a lawyer and urban planner, was in private legal practice in Waterbury for over 20 years, serving on its board of aldermen and City Planning Commission. He was a professor of urban planning, first at UCLA, USA, where he was also chair of the Los Angeles City Planning Commission, and then at Columbia University, USA, where he is now emeritus. He is active in the Planners Network, the New York City Community Land Trust Initiative, and the Participatory Budgeting effort, and he continues to be concerned with social theory and planning ethics. He has a blog, *Urban and Political Issues,* at pmarcuse.wordpress.com.

Luigi Mazza has been an active planner mainly in the urban planning field. He is also the founding editor of the journal *Planning Theory,* and a member of the boards of the *Town Planning Review, European Planning Studies, disP The Planning Review, Spatium International Review* and *Planning Theory,* all of which have published his articles. He is emeritus professor at the Politecnico di Milano.

Barrie Needham studied economics at the University of Cambridge, UK, and his first work was with a planning consultancy in London. Then followed university appointments in London and in Birmingham, and in 1978 at the University of Nijmegen in the Netherlands, where he was appointed Professor of Spatial Planning in 1994. In 2007 he took retirement as Emeritus Professor. His main research interest is the interaction between land-use planning and landed property.

Laura Saija is an Assistant Professor in City and Regional Planning at the University of Memphis, TN, USA, with a PhD (2006) in city and regional planning and design from the University of Catania, Italy. Her research focuses on action-research in planning, with a special focus on the theory and practice of ecological approaches to planning and design, i.e. approaches able to improve the relationship between humans, other living communities and their life environment.

Gerhard Schimak, born and raised in Austria, studied architecture at the Vienna University of Technology and worked there as a project and research assistant in the field of urban and regional planning. Later he became Assistant Professor and then Honorary Professor for Regional Planning and Development, his main field of scientific interest. For nearly 13 years he was Deputy- and Vice-Rector of his university. For the last four years, in retirement but still teaching, he was a member of the Executive Committee of the Association of European Schools of Planning.

FRONT COVER IMAGE: A SHORT DESCRIPTION

Beatrix Haselsberger

The book's front cover image is composed of two distinctive elements. First (in the background) the *Josephinische Landesaufnahme* (Josephinian Land Survey) of the Vienna region and second (in the foreground) the art work "Intertwined" by Amy Casey, a young artist based in Cleveland (Ohio, USA).

The old map of Vienna and its surroundings, the Josephinian Land Survey, has been chosen because it is the first comprehensive cartographic mapping of the entire Habsburg Empire. It was conducted between 1763 and 1787, for military purposes, at a time when scientifically based knowledge about society was starting to be considered relevant to improving people's living conditions. In the book's front cover image, this old map symbolically represents a time and situation long before the key thinkers writing in this book were born and spatial planning emerged as a distinctive discipline. Thus, in a way, this old map, which shows the Vienna region at its eighteenth-century stage of development, represents a sort of bedrock of today's spatial planning. Moreover, if we compare this first military mapping survey of the Habsburg Empire with all subsequently conducted maps, we can clearly see that our world is constantly changing. The segment of the Vienna region has been selected because Vienna has had a formative influence on the entire book project. It was in Vienna that the idea for this book was born in 2012. It was in Vienna that 14 of the 16 authors met for an entire week in 2014. It was in Vienna, at the Department of Spatial Planning of the Vienna University of Technology, that I—as the editor of this volume—spent four years pulling the strings in the background to bring this book project to a successful end.

At this point it needs to be stressed that a map is always a simplified representation of a spatial reality at a certain moment in time. The art work by Amy Casey has been added to the book's front cover image to symbolise the planning thoughts of many generations (including those of the 16 key thinkers writing in this book), which travelled through time and space and led to the spatial situation as we know it today. In addition, in my view, Amy Casey's abstract art work provides a means to understand some general aspects of spatial planning. First, there are many different types of spaces (including natural ones), which are intertwined and dependent on each other. This diversity of spaces is illustrated by the example of the urban–rural interrelationship. Second, there are many different types of land uses, which need to be accommodated in space, which can also be seen in the underlying map of the Vienna region. All these land uses are very much intertwined, as Amy Casey's art work emphasises.

For me, the book's cover image conveys the significant message that we—the current and future generations of spatial planners—should seek to meaningfully adopt existing planning ideas in our specific time, context and situation, as well as to develop planning ideas for our continuously changing world.

Credits

Art work "Intertwined" from Amy Casey, http://www.amycaseypainting.com/
Josephinische Landesaufnahme (Josephinian Land Survey), 1763–1787, B IX a 242, Lower Austria, section number 71, Austrian State Archive, section War Archive.

I wish to thank the Department of Spatial Planning of the Vienna University of Technology, Austria, for covering all the costs related to the compilation of the book's front cover image.

ACKNOWLEDGEMENTS

Beatrix Haselsberger

This book was over four years in the making. While in the beginning it involved a manageable amount of work, which I was able to do in the interstices of my life as a researcher, over time it became a full-time job. Without support from the Austrian Science Fund, I would never have managed to bring this book project to a timely end, and I want to express my deep gratitude to this funding agency. I should mention that in 2012 I was awarded a Hertha-Firnberg research grant for a project with a slightly different focus. Luckily the Austrian Science Fund was extremely flexible, so I was able to combine my original research project with this book project.

It is impossible to thank everybody who, directly or indirectly, has influenced me in this book project. But I would like to acknowledge those who were directly involved in it in one way or another. First and foremost I would like to thank all the authors. I know that it was not easy to write a contribution for this book, as it implied sharing private things with a broader audience. I also know that I have been a very strict editor, which in some cases led to very emotional conversations between us. I think that in the end we are all happy with the result, as we managed to allow planning knowledge and ideas to travel between generations. I have been helped in my editing job by three wonderful colleagues. Paul Benneworth helped me a lot in the initial phase, but he had to step down for private reasons after 19 months. Julie Knight (Porter) joined the book project a bit later than Paul. Unfortunately, Julie's move to the US, together with her new job, did not allow her to continue working on this book, and she had to resign after 11 months. Laura Saija joined the book project together with Julie, but from the beginning Laura was in the unpleasant situation of needing to find a job in one of the planning departments in Italy. After two years she gave up searching in Italy and moved to the US. Laura's new department in the US enabled her to continue helping me with this book, in particular in the very demanding concluding phase. As the entire book project was set up as an intergenerational dialogue, I benefitted greatly from discussions and debates with the editorial advisory board. In this dialogue John Friedmann, Patsy Healey, Judith Innes and Mike Batty represented the views of the retired or soon-to-be retired elders of the planning discipline, while Paul Benneworth, Julie Knight, Laura Saija and I represented the voices and interests of future planning generations. I want to use this opportunity to congratulate the four Planning Thought Award winners—Sabrina Lai, Kathrine Quick, Chris Maidment and Juho Matti Luukkonen—who were selected from 39 amazing applications. The four award winners have, alongside others, acted as reviewers for this book and in so doing have helped to challenge the elders of the planning discipline to come forward with messages that have contemporary and future salience. Three more people have contributed a lot to making my job easier. Hartmut Dumke set up and administered our book project website; Leanne Benneworth language edited every contribution in this book; and Amy Casey designed the art work for the book's front cover image. I would also like to thank the publisher Routledge and three persons in particular. I am very grateful for Nicole Solano's patience and honesty while negotiating the details of the book contract, and I would like to thank Judith Newlin and Krystal LaDuc for their consistent support since I signed the book contract.

In May 2014, 14 of the 16 authors came together for a week at the Vienna University of Technology in Austria. What was originally meant to be just a book workshop meeting became a big event, which was made possible by support from many sponsors. I would like to explicitly mention the financial and administrative support from Johannes Fröhlich, vice rector of the Vienna University of Technology. Thanks to him, this book event became one of the core activities of the 200-year anniversary celebration of the TU Vienna and was sponsored very generously. Further sponsors of this event were the Department of Spatial Planning at the TU Vienna (Michael Getzner), the deanship of Architecture and Spatial Planning at the TU Vienna (Rudolf Scheuvens), the dean of Study Affairs of Spatial Planning at the TU Vienna (Arthur Kanonier), the City of Vienna (Andreas Trisko, Kurt Mittringer, Thomas Madreiter, Hubert Christian Ehalt), the publisher Routledge (Jonathan Manley), the journal *Town Planning Review* (Cecilia Wong and David Shaw), the journal *Planning Theory and Practice* (Heather Campbell), the Regional Studies Association (Sally Hardy), the Association of European Schools of Planning (Gert de Roo), the AESOP-ERSA Lecture Series (Iza Mironowicz), the Austrian champagne producer Madl (Christian Madl), the Austrian winery Böheim (Stefanie Böheim), the Austrian winery Fuchs-Steinklammer (Stefan Fuchs), the Austrian winery Allram (Magdalena Haas), the Austrian winery Taferner (Karoline Taferner) and the Austrian winery Sabathi (Hannes Sabathi). I could not have run this event without the help of many people. My special thanks go to all the volunteers who so passionately assisted me in organising and running this event, namely Andreas Dillinger (head of the local organisation team); Robert Kolerovic, David Schwab, Gabriel Neuner, Markus Neuhaus and Johannes Suitner (taking care of all the conference delegates and speakers, including preparatory and subsequent work); Andreas Koiser and Hans-Christian Hofmann (organising and coordinating the wine-tastings); and Michael Kölbl (sound check, filming and video production). I also want to thank Thomas Dillinger for his support, as part of which I was able to occupy our centre's facilities for an entire week and draw on help from our student assistants. Our event was well reported in several national and international publication outlets thanks to Martina Koll-Schretzenmayr (*disP The Planning Review*), Michael Hebbert (*Planning Perspectives*), Cecilia Wong and Brian Webb (*Town Planning Review*), Frank Peck and Gail Mulvey (*Regions* magazine), Michael Palfinger (the Austrian newspaper *Wiener Zeitung*) and Florian Aigner and Nicole Schipani (Public Relations Office at the TU Vienna).

Last but not least, I wish to express my gratitude to my partner, Roman Eckstein, himself by education and passion an ecologist. With him I spent endless hours discussing the thoughts developed in this book. To him I am deeply grateful.

Vienna (Austria), February 2016

Note

Funded by the Austrian Science Fund (FWF), Project Number T591–016.

PART 1

Introduction

1

ENCOUNTERS IN PLANNING THOUGHT

An Introduction

Beatrix Haselsberger

This book represents an inspiring piece of oral history. It tells a compelling story about how planning ideas evolved, developed, circulated and moved through time and space over the last half-century. The 16 key thinkers in the field of spatial planning who contributed to this book have, over the course of their careers, made significant contributions to spatial planning discourses around the nature, purposes and processes of spatial planning. Together they have built a sizeable body of writings, on which the education of thousands of contemporary spatial planning scholars, students and practitioners is and was based. Most of the book's authors have elaborated and implemented programmes of study for spatial planning at their home universities. They helped to establish spatial planning as a distinctive discipline within the social sciences. In this book these distinguished spatial planners unpack the secrets of what they have done, why, and when, as they matured and built their ideas in an autobiographical way. None of this personal information has previously been published in such a compact and accessible way. With this book the reader gains new insights into classic planning thoughts, which do not come from only reading scientific articles. The intrinsic quality of autobiographical essays allows the reader to delve comprehensively and with ease into the issues concerned. It is this background information which enables us to better understand planning ideas and consequently some of today's established spatial planning concepts and theories. But, most importantly, it provides us with a means to understand how planning ideas can be adopted meaningfully in a different time, context and situation.

This book is targeted at readers with an interest in spatial planning, meaning the scientific study of environmentally sustainable development, organisation and functioning of anthropogenic spaces in order to secure sociocultural needs. For those who are newcomers to the field, it provides an easily accessible foundation on various planning ideas and experiences. At times of information overload, it allows young and mid-career planners to gain a better insight into the comprehensive legacy of what has been achieved so far in spatial planning. From a more personal perspective, the autobiographical essays in this book offer valuable insights into what it implies to build a career in spatial planning and how to get one's voice heard. For spatial planning educators teaching courses on the history and theory of spatial planning,

4 Beatrix Haselsberger

this book provides an enriching teaching resource. It will help and encourage them in their efforts to inspire students of spatial planning. For those from related professional fields, such as geography, architecture, public policy, sociology or ecology, it offers food for thought about potential interrelationships and interdependencies emerging from the interfaces of the differing disciplinary perspectives. In addition, the essays in this book provide some hints as to how far and in which ways the different disciplines can help to enrich each other. For professionals and members of municipal planning departments, it offers a unique and easy-to-read reflective history of spatial planning. This retrospective assessment gives a glimpse of past planning successes and failures, including their long-term consequences, which in some cases are still perceptible today. Finally, for those already established in the spatial planning field, the book seeks to grasp and reinterpret, with twenty-first-century relevance, influential planning ideas by offering intriguing insights into the authors' lives and the thought processes that accompanied the development of these ideas over the years.

The oral histories of the persons represented in this book offer an understanding of the transformation of spatial planning over the last five to six decades in the context of an ever-changing world. Reinterpreting these oral histories with a twenty-first-century lens requires revealing the original purpose of those planning ideas which triggered and then shaped this transformation. For clarification, planning ideas are the nucleus of planning's entire body of thought, and encompasses any space-relevant integrative knowledge, such as planning theory, planning practice, sustainable planning approaches, planning decision-making strategies and so forth. Making sense of planning ideas implies seeing them in context as well as looking at their history and their development over time. This in turn requires looking at the history of the person who generated the idea, as well as the geographical and social frameworks that have influenced the person's way of thinking (such as particular places, preconceived political frameworks and value systems, national and international networks, cultural and ethnic backgrounds, expectations from institutions, professional experiences, international development, mega projects, and events). The essays in this book are doing exactly this; they unravel planning ideas in context, and most importantly they are written by the persons who have generated or contributed to generating these ideas. Placing the planning ideas of selected planning pioneers into the centre of discussions, as in this book, allows us to better understand the overall resonance of major spatial planning achievements. Together, the essays form a solid base on which to understand the most salient elements to be taken forward by current and future generations of spatial planners.

The second half of the twentieth-century saw the retirement of the first generation of spatial planning educators who led the formation of academic spatial planning into an intellectual field within the social sciences. *Encounters in Planning Thought* was born out of the need to capture the planning thoughts and reflections from 16 distinguished influential thinkers in spatial planning. The authors were selected based on personal criteria. First, the authors had to have made a significant contribution to discourses around the nature, purposes and processes of spatial planning, which I had come across either in the frame of my spatial planning education in Austria, through reading (mainly in English), or at conferences. Second, the authors had to be older than 62. This is the age when females can retire in Austria. At the time of writing this introduction, the average age of the authors is 75. I am fully aware that within this frame one selection of authors can hardly ever represent a universal sample of key thinkers. There are many other distinguished spatial planners out there who have contributed significantly to enhancing spatial planning over the last five to six decades. But they might not have published a lot in English, or they might have attended other conferences than I, or they might have been engaged in more specific fields of spatial planning, such as urban planning. I am also aware that the selection of the authors is not gender balanced. This results from discrimination against women in academia some five to six decades ago and reflects the time when the authors represented in this book entered the field.

Each author in this book provides a fascinating and inspiring unravelling of his or her own intellectual journey in the context of events, political and economic forces, and prevailing ideas and practices, as well as their own personal lives. The context which the authors provide in their essays allows us to deepen our understanding of the powerful ideas and contributions that these individuals have made, most of which still shape the field of planning and influence other fields and disciplines. While each author tells the story in his or her own very personal voice, all of them write in the first person singular and look back from today's point of view when explaining what they have learned and discovered over the course of their intellectual journeys. In their essays, the authors portray the evolution of their planning ideas. They unpack why they were interested in entering spatial planning and how they came to write and do what they did. They speak about the challenges they had to face and how they coped with them. They shed light on influences that have shaped their ideas, including personal life circumstances, places, political frameworks and value systems, networks, cultural backgrounds, institutions and professional experiences, linking these to the content of their ideas. Each of these essays reads as a fascinating personal story, often with dramas, setbacks and successes.

The idea for this book was born in February 2012. At that time John Friedmann, a born Viennese, was in Vienna for an entire week. It was the first time that I had met John in person. I had previously known him only through his writings and a handful of e-mail conversations. John's stay in Vienna left a mark on my perception of spatial planning. In the frame of many fairly personal conversations, I gained a lot of insight into what had motivated him in the different phases of his career. Most importantly, I found that I had to some extent misinterpreted his writings, simply because I was not able to meaningfully transfer his messages into the current time. This was an awkward but enriching experience. The evening before John left, he told me how much he had enjoyed our intergenerational discussions and that for him it was enriching to look back from today's point of view and unravel how it all came into being. This extraordinary experience triggered my interest and curiosity in exploring more widely what lessons I could learn from past planning experiences for my future role as a spatial planner. With this in mind I elaborated the first-draft concept for this book. The first person I discussed it with was Patsy Healey. Patsy was very enthusiastic about this idea and she motivated me, in her encouraging and supportive way, to go for it.

From the beginning, the book was set up as an intergenerational dialogue, aiming to facilitate an open and transparent dialogue between different generations and cultures. This was realised through two different platforms. First, the entire book project was guided and accompanied by an intergenerational and intercultural editorial advisory board. On this board John Friedmann, Patsy Healey, Judith Innes and Michael Batty represented the views of the retired or soon-to-be retired elders in the field of spatial planning. Paul Benneworth, Laura Saija, Julie Knight and I represented the voices and interests of early-to-mid-career spatial planners. Second, over the last four years the book project involved in a broader intergenerational and intercultural dialogue between its authors and potential readers. As part of this, the Planning

6 Beatrix Haselsberger

Thought Award—dedicated to early career planning scholars—was established. Out of 39 impressive applications, four awardees (Sabrina Lai, Kathrine Quick, Chris Maidment and Juho Matti Luukkonen) were selected and invited to contribute to the discussions at the various book events as well as to act as reviewers for the book essays. All of these initiatives sought to ensure that the authors' contributions have a resonance, interest and value beyond mere retrospection and provide a solid source of information for current and future generations of spatial planners, as well as enriching the debate about the future of spatial planning.

In May 2014, 14 of the 16 book authors came together for an entire week at the Vienna University of Technology in Austria to present and discuss their first-draft essays, which they wrote according to the guidelines provided by me, the editor. The main objective of the Vienna Symposium was to involve as many different reader groups as possible in this early stage of the writing process. Several discussion formats were used:

- Three evening lectures (with around 200 participants each), where all 14 authors present in Vienna, plus the late Peter Hall via Skype, gave a 20-minute presentation of their essay and then contributed to a lively discussion with the audience. All three evening lectures (which took place on three different days) were fully booked within three weeks of being announced. The audience represented countries such as Australia, Austria, Belgium, Canada, Czech Republic, Finland, France, Germany, Great Britain, Greece, Hungary, Israel, Korea, Luxemburg, Norway, Poland, Romania, Slovakia, Spain, the Netherlands and the US.
- A world café with 12 master's and PhD students from the Vienna University of Technology, six young planning professionals from the Vienna city planning department, the four winners of the Planning Thought Award and the authors. The students and the young planning professionals identified the table topics after having read the authors' first-draft essays. The award winners moderated the world café tables.
- Eighteen intergenerational dialogues, where students and young planning professionals provided the authors with detailed feedback on their first-draft essays, helping the authors to recognise the difficulties younger generations faced when interpreting their established planning theories and concepts. This exercise helped the authors in preparing the second drafts of their essays.
- Eight workshops, where the award winners challenged the authors to respond to current challenges based on what they had written in their first-draft essays.
- Several book workshops involving just the authors, the editorial advisory board members and the editor, where we reached joint understandings of the purposes of the autobiographical essays and the most effective ways to present the material in later drafts.

A roundtable at the Association of European Schools of Planning (AESOP) 2014 conference in Utrecht, the Netherlands, a roundtable at the Association of Collegiate Schools of Planning (ACSP) 2014 conference in Philadelphia, Pennsylvania, and a keynote panel discussion at the AESOP 2015 conference in Prague, Czech Republic, were fruitful follow-up events, triggering lively discussions between selected authors and the audience.

Thanks to the fact that English has become the *lingua franca* in the scientific world of spatial planning, the intergenerational and intercultural exchange of planning ideas was possible, irrespective of any language barriers. Nonetheless it has to be acknowledged that, on the one hand, this fact should not create an international preference for planning ideas from countries where English is the first language. Spatial planning is contextual and has to remain so. On the other hand, not everything can be easily translated into English, as every country has its own country- and context-specific expressions. Similarly, the way the English language is used in different countries around the globe is not standardised. This can lead, in some cases, to misunderstandings or misinterpretations. Even in those countries where English is the official language, such as the UK and the US, differences in the use of the language regarding spatial planning can be found. All the essays in this book are written in English, but the way the English language is used differs from context to context as well as from author to author. Therefore, most of the essays in this book are rounded off with a terminology glossary.

In this book you will learn more about the many different perspectives on what spatial planning was, is and should be, as each of the authors has worked in different countries, has chosen a different field of specialisation and has operated in different institutional settings. With the help of autobiographical accounts it has been possible to make this wisdom available for a broader audience and in particular for the current and future generations of spatial planners. The innovative working approach applied for doing so is explained by Laura Saija in the subsequent introductory chapter. The 16 autobiographical essays written by selected key thinkers in spatial planning form the core of this book. This core part begins with the essay from the oldest author (John Friedmann) and ends with the one from the youngest (Charles Hoch). Each of the essays recounts a self-contained autobiographical story of the author's intellectual transformation. Considering that there is no generally valid recipe for tackling particular planning challenges, every single experience and intellectual transformation is worth studying. There is no suggested order which the reader should follow when reading this book. What I recommend, however, is that the reader should look at the terminology glossary for the respective essay before diving into the essay itself. The book is rounded off with my personal epilogue, where I address the question of what can be learnt from past planning experiences for the future of spatial planning. I hope to encourage a debate that enhances the chances of spatial planning flourishing in a world which is constantly changing.

Vienna (Austria), February 2016

2

AUTOBIOGRAPHY AS
A METHOD OF INQUIRY

Laura Saija

As mentioned in the introduction, this book is a collection of autobiographical essays written by some of the most established and widely quoted planning scholars of the second half of the twentieth century. Our authors' fame alone would be enough of an argument for publishing a book with their personal accounts of the evolution of their research and ideas. However, this book is more than just a collection of individual autobiographies. Rather these accounts are the outcome of a multistep process of inquiry that began with specific research questions that the editor asked each author to address. Thus autobiography is for us a research methodology that allows the exploration of planning ideas in a way that differs from most planning literature.

Beatrix Haselsberger and I, along with our generation of planners and planning scholars, developed our interest in planning research during the turn of the century, in the late '90s and early 2000s, facing big changes in how theory, knowledge and scholarship are defined in the realm of both science and humanities.

Most of the authors' names were on my compulsory reading lists in classes that I attended as a graduate planning student both in Italy and the US. These names started to become faces and voices over the years, mostly through international planning conferences and seminars. However, the perception that I had, together with many of my fellow scholars witnessing animated conference discussions and reading ferocious critiques of one scholar against the other, was that we better be careful about whom we support.

One might say that a certain level of disagreement between different schools of thought characterizes every era as well as every field of human knowledge. One could also argue that disagreement, even harsh conflict, could be considered a healthy mechanism through which research progresses. What I am referring to though is a deeper, more fundamental level of disagreement, which often implies non-communicability. Planning scholars of my generation have moved through the early steps of their intellectual journey in the middle of the centennial transition from the twentieth to the twenty-first century, which implied a shift from modernity to post-modernity, from normal science to complexity, from certainty to uncertainty, from blind faith in progress to the awareness of living in a limited world.

In the face of such a transition, a common attitude is the acknowledgement of episte-mological diversity among scholars, accompanied by the acceptance of a certain degree of non-communicability between schools of thought that will keep moving on their own. This attitude is mirrored by planning theory readers, which have often attempted to offer a roadmap among the various, sometimes conflicting research and planning paradigms (see, for instance, the collection in three volumes edited by Hillier & Healey, 2008).

Encounters in Planning Thought does collect contributions from scholars inspired by very different epistemological paradigms, but its aim is to go beyond celebrating the diversity of approaches. It does reflect a need to capture what makes us a community of ideas and practices, despite or because of our diversity. Many of us need to understand, to grasp a *field* that is made out of what researchers have done in a certain time frame. We do not aim to find unity and convergence, but we believe that scholars, through their decades-long discussions and disagree-ment, have generated a field that needs to be explored as such.

This book is an occasion to explore the centennial transition, especially the issue of dif-ferences between planning ideas and approaches, from an underexplored ground that all the authors, despite their differences, share: the ground on which they all *walked*, planet Earth, committed to the search for a meaning for their big passion—planning.

The authors of this book entered the field from very different places and mindsets, depend-ing on their country of origin and residence or other life circumstances. How did they make their choices about what to look at, and what to care about? How did they choose what was important to know?

This book begins from the assumption that there is a connection between such contingen-cies and authors' epistemological, methodological, and thematic preferences—a connection that is worth exploring, looking at the *place* where it develops: the βίος (*bíos,* for ancient Greeks the way of life proper of human beings).

Psychologists Atwood and Stolorow (1993), complaining about the fragmentation of their own field,[1] developed a similar conclusion and end up exploring Freud, Jung, Reich, and Rank's biographies in search of the subjective origins of what they considered the most influ-ential amongst psychological theories. In their case, such a biographical method is used to develop a general theory that looks at the individual mind as a "psychological product crys-tallizing from within a nexus of intersubjective relatedness" (p. 178). Despite the similarities, unlike Atwood and Stolorow this book is not searching for a general theory and uses an auto-biographical method instead of a biographical one. This chapter briefly explains the reasons behind this methodological choice.

Traditionally, autobiography is defined as "a retrospective prose narrative produced by a real person concerning his own existence, focusing on his individual life, in particular on the development of his personality," characterized by the "identity between the author, the narra-tor, and the protagonist" (Lejeune, 1982, p. 193; quoted by Anderson, 2001, p. 20). According to Gusdorf (1956, published in Olney, 2014), autobiography is a characteristic genre in Western culture, since it originates from humanity's effort to free itself from myths and traditional dog-mas, acquiring the ability to make history: "The man who takes the trouble to tell of himself knows that the present differs from the past and that will not be repeated in the future; [. . .] he believes it a useful and valuable thing to fix his own image so that he can be certain it will not disappear like all things in the world" (p. 30). In this perspective, the great tradition of autobiographies—that starts with the medieval *Confessions* of Saint Augustine and flourishes

10 Laura Saija

throughout modernity—is based on the principle that individuals consider themselves worthy of future remembrance because of the extraordinary and/or typical nature of their lives.

The very origins of autobiography, together with the fact that this book collects essays written by people that are out of the ordinary—if we apply all the indicators of academic success—might generate the misunderstanding that this book aims at celebrating a romantic notion of their selfhood. Instead, this book uses autobiography as a method of inquiry, reflecting a change in sensitivity toward this genre that occurred during the twentieth century and related to significant differences in the way both humanities and science conceptualize the mind-body relationship.

Many fields of knowledge have recently challenged the traditional dualism (separation) between mind and body as well as reason and emotion. The birth of psychoanalysis and the challenges toward scientific objectivity are only a few signs of the twentieth-century discovery of *self* and of the fact that the mind is not entirely *rational* and *conscious*. This broad discourse affects all humans, including scientists, who progressively lose their aura of neutrality, objectivity and rationality.

For instance, in his famous book *The Sociological Imagination*, C. W. Mills (1959) addresses researchers, warning them

- not to be captured by the huge amount of data that is available to them nowadays (which sounds quite an anticipatory note on the big-data phenomenon that researchers have to deal with today);
- nor to get lost in their rational abstract reasoning, which might result in exhausting their moral energy.

He clearly refers to the risks concealed in the major Western epistemological traditions, which have both conceived the researcher as a knowing subject, the *I*, clearly detached from the object to be known. On the contrary, Mills suggests the need for research to develop a special *quality of mind* that calls into play researchers' selfhood:

> What [researchers] need is a quality of mind that will help them to use information and to develop reason in order to achieve lucid summations of what is going on in the world and of what may be happening within *themselves*. [. . .] a quality of mind essential to grasp the interplay of man and society, of biography and history, of *self* and the world.
> *(Mills, 1959, p. 5, 6; author's italics)*

Mills's work is one of the first bricks of a large building that is being erected in the name of a reconciliation between rigorous research and personal experience. A building where a chemist shows the significant role that personal knowledge—"intellectual powers and their passionate participation in the act of knowing" (Polanyi, 1962, p. 17)—can play in non-subjective and rigorous scientific discoveries, "bridging the disjunction between subjectivity and objectivity" (Polanyi, 1962); a building where neuroscientists can be inspired by continental phenomenology in stating the inseparability between the object-knowledge and the self-knowledge of being in the world (Varela et al., 1993). In other words, the methodological choice of this book reflects the increasing awareness that scientists and scholars, even the most famous ones, are *embodied minds* (borrowing Varela's expression), i.e. people whose thoughts and interests

Autobiography as a Method of Inquiry **11**

are intertwined (constantly influencing and influenced by, shaping and shaped, etc.) with their place of birth, what they've seen, touched, smelled, the people they've interacted with, etc.

If researchers, like everybody else, are not just rational and objective creatures but drawing from their own experience, then one could question the factual validity of their personal memories, together with their self-representation in different time and space frames. In this perspective, then, autobiographies lose their absolute representational power. In the meantime, though, they acquire a new power, that is exactly what is put to use in this book: the power of a research method that, through self-reflection and self-representation, allows them to explore and share the mind-body nexus.

The recent evolution of planning research and planning theory, which the authors of this book have significantly contributed to, has been characterized by an analogous increase in the appearance of researchers' selves (personal views, autobiographical references, etc.). Several scholars have discussed the importance of stories and storytelling in planning practice (Eckstein & Throgmorton, 2003; Sandercock, 2003). With this sensitivity, they make frequent use of autobiographical narratives in their scholarly work (see Sandercock, 1998, amongst many others). Flyvbjerg encourages researchers to shape research around the concept of Aristotelian *phronesis,* a form of knowledge connected to practical wisdom developed through experience with a higher ethical stance than *episteme* and *techne*, making a clear appearance in its own academic writing (Flyvbjerg, 2002). A systematic use of an autobiographical style characterizes emerging approaches to research where the researcher is personally engaged in the processes of planning and the changes his/her research talks about (see Saija, 2014, for an in-depth discussion of the need to use autobiographical narratives in action-research scholarly writing).

While the interest in storytelling has something in common with the way autobiographies are intended here, this book also recognizes the fact that a significant portion of the planning scholars contributing to this volume would probably not consider themselves to have been influenced by the *story turn* in planning or in general by postmodernism. As a matter of fact, autobiographical writing allows each of the authors to give a different interpretation of the connection between their scholarly work and their personal dimension.

The editor gave each author the opportunity to interpret the autobiographical task with a significant level of freedom. Research questions were shared, together with the request to use the pronoun I as much as possible in describing the context (places, time frames, and historic events, personal and professional interactions) of their published work, and left them free to decide what to narrate. Some of them have reflected on how personal events have impacted their thinking more than others; some give space to the way they have experienced the outside world (the city, the region, the world), while others have paid more attention to dynamics inside universities' walls. Some have made an effort to reflect on their entire intellectual journey since childhood, while others have focused on a portion of their life and/or career. All of them have made very different linguistic and stylistic choices. These differences are most likely related to the nature of their research and therefore we think might help the reader to understand their work better.

Autobiographical writing is still a relatively underexplored style in academic writing that we think will be the center of a long debate. We hope such a debate will benefit from this specific autobiographical attempt to explore an epistemological middle ground originating from the need to both accept the fallacy of modern rational absolute certainty but also overcome the postmodern impossibility of moving beyond self-uniqueness and self-perceptions. In this

12 Laura Saija

book, rational scholars explore the link between their ideas and their *self*, while postmodern scholars start from their *self* to find a surprising common ground with their rational colleagues. They all answered the call of the new generation of planning scholars, who are engaged (could it be different?) in the never-ending search for a collective identity, one that is able to hold together fundamental differences while giving us the feeling that we might be heading somewhere important.

Note

1 "Modern history of psychology has been marked by the elaboration of divergent theoretical approaches [. . .] this proliferation of theories has not been accompanied by a formulation of principles to guide the assessment of their interrelationships or relative values, and the field as a whole has consequently undergone a process of relentless diversification and fragmentation" (Atwood & Stolorow, 1993, p. 3).

References

Anderson, L. R. (2001). *Autobiography*. London: Routledge.

Atwood, G. E., & Stolorow, R. D. (1993). *Faces in a Cloud: Intersubjectivity in Personality Theory* (revised ed.). Northvale, NJ and London: Jason Aronson.

Eckstein, B. J., & Throgmorton, J. A. (2003). *Story and Sustainability: Planning, Practice, and Possibility for American Cities*. Cambridge, MA: MIT Press.

Flyvbjerg, B. (2002). Bringing Power to Planning Research: One Researcher's Praxis Story. *Journal of Planning Education and Research, 21*(4), 353–366.

Hillier, J., & Healey, P. (2008). *Critical Essays in Planning Theory* (3 volumes). Aldershot, England: Ashgate.

Lejeune P. (1982) The Autobiographical Contract. In Tzvetan Todorov (Ed.), *French Literary Theory Today* (pp. 192–222). Cambridge: Cambridge University Press.

Mills, C. W. (1959). *The Sociological Imagination*. Oxford, England: Oxford University Press.

Olney, J. (2014). *Autobiography: Essays Theoretical and Critical*. Princeton: Princeton University Press.

Polanyi, M. (1962). *Personal Knowledge: Towards a Post-Critical Philosophy* (Corrected ed.). Chicago: University of Chicago Press.

Saija, L. (2014). Writing about Engaged Scholarship: Misunderstandings on and the Issue of Quality Action Research Publications. *Planning Theory & Practice, 15*(2), 187–201.

Sandercock, L. (1998). *Towards Cosmopolis: Planning for Multicultural Cities*. Chichester and New York: Wiley.

Sandercock, L. (2003). Out of the Closet: The Importance of Stories and Storytelling in Planning Practice. *Planning Theory & Practice, 4*(1), 11–28.

Varela, F. J., Thomson, E., & Rosh, E. (1993). *The Embodied Mind: Cognitive Science and Human Experience*. Cambridge, MA and London, England: The MIT Press.

PART 2

16 Autobiographical Essays from Key Thinkers in Spatial Planning

3

PLANNING AS A VOCATION

The Journey So Far[1]

John Friedmann

Intellectual and Moral Foundations

Expelled from Austria and a perpetual traveler, I have never succeeded organically to be part of the society in which I happen to be living. English was my second language, acquired through persistent study and practice, and yet a German word or phrase will occasionally come to mind before I can think of its English equivalent. At the end of World War II, when I briefly returned to Vienna as a member of the American occupation forces, I could not connect with even my closest boyhood friend, who had remained there after 1940. I had returned as a conqueror, and we had nothing to say to each other. On the other hand, neither could I share much with my dorm mates at the Mt. Hermon School for Boys, a boarding school delightfully located in western Massachusetts overlooking the Connecticut River, and my musical education was limited to Mozart and Debussy; I knew nothing of American pop and other teenage icons. Furthermore, at Bowdoin College in Brunswick, Maine, where I spent the academic year 1943/44 prior to induction into the American army, I found myself *persona non grata* by the fraternity brothers with whom I lodged because of my supposedly Jewish ancestry. A perpetual outsider, I could never find an organic connection to my adopted country.

I completed my formal education at the University of Chicago in 1955. The years I spent there had turned out to be truly formative. My first work after receiving the PhD in the interdisciplinary program of research and education in planning took me to Brazil, a country whose language I didn't speak and whose geography was a complete mystery to me. Still, my three years there were the beginning of a lifelong engagement with international development. My destiny was to become a sojourner. Sometimes my travels were only brief interludes, others lasted for years. Here is a list of the places where I lived for a while, not counting my first 14 years in Vienna: Germany, Brazil, South Korea, Venezuela, Chile, Japan, the United Kingdom, Australia, and Canada. In none of them did I ever feel settled or "at home."

This identity status has shaped me, I now realize. What follows is an attempt to describe some fundamental parts of my intellectual enterprise once I had learned to embrace my ambiguous social position. Perhaps Karl Mannheim, who invented the "Sociology of Knowledge"

16 John Friedmann

and had written the first serious book on democratic planning, was right when he thought of intellectuals as free floating (*freischwebende Intelligenz*) (Friedmann, 1960). He imagined them as unmoored from social class and habitus, but perhaps also from commitments to ideologies, political parties, social movements, and all the rest. As an unmoored intellectual, I would need to construct my own philosophical foundations for how to live correctly in the world.

Late one night in 1956 or '57, sitting at my desk in Santiago da Bahia, Brazil, and only the sound of the ocean in my ear, I made what I can only describe now as an existential decision: I would make myself into an intellectual in the European sense of the term. I loved the life of ideas, wanted to get to the bottom of how they evolve and work their way into the everyday world of affairs, and with the degrees the University of Chicago had bestowed on me, I would do so as a planner. In short, what I implicitly rejected with this decision was a form of planning conceived as a narrowly bounded profession. I imagined it instead as an unbounded enterprise—unbounded at least by institutional conventions—not for its own sake but as always engaged *with* and *in* the world. Small wonder, then, that I fastened onto planning theory as a still unexplored terrain, even as I engaged with practical issues of, for example, regional development policy, which was the specific area of my expertise.

As a planning theorist, a central preoccupation was also the perennial challenge: "What is planning?" So formulated, the question is of course unanswerable. There are no metaphysical definitions of either being or becoming a planner and unadorned by any adjective we can make of planning whatever we will, depending on one's circumstances and dispositions. But to be a planner—at least this much I knew—is to be oriented towards the future. As well, the word suggests some form of *action* that, however small, will help pave the way into the future step by step.

It took me years before I could resolve the puzzle of my original question. I regarded city planners as regulators of urban space and urban designers as artists of spatial organization. As a regional planner, which was my specific métier, I imagined some sort of market intervention by the state in the spatial allocation of investments. Yet, whenever I thought about planning *without* a qualifying adjective, it had to be more broadly conceived. Following Hanna Arendt, I proposed acting to mean "setting something new into the world": an innovative act, a new beginning (Friedmann, 1987). This relatively simple definition, however, entails five important operations: (1) a *strategy and tactics* about how to proceed, (2) an *ethical judgment* by which the action itself can be justified, (3) the assumption of *responsibility for the consequences of action,* which inevitably entails risks (not all consequences can be foretold), (4) an ongoing *politics* to shepherd and guide the process of innovation as it begins to take hold, and (5) a *process of feedback* about the flow of events that allows for correction and social learning in the ongoing processes of change. The original question—what is planning?—thus demanded a complex philosophical answer.

Although I had embraced planning as a life project, I was also a stranger in the world, a traveler, who needed something other for its full realization, not any *prêt-á-porter* ideology. What might be the metaphysics of planning? Its epistemology? Did planning have moral foundations? Was it perhaps subsumed under a broadly conceived philosophy of practice? It is to these questions that I now turn.

A Metaphysics for Planning

I confess a weakness for Chinese philosophy. Indeed, in my book on transactive planning (Friedmann, 1973, pp. 185–189), I included a short section entitled "The Tao of Transactive

Planning." Some critics contemptuously dismissed this as a modish conceit from la-la land (I was living in Los Angeles at the time). But I was serious. Here, I will merely summarize my Daoist view by referring to the *yin-yang* dialectics that animates the universe.[2] In Daoist beliefs, the cosmos is in constant movement, pervaded by two energy flows (*qi*) that together constitute a unity of opposites. In contrast to Western thinking, which obliges one to choose between two opposing propositions (they cannot both be true), and in which dialectics takes the form of a confrontation, Chinese tradition holds that opposites, though in principle needing to be harmonized, are nonetheless in a continual state of tension: the *yin* force (which also contains some of its opposite energy) and the *yang* force (which likewise contains elements of *yin*)—neither force being entirely "pure" so that transformation is an ever-present possibility—alternate in their relative strength. The *Chinese Book of Changes (I Ching)* traces these dynamics via an ingenious system of 64 hexagrams. In this constant play of energies, no situation ever remains the same but is undergoing often subtle changes favoring one force over another.[3]

I believe that this metaphysics has a great deal of explanatory power, especially when studying Chinese historical experience. But I believe it to be useful also in the Western world where we are more accustomed to think in terms of either/or rather than both/and. It is particularly applicable in planning conflicts. I don't want to draw too sharp a distinction between Western and Chinese ways of thinking and acting because clearly we who live in the West also know how to negotiate and compromise in order to move forward. But the *yin-yang* dialectics is a built-in characteristic of many Chinese institutions and practices in ways that are not in our world.

An Epistemology for Planning

At the University of Chicago (1949–55), I was thrown headlong into agitated discussions about the place of values in the social sciences. We debated Max Weber's thesis of a value-free sociology dedicated to arriving at statements whose truth value could be vouchsafed. And what was knowledge, the winning side maintained, if not a form of truth-telling? Truth-telling, they argued, required a stripped-down operational language, with precisely bounded concepts shorn of linguistic embellishments that might express the writer's feelings about the matter at hand. Truth-telling, they claimed, involved uncontaminated factual statements that could be mapped directly onto the world.

On the other hand, my fellow students and I were aspiring to be planners who, as the cliché had it, wanted to "change the world." And if this was so, if we adopted the prevailing positivist position, what would happen to social justice or a more inclusive development? And didn't the exciting new study of socio-economic development have, as one of its great practitioners put it, an inherent "bias for hope" (Hirschman, 1971)? Did positivistic science even allow for a category called "hope"? In our theory classes, we read the great John Dewey: In his large corpus on pragmatism, there was scarce mention of "truth" and "truth-telling" (Healey, 2008; see also Bernstein, 1971; Rorty, 1979). Instead of a never-ending search for truth, Dewey emphasized experience as a source of knowing.

Acquiring knowledge, then, was something like a trapeze act without a net. It required initiating actions where nothing was ever guaranteed. In 1955, with a PhD in hand, I set out for Brazil as a missionary of the new technology of regional planning. It would take me 20 years

18 John Friedmann

before I could confidently speak of a distinctive epistemology for planning.[4] In *Retracking America,* I listed my then current understanding of social-scientific knowledge from a planning perspective, which I had learned, as Dewey had taught us, from reflecting on years of personal experience as a "planner" (Friedmann, 1973, pp. 129–130):

- Knowledge is cumulative only within the assumptions of "normal" science.
- Knowledge is not the accumulation of "solid" facts but arises from the interplay of theories and counter-theories, each drawing on its own set of data and interpretations.
- The more general the knowledge about a range of phenomena, the fewer details it encompasses. But the reverse is also true: the more detailed the knowledge, the narrower its focus. You cannot encompass both at the same time.
- Different kinds of knowledge are not always directly convertible into each other.
- The larger the number of variables within a single explanatory model, the greater is the effect of random occurrences on the results obtained.
- Reality, and consequently knowledge of reality, is literally inexhaustible. We never have enough time to exhaust all possibilities for improving our understanding of a complex phenomenon. At any given moment, therefore, knowledge of reality is an infinitesimally small heap of sand on the "plains of common ignorance" and is tied to the ephemeral and narrow range of the phenomena to which our attention has temporarily turned.

It was this understanding of the limits of a *scientific* knowledge of society that led me to propose an epistemology of *mutual learning* that involved a variety of potential actors and planners who had come together in a common undertaking. It took me another five years before I dared to venture a formal critique of Karl Popper's theory of *objective* or *scientific knowledge* (Friedmann, 1978).[5] From a perspective of planning as innovation in the public realm, I argued that our primary task is to venture new beginnings, each intervention generating a stream of new "facts" as the consequences of more or less risky actions begin to materialize. Social practices (one of my terms for planning in that chapter) proceed through a process of *social learning*. I counter-posed this to Popper's advice that scientists had an obligation to do their best to *falsify* hypothetical statements about the world. Take his famous example of the swans: If, per hypothesis, all swans are said to be white, discovering a single black swan would invalidate the hypothesis; the science of swans would have to be revised. But truth by falsification is not the business of planners nor of planning as a collective endeavor. If black swans were a threatened species, our job might well be to find ways of protecting them.[6] Falsification of universal claims is not the business of planners.

A Moral Foundation for Planning

To choose a vocation—in this case, planning—implies a personal commitment to an intrinsically meaningful way of life. I had come into planning with only the haziest idea of what was entailed by my choice. My father was a professor of history; following in his footsteps was an attractive option, but after three years in the army and two years studying social science at the undergraduate level, I was drawn to what I thought was a more socially engaged calling. The year was 1949, and Chicago admitted students to graduate work after only two years of undergraduate studies. After taking a battery of tests, I was admitted to the planning program with the promise of a master's degree at the end of three years. It would take a great deal more experience and reflection, however, before I fully understood what it meant to be a planner. After I had become head of the urban planning program at UCLA in 1969, I began to work on *Retracking America,* my first major foray into planning theory (Friedmann, 1973). Until then, I had drifted from job to job, country to country, as opportunities appeared. But what I had learned from working in Brazil, Korea, Venezuela and Chile didn't come together to make sense until the writing of a book that on publication proved to be an academic success, with over 20,000 copies sold, followed by a reprinting (with a new preface) by the Rodale Press.

I called this way of planning "transactive", because central to it was the idea of open communication, or interpersonal dialogue, that is to say a *dialogic relation* between planners and those with whom they work (I called them "clients," a rather unfortunate word as I now look back on it). I wrote that transactive planning involved "processes of mutual learning that are closely integrated with an organized capacity and willingness to act" (Friedmann, 1973, p. 247). And in a glossary of new terms, I defined dialogue as "a form of person-centered communication, generally requiring face-to-face interaction" (p. 244).

I had learned about dialogue from Martin Buber's work (1965). Buber was a Viennese Jewish philosopher for whom a genuine encounter between two people—listening and responding to each other's concerns and needs—had a quasi-religious meaning. His dialogue, as I understood it, foreshadowed Jürgen Habermas's more secular concept of "communicative action" (1979), which has greatly influenced the communicative paradigm of planning that was to evolve in North America during the 1980s and '90s, with contributions by John Forester, Judith Innes and others (Innes & Booher, 2010). Be that as it may, I now believe that, given its emphasis on small action groups within, or indeed outside, the institutional framework of the state, interpersonal dialogue is capable of providing a moral foundation for planning. You might ask why dialogue should be so considered. I turned to address this question in my next book, *The Good Society,* which appeared in 1979.

A Broadly Based Philosophy of Radical Practice

The 1970s turned out to be a decade-long transition both for me personally and for the world at large. I will discuss this at some length in the section "An Historic Break". Suffice is to say that it was a period when the interventionist welfare state that had dominated policymaking in the post-war era was morphing into the neo-liberal state of today, bringing in its wake a profound economic and social restructuring. My literary exploration of a "good society" was an attempt to develop a new vision for a society engaged in radically transforming itself. The book that emerged was not a systematic effort to analyze what was happening. Its aphoristic, semi-poetic style foreshadowed a postmodern sensibility. I was looking for ways to express a philosophy of countervailing actions that we might want to take even as the old order was collapsing all around us.

The planning style it propounded was interpersonal, no longer geared to institutionalized planning but carried forward through the committed work of small action groups and larger social movements. The era I was writing about was awash with social movements: feminist, anti-war, black power, antipoverty, and the so-called third sector of organized civil society manifest in hundreds of thousands of non-governmental and other voluntary and community organizations that had sprung up to fill the vacuum left by a retreating state. Dialogue, the defining relationship of the good society, is a form of both genuine speech and deep listening, with the potential power to transform those who practice it. Dialogue also limits its size, which I argued are groups composed of 7±2 individuals. Small action groups have only a temporary existence, but they are the yeast that nourishes larger social movements, confirming the non-violent powers of an organized civil society. I thought of it as a process of transformative change from the ground up, and called its practice radical.

To my delighted surprise, the manuscript was accepted and published by the MIT Press, but it was not the commercial success I had hoped for (Friedmann, 1979a). Reading *The Good Society* today, I am startled by how prescient this text now seems in light of contemporary urban social movements such as Occupy Wall Street or the people's movements in Egypt and Turkey, mediated by cell phones and other social media. I think of these largely spontaneous actions of a rebellious civil society as materializations of the "good society" in a struggle that, despite provocations, is essentially non-violent. Their organization is cellular. Their objectives are clear: Protest injustice, an oppressive state, an unresponsive bureaucracy and a way of being that prefigures a new world.

Some readers may think that what I have described here as radical practice cannot (should not?) be called planning. But as a form of radical practice, who would deny that in the neo-liberal and violent world of today it is precisely these movements that are often the principal sources of positive change and perhaps our one best hope for a better society?

Apprenticeship Years

Once anointed with a PhD, many might feel ready to take on the world. But in fact, the doctorate simply marks the end of a stage in life and a new beginning. I now think of the years from 1955 to 1969 as my apprenticeship years, my *Wanderjahre*. I was learning all the while, and though I held down responsible jobs, each of these posed different challenges and of which no one had informed me during my graduate studies. In short, I learned by doing, often pretending to know when I did not, and always ready to abandon notions for which I could claim no basis for the limited truths of my own experience. The very idea of planning in capitalist societies was new, and it was economists who were among the leading proponents of this new "soft" technology.

The Second World War had erased dark memories of the Great Depression, and national states everywhere were charged with managing the economy: In the United States, the welfare state created during Roosevelt's New Deal favored planning as a means for transiting from a wartime to a peace-time economy with a particular focus on metropolitan regions; in Western Europe, the state was charged with reconstruction; and the newly decolonized states, with Nehru's India in the lead, embraced ideas of a planned economy. The Dutch economist Jan Tinbergen had created the first macroeconomic model which underlies national policy-making and was awarded the Nobel Prize. The United Nations Economic Commission for Latin America, under the leadership of the Argentinian economist Raúl Prebisch, promoted an endogenous model of industrialization via import-substitution, and economic aid from the United States soon required the submission of national plans to the so-called Alliance for Progress as a basis for allocating foreign aid to Latin American countries. In France, the noted economist Jean Monnet worked assiduously in partnership with Robert Schuman and others towards a European economic union. And Harvard econometrician Wassily Leontief invented input–output analysis as a tool for economic planning. He, too, was crowned with the Nobel Prize.

Unsurprisingly, this grand vision of a planned economy in democratic, capitalistic countries was a contentious affair. At the University of Chicago, one of my professors, Julius Margolis, had taught us the fundamentals of social accounting, while Rexford Tugwell, the founding director of our program and former governor of Puerto Rico, dreamed of planning as a Fourth Power alongside the legislative, executive and judicial branches of the federal government. But only a few steps away, on the floor above the offices of the planning program, the young Milton Friedman lectured to spellbound crowds of students with his rhetoric of a free enterprise economy liberated from statist constraints. His ideological comrade-in-arms, Friedrich Hayek, whose anti-planning polemic *The Road to Serfdom* (1944) had caused a storm of contention in post-war Britain, had recently joined the university's prestigious Committee on Social Thought. He, too, eventually received a Nobel Prize, though not until 1974, when the prize was shared with another polymath, the Swedish Gunnar Myrdal, who had served as the first executive secretary of the United Nations Commission for Europe (1947–57) and was a persuasive advocate of planning in all its forms. In the mid-seventies, to plan or not to plan appeared to be the question at stake.

I mention these distinguished names to make two points: first, to show that in the post-war era, planning and specifically some forms of national economic planning and/or long-range policymaking, based on the instrumentalities of national accounts, was the intellectual environment in which my own ideas on planning were formed; and second, to foreshadow what I call here the "historic break," as the two champions of the neo-liberal revolution—Milton Friedman and Friedrich Hayek—finally came into their own during the 1970s, prevailing in the Anglo-America of Margaret Thatcher, and Ronald Reagan. With the gradual retreat of the state and the rise of institutions such as the World Bank, the International Monetary Fund, and the World Trade Organization, all of them based in Washington DC, the focus of planning had to be rethought. The well-known slogan that encouraged us in the late '70s and '80s to "think global, act local" is emblematic of this shift.

My personal experiences and thus also my evolving views on planning had been shaped by my work in Brazil, South Korea, Venezuela, and Chile: All of them, except for Venezuela, would today be considered, to use a current phrase, emerging economies. But we tend to forget that their successful spurt of economic growth was for the most part generated under the iron hand (*mano dura*) of military rule, with a law-and-order state that was enthusiastically supported by a succession of American governments that aimed at global hegemony and were dedicated to the creation of safe spaces for private capital accumulation. I turn now specifically to my own academic work as a planner.

Regional Development Planning

My artist daughter was born in 1959 during our stay in Korea. I worked in the development policy section of the US Operations Mission (USOM) from 1958 to 1961. As my two-year term came to an end, I was offered another appointment, this time to the US aid program in Turkey. But with a new baby and wary of yet another cultural immersion, my wife and I decided against it. Once we returned to the States, I would look for a job in the academy. After several false starts, I learned of an opening at MIT's Department of Planning in the School

22 John Friedmann

of Architecture and Planning. The department, led *de facto* by Lloyd Rodwin, whose interests were—in many respects—similar to my own, was looking for someone to teach in the area of regional planning as well as engage in research in connection with an exciting collaborative project that was about to be launched in Venezuela. The government of Venezuela had created the Guayana Development Corporation (CVG) to plan and build an urban-industrial "growth pole" at the confluence of the Orinoco and Caroní Rivers in the eastern part of the country. The corporation's president, a colonel (later general) in the Venezuelan army, with an engineering degree from MIT, had invited the Joint Center for Urban Studies at MIT/Harvard to help with this ambitious undertaking: constructing a hydroelectric dam, setting up a large steel works, and designing a new city for its workers, employees, and others yet to come. Assistance would take two forms: on-site consulting and project-related research. A two-year stint with the regional studies division of the Tennessee Valley Authority, my Brazilian background, and my experience in Korea had made me a logical choice for the position, which I happily accepted. The next four years were spent inventing the new subdiscipline of regional development planning.

I threw myself into this challenge. Regional studies had recently been boosted in the English-speaking world through Walter Isard's path-breaking research on spatial economics, which he called regional science (Isard, 1960). An economist with a penchant for mathematical modelling, Isard had founded a department dedicated to the new discipline at the University of Pennsylvania. When I learned that William Alonso, his first PhD, had just been appointed to an associate professorship at Harvard's Graduate School of Design, we met to plot out a book of readings, which ended as a somewhat lengthy 700-page exercise, collecting an eclectic selection of articles around five major topics: space and planning, location and spatial organization, theory of regional development (including resources, migration, and urban history in developed countries; and problems of the rural periphery), national policy for regional development, and a guide to the literature. The MIT Press accepted our manuscript—I forget how we managed to do it all in this pre-Internet era—and in the end, it turned out that we had won the lottery: Before this edition went finally out of print, more than 20,000 copies had been sold, and the publisher asked us to prepare a second edition (Friedmann & Alonso, 1964).

As we complied, here is how we introduced the new volume:

> In the few years that nations have sought economic development as an explicit policy goal it has become clear that the arithmetic of macro-economics has need of and is made more powerful by the geometrics of regional considerations.
>
> *(Friedmann & Alonso, 1964, p. 1)*[7]

With 90 percent new material, the second edition carried a brand-new title: *Regional Policy: Readings in Theory and Applications* (Friedmann & Alonso, 1975). In my literature review (chapter 37), I put on a brave face when I wrote: "A decade's work has yielded a rich harvest. It has not only strengthened the theoretical foundations of regional planning but has extended knowledge from policy analysis and the evaluation of actual experiences with regional planning in a variety of national settings" (p. 791).

I say brave because it was sheer bravado to claim that regional development planning would survive another decade, and that by 1984, perhaps, a third edition would be in the

Planning as a Vocation **23**

offing. In fact, when we assembled the second edition, it hadn't quite dawned on us that the world was already gearing up to the coming neo-liberal revolution, and that state-led planning would be one of its first victims. I don't know how many copies of *Regional Policy* were eventually sold, but I doubt it was much more than 10 percent of the sales of the successful first edition. As one critic observed, by the mid-seventies, regional planning had begun to "sound boring." Four decades later, I described it as the "last hurrah" of an era that was about to disappear forever (Friedmann, 2001, p. 392). We had failed to notice the rise of environmental consciousness that would evolve its own brand of regionalism and had skirted other forms as well, such as the resurgence in many parts of the world of cultural regionalism as a political force.[8]

But let us leave this funereal mood and allow me to dial back to the preceding decade and my involvement with the Guayana project, which eventually led me to write *Regional Development Policy: A Case Study of Venezuela* (Friedmann, 1966b).[9] Ciudad Guayana was a steel city that successfully promoted Venezuela's eastern region as a vital link in the country's space economy. Today, it has a population of about one million. At the start of this research, however, I had a serious confrontation with Professor Rodwin, the co-director of this collaborative project and my *de facto* boss.[10] He had asked me to concentrate my research on the Guayana region only, but I argued that since this region was still largely uninhabited it would make more sense to undertake a nationwide policy study of regional development that would provide a broader context for the Guayana project. Rodwin did not like to be contradicted while I, as usual, was stubborn and stuck to my guns. In the end, extending the scope of my study to the whole of the national territory turned out to be correct, but in Rodwin's view, I had been wilful and insubordinate. At the end of my four years at MIT and despite my many publications, I failed to get tenure and resigned.

Planning as a Political Practice

The time had come to put my skills as a regional planner to a test. A year earlier, the Ford Foundation had started a demonstration program of building community facilities as an integral part of public housing programs in Santiago and elsewhere. The idea had originally come at the behest of the American aid program, an arm of the State Department. What I did not know at the time was that this was a policy move by the US government to counter the growing civil unrest and sense of disaffection among working-class Chileans at a time when the then current government of Jorge Alessandri—scion of one of Chile's most prominent political families and an arch-conservative—was drawing to a close. The perennial fear during these Cold War times was a Communist takeover, with Chile—according to the American domino theory of history—the first potential domino. In the presidential elections of 1964, a center-left coalition of the Christian Democrats had voted Eduardo Frei and his Christian Democratic Party into power in expectation of a six-year period of fundamental economic and social reforms. The modest community facilities program was meant to reinforce the Frei agenda (to the extent that it was known in Washington) and thus "save the world for democracy." This was actually a ridiculous notion, made worse by a cumbersome process of delivering assistance services. Dysfunctional from the start, and despite spending a lot of money, the program never properly got off the ground.

24 John Friedmann

In February 1965, foundation representatives obtained an interview with the new president. A memorandum of conversation records the basic understanding reached on this occasion. Paragraph 2 of this memorandum is reproduced below:

> The President has a special interest that the advisory service solicited be principally be oriented towards the formation of administrative and learning institutions, the training of personnel, and the collection of basic information that will make it possible to put the programs that interest us on a solid foundation. These advisory services may be made operational through specific agreements with each of the interested institutions, but should be related to each other, as may be advisable, in order to maintain the unity of purpose which they are seeking.
>
> *(Friedmann, 1969, p. 9)*[11]

The institutions President Frei had in mind included the newly created National Planning Office (ODEPLAN) for regional planning; the newly restructured Ministry of Housing and Development (MINVU) for urban policy, community facilities, rural housing, and related services; the National Council for Popular Promotion working directly out of the presidential office; and the Catholic University of Chile, where the creation of a teaching and research Center for Urban Development (CIDU) was to be brought into being. But the important thing was the president's phrase concerning "unity of purpose." The foundation had recruited me to shut down what still remained of the old program and to coordinate the various undertakings of the new commitment. We knew that time was short: Eduardo Frei was constitutionally prevented from serving a second term, and his term of office would end in 1970. Effectively we had a mere four years to obtain agreements with the various participating institutions, recruit personnel and provide such program assistance as might be requested.

In the eyes of our hosts, we must have done well. When I left Chile in 1969, I received an honorary doctorate from the Catholic University (the second only after the poet Pablo Neruda) and a medal from the government. But in my own assessment, we had barely begun our work. The details can be found in my final report to the foundation (Friedmann, 1969). Here I will limit myself to summarize what the experience had taught me. Much of what I learned is incorporated (though without specific attribution) in *Retracking America,* discussed above. To be more specific, it was in the course of my continuing reflections in Santiago—one part of me critically observing what the other part was doing—that the crucial discovery came to me as I awoke one morning and had the insight that planning could be theorized productively as the linking of knowledge to action, a formula that would eventually replace the traditional but still popular self-understanding of planning as a form of rational decision making.[12] The second discovery was that planning as innovation necessarily involves a process of continuous mutual learning by all concerned. And the third was the critical importance for successful practice of dialogic interpersonal relations.

This was not all I learned, however. The major practical lesson for me was the insight that planning is an intensely political practice in the sense of being fully immersed in a highly politicized context. This is still not a lesson taught in planning schools, where students typically learn a set of technical skills devoid of any notion of the political context in which these skills might be deployed. But a stripped-down rationality simply won't work in the political sphere. Planning, and especially innovative planning, is also a form of political practice, or it remains an empty gesture (Abers & Keck, 2013). The implications of a planning embedded in the political sphere are indeed of major importance. Without strong support from politically powerful groups no plan is ever likely to succeed. Planners must therefore be thinking constantly about how to mobilize support, align with sympathetic political factions and consider various strategies of action. Yet even with extensive societal support, the winds of politics blow hot and cold from different directions. In Chile and within the span of a single decade, liberal Christian Democrats had replaced a Tory president who would, in turn, be replaced by a Popular Front coalition, only to be finally pushed aside by a military coup that was closely aligned with American corporate and political interests. The politics here were essentially global but with specific national characteristics (a six-year presidency, a landed oligarchy, the influence of the Catholic Church, etc.).

Chile, however, is not unique in this regard, and any other place might serve as well to illustrate the primacy of politics in planned undertakings. Under these conditions, long-range planning becomes virtually impossible, since every political constellation holding power will try to wipe the slate clean of the past and put their own people into controlling positions, click "delete" on the previous regime's agenda, and send oppositional figures into exile, prison, or retirement. I had a similar experience in Brazil, where my work at the Federal University of Bahia quickly unraveled after a military coup in 1964 sent many of our former staff into exile abroad, and I had also watched South Korea come under the sway of military rule under General Park Chung-Hee. It was these serial experiences that finally persuaded me to return to the academy in my adoptive country. Harvey S. Perloff, my dissertation advisor at the University of Chicago and a long-time friend, had just been appointed dean of the School of Architecture and Urban Planning at UCLA and invited me to join his faculty and head up a new planning program. And so, in June 1969, my family and I moved to Los Angeles.[13]

An Historic Break

Without historical perspective, it is all but impossible to understand the meaning of the present. But when history—time—speeds up, which is the case in today's urbanized world, how can we get a proper perspective? All we can do is grope our way through the landscape of the present shrouded in fog and illusions. This is more or less what happened to us during the 1970s. We perceived what was happening—deindustrialization, the shift from the Atlantic Ocean to the Pacific—but what did it all mean? And even if we knew, what, if anything, could anyone do about it?

Before proceeding, I should say a few words about my own situation, which was about to undergo its own "historic break" with the past. In the mid-seventies, my wife and I separated, eventually to divorce. We had originally met in Germany and married after the war, but the marriage had not been going well for some time. For the next decade, I lived by myself until, through an intermediary, I got to know Leonie Sandercock, who was then a professor at Macquarie University in Sydney, Australia. We had met briefly on two prior occasions, but in the 1980s started a correspondence that ended with Leonie coming to Los Angeles to enroll in the UCLA Film School screenwriting program while teaching on a visiting basis in the urban planning program. Our lives have been entwined ever since and on my retirement from UCLA I accompanied her back to Australia, where she had accepted a professorship at the Royal Melbourne Institute of Technology.

26 John Friedmann

But to return to my intellectual trajectory: In 1975, two eminent Yale economists published a book that foretold (in theoretical language) what was about to happen or perhaps was already happening (Paauw & Fei, 1975). With the Philippines as a case study, they argued that countries in South East Asia which they referred to as "open dualistic economies," should abandon their misguided policies of import substitution and turn their economies around by promoting industries that would be attracted by cheap and docile labor as well as capital subsidies to produce commodities for export markets in the West. I decided to write what I thought was a withering critique of this thesis and tried to publish it in a well-known Dutch journal, *Development and Change*. It took me nearly a year to persuade the editors to accept my review, and they finally agreed under the condition that appended to my review would be a series of comments by three of the best-known development economists in the business: Martin Bronfenbrenner, Gustav Ranis, and Hans Singer (Friedmann, 1979b; reprinted in Friedmann, 1988). As it turned out, it was a fist fight with the gloves off. My review was hard-hitting and so were the three commentaries, one of which dismissed my essay because I was a planner, not an economist, and what would I know about questions that were properly in their domain?

This is not the place to rehearse these arguments, though parenthetically it might be noted that, despite the good advice, the Philippines did not turn out to become one of Asia's "little tigers". But from my essay and the commentaries attached to it one could begin to sense that a historical turn was about to happen, that what we now call the neo-liberal revolution would unleash an avalanche of changes that would transform the world as we knew it. For those who were born after 1980, let me recall them briefly.

The revolution was called neo-liberal because it championed the libertarian philosophy of Friedrich Hayek and Milton Friedman, two of the leading ideologists of this anti-planning movement. But here is a correction: Ideas alone don't change the world; the times must also be prepared and ready to change. Another name for this period could therefore be "the recapitalization of capital," meaning that rates of return on capital were shrinking (Marxist economists were calling this a "crisis of accumulation"), and a new global division of labor would be one of the ways by which profits could again be energized. But in order for this to happen, the Keynesian welfare state with its focus on the nation would have to be replaced or at least made to retreat, allowing market forces to fully deploy their logic on a global scale. Economic growth was now set equal to development (serious proposals for prioritizing basic human needs had been rejected) and the Gross Domestic Product became the universal yardstick of positive change.[14] No one thought of looking further for the full extent of human, environmental and social consequences of hyper-rapid economic growth.

As the national state began to shed some of its traditional functions, it encouraged local governments to pick up the pieces. In the United States, this process involved mandating local governments to provide certain key services without actually funding them (these were dubbed "unfunded mandates"). Most significantly, local governments began to see themselves as competing with all other places in a race to attract footloose capital, and so came to be called entrepreneurial, setting city against city, province against province. Capital itself was decontrolled, and the financial sector was disarticulated from the "real" economy of production. Once controls had been lifted, there was little to stop corporations from reconcentrating into gigantic conglomerates on the model of Japan's *zaibatsu*, whose size would allow them to operate effectively on a global scale. The result was that many industrial firms simply packed up their machinery and moved from former industrialized regions to beckoning countries in coastal Asia, not just the little tigers of South Korea and Taiwan, but also to Indonesia, Malaysia, and Thailand, and after 1980 to China as well, which after Mao's death and under the leadership of Deng Xiaoping had opened its economy to the world.

Inevitably, my own work was profoundly affected by snowballing globalization. In the following pages, I will briefly discuss some of my major publications from the 1980s and '90s on three topics: world cities, rethinking poverty, and 200 years of planning history.

World Cities

With a few notable exceptions, American planners and the planning profession generally have shown scant interest in global issues, urbanization in other parts of the world, or comparative studies of urban planning. It was European planners, aroused by growing European economic integration, who were the first to write about their growing awareness of national differences in planning institutions and initiated comparative research on what they called a variety of planning cultures (Keller et al., 1993, 1996). In what ways was planning practice similar and, more importantly, different across the expanding map of the European Union? Knowing about these similarities and differences, cities might start to learn from each other's experiences. Or, in order to prepare planners for practice across the EU, planning education might need to be modified to take these differences into account. It took more than a decade for the idea of different planning cultures to gain traction in the US, with a prize-winning essay by myself (published, however, in Europe!) followed by a collective volume edited by Bishwapriya Sanyal (Friedmann, 2005; Sanyal, 2005).

The original stimulus for my essay had been the first World Conference of Planning which was held in Shanghai in 2001. Although I was unable to attend—Leonie and I were moving to Vancouver—I noticed that some of my colleagues were eager to propagate a view of planning as a universal profession, which, despite some adjustments in translation, could basically be a standardized American model, conveyed in the *lingua franca* of the day, i.e. English.[15] This universalization of Anglo-American planning theory and practice seemed to me a fundamentally misguided project and motivated me to write my essay. In the end, however, even I could not abstain from speculating about an emerging "global planning culture" that, I thought, should be based on three assumptions: that the expansion and consolidation of global capital would continue into the foreseeable future, that the rural-urban global transition would be all but complete over the next several decades, and that city-mediated, increasingly transnational relations would continue to be strengthened (Friedmann, 2005, ch. 3).

I had gradually come to this view of the world and of what we could look forward to in the medium term, beginning with my first essay on world city formation (Friedmann & Wolff, 1982), which had evolved from a UCLA seminar on "The Future of the City." Its first paragraph outlines the project.

> Our paper concerns the spatial articulation of the emerging world system of production and markets through a global network of cities. Specifically, it is about the principal urban regions in this network, dominant in the hierarchy, in which most of the world's active capital is concentrated. As cities go, they are large in size, typically ranging from five to fifteen million inhabitants, and they are rapidly expanding. [. . .] These vast, highly urbanized—and urbanizing—regions play a vital part in the great capitalist

undertaking to organize the world for the efficient extraction of surplus. Our basic argument is that the basic character of the urbanizing processes—economic, social, and spatial—which define life in these sprawling cities reflect, to a considerable extent, the mode of their integration into the world economy.

(Brenner & Keil, 2006, p. 58; orig. Friedmann, 1982)

We concluded with some suggestions for how the concept of a world city might find appropriate planning responses. Together with a companion piece a few years later (Friedmann, 1986), world city research became a major research focus globally, chiefly in geography. A decade later, two geographers convened an international conference to highlight ongoing research from a variety of disciplinary and ideological perspectives (Knox & Taylor, 1995), and another decade on, research had sufficiently matured to warrant a compilation of a textbook of readings (Brenner & Keil, 2006): "World city" was becoming a normalized concept.[16] By then, however, the concept had already become somewhat dated, as more and more cities in both the North and South had in various ways been incorporated into the global system. The British geographer Jennifer Robinson called them "ordinary cities" and asked researchers to shift attention from the well-known global hubs to the less known cities, especially in the Global South (Robinson, 2006).

Rethinking Poverty

A few days before beginning the present essay, I received a parcel in the mail from an address in Cairo which I didn't recognize. It looked like a book and curious what it might be, I unwrapped it. The text was in Arabic, and on one page I discovered that it was a translation of my 1992 book, *Empowerment: The Politics of an Alternative Development*. This made me wonder why the National Centre of Translation in Egypt would have wanted to make my book available throughout the Arab world at precisely this time.[17] I thought that it may have had something to do with the beginnings of the popular movements in Egypt and other North African countries which the media had called the Arab Spring. In fact, I have been astonished at the number of translations of this same text that had previously appeared in Japanese (1995), Portuguese (1996), and Italian (2004). What had aroused this growing interest in my perspective on an alternative development dating back to the early 1990s?

The book is an attempt to rethink development strategies for the alleviation of widespread poverty, primarily in the Global South.[18] Parenthetically, it was also meant to be an alternative to the many proponents of the export-oriented model of Paauw and Fei discussed above and so ardently defended by the doyens of development economics. Two theoretical chapters set out to challenge the prevailing views. The first I called the whole-economy model, which took the household rather than the individual as a unit of decision making. The model integrated two "economies" with regard to which any marginalized household had to make decisions about the disposition of its resources between the monetary economy articulated through markets and the moral economy based on the production of use values within the household itself in its community setting (Friedmann, 1992, ch. 3).

The second theoretical chapter—rethinking poverty—was a model of access to what I called the bases of social power, in which the household economy is at the center. I argued that poverty is not usefully defined by low income but rather should be understood as a multifaceted set of *resources* to which households have variable access, including defensible life space, surplus time over subsistence requirements, social networks, social organizations, knowledge and skills, appropriate information, instruments of work and livelihood (including good health), and financial resources. Good access to these bases of social power would enable households to make their own choices in the pursuit of life. Significantly, however, state assistance in such matters as housing, financial resources, the costs of public transportation, education, and health could substantially improve a household's capacity to help itself.

In addition to these theoretical chapters, *Empowerment* also included two chapters on political claiming. The first concerned claims for an inclusive democracy and appropriate economic growth with an emphasis on informally organized market-based activities; the second was about claims for gender equality and environmental sustainability. A concluding chapter addressed questions of political practice, where I argued that a precondition for a politics of claiming was a measure of empowerment achieved through greater access to the bases of social power, which would then enable mass movements to convert such gains in social power into effective political practices. One of the forms of its historical manifestation is precisely this conversion that brings civil society out into the street, and where, once televised, it suddenly becomes visible to the world. This may well be one of the reasons why this small academic book continues to enjoy popularity in the Mediterranean world.

Two Hundred Years of Planning History

The third work in what in retrospect turned out to be the most productive period of my life was what some have called my *magnum opus,* the writing of which extended over several years. I had lived with the new definition of planning—the linking of knowledge to action—since the late sixties and now wanted to explore what Michael Foucault would have called its archaeology, that is how this specifically European idea had evolved through the writings of a range of influential authors, some of whom had reached far across their own specialties to shape the world as we know it. The planning I was interested in was, as always, "in the public domain", and this phrase became the lead title of my new book (Friedmann, 1987).

From the start, it was clear to me that I would have to trace the story of planning to the period we call the Enlightenment in both France and the United Kingdom. But as I continued my research, I came to realize that I would also have to carry it forward into the period of historical rupture through which we were living at the time. I started by creating an elaborate chart, a veritable panoply of new thinking, in which I traced the origins of planning as a way of mastering the future across the political spectrum. Its beginnings I located in the field of sociology writ large, from its immediate precursors in such figures as Saint Simon and Auguste Comte, on through Emile Durkheim and Max Weber to Mannheim, Popper, and Etzioni. From early on, the thinking of these men intersected with the birth of the engineering sciences in the early 1800s, a fact that has had an abiding influence on the more technocratic branches of planning from scientific management to applied systems analysis and for a long time prevented us from thinking of planning as essentially a political practice. A second stream of influence began with the early political economists such as Adam Smith and J.S. Mill that would soon branch out into a number of important schools, ranging from neoclassical microeconomics to the welfare economics of Pigou and Sen and institutional economics originating in Germany (a late developing country) to Veblen, and on to the recent work of Tinbergen and

30 John Friedmann

Leontief to which I have already alluded. John Dewey's pragmatist writings were a welcome philosophical leavening to this array of thinkers that would eventually inspire many successful planners to adopt his important idea of experiential learning. Finally, on the political left, I named a variety of influential thinkers across the ideological spectrum—utopians, anarchists, and a diverse assortment of "radicals"—citing such names as Robert Owen, Pierre-Joseph Proudhon, and Peter Kropotkin, all the way to leading feminists and critics of recent decades, including Dolores Hayden, Ivan Illich, and Murray Bookchin. Not to be forgotten in this ancestral hall of radical ideas were Marx and Engels along with their modern Russian and Chinese interpreters, respectively Lenin and Mao, the charismatic champions of five-year national plans designed to propel their countries at top speed into the twentieth century.

Onto this impressive roster of creative political thinkers, I overlaid four major traditions of innovative planning: *social reform, social learning and policy analysis*—all three representatives of state-led planning—and a fourth tradition of *social mobilization,* which I called radical because it represented the eruption of civil society into the public realm. Chapters were devoted to discussing each of these traditions through the contributions of their respective authors.

On publication, my colleagues in the planning academy were startled. Where in this account were the heroes of urban, regional, and community planning? Why hadn't I identified a "distinct literature that addressed urban planning per se"? Why wasn't there what might have been a fifth tradition concerning the aesthetics of urban design? Still others worried about what I had called "radical" planning: They thought that a planning with contributions by civil society was a bridge too far. Community mobilization and the decolonization of state-led planning were odd if not downright dangerous ideas to bring into the classroom, some critics averred, along with terms such as resistance, counter-planning, and counter-hegemonic practices. In the end, many objected to the whole idea of a *transformative* planning. They simply wanted to carry on with what they already knew. Even so, and despite this puzzlement about my approach and the range of ideas it covered, the book continues to be in print after more than a quarter century. It has been translated into Italian, Spanish, and Farsi (Persian), and copies were bootlegged in Taiwan. *Planning in the Public Domain* has apparently acquired the status of a classic in the field.

After retiring from UCLA at the age of 70, I decided to cross the Pacific and relocate in Melbourne, Victoria, where Leonie had accepted a position as chair and professor at the Royal Melbourne Institute of Technology. We remained in Australia until 2001, when we returned to North America so that Leonie could take up a professorial appointment at the University of British Columbia. The millennium had arrived with its new challenges, and I gratefully accepted an honorary position in UBC's School of Community and Regional Planning, where I continue to teach and do research.

Final Reflections

Planning understood as city-building is an ancient art. In the global era of urban expansion, this art is practiced in most parts of the world, and planners have been joined in this endeavor by architects, engineers, sociologists, geographers, and many others. Planning is still an art of sorts, but over the last century it has increasingly become a professional field. As such, it is variably understood. China, which is the leading city-building country in the world today, employs tens of thousands of planners whose social prestige is generally held in high esteem.

In the United States, Canada, and the United Kingdom, the profession has struggled to gain recognition. It has somewhat succeeded in this, but its public status is near the bottom of the professions, while on the European continent, professional status has yet to be achieved in most if not all countries. Part of the problem has been the lack of a specific role or range of capabilities whose performance might be clearly understood by the general public. People still expect planners to draw up (spatial) plans, although these "plans" rarely serve as a practical guide to city-building; most of them gather dust and are forgotten. As far as my own work goes, the last "master plan" I drew up was in graduate school almost 70 years ago. This is clearly not where my heart is.

Since my degrees are all in planning, I have no trouble defining myself as a planner or rather planning academic, and the work that I do is therefore "planning" by default. But I suspect that in today's world, this is small consolation for young academics and graduate students who look enviously across the fence at other professions whose practitioners pull down six-digit salaries working for the private sector.[19] The situation is paradoxical, however. Although planners always bemoan their relatively low public standing, I am impressed by the quality of our students, who continue to compete for entry into this low-status field, mostly I suppose for ethical reasons, to make the world a better place. Students tend to be champions of all the things that need doing in terms of social justice, environmental stewardship, a people-centered and sustainable development of our cities, bio-regionalism, and similar valued objectives. A graduate planning education seems to offer them some tools for reaching these ideals.

With these things in mind, I have at different times and in different places done things and written things with the intention of promoting these values, which I consider central to our field. Always restless and peripatetic, I have moved through the world in both its geographic and cognitive sense. And I came to think of planning as an historical project that neither began with nor will end with me, but will go on forever, as action comes to be joined to knowledges of every sort in the solution of the multiple challenges facing humankind. The specific context for inserting ourselves into what Patsy Healey calls the flow of life is therefore always a different one, with the result that planning does not lead to cumulative knowledge as in the sciences but takes us on a path of continuous social learning. Perhaps it is this hope in a better future for all of us earthlings that ultimately keeps us going.

Notes

1 I have used the first part of this title, which echoes Max Weber's famous essay, "Politics as a Vocation" (1946), half a century ago in a two-part essay that appeared in *Plan Canada* (Friedmann, 1966a).
2 There are many Chinese sources which talk about this in various contexts. See e.g. Jullien, (1995), Farquhar and Zhang (2012).
3 The following quotation from Jullien (1995) may help the reader to grasp the deep meaning of Chinese metaphysics: "As Aristotle declared, contraries 'cannot act upon each other', 'do not change into each other', and 'are mutually destructive'. In logical terms, they are mutually exclusive. In contrast, the entire Chinese tradition insists that contraries both oppose each other and 'contain each other mutually': within *yin* there is *yang,* just as within *yang* there is *yin;* or, as one might say, as the *yang* penetrates the density of the *yin,* the *yin* open up the dispersion of the *yang.* Both constantly proceed from the same primordial unity and reciprocally give rise to each other's actualization. [. . .] In China all the energy fuelling actualization is constituted by both *yin* and *yang* [. . .] they together form all that exists" (pp. 250–51). The symbol of the cosmos is the writhing Chinese dragon.

32 John Friedmann

4 It could be argued that planning as a way of doing doesn't require an epistemology. But if planners link knowledge to action, which is the claim, they have to justify their position on any particular matter, and usually do this by flaunting their "expertise" and graduate degrees. But what good are these in a world that is in constant motion?

5 The social sciences in the English-speaking world all too often try to imitate physical science as the true model of scientific thinking. The German word for science is *Wissenschaft,* a more pliable and inclusive term that encompasses the humanities as well.

6 For further discussion of this article, see Friedmann (2011, ch. 2).

7 Today I would have substituted spatial considerations for "regional".

8 In 1979, Clyde Weaver and I published another regional planning book (Friedmann & Weaver, 1979) on the development of this subfield from its origins in nineteenth-century France and Great Britain. But history had rushed on, and our book, useful in its survey of origins and mid-century developments, had failed to spot that the era of state-led planning had already ended, and the final part of this volume, which we imagined as visionary, fell on sterile ground.

9 Other books that grew out of the Guayana project include Rodwin and Associates (1969), Peattie (1970, 1987), Appleyard (1976).

10 The other co-director was Martin Meyerson at Harvard, whom I remembered from my Chicago days as a physical planner. In 1971, he became president of the University of Pennsylvania.

11 The reference to Friedmann (1969) is my final report to the Ford Foundation in whose files it can undoubtedly be found. A small number of copies were printed, but to the best of my knowledge, library copies do not exist.

12 The perceptive reader may wonder about the difference between these two formulas. Decision making implies but doesn't necessarily lead to action (implementation is treated, if at all, as a separate question), and it's not clear whether in this self-definition, planner and decision maker are understood to be one and the same or two different roles. In some views, planners are seen as "rational", while politicians are described as motivated by concerns other than efficient instrumental relations between ends and means. On the other hand, with "action" defined as innovative ("setting something new into the world"), the planner's role is not necessarily separate from making decisions, and the question of whose and what sort of knowledge is relevant for action is left open. The two models of planning described by these definitions in fact lead to very different agendas, with their "rationality" always in question (in relation to what and whose ends?), whereas action correlatively involves both ends and means.

13 Harvey Perloff's distinguished career is celebrated in Burns and Friedmann (1985).

14 Eventually this was supplemented with the Human Development Index, but this too was heavily weighted by the inclusion of per capita income. And further, the unit of analysis was inevitably the national economy rather than smaller territorial units (province, city, metropolitan region).

15 Americans often imagine themselves as the universal culture *tout court.* But this is a dangerous illusion. We are strong on both planning and urban theories, but our cities display little evidence of this other than as planning that is mediated by market forces.

16 The term "world city" in itself was not new. I grew up in Vienna, which had fancied itself as a *Weltstadt* long ago, when it was still the capital of the Habsburg empire. Peter Hall appropriated the term for a book, which however was primarily concerned with the descriptive geography of a number of large "international" cities linked to trade (Hall, 1977). Our use of the term was in the context of the rapidly globalising geography of the 1980s.

17 The translation into Arabic was copyrighted in 2010.

18 This term was still unknown in the 1990s.

19 According to the US Bureau of Labor Statistics, the median income of city and regional planners in May 2012 was, in rounded figures, $65,000, in comparison with geographers' $72,000, architects' $73,000, civil engineers' $79,000 and economists' $92,000 (http://www.bls.gov/ooh/life-physical-and-social-science/urban-and-regional-planners.htm [visited August 13, 2014]).

References

Abers, R. N., & Keck, M. (2013). *Practical Authority: Agency and Institutional Change in Brazilian Water Politics.* New York, NY: Oxford University Press.

Appleyard, D. (1976). *Planning a Pluralist City: Conflicting Realities in Ciudad Guayana.* Cambridge, MA: MIT Press.

Bernstein, R. J. (1971). *Praxis and Action.* Philadelphia, PA: University of Pennsylvania.

Brenner, N., & Keil, R. (Eds.). (2006). *Global Cities Reader.* London: Routledge.

Buber, M. (1965). *Knowledge of Man: A Philosophy of the Interhuman.* Edited with an introduction by M. Friedman (M. Friedman and R. G. Smith, trans.). New York, NY: Schocken.

Burns, L., & Friedmann, J. (Eds.). (1985). *The Art of Planning: Selected Writings of Harvey S. Perloff.* New York, NY: Plenum Press.

Farquhar, J., & Zhang, Q. (2012). *Ten Thousand Things: Nurturing Life in Contemporary Beijing.* New York, NY: Zone Books.

Friedmann, J. (1960). Intellectuals in Developing Societies. *Kyklos, 8(4),* 513–541.

Friedmann, J. (1966a). Planning as a Vocation. *Plan Canada,* Part 1, April 98–124; Part 2, August 8–26.

Friedmann, J. (1966b). *Regional Development Policy: A Case Study of Venezuela.* Cambridge, MA: MIT Press.

Friedmann, J. (1969). *Urban and Regional Development in Chile: A Case Study of Innovative Planning.* Santiago, Chile: The Ford Foundation Urban and Regional Development Advisory Program in Chile. June 1, 1969. Hectographed limited edition.

Friedmann, J. (1973). *Retracking America: A Theory of Transactive Planning.* Garden City, NJ: Doubleday and Anchor Books.

Friedmann, J. (1978). The Epistemology of Social Practice: A Critique of Objective Knowledge. *Theory and Society, 6,* 75–92.

Friedmann, J. (1979a). *The Good Society.* Cambridge, MA: MIT Press.

Friedmann, J. (1979b). The Crisis of Transition: A Critique of Strategies of Crisis Management. *Development and Change,* with comments by H. W. Singer, M. Bronfenbrenner, and G. Ranis, and a rejoinder by J. Friedmann, *10(1),* 125–176.

Friedmann, J. (1986). The World City Hypothesis. *Development and Change, 17(1),* 69–84.

Friedmann, J. (1987). *Planning in the Public Domain: From Knowledge to Action.* Chichester: Princeton University Press.

Friedmann, J. (1988). *Life Space and Economic Space: Essays in Third World Planning.* New Brunswick, NJ: Transaction Books.

Friedmann, J. (1992). *Empowerment: The Politics of Alternative Development.* Cambridge, MA: Basil Blackwell Publishers.

Friedmann, J. (2001). Regional Development and Planning: The Story of a Collaboration. *International Journal of Regional Science, 24(3),* 386–395.

Friedmann, J. (2005). Globalization and the Emerging Culture of Planning. *Progress in Planning, 64(3),* 183–234.

Friedmann, J., & Alonso, W. (Eds.). (1964). *Regional Development and Planning: A Reader.* Cambridge, MA: MIT Press.

Friedmann, J., & Alonso, W. (Eds.). (1975). *Regional Policy: Readings in Theory and Applications.* Cambridge, MA: MIT Press.

Friedmann, J., & Weaver, C. (1979). *Territory and Function: The Evolution of Regional Planning.* London: Edward Arnold, Ltd., and Berkeley, CA: University of California Press.

Friedmann, J., & Wolff, G. (1982). World City Formation: An Agenda for Research and Action. *International Journal for Urban and Regional Research, 6(3),* 309–344.

Habermas, J. (1979). *Communication and the Evolution of Society.* Boston, MA: Beacon Press.

Hall, P. (1977). *World Cities.* London: Weidenfeld and Nicholson.

Hayek, F. (1944). *Road to Serfdom.* Chicago, IL: University of Chicago Press.

34 John Friedmann

Healey, P. (2008). The Pragmatic Tradition in Planning Thought. *Journal of Planning Education and Research, 12(3)*, 277–292.

Hirschman, A. (1971). *Bias for Hope.* New Haven, CT: Yale University Press.

Innes, J. E., & Booher, D. E. (2010). *Planning with Complexity: An Introduction to Collaborative Rationality for Public Policy.* London: Routledge.

Isard, W. (1960). *Methods of Regional Analysis: An Introduction to Regional Science.* New York, NY: Wiley.

Jullien, F. (1995). *Treatise on Efficacy: Between Western and Chinese Thinking.* New York, NY: Zone Books.

Keller, D. A., Koch, M., & Selle, K. (Eds.). (1993). Special Issue on Planning Cultures in Europe. *disP— The Planning Review, 29(115).*

Keller, D. A., Koch, M., & Selle, K. (1996). 'Either/or' and 'and': First Impressions into a Journey into the Planning Cultures of Four Countries. *Planning Perspectives, 11*, 41–54.

Paauw, D. S., & Fei, J. (1975). *The Transition in Open Dualistic Economies: Theory and Southeast Asian Experience.* New Haven, CT: Yale University Press.

Peattie, L. (1970). *View from the Barrio.* Ann Arbor: University of Michigan Press.

Peattie, L. (1987). *Rethinking Ciudad Guayana.* Ann Arbor, MI: University of Michigan Press.

Robinson, J. (2006). *Ordinary Cities: Between Modernity and Development.* London: Routledge.

Rodwin, L., & Associates. (1969). *Planning Growth and Regional Development: The Experience of the Guayana Program in Venezuela.* Cambridge, MA: MIT Press.

Rorty, R. (1979). *Philosophy and the Mirror of Nature.* Princeton, NJ: Princeton University Press.

Sandercock, L. (2010a). From the Campfire to the Computer: An Epistemology of Multiplicity and the Story-turn in Planning. In L. Sandercock & G. Attili (Eds.), *Multimedia Explorations Urban Policy and Planning: Beyond the Flatlands* (pp. 17–38). Dordrecht: Springer.

Sandercock, L. (2010b). Mobilizing the Human Spirit: An Experiment in Film as Social Research, Community Engagement and Policy Dialogue. In L. Sandercock & G. Attili (Eds.), *Multimedia Explorations Urban Policy and Planning: Beyond the Flatlands* (pp. 57–84). Dordrecht: Springer.

Sanyal, B. (Ed.). (2005). *Comparative Planning Cultures.* New York: Routledge.

Weber, M. (1946). Politics as a Vocation. In H. H. Gerth & C. Wright Mills (Eds.), *From Max Weber: Essays in Sociology* (pp. 77–128). New York, NY: Oxford University Press.

4

FROM UTOPIAN AND REALISTIC TO TRANSFORMATIVE PLANNING

Peter Marcuse

My path to a career in urban planning had many bends and did not start professionally till midlife, but I believe began to head that way much earlier. Looking back on it, I see a running tension between a desire to change the world in a big way and a need to find a specific role in that process where I could make a concrete contribution, necessarily with much more limited objectives but based on a professional activity in which I would find satisfaction and have some claim to credentials in the effort.

Personal Background

My course was undoubtedly colored by my background as a child, emigrating from Nazi Germany (I was born in 1928 and emigrated to New York City in 1933 via Zurich and Paris), and the wartime experience in a family heavily involved in the wartime struggle against fascism from the vantage point of the United States. In college the atmosphere was strongly antifascist, with a focus on the possibilities of a new world after the end of the war. I focused on issues of social justice and wanted to get into politics to make a difference. After a summer 1948 trip to a Europe recovering from the war, I concluded that my role was at home and in politics, thought a law degree would help, and entered and graduated from Yale Law School in 1952. I then stayed in private practice law, with a few side steps, for 20 years.

Immediately after graduating, I served as director of research for the Connecticut State legislature's Temporary Commission on Housing, helping make the argument for fair housing legislation, writing a report strongly advocating such legislation for the state. It passed. As a lawyer, I then got a job with the attorney for the Connecticut State AFL-CIO Labor Council in Waterbury, Connecticut, an industrial town then the center of the brass industry in the Naugatuck River valley. I did labor, workmen's compensation, civil rights, and civil liberties work, and represented defendants in civil rights–tinged criminal cases. I represented labor unions, helped incorporate a nonprofit housing corporation, and helped develop private inter-racial housing in the city.

36 Peter Marcuse

I was active in local politics and was elected to the board of aldermen, and I promoted public planning and affordable housing. In Freedom Summer (a major program of the civil rights organizations in 1964, to send useful northerners south to help in the desegregation and voting rights efforts there) I went south briefly, to Mississippi, with the Lawyers Constitutional Defense Committee, and later I litigated racial gerrymandering cases in Alabama. Back in Waterbury, I helped organize New Opportunities for Waterbury, the city's antipoverty agency, and became its chair. Defeated for the board of aldermen, I was appointed to the city planning commission.

By the 1970s deindustrialization was taking its toll, the brass industry relocated west, and the civil rights movement was stabilizing. Through my service on the planning commission, I became more interested in the planning field, which seemed to combine my interests in housing and civil rights—the labor part of my practice was becoming less fruitful as the large brass manufacturing plants moved. I enrolled in Yale's planning program part time and got a master's in urban studies there in 1967.

Thinking it over, I decided professional knowledge of planning substance as well as legal forms was a useful new direction to go in, left my law firm, and entered the newly funded social policy planning program at the University of California at Berkeley's Department of City and Regional Planning, where I got a PhD in planning in 1975.

My Career in Planning

That began an entirely new career for me, professionally, although carrying forward the same value-laden political concerns I had from earlier work. If one categorizes, as I later did (Marcuse, 2011), the main currents in planning in which I was involved, and presents them in the order they appeared in the history of planning, although not in my own evolution where they largely ran concurrently, they would be as follow:

I. The current in planning history, utopian, broadly political and socially liberal (nineteenth-century)
II. Technical/mainstream urban planning, housing–technicist (first half twentieth century on)
III. Social planning, broadly liberal (1945 on)
IV. Critical/radical/transformative (1973 on)

Intellectually, my approach to planning evolved in a way ahistorically, not recapitulating the historical development in my personal chronology. The first paper I ever wrote, as my high school thesis in 1943, was on Sir Thomas More's *Utopia*. From there it went schematically, seeing the law as a route to radical social transformation; that proving abortive in the 1960s turning to social policy as an alternative personal route; realizing the importance of technical competence as a way of legitimizing a role in ongoing social movements; ending with the conviction that radical transformative approaches were what would in reality be most productive.

How that did or did not play out over time the following chronological account will show!

The program at Berkeley, my formal entry into the planning field full time, was clearly within the social liberal (III above) current and responded to an upwelling of liberal (in the US sense, not the European) and radical activity in the mid-sixties, putting together issues about which I had always been concerned—labor, civil rights, social justice, peace, public space,

From Utopia to Transformative Planning **37**

segregation—but in a reformist framework. The radical was reflected more in the militancy of street activities than in the organized pursuit of radical or utopian goals. I have only now begun to be clear in my own mind what the basic difference between liberal and radical or critical planning really is (see below). Herb Gans and Paul Davidoff were my heroes. The founding of Planners for Equal Opportunity, of which I was an early member (Thabit, 1999), made socially oriented planning a high-profile issue within the then American Institute of Planners, the professional organization of planners.

My dissertation for the PhD at Berkeley was on a then newly developing aspect of the federal public housing program, trying to adapt the existing structure of public rental housing to also produce single-family homeownership opportunities for lower income households. My position tried both to suggest how that might be accomplished, and yet to put a major emphasis on its limitations. It somewhat gingerly put forward a radical critique of the focus on homeownership as an end in itself that underlay so much of US housing policy from the beginning.

I was never seriously interested in the dominant technical aspects of planning, those dominated by architects and largely focused on physical design, transportation or building engineers, or quantitative evaluators. While at Berkeley, I worked at the University's Housing Law Project, an antipoverty-funded technical assistance project targeted at technical assistance for legal services attorneys doing housing-related work; "law" and housing were my technical fields of specialization within the broad field of planning.

The first piece I published in a professional planning journal (Marcuse, 1976) was based on my experience in practicing law, where I had instituted a Friday afternoon required session in our law firm, dealing with issues in legal ethics as they might be involved in any of the various cases our firm handled. The piece was entitled "Professional Ethics and Beyond" and compared the ethical requirements imposed on lawyers with the—I thought much fuzzier but more socially oriented—requirements adopted by planners for their own professional self-regulation.

My first job after getting my PhD was in the planning program at the University of California at Los Angeles, then under the progressive deanship of Harvey Perloff. I was able to put into practice my hope to have direct political influence, at least on the social direction of urban planning, by getting into Tom Bradley's campaign for mayor of Los Angeles, the first by a person of color, and I wrote several speeches for him. I was subsequently appointed to the Los Angeles City Planning Commission and a year later elected its president. But I was disappointed in what I was actually able to accomplish in that role. The activities of our commission largely consisted of hearings on various developers' proposals for suburban-type divisions in the San Fernando Valley in northern LA, and very superficial contact with the professional work of the staff on the new city plan, which amounted primarily to the formulation of a physical plan for multiple nuclei for the business districts of the spread-out city. The limits of the technical approach to planning involved in the commission's work became increasingly clear. The big issues were all political, not technical. The commission was only tangentially involved. The debates around the plan's passage, such as there were, took place in the city council.

The period was one in which new ideas were bubbling around Lyndon Johnson's War on Poverty, which he had rushed through Congress in the aftermath of John F. Kennedy's assassination. Social policy planning was seen in that context as a legitimate arena for technically trained planners; "maximum feasible participation of the poor" was a guiding principle of the US federal government. I had had experience with the process in my political role back in

Waterbury, and it had helped get me into the PhD program designed to teach it at Berkeley. But it remained a subsidiary and struggling field within professional planning circles and was largely simply grafted onto existing modes of work and thinking.

When I began my first job teaching planning in 1972, at UCLA, I pushed to move the substance of planning away from a what I later called the technicist approach to planning—seeing planning as a tool whose perfection was an end in itself—to one that saw planning as one means to a good society, cities being perhaps a key physical manifestation of what that society might look like. John Friedmann ran a course called "The Good Society," and I thought that was the right way to go. It was not a utopian approach, in the sense of the utopian current mentioned above, but rather a development of Berkeley's social policy approach, trying to portray its result within the existing structures of society.

The crucial point in the evolution of my thinking about planning and the social role of its professional activity came in 1975, with the publication of two books: David Harvey's *Social Justice and the City,* and Manuel Castells's *The Urban Question,* linked, although at that time not so obviously, to the work of Henri Lefebvre. Harvey and the early Castells made clear to me the broader link between the kinds of political questions, generally about social justice, and the details of what the planning profession could accomplish. They suggested the outlines, at least, of what a radical, transformative, verging on the utopian set of guiding principles for good planning might look like.

The story from there on is one in which the changes, issues, programs, and actions in the wider field of urban development and social change interacted with this evolution of my own thinking and actions.

The early '70s were a time of real ferment within the planning field. The '60s had seen action in the streets and a direct link between broad political action, social movement organization, and radical theories. As the militant strength of the, generally New Left–related, activist-increased effort was increasingly met by a conservative counteroffensive, the thrust of social justice efforts in planning became more focused on narrower but more concrete issues, and my work followed suit. That tension was visible everywhere. California and New York were positioned on the very liberal end of it.

When, for family reasons, I decided to return to the East Coast in 1975, I was offered a job as chair of the planning program at Columbia University, I believe primarily for my potential to bring Columbia's program into the swing of the then still vibrant movement towards progressive social and political engagement. I believe my planning-related activities then began to move in two directions: One was deepening my competence and contribution to actual liberal planning policies, the technical current, the other was exploring theoretically the more utopian potentials of planning, with some focus on planning history and comparative international planning practices. In the terms of the sketch of the historic currents in planning suggested at the beginning of this paper—the utopian, technical, liberal, and radical—I sought to combine the technical with the liberal in part of my activities, and to move towards the critical with the other, more theoretical, part.

On the more theoretical end of the critical, I had the opportunity to conduct a Ford Foundation–subsidized tour of German housing developments shortly after my return to New York City, and it began a lifelong interest in comparative housing policy and the history of governmental housing policies around the world. It resulted in an article that received fairly wide attention (Marcuse, 1978), which argued, critically I thought, that housing policy was rarely the result of the benevolence of rulers, but rather it served other purposes for those in power, from social stability to economic needs to the protection of public health in private housing.

The importance of paying attention to the technical component of planning was clear. I had written about rent control, and made friends with rent control advocates in the tenants' movement. I was thus (I believe) retained to do a major research study on rent regulation for the city, and I developed the figures for the city's 1978 Report on Housing Conditions based on the Census Bureau's Housing and Vacancy Study, a detailed on-the-ground survey of 18,000 households in New York, with careful statistical tabulation of the results. It was my task to write up those results in language understandable to the city's legislative body and executive. I relied on a colleague to do the heavy statistical work, calculate margins of error for each tabulation, etc., but I framed the results in what I felt to be policy-relevant terms: Were high rents a particular burden on low-income households? On minority households? Did they require them to move more often? Were such households in disproportionately low-income and high-minority districts, i.e., segregated? Did increases in rents exceed increases in the rate of inflation and in cost-of-living indexes? The report was, as might be expected, well received by liberal politicians and tenant advocates, but neglected by landlords' groups.

Other technical but policy-related work followed, some at the request of government agencies or advocacy groups, or independently funded. The work consciously reflected my understanding of the most critical issues facing low-income and minority households in New York City.

The housing shortage and its relation to the level of rents had led to the work for the city on rent control. It also intersected with what was developing as a major problem, not only in New York City but also elsewhere: the outright abandonment of older housing in neighborhoods where the ability to pay profit-producing rents was simply lacking. Many blamed rent control for the result, and I developed a theoretical analysis of the relationship between rent control and housing abandonment that played something of a role in both the political fight to keep rent control and the theoretical debates about abandonment, where I pressed the critical view that it was a logical result of a housing market distributing housing based solely on the market and the ability to pay (Marcuse, 1982). The practical and the theoretical went nicely hand in hand.

As the economy recovered and investment returned to areas of abandonment, the process of gentrification became prominent, and my work followed suit. On the technical end, I was able to use my legal background to develop practical recommendations for legislation dealing with the displacement that was a hallmark of gentrification. Theoretically and critically, I was able to relate it, including its location, to the longer historical process of residential development in New York City, incorporating also theoretical work of Neil Smith on the nature of gentrification (Marcuse, 1985).

The interest in tenant participation in housing and its purposes combined with the broader interest in social change that had led me to planning to begin with both led me to look for ways of combining technical competence with political action. New York City had a system of community boards, one in each of the city's 56 community planning districts, in which 50 local or locally employed residents were named by elected city officials to a board that was given broad scope to examine neighborhood planning issues, although with limited formal power to do more than recommend for or against desired land-use related changes and express the community's priorities for other city community-related actions. I was appointed

40 Peter Marcuse

a member of Community Board 9 Manhattan, the district in which Columbia University was located.

The community board work was very hands-on in terms of practical politics, but it raised interesting questions about citizen participation in planning, and more broadly and critically, how planning and governmental action generally might be made more democratic and responsive to informed citizen input. It resulted in some published articles but also influenced my teaching, particularly in the direction of encouraging students to become directly involved in the planning controversies of their neighborhood, and in class studios we developed some zoning proposals that had a strong social justice orientation.

International Work

When a sabbatical came up I had the opportunity to get a Fulbright grant for a year's study abroad, and I had to resign from the community board to do so. Spending most of the year in Germany and becoming familiar with its approaches to planning and housing provision was an eye-opener and perhaps led to an important twist in my approach to planning. On the one hand, the German lesson illustrated the crucial role of national-level policy, both in planning and in economic development, for all actions dealing with physical, social, and economic development. At the same time, however, it forced a realization of the limited ability of technically refined planning measures to produce social justice.

That first German experience thus fed into a gnawing set of doubts about the usefulness of professional planning in the long run. Clearly planning could accomplish important changes, in the short run, that could make many people's lives better, could promote social justice, could protect the environment, could influence (although here doubts increased) economic development. But its influence on the big picture was limited.

To get a closer look at what big-picture changes might mean for planning and social justice, we were able to spend a year in the German Democratic Republic, East Germany, in 1989–1990, the year of Gorbachev in the Soviet Union, Honecker in the GDR, and then the big shift back to West Germany's more familiar and conventional policies when the wall came down. The lesson was the same: The big picture determines the little picture; planning plays an important but realistically subsidiary role in what happens.

Broader international experience strengthened that realization, particularly watching events from a visiting position at the University of the Witwatersrand in South Africa a bit later, the year Mandela was sworn in as president after being released from prison. Apartheid had stark planning consequences; planning was a negligible tool in altering it. And its independent role in changing the political climate was not remarkable.

The growing professional discussions on the role of globalization increased the sense of the limited role of technical solutions in the solution of societal problems, particularly those involving social justice. Social science research increasingly made clear the major role that global events and global relations played in determining national and, it was increasingly clear, local policies, including those affecting the built environment, planning's bread and butter. Planning was only a bit player in a global world, and addressing global issues with the tools of planning was not very productive. When I published a piece dealing with the relationship, I referred to the danger of glossy globalization (Marcuse, 1997) and spoke of the abdication of any effort on the part of planning to bend its arc in the direction of social justice

(Marcuse, 1983). "Technicist" is perhaps a bastard word, but I use it to denote that approach that sees technical competence as an end in itself, and leaves the determination of the goals it is to serve to others, without question and without concern.

Yet planning was on the right side of things, and there was always an element impacting social justice in everything in it. The profession has always had these two currents, the technical and the social, reflected in the division between conventional planning, on the one hand—increasingly sophisticated in its technical tools, its professionalization, the scope of the activities in which it claimed a role—while guiltily recognizing the importance of social justice, if only as an overlay, on the other.

I have traveled widely in my career as best I could, exploring issues of social justice and their global ramifications in countries on all five continents. In 2003 I retired from full-time teaching at Columbia, but I have remained active in campaigns around housing and planning issues, most recently campaigns to explore the possibilities of (1) community land trusts in housing and (2) participatory budgeting in capital planning. I have also turned to more theoretical work focusing on the ethics of the planning profession and more broadly on strategies for transformative social change through social policy and social movement organization.

The field of planning has changed dramatically in the last three-score years, but it has done so in response to major changes in the social, economic, technological, and cultural structure of society.[1] I would see the turning point being in the 1960s, with a deepening of those changes shortly after the turn of the century. Before World War II and its immediate aftermath, the crucial lines of cleavage and conflict in the industrially advanced countries were around the workplace: wages, hours of work, unionization, job security, seniority. Planning was not directly involved in them, to the extent that it affected the costs of living for employees, i.e., housing costs, health conditions, location, and related transportation costs, most directly, and recreation indirectly.

As manufacturing developed technologically, both in advances in automation and manufacturing processes themselves and in the organization of production, and as the increasing concentration of capital and transportation and communication developed and produced the newly technically feasible globalization of production, the nature of workplace conflicts also changed. Wages, the brutally concrete conditions of labor, continued to be a flash point, but dissatisfaction with the impact of working relations on the broader aspirations of workers, and particularly of young people and students, also changed. Material relations improved, and the issues began to revolve more around developmental opportunities; the freedom of personal development, choice, and study; and the desire to live a full life outside of the workplace itself (as well as within it). For those with the social concerns that had prompted many to become involved in labor-based issues and direct political action—e.g., around the war against fascism and then the war in Vietnam, and in combination with the possibilities of direct action for broad social change—planning was a dependent interest, interesting not so much for its inherent importance but rather because of its relation to these other broader concerns.

Planning, Politics, and Social Change

But the links between the concerns of planning and those of broader social change grew steadily stronger in the 1960s/1970s. The civil rights movement was a clear arena for involvement with those issues. Residential segregation was an important issue in racial injustice, as was

42 Peter Marcuse

workplace discrimination. Housing and planning moved from specialized concerns involving narrow issues, to some extent appropriately left to architects and engineers and public administrators, to being a field of social conflict, and many young people moved into planning for that reason.

A related development was the increasing importance of planning-related issues. As the productivity of the economic system grew rapidly, based on technical progress, globalization of organization and control, and the slow elimination of abject poverty and the harshest forms of material need and social control, the path to improvement for the wide majority seemed open. It seemed to lie along the lines of individual betterment, increased availability of consumer goods (made available to all), and increased urban life possibilities outside the workplace and in the community. In many situations globally, community control and individual autonomy, rather than influence on working conditions, seemed a more immediately feasible path to betterment. The emphasis on what was important in life shifted from the factory to the home and the community, from the economic to the social relations of production, from production to distribution.

The shifting focus of social concerns, and with it the shifting ways in which action for social change could be organized, changed as a consequence. The workplace had formed a natural base for social organization for change. Outside of the workplace, the place to pursue individual progress seemed ever more individual, in the private pursuit of prosperity, affluence, material goods, and material relations. The deep dissatisfactions with the restrictions of the workplace in the highly productive advances of mass production, frustrated by the difficulties of workplace organization, were diverted to issues of life outside of work, in residential rather than workplace communities. That shifted the focus of efforts for fundamental social change from the workplace to the community, and for some seeking a professional path into involvement in social change, a shift from labor support to community support, and thus to involvement in planning, specifically urban planning, as in the developments of the '60s and '70s, cities themselves were shown to be where the action was.

Thus I would see the '60s and '70s as a major turning point in the field of battle, and one in which the tools of planning could play an increasingly important role as residential life, on top of and often subtly replacing the activities of working life, became more and more vital for more and more people. It was a shift from the starkly material to the broader psychological, moving the sites of social interaction from the factory to the community. In terms of social psychology, it was reflected in the separation out of collective concerns from individual hopes and aspirations, and thus the increasing one-dimensionality of the individual as a social being.[2]

The second turning point—actually less a turning point than a sharp new influence on the changes already underway—was the growing role of consumption as an economic force, and of the built environment, and particularly its residential and consumption-related uses, as a locus of investment. As the possibilities of profit in manufacturing, and more broadly in production, were more and more fully exploited through technical advances and globalized operations and control, new avenues for investment of the profits being produced were pursued.[3] The built environment provided a major opportunity in two areas, both relevant to planning. One was in investment in land appropriate for commercial/business use, particularly for financial sector firms. The other was in residential housing, where demand could not only be stimulated by extensive direct and indirect advertising and media presentations, but also fostered by extending credit, where profit could be made not only on the sale of the item being financed but also on the receipt of interest payments on the amounts loaned, and potentially on the resale of the financed property if there was a default on those payments. The interest of the real estate industry in the large and continuing increase in housing, fueled by extensive speculation, was a natural part of this picture, with an increasingly important role in the process of financialization in the most industrially developed countries.

Planning had a significant role to play here, but the question was for whom, in what direction. Local government generally played a supportive role to the industry, providing infrastructure, zoning permissions, transportation accessibility through roads and mass transit, and favorable discretionary decisions fostering profitable development. The boom in megaprojects is one result. The real estate industry, broadly defined, played an increasingly prominent role not only in influencing specific planning decisions, but also in electing local governments basically supportive of their quest for growth, essentially largely convincing the local leadership to equate economic growth with desirable cities and successful political leadership. National government, on the other hand, was seen by the local real estate players in a different light. Its role was largely regulatory, particularly when an economic crisis fixed attention on the role of national forces in banking and financing and development. National government had been responsive to strong public pressure to help subsidize the meeting of social needs, for instance in the provision of affordable housing, infrastructure, and welfare policies. But that kind of investment more often than not got in the way of other uses of such funds, as when it went to publicly owned housing for poor households rather than guaranteeing risky mortgages for middle-income households. And it was of course financed by taxes with an element of progressivity, increasing the business community's opposition.

Putting all this together, the dominant private powers adopted a clear political policy approach: Shift power away from the federal government to local government, decrease the public regulation of private market–determined development and trading in investment in the built environment, and in general downplay the usefulness and even legitimacy of the intervention of government in private building (commercial and residential) activities in the built environment.

Thus public planning became a conflict-laden activity, in which problems were generally not defined as how to produce the "best" plans for the public good, for the benefit of users and the implementation of social justice, with all participants looking to technical knowledge and experience to provide answers. Instead, planning was an arena of conflict, a constant clash of interests between private and public, between business profit-seeking and individual human-development-seeking, between valuing exchange values versus use values. And this is where the formal activity of planning as it is of necessity engaged in, willy-nilly, by the majority of planners, is today.

Planners themselves have not been merely passive observers of these conflicts. The clash of interests into which their work took them produced reactions among them. Urban inhabitants were not all quiet victims of what other forces imposed on them and their neighborhoods, but they rallied against many of the most obvious pains inflicted in the process, from the imposition of unaffordable costs on such adequate housing as was available to them, to the resistance to displacement, whether by urban renewal or gentrification. Community control and participatory decision making was a popular and articulate goal. Conflicts of interests were brought out into the open, and planners found themselves in the middle of the shifting balance that the four major currents in planning outlined at the beginning of this account reflect—the balance among the utopian, the technical, the social/liberal, and the radical/transformative, reflecting the impact of conflicts of forces far larger than those that planners work with in their everyday practices. But they need to take positions in these conflicts, and work out how their own work can influence them, if they are to be true to their profession's potential for human betterment.

Some Prosaic Practical Suggestions

Urban planning attracts many young people to it as a way of improving the world, and particularly urban life, through focused thought and professional competence, combining theory with practice, with social justice a leading value. I certainly came to the field with that expectation, and what follows is addressed to those with a similar orientation.

1. Realize that planning is a very diverse field, and that the technical capacity, the skills you have honed, the principles you have professed, the results you have hoped to accomplish, are those of "planning" writ large; that the field is not homogeneous; that it is not moving smoothly from one new approach to the next as its practitioners learn from the experiences they have gained in practice or the ideas they have garnered from the study of theory. Planning, indeed, has a progressive social core, but its manifestation is often subdued under pressure of circumstances beyond its control.

Planning is thus a field in which there are large differences in the tasks undertaken, the skills needed, the technical knowledge required. But there are also often huge differences in the clients served, the goals pursued, the freedom allowed to the planner, and the scope of the work. Its social heart may be constantly throbbing, but its arms and legs may go in their own directions.

Each planner's role will depend on a number of factors, which can be named and recognized at the outset of a career and kept in mind throughout it. Key, to put it crudely, is the simple question of the client, who is paying for the work the planner is to do. Government agencies have a set of expectations, and government agencies may well disagree with each other, their political leaders with their technical staffs, their old-timers with their younger entrants, those with different beliefs and backgrounds with each other. Private developers have quite different agendas, different roles to play, different definitions of goals to be achieved—in general, the work will be much more market dependent and will be evaluated in the market rather than—although not necessarily in conflict with—by social concerns. Nonprofit clients will have different expectations from profit-oriented ones, community-based or advocacy clients from charitable ones.

Realize that planning should not be a peaceful career.

2. All clients will look for professional competence and professional conduct in any planner they pay. The minimum standards and rules of conduct for professional planners are embodied, for the United States, in the AICP's Code of Ethics and Rules of Conduct (more on that below). Some specialization is useful, but planning is a broad field, and the details of what is needed for any particular work will likely be learned on the job; knowing where to look and how to learn is an essential part of a planner's work.

3. But if young people are attracted to planning with the hope of contributing something positive to society, including a basic concern for values such as social justice, environmental quality, the desire to make the built environment respond well to basic social needs, then they have an additional burden beyond meeting the standards of the AICP Rules of Conduct. The AICP Code of Ethics also speaks of such values as aspirations of the planner. And indeed they should be. But they are only variably observed, and not in a way enforced by the profession if ignored.

4. But then what does it mean if these aspirations are to be part of the actual work of a planner? What I have learned is that it is a deceptively easy thing to do in any simple case, if seen within the context of what a planner can realistically accomplish. It simply means that at the beginning, when controversies exist as to basic values, the planner should be on the right side, and should try to push the inevitable compromises in the direction of his or her values, pressing to make socially oriented aspirations binding and enforceable.

That's all rather pragmatic, rather than theoretical or philosophic, advice. When we get to its linkage to the substance of what planners do, or try to do, the picture becomes more complicated and relies more on an extensive background analysis of the role of what the planner is doing in the real world of social justice, economic prosperity, environmental quality, and human values. I would summarize my personal conclusions on what the content of planning should be, and what the planner should strive to do in whatever capacity and by whomever he or she is employed, in one word: *transformation*.

Conclusion: Transformational Planning Is Needed, with Some Examples

Returning to the opening taxonomy of the four key currents in planning, the term *transformative planning* needs some explication.

Reluctantly, I have realized over the course of my career that there is no easy relationship between, on the one hand, the insights I pursued in my most interesting writings, which tend to explore rather critical views of that which is, and, on the other hand, what can actually be accomplished in terms of daily practice in the real world. In academia, it is analogous to the split between the content of most of the courses we teach "about" planning, and the studio we run in which we try to "do," on a small scale, actual planning. The two have often, in my own experience, run on parallel tracks—parallel in the sense of moving in the same direction but never meeting. The theoretical work can be both more interesting and more illuminating than the day-to-day run of professional planning, and even its advocacy and policy and political aspects are dealt with more theoretically than in practice. The problem has a directly political aspect; it will be in the more theoretical aspect that what is critical and radical politically will emerge, an aspect that can simply be put aside as an annoying, irrelevant distraction in real-life practice.

Yet leaving the theoretical, the historical, analytic, value-laden, perhaps philosophic, to develop without relation to the day-to-day work might be an indication of the need to find a different line of work, where principles can play a bigger role. I think that is an honest but wrong conclusion.

Rather, I think the principled planner (to whom this is addressed) can see, in almost anything he or she does, the outline of what more really needs doing, of what beyond the immediately

46 Peter Marcuse

feasible is the ultimately desirable, what principle would dictate really should be. That involves bringing out the hidden dimension of the alternatives underlying the one dimension of the actual. And then shaping the actual and realistic goal so that it points in the direction of the hidden dimension, the ultimately desirable, and makes them visible—puts them into play, even if they are not currently implementable. I would consider such an approach, combining doing what can be done now with raising what should be done in the future, transformative planning. I commend the approach.

I call this "transformative planning" and locate it, on the opening paradigm, between the social/liberal and the critical/radical.

Planning practice can thus have a broader educational and political impact in moving towards, although not achieving, the ultimate goal. Such transformative planning aims at immediate results but opens a door to the future pursuit of what more is critically needed, keeping the image of that ultimate goal as the second dimension of the one-dimensional world[4] to which day-to-day practice is in danger of confining us. It takes the trite adage "the best is the enemy of the better" and makes it read "the best is at the heart of the better" (see Marcuse, 2009). It does so while actively pursuing the good and the better.

Some brief examples, from current issues in the United States follow.[5]

Community land trusts (CLTs): A shortage of decent housing affordable for families of low income is perennial, is inherent in the way housing is produced and distributed in a largely unregulated market economy (critical theory tells us). It becomes acute in times of economic crisis, when mortgage foreclosures surge and homelessness becomes more widely visible. The immediate answer is to deal with foreclosures and evictions, to modify the terms of mortgages, to limit rents for poor households, to have government intervene to modify the pain and suffering caused. Planning can play an important role in developing an efficient and fair process for such modifications. But ultimately the problem is deeper. At least one important part of it is speculation in land, and its relationship to the housing bubble that incubated the crisis.

One proposal is to create community land trusts to take ownership of the housing involved. CLTs are entities that are controlled by residents and neighbors and sympathetic friends, advocates, and officials, as a nonprofit vehicle into which title to foreclosed-on properties, or rental properties economically unfeasible at affordable rents and often in tax arrears, can be transferred. The trust separates ownership of the land from that of the building(s) on it, leases the land to residents needing housing, or sells the right to build on it to potential needy residents, with restrictions on resale.

It is a workable idea that can make an immediate contribution to addressing a severe immediate problem, and it deserves all the support from planners that it can get. But principled planners know that the problem is deeper. Their critical analysis tells them that the ideal of individual homeownership in single family housing as the American ideal is treacherous, ultimately unjust, environmentally unsustainable, and economically inefficient. They can point this out as they work on developing community land trusts. In obtaining support for the idea, on the ground, they can point out its immediate advantages in expanding the availability of affordable housing. But they can also point out that ultimately the system needs changing. They can point out, as they sell the concept, that really land is in limited supply, its value is socially created, and making profits on its sale and resale has no economic or moral justification. They can point out that an active public role in determining land uses can be both more efficient than the prevailing market-based system, and can pursue goals of social justice that the market does not pursue. Done well, that might be transformative, with practical results in future debates.

Rent control: In many places local laws address the problem of maintaining an adequate supply of affordable housing by regulating the level of rents and rent increases. Planners play an important role in developing formulas to calculate limits, relating them to cost of living increases, management costs, utilities costs, landlords' profit levels, etc. They also use theoretical work to deal with arguments that rent controls reduce the housing supply, unfairly restrict landlord profits, etc.

But ultimately the problem is more complex, in both areas. Would fixing the limits, which now permit appeals from restrictive limits when landlord incomes are kept so low that they result in losses to landlords, not also take into account tenants' incomes, and hold rent levels low to keep tenants from going broke or homeless? But raising that question transcends the limits of the immediate debate and opens the door to the question of the justification for the private provision of housing as a vehicle for profit, including growing profit for the financial sector, and the question of the role of government. Is there or should there be a legal and enforceable right to housing, and if so what is the role for private profit-making in housing? Again, done well, that might be transformative, with practical results in future debates.

Participatory budgeting: Governmental budgets, almost universally, are decided on through a representative process, at the highest level of whatever governmental entity is involved for the given jurisdiction. Participatory budgeting is a scheme to bring decision making on specific parts of such budgets down to the grassroots level, to permit thoughtful and informed public participation in how much should be spent on what. At least in the United States, it has been limited to capital expenditures, and then only in specific areas or up to specific dollar amounts. In New York City, it applies only to a small portion of the capital budget, and each city council member is given wide discretion on expenditures. Community groups, at carefully structured assemblies and work sessions, present proposals and residents examine them, debate them, and set priorities, which are important inputs into final decisions as to the amounts involved. Planners clearly have a practical role to play in evaluating proposals and informing discussions about their merits or defects.

But ultimately the problem is a broader one. How can key governmental decisions, and not only budgetary ones, be democratically resolved with real power in the hands of an informed citizenry? The practical problems are severe: How can one efficiently involve, presumably, some 8,000,000 residents, or any sizable fraction of them, in debates that normally take hours, days, and months of the time in the city councils and legislative bodies that currently make the decisions? Facilitation of the process is a challenge for professional planners, who are just learning their roles in the process. But shouldn't it in fact be applicable to all budgetary decisions, and even, ultimately, to all public decisions in a true democracy? Doesn't it involve challenges to the existing distribution of power and control that will be bitterly contested, and involve not only conflicts of interest but of principles and moral values as well? Again, opening the door to such questions, done well, might be transformative, with practical results in future debates.

Professional ethics in planning: If planning is a true profession, it will have, and must have, and does have, a code of ethics governing its members' conduct. In the United States the American Planning Association and American Institute of Carried Planners do indeed have such a code, with rules of conduct governing the professional behavior of its members, requiring them to avoid misrepresenting their competencies, to faithfully serve their clients, to be honorable in completion with other planners, present information transparently and fully, and avoid

48 Peter Marcuse

conflicts of interests. Planners in practice have paid attention to developing those rules and debated their contents and the procedures for their enforcement.

So ultimately the problem is a broader one. The code also contains provisions under the heading of "Aspirations," a statement of principles, such as to serve the public interest, protect the environment, provide opportunities for those that have the least, etc. These are not rules of conduct, and there is no provision for enforcement; they are statements of broad goals, aspirations. Should they be spelled out and made binding? Should they be allowed effectively to limit substantively what planners might work on, what goals their plans should pursue? Difficult questions. The South African national organizations of planners and architects debated long and hard as to whether their members should participate in the planning of segregated African townships. Raising questions, for instance, around gated communities in the United States, which efficiently segregate by income and implicitly if indirectly by color, can make life very uncomfortable for planners and for citizens. When the issue was raised about Israeli planners planning settlements in the West Bank, it provoked heated but healthy debates here. Again, opening the door to such questions, done well, might be transformative, with practical results in future debates.

Final Thoughts

Planning is a wonderful profession. It is perhaps the only profession for which service of the public good is the direct and explicit primary goal of the professional activity itself. Other professions certainly see their work as also serving the public good. Law, for instance, can certainly be used to serve the public good, and the judicial system is certainly designed to serve that end. But what an individual lawyer does as a lawyer may or may not go in that direction; for many, it is simply irrelevant. It is the particular client that must be served. In what other profession could you imagine a requirement that, when the work is done, it must be delivered with an environmental impact assessment, let alone a social welfare assessment? Philosophy, in the classic tradition, also aims to understand and further the good life, but only as theory. For planning that ought to be the goal of all action.

Planning still has a way to go to make good on its aspirations, both in its theory and its practice. It won't reach its full potential in the short term, and getting there will be a perhaps permanently ongoing process. The conditions making it possible for it to advance toward its objectives are conditions over many of which planning has little influence; planners need to be modest in the acknowledgement of their limitations. But one makes the path by walking. And planners are, after all, citizens as well as planners, and as such they can not only inform the political processes but play a role in them directly, and they should do so.

Planning is a tool that contains its own goal. Its underlying goal is, at least as I see it, to help develop the built environment, with all its social, economic, and political aspects, in the direction of full development of human capacities and human lives in a sustainable natural environment with social justice as a guiding principal. Planning will still need a lot of pushing and shoving, theoretical clarity, and practical experience to move steadily in that direction, but it's the right way to go.

Young planners will not always have an easy time of it, but if they keep their principles and those underlying their profession and pursue them in both theory and practice, they'll always be on the right side of events.

As to advice for young planners: Plan what you can, fight for what's right, be proud of your profession and keep it something to be proud of—and enjoy!

Notes

1 Obviously, there is a whole range of developments in the post–World War II period for which much more room than available here is needed. Most conspicuous by their absence seems to me political developments in the political sphere related to the Cold War, the dominance and decline of the threat of radical change from inside or outside, the growing importance of environmental dangers, and the directions of intellectual and cultural change. But I believe what is described as follows is fundamental, if not complete, to describe the changes in the context in which planning and planning thought has operated.
2 I assume the influence of my father's work, particularly Herbert Marcuse, *One-Dimensional Man, Essay on Liberation,* and other writings, is apparent!
3 The following argument obviously owes a major debt, directly, to the work of David Harvey and indirectly to many others working along similar lines.
4 That concept of course harkens back to Herbert Marcuse's *One-Dimensional Man.*
5 See my Blog #30 Transformative Proposals in Nine Areas at https://pmarcuse.wordpress.com for other examples.

References

Castells, M. (1979). *The Urban Question: A Marxist Approach.* Cambridge, MA: MIT Press.
Harvey, D. (1973). *Social Justice and the City.* Athens, GA: University of Georgia Press.
Marcuse, H. (1964). *One-Dimensional Man: Studies in the Ideology of Advanced Industrial Society.* Boston: Beacon Press
Marcuse, H. (1969). *An Essay on Liberation.* Boston: Beacon Press.
Marcuse, P. (1976). Professional Ethics and Beyond: Values in Planning. *Journal of the American Institute of Planners, Vol. 42, No. 31,* 264–274.
Marcuse, P. (1978). Housing Policy and the Myth of the Benevolent State. Social Policy, Jan-Feb., pp. 248–263. Reprinted in R. Montgomery & Mandelker, D. (Eds.). (1979). *Housing in America: Problems and Perspectives.* Indianapolis: Bobbs-Merrill and in R. Bratt, Hartman, Ch. & Meyerson, A. (Eds.). (1986). *Critical Perspectives on Housing.* Philadelphia: Temple University Press.
Marcuse, P. (1982). Housing Abandonment: Does Rent Control Make a Difference? Paper presented at Conference on Alternative State and Local Policies. Washington, DC.
Marcuse, P. (1983). On the Feeble Retreat of Planning. *Journal of Planning Education and Research, Vol. 3, No. 1, Summer,* 52–53.
Marcuse, P. (1985). Gentrification, Abandonment, and Displacement: Connections, Causes, and Policy Responses in New York City. *Journal of Urban and Contemporary Law, Vol. 28,* 195–240.
Marcuse, P. (1997). Glossy Globalization. In P. Droege (Ed.), *Intelligent Environments* (pp. 29–48). Amsterdam: Elsevier Science Publishers.
Marcuse, P. (2009). From Justice Planning to Commons Planning. In P. Marcuse, J. Connolly, J. Novy, I. Olivo, C. Potter, & J. Steil (Eds.), *Searching for the Just City: Debates in Urban Theory and Practice* (pp. 91–102). Oxford: Routledge.
Marcuse, P. (2011). The Three Historic Currents of City Planning. In G. Bridge & S. Watson (Eds.), *The New Blackwell Companion to the City* (pp. 643–655). Oxford: Wiley-Blackwell.
Marcuse, P. Blog #30 Transformative Proposals in Three Areas. Retrieved at https://pmarcuse. wordpress.com
Thabit, W. (1999). Unpublished History. Retrieved at http://www.plannersnetwork.org/wp-content/ uploads/2012/07/A_History_of_PEO.pdf

List of Abbreviations

AFL: American Federation of Labor
CIO: Congress of Industrial Organizations
CLT: Community Land Trust
UCLA: University of California Los Angeles

Terminology Glossary

City Council: The legislative body for a municipality.

Community Board: An official body with 50 members appointed by elected officials of the city for each of 59 districts into which the City of New York is divided for limited administrative and advisory purposes.

Fulbright Grant: Funding from the federal government for studying outside the United States.

State AFL–CIO Labor Council: A council composed of representatives of all unions in the region belonging to the national AFL-CIO federation.

5

VISIONS OF CONTEMPORARY PLANNING

Stories and Journeys in Britain and America

Peter Hall*

My First Memories

I must have been about two and a half when my father lifted me up to peep over the wall near to our flat in West Kensington, to see the Piccadilly line trains coming out of the tunnel next to the District line ones. I became instantly fascinated by the tube, and in particular by H. C. Beck's legendary map, which had made its first public appearance that very year, 1934. A little later, at the age of about five, I spent many obsessed hours with coloured crayons, copying it out. I suppose that in 1938 I must have been the only six-year-old in London who knew all the tube stations by heart. It was a very useful training for life, which did give me a kind of respect for rote learning.

The point is that the tube in the 1930s had a truly magical quality for any child, and for more than a few parents. Charles Holden had been commissioned to redesign many of the central stations and to design the new stations along the extensions. Still almost brand new, they seemed like modern palaces. The huge, brilliantly lit entrance halls, the extraordinary indirect lighting on the escalators, the clean lines of the station platforms, the rivers of people flowing through the system all made an impression of power, of simplicity, that was overwhelmingly the magical memory of my childhood. Above all I remember the smell. Few now can recall it. It has gone, vanished from the world. It hit you like a wall as you entered the station: warm, enveloping, rich, pungent. I suspect in retrospect that it was a product of poor personal hygiene and excessive tobacco consumption; in those days, six cars in eight were reserved for smokers. But the smell has long gone. They have not yet even been able to put the tube smell into the new London Transport Museum; technology has still not risen to every challenge, if it ever will.

Of course I only found out later, years later, the name of the true architect of the tube system: the legendary Frank Pick, who with Albert Stanley (Lord Ashfield) conceived and commissioned the extensions of the system and its integration into the then quite new London Transport, created the year after I was born. What I also did not realise at the time was the connection with all that was happening around me. We had moved to Wimbledon, but each weekend we would go house-hunting in our Model Y Ford 8 through the outer south London suburbs, through Worcester Park and Motspur Park and Cheam and Ashstead, past rows of half-finished semi-detached houses, and through scores of builders' show houses fully equipped with what passed in those days for all mod cons. Alan Jackson's marvellous book, *Semi-Detached London,* gives the flavour of that world in the making.

What I was actually living through, as a child of six, was *The Making of Modern London:* the title of Gavin Weightman's memorable book and television series. This childhood world was the creation of Pick and his great competitor south of the river, Sir Herbert Walker, creator of the vast Southern Electric System, the greatest commuter network in the world. Pick really was the person who, more than any other, totally transformed the way we live in London and created the London we know. In adulthood, Pick became the first of my great role models for he quite consciously created that London. Of course, we may hate the world Pick made; and, quite unbeknown to this six-year-old, a significant minority of people were hating it very much and were giving evidence to Sir Anderson Montague-Barlow's Royal Commission on the Geographical Distribution of the Industrial Population to try and stop all this. These people were much grander than the ordinary people like my father, who were putting down their humble £5 deposits (yes, £5 deposits) to acquire their brand-new semis. They succeeded, as the great and the good so often do: After the war, they did what Canute had never succeeded in doing, and stopped the growth of London. There was a real planning system, at last, and one of its main aims was to secure an end to the growth of Semi-Detached London.

It seems incredible, when one thinks about it: All those thousands of private dreams, all those £5 deposits, all those new worlds were just abolished, like that. And, years after, when I came to research the whole phenomenon and its effects, we found that ordinary people had indeed lost out as a result: In the 1960s they were paying more, for less housing, than my mother and father had to pay in the 1930s. And it was all because we had a real planning system, quote unquote. But to understand how this could be, we have to start where I have started, in the years of my childhood.

Uprooted to Blackpool, the War and Early Intellectual Influences

A year after our house-hunting, like so many other Londoners, we found ourselves uprooted, and I spent the rest of my school years in Blackpool, on the far north-west shores of England, which in those days seemed an infinitely distant place from London. However, the point was the extraordinary spirit, among everyone, to fight the war and then to rebuild a better world. It is absolutely impossible to recapture that spirit now, any more than it is ever possible to bring back the value systems that motivated people in past ages; despite our current passion for wallowing in nostalgia, you can only get the most distant whispers from old documentaries and a few imaginative reconstructions. Best of all, though, from the wartime issues of *Picture Post,* above all that classic special issue in the darkest days of 1940 called *Why We Fight.* It was a series of double page spreads; I can remember them to this day. One, showing an English country lane, was entitled *Sunday Afternoon in England.* The other, entitled *Sunday Afternoon in Germany,* was an air view of thousands of goose-stepping Nazis. That was some of the greatest picture journalism of all time, which inspired my own contemporaries, like the late Derrick Amoore, who went on in the 1950s to create the traditions of BBC and ITV journalism.

What happened, by the war's last years, was a huge pent-up desire to come back and rebuild Britain. It was brilliantly seized by Patrick Abercrombie, my distinguished predecessor in the

Bartlett chair, in his two great wartime plans for London. Abercrombie is the only other person in the entire history of London, apart from Pick, who almost single-handedly reshaped it forever. He had been a founder member of the Council for the Preservation of Rural England in 1926; and he was a key member of the great and good who had campaigned against the growth of the suburbs. Other people could have been commissioned and could have produced plans. But it was Abercrombie who stamped his intellect and personality on the entire enterprise and gave it that cartoon-like simplicity, captured in the famous diagrams of the neighbourhood units, the green belt, the new and expanded towns.

Any planner wanting to know how to win the hearts and minds of the people should go back, again and again, to those diagrams. I remember, at the age of 13, the popular Penguin edition of the Greater London Plan, which became a bestseller. It was that mood which swept the Attlee government to power; that spirit which guaranteed that the Abercrombie vision would come to pass. Almost unbelievably, it all happened: The growth of London was stopped, the green belt was established, eight new towns were started. And all in conditions of the most unbelievable privation and hardship: savage food and clothes rationing, much more so than in wartime; freezing winters; power cuts; the virtual paralysis of the economy. It took persistence as well as vision, but in those days people had both.

I was distant from these events, still up on the Lancashire shores. But there is one point from that bleak teenage experience that I do think was significant. I come from one of the smallest generations ever to have been born in Britain; the birth rate reached an historic low point in 1933. And, the year I passed the 11-plus into grammar school in 1943, exactly 25 per cent passed, not far short of half the proportion (50 per cent) who passed on to *university* 70 years later! But only a fraction of those who passed the 11-plus actually went on to university. There, like others of my generation, I received an Etonian-quality education, entirely free of charge, in a northern grammar school. Despite the disruptions of the war years, we were taught in classes which now seem almost indecently small. The man who taught me the craft of history, Donald Murdoch, had joined the Communist Party (CP) in the late 1920s in Oxford, and left it in the 1930s as a result of the Stalin show trials and the Spanish Civil War to become an unrepentant Trotskyist. His lessons interspersed a Marxist interpretation of the English Civil War with bizarre anecdotes about the CP of the 1930s.

In these last years of high school, he introduced me to many writers who became my intellectual role models for life: the late Arthur Koestler (1940) whose *Darkness at Noon* is still the greatest and most moving account of an intellectual coming to terms with totalitarianism, and whose autobiography (which came a little later) is a sparkling account of the life of a Communist intellectual in the 1920s and 1930s; another Central European Marxist émigré, Franz Borkenau (1940) whose book *The Totalitarian Enemy* brilliantly equated Nazism and Stalinism; the great American sociologist and one-time Trotskyist James Burnham (1941) (whose brilliant *Managerial Revolution* is little read nowadays, despite its continuing relevance). And Joseph Schumpeter (1941) whose *Capitalism, Socialism and Democracy* came to the same conclusions, and which I then found less interesting, though I have since come to see it as a twentieth-century equivalent to *Das Kapital,* distinguished from the original by the fact that its analysis was actually correct. Then an unacknowledged hero in an undiscovered country but more, much more, of him later.

Those years in Blackpool before university were years when I began to read more formal as well as personal accounts of living in cities. Above all, there was George Orwell. I started to

54 Peter Hall

read him at the age of 16, after *Animal Farm* but just before the publication of *1984*. I never admired him much as a novelist, but as a sociological and political essayist, he was of the first order. No one who has absorbed Orwell when young could ever produce the kind of jargon-ridden claptrap which sadly passes for academic writing in the social sciences, then as now, except that now there is so much more of it. And no one influenced by Orwell could fail to see his point that so much bad writing is a deliberate attempt to obfuscate the real issues, to use bad language in order to conceal bad thought.

There was another book I read in the last two years of high school and this, indirectly, was the most influential of all: Lewis Mumford's (1938) *The Culture of Cities*. It still reads brilliantly, though one can see at my age of 82, as one could not at 16, that its scholarship is suspect and its basic argument—that urban culture reached a high point in the medieval city state—dangerously sentimentalised. But what Mumford did, as no one has ever done since, was to integrate the entire history of urban development within a brilliant, almost cartoon-like socio-economic framework so that one could see, for instance, exactly why the nineteenth-century industrial city was a necessary result of early capitalism, or the early twentieth-century metropolis was a product of finance capitalism. To that extent, it was quasi-Marxist. But it also had a second half, an extraordinary vision of the possibility of a future regional planning system designed for the re-creation of those medieval communities on the basis of twentieth-century technologies. Even then, I found it all a bit starry-eyed; and, of course, the irony is that virtually none of this vision ever came to pass in Mumford's own homeland. As we now know from his letters to Frederic Osborn, he later came to believe that America had failed while we had actually caused the vision to happen.

And So to Cambridge, to Geography

At university in Cambridge, there were other intellectual role models, now with human faces. Those years have been monstrously media-hyped as the golden age of Cambridge, the *Glittering Prizes* years. I did not see them that way then, nor do I now: Much of that world was smart and superficial and self-promotional. But there was a more serious Cambridge; and here there were two influences, rather strangely contrasted and even contradictory. One was the broad historic humanist Cambridge tradition, so powerfully epitomized by the Edwardian world of Keynes and Russell, and so brilliantly conveyed in Keynes's (1938) marvellous essay, *My Early Beliefs,* which would also go on to my list of compulsory readings. The values he describes there—humanist values based on discourse among friends—were the values of the circle in which I lived and moved. But Keynes was a role model in another sense, and it was a remarkable one: of a person who somehow juggled the jobs of top academic economist, college bursar, personal financial speculator on the grand scale, patron of the arts, and socialite. The many anecdotes about Keynes always reminded me of another great academic, the geographer Lionel Dudley Stamp, who created the National Land Utilisation Survey and masterminded the Scott Committee inquiry on rural land-use in 1942, who once said to me that if you ever wanted to make sure you would get a job done, you should find the busiest person you knew and recruit.

There was another dominant voice, and the irony is that he was bitterly opposed to everything that Keynes and his group stood for: It was the unmistakeable voice, known to almost everyone in the Cambridge of that time, of Frank Raymond Leavis. It was the English Tripos that set the intellectual tone of Cambridge in those days, and it was Leavis's famous lectures in

Visions of Contemporary Planning 55

the Mill Lane lecture rooms which set the tone for the Tripos and for all those non-students of English who invaded the hall to overflowing. His insistence on the seriousness of literature, on its moral significance, became our creed. We should also not forget that Orwell called himself a socialist, and I can hardly remember anyone, at school or at university, who called himself anything else. We were avid readers of what was still proudly called the *Manchester Guardian,* which came from Manchester's Cross Street via an agonisingly slow night-train that trundled across the Fenlands, rather like a foreign newspaper (which I suppose in a way it was). The paper was still extraordinarily Manchester oriented, but it also campaigned tirelessly, as did the *Observer* on Sundays, for the great liberal causes that were our obsessions in those days.

Geography at Cambridge in 1950 was at first very much an anticlimax. This was still old-fashioned geography: a mélange of the physical and the human, without much insight into either. We had field trips to the neighbouring Gog Magog Hills, where we heard that we were standing on the highest ground from there to the Urals. We did fieldwork there in wretched weather, on our bicycles, measuring the water table from local wells, and almost subconsciously I absorbed a sense of the relationships between the physical environment and the human response to it. Year two was the great escape, into specialisation: economic geography plus historical geography, a combination that proved uniquely fruitful for subsequent work. And, that year, Gus Caesar arrived as fellow and director of studies in geography at my college, St Catharine's. And he was the greatest single influence of all. For he taught a generation of us—"Caesar's Praetorian Guard"—not only relentless logic, but also a belief that geography could be actively applied to change the world. As Marx memorably said, the point was not merely to understand the world but to change it. What Marx did not say was that to change it effectively, you had better first understand it.

Immediately (no master's degrees in those days), the intellectual trail led in 1953 to a PhD in the historical-economic geography of industry in London, borrowing theory from Alfred Marshall (who invented the new economic geography in 1890 only for his fellow economists to forget all about it for the next one hundred years until Paul Krugman reinvented it) and a few near-contemporaries who were just then beginning to apply it to real-world research: in particular, the economist P. Sargant Florence and the geographer Michael Wise, working together at the University of Birmingham. Still missing from the intellectual lexicon, except through fragments, was the whole body of location theory developed by German economists and geographers who had borrowed from Marshall and were busy applying it through empirical research. The pioneer, Johann Heinrich von Thünen, was a Mecklenburg farmer and contemporary of Ricardo, whose astonishing *Der Isolierte Staat* (1826) was finally translated in a joint effort by my wife and myself as we were getting amicably divorced (Hall, 1966a); Alfred Weber's work on industrial location had been half-translated in Chicago in 1909, but the accompanying empirical studies lay buried in the original German to this day; the astonishing synthesis by the Kiel economist August Lösch, *Die Räumliche Ordnung der Wirtschaft* (1940), had also been translated into English in 1954; Walter Christaller's *Central Places in Southern Germany* (1933), which had provided an essential foundation for Lösch, appeared in English the same year as von Thünen in 1966. So my theoretical basis was, to say the least, fragmentary—but no one knew then.

Be that as it may, the PhD was eventually approved in 1959 and turned into my first book, *The Industries of London* (Hall, 1962). It described a world, still surviving, of small-workshop industries dependent on what was then called Marshallian agglomeration economies, later renamed clustering. The industries have long gone but the theory remains, embodied in the

56 Peter Hall

thousands of successor workshops that now cater for the knowledge economy. In all today's hype surrounding high-tech start-ups at places in London like Silicon Roundabout, no one ever seems to remember that the phenomenon was alive and well, observed by Charles Booth, 80 years before the advent of either the silicon chip or the roundabout.

A New World: To Scandinavia, and from Geography to Planning

What was central to those mid-1950s years when I became an adult was the huge generation gap and the sense of impotent outrage which we all felt against Britain and traditional British institutions. If you look at the major literary events of the time, like John Osborne's *Look Back in Anger* or Colin Wilson's *The Outsider* or Dennis Potter's *The Glittering Coffin,* it is amazing how even the titles capture the spirit. And, it must be said, Leavis himself was a symbol: A perennial self-declared outsider, raging against the smart Cambridge establishment, his appeal lay precisely with that generation of grammar school boys (and one or two grammar school girls) who felt repelled by the smartness and the superficiality of so much of the Cambridge world. But I doubt that anyone under the age of 70, 75 even, could ever capture the spirit of Osborne's great play *Look Back in Anger* when it first appeared at the Royal Court Theatre in May 1956. It was the cry of a generation. I do not believe that I shall ever again sit in a theatre and experience anything like the electricity that went through the audience. And, a few months later, it burst out in action, as we all found ourselves in Whitehall, facing down the mounted police at the time of the Suez Crisis. The country was totally divided, young against old, left against right, in a way that has never truly been seen again, even in 1968, even in 1984, never in any years since, even now in the present age of so-called austerity.

I think it is impossible ever to convey, now, any sense of how utterly clapped out and dreary a country Britain was in those days. The country had effectively stood still through a quarter century of depression, total war and post-war economic crisis. The first shoots of recovery were just beginning to break through, in those key years 1955–6, in the form of brighter clothing, new music (rock 'n' roll) and the new espresso bars. But Manchester, Liverpool and Birmingham were still nineteenth-century Dickensian horrors under their smoke-filled skies. Official counts, just at that time, registered 88,000 houses unfit for habitation in Liverpool; 68,000 in Manchester. And by uninhabitable I mean uninhabitable; these were no statistical artefacts. I saw those houses for myself. Times without number, as a child and teenager visiting relatives in Manchester, I travelled through the densely packed terraces of Hulme, jet black under their coating of soot; they were swept away in the great rebuild of the 1960s, the greatest single urban renewal project in Europe at that time, and their successors in their turn are now being torn down even faster. We wonder, now, how cities could have made such mistakes in their rebuilding as in Manchester's Hulme flats. I can tell you, and so can any of us who saw with our own eyes what came before the Hulme flats: It was desperation, sheer gut desperation, to pull down housing that was truly, deeply abominable. And no amount of sentimentalising about working-class neighbourhood culture can expunge that fact.

That was the background when, in the summer of 1955, I first had a real sense of vision of what an alternative society could look like. With a fellow student I went on a three-week railpass trip around Scandinavia, Esbjerg back to Esbjerg. So, when I went to Copenhagen and then to Stockholm, it was truly like a Promised Land. In Stockholm we stayed in the hall

Visions of Contemporary Planning **57**

of residence of the veterinary school, set among forests and lakes, five minutes from the tram terminus and fifteen minutes from the centre of the city. I marvelled at the calm simplicity and elegance of the building, the furniture, even the cups and saucers and knives and forks. It was the same everywhere one went: the cheap cafeterias where we ate, even the cheap chain stores where we bought souvenirs; this was a country where bad taste had simply been abolished, if it had ever existed. We rode on the *Tunnelbana,* then almost brand new, to the new satellite town of Vällingby, and then to Hässelby Strand. Ten years later exactly, I went back and saw it all finished. It looked as much like a dream world as ever. It looks slightly more faded now, but of course it is more than 60 years old. I must say that all those Swedish suburbs of the '50s and '60s have stood the test of time amazingly well. They show that good planning concepts, well executed in good materials with good workmanship, will withstand both the physical ravages of time, and the unforeseen forces of social change.

The real irony, the sad fact, is I think this. So many of my generation, in our different ways, vowed to try to build a Sweden here in Britain. We wanted to realise the ideals of social democracy, of a vigorous capitalist economy mediated and mitigated by a welfare state. We wanted to create cities of Swedish or Danish quality. We wanted above all to expunge the ugliness, the sordidness, that disfigured our own cities—to create homes and neighbourhoods where good proportion and simple design would be a part of everyday life. And I am not sure that we have even half-succeeded. Whenever I revisit Scandinavia, I am profoundly uplifted by the potential of good urban planning, and equally cast down by our relative failure here in Britain. But we did try. And we were given our chance, amazingly soon. A generation of us, newly and precariously established in our junior perches in academia and in the media, worked to lay the foundation for what we imagined would be a social democratic revolution.

I arrived into my first academic position as an assistant lecturer in geography at Birkbeck College (The University of London) in 1957. I found myself lecturing on German geography, visiting the country to understand it and then leading field classes. I became deeply appreciative of the tradition of *Landschaft,* gradually understanding the concept of how human settlement had adapted to the limitations and potentials of the natural environment and then had gone on to shape it. In parallel, lecturing on historical geography, I seized on a new book from a professor at the University of Leicester, W. G. Hoskins, who in 1955 published *The Making of the English Landscape.* At Leicester, Hoskins was pioneering a totally new approach to English local history, consciously or unconsciously adapting the German tradition. Oddly, his book, still in print more than 60 years later, was essentially a profound essay in human geography. It revolutionised both historical and geographical research. But equally oddly, human geography was just about to lurch into an entirely different direction, with equally momentous consequences.

Here enters one particular influence in my life: the brilliant, mercurial John Vaizey, who arrived as research fellow at St Catharine's in 1954 and began to organise some of us into a discussion club. As well as being the funniest raconteur I have ever met, he was ruthlessly irreverent and savage in his opinions and prejudices. Above all, he was merciless in his attacks on what he called cant and humbug, received opinions that had no good foundation. It was John who turned me from geography to planning, when in 1961 he suggested that I write a book about the future of London, and even suggested the title, *London 2000* (Hall, 1963). Also at that time, at John's instigation, I began to write for Rita Hinden's *Socialist Commentary,* and in 1961 I began to play an active role in the Fabian Society, working with a remarkable

58 Peter Hall

young general secretary called Shirley Williams, beginning to advise the shadow ministers who were soon to be swept into power as members of Harold Wilson's 1964 government. After Wilson's victory, I remember the afternoon session in the library of the Reform Club, where John advised me immediately to emigrate, since Wilson's first act as prime minister would be to ask the queen to welcome the Red Army at Tilbury. Wilson did become prime minister, the Red Army inexplicably failed to appear, a "week" proved to be (as Wilson memorably said) "a long time in politics", and in no time John was advising Tony Crosland on the creation of the binary system of higher education, with parallel and equal streams of general and specialist polytechnic education.

Meanwhile Bill Rodgers, who became regional minister in the newly formed Department of Economic Affairs run by George Brown, became a good friend. We all believed that we were going to create that brave new world, almost instantly. We were very sure of how we were going to do it. Within a year I was a member of the new South East Regional Economic Planning Council, drafting a new regional plan all in the ridiculous space of a few weeks: It was that *Weekend Telegraph* plan, derived from those great Scandinavian models, officially resuscitated. We really felt that we were going to change the world.

And in a way we did. If I have anything to look back on with some satisfaction, it is the work I did with Tom Hancock as part of the team on the original master plan for Peterborough, and the visionary plan for the new town in Mid-Wales that tragically fell foul of local parochial politics and was never built, or the more peripheral and conceptual work I did with Richard Llewelyn Davies on the original design concept of Milton Keynes. These are visions, too; and the people I worked with then remain among my personal role models. I think of Richard Llewelyn Davies, who so amazingly juggled a hundred different full-time commitments—as my predecessor as Bartlett Professor, as partner in one of Britain's most distinguished planning practices, as prime mover and finally chair of the governors at the old Centre for Environmental Studies. I think too of the team we assembled to produce the Mid-Wales plan, all under 35, all of them almost unknown: Christopher Foster on economics, Alan Wilson on urban modelling, John Goddard as my assistant. We were derided because in our analysis we suggested that it was possible to build a town on the foundation of a service economy, without a strong basis in manufacturing. To be specific, we suggested a tourism and retirement community. People, especially in the Labour Party of the mid-1960s, thought that was frivolous if not mad. Now, 50 years later, with virtually the whole of the British workforce in services, it is quite evident that we were right. But that did not help us, for as many have done before, we fell foul of Welsh politics.

The American Dream and the Idea of *Nonplan*

Joseph Schumpeter, who had already appeared in my reading in my later high school years, once said that in the history of ideas the critical point was the first imaginative leap, the sudden connection; the rest consisted of putting the intellectual top dressing on it, which might take years. I believe that like so much else of Schumpeter, that is profoundly true. In my case, in April 1961 I had made a trip down the Blue Ridge Mountains of Virginia, driving the famous Skyline Drive which had been engineered by the Works Program Administration as part of FDR's plans to counter the Great Depression. I saw for the first time how it was possible to integrate a scenic parkway into a National Park and to make this the base for a huge tourist development in an area which had been extremely remote and desperately poor. That provided the basis for an article in *New Society* in 1967, "The Great British Parkway Drive In" (Hall, 1967) and also a basic insight for the Mid–Wales plan. I came to believe then, and for many years after, what I believe many of my generation believed: that America, simply because it was so much more affluent, was a kind of harbinger of things to come. Nothing I have seen in the intervening 50 years has really shaken me from that view.

The most definitive American experience, though, came a year and a half later, September of 1966, my first visit to California. I landed at the helipad in Berkeley and was greeted by Mel Webber, whom I had never met but with whom I had corresponded since I had reviewed his definitive essay on the nonplace urban realm a couple of years earlier. It was the beginning of an intellectual comradeship that extended over nearly 40 years, and that finally took me to join him as a colleague in Berkeley. Berkeley was the high-water mark of a certain self-created myth centred on California's view of itself. The state was in the middle of its extraordinary boom years, fuelled by 10 years of Cold War, by defence contracts and by the rise of Silicon Valley on the other side of the San Francisco Bay. Under the benign governorship of the late great Pat Brown, California was pumping its wealth into a huge investment programme: into the brand new freeways that were everywhere, and multiplying into massive expansion of the university system that would make it the greatest in the world (Innes, 2017).

It was also the time of the Beach Boys and the beginnings of Flower Power; that September, I heard a concert in the Berkeley Greek Theater by a band called Country Joe and the Fish, who were so unknown and so quintessentially Californian that they distributed a record for free, with a notice on it saying please send us a dollar. Again, as with Britain in the 1950s, I am conscious of suffering from a catastrophic inability to convey any idea of how California felt in those days, when it was somehow at the leading edge of the entire Western world. I doubt whether any part of the world, ever since, has ever packed such an extraordinary emotional punch, a feeling of a place that was leading the world in technology, in economic achievement, in the forging of a new and different lifestyle. On that trip I first visited Los Angeles and drove, mesmerised, around the freeway system. The Santa Monica freeway was a year old. I came back and wrote an article about it, calling it "The Patterns of Cities to Come" (Hall, 1966a). Peter Banham, then reader at the Bartlett, phoned to ask if I was planning to turn it into a book because if not, he proposed to write one. I said no, I wasn't, and he went on to produce *Los Angeles: The Architecture of Four Ecologies* (Banham, 1971).

The Los Angeles experience had profound effects, not only on Peter Banham and myself, but on an entire generation of us. One immediate result was that Mel Webber, on sabbatical at the newly established Centre for Environmental Studies in 1967, was brought in by Richard Llewelyn Davies as part of that seminar group, and later as consultant, on the planning of Milton Keynes. I believe that Mel was the true spiritual father of Milton Keynes and that it does indeed embody the essence of what I will call the Berkeley-style of planning in the mid-1960s. When the Milton Keynes Master Plan came out, the editorial in *The Times* was headed "Los Angeles, Bucks"; that was a slight simplification, but it captures something important. We were soon attacked, and are still being attacked, for producing a city that was car-dependent, unsustainable and in every way the work of the devil; but meanwhile Milton Keynes has grown to be perhaps the most successful, certainly the best-known, and interestingly the highest-ranked new town in Britain for quality of life. That should give some pause for thought, perhaps. Indeed it does not look like a "new town" and this must also be part of its great success!

60 Peter Hall

There was however another result. By then, indeed since 1964, I was established as a part of the regular team of outside correspondents who wrote for the magazine *New Society,* which had been founded in 1962 by Tim Raison and edited since 1964 by Paul Barker. *New Society* would really deserve a lecture or two on its own rather than a couple of sentences. It was the result of the explosion of the social sciences in the universities in the 1960s, an explosion which was fundamentally changing the education of planners through the new planning courses, the first of which—the master's in regional and urban planning studies—I helped set up at the London School of Economics (LSE) in 1966. Underlying that explosion, and the magazine, was the basic idea that disinterested study of society really could contribute to the making of social policy.

But part of the ethos of the magazine, under Paul's wonderful editorship, was a creative iconoclasm that partly stemmed from Paul's parallel interest in the arts. Only that, I think, could possibly explain the manifesto that appeared in the magazine in 1969, jointly written by Paul, Cedric Price, Peter Banham and myself, under the title "Nonplan: An Experiment in Freedom" (Banham, Barker, Hall & Price, 1969). It argued that the planning system was stultifying creativity and experiment in building and design and living styles, and that there should be experimental nonplan zones in various parts of the country: The Isle of Wight was one, Sherwood Forest another. It stemmed in large measure from the experiences of the two Peters in California, and it caused a terrible furore in the official planning system. It articulated the growing doubts about planning and the planning system. The policy research group PEP (Political and Economic Planning) then obtained Ford Foundation funding to launch a major inquiry into the operation and effectiveness of the 1947 planning system in England and asked me to take overall charge. We assembled a strong team comprising Ray Thomas (later at the Open University), Roy Drewett (who died tragically young) and the American sociologist Harry Gracey. After four years of massive effort, and not a little internal conflict, the result was the mammoth two-volume book *The Containment of Urban England* (Hall, Thomas, Gracey & Drewett, 1973). Its main message, stemming from my deep doubts about the system, was that planning had produced perverse and unintended effects. It had physically contained London and other great cities, but it had increased the separation of home and work, and—the most momentous conclusion, which would echo down succeeding decades—it had caused inflation of land prices and thus housing costs. There was an important secondary message, the one Ray Thomas wanted to make the main one: The new towns had worked because in them these effects did not obtain. In effect we were preaching a pure Town and Country Planning Association (TCPA) message: If all urban development had taken place on the new towns model, it would all have been fine, but, as we discovered, it was very far from fine.

The doubts continued to grow. In 1975 I published a basic textbook of planning (Hall, 1975), which has gone through many successive editions over 40 years and has been translated into several languages, most recently Chinese (Hall, 2011). In a sense it represented the equivalent of a late nineteenth-century Liberal Party ("Whig") view of history, a view of constant progress from darkness to light in which everything eventually turned out to be the best of all possible worlds. Its apogee was the systems view of planning as embodied by authors like Brian McLoughlin and George Chadwick, in which rational planners set rational objectives, generated alternatives, used the then new computer modelling techniques to simulate their future consequences, and evaluated them using rigorous economic techniques.

Visions of Contemporary Planning **61**

But all too suddenly, as the book was being completed and going through production, this entire world turned upside down (Faludi, 2017). A new generation, inspired originally by protestors against the Vietnam War in America and by protestors against everything on the streets of Paris (*"Je suis Marxiste, tendance Groucho"*), questioned the very fundamentals of this view, which they saw as driven by a military-industrial complex embodied in the fictional Dr Strangelove. Large-scale top-down strategic planning was out, small-scale community action was in. Battles were fought everywhere: in London, against plans for hundreds of miles of motorways and against the comprehensive reconstruction of Covent Garden. The new heroine was Jane Jacobs, who a decade earlier in New York had anticipated the change by questioning urban motorway proposals in New York's Greenwich Village, and who went on to argue the case in a book that became an instant classic, *The Death and Life of Great American Cities* (Jacobs, 1961). So in an important sense *Urban and Regional Planning* (Hall, 1975) was outdated the day it appeared, and accommodating the twists and turns of planning theory has proved to be a major travail in the revisions that followed.

Innovation and Enterprise in Parallel to Great Planning Disasters

Meanwhile, in 1975 came one of those blinding Schumpeterian flashes. I was invited to Hong Kong to advise on the setting up of an urban studies and planning programme within the university. Apart from a brief visit to Japan in 1970, this was the first visit I had made to the Far East. I was totally mesmerised by the energy, the power, the achievement of the place. Most surprising for me was the achievement: Expecting a third world sort of country, I found a city that in many ways was more advanced than London. And Singapore, to which I paid a flying visit, was even more impressive: It was a kind of 1960s planners' dream, a British city that never was. On the long flight home, for hour after hour I was haunted by a transmogrification of that famous phrase of Khrushchev; I kept repeating to myself, *they'll bury us.*

Reflecting for days and weeks after that first trip, I came to an insight that later I found reflected in the writings of Schumpeter: that the reason these societies were so successful was that they gave scope for enterprise, that is for innovation, and that enterprise was not merely the only successful way of achieving economic growth, but also the only way many people would gain personal satisfaction in their own lives. In other words, despite all the strictures that have justifiably been made about it, capitalism was not only a tolerable system, but actually an admirable one in the way it released human energy and the human spirit. I saw that this was essentially what I had so much admired about America a decade earlier, and I also saw how the lack of it was responsible for the almost cosmic despair that had settled on me on my rare visits to the USSR and the socialist countries of Eastern Europe in the middle and late 1960s. To me, almost as ghastly as the Gulags was what survived their disappearance after Stalin: this crushing of the human spirit, the deadness and the meanness that characterised that system.

One result of these cogitations, in June 1977, was an address to the annual conference of the Royal Town Planning Institute in Chester. I remember it particularly well because, committed to a dinner in Reading the night before, I found that the only way to get there was by driving through the night. The delivery was probably less than coherent, but it seemed to make the delegates sit up. It was the year of publication of three famous consultants' reports on the problems of the inner cities and a Labour government white paper on the subject. I argued

62 Peter Hall

that, if we really wanted to revive the true urban basket cases, the only way might be in effect to make them into mini Hong Kongs. We should declare them effectively outside the UK and then invite all and sundry to locate there; the Chinese, in particular, would come in their tens of thousands. I was at some pains to point out that this was a highly academic flight of fancy, and that I did not expect any British government of any complexion to take the idea up in a hurry. The speech did not endear me to my colleagues and friends in the Fabian Society; and I found myself increasingly distanced from them politically. Meanwhile the conservative minister Geoffrey Howe had suggested we have lunch, and he revealed that he had been having similar ideas. I fear though that the enterprise zones, when they eventually arrived, were a rather long way from my original highly academic vision.

The final break with Labour policies, for me, came one day in the House of Commons, at a meeting of the Home Policy Committee on Transport. It was totally packed with gentlemen in dark blue suits with little badges in their buttonholes, signifying membership of the then NUR (National Union of Railwaymen) or ASLEF, a name I always savour because it stands for the Amalgamated Society of Locomotive Engineers and Firemen, indicative of a certain nostalgia since the last steam train ran on British Rail in the mid-1960s. The delegates quickly decided that the Labour government under Tony Crosland as transport minister (whom they deeply distrusted as a closet Tory) was spending far too much on the roads and that this money, predictably enough, should be transferred to the railways—and that, in particular, the plans to build the M25 orbital motorway around London should be abandoned forthwith. I uttered a feeble protest to the effect that this would fail to deal with the manifest congestion on the existing North Circular, to which came the immortal reply that, under proper Labour regional policies, all this traffic would be in the north of England.

It was at that point that I effectively lost all contact with the Labour Party and its policies, since at the time, still on the South East Planning Council, we were month by month repeating, to the point of tedium if not nausea, our total support for three basic policies: completion of the M25 as top national priority; Stansted as London's third airport; and a development corporation for Docklands. Predictably, we got virtually nowhere on any of these counts with Peter Shore as environment minister in the dying days of Jim Callaghan's government. Two months after the arrival of Thatcher in 1979, Michael Heseltine as secretary for the environment summarily dismissed us. Over the following 13 years, the Thatcher governments faithfully carried out all three of our basic recommendations: the LDDC (London Docklands Development Corporation) was in place in 1981, the M25 was finished in 1986 and Stansted was opened in 1992.

Yet the experience proved salutary because it led me to question the whole basis of the rational approach to planning. In the 1970s, in Britain and elsewhere, the media recorded a series of extraordinary sagas in which major projects were either abandoned or reversed, or completed projects came to be derided as costly white elephants. In Britain the government went in a series of policy circles over the location of a third London airport, from Stansted to Cublington to Maplin and back to Stansted again. The London motorways came and went. Sydney built an opera house that escalated in cost from $7 million to $102 million Australian dollars, and finally could barely house opera. San Francisco built a rapid transit system that was questioned by critics. The same story was repeated in almost every major city in the world.

I decided to retell these stories, journalist-style—the easy part—and then to try to find academic theory that helped explain them. In the search, I discovered public choice theory, the invention of a few little-known American economists and political scientists such as Charles

Lindblom, Mancur Olson and James Buchanan (Lindblom, 1959; Buchanan & Tullock, 1962; Olson, 1965). Their work illuminated the remarkable ways in which democratic societies reached collective decisions. Their struggles helped explain outcomes in a remarkably illuminating way. But they also showed how extraordinarily imperfect, even in the most exemplary democracies, were the processes. *Great Planning Disasters* (Hall, 1980) duly appeared, but meanwhile, having fallen hopelessly in love at first sight with California in the 1960s, in 1979 I had decided to move there. I remember the day. I was in Manchester for the conference of the Institute of British Geographers. The sky was leaden and the Fallowfield Hall of Residence, where they had housed us, was a more than usually dreary example of that uniquely sordid British art form. It was the second winter of discontent, and all the tanker drivers in the north of England were going on strike. I was sitting in a motionless queue for petrol, wondering whether I would get back to London or be forced to sell the car for scrap. I suddenly decided that I had had enough. I got to the nearest telephone and called to say I was a candidate for the vacant job in Berkeley. A year and a half later, I took up residence there.

The "Unreal" Real America

For me the move to Berkeley was the consummation of my long affair with America and with California. It plunged me into an extraordinary encounter with American society in one of its most exhilaratingly dynamic eras. Silicon Valley—the name had been coined by a journalist in 1971—was burgeoning. Steve Jobs and Steve Wozniak had invented the Apple 1, the first commercially successful personal computer, four years earlier (in 1977). The San Francisco Bay Area offered a unique combination of innovation and zaniness: Next door to the house we first rented, a parked truck advertised *Trans-Time Inc: Cryogenic Suspension,* which would freeze you just before you expired of your terminal illness, to wait for the medical advance that would bring you back to the land of the living.

In this new atmosphere of liberation, it seemed logical to inquire about the process of innovation and how it related to the genesis and growth of new industries, indeed new cities. By chance, I stumbled upon a then-new English translation by a German academic, Gerhard Mensch (1979), *Stalemate in Technology.* He set out to produce detailed supporting evidence for a thesis set out long before by Schumpeter (1939) in his magnum opus *Business Cycles*: that since the first industrial revolution in the eighteenth century, the capitalist economy had grown through 57-year-long waves of alternating growth and depression, first identified by an obscure Soviet economist, Nikolai Kondratieff, who had died in the Gulag for the sin of inventing something that seemed to explain a facet of capitalism. Schumpeter attributed the origin of these waves to fundamental technical and organisational innovations that turned inventions into commercially profitable industries: the first Kondratieff, from 1785 to 1842, based on cotton textiles and wrought iron; the second, from 1842 to 1897, on steel, railways and steamships; the third, from 1897, on electricity, cars and chemicals. Mensch was able to suggest that this wave had ceased in 1954, four years after Schumpeter's death, to be succeeded by a fourth Kondratieff based on electronics and aviation; further, he painstakingly showed how the process of transition, from invention to innovation, dramatically speeded up at the start of each wave, as capital sought out new and profitable opportunities. Further, Mensch produced mathematical evidence that the next key date for this occurrence would be that fateful year, 1984. It was and is a remarkable piece of scholarship, and it made me a

64 Peter Hall

Schumpeter worshipper and obsessive Kondratieff watcher, seeking evidence for a coming fifth Kondratieff (Hall, 1981, 1983).

Logically I began to ask what exactly it was that had made California so dynamic an economy in the years since World War II, and why it was that the British economy seemed to have suffered such long years of structural decline—going back, on any reasonable account, to the 1880s. That led me to read or re-read the canon of Schumpeter's (1939) work, above all his 1100-page tome on *Business Cycles*, published just before World War II. The result was an article in *New Society*, "The Geography of the Fifth Kondratieff Cycle", published in 1981, and a short piece on the 100th anniversary of Schumpeter's birth, which came out in 1983. I suppose that just as parents secretly have favourite children, so authors have favourite works: these two articles, in particular the second, are my own personal favourites. I think that in the three pages that Paul Barker allowed me, I said a lot about what anyone needs to know about the career and work of this extraordinarily exotic and brilliant man, whose career sounds like something from a Hollywood silent movie of the 1920s: one of many experiences he had was that in his first academic job he fought a duel with the librarian over the students' access to books; he married an aristocratic Englishwoman, but it lasted six months; and so on. And behind all this facade of an Austrian cavalry officer, he produced the only truly profound accounts of the operation of the capitalist system that have ever been written, showing that Marx, whose work he so much admired, was fatally flawed, as was Keynes. He demonstrated to his own satisfaction, and those of many others who follow him, that the capitalist system marched to three different clocks of which the most critical, was the Kondratieff. He was widely ridiculed for this, in his own time and since. But, dying in 1950 at the early age of 63, he had the last laugh. The great second Wall Street crash came in October 1987: four months after he had predicted it! Not bad, really, for something he published in 1939.

His writing and my view of his importance led to collaboration with my Berkeley colleague Ann Markusen; we first held an edited symposium on these themes (Hall & Markusen, 1985) and then produced two major pieces of funded research with graduate students (Markusen, Hall & Glasmeier, 1986; Markusen, Hall, Campbell & Deitrick, 1991). In parallel, constantly commuting back to my old base in the University at Reading, I directed two deliberately comparable studies of high-technology development, one in the United Kingdom, the other international (Hall, Breheny, McQuaid & Hart, 1987; Hall & Preston, 1988). And finally, I embarked with John Brotchie—a uniquely stimulating researcher from CSIRO Australia—on the first of an entire series of symposia resulting in books comparing high-technology-based development across the world (Brotchie, Newton & Hall, 1987).

Further, the books used a very similar research approach, combining quantitative evidence about the location of the new growth industries with a qualitative-historical account of their genesis and growth. Throughout my research life, I have always found this productive, and nowhere more so than in this golden period of my research. What the research very clearly showed was that the process was dependent on a unique set of historical circumstances at particular periods of time—particularly World War II and then the following Cold War era, in which government research agencies propelled and stimulated new technologies for strictly non-commercial reasons, using non-commercial criteria.

Logically, the question arose: If national defence could propel technological innovation, could the civil state achieve the same result in conditions of peace? Manuel Castells, another star in that extraordinary Berkeley firmament, asked me to join him in a major global investigation, funded by the regional government of Andalucía in southern Spain. The historic occasion that prompted this was that Catalonia had won the 1992 Olympics; a Socialist government in Madrid had responded with a major international expo in its other power base in Andalucía; enormous investment was being pumped into this rather backward region in the far southern tip of Spain; and the challenge—indeed, Manuel's dream—was to use it to lay the base for a European Silicon Valley. We fanned out and toured the world seeking appropriate parallels, while a team in Seville worked on developing the expo site—on a remarkably undeveloped island opposite the city centre—for the event itself and its subsequent adaptation. This was a truly audacious exercise in applying global research to a hugely ambitious enterprise in regional economic transformation (Castells & Hall, 1994). But politics intervened: Half the site was sold off for a theme park, while the other half has welcomed high-tech firms that have failed to achieve the necessary transformation. It was a colossal disappointment, but 20 years later we again came together, with MIT's Bill Mitchell, to try to achieve a similar result in the Aragon capital of Zaragoza; *etopia,* the city's new Centre of Art and Technology, opened in mid-2013.

Take Me Back to Dear Old Blighty

After my return to England and on taking the Bartlett chair at UCL in 1992, at the overripe age of 60, I spent much of the following decade completing a book that was always intended as some kind of ultimate synthesis of my thinking about cities: *Cities in Civilization* (Hall, 1998). The idea had come from my long-term literary agent Michael Sissons, who felt that this was the book I had always been waiting to write. I was initially sceptical because I desperately wanted to avoid the pitfall of producing a glossy coffee-table book of the *Wonders of the World's Great Cities* variety. But then the key offered itself: This was to be an extension onto a much larger canvas of the basic ideas that had been developing in all those books on innovation. Now however the theme was to extend far beyond technical innovation into artistic creativity and also—as a logical continuation from *Cities of Tomorrow* (Hall, 1988)—urban innovation.

The direct inspiration came from reading the work of Swedish colleagues, some of it buried in the original Swedish—Gunnar Törnqvist, a valued geographer at the University of Lund, and Åke Andersson, a stimulating economist-controversialist from Stockholm—who were arguing for the unique role of great cities in the history of creative endeavour (Törnqvist, 1983; Andersson, 1985a, 1985b). I was well satisfied with the resulting book, but much less satisfied with its reception. It appeared as what the publishers call a "trade" book, designed to feature briefly and prominently at the front ends of bookstores before being banished to the remainder section and finally to obscurity. There, it received respectful reviews but was clearly never destined for bestseller status. More bizarrely, it was virtually ignored by academic reviewers, presumably because the publisher never supplied review copies. Maybe, 40 years earlier, it had been possible to bridge these two worlds of publication—as *London 2000* (Hall, 1963) had shown. But by 1998 a Chinese wall had arisen, and *Cities in Civilization* (Hall, 1998) found itself in a kind of stateless limbo, unable to gain citizenship on either side. There was however an unexpected happy sequel which I will reserve for later.

Satisfying as California proved from an academic point of view, I could not keep away from these shores for long, and from 1983 to 1988 I was back for half of each year. It was the high-water mark of Thatcherism, and *Nonplan* ruled the day with a vengeance. Meanwhile, inside the Labour Party, the worm had turned. A key group, including old friends like Bill Rodgers and Shirley Williams, gathered for that fatal meeting in Limehouse that split Labour and led to the declaration of the Social Democratic Party. I got a call from Michael Young. In that typically hesitant, *tentative* voice of his, he announced that he wanted to create a think tank, a Fabian Society for the Social Democratic Party. Further, it was to be called the Tawney Society, in memory of R. H. Tawney. When the launch took place there were howls of anguish from the Labour Party, who said that the memory of Tawney had been hijacked. It all got huge publicity, just as Michael intended. We went on to publish a series of pamphlets, which essentially helped shape the entire political stage of the late 1980s and 1990s. Privatisation, freedom of choice, deregulation—if you want to find their origins, look to the collective contribution *The Middle of the Night*, published in 1983. What we tried to do there was to redefine, in terms of the mid-1980s, the dilemma that Tony Crosland had so brilliantly posed in his book *The Future of Socialism* in the 1950s: how you can create a society that is entrepreneurial and dynamic while at the same time providing a platform of equal opportunity and a safety net of services for the least fortunate. This is a permanent and basic dilemma of modern societies which continues to this very day, although the details may change. Today we see a strange return, in so many ways, to the conditions of the 1880s, also a time of wretchedness and homelessness and beggars on the streets, which prompted the first true social scientific inquiry, that of Charles Booth, as well as the reforming pamphlets of the first Fabians, Sidney and Beatrice Webb, who symbolised the spirit of those times.

During my life, I have spent a lot of time thinking about how cities are structured through their networks, through their transport and through ways in which innovation, enterprise and segregation are all influenced by such connectivities. One person who had been thinking about such things was another British geographer-emigré to the United States, Brian Berry, a graduate of UCL, who in 1991 published an important—but neglected—book arguing that Kondratieff theory explained not merely booms and slumps, but also cycles of urban development, each of which is based on a fundamental advance in transportation or communication technology. I happen to like that, because it seems to me transparently evident that it does explain some remarkable facts, such as the first railways of the 1830s which we see symbolically represented at the start of George Eliot's novel *Middlemarch;* the burst of urban metro and tube systems we had worldwide about 1900, at the start of the third Kondratieff upswing; or the surge in motorway building in the late 1950s, the take-off point for the fourth. The bad news here was that the fifth Kondratieff was scheduled to start somewhere in the region of 2007–2011, which proved to mark a major global slump: perhaps the darkest hour before the Kondratieff dawn. It is of course an open question as to whether the rapid growth in low cost IT industries and the all pervasiveness of individual services fostered by Web 2.0 that now seems to be propelling the growth of some Western nations is a genuine upswing of the cycle.

A key to all this was the paper by the economist Colin Clark (1957), published in the *Town Planning Review*, "Transport, Maker and Breaker of Cities". Clark showed how successive waves of change in transport technology had profoundly shaped the ways in which cities grew and changed. In particular, they led to a progressive flattening of the density gradient from centre to edge: Electric commuter railways, then motorways, allowed cities to spread and to sprawl. The question therefore was what would come next. And there was already one answer. Whatever the timing, we can already be pretty sure about the technologies that will carry it, as we could have been sure about 1820 or 1880 or 1940, about ten years before the start of previous Kondratieff waves. They will be high-speed trains, information technology applied to the management of highways, and the web. And we can be sure that they will have effects on urban growth as profound as the London tubes and the Los Angeles freeways in their eras.

The first time that I became absolutely convinced of this, a true Schumpeterian moment, was in 1990 when I first rode on the *TGV Atlantique* from Paris down to Le Mans. There is an electric moment on this ride, when the train emerges from a long tunnel and begins to run parallel to the motorway. Suddenly, you see a line of broken-down trucks. But they are not broken down: They are travelling at 60 mph. And then you pass the cars, travelling at 80 or 85, at two and a half times their speed, leaving them somehow suspended weirdly on the highway, for all the world as if they have all suffered collective clutch failure. The point is this: When you actually experience this, you absolutely know, as in Stockholm in 1955 or Los Angeles in 1966 or Hong Kong in 1975, that here is something new and definitively different, which is going to change our world beyond any possibility of doubt.

So my return to London marked what in some ways were personally the most satisfying years of all. I was able to combine my teaching and research in UCL with advice to three successive secretaries of state for the environment, in particular on the launch of the East Thames Corridor, later Thames Gateway, and the Channel Tunnel Rail Link, later High Speed One. Through a series of cliffhanger episodes that sometimes seemed to resemble a cheap television thriller, during the summer of 1991 our team at the Department of the Environment managed to snatch victory: We got the line diverted through the corridor to give it the potential to feed the development, at last rectifying the imbalance that occurred half a century ago when an almost accidental wartime decision put London's first airport to the west of the city; we nursed it through successive stages to the firm route announcement in 1994. And at that point, bowing out from officialdom, I played an active role with one of the private promoters who finally won the competition to build and operate it.

But that success led to a reflection. There was one point that even Clark had failed to grasp: that, as cities grew and spread, they would mutate into polycentric mega-city regions. At the Institute of Community Studies in Bethnal Green, which I had taken over from the legendary Michael Young (then 85) in 2001 while retaining my teaching post at UCL, we started on a major comparative study, by eight research teams in eight major European "mega-city regions"—London, Paris, Central Belgium, Randstad Holland, Rhine-Ruhr, Rhine-Main, Central Switzerland and Greater Dublin—asking how far and in what ways they were becoming more polycentric in their urban structure and functions. It was in a sense a return to that question explored more cursorily in *The World Cities* (Hall, 1966b), 40 years earlier. And the results, published in *The Polycentric Metropolis* (Hall & Pain, 2006), staggered the researchers: Randstad Holland, that archetype of the polycentric urban region, was not merely as polycentric as we all thought, but it was splitting into a more successful northern half around Amsterdam and a less successful southern half around Rotterdam, while the vast Greater South East Region was less dominated by London than we had believed.

As always in such research, there was a major disappointment: We could find no good data on the geography of information flows. But serendipity remarkably intervened. As we were completing the manuscript, in 2005, I was working in my study at home when the phone rang and a voice said: "I am phoning to tell you that you have just won one million Swiss francs, *and this is not a hoax*". I was reassured that he did not ask me for my credit card details, and even more so when a letter arrived telling me that I was the recipient of the 2005 Balzan Foundation

68 Peter Hall

Prize, for work on the social and cultural history of cities since the sixteenth century—clearly a belated recognition for the *magnum opus*. Half the money must be spent on supporting young researchers. It duly went on supporting one of those researchers to help me finish *London Voices* (Hall, 2007), but in bigger measure to support three years of research by two PhD students at UCL, Basak Demires Ozkul and Jonathan Reades, to work on deeper quantitative research on the geography of the polycentric metropolis: she on changing home-to-work relationships in the UK, he on telephone traffic in the UK. Both resulted in outstanding PhDs which are still yielding new and original publications.

And in Conclusion

Meanwhile, in March 2012, I had passed one of life's great milestones: my 80th birthday. The Chinese adage has it that those who reach that point are blessed by heaven. Others might have reservations. Real old age—old, as distinct from the young old of the 60s and 70s—brings with it the steadily growing realisation of declining physical powers. Knees creak, legs are unsteady, regular medical checkups show unwelcome results. The guide to that world is the great poet W. B. Yeats. Remarkably, the poems where he so ineffably recorded his own decline were published in a collection, *The Tower,* in 1928 when he was only 63. But bodies aged faster then, and he was wracked by heart failure: a Celtic genetic inheritance. But in these two great poems *The Tower* and *Sailing to Byzantium,* he gained a profound insight: the paradox that, while the body decays, the mind may remain sparkling bright. In my ninth (and, barring an unlikely medical miracle, final) decade, I find that an inspiration for a few future years of rewarding work.

Note

* Peter Hall passed away on 30th July 2014 some two months after he presented this paper using the medium of Skype on 19th May 2014 in Vienna. Michael Batty, who knew him from 1969, first as his research assistant, then as one his lecturers at the University of Reading in the 1970s and lastly as his erstwhile colleague at UCL, edited this version of the paper from Peter's early draft. There will be differences that others may find with his interpretations of the original draft.

References

Andersson, A. (1985a). Creativity and Regional Development. *Papers of the Regional Science Association, 56,* 5–20.

Andersson, A. (1985b). *Kreativitet.* Stockholm: Prisma.

Banham, R. (1971). *Los Angeles.* New York, NY: Harper and Row.

Banham, R., Barker, P., Hall, P., & Price, C. (1969). Non-Plan an Experiment in Freedom. *New Society, 13,* 435–443.

Borkenau, F. (1940). *The Totalitarian Enemy.* London: Faber and Faber.

Brotchie, J., Newton, P., & Hall, P. (Eds.). (1987). *The Spatial Impact of Technological Change.* London: Croom Helm.

Buchanan, J. M., & Tullock, G. (1962). *The Calculus of Consent.* Ann Arbor, MI: University of Michigan Press.

Burnham, J. (1941). *Managerial Revolution.* New York, NY: John Day.

Castells, M., & Hall, P. (1994). *Technopoles of the World.* London: Routledge.

Christaller, W. (1933). *Central Places in Southern Germany* (J. Gustav Fischer, trans.). New York, NY: Prentice Hall, Englewood Cliffs.

Clark, C. (1957). Transport, Maker and Breaker of Cities. *Town Planning Review, 28*, 237–250.

Faludi, A. (2017). Understanding and Improving Planning Processes and Planning Institutions: A Moving Target. In B. Haselsberger (Ed.), *Encounters in Planning Thought: 16 Autobiographical Essays from Key Thinkers in Spatial Planning* (pp. 88–106). New York: Routledge.

Hall, P. (1962). *The Industries of London since 1861.* London: Hutchinson.

Hall, P. (1963). *London 2000.* London: Faber and Faber.

Hall, P. (1966a). The Patterns of Cities to Come. *New Society, March 10.*

Hall, P. (1966b). *The World Cities.* London: Weidenfeld and Nicholson.

Hall, P. (1967). The Great British Parkway Drive In. *New Society, August 3.*

Hall, P. (1975, 2011). *Urban and Regional Planning.* Middlesex: Penguin, Harmondsworth. (China Architecture and Building Press, Beijing, PRC, 2011).

Hall, P. (1980). *Great Planning Disasters.* London: Weidenfeld.

Hall, P. (1981). The Geography of the Fifth Kondratieff Cycle. *New Society, March 26.*

Hall, P. (1983). The Third Man of Economics. *New Society, December 1.*

Hall, P. (1988). *Cities of Tomorrow.* Oxford: Blackwell Publishing.

Hall, P. (1998). *Cities in Civilization.* London: Weidenfeld and Nicolson.

Hall, P. (2007). *London Voices, London Lives.* Bristol: Policy Press.

Hall, P., Breheny, M., McQuaid, R., & Hart, D. (1987). *Western Sunrise.* London: Unwin Hyman.

Hall, P., & Markusen, A. (Eds.). (1985). *Silicon Landscapes.* London: Allen and Unwin.

Hall, P., & Pain, K. (2006). *The Polycentric Metropolis.* London: Earthscan.

Hall, P., & Preston, P. (1988). *The Carrier Wave.* London: Unwin Hyman.

Hall, P., Thomas, R., Gracey, H., & Drewett, R. (1973). *The Containment of Urban England (Vols. 1–2).* London: George Allen & Unwin.

Hoskins, W. G. (1955). *The Making of the English Landscape.* London: Hodder and Stoughton.

Innes, J. E. (2017). From Informing Policy to Collaborating Rationally. In B. Haselsberger (Ed.), *Encounters in Planning Thought: 16 Autobiographical Essays from Key Thinkers in Spatial Planning* (pp. 145–164). New York: Routledge.

Jacobs, J. (1961). *The Death and Life of Great American Cities.* New York, NY: Random House.

Keynes, J. M. (1938). *The Collected Writing of John Maynard Keynes.* London: Macmillan.

Koestler, A. (1940). *Darkness at Noon.* New York, NY: Schribner.

Lindblom, C. (1959). The Science of Muddling Through. *Public Administration Review, 19(2),* 79–88.

Lösch, A. (1940). *The Economics of Location* (J. Fischer, trans.). New Haven, CN: Yale University Press.

Markusen, A., Hall, P., Campbell, D., & Deitrick, S. (1991). *The Rise of the Gunbelt.* Oxford: Oxford University Press.

Markusen, A., Hall, P., & Glasmeier, A. (1986). *High-Tech America.* Boston, MA: Allen & Unwin.

Mensch, G. (1979). *Stalemate in Technology.* Cambridge, MA: Ballinger Publishing Company.

Mumford, L. (1938). *The Culture of Cities.* New York, NY: Harcourt and Brace.

Olson, M. (1965). *The Logic of Collective Action.* Cambridge, MA: Harvard University Press.

Schumpeter, J. (1939). *Business Cycles.* London: McGraw-Hill.

Schumpeter, J. (1941). *Capitalism, Socialism and Democracy.* London: George Allen and Unwin.

Törnqvist, G. (1983). Creativity and the Renewal of Regional Life. In A. Buttimer (Ed.), *Creativity and Context* (pp. 91–112). Lund: Gleerup, Lund.

von Thünen, J. H. (1826). *Von Thünen's Isolated State* (P. Hall, trans.). Oxford: Pergamon Press.

Weber, A. (1909). *Theory of the Location of Industries* (trans. Carl J. Friedrich). Chicago, IL: The University of Chicago Press.

List of Abbreviations

ASLEF: The Amalgamated Society of Locomotive Engineers and Firemen, dating back to 1872
CES: The Centre for Environmental Studies
CP: The Communist Party

70 Peter Hall

CPRE: The Council for the Preservation of Rural England
CSIRO: The Commonwealth Scientific and Industrial Research Organisation (Australia)
HS1: High Speed One, a fast rail line designed primarily for the Eurostar railway
LCC: London County Council
LDDC: The London Dockland's Development Corporation
NUR: The National Union of Railwaymen, dating back to 1913
RTPI: The Royal Town Planning Institute
TCPA: The Town and Country Planning Association
UCL: University College London (a college of the University of London)

Terminology Glossary

Barlow Commission: Sir Montague-Barlow's Royal Commission on the Geographical Distribution of the Industrial Population, reporting in 1940.

Beck Map: The abstracted London tube map developed by H. C. Beck in 1931, which has influenced how we draw metro and subway maps around the world.

Birkbeck College: The extramural college of the University of London.

Creative Destruction: The process of development of new technologies identified by Joseph Schumpeter in the 1930s and linked to Kondratieff waves.

Enterprise Zones: Small zones in British cities where industries might locate and be subsidised through tax breaks, sometimes linked latterly to science parks, and suggested by Professor Sir Peter Hall.

Fabian Society: A left-wing society of intellectuals in the UK Labour Party, concerned with rational and democratic policies and philosophies, founded in 1884.

Grammar School: The schools that segregated boys and girls from ages 11 to 18 and filtered out the most talented 20 per cent of the age group through a national examination called the 11+.

Greater London Plan: Abercrombie's plan for the metropolis developed in 1944.

Kondratieff waves: Long cycles of technological development of about 50 or so years in duration originally identified as key to economic development by Kondratieff in the 1920s in Russia.

Manchester Guardian: The most liberal of the serious UK newspapers (the broadsheets) originally published and printed in Manchester from 1921 until 1959 when it became a national newspaper *The Guardian*.

Milton Keynes Plan: The last of the new town plans commissioned in late 1967 and closed in 1992.

New Society: A weekly serious magazine on contemporary society from the perspective of the social sciences, published from 1962 to 1988.

Private Eye: A satirical magazine that has commented on British life from 1961 on.

Southern Electric System: The commuter rail system in London, south of the river, developed as a complementary system to the tube.

Tawney Society: A society of enlightened intellectuals which existed from 1981 to 1986 on the left of British politics, originally spawned in memory of R. H. Tawney and focussed on the establishment of a new political party, the Social Democratic Party (SDP).

6

AN ANCIENT FUTURE

Luigi Mazza

My personal intellectual journey is that of a self-taught man who trained as a planner through practical experience. The tools I believe served me most during my formative years were "learning by doing" and the behaviour of "the reflective practitioner". Professional practice made me face problems that had theoretical implications, and my theoretical concerns helped me to frame and reconstruct any problematic situations. Together with an uninterrupted interface with professional practice, another leading factor in my personal development proved to be the relationship I entertained with politics. My impression is that taking part in political action, as a member of a political party, helped me a great deal in appreciating the bonds that tie planning to its contexts and to the stakeholders involved. More to the point, my active engagement in politics assisted me in recognising the advantages and limits implicit in the application of participative processes, before such themes became the subject of intense theoretical and practical debates.

Setting the Scene

In 1961, having been awarded my graduate degree, I was eager to begin my career as a practising architect and such a prospect filled me with joy when, completely unexpectedly, I was invited to prepare the local land use plan for the city of Alessandria (Italy), my home town. Although I did not have the faintest idea of how to prepare a land use plan I was, for several reasons (mostly political), not in a position to decline the job offer. Hence, not without worries, I franticly began to read all the textbooks I could get my hands on, and in this way I began my career as a self-taught planner.

Looking backward, I would say that I faced the bulk of the planning problems and the "theoretical knots" which have stayed with me for almost half a century, during this first commission. Nowadays, by adopting a long-term perspective and after having worked on many planning schemes and land use plans, I feel confident in stating that the substantial issues and problems spatial planning is called upon to address have not changed much. For this reason, I am becoming more and more convinced that what lies at the heart of spatial planning not only has deep roots in ancient history, but also remains substantially unaltered with the passage of time.

The next sections of this essay focus almost completely on my first professional experience: the land use plan for the city of Alessandria. This experience provides the main thread guiding the narrative. Alessandria is a city, located in the north-western region of Piedmont in Italy. It covers an area of around 125 square miles, divided into 9 wards and 14 neighbourhoods, with a population at the time of approximately 100,000 people.

An Unforeseen Professional Appointment

Practice and Theory

To say that professional practice played a key role in my prolonged training process as a planner is not equivalent to stating that everything important that occurred to me professionally had its origins in practice. For example, with regard to the drafting of my first land use plan, a decisive factor proved to be the book *Traffic in Towns* (Ministry of Transport, 1963). The book, also known as the Buchanan Report, can be regarded as a true planning handbook; it provides the reader with a rich conceptual toolbox and a method which can be used to analyse the city and to design and redesign its form. The urban structure proposed in the plan for Alessandria explicitly acknowledges the intellectual influence exerted by Buchanan. Studies and research exploring the city's history, particularly in the nineteenth century (as for example Dyos & Wolff, 1978; Dyos, 1982), provided another important source of inspiration, as they offered a different way to grasp the opportunities and limitations of the area to be covered by the plan.

The interface between practice and theory, as I experienced it, took different forms. Professional practice kept generating new opportunities for theoretical considerations. When it is practice engaging theory, to a certain extent the opportunities for theoretical reflection are triggered by practical instances, particularly when practice was necessary to earn a living and therefore could not be programmed and directed as a research project. I accepted many projects because I needed the money, and that made me face problems that probably I would have ignored, or avoided, if guided only by my inquisitiveness or a specific theoretical concern. Moreover, to progress from practice implies facing different themes that are not linked by any explicit theoretical connection, and this in turn means that, in the short term, work can hardly have a cumulative effect.

The continued interaction between theory and practice was interrupted more or less ten years ago, when for the first time, I had a chance to dedicate a six-month period to my studies in the quiet of the British Library's reading rooms. During those six months, I became aware of the work of the British idealists (e.g. Vincent & Plant, 1984; Boucher & Vincent, 2000), an encounter that was to challenge some of the views on planning which I had held for a long time.

Technical Knowledge and Politics in Spatial Planning Processes

In the second half of the nineteenth century, a debate arose between the two economics schools of Oxford and Cambridge on the status of political economy vis-à-vis politics (Hall, 2017). In extreme synthesis, in Oxford, in line with its old reformist tradition, it was argued that economic policy is necessarily intertwined with politics and inseparable from it. In Cambridge it was argued that political economy and politics should have clear and separate domains, and that such a distinction was beneficial to both disciplines. The point of view of the school led by Alfred Marshall was that political economy should be a discipline independent from the aims of politics, and as such it could serve, and be functional to, different political objectives.

This debate always springs to my mind when I hear people claiming that since planning is inherently a political activity, distinguishing between spatial planning issues and political factors cannot be done. The fact that so many people share this view is not surprising if we consider that planning problems, and their solutions, mainly concern substantial political issues. This proves to be the case 99 per cent of the time, even when the actors involved in the process are not fully aware of it and are convinced they are looking for technical issues. As discussed in more detail later in this essay, when I presented detailed images of the draft plan for Alessandria to the councillors, I had to face the—entirely political—problem of stating who was to gain and who was to lose from the plan.

I realise now that in answering the barrage of questions coming from elected members, the points I made were all political. I justified the decisions taken as directed towards the "public good", rather than towards some of the individual interests that were close to the heart of many councillors. That was at a time when the mismatch between common good and individual interests had a great ascendency amongst the public; arguments in favour of individual interests would not be tolerated unless they could be cast to show advantages for the community as a whole. No doubt I was using a bit of rhetoric in defending the choices articulated in the plan by referring to the public good. My critics could have demolished my claim simply by stating that there is no such a thing as the "public good", but in those years that would have been a counterproductive remark to make. I understood that many of my arguments worked because what I was putting forward were political claims, which in turn sounded credible mainly because public opinion largely shared my political assumptions. In other words, the choices embedded in the plan held because they were supported by a positively biased public opinion. Technical arguments did not appear that fundamental to the debate, and when they were presented they only provided some added value.

With such premises, the interaction with politicians necessarily manifests itself as a relationship among equals. Planners provide contributions that are first and foremost political while politicians feel the urge to intervene on technical issues, because when decision-time comes everything is argued technically. I am of the opinion that although such an exchange of views has to occur within governance processes where the different stakeholders involved are asked to take decisions, the role of the planner should be that of contributing to the process through technical claims that highlight the main features, and rationale for, the various options available. To sum up, my thesis is that there is a form of disciplinary knowledge that can be used in governance processes. This form of knowledge, by itself, does not offer the "right" answers, but it is functional for their validation and their justification.

In the last few decades planners have largely focused their attention on procedural knowledge. For some time now, the issue of "how" decisions are taken has been at the centre of the debate, while the issue of "what side" of the decisions taken has been less considered, even if the boundary between the "how" and the "what" is not always clear-cut (see also Marcuse, 2017).

At the beginning of my career I found myself in a position of ambiguity, for throughout the Alessandria plan-making process I spoke and behaved as if I was a politician. My "clients" were the first to encourage me to speak as if I were an elected member of the local authority, rather than the chief planning consultant. Within the context of public debates, consultation exercises and council meetings, to be a political party member and to act as an elected member commanded authority, much more so than if I had to rely on my (supposed) technical competence.

Instances where the planning consultant ends up behaving like a politician with full approval of the client group are not rare. My role was appreciated because I could build a technical argument capable of supporting local government policy. These were policies I did believe in and that I could sometimes articulate better than local elected members. In such instances, the planner finds him/herself in the comfortable position of being able to say or hint at something that even the skilful local politician is not fully aware of. Or to state what politicians would rather have the planner saying, in order to use technical arguments to justify decisions that may have an adverse impact on their electors.

There are also a lot of cases where the planner is brought in to act as a third party. In the early 1970s I was selected as the lead consultant in charge of drafting a land use plan for a medium-size city on a lake, mainly because I did not belong to the party that won the local election. The local branch of the party was internally divided, and it was believed that, as an outsider who had openly manifested support for the opposition, I would not favour any particular faction. In that case I was chosen, and I was going to be assessed, not with regard to my technical skills but on the grounds of my integrity and my ability to mediate between diverging interests. I came to realise that at times conflicts internal to the local authority, over decisions to be taken in the context of the local plan, were in reality internal party conflicts over power. The decisions to be taken in order to steer the production of the local plan become an opportunity, and a means, for different local groups within the same party to test each other. Local statutory land use plans provide excellent opportunities for regulating internal disputes and settling scores.

Before the work on this city's plan began, I was called in for a meeting with the chairman of the regional assembly; during the meeting it became clear to me that it had been him who had insisted the job was awarded to me, but there was more to come. The chairman informed me that he was perfectly aware that the trunk road, then being constructed to run along the shores of the lake (the focal point of the city) was a technically flawed solution. Yet, this was the decision through which his group had gained ascendency and managed to establish itself as new leading faction within the local branch of the party. Hence, reversing this decision was not an option, and he concluded by saying that if I respected his position, then I could do whatever I thought appropriate with the rest of the plan. He added that if I experienced problems with my client group, I was to inform him and he would support me by intervening at the political level. I did not encounter any "problems", and therefore I do not know whether his support would have materialised. Nonetheless, that meeting confirmed to me that often a planning issue is in reality an opportunity for a political challenge, perhaps within a party, and that the urban problems at stake are often perceived simply as a resource for the challenge.

Going through this type of experience convinced me that a planning consultant, regardless of the job he/she has been asked to do, is always at risk of being used by politicians to settle their own disputes. To defend their professional integrity, the consultant's only resource is their own technical skill, which allows them to take a clear position with regard to the key decisions at stake. If the position of the planning consultant is substantially in line with the client group, he/she will be able to demonstrate that decisions were not taken to please the commissioning side, nor as a form of political pledge. However, if the consultant's position is not in line with the client's, he/she may try to convince them by making use of sound technical arguments. If this fails, the only solution left is to decline the work. If the planner is employed in the public sector and does not want to lose the job, he/she may enact a form of passive resistance and attempt to block, or at least delay, the implementation of the decision he/she does not agree with. In any case, the planner's means of offence, as well as defence, is the technical knowledge he/she brings to the table.

To argue that it is impossible to make a distinction between spatial planning and politics implies denying the existence of planning technical knowledge and hence of planning as a discipline. One point often mentioned when arguing this is that key decisions related to spatial planning are the result of political decision-making processes where many stakeholders are involved, with planners among them. Yet, it is when planners apply their technical knowledge that their contribution differs from other actors. The distinction between politics and spatial planning becomes more clearly identifiable if we use the term "spatial governance" to refer to all decision-making processes, and use "spatial planning" to refer to planners' technical knowledge. This way, spatial planning appears as one form of sectoral knowledge—one among others, each characterised by its own aim, and all functional for "spatial governance" and its objectives. In their work, planners intervene making use of their technical skills to put forward and defend the options they find most appropriate—or to put it differently, the options they think are functional to the achievement of their own or their clients' political objectives. To claim that separating politics from spatial planning is not possible leads to the conclusion that the role of technical knowledge is negligible. I think that such a perspective is not completely unrelated to the degree of uncertainty planning as a discipline is currently experiencing. Without a discipline to refer to, it may be convenient to hide behind the screen of politics by reducing everything to "spatial governance". The latter, however, does not constitute a discipline but rather a political process grounded on procedural knowledge, which has the analysis of decision-making processes as its main culture of reference. To make a distinction between spatial planning and politics equates to making a distinction between spatial planning and spatial governance.

Participation and Manipulation

During my first professional experience, not really knowing how to conduct myself in the drafting stages of the plan for Alessandria, I decided to apply what I had learned from political experience and set up a local forum in each ward and neighbourhood. The fora's main aim was to gather information on the needs and aspirations of the local residents, but also to collect their recommendations. It was one of the first times in Italy that a plan was prepared with the broader involvement of local residents, and the members of the local community showed their willingness to join forces. In almost every meeting I attended, I learned something new about the city and its resident population. In one forum in particular, I learned something I think worth sharing about decision-making processes.

I already had a chance to spend some time, and attend a meeting at a local forum, in a working-class neighbourhood located outside the city centre and separated from it by railway lines. On that occasion we discussed the lack of access to local services and facilities, including issues related to the lack of primary and secondary schools and the poor provision of public transport options to and from the city centre and to and from the railway station. This time I presented my proposal for the area, which hinged on significantly increasing, almost doubling, the size of the neighbourhood. This way the investment needed to deliver improved local services and infrastructure could be justified. The audience attending the forum surprised me by unanimously rejecting my proposal. They explained that in order to increase the population, new homes would have to be built; dwellings accessible to families with higher incomes than those of current residents. There would be population growth, but the newcomers would end up altering the political and social makeup of the neighbourhood, whilst for the residents its social and political composition was more important than obtaining more infrastructure and better local services. However, the surprises did not end there for me. Following a debate in which I tried to understand the origin of such hostility towards my proposal, and to defend it by illustrating the many advantages I thought it would yield to local residents, after having asked to put on record their dissatisfaction, the local residents decided to approve the proposal. This was due to the fact that the proposal was perceived as being the choice made by the party, and as such it should be respected. Those were years in which it was believed that the party, understood as a collective entity, had the ability to see and frame issues according to a wider perspective than that of individuals, including those directly involved, and that the party would ultimately take decisions in the best interests of all.

In that instance, I began to ask myself what the role of the public good was within the context of planning processes, and above all, if a definition could be provided for it, how and by whom. It was clear to me that the definition of "general interest" articulated by party politics was more credible than anything that technically trained individuals could have come up with through their analyses. I also became aware, once more, that the input coming from politics was a key ingredient in planning processes.

Through my presence at meetings organised for other fora, I came to realise that my technical skills, albeit limited, were enough to build arguments in favour of one proposal or another, and that it was not too difficult to convince my audience one way or the other. This was quite unlike party meetings, where the debate on a political matter was unrelated to the level of education but rather depended upon one's ability to extract from everyday experiences the reasons for supporting or fighting a certain decision. In other words, it almost appeared as if my belonging to a political party and my technical competence combined were enough to convince, and almost coerce, my audience into agreeing to my proposals.

After that professional experience, I opted for different forms of participative processes, always attempting to give stakeholders the information needed to enable them to make their own choices. For example in 1971, as part of the drafting of a land use plan for an industrial city in the metropolitan region of Milan, I had a leaflet prepared and delivered to all households. The booklet contained an explanation of the rationale for the plan, with particular attention paid to the need for compulsory purchase of the land necessary to deliver new services and infrastructure. In order for it to be easy to follow, the leaflet made use of graphics and cartoon strips. During debates, many families used common sense as a weapon in an attempt to rebut the technical arguments presented, but they were not always successful. My perception is that there was a divide between planners and their audience, and the concrete possibility of manipulating the beliefs of those who attended the meetings.

Going back to the plan for Alessandria, the local fora provided support for the planning process more than an opportunity for residents to inform the technical decisions to be taken, and the fora proved useful as they provided a place to exchange information. They offered planners the opportunity to correct any of the possible mistakes made and to inform the local residents what was envisioned for their area. I also realised that many residents attended the meetings after a long day at work. They were tired and had only had a quick supper in order to be able to join the meeting. Because of my political passion and pedagogical instinct, I would never have renounced the local fora, but nowadays I must recognise that outcomes seldom went further than the exchange of information, and only rarely did debates have "traction" in the way that they did during party meetings. When political parties operate properly, they are a much more effective and selective tool for participation. No public meeting or forum set up to contribute to the drafting of a land use plan has the capacity to elaborate information and provide structured inputs equal to that of a party meeting on the same subject. But, nowadays, political parties have almost disappeared; they have become almost entirely electoral machines and have lost the wide range of in-house skills they once had. To conclude, the problem of participation in planning, in reality, is the problem of open participation in politics. It is not an exaggeration to state that problems of participation in planning processes are in reality the same problems of a malfunctioning democracy, and that consultation events organised to discuss decisions related to plan-making processes work best when they are conceived as opportunities to be involved in politics, as people used to be in the past.

Ideology and Experience

Nonetheless, we often assume that residents do know and perceive their city based on true evidence as experienced in their everyday life. As part of the preparatory studies for the plan for Alessandria, I commissioned a survey to assess the most sought-after locations for new dwellings. It was naïve of me to do so, as in a small town such as Alessandria families in need of dwellings rarely have a strong bias. In order to get a house at a decent price, most of them are willing to move almost anywhere within the city boundaries. The survey did not give the results we expected, and it taught us that we might construct realities on the basis of false preconceptions.

The area of the city where many wealthy families lived was mainly composed of low-rise detached houses with one or two floors. The houses had small yards with a few flower bushes and some trees. The neighbourhood had only a minimal provision of green spaces. Anything could have been said of that neighbourhood, but not that it was very green. Regardless of this fact, the great majority of the interviewees pointed to that neighbourhood as the leafiest in the whole of Alessandria. The implication was that, being one of the wealthiest neighbourhoods in town, it ought to have an excellent provision of green space.

If, during a meeting, I had stated that the lack of green space was a fundamental feature of that neighbourhood, I would have astonished my audience, as if I was speaking of a city different from the one they knew. I therefore learned that the relationship linking a city to its inhabitants is mediated by ideological filters, which one needs to be aware of when advocating change, or when depicting an image of the city as it appears from survey evidence.

This way I came to realise that although planning work clearly involves the assimilation of "objective" data, such as the information needed to assess transport congestion or commercial demand for land, it also calls for an assessment of a whole range of more subtle ideological dimensions. These can have strong bearings on the attitude of local residents towards their city

78 Luigi Mazza

and the plan. The problem here is how to gain an understanding of such aspects, when only sociological and anthropological studies could treat the subject properly, and the necessary time and resources are rarely made available.

One Lecture on Planning

As mentioned above, one reading that proved decisive while I was trying to orient myself in the preparation of the land use plan for Alessandria was the *Traffic in Towns* report (Ministry of Transport, 1963). The Buchanan Report helped me to explore the links between land uses and transport demand, and the importance of this relationship with regard to the urban form. It also helped me in interpreting long-distance road networks within the context of orthogonal grids. The division of the city into environmental areas introduced a simplification at both analytic and project levels that proved very useful for a novice. Nowadays, such forms of simplification may be deemed excessive. However, despite the fact that they work against the principles underpinning the mix of activities and land uses, I still believe that they maintain their usefulness as tools that can be applied to understand contexts and situations. If the structure presented in the plan for Alessandria displayed a certain degree of clarity and elegance, this was mainly due to the application of the Buchanan Report's principles, or at least to my attempt to adapt them to the particular shape of the city and the existing pattern of the primary and secondary road networks.

Together with traffic surveys, origin and destination analyses and the detailed mapping of existing land uses necessary to proceed with the plan, a large number of other studies were also undertaken. These generated thousands and thousands of pages of data and diagrams, which in the end proved almost useless for the preparation of the plan. However, this was not the only lesson I learned from this professional experience. The dressing down I got during the debate on the plan that followed the presentation I made to the full council proved to be much more incisive.

The presentation of the plan to councillors included a whole series of slides illustrating the new urban form, and more specifically detailed bird's-eye views that were easy to understand and allowed for an easy comparison with the old parts of the city. Thanks to the many images shown through the projector, councillors followed the presentation attentively. When the lights went on again, after some general muttering and small signs of approval, a councillor, who was a university professor and held the post of undersecretary at the Ministry of Public Works, asked to speak. He said: "Dear architect, thank you for the beautiful pictures shown to us, can we now speak about the plan?" The meaning of that remark was clear; after the "rhetoric" of the images, we would like to know the facts. As if he doubted I understood the first time around, he then added that he wanted to know in detail: "Which new areas were earmarked for development? How much you could build on them? And according to which conditions?" Even if he did not say so explicitly, the meaning was straightforward: According to your plan, who are the winners and who are the losers? Who owns the areas you can build upon, and who owns the land allocated to social housing and local services? Fifty years have passed since then, and those words still resonate in my mind as if I heard them yesterday. It was the first planning lecture I received, and it taught me that for almost everyone the uplift in land values driving capital gain was *the* issue. The comment from the councillor kicked off a debate that resulted in the council asking for major revisions to the plan presented.

An Ancient Future 79

The extended shape of the city allowed us to propose surrounding the existing built fabric with a linear park that went from top north, all the way down south, and which would have enveloped all of the west side of the city (see Figure 6.1). The park was then to come back up the eastern side, and here rejoin the banks of the Tanaro River, one of the two tributaries that surround the city. The park was conceived as a long uninterrupted strip of land of variable width to be used for recreational purposes. In the plan it was suggested that teachers could take

FIGURE 6.1 Primary road network prepared for the Plan for Alessandria, 1968

Source: Author's archive.

80 Luigi Mazza

their pupils outdoors to show them the history of the city and how this grew in time (although I yet had to read Geddes's writings [e.g.: Geddes & Brandford, 1917; Geddes, 1925, 1973], he was already showing himself in my practices).

The analysis of traffic conditions pointed to the need to build a new north–south circular road, which could absorb the through traffic not directed towards the city centre and distribute it onto the external trunk road network. The ring road was to form the new city boundary on the east, and the new commercial and residential areas were to be located between the road and the linear park. The road was designed to run close and parallel to the new growth areas and included secondary distributors providing access to the various parts of the city, hence allowing for U-shape journeys according to the pattern: secondary distributor, into primary distributor (i.e. ring road), into secondary distributor. Vehicles were expected to move freely north to south and vice versa, without the need to pass through the city centre or to cross the barriers represented by the railway tracks converging into it. However, for the scheme to be successful, it was important that secondary distributors were designed as short routes in and out, to encourage motorists to undertake journeys that were longer in distance but swifter in time. This is why it was so important for that segment of the new circular road to run parallel to and not far from the new growth areas. The landowners with interests in the area, particularly those closer to the city centre, did not believe that the U-shaped circulation pattern was a good idea, and they were keen to push the ring road further out. This, in turn, would have meant allocating more land for development between the city boundary and the ring road, which was to become available for more development in the future if needed.

The council debate on the plan focused almost entirely on the possible alignments for the ring road. I was dumbstruck, as all the data we had showed that the areas earmarked for development were more than enough to cater for future demand, and there was no real need to increase them. However, landholdings were concentrated in the hands of a few powerful owners. Moreover, previous councillors had got into the habit of taking decisions on the areas to be allocated for future development on the basis of informal agreements with landowners—something confirmed by the fact that, in order not to interfere with such agreements and be able to decide *ad hoc* solutions as needed, a plan prepared a few years before was still sitting in the drawer, and never got a chance to be adopted. The councillors' behaviour should not surprise. The city obtained substantial advantages from such "deals": land for social housing and public services was given for free to the council, in exchange for planning consent being granted for other land they owned. The new cabinet decided to prepare a new land use plan to break the tradition of informal agreements, and this succeeded in generating a certain degree of discomfort among landowners. The drafting of a new plan was a measure strongly advocated by the new council cabinet, as they wanted to signal a wind of change that would bring an end to certain relationships and certain ways of making deals. It is possible that the demand to push the alignment for the proposed ring road outwards, in order to increase the land available for new builds, was motivated by the willingness of the landowners to flex their muscles in front of the recently elected members. Regardless of the signals sent out, the landowners attempted to continue on the path of informal agreements and contacted the councillor who held the environment portfolio. However, when this attempt became public knowledge during the meeting, the councillor was forced to resign rather dramatically. There was no need for me to prove I had no part in such informal negotiations, as the plan spoke for itself.

Regardless of the "wind of change", the resourceful landowners had links with other councillors, and the claim related to the need to push the ring road further out was supported by many elected members and was voted upon and passed. The land allocated to growth areas was increased accordingly, and the hypothesis of U-shaped journeys thrown in the bin. Amid such conflicts, clashes of economic interests, and rivalries between political parties and within the ruling party, I, acting as the lead consultant, found myself between the proverbial hammer and anvil. Nowadays, almost half a century later, a good chunk of the areas earmarked for development still lay vacant. This is a poor consolation if we think that the main feature of the plan was rejected and the ring road built further out, as requested by the landowners.

I was aware that although it was easy enough to point to the speculative drive as a key issue, it was not at all easy to set against it other issues that had come to the fore during plan-making, e.g. the matter of the urban form. Moreover, it was not easy to address the matter of the "unearned increment" in relation to the definition of "general interest", unless one was willing to treat the matter rather simplistically. The pragmatic request "to speak about the plan" had little to do with the matter of the "common good". Rather, it was directed towards knowing how the plan dealt with individual interests, which could be cited by surname, and which were politically represented within the council. What appeared important to me was that the relationship and the possible conflicts between individual interests and the general interest had the opportunity to come freely to the surface. This way they could be identified and dealt with without excessive hypocrisy. This was one more objective the plan had to contend with.

Control of Space and Social Control

Space and Citizenship

From the events of the neighbourhood forum where local residents opposed growth, where they were concerned this would have altered the socio-economic (and political) profile of their area, I learned that the plan is not only a tool used to manage the development of the city, the construction of new roads and the siting of buildings, but above all it is a tool that transforms social relations. At the end, the participants to the forum agreed to the proposal and some years later, following the approval of the plan, the neighbourhood was increased in size, in a project I had the chance to prepare myself. Around ten years ago, I was invited to give a lecture in Alessandria and was asked if I wished to take a tour of the new section of the neighbourhood, now fully built and inhabited. The neighbourhood had changed its look, as suggested by the person acting as guide that part of the city now "resembled the houses of the Nordic cities you sometimes see in the magazines". The buildings faced large, rectangular, green public spaces; they were no higher than three storeys, and they were surrounded by a double line of trees. My guide was unaware that the idea for the layout occurred to me after thinking about the military barracks set around large rectangular spaces originally designed for army training, which used to be located on the outskirts of the old neighbourhood. Regardless of the fact that that space was once part of a military facility, the environs were pleasant, and once the military structures were demolished I did my best to preserve the memories of a space that was simple and yet pretty.

The new neighbourhood looked airy and, perhaps thanks to the fact that it was a sunny day, lively. I wondered what those who, 30 or more years earlier, resisted the expansion plan would have thought. Not only had access to services and facilities improved, but the neighbourhood as a whole looked more appealing than I had hoped when the plan was adopted. I asked myself if and how social bonds had changed. Regrettably, I do not have an answer to these questions, but the available green spaces encouraged youngsters and adults to play and exercise; pedestrian movements were protected from heavy traffic; kids could safely walk to the new school built in close proximity; and the elderly could get to the community centre. Buses to and from the city centre were more frequent than before, and hence people who worked or studied in other areas of the city, or had to reach the station to catch a train, benefitted from reduced commuting times. It could be said that the opportunities for social and civic action were now enhanced and with them the political rights of the local residents. In other words, their citizenship conditions had improved.

We can use "citizenship" to refer to a social "status", made of rights and duties, but we can also use the term to point to a social process understood as a bundle of practices: the experiences and activities of citizens constantly committed to drawing and redrawing the boundaries of such rights and duties. Citizenship understood as a social process is a project as well as a way of life that entails a redistribution of resources, among them space, which is prime. My impression is that the residents of the old neighbourhood, hostile towards the expansion scheme, had a strong sense of citizenship and were rightly fearful of seeing this compromised by the arrival of new families from different backgrounds. For them, citizenship was a social process to be performed by fighting the weariness of a working day and attending the evening meetings of the neighbourhood forum. Maybe the changes made had improved their conditions and given them more resources to better understand and defend their social and political rights. More than anything else, I think it was important to show that things could change for the better. The change happened intervening in space. Space reveals itself as a mediation tool used by the practices aimed at redesigning citizenship conditions, with such practices using space to construct and represent a given social order.

The Poetics of Urban Space

I think Henri Lefebvre, more than others, grasped the importance of urban space in the construction of citizenship. He was the first to put forward the unorthodox idea of "a right to the city" as a practice leading to the democratic production of a social space. This was aimed at overturning the decision-making processes characteristic of the capitalist city, and at providing new rights to citizens, additional to the classic ones belonging to the welfarist tradition (Lefebvre, 1991).

Buchanan gave us a method to deconstruct the urban fabric, where the different land uses and functions can be used as guiding principles to reconstruct environmental areas and transport networks (Ministry of Transport, 1963). The differences are the key factor, which lead to and provide the rationale for, the separation of the parts and then their reconnection through transport networks. In the schemes imagined by Buchanan, the city centre seems to be missing. As a matter of fact, centrality should to some degree be averted, as it is at the origins of congestion and conflicts. What we could refer to as Buchanan's "physical functionalism", centred on the flows of people and goods, we can juxtapose with the "social functionalism" proposed by

Lefebvre, which focuses on social relations and interactions. Lefebvre recommended recomposing the urban fabric in a way that accentuates "centrality", and where "fluidity" and "continuity" are constantly at work, knitting together the different parts of the city. This is how the creation of the lifeless suburbs can be averted, by linking outer areas to the city centre in a fluid and continuous fashion. Lefebvre is constantly looking for a mixture, and the parallel occurrence, of multiple land uses and functions. This is something that surely does not support the smooth circulation of vehicles, but it succeeds in bringing to the fore the richness of the city conceived as a place of encounters.

The linear park I had in mind for Alessandria was an attempt on my part to link together the various neighbourhoods of the city in a continuous and fluid fashion, and it was meant to symbolically represent the seamless nature of the urban space. It was a pity I had yet to read Lefebvre, as I could have borrowed some of his arguments to present the project to councillors more convincingly, and perhaps this project would have been realised.

What I found striking in Lefebvre's approach was his attempt to overturn the processes of control and development of the capitalist city through a democratic practice leading to the production of a social space. This is what, on a small scale, I tried to achieve in Alessandria with the park and the "leopard spot" distribution of local services scattered across the city. Years later, I think I came to a better understanding of his remarks on social needs in everyday life and on other specific needs that are not satisfied by commercial and cultural services. Among them, the need for creative activities, arts and knowledge, access to news, symbolism, imaginary, sexuality, fun and games and physical activities. And, finally, the need for the city, and for urban life, which are needs "of quality places, places of simultaneity and encounters". In other words, places where the interactions are genuine, not guided by the exchange of value, commerce or profit. I have to say, as regard to his observations on human needs, I always felt them on my skin as the desire to experience the vibrancy and "buzziness" of the urban environment.

How to offer citizens new rights, additional to the classic ones made available by the welfarist tradition, is a question prompted by Lefebvre, which I reflected upon many times in my professional career. It often led me to propose schemes that were high density in terms of both population and functions, which often faced resistance and hostility. High-density schemes are in fact frequently associated with the maximisation of profits, often rightly so. Yet, high-density schemes can be compensated with a wealth of public open and green spaces. How to design and allocate such spaces then becomes essential. After 1999, when I was a consultant to the Milan City Council, we approved a number of high-density agglomeration schemes conditional on the ability of the developer to deliver substantial public green spaces and new services to local residents. We did not manage to achieve great results in every instance, mainly because, numbers aside, it is not always easy to find good urban designers and master planners.

A different but related difficult-to-solve issue is the extent to which we are able to ensure an adequate mix of population and activities in the more peripheral areas of the city. Lefebvre dwelled at length on this aspect of urban change. He was of the opinion that in order to transform the outskirts of our cities and bring them closer to the city centre, it was necessary to infuse in them the two urban features he identified as fundamental: centrality and simultaneity of opportunities and encounters. Since there is no centrality without an environment densely populated with activities and people, the suburbs need to become denser, provided this does not simply mean piling up people on top of each other, as many developers would be tempted to do.

The unavoidable juxtaposition between city centre and the outer areas becomes acceptable if the relationship between the two, from a functional point of view and above all in terms of its symbolic value, is spatially fluid and seamless. The spatial fluidity implies the creation of a permeable city and the defence of public spaces against their functional and symbolic privatisation. The visual and functional continuity of space is a real and abstract link that allows us to overcome the fragmentation of space and to connect the core to the periphery. From this perspective, urban public spaces—roads, squares, green spaces, etc.—are important, as they act as a connecting layer operating within the city, as places of encounters and social relationships. To guarantee the presence of such features in the peripheral areas of a city like Milan, for example, is not easy. The intervention has to occur on a consolidated piece of urban fabric, and thus working on a few big but isolated regeneration schemes would not succeed in bringing about change.

There is no urban realm without a centre, without a place where everything that can develop or be produced in space is concentrated, without a place of real or possible encounter of all subjects and objects. According to Lefebvre, to exclude groups, classes and individuals from the urban realm equates to excluding them, if not from society then at least from the civilisation process.

One of the greatest difficulties with regard to the retrofitting and densification of peripheral areas has to do with whether it is possible to create local centres that can provide similar services and infrastructure to those available in the city centre. A policy leading towards densification is feasible only if the area around the periphery has a population that is dense enough to express a demand for services that reaches a certain critical mass. It is a circular process, with population and activities mutually engaged in the densification process. At this point, we can note an inconsistency between an idea of a *right to the city* that focuses on the satisfaction of aspirations that are substantially independent from the capitalist means of production and consumption, and the need to retrieve, to a large degree, such means in order to achieve the desired outcomes.

The problem I frequently came to face while practising as a planner is how to come to terms with and contain the social and spatial fragmentation of the city, to recreate a spatial and temporal unity that encourages new forms of socialisation. In the scheme for the new neighbourhood in Alessandria, this aim was pursued by forbidding individuals and groups from privatising open spaces, and by laying out the dwelling units around a wide open space—something similar to a big courtyard where residents could meet and undertake joint activities.

Lefebvre's principles could be assimilated as principles laying the foundations of a poetics of urban planning, which have the potential to be debated and applied independently from the cultural perspective adopted by the author. I believe many would share the view that the urban realm is important in the construction, practice and experience of citizenship, and I think that Lefebvre's principles could be used to ensure that the urban form is functional to the betterment of citizenship conditions.

For Lefebvre the *right to the city* is the right to the centre, the concrete location of real and symbolic power, of culture, information and representation. The *right to the city* affirms once again the right to make encounters and to "concentration", so that places and objects can satisfy needs not often acknowledged by the technocratic culture—among them, the need for a social life and for the centre, the need for a symbolic function and for fun and games. Social needs and unclassified needs cannot be objective, as they are a part of time and only poets can adequately convey it: desire.

An Ancient Future

In my career I was lucky enough to work on a variety of different issues, dealing with different forms of planning action, some interesting and effective, others less so. For the sake of brevity, I made here only passing reference to other professional experiences, deciding instead to focus on one specific planning experience, which also happened to be my first. I decided to do so for two main reasons. First because, since ancient times, arranging and controlling space is the form of planning with which, so to speak, everything began. Although many aspects of politics, society, economics and culture may well change in the future, my opinion is that societies will inevitably have to control and order space. *Spatial governance* and *spatial planning* will therefore always be necessary; their future is an ancient one. Investigating the nature of and features characterising our need to control and order space, and the relationship these have with a given political order, would help us to improve the technical solutions we are able to offer. Second, no other form of planning can be enacted without a modification of the spatial state of affairs; hence *spatial planning* and *spatial governance* are a sort of necessary conduit for all other forms of sectoral planning.

This said, the account provided in this chapter would not be complete without addressing my involvement in *planning theory*. During my initial years in practice, I experienced considerable difficulties in appropriately framing the planning problems I was confronted with, and this was at the origins of the need I felt for a form of theoretical knowledge capable of providing a frame of reference and increased certainty for the plan-led actions I was engaged in. I hence got in touch with Oxford, where Patsy Healey and her colleagues were developing important studies on the subject, and in 1981 they organised the Conference on Planning Theory. The exchange of ideas generated by the event proved very stimulating; one of the results was the second international conference held in Turin in 1986 under the title Planning Theory in Practice (see also Healey, 2017). Another outcome was the drafting of the agreements for the 1987 creation of the Association of European Schools of Planning (AESOP) (see also Kunzmann, 2017). Above all, such activities allowed me to harness an idea of planning that went beyond Italian experiences and to assess aspects and problems that up to then I had not personally encountered. In order to give continuity to the debates that took place during the Turin conference, while also strengthening the relationship between the two sides of the Atlantic, in 1988 I became actively involved in the publication of the *Planning Theory newsletter*. This was originally conceived as a place to collect contributions to debates on themes we proved to be so passionate about during those years. In 1991, it became the *Planning Theory newsletter* journal, which was issued up to the end of 1997. Then, because of a range of different problems, we had to wait until 2002 for a new series of *Planning Theory* to be published, which is the format still in use at the time of this writing.

This proved to be an exciting period, during which planning theory ventured into what were uncharted territories. This was a result of the get-together and cross assessment of the European and American planning cultures, and of a rich—perhaps with the benefit of hindsight even too rich—interdisciplinary fertilisation. Concerning myself, I always felt the urge

86 Luigi Mazza

to link theoretical thinking with practices, to contribute to the growth of planning knowledge while averting a situation of diverging priorities (or imbalances) between the interests of academia and the demands placed on planning by society and governments.

Although I read, and to a certain extent interacted with, the theoretical research of the last few decades, my interest gradually faded. My attention shifted from a general theory of planning towards a theory of spatial planning, while I became more and more interested in planning history and the theory embedded in spatial planning practices adopted in the last two centuries. The attempt I made (an effort I am still engaged in) is to reconstruct a form of knowledge capable of legitimising planning activities. From such studies, and my practical experiences, I became more and more convinced that the essence of spatial planning is control of space. All of my experience begins and ends with this belief. In this sense, spatial planning has an ancient future in that it is grounded in experiences that unfolded together with the first forms of social life and which have reached us, travelling through time, with only few variations. Practices related to control of space will continue into the future, as it is impossible to conceive a model of society where control of space is not exerted (Mazza, 2015).

Despite the fact that many problems we deal with are ancient problems, a large number of them remain unresolved. We do not have at our disposal a shared and codified technical language that could be used to avoid excessive misunderstandings and which would allow us to build a well-structured and cumulative form of knowledge. Spatial planning is nowadays characterised by a large number of aims and objectives, not always clear or coherent with each other. This would suggest that we lack a discipline able to grow over time through a critical debate among experts. Moreover, regardless of the abundant contributions of planning historians, including some recent, few of them addressed matters related to planning techniques. In order to build and develop spatial planning as a discipline, we would need at our disposal a comparative history of planning techniques applied in the last 150 years or so, which would help us to understand what has been done so far, with what degree of success and failure, and how to make progress.

We are still piggybacking on the contributions of authors such as Ildefons Cerdà, Ebenezer Howard, Patrick Geddes, Patrick Abercrombie and Colin Buchanan. If we think that spatial planning is a technical resource that is unreplaceable, it is rather odd that after more than a thousand years the technical knowledge attached to this practice is still underdeveloped. It is necessary to design new rules and spatial models to be applied in professional practice, taking into consideration new contemporary needs and without becoming too intimidated by the dominant political cultures. To conclude, for people willing to study planning the agenda is crammed with issues; you only have to take your pick.

References

Boucher, D., & Vincent, A. (2000). *British Idealism and Political Theory*. Edinburgh: Edinburgh University Press.

Dyos, H. J. (1982). *Exploring the Urban Past*. Cambridge: Cambridge University Press.

Dyos, H. J., & Wolff, M. (Eds.). (1978). *The Victorian City: Images and Realities, vol. 1–2*. London: Routledge & Kegan Paul.

Geddes, P. (1925). Talks from My Outlook Tower: A Schoolboy's Bag and a City's Pageant. *Survey, 53(February 1)*, 525–554.

Geddes, P. (1973). *City Development: A Report to the Carnegie Dunfermline Trust. A Reprint*. Shannon: Irish University Press.

Geddes, P., & Brandford, V. (1917). *The Coming Polity: A Study in Reconstruction*. London: Williams and Norgate.

Hall, P. (2017). Visions of Contemporary Planning: Stories and Journeys in Britain and America. In B. Haselsberger (Ed.), *Encounters in Planning Thought: 16 Autobiographical Essays from Key Thinkers in Spatial Planning* (pp. 51–70). New York: Routledge.

Healey, P. (2017). Finding My Way: A Life of Inquiry into Planning, Urban Development Processes and Place Governance. In B. Haselsberger (Ed.), *Encounters in Planning Thought: 16 Autobiographical Essays from Key Thinkers in Spatial Planning* (pp. 107–125). New York: Routledge.

Kunzmann, K. R. (2017). Places Matter: Creativity, Culture and Planning. In B. Haselsberger (Ed.), *Encounters in Planning Thought: 16 Autobiographical Essays from Key Thinkers in Spatial Planning* (pp. 202–221). New York: Routledge.

Lefebvre, H. (1991). *The Production of Space* (D. Nicholson-Smith trans.). Malden, MA: Blackwell Publishers.

Marcuse, P. (2017). From Utopian and Realistic to Transformative Planning. In B. Haselsberger (Ed.), *Encounters in Planning Thought: 16 Autobiographical Essays from Key Thinkers in Spatial Planning* (pp. 35–50). New York: Routledge.

Mazza, L. (2015). *Planning and Citizenship*. New York and London: Routledge.

Ministry of Transport. (1963). *Traffic in Towns: A Study of the Long-Terms Problems of Traffic in Urban Areas (The Buchanan Report)*. London: HMSO.

Vincent, A., & Plant, R. (1984). *Philosophy, Politics and Citizenship: The Life and Thought of the British Idealist*. Oxford: Blackwell.

7

UNDERSTANDING AND IMPROVING PLANNING PROCESSES AND PLANNING INSTITUTIONS

A Moving Target

Andreas Faludi

Throughout my entire intellectual journey I was always concerned with planning processes and planning institutions. But why? One reason was my reaction to an architecture-cum-planning course in the 1960s, which I found uninspiring. This sharpened my understanding that planning is much more than "just" the designing of spaces. Over the years I understood that planning is a process which shapes minds and not just places. All the different planning institutions, including now those at the European level, play a decisive role in this regard. For this reason, I have always argued that good planning has first of all to unravel the planning environment, including the problems we face now and in the future, in order to make the right decisions. The project of which this book is the product has formed the occasion for reflecting on the pursuit of this moving target, from both a personal and a scientific point of view. My move from Austria to the UK has been decisive, and the UK is where I became the planning theorist as which I will remain known. This and a dose of good luck have taken me—thanks to the gracious support of Raya, my partner—around the world where, amongst others, I met all the authors of this book, mostly on their home turfs. But how did everything begin?

Setting the Scene

None of this was foreseeable. A Hungarian citizen, my father had fled to his country of origin on the day the Germans invaded Austria, and my Austrian mother had followed him to the relative calm of Budapest. After the Nazi takeover of Hungary, when I was four, my father perished. Somehow, my mother and I went unscathed until one day a Red Army officer shook hands with people crawling out of their shelter to welcome their new masters conquering Budapest in house-to-house fighting. After this was over, my mother decided to return to Vienna. With papers long in coming I attended school in Budapest until, in late 1946, I found myself, with only a smattering of German, in Vienna. There I spent my formative years, until after my PhD.

Other children had lost fathers too and been tossed around, so I was no exception. In Hungary, and for good reasons, my mother had told me a half-truth: that my father had been called up. A converted Jew, he had served in a Hungarian labour battalion, only to be massacred by the German guards during the retreat from Yugoslavia. The difference compared to children who lost their fathers on the German side occurred to me as an adolescent living in the household of my mother's second husband, a writer. At home, returnees who had supported the Allies mingled with Nazi opponents who had survived by keeping their heads down. Maybe this was why the slow revelation of my father's fate did not hit me like a brick, but it was responsible for my lifelong passion for history, starting with that of the Second World War. The desire to also understand geography and cultural context has never left me.

Vienna was an intellectual shadow of its past. Rather than liberators from the Nazi yoke, the Allies were seen as occupiers, but with a difference. The US Army treated us schoolchildren to Christmas dinners, and there were CARE parcels and Marshall Aid. The Soviets deported people and ran key industries for their profit, claiming, not always without justification, that they had been German property. But they refrained from imposing a Communist regime and, during a period of thaw, Austria miraculously gained its freedom. She lived up to her declared neutrality, nonetheless welcoming refugees fleeing from Soviet tanks crushing the Hungarian Revolution. World history happened on our doorstep, a formative experience for a 16-year-old. For us literally living on the edge, the lands beyond the Iron Curtain had been *terra incognita*. From where we lived, an oil well burning in Slovakia, then still part of Czechoslovakia, once seemed like sending signals from outer space, but in 1956 the border was open and real people swept across. My mother spoke Hungarian—mine had gone—and we were flooded with relatives, friends of friends and people looking for places to lay their heads. Later, on our travels, Raya and I would occasionally catch up with them.

Quickly, the Russian Bear crushed the revolution. The menace was clear, but I did not buy into a mindless Cold Warrior mentality. The home environment had taught me to see things from various angles. In this state of mind, and with mild amusement, I did my national service. Our non-commissioned officers unashamedly admired the *Deutsche Wehrmacht* in which some had served, and there were also some trained by the Americans. Covertly, the US had built up a small Austrian force to support NATO operations if needed. These troops formed the nucleus of the new Austrian army. Such enlightened instructors whispered into our ears what I would now describe as their doctrine: We were to hold out against the inevitable Warsaw Pact assault, using whatever weapons the occupiers had left behind, until NATO came to our rescue. It was only later that neutrality was given a positive spin, turning it into a defining characteristic of Austrian identity.

I had found school rather dull in comparison with the home environment. At university, I was drawn more to the few leftist students than to the conservative majority, the latter maybe a unique Austrian phenomenon. Students are supposed to be more liberal, if not rebellious, than the population at large. The third of students who were far right, including beer-swinging and duelling corpora members with Nazi sympathies, were really obnoxious.

The course I chose was architecture. I had no immediate role models, but my mother and a teacher had both encouraged me in the belief that I had inherited artistic talent from my father, a painter. I had seen a Le Corbusier exhibition. Architecture at the time covered the whole spectrum from interior design to regional planning, and I was looking forward to the curriculum allowing me to work on something like the *Plan Voisin*.

School had been unexciting, and so was the study of architecture. I had more talent for writing than for drawing. The home environment rather than my father's artistic gifts had shaped my capacities. Planning promised to be an outlet for my developing interest in the social sciences. My planning professor disabused me about Le Corbusier and focused our minds on more down-to-earth planning practice. There was no reflection on the role that had developed for planners in Austria, essentially that of a bureaucrat, or on the institution of bureaucracy itself, let alone on the political context. We were educated and evaluated through studio practice, working on real projects. I continued to use this method once I became a teacher myself, albeit with modifications intended to simulate the context in which planning took place. At the time, however, the pedagogy was authoritarian. We looked over the shoulders of our teachers sitting in front of our drawings criticising our work, invoking no obvious method. This surely contributed to my yearning for theory in the planning curriculum. Anyhow, dangling the prospect of a PhD before my nose, the professor handpicked me as his assistant. I was dazzled to the point where I declined a postgraduate Fulbright grant at the Massachusetts Institute of Technology.

Architects rarely did PhDs. Watching the professors with their coterie of assistants, seemingly free to pursue whatever line they wished, I had the wild idea of becoming one, an ambition that I have fulfilled. I hoped that writing a PhD would provide me with the intellectual challenge I had been looking for. My favourite topic had been planning in the Third Reich, but it was naïve to think someone, for instance my professor, would be willing to supervise me: too many of those involved were still in positions of authority. The PhD became a descriptive study of a small town in the hinterland of Vienna. The supervision was ungratifying, but I completed the PhD in good time and returned to my earlier ambition of studying abroad. A cousin of mine had had a Fulbright grant and some 17-year-olds I knew had spent a year in the land of plenty, as we then thought of the United States. Turning down the previous offer made reapplying to Fulbright out of the question. Plans for a year in a French-speaking country had dissipated along with my school-day French. I cast my eyes to the UK, where I wanted to do some sociology. Not that I knew what exactly to expect, but the few books I had read and the one course that I had taken as an external student made this seem an exciting prospect.

I had been at a UK voluntary agricultural camp and tramping around the country before, but that was not why I applied for a British Council scholarship. Maurice Broady, an enthusiastic sociologist at the University of Southampton, agreed to sponsor me. The British Council selection board in Vienna was surprised at someone they thought was an architect wanting to do sociology. Fortunately the chairman had heard about problems in new towns and found it reasonable for architects to wish to know "what people want". I got the scholarship.

The Different Phases of My Intellectual Transformation

I divide my intellectual development into four phases. The first phase concerned developing planning theory as presented in my two books published whilst in the UK (Faludi, 1973a, b). After almost seven years in the UK, I moved to the Netherlands. Comparing development regulation in the UK and the Netherlands, I recalibrated my views. Under the influence of the IOR School—a term to be explained later—and Popper's philosophy of science, I entered the second phase, in which planning theory became planning methodology and my view of planning became "decision centred". Surprisingly though, a longitudinal study of Dutch national planning revealed it as an, admittedly rare, example of great ambitions being fulfilled. Grappling with this finding, I concluded that the Dutch planning community had successfully

A Moving Target **91**

propagated a planning doctrine shaping the minds of professionals, politicians and the public alike. This kind of sociological explanation led to the third phase in the development of my views on planning theory; in Faludi (1998) I described this as planning theory "mark 3". Finally, in my fourth and continuing phase, I shifted my attention to the European Community, now the European Union (EU), and its tentative steps towards European planning.

Phase 1: Building a Planning Theory, 1967 to 1973

When we arrived, the UK was caught in a downward spiral. A Labour government was struggling to maintain the welfare state. With few exceptions—London, of course, but also Oxfordshire where we would settle later—the country was impoverished. The countryside was beautiful, but Southampton seemed dull. I knew what to expect, but I had gone there for the academic experience. Southampton University gave me a taste for seminars. Night-long discussions with friends had been my only preparation for the rigorous exchanges involved. I soon gave up any thought of returning to Austria, but what to do after the grant expired? One plan was botched by the unlikely failure of the timely arrival of a telegram[1] meant to confirm that I had a position at a German university. By the time it did arrive, the deadline for responding to another offer had passed and I had accepted a role as a lecturer at the then Oxford College of Technology, now Oxford Brookes University. The UK Town Planning Institute (TPI, later to become the Royal Town Planning Institute know as the RTPI), which approved planning courses, now required the teaching of planning history and theory, and my brief exposure to the social sciences, including some planning literature, must have appeared promising to the selection board. Whilst following a potted undergraduate sociology course at Southampton I had, on the advice of my sponsor there, spent the year studying US planning theory. This gave me the courage to leap into the void.

Why did they appoint me at Oxford College of Technology? The TPI had expressed a preference for undergraduate planning courses, which suited me down to the bone, and I had said so before the admission board. Faced with a rare example of an applicant with a PhD, the board took the plunge, appointing a foreigner with only a few months' experience in the country. It turned into a very fruitful five years or so at what would soon become a dynamic institution. Colleges of technology, some of which—like Oxford College of Technology—became polytechnics, responded flexibly to the TPI's preference for undergraduate planning courses.

The UK government promoted polytechnics to provide cost-effective higher education, and there was a strong demand for planning professionals at the time. When I joined in 1968 there were 11 staff. By the time I left there were 35 of us, and we held our own against the universities. My preference for undergraduate planning education became stronger still, and I developed ideas about how to integrate lectures and studios. The latter I diverted away from focusing on plans to role-playing and simulation exercises supported by reports on generating and evaluating alternatives. For this purpose I had electric typewriters installed in studios. The stimulus had again been from the US: I had attended an American-Yugoslav summer school at Ljubljana where John Dyckman and Ira M. Robinson, amongst others, had exposed me to thinking about the planning process.

Why all this US input? At Southampton, Maurice Broady had contrasted the encouragement of citizen participation in the US with what he saw as government-knows-best in the UK. He had suggested that I should compare US and British planning theory. As a preliminary,

92 Andreas Faludi

I had to decide for myself what planning theory was. In the *Journal of the American Institute of Planners,* as it was then called, I found literature from social scientists who had been flocking into planning, many from the first social science–based planning course at the University of Chicago. These sources, eventually to figure in *A Reader in Planning Theory* (Faludi, 1973a), had discussed the roles of planners in their various institutional settings and also how one should look at planning, with Paul Davidoff and Thomas A. Rainer ("A Choice Theory of Planning", 1962) making a splash. There were also Edward C. Banfield ("Ends and Means in Planning", 1959) and Martin Meyerson ("Building the Middle-Range Bridge for Comprehensive Planning", 1956), each with his own take on the rational planning process derived from their magnificent study of the Chicago Housing Authority (Meyerson & Banfield, 1955). John Friedmann's work, discussed at the Southampton seminars, had given me yet more cues. Having been exposed to the starkly different South American context, Friedmann had also factored the "decision-making environment" into the equation ("A conceptual model for the analysis of planning behavior", 1967). At Southampton, I had never been able to explore the UK context, so the comparison which Maurice Broady had suggested never came about. US planning theory had been enough to digest in the few months that I had. Later, with the stimulus of the Oxford environment, I was able to produce my own synthesis of how I understood planning, which became *Planning Theory* (Faludi, 1973b).

My book discussed planning as a rational process and planning agencies as analogous to the human mind. It presented hypotheses for empirical research. Friedmann (1967) and others, such as Dror (1963) and Bolan (1969), had done the same: advance conceptual models to guide empirical research. In the absence of any established empirical theory, my book ventured into making recommendations for bringing rational planning into practice and for planning agencies to be more open to a plurality of opinions and interests. It speculated about "multi-planning agencies" and about a "planning society" embracing change. I also made suggestions as to why the UK environment seemed more conducive to planning. From all this I concluded that institutional issues were not only different from but also of more general import than any theoretical propositions invoked in dealing with neighbourhood planning, urban renewal or regional development. My year spent exploring US literature had thus laid the foundations for focussing on the planning process and planning agencies.

"Andreas, there is a book in this", was famous urban sociologist Ray Pahl's comment when I showed him the lecture notes for my Oxford course. He tried to persuade Penguin Press to publish a book based on them. The wry reply was that the average reader on the train from London to Birmingham would not care to read it. More encouragement came from Peter Hall, who gave constructive comments on my first submission to *Regional Studies,* of which he was then editor. Through publishing "The planning environment and the meaning of planning" (Faludi, 1970) and eventually the book that Ray Pahl had encouraged, I became a planning theorist.

Before discussing criticisms, how could the inexperienced foreigner that I was do this? When asked about what he was afraid of in politics, former UK Foreign Secretary Harold Macmillan is reputed to have said to his interlocutor, "Events, dear boy, events", but events can also be fortuitous. I owe the publication of the two books to two events. Pergamon Press was right opposite Oxford College of Technology. There, a new editor was given notes on a potential planning series. He ambled into my head of department's office asking for advice. The head of department's reply was that the publisher would have to retain him and a young member of staff: me. The retainer was £50 sterling, a princely sum at a time when my monthly take-home pay was one hundred plus. We took the curriculum of the TPI, and I scoured the library for lacunae in the literature. One was literature of the kind that I had come across in the *Journal of the American Institute of Planners*.

Here I need to describe the UK context, where planners were expected to be members of the TPI (as indicated, soon to be RTPI). This was a self-organising "qualifying association", protecting its members against unqualified competitors by admitting only those having passed a stiff exam (see Hague, 2017; Healey, 2017). Having done so, planners affix the letters MRTPI, for "Member of the Royal Town Planning Institute", to their names. Qualifying associations took to granting exemptions to graduates of recognised courses. However, uniquely, the TPI had been set up by the "parent professions": architecture, civil engineering and surveying, with architecture the dominant profession. Only those qualified in one of these could become town planners, but in recognition of new challenges and a shortage of planners, geographers and others had recently been allowed to enter the profession through postgraduate courses. As with those who had worked their way up through the TPI's examination system and were neither architects, engineers nor surveyors, their only professional qualification was planning, so they considered themselves "generalists" but were looked down upon by those with double qualifications, the "specialists".

The TPI was self-governing, and in the mid-1960s tension erupted. Busloads of "generalists" arrived at a general assembly and staged a coup, as Brian McLoughlin, an eyewitness, recalled in an interview. The TPI's educational policy started promoting undergraduate planning courses as the preferred avenue for obtaining a qualification in planning without having obtained another professional qualification first. The TPI insisted on "planning theory" in the curriculum, but there was no relevant UK literature. In the 1980s, Peter Hall (1983) would still note that the theoretical impetus in planning had come from the US, which is no longer the case now. Among the imports then were the systems view and operational research and, as far as I was concerned, the US literature that I had read at Southampton. The Pergamon series provided an avenue for creating a comprehensive UK literature of which my books were part.

My becoming part of this exciting enterprise was the result of yet another occasion when fate smiled on me: I was invited to join the editorial board of the new planning series. The chair was George Chadwick, whose *A Systems View of Planning* (Chadwick, 1970) became volume 1 of an eventual 37 volumes. I had the temerity to criticise both it and Brian McLoughlin's (1969) *Urban and Regional Planning: A Systems Approach* (Faludi, 1973c). George's wry comment, which I would learn to sympathise with when my own works came in for criticism, was that he would have wished to be taken up on what he had said rather than what he had not said. John Friend, whose seminal book with Neil Jessop (Friend & Jessop, 1969, second edition 1977) had come out in 1969, was amongst the board members. His work, a genuine UK contribution to the planning literature that has never been fully appreciated by academia, is discussed later, as it put me on a course towards reformulating planning theory in the 1980s.

The notes submitted unsuccessfully to Penguin formed the basis for a this-time successful submission to the Pergamon board. Whilst still in the process of writing *Planning Theory,* they asked me to do a volume of readings. I had the articles which I had collected at Southampton to hand, and so *A Reader on Planning Theory* (Faludi, 1973a) came shortly before *Planning Theory* (Faludi, 1973b), both appearing just before I headed for the Netherlands.

94 Andreas Faludi

What did reviewers make of the books? Conventionally, the emphasis in UK planning education had been on *Principles and Practices of Town and Country Planning* (Keeble, 1951), so the focus on procedures raised eyebrows with planners steeped in this tradition, but they did not go public; others did. So, as with anyone who makes an intellectual statement, I became the target for critics, radical and otherwise, but gratifyingly most of them at least acknowledged the intellectual ambition of *Planning Theory*. Before that, the reader was generally welcomed as the first of its kind—a "Stout milestone", said Peter Hall (1973). Concerning *Planning Theory,* Patsy Healey (1975), my successor at Oxford Polytechnic, identified parallels with McLoughlin and Chadwick but raised concerns, amongst others, about the analogy between planning agencies and the human mind. In the early 1970s, neo-Marxists such as David Harvey, whose *Social Justice and the City* (Harvey, 1973) came out concurrently with my book, had great impact. In this vein, Jennifer Thornley (1974) reviewed the reader. Invoking a distinction made by Harvey, explaining and maintaining the *status quo,* as the reader apparently did, she deemed the work "counter-revolutionary". To qualify as "revolutionary", it would have had to explain the reality it sought to represent and to dialectically encompass in itself conflict and contradiction.

The general mood in this Marxist camp was that planning was ephemeral. Capitalism determined urban and regional development, so why bother about procedures? Later I would suggest that there were object-centred, control-centred and decision-centred planning theory paradigms, each with a different focus. Patsy Healey, along with Glen McDougall and Michael Thomas as the editors, included that paper from the proceedings of an Oxford conference in *Planning Theory: Prospects for the 1980s* (Healey, McDougall & Thomas, 1982), but they themselves were critical. My account of the controversy concerning "procedural" planning theory is to be found in chapter 5 of my follow-up, written at Berkeley in the mid-1980s: *A Decision-Centred View of Environmental Planning* (Faludi, 1987). I recall Judith Innes, to whom I showed the draft chapter at Berkeley, voicing surprise about how tough debates in Europe were.

At least *Planning Theory* gained notoriety and *A Reader in Planning Theory* was even a commercial success, with print runs going into twenty-thousand and more. To my surprise, this was not mainly in the UK—where few planning courses had access to the material from which I had culled most papers—but in the US, where it became a course textbook. *Planning Theory* was referred to less often in the US. John Friedmann, whose *Retracking America* (Friedmann, 1973) had come out concurrently, gave me a backhanded compliment in his review. I was the "last of the rational planners". The book was the ". . . epitaph on a mode of thinking about planning that may rapidly becoming obsolete" (Friedmann, 1974). He criticised the book for being "Anglo-American". Apparently, my acculturation had been successful. The book also failed to pay attention to non-rational elements, stopping short of considering the ongoing stream of actions that make any distinction between planning and implementation appear artificial. *Planning Theory* explored the notion of a planning society, and Friedmann extolled this as far as it went, but in his view I had failed to come to grips with the question of power.

Being the butt of criticism, authors tend to feel misunderstood. I felt this particularly with Friedmann's review. Although we had encountered each other only briefly at that time, his writing had been influential for me. We had also been inspired by some of the same sources. Karl Mannheim, who Friedmann discusses in his recent review of Austrian thinkers (Friedmann, 2014), has also influenced me. Another influence was Edward C. Banfield, Friedmann's teacher at Chicago. Banfield had been one of my sources for the rational planning model. In his review, Friedmann acknowledged such commonalities, saying that in the past he had been guilty of a similar quixotic pursuit of societal consensus arrived at through amicable discussion and mutual give and take. His experience had of course been vastly different from, and broader than, mine. Nonetheless I felt that a sympathetic reading might identify parallels between *Retracking America*—emphasising planning as an interactive process involving mutual learning—and *Planning Theory*. Under the influence of, amongst others, John Friend, my view of planning as an interactive process would become firmer still.

Phase 2: A Decision-Centred View of Planning, 1974 to 1987

The debate on *Planning Theory* started when I was in the Netherlands. What had taken me there? Well, once more fate had smiled on me. The book and its companion reader, both still in press, had encouraged Delft University of Technology to offer me a chair. We settled in the Netherlands, a prosperous country seemingly able to afford its welfare state, its crisis still being 10 years away. Planning enjoyed a high reputation, and the fame of Delft University of Technology had reached me in Vienna. Planning was a specialisation within architecture, so on the face of it I was back to square one. However, there had been a call for developing the discipline, and in this respect my work must have seemed to have promise.

I encountered a new educational context stimulating me to recalibrate my teaching and research. The planning profession in the Netherlands was not organised as in the UK; in fact it was not organised at all. There was no question, therefore, of recognising courses as prerequisites for practising planning. In fact, there was no educational policy other than what the planning courses came up with and what the university authorities, independently or jointly, accepted as such. As far as the highly respected practice was concerned, it was architects and civil and agricultural engineers that dominated. Geographers were supposed to do survey research. Drawing on international literature, some of them laid claim to a new discipline of "planology" (see Needham, 2017). Hearsay had it that my coming to Delft had raised eyebrows, therefore, with "planologists". "What was Delft up to appointing somebody with my profile?" was the blunt question put to me by the first incumbent of a chair in planology, Willem Steigenga, whose successor I later became.

Upon my arrival with the two Oxford Polytechnic graduates I was allowed to bring with me, I found Delft had decided to refocus on design! The saving grace was that I came with a grant from the Centre of Environmental Studies in London. It was for comparing, together with colleagues from Oxford Polytechnic, Dutch and English local planning. Apart from seeking an opportunity to learn about planning in my new home country, my idea had been that English and Dutch planning would provide a testing ground for the hypotheses on planning behaviour in *Planning Theory*. Once tested, I hoped that they would provide building blocks for an empirical theory. This reflected my idea of turning planning theory into a social science discipline with a body of empirical knowledge. This intention, announced in *Planning Theory*, earned me the doubtful distinction of being a "positivist".

However, during preliminary explorations the team persuaded me against testing my preconceived hypotheses. We opted for a qualitative approach with a minimum of preliminary assumptions, centred on two case study towns. They were Leiden in the Netherlands and Oxford in England. These were scoured for routine examples of projects that had gone through, amongst others, the standard system of planning regulation. The assumption was that each project was promoted by some actors, with others trying to control or even block it. All this was supposed to happen within social, political, financial and legal constraints. Importantly, we looked at projects first, then to the conditions under which they took shape, including any relevant formal or informal plans. We assumed that by doing this the effectiveness of planning, or rather the lack of it, would become plain.

The case studies were my introduction to Dutch planning. In addition, my inspiration from US literature was supplemented by the "IOR School", called after the UK Institute for Operational Research of which John Friend, fellow member of the Pergamon board, was the leading light. So here I need to introduce this school, which influenced our English-Dutch comparison (Thomas et al., 1983). The foundational text, *Local Government and Strategic Choice: An Operational Research Approach to the Process of Public Planning* (Friend & Jessop, 1997), first published in 1969, was the outcome of qualitative research. Its initial impact in the United Kingdom was pronounced, with Peter Hall giving it a glowing review. So was its influence in the Netherlands, and I am glad to say that I had a hand in this. I already had some exposure to the people from the IOR School because I had helped them with a project for the German government arranged through the agency of Fritz Scharpf, then a professor of public administration at Konstanz in South Germany. In the process I was offered, and turned down, a senior lectureship there—the last occasion on which I contemplated entering German academia.

I should add that UK interest in the IOR School has declined, and the advisory work of John Friend, together with Allen Hickling, took place outside mainstream planning. This decline was more than matched by interest in what is called "soft OR" (Faludi, 2004, see 1st ed. 1987; Friend & Hickling, 2005). The reason we drew on the IOR School in interpreting the outcomes of the Dutch-English comparison was the unworkable legal requirements in Dutch local planning. Unlike English planning at the time, but much like US Zoning, Dutch planning puts great store in binding statutory plans providing "legal certainty". But planning cannot live up to this ideal. Rather, it creates a make-believe world that is in stark contrast with a muddled practice. As evidenced by our research, as in what in the US is called "spot zoning", granting exceptions to plans was the rule. One of the conclusions was thus that planning systems and practices needed to openly embrace flexibility, for it is these decisions about development projects which really matter. According to the IOR School, what is important is to help decision makers with situations they face here and now. Planning should be ". . . not so much concerned with the description of the future—a future over which there is only limited control—but with providing a firmer case for action which there is power to take now. Planning is not so much concerned with producing a plan as with gaining a better understanding of the problems with which we are faced now and in the future, in order that we can make better decisions now" (Friend, Wedgewood-Oppenheim et al., 1970, p. 16). This quote, which should appeal to John Friedmann expounding planning as ongoing action, shows the affinity of the IOR School with collaborative planning and planning as learning. The underlying philosophy has remarkable similarities with alternative dispute resolution and communicative planning. The literature on the "argumentative turn" (Fischer & Forester, 1993), "communicative planning" (Healey, 1996) and collaborative rationality (Innes & Booher, 2010) has ignored this parallel. Nonetheless, the rebuttal of the critique of communicative planning by Judith Innes (2004) brings out the family resemblance of this apparently academically more respectable school to the strategic choice approach. The latter represents a practical way of approximating rational decision making. This is the result of its wholehearted acceptance of, and its manner of dealing with, uncertainty, making it what Rittel and Webber (1973) describe as a second-generation approach, which I describe as planning theory "mark 2". In dealing with uncertainty, strategic choice puts essential aspects of planning, such as engaging in research, political choice and coordination into a unified perspective (Faludi, 2004).

On this basis, I reinvented myself as a theorist of a pragmatic approach. By this time, I had moved to the University of Amsterdam where I succeeded Willem Steigenga, who had passed away all too early, in the foundational chair in "planology". I took various initiatives applying the message of the IOR School in the Dutch context, at the same time attempting to relate it to mainstream planning thought, including my own ideas. The radically new element encapsulated in the quote above was to focus not on plans but on decisions. The outcome was the "decision-centred view of planning" (Faludi, 1987), shifting attention from plans to what I call operational decisions, the only ones that effectuate change. Inspired by Popper's critical rationalism, I recast planning theory itself as planning methodology, with rationality a rule on *a par* with falsifiability for determining whether or not to accept decisions (Faludi, 1986).

The decision-centred view has implications for the "object" of planning. Previous views, including my own, had been that this was a material object. But the 1969 edition *Local Government and Strategic Choice* describes the object of planning already as ". . . the powers for dealing with . . . situations" (see Friend & Jessop, 1969, p. 120). Under this view, planning is the arranging of ongoing decisions as to the use of those powers into packages that make sense from some overall point of view. The link with what is conventionally described as the object of planning is indirect: The immediate object is the set of decisions at hand. These decisions need to be arranged into coherent packages (Mastop & Faludi 1997).

Critics of procedural planning theory alleged it neglected the object of spatial or, the term then in use, physical planning, but now I could say something about that object.. I started considering this object as the "environment". The Dutch language, in which some of these discussions were held, has two words for it: *milieu* and *omgeving*. The former stands for environment in the sense of water and ambient air, nature preservation and so forth. *Omgeving* is what in the UK used to be referred to as the physical environment, the object of "physical" planning, alongside "economic" and "social" planning. But physical planning and physical environment were uncommon terms in the US, where I wrote *A Decision-Centred View of Environmental Planning* (Faludi, 1987), so I opted for "environment" in its comprehensive sense. I proceeded to identify the handles for managing it, which were thus the potential objects of decision making. In so doing, I took a leaf out of a book in German (Bökemann, 1982) on the theory of spatial planning. Bökemann focuses on the land regime superimposing itself on parcels of land and their owners. These parcels of land I described as "land decision units". Following the IOR School, I defined the object of planning in terms of the powers of influencing what happened with and on these units. Always inspired by Bökemann, I broke land decision units down into their component parts: their boundaries defining them, the resources on them, their positions in relation to other units and the legal titles on them. The object of environmental planning was then the sum total of possible decisions as regards the boundaries of land decision units, the resources on them, access to, and/or the legal titles on them.

Phase 3: Planning Doctrines Shape Minds, 1988 to 1994

The reception was mooted, and this is where I let matters rest, focusing instead on the "decision-centred" view as an interactive process, taking a "sociological turn" (Faludi, 1998). This took me along two related tracks. One was to pay more attention to the context of planning as decision making, in particular the ideas framing planning thought and action. The second was to see the role of planning itself as framing rather than determining subsequent decision making.

The first study of planning in the Netherlands, taking an approach as in the sociology of science by Peter de Ruijter (1987), invoked the concept of a "programme" binding a coalition together, one which he likened to a social movement behind the formation of the "Netherlands Institute for Housing and Planning". De Ruyter took his cues from Thomas Kuhn. Studying planning in late nineteenth-century Amsterdam, Arnold van der Valk (1989) identified a coherent body of thought with substantive and procedural precepts on "systematic town extension", to which planners in Amsterdam referred. In a celebrated work, another former student of mine, Maarten Hajer (1995), invoked the notion of hegemonic projects consisting of discourses, systems of positions and practices and strategic actions. In a study of the relative success—yes, success there was—of Dutch national planning (Faludi & van der Valk, 1994), we called this a "planning doctrine". This concept delineates an arena for discussion and action by providing the code (Faludi & Korthals Altes, 1994, p. 10) in which situations are defined, not only by the planners but ideally also by those responsible for follow-on decisions. Our proposition was that Dutch national planning owed its success in shaping development not to the firmness of any plans, but to the strength of the underlying doctrine. It shaped the minds of planners, politicians and relevant publics who accepted it as a valid frame. The doctrine comprised a synthesis of views as to what the country should look like and how planning could help in pursuing this ideal. In taking a leaf out of the book of the sociology of science—hence sociological turn—planning theory in this phase took on a new quality.

The second track taken under this sociological turn concerned what we called the performance of plans. I took my cues from the central point of the decision-centred approach I had developed: It is not the implementation of preconceived plans that counts but the quality of day-by-day decisions. Inspired by Barrett and Fudge (1981), my argument was thus that evaluation of planning action should focus on whether strategic planning provided decision makers with intelligence as to the likely ramifications of their intended action (Mastop & Faludi, 1997; Faludi, 2000). If and when and where this happened, it was possible to say that strategic planning had effects. Strategic planning thus "shapes minds, not places", we claimed, which is why this is another instance of a sociological turn in planning theory. Our work had increasing resonances with the "communicative turn" in planning theory, as indeed did the work of the IOR School, though in both instances this connection has been ignored by most planning academics.

Phase 4: Planning Challenges in Europe, 1995 to . . .

Some years before the turn of the century I arrived at a crossroads. Should I continue studying the fate of Dutch doctrine? Responding to the mood of the time, a succession of right-of-centre governments have dismantled a good part of the institutional setup, and doctrine has dissipated since. In retrospect this could have been an opportunity to explore the analogy, one we had invoked only as a contingency, between a potential "doctrinal revolution" and "scientific revolutions" according to Kuhn (1962). It was not to be because by the time the crisis hit Dutch planning I had already engineered a career change. By this time, the project of European integration was developing rapidly, affecting concepts of regional development and spatial planning. I was alerted to ideas about planning emerging at the European level by a former student of mine who became a well-respected participant in the process, as well as by the parallel works of Klaus Kunzmann and Louis Albrechts, both of whom I already knew well. Also, my work on Dutch national planning provided a good foundation for exploring how planning ideas were unfolding at this scale. And my "European" background was a useful asset in this project. So, after 21 years at the University of Amsterdam I became a professor of spatial policy systems in Europe at Radboud University Nijmegen in 1999. There I taught European planning, giving me the incentive to continue with something that I had already started doing: empirical research into its processes and institutions of a kind that I have been engaged in ever since.

Initially I thought that, speaking German, I would have unique access to German thinking on the matter. Holding the presidency of the Council of Ministers of the European Union (EU) in 1994, Germany exerted its influence early on in the process. It continues to do so because of the sheer weight of its professionals, operating mainly from a base at the Federal Institute for Research on Building, Urban Affairs and Spatial Development within the Federal Office for Building and Regional Planning, also known by their German acronyms as the BBSR and BBR in Bonn. But Germany's concern was not only improving European planning. It was also defending the turf of German planning against what they perceived, and continue to perceive, as an invasive European Commission.

Little did I know at the time that I would also have to brush up my school-day French, which had been buried under the English and then Dutch languages. Nor did I know that looking into things European would become as intellectually challenging as it has been.

Initially I suppose I was a naïve "Euro-federalist", assuming that Brussels was benevolent and member states narrow-minded—which they sometimes are, of course. My research since has taught me, if not to switch sides and support the member states, then at least to appreciate that federalism or, as it is also called, supranationalism may not be an answer. In due course, I would also question the concept of the nation-state, and with it that of a putative "United States of Europe" as such. Maybe the historic construct of a state with a territory over which it claims jurisdiction is the problem!

Such thoughts arose from reflecting on what I observed following European practitioners from a range of countries. I should not give the impression, though, that in so doing I followed any systematic comparative method. This was a pragmatic process relying on the snowball effect of me becoming familiar with, in some cases friends with, practitioners and also fellow academics interested in European planning. I was building myself a network on which I could draw for information and inspiration. It has become something of a passion to learn what European integration means in itself. Later, I also explored what it means for the concepts of territory, nation-state territoriality and the nation-state as such which may—just may!—metamorphose into something less dominant, overbearing and exclusive than it is today—that is, if rising external and internal security concerns do not reinforce the apparent rationale for its existence.

100 Andreas Faludi

Whether under the flag of European spatial development or, as is presently the case, of an EU policy of promoting territorial cohesion, the practical achievements of European planning are below expectations. Anyhow, the naïve Euro-federalist that I had been, believing that Brussels needed planning powers commensurate with the EU scale, was disabused by the observed reality of the making of the European Spatial Development Perspective, or ESDP, the object of a case study (Faludi & Waterhout, 2002). That reality pointed more to an "intergovernmental" EU. But soon I discovered there were other views of what the EU was, or could be. These views were more congenial to what we observed on the ground, where there was much networking leading to mutual learning, creating a slow but insistent dynamics that changed perceptions (Faludi, 2010, 2014). This was of course inspired by the sociological turn taken in phase 3 of my intellectual journey. I also began to put more store by earlier ideas concerning the evaluation of the performance of strategic planning, of which the ESDP was of course an example. I looked at what they told decision makers about the concrete decisions they faced. But it was clear that a European "planning doctrine" was "a bridge too far" (Faludi, 1996). Even in terms of learning and so forth, European planning has had only a limited influence. Meanwhile I, for one, have learned about European integration and take some consolation from its history: The patient but tenacious pursuit of good ideas is of the essence in this process. So European planning could be a long-term goal to be achieved in the face of persistent opposition.

I also began to think that there is more to consider than the alleged short-sightedness of decision makers. In the literature, there is a lively debate on the nature of space, whether absolute or relative. Both John Friedmann (1994) and Patsy Healey (Graham & Healey, 1999; Healey, 2010) have criticised a "Euclidean" absolute view of space as a basis for planning. The debate is important for European planning. Political decision makers and their planning advisers are stuck in the absolute view of space, if for no other reason than because absolute space complements territory as a fixed expanse of land: a land decision unit, albeit on a large scale. Politicians and planners, and researchers, are thus constrained by variations of "methodological nationalism", the ". . . tendency within political science to focus on the nation-state as the main unit of analysis in studying social and political life" (Jeffrey & Schakel, 2013, p. 299). It constrains them to reproduce the assumption that the nation-state is the boundary condition for defining social problems and phenomena.

Extensive and complex debates on this take place within human geography, where a "relational" view of space in a networked world is opposed to a "territorial view" asserting the continuing relevance of administrative boundaries. But there is helplessness in face of the monopoly of such units on the production of democratic legitimacy through elections. Bound to pursue the interests of their territorial constituencies, elected politicians cannot take due account of spatial interdependence. In the UK, the relevant academic debate is particularly virulent, but the conclusion is always to seek compromise between relational and territorial views (Harrison, 2013). Rare are the examples of the principle of territorial representation as such being questioned. Sabel and Zeitlin (2010) at least lay bare untenable assumptions of the "principal-agent" theory underlying it, but they do not address the territorial dimension. Rehfeld (2008) proposes random rather than territorial constituencies for the US. As a constitutional theorist, he does not discuss the geography literature. Nor does Rehfeld question the nation-state as such, only the subdivision of the US into congressional districts. However, it is possible to question at all levels the continuing monopoly of territorial jurisdictions on the production of democratic legitimacy. Cross-border and transnational relations, including those between the EU and its "near neighbourhood", but also trans-Atlantic and even worldwide, mean that we should rethink how to represent networks in the electoral process.

However, undoing territorial institutions is an unrealistic prospect in the short term. Having admitted that much, I arrive at a further conclusion. It is that representative democracy itself is a human construct and thus not beyond criticism. First, there is much variation in the ways in which it is organised. Second, it creates a "territorial-administrative complex" which, like the "military-industrial complex", skews decision making (Faludi, 2017). As a consequence, it does not necessarily pursue any genuine common interest. The interests of elected representatives and their bureaucratic support troops may prevail. Third, and once again as with all human constructs, the territorial-administrative complex can change. Like the medieval—non-territorial—feudal order having slowly but persistently been replaced by the system of nation-states, so with that system itself: It can be improved and in the process modified, perhaps beyond recognition.

Retrospect and Prospect

Should I have done things differently? I never regret having abandoned architecture, but if I had not done the course I would not have become the protagonist of planning as an independent programme of study with planning theory as a core subject, views which I still hold strongly. Importantly, I would not have done the student internship with an architectural firm in Israel that ultimately led to the lifelong partnership that my wife and I continue to enjoy. Why, then, Israel? As a boy I had read about a Swiss globetrotter pretending to be an illegal Jewish immigrant to Palestine in the 1930s, so it was mild adventure rather than my roots that I sought in Israel, which was still small and romantic. Romance there was when I met Raya, whose parents had managed to reach Palestine before the war. In our case, and not without initial detours, just when the PhD was finished romance became a lifelong partnership. Raya and I went on an inadequate grant to experience Spartan living conditions in Southampton.

It had always been my ambition to go, albeit temporarily, abroad. It turned out to be a permanent life away from where either of us had roots. So we became a family with a multiplex identity, which is not uncommon now. I would not brag about it, but I continue to find this satisfactory. Anyhow, thanks to repeated assignments to teach European planning at two of its universities, we have rediscovered Vienna as the vibrant place it is now, thanks, amongst other things, to having regained its position—not entirely unproblematic, of course—in the heart of Central Europe. But we have lived in Delft for longer than anywhere else, and that's where we call home.

Home could have been Woodstock, where we lived in pastoral surroundings. But however much we enjoyed life in England, the UK in general and academic life in particular have become even tougher there than they are elsewhere. And what my career prospects would have been is anybody's guess. In the eyes of the profession I was not qualified as a planner. Maybe this could have been overcome, but I would certainly never have become modestly expert in interpreting Dutch, let alone European, planning. I learnt that grabbing opportunities where they present themselves is important!

As to Dutch planning, as reported it is becoming less assured of itself, but it would require in-depth research to unravel whether there has been a doctrinal revolution, analogous to Kuhn's scientific revolutions, which we already saw as a theoretical possibility at the time of writing about doctrine. My guess is that it has, but I am in no position to do, nor indeed disposed to do,

102 Andreas Faludi

the work needed to support this hunch. But I have no regrets about having been involved in inquiring into Dutch planning for my first, give or take, 20 years in the Netherlands. Amongst other things, this is because it provided me with an entry to the work on European planning, which I continue to be involved in.

How do I look back on my role in developing planning theory? Presently, there is a journal *Planning Theory*. It shows the field as highly diversified, maybe to the point where the purpose of planning theory is becoming unclear. There is no longer a central concern for it to form the core of the planning curriculum, which drove the UK debates of the 1960s and 1970s. In fact, planning education itself has become more diversified, with less emphasis on giving graduates a planning identity. I would applaud it if the present generation would return to the issue of the identity of planners and the theory on which it rests. This is not meant to signify a commitment to town planning as a separate profession. I have been known to be inimical to this idea. No, this is meant as a plea for planning as a more general orientation towards *Planning in the Public Domain,* the title of one of John Friedmann's books (Friedmann, 1987).

If I am no longer involved, then it is because I have moved to new pastures. From our beloved Delft, according to my ability I participate in the exploits of the up-and-coming generation of working on European planning. They need to reinvent established institutions, which involves deconstructing existing ones. Surely, this is a long process, but exciting and an area within which it is worthwhile to make one's mark.

Among the vehicles are the congresses of the Association of European Schools of Planning; I organised the first congress in Amsterdam in 1987. Towards the end of the 1990s, I took the place of the late Dick Williams (Williams, 1996), to whom all scholars of European planning owe an intellectual debt, and have co-chaired the relevant sessions for many, many years. I continue to be an elder statesman in the vibrant community of younger colleagues sharing an open but duly critical attitude towards European planning. Academic interest seems to be greater than in the field itself, where great ambitions have been replaced by a frantic search for sources of funding. Still, the multivarious learning resulting from cross-border and transnational exchanges should provide a basis for renewed ambitions and relevant initiatives in the future.

What I have learned is to relentlessly search out and help to repair the failings of existing systems, including those involved in European integration. In so doing, one must of course dare to break taboos, including, where it relies on concepts of yesteryears, that of the nation-state, the homogenous region or the unitary city being the primary unit of analysis and action. And I have learned not to be afraid to move to new situations if and when the opportunity arises, not to flinch from assuming a new identity, intellectual or otherwise, acquiring new languages and settling into new homelands. Your previous identities, languages and cultures form the rich sediment upon which to graft new life, hopefully making for a fertile cosmopolitan mixture.

Note

1 Sending a telegram was an expensive method of rapidly conveying messages which with the arrival of Internet has become obsolete.

References

Banfield, E. C. (1959). Ends and means in planning. *International Social Science Journal, 11,* 361–368.
Barrett, S., & Fudge, C. (Eds.). (1981). *Policy and Action: Essays on the Implementation of Public Policy.* London & New York: Methuen.

Bökemann, D. (1982). *Theorie der Raumplanung*. Munich: Oldenbourg.

Bolan, R.S. (1969). Community decision behavior: The culture of planning. In A. Faludi (1973) *A Reader in Planning Theory* (pp 371–394). Oxford: Pergamon.

Chadwick, G. A. (1970). *A Systems View of Planning*. London: Pergamon.

Davidoff, P., & Reiner, T. A. (1962). A choice theory of planning. *Journal of the American Institute of Planners, 28*, 108–115.

de Ruijter, P. (1987). *Voor volkshuisvesting en stedebouw: Voorgeschiedenis, oprichting en programma van het Nederlands Instituut voor Volkshuisvesting en Stedebouw 1850–1940*. Utrecht: Uitgeverij Matrijs.

Dror, Y. (1963) The planning process: A facet design. In A. Faludi (1973) *A Reader in Planning Theory* (pp 323–343). Oxford: Pergamon.

Faludi, A. (1970) The planning environment and the meaning of planning. *Regional Studies, 4*, 1–9.

Faludi, A. (Ed.). (1973a). *A Reader in Planning Theory*. Oxford: Pergamon.

Faludi, A. (1973b). (Reprinted with a new foreword by the author in 1984) *Planning Theory*. Pergamon: Oxford.

Faludi, A. (1973c). The systems view and planning theory. *Socio-Economic Planning Science, 7*, 67–77.

Faludi, A. (1986). *Critical Rationalism and Planning Methodology*. London: Pion Press.

Faludi, A. (1987). *A Decision-centred View of Environmental Planning*. Oxford: Pergamon.

Faludi, A. (1996). European planning doctrine: A bridge too far? *Journal of Planning Education and Research, 16*, 41–50.

Faludi, A. (1998). From planning theory mark 1 to planning theory mark 3. *Environment and Planning B: Planning and Design, 25th Anniversary Issue*, 110–117.

Faludi, A. (2000). The performance of spatial planning. *Planning Practice and Research, 15*, 299–318.

Faludi, A. (2004). The impact of a planning philosophy. *Planning Theory, 3*, 225–236.

Faludi, A. (2010). *Cohesion, Coherence, Cooperation: European Spatial Planning Coming of Age? (RTPI Library Series)*. London: Routledge.

Faludi, A. (2014) EUropeanisation or Europeanisation of spatial planning? *Planning Theory and Practice, 15*, 155–169.

Faludi, A. (2016) European integration and the territorial-administrative complex. *Geografiska Annaler: Series B, Human Geography, 98*, 71–80.

Faludi, A., & Korthals Altes, W. (1994). Evaluating communicative planning: A revised design for performance research. *European Planning Studies, 2*, 403–418.

Faludi, A., & Korthals Altes, W. (1997) Evaluating communicative planning. In D. Borri et al. (Eds.) *Evaluating Theory-Practice and Urban-Regional Interplay in Planning* (pp. 3–22). Oxford: Carfax Publishing Company.

Faludi, A., & van der Valk, A. J. (1994). *Rule and Order: Dutch Planning Doctrine in the Twentieth Century*. Dordrecht: Kluwer Academic Publishers.

Faludi, A., & Waterhout, B. (2002). *The Making of the European Spatial Development Perspective: No Masterplan (RTPI Library Series)*. London: Routledge.

Fischer, F., & Forester, J. (Eds.). (1993). *The Argumentative Turn in Policy Analysis and Planning*. London: Duke University Press/UCL Press Limited.

Friedmann, J. (1970). A conceptual model for the analysis of planning behavior. In A. Faludi (1973) *A Reader in Planning Theory* (pp 345–370). Oxford: Pergamon.

Friedmann, J. (1973). *Retracking America: A Theory of Transactive Planning*. Garden City, NY: Doubleday Anchor.

Friedmann, J. (1974). Review of 'Planning Theory'. *Regional Studies, 8*, 311.

Friedmann, J. (1987). *Planning in the Public Domain*. Lawrenceville, NJ: Princeton University Press.

Friedmann, J. (1994). The utility of non-Euclidean planning. *Journal of the American Planning Association, 60*, 377–379.

Friedmann, J. (2014). Austrians in the world: Conversations and debates about planning and development. *European Spatial Research and Policy, 21*, 11–22.

Friend, J. K., & Hickling, A. (2005, first edition 1987). *Planning under Pressure: The Strategic Choice Approach*. Oxford, Boston, Johannesburg, Melbourne, New Delhi & Singapore: Butterworth-Heinemann.

Friend, J. K., & Jessop, W. N. (1969, second edition 19779). *Local Government and Strategic Choice*. Oxford: Pergamon.

Friend, J.K., Wedgewood-Oppenheim, F. et al. (1970) *The Logimp Experiment: A Collaborative Exercise in the Application of a New Approach to Local Planning Problems*. London: Centre for Enviromental Studies.

Graham, S., & Healey, P. (1999). Relational concepts of space and place: Issues for planning theory and practice. *European Planning Studies, 7*, 623–646.

Hague, C. (2017). Challenging Institutions That Reproduce Planning Thought and Practice. In B. Haselsberger (Ed.), *Encounters in Planning Thought: 16 Autobiographical Essays from Key Thinkers in Spatial Planning* (pp. 222–241). New York: Routledge.

Hajer, M. A. (1995). *The Politics of Environmental Discourse: Ecological Modernization and the Policy Process*. Oxford: Oxford University Press.

Hall, P. (1973). Stout milestone: Review of a reader in planning theory. *New Society, 29 March*, 713.

Hall, P. (1983). The Anglo-American connection: Rival rationalities in planning theory and practice, 1955–1980. *Environment and Planning B, 10*, 41–46.

Harrison, J. (2013). Configuring the new "regional world": On being caught between territory and networks. *Regional Studies, 42*, 55–74.

Harvey, D. (1973). *Social Justice and the City*. London: Arnold.

Healey, P. (1975). Review of 'Planning Theory'. *Town and Country Planning, 1*, 43–44.

Healey, P. (1996). The communicative turn in planning theory and its implications for spatial strategy formation. *Environment and Planning B: Planning and Design, 23*, 217–234.

Healey, P. (2010). *Making Better Places*. London: Palgrave.

Healey, P. (2017). Finding My Way: A Life of Inquiry into Planning, Urban Development Processes and Place Governance. In B. Haselsberger (Ed.), *Encounters in Planning Thought: 16 Autobiographical Essays from Key Thinkers in Spatial Planning* (pp. 107–125). New York: Routledge.

Healey. P., McDougall, G., & Thomas, M. J. (Eds.). (1982). *Planning Theory—Prospects for the 1980s*. Oxford: Pergamon.

Innes, J. E. (2004). Consensus building: Clarification for the critics. *Planning Theory, 3*, 5–20.

Innes, J. E., & Booher, D. E. (2010). *Planning with Complexity: An Introduction to Collaborative Rationality for Public Policy*. London: Routledge.

Jeffrey, C., & Schakel, H. (2013). Editorial: Towards a regional political science. *Regional Studies, 47*, 299–302.

Keeble, L. (1951). *Principles and Practice of Town and Country Planning*. London: The Estates Gazette.

Kuhn, T. S. (1962). *The Structure of Scientific Revolutions*. Chicago: Chicago University Press.

Mastop, H., & Faludi, A. (1997). Evaluation of strategic plans: The performance principle. *Environment and Planning B: Planning and Design, 24*, 815–832.

McLoughlin, J. B. (1969). *Urban & Regional Planning: A Systems Approach*. London: Faber and Faber.

Meyerson, M. M. (1956). Building the middle-range bridge for comprehensive planning. *Journal of the American Institute of Planners, 22*, 58–64.

Meyerson, M. M., & Banfield, E. C. (1955). *Politics, Planning and the Public Interest: The Case of Public Housing at Chicago*. New York: The Free Press.

Needham, B. (2017). A Renegade Economist Preaches Good Land-Use Planning. In B. Haselsberger (Ed.), *Encounters in Planning Thought: 16 Autobiographical Essays from Key Thinkers in Spatial Planning* (pp. 165–183). New York: Routledge.

Rehfeld, A. (2008, first edition 2005). *The Concept of Constituency: Political Representation, Democratic Legitimacy, and Institutional Design*. Cambridge: Cambridge University Press.

Rittel, H. J. W., & Webber, M. M. (1973). Dilemmas of a general theory of planning. *Policy Sciences, 4*, 155–169.

Sabel, C. F., & Zeitlin, J. (Eds.). (2010). *Experimentalist Governance in the European Union: Towards a New Architecture*. Oxford: Oxford University Press.

Thomas, H. D., Minett, J. M., Hopkins. S., Hamnett, S. L., Faludi, A., & Barrell, D. (1983). *Flexibility and Commitment in Planning*. The Hague, Boston & London: Martinus Nijhoff Publishers.

Thornley, J. (1974). Review of: 'A Reader in Planning Theory'. *Urban Studies*, *11*, 111–112.

van der Valk, A. J. (1989). *Amsterdam in aanleg: Planvorming en dagelijks handelen 1850–1900 (Planologische Studies 8)*. Amsterdam: Planologisch en Demografisch Instituut, Universiteit van Amsterdam.

Williams, R. H. (1996). *European Union Spatial Policy and Planning*. London: Chapman Publishing.

List of Abbreviations

CARE: International organisation aiming to reduce hunger and show solidarity with the people of war-torn Europe, now worldwide.

ESDP: European Spatial Development Perspective

EU: European Union

IOR: Institute for Operational Research

MRTPI: Member of the Royal Town Planning Institute

NATO: North Atlantic Treaty Organization

RTPI: Royal Town Planning Institute

TPI: Town Planning Institute

Terminology Glossary

Alternative Dispute Resolution: Deliberation method to resolve issues.

British Council: UK government agency giving grants to visiting scholars.

Brussels: Code for the administration of the EU, most but not all of which is headquartered at Brussels (imprecisely named Europe's capital).

Central Europe: Group of European states in the heart of the continent.

Centre of Environmental Studies: UK agency stimulating planning debate and research in the 1970s.

Communicative Turn: Social sciences abjuring positivism in favour of participatory approach to research with implications for policy and planning.

Council of Ministers: Ministers of EU member states deciding on proposals made by the European Commission.

Euro-federalist: Advocates of a "United States of Europe".

European Commission: European commissioners appointed by member states, proposing EU legislation to Council of Ministers, and administering it once passed.

European Community: Quasi-federation of European states eventually numbering 12 in 1993.

European Spatial Development Perspective: Strategic vision of European space and development jointly prepared by EU member states and published in 1999.

European Union: Name of European Community, with presently 28 European states (due to become 27 if and when the United Kingdom consummates the so-called Brexit, meaning its leaving the European Union) in pursuance of the outcome of the referendum on the matter held on 23 June 2016.

Falsifiability: Rule for distinguishing scientific propositions from others by twentieth-century philosopher of science Sir Karl Popper.

Fulbright: US foundation giving grants to visiting students and scholars.

Hungarian Revolution: 1956 uprising against Communist rule.

Intergovernmental EU: Restricted view of EU giving primacy to member states and, as such, a counterpoint to federal ideal.

IOR: Institute for Operational Research, part of the Tavistock Institute of Human Relations in the 1970s.

Iron Curtain: Border dividing Central and Eastern Europe from the West until its fall in 1989, named as such by Sir Winston Churchill.

Journal of the American Institute of Planners: US scientific journal, now *Journal of the American Planning Association*.

Marshall Aid: US aid to reconstruct (Western) Europe.

106 Andreas Faludi

Military–industrial complex: Designation by former US President Dwight D. Eisenhower, describing a self-serving coalition working towards continuing rearmament.

Near Neighbourhood: States with some chance of joining the EU in future.

Penguin Press: UK publishing house.

Pergamon Press: Former UK publishing house.

Planology: Dutch name for the social science discipline of planning.

Principal–agent theory: Political representatives bound by wishes of constituencies.

Regional Studies: UK scientific journal.

Relational view of space: Space defined in terms of spatial relations.

Royal Town Planning Institute: Honorific title subsequently awarded to Town Planning Institute.

Scientific Revolutions: Switch from one dominant paradigm in a scientific discipline to another.

Strategic choice approach: Package of techniques to deal with multiple uncertainties and complexity developed by the IOR in the UK.

Third Reich: Nazi Germany 1933–1945.

Territorial view of space: Space defined by administrative boundaries.

Town Planning Institute: Qualifying association of professional planners in the UK.

United States of Europe: Post-war ideal of unifying Europe advanced by Sir Winston Churchill in a 1946 speech at Zurich.

Voluntary Agricultural Camp: UK camps for holidays spent working as a farm labourer.

Zoning: US statutory land-use planning.

8

FINDING MY WAY

A Life of Inquiry into Planning, Urban Development Processes and Place Governance

Patsy Healey

The Planning "Project"

After many decades of engagement with the planning field, I have come to understand planning as a sociopolitical project centred on collective endeavours to shape place qualities to promote better trajectories than might otherwise occur. For me, places are locales, landscapes, territories which we inhabit, imagine and seek to shape. Planning, understood in this way, is a form of "place governance", sociopolitical practices concerned with the development and management of places. Such a project is not just any form of place governance, but one with a particular orientation. It takes a dynamic focus, recognising how place qualities evolve and change through the actions of many webs of relations. It is future oriented, in the sense of searching for ways of making place qualities better than in the past. It emphasises how places are experienced and valued by the diverse and often conflicting many who have a stake in a place, not just the powerful few. In searching for ways of making places more liveable and sustainable for these many, such a form of place governance gives recognition to the complexity of temporal and spatial interdependences and the multiplicity of knowledge claims and forms of knowledge which may be asserted when place qualities are argued over. It also stresses the value of open and transparent reasoning when addressing collective action issues and in this way helps to enrich the public realm of a political community.[1] In taking this position, I emphasise a strong normative commitment. This does not mean that I expect the planning project as translated into practices to appear in such a form. Instead, for me it represents a form of place governance to be struggled for and an evaluation framework to judge how governance practices are evolving (see Healey, 2012).

I also approach thinking about the planning project with particular personal "sensibilities". But what are these and where have these come from? In this account, I try to provide some clues. Using an organising idea I found in anthropology many years ago (Geertz, 1966), I group my sensibilities into ways of thinking and ways of acting. In terms of ways of thinking, I am deeply fascinated by how social formations, in interaction with their specific histories and geographies, evolve in time and space, leaving legacies for future generations in the landscapes

108 Patsy Healey

and cultures, the politics and economics, that they leave behind. I seem always to have known that we humans live in a variety of thought worlds and practice traditions, and understand, value and organise in different ways. Perhaps for this reason, I have found inspiration in social anthropology and in literature. And although I know we humans are complex thinking and feeling beings, struggling to find ourselves as individuals, I am conscious that we are also bound into sociocultural contexts which we can partly know but never completely discard, and that our webs of relations, with each other and the natural world, are shaped by these sociocultural contexts as well as by the exigencies of present circumstances.

Yet, as humans, we are not passive receivers of our particular inheritances. We are active beings, and in our acting, we continually search for ways to improve our condition, or fall into depression at our failures. What varies among us is the terrain within which we seek such improvement and the ambition of our efforts. Like many, I was attracted to the planning project because it seemed to promise that social groups could, through collective action, organise to improve our societies so that resources and opportunities were more justly distributed and social conflicts could be addressed in less violent ways. My interest in planning was therefore in organising to facilitate transformative change in living conditions in places. Yet in our acting we have not only to recognise that what is seen as an improvement for one may not be the concern of another. In acting to change the way things go on, therefore, those embarking on such actions need to relate their strategic intentions to a respectful sensitivity to how such changes are likely to work out in the flow of life—the micro-practices, meanings and relations of the political and social communities in whose name such action is being mobilised and institutionalised.

In summary, these sensibilities have led me towards concepts and theories which emphasise a relational perspective on social formation rather than an individualistic one, an interpretive perspective focused on meanings as well as materialities and an awareness of the multiple institutions, with their norms and modes of practice, within which any effort in place governance with the kind of orientation I have sketched above will be situated. My own life in planning has not just been a contemplative one, observing the ways of thinking and ways of acting of others. I have also been a kind of institutional activist, involved with others in initiatives to create, develop and change organisations, their cultures and practices. For me, and perhaps for many planning academics, the interaction between a contemplative life and an activist one has been a crucial crucible in which my understanding has developed.

Early Life: From Childhood to a Planning Doctorate

The understanding outlined above is the product of a life's journey of intellectual exploration, empirical research and personal experience. I was born in 1940, into a world at war, and for many years was haunted by the fear that war and disaster could break out again at any moment. I echoed, I suppose, my parents' own anxieties. I came from the English professional middle classes, and a family with a nonconformist[2] and scientific-atheist background, but went to a school for the daughters of missionaries. This conjunction taught me that there were different ways of understanding the world. I learned the important lesson that people may have different views but that what really mattered was to develop a tolerant appreciation of difference while searching for the common humanity we share with others. My father, an academic mycologist, promoted such tolerance rhetorically but was not consistent in his practice, energetically dismissive of what he saw as the delusions of religion. Yet from him I learned how to explore and observe the world in its multiplicity of manifestations as you go about in it.[3] He also showed me that you could expand the range of exploration through books. I read voraciously and eclectically. And I imagined that I could travel in space and time, trying to turn the tide of history before it happened. As I got older, and more children appeared in my family, I began to take on the more mundane idea of my future which my parents had in mind—a reasonably educated wife and mother. Yet I retained the mission, imbibed from school and home, that we each have a responsibility to struggle to improve the world we find ourselves in.

It was assumed all of us children would go to university. In a rather arbitrary manner, I chose to study geography with social anthropology as a subsidiary. But I hit geography at University College London in the late 1950s, when my course was dominated by a form of descriptive regionalism, with very little discussion of ways of thinking or modes of analysis. I was enriched intellectually by the social anthropology subsidiary I took, which introduced me to a literature about social groups in different times and places, as well as women scholars, of whom I particularly remember Mary Douglas. But I also got energetically drawn into left-wing student politics, a natural direction for naïve progressives like me, searching for ways to throw off the imperial traditions of British history and suspicious of the dominant rhetoric of Cold War politics. What I encountered was a complex world of sectarian groups, each with their own interpretations and agendas. Which group you belonged to seemed to matter more than promoting the wider objective of helping to shape better futures. I learned from this experience to be cautious of being dragged along by the fashions and "isms" of political and intellectual thought. Now, after a lifetime of observing the ebb and flow of intellectual and political discourse, I know that an explorer can never really "belong" to a specific perspective, as that assumes you have intellectually "arrived" at a position from which you can broadcast to the world. Exploration is about continual searching, learning and moving on, rather than arriving.

However, by the time I finished my geography degree, I was set on a pathway which had little to do with these experiences. I contemplated doing a graduate planning course in London, but instead got married to a fellow student (an ecologist who gave me the surname Healey) and followed my husband to South Wales as he did his PhD and launched his scientific career. I trained as a teacher, which gave me an early encounter with the writing and influence of John Dewey, and then I taught for three years. With a PhD, my husband got a lecturing post in London, and I found a teaching job in a large early comprehensive school.[4] The destined motherhood role never came (very fortunately, in retrospect), and I began to feel very frustrated with teaching geography. I was not quite clear why at the time, but in retrospect it was probably because my cast of mind was more interested in intellectual exploration than in school-level education. It comes to many of us from time to time to realise that we have become stuck in one pathway, and we need to pull ourselves out and search for another. My struggle took about eight years, ending in a completed PhD and an academic position as a planning lecturer. At the time, I had no idea that I had the capability to be an "intellectual". Instead, I searched the London job market, applied for many jobs and eventually became a trainee planning officer in the London borough of Lewisham.

In the UK, local authorities (the term we use for municipalities) were required to produce development plans and regulate development. They also had powers and resources to undertake major development projects. I had no knowledge or experience of local government at the time and became fascinated with the complex practices which I came across—from the planning ideas that circulated around, the activity of collecting land use information for development plan-making, and the informal ways that organisational knowledge circulated. I was also struck by how difficult people found it to explain why they were doing what they did in the way that they did. My employer sent me on a part-time planning course at the then Regent Street Polytechnic (now Westminster University), which had rapidly expanded to train the large numbers of planners needed for the newly created 33 London boroughs. In 1965, the London County Council, which in the post-war period had an international reputation for its innovative development plans and projects, had been reorganised and expanded into the Greater London Council (GLC) as an upper tier authority, encompassing the boroughs within it.[5] The course I was sent on seemed to have little coherence or direction, consisting of a miscellaneous collection of subjects of very uneven focus and quality, taught largely by part-timers. What was most stimulating was the project work, where we students—a diverse mix of ages and backgrounds, working in different London borough planning offices—got together. We developed our own critical assessment of the course, while learning a lot about each other and our various understandings of planning work and the planning project. But we were quite unaware of the paradigm shifts in understanding the planning project which were underway at the time in places such as the Manchester planning school (see Batty, 2017).

By the end of my twenties I had planning experience and a planning qualification (a diploma in town planning), but I still felt that I had little understanding of what this planning activity was all about or how the practices of London borough planning related to the trans-formative goals so often associated with the planning project. Given my academic parent and husband, I thought that doing a PhD would help me to develop this understanding, although at the time very few planners I came across would have thought the same.[6] So I went along, very tentatively, to the London School of Economics (LSE), to see if I could do a PhD part-time. Peter Hall, and subsequently Derek Diamond, had developed a master's programme in urban and regional planning, and I thought I could do a PhD in that environment (see Hall, 2017). Somewhat to my astonishment, I was welcomed into the group—I had a geography degree, but I think it was my practice background that helped me.

My PhD and Its Role in My Academic Life

My PhD experience was quite unlike the structured programmes promoted by the end of the century. It was essentially an effort in unguided exploration, in the LSE Library and then in fieldwork in Venezuela and Colombia. My theme was "planning and change"—a vast canvas but one which reflected my unfocused sense that the planning project should somehow be related to helping to transform urban development processes in ways which could promote more liveable and fair environments for inhabitants. Seeking new experiences,[7] I had by then moved from the London borough of Lewisham to the Greater London Council, where I met planners from many parts of the world, including Venezuela. My ecologist husband at this time had a fellowship to spend time on an island in the Panama Canal, giving me the oppor-tunity to go to Latin America. This led to the idea of a PhD research project on the relation of planning activity to the challenge of rapid urban change. As a foundation for this, I spent hours searching the planning literature (especially the *Journal of the American Institute of Plan-ners,* now *JAPA*), the literature in anthropology, sociology, geography, economics and political science on societies "in development", and the emerging "development studies" literature itself. I found the last most helpful, as it viewed development in a multidimensional way, with at least some sense of how social formations evolved through time. I particularly enjoyed Albert Hirschmann's *Development Projects Observed* (1967). But I was also confronted with a range of different theoretical perspectives and debates, as well as methodological and stylistic preferences.

My research focused on processes of urbanisation in two cities in both Venezuela and Colombia and the relation of planning activity to these processes (Healey, 1974). Through detailed fieldwork, I came to understand the importance of landownership systems, development investment activity and political processes. In Venezuela, by the early 1970s cities were being built by a mixture of public and private sector development and a very active informal sector, which constructed at least 50% of the additional housing provided in the years of my study. Why did we not see such an unregulated urbanisation in nineteenth-century Britain, I wondered, a question which led me to appreciate the significance of historical landownership systems in affecting the form and practices of both the property development industry in a country and the way planning systems worked. In both Britain and Venezuela, landownership was concentrated among a relatively small class of people, as neither country had experienced any significant land reform movement. Historically, however, many Latin American cities had allocations of municipal land which, in Venezuela, provided a resource energetically exploited by squatters (Healey, 1974).

I also "found" the emerging "canon" of planning theory. This was evident in part in the planning literature, where I encountered most of the papers which Andreas Faludi later collected in his influential reader (see Faludi, 2017). But I also found it empirically, as, especially in oil-rich and newly democratic Venezuela, planning and development consultants from different countries and planning traditions were promoting their advisory wares. I had already come across the work of John Friedmann, as he had written about Venezuelan economic planning in the 1960s (Friedmann, 1966). In addition, I found British and American ideas of new town planning, French ideas about community development and US concepts of rational planning processes, all struggling for the minds and practices of a young democracy.

Having two cases in each of two countries (Venezuela and Colombia) showed me clearly that each situation had its own particular histories and geographies. These created distinctive potentials and constraints, a conclusion which has made me sensitive to the many overgeneralisations we find in the academic literature. Further, the relation between planning ideas, governance practices and urban development processes was not a straightforward one. It was refracted through complex sociopolitical relationships and institutional forms, producing all kinds of contradictions, development coordination problems and unexpected side effects. I found myself challenging the ideas in some of the development literature that "developing countries", through learning from Western experience, could advance more rapidly towards the affluence and apparent social peace achieved in Western democracies. Instead, what I found were complex interactions between broad economic, political and cultural forces, and the specific histories and geographies of the urban areas I was studying.

When I look back,[8] I can see that this PhD work laid out the terrain around which my academic interests and sensibilities have ever since revolved. It helped me too to see my own country from the outside, to learn to appreciate its own specificities. Also, without realising it, I had attempted a more narrative style for writing up my PhD. My external examiner, political scientist W. J.M Mackenzie, told me in my viva that I should write an administrative novel.

112 Patsy Healey

At the time, I had no idea what he meant, but now I see that this was a comment on a way of writing up multistranded qualitative research about institutional dynamics. Through the PhD, I found my academic focus and voice. Through observing ideas in practice, as well as reading the formal literature, I grounded my understanding of planning theory. But as many do, I also "found" myself—through moving outside my own country into very unfamiliar environments, through encountering different fields of knowledge, but also through leaving my marriage and coping with the tragic aftermath.[9]

Creating an Academic Life at Oxford Polytechnic[10]

I was at "Oxpoly" from 1973 to 1987, a period of major change in UK politics and public policy. During this time, I was energetically involved in shaping planning education and the planning profession, whilst also pursuing a research agenda and continuing my intellectual explorations. For me this was a very productive period, during which I became involved in national and transnational arenas. I was also fortunate to find myself in a planning school which, with a young and lively group of staff and very engaged students, pushed to innovate in planning education.

In the UK in the 1960s, the planning school at Manchester University had been in the lead intellectually, with younger academics and students challenging the old regionalist and consultancy-driven education programme with conceptual and analytical ideas drawn from rationalist planning, regional science and systems theory (see Batty, 2017; Hague, 2017). By the 1970s, however, a vigorous team of young staff at Oxford Polytechnic was challenging this paradigm with a political economy perspective and redesigning the structure and content of planning programmes. Andreas Faludi had greatly strengthened the intellectual ambitions of the school and introduced the rationalist planning canon during his time there, and I found myself replacing him in 1973. I joined a group of staff[11] already engaged in critical debate about the nature and purpose of planning. By this time, and thanks I think to Andreas's initiative, a group of planning academics interested in planning theory had begun annual meetings, so we had some depth of debate to draw upon.

Immersion in Planning Education

I found the discipline of teaching very productive. Designing and delivering a course provided an opportunity to reflect on and consolidate my own thinking and then convey it to others in an understandable and relevant way. But at Oxpoly, I was not just teaching. In the mid-1970s, a group of us took on the project of redesigning the undergraduate planning programme from a four-year structure leading to a bachelor's degree to a '3+1' structure, with a bachelor's and master's degree. This created the possibility for students to follow different specialist master's programmes, a pattern that has since expanded across the UK. By the late 1970s, Oxford Polytechnic was recognised as a centre of innovation in planning education, influencing the professional institute, the Royal Town Planning Institute (RTPI), in its policy towards the planning programmes it approved (see also Hague, 2017). The RTPI required members to have qualifications and experience in the planning field. During the 1970s, the RTPI was moving from a system of examination directly by the Institute to reliance on education in formally recognised planning programmes in a polytechnic or university setting.

Developing a Research Profile

In my PhD I had discovered a taste for empirical research, which was an undeveloped tradition in UK planning schools at the time. So I began to formulate a new research project. I had found different planning ideas influencing the way planning was thought about and practised in Latin America. I wondered about the ideas which influenced the practices of London borough planning departments, where I had worked previously. With the help of sociologist Joe Bailey, my conceptual apparatus and methodological confidence was enlarged as I came across social interactionism, phenomenology and ethnomethodology.[12] Through these explorations, I began to develop an interpretive way of understanding the meanings and practices mobilised in urban planning situations. I also became more sophisticated in using qualitative research methods. I drafted a research proposal which I called "Planners' use of theory in practice", which I presented to the then-existing Centre for Environmental Studies. Marxist political economists such as Doreen Massey were based there at the time, and my proposal got some criticism as not sufficiently grounded in structural concepts. But I was fortunate that Brian McLoughlin was also there.[13] He was very sympathetic to someone who, like him, had worked in the planning field and was keen to research planning practices. I got the research money, which allowed me to work with the late Jacky Underwood, who had also worked as a planner in a London borough. The project involved interviews with senior, middle-level and junior planners in the 33 London boroughs, and Jacky spent six months as participant observer in the London Borough of Haringey. Jacky's work was written up into a fine monograph, *Town Planners in Search of a Role* (Underwood, 1980), and we summarised the work in a long paper in *Progress in Planning* (Healey & Underwood, 1978). We showed how different conceptions of planning were being played out in debates and practices, interacting with the particular political and development situations in each borough.

By the late 1970s, the RTPI was beginning to appreciate that a planning school needed to develop a significant research dimension, a factor which has become increasingly important in assessing the performance of universities and departments nationally in the UK. I was encouraged by our head of school to work with Martin Elson, a rural planning specialist. This led to a stream of work on development plan-making, at a time when the whole planning system in the UK came under challenge. The 1979 Thatcher Tory government had a visceral antagonism to planning, which was associated in the minds of the newer neoliberal Tories with socialism. But the Tories also had a voter base which was deeply concerned about defending rural and suburban England from too much development, and expanding green belt[14] designations as a way of doing this. The planning professionals in the national civil service had funds to commission research on how the planning system was working and commissioned us to research how development plans were being implemented. This focus was a fortunate opportunity for me, as I had concluded from the London boroughs' study of planners at work that I needed to shift attention to a wider context and explore how planning tools and institutional practices were interacting with the political and development dynamics of specific situations.

Martin and I, and colleagues at the School for Advanced Urban Studies (SAUS) at Bristol, were already looking at the local plans being produced at the time, and at the various green belts designated across England.[15] The project on development plan implementation required us to struggle with our funders over how to conceive of the way a British development plan, a non-legal instrument, could influence development activity, and over our preference for a

114 Patsy Healey

few in-depth case studies rather than many rather superficial ones.[16] We showed through this work that development plans did have an influence, particularly where the main development activity was driven by the private sector. Despite continually criticising the planning system, private sector developers actually valued the way that plans structured development opportunities. Our findings thus challenged the prevailing political beliefs.[17] Eventually, we turned our research into a book, with research associates Paul McNamara and Joe Doak, on the British planning system, *Land Use Planning and the Mediation of Urban Change*. We focused, in a proto-institutionalist way, on the practices of the British planning system, which we understood as "the collection of institutional arrangements, powers and resources which in Britain constitutes an explicit programme for the management of land use and environmental change" (Healey et al., 1988, p. 2). We sought to identify the ways in which different groups struggled to insert their values and interests into how the system worked, and how this varied between different localities and different kinds of urban development challenge.

Transnational Encounters

By the mid-1980s,[18] I was also deeply involved in academic management at Oxford Polytechnic, becoming head of school in 1978, and then dean of the Faculty of Architecture, Planning and Estate Management. For a few years, I was a member of the Council for National Academic Awards (CNAA—the degree awarding body for polytechnics until their conversion to universities in the late 1980s), the RTPI and the UK social science research funding body, the Economic and Social Science Research Council (ESRC). All these involvements, though time-consuming, were very educative about the organisational practices and power dynamics of academia. But I was also growing intellectually, through some very significant encounters. In 1982, I met John Forester at a seminar organised by the late Mike Breheny and Alan Hooper at Reading University on "rationality in planning" (Breheny & Hooper, 1985). John shared my fascination with what "practising planning" involved, and our interaction increased from then on. In 1985, I went for the first time to a US planning school, UC Berkeley, where I met my now very good friend Judith Innes, who educated me on how to get about in US planning academia. We also shared many intellectual sensibilities and have exchanged ideas and papers ever since. It was she who told me that I had to go to the American Collegiate Planning Schools (ACSP) annual conference, which I did later that year. It was here that Klaus Kunzmann and I met up and began to develop ideas for what became the Association of European Schools of Planning (AESOP) in 1987 (see Kunzmann, 2017).

At Oxford, we also maintained a strong position in the planning theory field. Glen McDougall, the late Mike Thomas and I felt we should continue the tradition initiated by Andreas Faludi in the early 1970s of holding seminars in planning theory. We organised a major conference in 1982, which brought together speakers from several different perspectives and led to a book which became much used in planning programmes (Healey et al., 1982). This planning theory interest and the connection with planning practice brought visitors from the Politecnico di Torino, who were doing a study visit around British planning schools. Luigi Mazza and colleagues became very interested in our focus, and Luigi came back for a longer period later on. This encounter resulted in the International Conference on Planning Theory in Turin in 1986, which brought together planning academics from across Europe and also from North America (see Mazza, 2017), creating a network of interactions which continued afterwards and became a significant part of the initial address list for the first AESOP Congress in Amsterdam in 1987.

Conceptual Exploration

Meanwhile, I was returning to philosophy, sociology and geography to strengthen my understanding of social dynamics in the public sphere. It was in this period that I really came to grasp what was involved in taking a relational, interpretive and institutionalist perspective on social phenomena such as planning practices. I began reading Habermas's work and was inspired by both his recognition of multiple rationalities and his concern with promoting alternative discursive qualities to the adversarial forms so dominant in the UK. I came across the sociologist Claus Offe, who offered a well-developed sensibility to the contradictory practices of public organisations; he also found considerable empirical support for his concept of an unachievable "restless search" for a stable form of administrative practice. Geographers David Harvey and Doreen Massey provided rich relational concepts for understanding the complex political economy of the financial sphere and the ebb and flow of property development investment, as well as the economic relations through which spatially uneven development outcomes come about.[19] All these reinforced my sense that it is important to look at planning ideas, policies, projects and practices as embedded in complex relations in dynamic evolution at multiple speeds and scales. For me, though, it was the approach to the interaction between structural dynamics and active agency of Giddens's structuration theory which helped me make the connection between the worlds of practice and their broader context.[20] I was struck not only by his emphasis on how agency created structures which shaped the way people as active agents thought and acted; he also presented three ways in which this powerful interaction was accomplished—through the flows of material resources, through regulatory practices, both formal and informal, and through framing ideas.[21]

Slowly, an idea grew in my mind to move beyond trying to understand the British planning system and its practices towards a broader conceptualisation of the planning project. I wanted to set this in a relational view of spatial dynamics, recognising the complex interactions of social forces and agency power. From a relational perspective, I realised that to understand the power dynamics of governance practices, it was important to look closely at the communicative dimensions of how issues were brought to attention, how knowledge was mobilised and how arguments were expressed and filtered. It seemed to me that any progressive agenda which sought to challenge and transform current practices had to penetrate into the fine grain of such sociopolitical practices. For me, what became *Collaborative Planning* was a way of drawing together all I had learned and come to grasp—from intellectual debates, to detailed empirical research, and to my own sense of what living in the world is about. By the time it emerged (Healey, 1997/2006), it was 10 years since I had left Oxford Polytechnic for Newcastle University.

Flourishing in Academia at Newcastle

Many people were surprised when I made this move—from the buoyant south of England to the "rustbelt" north, and from a lively young institution to what was then a rather complacent old university. The Newcastle programme had been little touched by emerging ideas about the nature of the planning project and the intellectual tools available for developing it.

116 Patsy Healey

But the challenge of transforming an academic department attracted me, with my interest in transformative practices. I had come to feel that the dominant interpretation of the planning project among my Oxford Polytechnic planning colleagues, exacerbated not surprisingly by the aggressive right-wing politics of the Thatcher government, was too focused on political critique of national government policy and too little on developing alternative planning ideas and inserting them into regulatory processes, technical analyses and organisational practices. The challenge at Newcastle, it seemed to me, was to sustain the department's involvement with place governance practices, while at the same time building an intellectually strong and research-focused dimension to the school. Looking back over 25 years, I think I can say that this project has by now been achieved, but it took much longer than I imagined and required the contributions and commitment of many colleagues over the years. It was a period of intense commitment and hard work. Here I will focus on five dimensions of this life which shaped my intellectual contributions.

Researching Land and Development Processes

Following the research on the implementation of development plans at Oxford Polytechnic, I had been working with colleagues at SAUS, particularly the late Sue Barrett, on urban land and property development processes. This revived the interest I had developed through my PhD but also balanced the understanding of the state's role in the promotion and regulation of development with that of the "market". We were particularly interested in the specific form of the British property development and investment industry, and sought to use an "institutionalist" understanding, grounded in Giddens's structuration theory and Harvey's analysis of the place of property investment in circuits of capital. We designed a major research project which, despite initial encouragement, was turned down by the ESRC. Refusing to be put off by this setback, we published a paper on our ideas (Healey & Barrett, 1990), which, somewhat to our astonishment, was later published in an economics text on key papers in institutionalist economics![22] By this time, we had also drawn together a network of property development researchers, including Rupert Nabarro, the creator of Investment Property Databank (IPD), and published further work on land development policy and practice (Healey & Nabarro, 1990; Healey, 1991b, 1991c). Meanwhile, the university had been very helpful in providing me with funding for a research project on land and property development in the Tyne and Wear conurbation, an area of industrial decline. These days in European language we would describe this urban complex as a "shrinking city". We called it a "weak" property market. With researchers Simin Davoudi and David Usher, and inputs from some local estate management practitioners and planning officers, we produced an account of the property development dynamics of the conurbation, which not only got academic exposure but proved useful to practitioners locally (Healey, 1994).[23] Before long, I was asked to become a board member of the Tyne and Wear Development Corporation (TWDC), which drew me further into the tensions and politics of urban development practices.[24]

Ethnographies of Urban Partnerships

But the Newcastle context also offered an opportunity to get involved in the emerging sequence of urban regeneration partnerships. Encouraged with public funding, these initiatives focused on involving local communities and the private sector in neighbourhood regeneration. With Newcastle colleagues,[25] we researched a stream of projects which recorded and evaluated the complex microprocesses through which ideas about what to do and how to do it played out. These experiences of close observation of sociopolitical practices became one strand of the foundation upon which I gradually built up a conception of the dynamics of governance capacity building. This later evolved into a major project funded by the ESRC on institutional capacity building in urban contexts led by Ali Madanipour, John Pendlebury and myself. Claudio de Magalhaes joined us as research associate, with his Brazilian practice experience and his property development–focused PhD. He greatly strengthened our methodological techniques (Healey et al., 2003). For me, these "close encounters" with governance micro-practices on the edge of established state processes helped to fill in my understanding of how state, market and civil society interactions could work out. They underlined that broad generalisations about power, politics and public policy barely capture the diversity, complexity, structuring constraints and transformative potential of these micro-practices. This realisation led me to search for a more effective analytical approach and vocabulary through which to understand governance transformation processes, though this did not mature until sometime later.

Strengthening My Conceptual Perspective

Meanwhile, a group of us at Newcastle University in the early 1990s were struggling with the wave of postmodernist (or post-positivist—the vocabulary was very unstable at this time!) intellectual innovation underway in the social sciences, carried to us especially through regional development geography, urban political economy and the sociology of science. We were a fluid group, but key participants were Ash Amin, Kevin Robins and Jonathan Murdoch, along with myself and Stuart Cameron with planning backgrounds. Within our department, graduate student Stephen Graham and new lecturer Simon Marvin were also vigorously developing a sociotechnical systems approach to urban networks. In a small minority in our separate departments, we got together to read and discuss regulation theory and the implications of "post-Fordist" regional development. We also began to look at actor–network theory. Overall, we were trying to come to grips with a relational, non-linear way of conceiving of cities as socio-spatial formations produced through time by the complex interactions, synergies and struggles within and between multiple webs of relationships, each with their own power dynamics, and their own specific spatial reach and temporal dynamics.[26]

The Collaborative Planning Book

These discussions helped me as I developed what became *Collaborative Planning*. They refreshed my understanding of how urban political economists understood the power dynamics, political struggles and distributive consequences of urban development processes, though, following Giddens, I sought to assert a much stronger role for active agency and historical contingency. I was also much less excited by Foucauldian ideas and actor–network theory than my colleagues, as my encounters with social anthropology and institutional sociology had already shown me dimensions which these ideas highlighted. This affected how I treated "power". Many critics of *Collaborative Planning* argued that my approach has neglected "power" and the way dominant forces structure social processes to their own advantage. I recognised these forces too, but

118 Patsy Healey

I also appreciated that power is as much about the energy to do things as about the ability to dominate others.[27] I was interested in the power dynamics in the many different webs of relations, how these interacted with each other and how in turn these interactions shaped the terrain through which future interactions evolved. I was guided by the Marxian concept that agency has power to make history, but not in circumstances of our own choosing.

So, in analysing and considering the potential progressive transformative contribution the planning project could play, I was interested specifically in how circumstances shaped how the planning project was understood and institutionalised and the shaping role it then played. Planning viewed in this way was at one and the same time a set of ideas or, following Foucault, discursive frames, a set of institutionalised regulatory practices and a way of deploying and shaping the distribution of resources.[28] How planning activity was enacted and the potential for progressive outcomes therefore depended on the nature of the ideas and debates around them (ways of thinking) and how these were performed (ways of acting). Located in complex interactions between multiple webs of relations, it was important, it seemed to me, to focus on the communicative dynamics of the relations and interactions, and the ways these lodged or displaced particular modes of thought and practice and through this affected struggles over resource distribution and regulatory power. To understand this, I drew on discussions about communicative rationality and interpretive policy analysis then developing among scholars including John Forester, Frank Fischer, John Dryzek, Judith Innes, James Throgmorton and Maarten Hajer.[29] My core referent was the changing UK and wider European context, where old forms of government which privileged technical experts and bureaucrats were breaking down as new groups struggled for voice, participation and control over place governance.

Building Academic Institutions

Throughout these years at Newcastle, I worked to change the culture of our department, to create a strong intellectual dimension while retaining the focus on practices. I was also very much involved in the early days of AESOP, becoming president from 1994 to 1996. During this time, I helped to introduce the "PhD Workshop" as a regular event,[30] as well as the "AESOP Prize" paper system. Both these initiatives reflected my concern that AESOP needed to be about planning research and scholarship as well as about teaching. AESOP, in effect, was creating research networking opportunities across Europe, and through this a group of us developed the idea to look at "innovations" in development plan-making in our various countries. We focused especially on spatial plans which sought to be strategic in shaping development activities. This became a lively research group, punctuated by seminars drawing in others, including Andreas Faludi and Louis Albrechts, which not only helped each of us to think about our own national situations, but developed our individual conceptualisations.[31] AESOP in effect became a kind of intellectual home for me, as we struggled with diverse intellectual perspectives, understandings of planning and experiences of planning systems.

All this time, I maintained an involvement with the RTPI. I was an elected council member from 1987 to 1992 and became chair of the institute's "Women in Planning" subgroup. I also led the revision of the institute's *Planning Education Guidelines* in the early 1990s. In both, we emphasised the importance of recognising diversity and social justice within the ethics of the planning profession. Working with Huw Thomas, we persuaded a group of planning practitioners to write an account of how they approached questions of ethics and values in their work. This resulted in a book, *Dilemmas of Planning Practice* (Thomas & Healey, 1991), which remains a rather rare example of planners talking reflectively about the ethical challenges they face. One of the planners involved was the late Ted Kitchen, then deputy chief planning officer at Manchester City Council. Prompted by an invitation to a seminar organised by John Forester (see Forester, 2017; Hoch, 2017), which required attendees to spend a day "shadowing" a planner, I spent an extraordinarily interesting day with Ted, observing what went on and the interactions he had, and reflecting with him on what had happened. A key insight I had from this was that a planning officer not only interacted with different groups, but that such officers carried the concerns of others into the fine grain of their communicative interactions.[32]

These institution-building activities, research teams and interdisciplinary intellectual encounters in Europe and the US, along with the experience of working with doctoral students from different parts of the world, combined with empirical research, all fed my further development. I remember the 1990s as a very stimulating and rewarding experience. I had become a well-regarded senior academic, a quite different and much more satisfying career path for someone like me than that mapped out for me 40 years before.

Rebalancing My Life

When I reflect back on this period of my life, I cannot quite imagine how I did it all. But by the end of the century, when I turned 60, I realised that such a hectic schedule was unsustainable. Two intuitions pushed me towards retiring. The first was a strategic concern with the future of the department, by now quite successfully enlarged into the School of Architecture, Planning and Landscape. I had played a major role—as head of department and then as research leader. I knew that lasting institutional change requires that cultures and practices endure beyond individual contributions. It was important for me that the research culture which was now emerging strongly could sustain itself and that a new generation could move into place to carry this forward. I therefore wanted to step into the background and divest myself of the many management obligations which I carried. This was linked to a strong feeling I had that, after years of intense focus on the planning field, I needed to widen my horizons and refresh my intellect. So I retired in late 2002, making use of a rare form of positive discrimination which allowed female UK university staff to retire at or after 60, rather than 65.

I had many planning commitments at the time, and it was a while before these all came to completion, but I did create space to do completely different things. But it soon emerged that what I really wanted to do was to continue developing my thinking about the activity of strategic spatial planning, honing the tools of my kind of "institutionalism" to this purpose. Being retired enabled me to act as my own research associate in investigating three cases of such planning activity, resulting in what I consider my "best" book, *Urban Complexity and Strategic Spatial Planning* (2007). I positioned strategic spatial planning as a governance endeavour aimed at making a difference to the dynamics of an urban agglomeration, not just a particular jurisdiction. Centred on three cases, examined over a long time span, I drew conclusions about the nature of strategy-making, about the spatial imaginations which animated such activity, about the kinds of knowledge mobilised in such processes and the implications for urban governance. I enjoyed this work tremendously, working on archival material, interviewing current actors in strategic planning processes and discussing cases with colleague planning academics and practitioners whom I knew from previous work. It was like doing a PhD again, but with

120 Patsy Healey

more full-time attention than I had been able to devote to my actual PhD, and with all the depth of knowledge I now had.

I continued to be actively academically engaged through the 2000s, publishing papers which marked the development of my thinking. I was also very involved as senior editor of the new journal *Planning Theory and Practice,* with the mission to "provide an international focus (and forum) for the development of theory and practice in spatial planning". A spin-off from this experience was an edited book with fellow editor Robert Upton about the way planning ideas "travelled" transnationally (Healey & Upton, 2010). I was also drawn back into the history of planning ideas, partly through coming across the work of pragmatist William James as part of my enlarged wider reading. This took me into an exploration of the influence on US planning thought of the pragmatist tradition, which was largely unknown as such among European planning academics (Healey, 2009). I realised I had a pragmatist perspective without knowing it, and that this tradition had been deeply influential in much of what I had read. This experience underlines for me the importance of conveying the history of ideas in our field. With Jean Hillier, I made a contribution in this area by reviewing the terrain of planning theory, as we worked together to collect and comment on key planning theory texts.[33] Finally, I attempted to draw together what "the planning project" has come to mean to me, written for a more general readership than the papers I had been writing. The result was *Making Better Places* (Healey, 2010).

At 70 years old, I came to the conclusion that writing books was just too hard! I thought I might carry on thinking about the history of planning ideas. But at this time, I became a trustee, and then chair until 2015, of a local development trust which had grown up in Glendale, in North Northumberland where I now live. This involves me in efforts to address the many challenges of a community with diminishing employment in agriculture, an ageing population and little opportunity for young people. Finally, I am back to "doing" planning work, drawing on all my planning and managerial experience. I still maintain some small engagement with my academic life, and I have also been able to draw university resources to work with our community on several issues. My main reflection now is that I wish I had had more opportunities to be fully involved in practices from time to time in my planning career.[34]

A Career in Perspective

In retrospect, my "voyage" in the planning field has been a meandering one. Reflecting now, I puzzle about how I came to my way of understanding the world and specifically of planning as a project and as an activity. The voyage has been an intellectual one, but this dimension cannot be divorced from the experiences I have had as I have journeyed through life, a journey which has taken me through many different places, cultures, agencies and encounters. However much we attempt to plan a life path, the experiences of living in the world hurl us about, opening here and closing there, in ways which can be both wonderful and tough. But it is through these experiences that we develop and enrich our sense of what matters and how to act.

Reflecting on this account, it is clear to me that my institutional involvements helped my intellectual development and vice versa. The range of activities helped to feed my strategic grasp and my sense of how ideas and ways of thinking interact with practices. I have also always found it helpful to think of planning as a project and a field of endeavour, drawing on many branches of formalised knowledge—many disciplines, as well as the knowledge of experience. I have come to understand the enduring value of the planning project as a form of place governance in the complex situations in which so many of us live, and also that the scope for generating such value is very dependent on both context and particular contingencies. As professionals and activists, we have a potential to expand that scope. The focus of our contribution as planning scholars is precisely to understand these interactions and contingencies, and to develop the craft of inquiring into when, how and why planning work is and could be done. I often feel that only at this late stage in my career have I really understood this craft and how to use it. Looking back, I can see that it has involved a great deal of interaction with other people, with many kinds of empirical experience, and a great deal of reading and writing.

In terms of developments in planning thought, I realise that I have lived through a major "paradigm shift" in philosophy and the social sciences. By the time this shift began to gather labels (postmodernist, post-positivist, etc.), I was already deeply embedded in the new direction. I seem early on to have had a leaning to such an understanding. But I have needed to make regular investments in keeping up with the waves of social theory that have washed across the various disciplines which have ideas and knowledge relevant to planning activity. Through these, I have found concepts and vocabularies through which to "interpret" the situations I have researched, and to develop policy and practice ideas. But ultimately, the inspiration for my thinking has always been the practical challenges which people face as they struggle to survive and improve their life conditions in particular places and times. In navigating social theory, we surely need positional markers to distinguish between ideas and arguments, and between ways of thinking about the world. Yet we need to avoid being so dominated by theoretical frameworks and propositions that we become blinded to the way the world speaks to us. Theories and conceptual frameworks provide vocabularies and probes to open up dimensions of the world we had missed before. For me, the scholarly side of planning activity does not require that we become philosophers or social theorists. Instead, our focus should be on the present and emerging challenges in the evolution of place qualities, and developing knowledge and ideas to help people as they try to shape that evolution to improve daily life conditions for the many. My intellectual project has been to explore these challenges from many angles and to help provide a useful literature to others involved in the same challenges.

Acknowledgements

I have been privileged to have many people comment on this text, and my thanks to all for drawing out from me what is often forgotten, hidden or taken for granted.

Notes

1 I try to articulate these concerns in Healey (2010).
2 In the UK, the term nonconformism refers to protestant religious affiliations which are outside the established Church of England. In the nineteenth century, my father's family were Unitarians.
3 Only later in life have I come to recognise how much of my personality comes from my mother!
4 In comprehensive schools, students of all ages and abilities are educated in the same institution from 11 to 18 years.
5 The GLC, and the metropolitan authorities created in the 1970s, were then abolished in 1986. The current Greater London Authority was created in 2000.

122 Patsy Healey

6 Andreas Faludi was of course one, and my first attempt to contact him was in writing in the late 1960s. At the time a PhD was unusual outside the main sciences, although this situation was changing by the 1970s.

7 I had also been denied promotion at Lewisham through what I vaguely perceived as gender prejudice.

8 An edited collection of my work has recently been produced by Jean Hillier and Jonathan Metzger (Hillier & Metzger, 2015).

9 My first husband died of cancer in 1972.

10 Polytechnics in the UK grew from local colleges of technology and related institutions. They were absorbed into the university system in the late 1980s. Oxford Polytechnic, then informally known as "Oxpoly", is now Oxford Brookes University.

11 Which included Michael Hebbert, Michael Thomas and Glen McDougall.

12 I found Silverman (1970) and Bailey (1975) particularly helpful.

13 He had left Manchester University and moved away from the attractive logic of the systems approach (McLoughlin, 1969).

14 Green belts in the UK are a form of urban growth boundary.

15 See Healey (1983) and Elson (1986).

16 The tension here was between a "performance" and a "conformance" perspective, later articulated in this way by Mastop and Faludi (1997).

17 See Healey (1991a) where I recount this story.

18 By this time, I was on my own again, having been married and widowed again during my Oxpoly years.

19 See especially Offe (1977), Harvey (1982), Habermas (1984), Massey (1984).

20 See especially Giddens (1984).

21 During the mid-1980s, Maarten Hajer spent time as a planning/political science graduate student with us at Oxford, greatly enlivening our discussions on these matters!

22 See Greenhut and Norman (1994).

23 This interest in the interaction of planning regulation and property development led to a research project on developer obligations, in which I collaborated with lawyer Michael Purdue, and ventured into yet another "discipline" (see Healey, Purdue et al., 1995).

24 The TWDC was set up by national government in 1988, as a deliberate challenge to local government capability. I was involved from 1991 to the end of its life in 1998.

25 Stuart Cameron, Rose Gilroy and Simin Davoudi.

26 One product of this group was *Managing Cities* (Healey, Cameron et al., 1995).

27 An idea Foucault captures in his power to/power over distinction.

28 Here I drew directly on Giddens (1984).

29 Most of these contributed chapters to *The Argumentative Turn* (Fischer & Forester, 1993).

30 Simon Marvin and Stephen Graham organised the first workshop.

31 This led to a book, *Making Strategic Spatial Plans,* edited by Abdul Khakee, Alain Motte, Barrie Needham and myself (Healey et al., 1997). Some of us reviewed our own national situations (see Motte, 1995; Vigar et al., 2000).

32 See Healey (1992). Because this was published in *JAPA,* the paper became quite widely known in North America.

33 This project arose in response to an invitation from publisher Ashgate; see Hillier and Healey (2008), Hillier and Healey (2010).

34 In the UK academic context, this has not been an easy opportunity.

References

Bailey, J. (1975). *Social Theory for Planning.* London: Routledge and Kegan Paul.

Batty, M. (2017). A Science of Cities: Prologue to a Science of Planning. In B. Haselsberger (Ed.), *Encounters in Planning Thought: 16 Autobiographical Essays from Key Thinkers in Spatial Planning* (pp. 242–259). New York: Routledge.

Breheny, M., & Hooper, A. J. (Eds.). (1985). *Critical Essays on the Role of Rationality in Planning*. London: Pion.

Elson, M. J. (1986). *Green Belts: Conflict Mediation in the Urban Fringe*. London: Heinemann.

Faludi, A. (2017). Understanding and Improving Planning Processes and Planning Institutions: A Moving Target. In B. Haselsberger (Ed.), *Encounters in Planning Thought: 16 Autobiographical Essays from Key Thinkers in Spatial Planning* (pp. 88–106). New York: Routledge.

Fischer, F., & Forester, J. (Eds.). (1993). *The Argumentative Turn in Policy Analysis and Planning*. London: UCL Press.

Forester, J. (2017). On the Evolution of a Critical Pragmatism. In B. Haselsberger (Ed.), *Encounters in Planning Thought: 16 Autobiographical Essays from Key Thinkers in Spatial Planning* (pp. 280–296). New York: Routledge.

Friedmann, J. (1966). *Regional Development Policy: A Case Study of Venezuela*. Cambridge, MA: MIT Press.

Geertz, C. (1966). Religion as a cultural system: Anthropological approaches to religion. In M. Bandon (Ed.), *ASA Monograph No. 3* (pp. 1–46). London: Tavistock Press.

Giddens, A. (1984). *The Constitution of Society*. Cambridge: Polity Press.

Greenhut, M. L., & Norman, G. (Eds.). (1994). *The Economics of Location*. London: Edward Elgar.

Habermas, J. (1984). *The Theory of Communicative Action: Vol 1: Reason and the Rationalisation of Society*. Cambridge: Polity Press.

Hague, C. (2017). Challenging Institutions That Reproduce Planning Thought and Practice. In B. Haselsberger (Ed.), *Encounters in Planning Thought: 16 Autobiographical Essays from Key Thinkers in Spatial Planning* (pp. 222–241). New York: Routledge.

Hall, P. (2017). Visions of Contemporary Planning: Stories and Journeys in Britain and America. In B. Haselsberger (Ed.), *Encounters in Planning Thought: 16 Autobiographical Essays from Key Thinkers in Spatial Planning* (pp. 51–70). New York: Routledge.

Harvey, D. (1982). *The Limits to Capital*. Oxford: Blackwell.

Healey, P. (1974). Planning and change. *Progress in Planning, 2(3)*, 143–237.

Healey, P. (1983). *Local Plans in British Land Use Planning*. Oxford: Pergamon.

Healey, P. (1991a). Researching planning practice. *Town Planning Review,* 457–468. (republished in Lo Piccolo F. & H. Thomas H. (Eds.). (2009). *The Ethics of Planning Research*. Aldershot: Hants, Ashgate).

Healey, P. (1991b). Urban regeneration and the development industry. *Regional Studies, 25(2)*, 97–110.

Healey, P. (1991c). Models of the development process: A review. *Journal of Property Research, 8(3)*, 219–238.

Healey, P. (1992). A planner's day: Knowledge and action in communicative practice. *Journal of the American Planning Association, 58(1)*, 9–20.

Healey, P. (1994). Urban policy and property development: The institutional relations of real-estate development in an old industrial region. *Environment and Planning A 26*, 177–198.

Healey, P. (1997/2006). *Collaborative Planning: Shaping Places in Fragmented Societies*. London: Macmillan.

Healey, P. (2007). *Urban Complexity and Spatial Strategies: Towards a Relational Planning for Our Times*. London: Routledge.

Healey, P. (2009). The pragmatist tradition in planning thought. *Journal of Planning Education and Research, 28(3)*, 277–292.

Healey, P. (2010). *Making Better Places: The Planning Project in the Twenty-First Century*. London: Palgrave Macmillan.

Healey, P. (2012). Re-enchanting democracy as a way of life. *Critical Policy Studies, 6(1)*, 19–39.

Healey, P., & Barrett, S. M. (1990). Structure and agency in land and property development processes. *Urban Studies, 27(1)*, 89–104.

Healey, P., Cameron, S., Davoudi, S., Graham, S., & Madanipour, A. (Eds.). (1995). *Managing Cities: The New Urban Context*. London: John Wiley.

Healey, P., Khakee, A., Motte, A., & Needham, B. (Eds.). (1997). *Making Strategic Spatial Plans: Innovation in Europe*. London: UCL Press.

Healey, P., Magalhaes, C. de, Madanipour, A., & Pendlebury, J. (2003). Place, identity and local politics: Analysing partnership initiatives. In M. Hajer & H. Wagenaar (Eds.), *Deliberative Policy Analysis: Understanding Governance in the Network Society* (pp. 60–87). Cambridge: Cambridge University Press.

124 Patsy Healey

Healey, P., McDougall, G., & Thomas, M. (Eds.). (1982). *Planning Theory: Prospects for the 1980s.* Oxford: Pergamon.

Healey, P., McNamara, P., Elson, M., & Doak, A. (1988). *Land Use Planning and the Mediation of Urban Change.* Cambridge: Cambridge University Press.

Healey, P., & Nabarro, R. (Eds.). (1990). *Land and Property Development in a changing context.* Aldershot: Hants, Ashgate/Gower.

Healey, P., Purdue, M., & Ennis, F. (1995). *Negotiating Development.* London: Spon.

Healey, P., & Underwood, J. (1978). Professional ideals and planning practice. *Progress in Planning, 9(2),* 73–127.

Healey, P., & Upton, R. (Eds.). (2010). *Crossing Borders: International Exchange and Planning Practices.* London: Routledge.

Hillier, J., & Healey, P. (Eds.). (2008). *Critical Readings in Planning Theory: (3 Volumes).* Aldershot: Hants, Ashgate.

Hillier, J., & Healey, P. (Eds.). (2010). *The Ashgate Research Companion to Planning Theory.* Aldershot: Hants, Ashgate.

Hillier, J., & Metzger, J. (Eds.). (2015). *Connections: Exploring Contemporary Planning Theory and Practice with Patsy Healey.* Farnham, Surrey: Ashgate.

Hirschmann, A. O. (1967). *Development Projects Observed.* Washington, DC: The Brookings Institution.

Hoch, C. (2017). Pragmatism and Plan-Making. In B. Haselsberger (Ed.), *Encounters in Planning Thought: 16 Autobiographical Essays from Key Thinkers in Spatial Planning* (pp. 297–314). New York: Routledge.

Kunzmann, K. R. (2017). Places Matter: Creativity, Culture and Planning. In B. Haselsberger (Ed.), *Encounters in Planning Thought: 16 Autobiographical Essays from Key Thinkers in Spatial Planning* (pp. 202–221). New York: Routledge.

Massey, D. (1984). *Spatial Divisions of Labour.* London: Macmillan.

Mastop, H., & Faludi, A. (1997). Evaluation of strategic plans: The performance principle. *Environment and Planning B: Planning and Design, 24,* 815–832.

Mazza, L. (2017). An Ancient Future. In B. Haselsberger (Ed.), *Encounters in Planning Thought: 16 Autobiographical Essays from Key Thinkers in Spatial Planning* (pp. 71–87). New York: Routledge.

McLoughlin, J. B. (1969). *Urban and Regional Planning: A Systems Approach.* London: Faber and Faber.

Motte, A. (Ed.). (1995). *Schema directeur et projet d'agglomeration: L'experimentation de nouvelles politiques urbaines spatialisees 1981–1993.* Paris: Les editions Juris Service.

Offe, C. (1977). The theory of the capitalist state and the problem of policy formation. In L. N. Lindberg & A. Alford (Eds.), *Stress and Contradiction in Modern Capitalism* (pp. 125–144). Lexington Massachusetts, DC: Heath.

Silverman, D. (1970). *The Theory of Organizations.* London: Heinemann.

Thomas, H., & Healey, P. (Eds.). (1991). *Dilemmas of Planning Practice.* Aldershot: Hants, Ashgate.

Underwood, J. (1980). *Town Planners in Search of a Role.* Bristol: School of Advanced Urban Studies, University of Bristol, Occasional Paper, No 6.

Vigar, G., Healey, P., Hull, A., & Davoudi, S. (2000). *Planning, Governance and Spatial Strategy in Britain.* London: Macmillan.

List of Abbreviations

ACSP: Association of Collegiate Schools of Planning
AESOP: Association of European Schools of Planning
ESRC: Economic and Social Science Research Council (UK)
GLC: Greater London Council
IPD: Investment Property Databank
JAPA: Journal of the American Planning Association
LSE: London School of Economics

RTPI: Royal Town Planning Institute (UK)
SAUS: School of Advanced Urban Studies, University of Bristol
TWDC: Tyne and Wear Development Corporation

Terminology Glossary

Development Corporation: Special purpose government agency, with powers to acquire land and organise the building of new towns and, since the 1980s, regenerate areas of existing towns.

Development plans, structure plans, and local plans: A key tool within the British planning system, though names have changed from time to time.

Graduate course: Course taken after a first degree—master's or PhD.

Lecturing staff: Academic staff.

9

EDUCATING PLANNERS

The Dream of a Better Future

Gerhard Schimak

The old lady shouted at my mother that she should quiet me down. It was 1944 in Vienna. I was some four years old and I remember the anxious faces of the people sitting in the cellar, which was lit by one petroleum lamp. At that moment I became very afraid, listening to the sharp thunder of (luckily quite distant) exploding bombs. That specific sound is still in my head and whenever I hear a similar noise, I remember the scene in the cellar.

(That is my earliest recollection as a child.)

Challenged to write the story of my professional life in the field of spatial planning, I tried to find an answer to how my interest in planning developed and how it became the main topic of my professional life. It was certainly influenced and guided by a lot of personal and academic experiences. I grew up with an early wish to build up my country and do something for society, along with an early fascination with maps and plans and an interest in strategies. This interest led me to the study of architecture with an emphasis on urban planning, and to work as an assistant professor at the Institute of Urban Design and Spatial Planning at the Vienna University of Technology, where I was first more of an observer, but increasingly had a growing influence on the programme of study for spatial planning which started in 1970, a new sort of a school of planning. My interest was also heavily influenced by my work with students, exploring with them the importance of creativity in planning.

Three accidents in my life, which totally changed my life and career and were unpredictable and unpreventable, led me to think about the question of uncertainty in planning and to scepticism about the role of calculative planning methods. I became aware that the search for certainty in dealing with the future is a human desire deeply ingrained in our mind and one of the basic motivations of planning. Emotionally, planning for me became an adventure: going into the unknown, over the border in your mind, the real fascination of my professional life as a "planner".

The context in which I grew up after the war—in a partially destroyed city under very poor living conditions, in a country which for 10 years after the end of the war was still occupied by Russian, American, British and French forces—certainly raised my early interest in politics, including my growing feeling of anger at this occupation. I was also living in Vienna only 50km away from the Iron Curtain, with relatives in the neighbouring Communist countries. On various occasions, confronted with the realities of such a system, this situation strengthened my view that democracy is important not only as a political system, but as way of influencing, and even being part of, everyone's life.

My university career culminated in 13 years as deputy and vice rector of my university, where I had the chance to "plan"—within my fairly wide range of responsibilities—the development of a university. But looking back, the impact of the war, the destruction, and the "building up" atmosphere are foremost in my mind.

Angst

In the final months of the war, my mother and grandmother moved to a room in a house belonging to family friends, in the countryside some 100km west of Vienna, to avoid the air raids in Vienna. There was an empty sawmill nearby, which was used as an SS military hospital and later as a Russian military hospital. I had a joyful time playing with the children of farmers in our neighbourhood. But again most of what I remember are strange incidents, like the deep thunder of a fleet of airplanes flying over our village and returning after a while. Then in the following night the red shine on the northern horizon, the burning city of Amstetten some 20km away.

The SS left with a last "greeting"—an enormous bang, as one of them threw a hand grenade into a field some 30m from the place where I played. Then everybody waited hopefully for the Americans, who had already been seen on a hill some 2km away. But they stopped there and after a few days of waiting, Russian tanks rolled into our small settlement. Again I remember the fear of all the people of the house, sitting in one room and waiting until the door opened and two Russian soldiers came in. My mother, who knew some Czech from her parents, greeted them in Czech. The guy in front looked astonished and then said only "Oh, Czech!", saluted, and they both went out. I did not know it at that time, but for us that was the end of the war. A small group of soldiers then lived in the ground floor of the house. They were very friendly, especially to us children. Interestingly from the present point of view they insisted they were Ukrainians, not Russians, and they told my mother that they would shield us from their "comrades". On a few occasions, they really did.

The contents and meanings of my "memory-pictures" from the time of the Second World War and its aftermath, still vividly ingrained in my mind, were explained to me by my mother years later. Maybe the context of angst and insecurity I felt in the people around me—even if I did not understand the reason for it at that time—was a kind of background motivation for creating security and grasping the future in my life.

Formative Years: To Serve the Public

In May 1945, when my family returned to our flat in Vienna we found a family of refugees from Slovenia occupying part of it. To have refugees in part of the flat was luck to a certain degree. The refugees left after a few months, while two of the four flats in the house were occupied by French families, who worked for the French occupational forces. One of these

128 Gerhard Schimak

families—a higher-ranking officer and his wife—had the house-owner's flat, with a huge garden full of trees and flowers. We children were never allowed to set foot in it and could only look through the fence into a mysterious realm: a kind of metaphor for the 10 years to 1955, when finally the Austrian State Treaty was signed and all the occupying forces—including our French neighbours—left our country.

One evening in January 1946, my mother called me to come to our kitchen. There was a man I didn't know sitting at the kitchen table. My mother told me that this man was my father. He had just returned from a British prisoner-of-war camp. I had never seen him before, and for me he was a kind of intruder into our small family. Of course the main issue was that he had survived the war, but I regret to say that the initial emotional distance between him and me never totally vanished until the last days of his life.

His total devotion to his job and his incredible correctness even in small details, which was sometimes not easy to live with, certainly had a formative influence on my approach to handling various jobs throughout my life. To a certain degree he was a person from a distant past, like one of the "officials" described in books about the Habsburg monarchy and its aftermath, by authors such as Joseph Roth and Stefan Zweig. These officials saw their work as a duty, which has to be fulfilled in the best possible and correct way, as a service to the country and its people. His sense of duty influenced my own view of planning as a kind of profession which offers, unlike many other professions, the opportunity to see and develop your own work as "serving the public interest".

Formative Years: We have to Build up our Country

With my personal life story of being born in a fascist time in occupied Austria, with the swastika and "Deutsches Reich" on my birth certificate, I grew up in the hunger years after the Second World War. As the only child in the family I got enough to eat, but I remember my mother putting dried peas into a pot with water, then waiting until all the worms in the peas had floated up to the surface to skim them off. Only one light bulb was screwed into the old chandelier in our living room, in order to save electricity. And I remember my excited feelings when a second light bulb was screwed in for celebrations like my birthday.

Unlike many German cities, Vienna was not carpet-bombed. The targets for bombing were mainly industrial areas and railway stations and lines, but there was a lot of collateral damage to the surrounding areas. There was also heavy damage caused by the fighting between the Russians and the retreating German army, particularly along the so-called Danube channel (a branch of the Danube going to the edge of the old city centre) where the retreating German army had blown up all the bridges and the armies shelled each other across the river for days. This started huge fires in the old centre. Even the landmark of Vienna, the gothic St Stephen's Cathedral, was severely damaged.

Living in a partially destroyed city fostered my growing feeling that we had to build up our country. This rather emotional feeling is still there in small recollections of joy, such as in 1953, standing with my parents and thousands of others for a brief glimpse of a passing low-loader carrying the newly cast 20-ton bell for St Stephen's Cathedral.

I also remember this feeling of "building up a country" from autumn 1955, sitting with my parents and others in an uncle's living room— he owned one of the first television sets in Austria—in order to see the live broadcast of Beethoven's *Fidelio* from the opening ceremony of the newly rebuilt State Opera in Vienna. I still wonder how much effort and money was spent rebuilding those old monuments in that first decade after the war. Of course they were symbols of our historical and cultural identity, which could not be allowed to be destroyed. I saw this same spirit much later in Warsaw, where the old city centre and the royal palace, blown up by the German army with the sole intention of destroying Polish culture, were recreated in every detail after the war.

I grew up in a time when—as I later realised—planning meant rebuilding the economy and recreating a democratic society after fascism, and only 50km from the sometimes shocking realities of the Communist world. This was evident after the Hungarian revolution in 1956, when schools were closed for a period to accommodate some of the 150,000 refugees who fled to Austria until the Russian army could close the border.

To Study "Planning"

My decision to study architecture was certainly influenced by this "building up" feeling, particularly as architecture also included urban planning and fitted my fascination with maps and plans.

At that time, education in architecture was a rather crazy mixture of teaching and especially of teachers. Some of them were really old-fashioned, but others led us into a structural and organisational approach towards planning—showing us students that there is no real difference between organising your own working table, a simple family home, and complicated structures such as schools, offices or theatres. The professor behind that educational approach was Karl Schwanzer, a well-known Austrian architect. He was a charismatic teacher, and he surrounded himself by very inspiring associate professors. One of them, whom we all admired, was Günther Feuerstein. He introduced us to a totally different view about architecture and art. I remember, for instance, his lectures about "naive architecture", ranging from how ordinary people decorate the entrances to their houses, up to naive designs such as the Watts Towers in Los Angeles. Yes naive, but also architecture. This education shaped some international careers, such as that of Coop Himmelblau.

For me, studying architecture was not only about learning a systematic and structured, rather rational approach to planning. It also widened my view of creativity as a feature not merely of artists, but as a part of all human beings—a view which I later introduced into my own teaching of planning. I also learned that there is not only the town, but an area around—regional research and planning. The region, as the much wider context of urban planning dealing with various development issues with natural, social, infrastructural and economic implications, became the main interest of my life.

Practice Years

After finishing my studies I wanted to find a job in regional planning, which was not yet a recognised profession in Austria. A letter to my former professor for urban and regional planning, Rudolf Wurzer, led to an invitation to work for him as a project assistant in his university institute. The next three years were a great experience of working on a wide range of research and planning projects. This was a physically exhausting time, sometimes with 36 hours of work, then 12 hours of sleep and another 36 hours of work.[1]

130 Gerhard Schimak

The work included developing plans for quite a few communities in different parts of Austria, work which also meant updating old maps, spending a week walking around a community and adding missing information onto the map by hand. I got also into many discussions with people who asked me what I was doing there. I got a lot of down-to-earth information and opinions—some funny, even crazy, some strange or emotional—about how these people saw what had happened or should happen in their communities: street talk about planning.

I worked on several land-use plans. I remember one for the community of Leonding, near the town of Linz. They had a serious problem connecting their community to a new development area across a main railway line. All the proposed solutions had major drawbacks. Sitting at my table with the community map in front of me, I suddenly had the idea of creating a totally different traffic solution, with a new bridge over the railway in another part of the community. After intensive discussion in the local council, it was accepted and a few years later built. Nowadays when I pass under this bridge on the train, I remember this is "my bridge". I still like this feeling of having planned something, convinced people, and it having been implemented. It is still there and it works.

I also had the chance to work on a land-use plan for the second-largest city in Austria, Graz, with a population of more than 300,000 and on regional development programmes such as the one for the Austrian province of Vorarlberg, the first such programme of that size in Austria. I was also involved in a really large study for a national spatial survey of Austria. Together with colleagues, I had to deal with a large group of specialists, their statistical material, and translating this into visual expressions of thematic maps to show the wide range of spatial features and problems in Austria. This work (Wurzer, 1970) raised, not only for me but—and this was really important—for the responsible politicians, awareness that spatial development needs a new kind of planning professional, not only with broad knowledge of many different fields, but also with a knowledge-integrating approach towards spatial development.

From Practice to Theory—and Back?

When, in 1971, I was finally asked by Rudolf Wurzer to become a research and teaching staff member at his institute, my personal workload changed dramatically. I was now formally on the more regulated staff conditions of the university. This gave me the chance to confront my experiences in practical spatial planning with the available literature on planning methods and theories. In some ways it was the path from reality into analysis of what I had done. I had learned at the university that spatial planning has to follow some procedures and methods: first doing a detailed survey of the planning area, then analysing the results, defining the problems to be solved, creating goals to be reached and using tools (from building plans to regional and national programmes) to implement the necessary spatial decisions. But practice experience made me aware that a plan or a programme is only a framework for implementation and that there has to be a constant process involving—and accepting—public participation and the political side, those who finally have to decide and implement the plan.

The Growing Doubts

The political dimension of planning had always been an important feature in Wurzer's projects. I participated in quite a lot of meetings with planning boards or commissions. But I remember also a tough aspect during our work on the land-use plan for the city of Graz. One of the features of the plan was fixing a route for a new motorway in the west of the city, most of it underground and covered, with a few connections to the city street network. I still believe that this was the best solution for efficiently distributing the incoming and outgoing traffic for a city of that size. But it raised a storm of protest from the people living there. The mayor of the city and his party agreed with our proposal, supported by all the traffic experts, but he lost the next election and had to step down. I remember my cynical feeling: "He lost his job and we planners are going to our next task to give the best possible professional advice to another politician."

The Scientific Challenge

The process of reading books and theoretical papers began to challenge my planning education. Looking back, the first "eye-opening" paper was Charles Lindblom's *The Science of "Muddling Through"* (Lindblom, 1959). He got into my rather idealised "survey-analysis-plan" education from a totally different and analytical viewpoint. His analysis of planning and decision processes mirrored, to an astonishing extent, some of my practical experiences. Even if I do not agree with some of his conclusions, his incremental approach became very important for me and was strongly supported later, not only by other theoretical literature, but also by some very personal experiences. In fact I defined myself in a discussion some time ago as a "target-oriented incrementalist", and this definition is still valid for me.

Next came reading Karl Popper's *The Open Society and Its Enemies* (Popper, 1975). This great dispute with Plato's theory of ideas tangentially includes an idea of planning as keeping open possibilities, again a totally different view from my education to use planning to create some certainty in the future.

With these growing doubts, I started teaching students of architecture in urban planning and, increasingly, students from the new spatial planning programme of study.

The Start of a "Planning School"

During my years as a project assistant I had the opportunity to follow closely the creation of a new programme of study for planning, and later as a research assistant I was appointed as a kind of secretary to the study commission which designed and fixed the programme of study. I became more and more intensively involved in the many details of this process, which gave me great insights into planning education issues.

Rudolf Wurzer was without doubt the founder of the study of planning at the Vienna University of Technology. He started there in 1959, as professor of urban design and spatial planning. As a former head of the Department of Spatial Planning in the Austrian province of Carinthia, his interest was quite clearly more in planning than in the architecture-oriented urban design. From 1964 until 1966 he was rector of the university and afterwards he headed the previously mentioned huge research project on spatial planning in Austria. With his experience, it was soon clear to him that it was neither sufficient nor possible to add a few more options about planning to the architecture course, but that a separate programme of study had to be established for the education of planners.

As rector, and with the wide political connections developed and strengthened during his work on the national research project on planning, he played a decisive role. And he

132 Gerhard Schimak

knew—that was one of his strengths—it was important not only to talk theoretically, but to create facts, which then draw the necessary decisions after them. He created an education for planners, yet this profession did not officially exist. The right to create official spatial plans and to get contracts for such a task was solely allocated to architects, as members of the legally established "Chamber of Architects". It was not until 1978, when an increasing number of educated spatial planners were on the market, that this law was changed to allow professional "spatial planners" to exercise this right (Schimak, 1980). The compromise was that the rights for architects were not changed.[2]

With his political connections,[3] Wurzer made sure that in a new National Law for Technical Universities "spatial planning" was included in the list of programmes of study for the Vienna University of Technology and immediately implemented a so-called study commission for the "new" study of planning. These study commissions were at that time highly disputed new institutions, because they consisted of (only) one-third full professors, one-third scientific staff and one-third students—a result of the "demonstration year 1968" and a way to establish student participation. Wurzer used the study commission extensively (Dillinger, 2012), creating a programme of study but also supporting his demands to establish new professors for various fields necessary for research and teaching in planning.

The Challenging Years

When planning studies started in October 1970 (as a three-year kind of master's course[4]), formal authorisation through a by-law for a programme of planning study had still not been given. Wurzer used a special exemption in the law, which allowed every student to create a personal programme of study from existing courses. Each student of planning had individually, but in fact based on the proposal of the study commission, to ask for approval for this so-called studium irregulare. This requirement resulted in a cumbersome process for students, teachers and the administration.

The three-year programme of study for the "studium irregulare" was partly based on theoretical ideas of what should be taught. But it was also heavily influenced by the programme of planning study at the University of Dortmund and a postgraduate programme at the ETH Zürich. In the early days, the main structure of lectures was partly provided by the founding Institute of Urban Design and Spatial Planning and some other existing institutes—mainly from the Faculty of Civil Engineering—and external lecturers. Slowly, some additional full professors were appointed, replacing external lecturers and contributing their own ideas about how and what to teach in their field (Schimak, 1993a; Wurzer 1994).

The programme of study was constantly changing. As a result, in the early years every student was forced to change (including a new approval) his/her "individual" programme of study every year: an administrative nightmare. However, it was also a nice example of how planners "plan" a programme of study for planning in a constantly changing environment.

Integrating Knowledge

Beside administrative nightmares, problems sometimes went much deeper into the teaching we had to provide, especially in the field of study-projects simulating practice.

At that time, the internal organisational structure of the university consisted of several faculties, split into a lot of mostly small institutes. Normally (with very few exceptions) every full professor had his own institute, supported by scientific and administrative staff. In the 1980s, a new rector criticised this structure at his inauguration, comparing it to medieval Italian "Duodez-principalities". I called them "chair institutes", the full professor sitting on the chair with his staff around his knees listening to him.

From the start, the programme of study for planning included a large planning project in a real community or region, to be provided cooperatively by two or more of the specialist institutes. The unspoken intention of such projects was a constantly emerging challenge for educational cooperation, wisely inbuilt by the study commission and one of the founding reasons for a programme of study aiming to educate people to be capable of integrative thinking.

Initially, this enforced cooperation created some real fights between full professors, who were of course all educated as specialists. In many cases, the teachers left their students to handle the knowledge-integration on their own. Yet this encouraged the students to learn a great deal about the integration issue in planning, which could not easily be done didactically and—as I see it now—simply could not be provided properly in the organisational structure of the university which existed at that time.

This challenge led to continual revision of how these projects were carried out. But this tremendously incremental process took until 2005 when, after a major structural reorganisation of the university providing the necessary organisational background, the programme of study finally arrived at an acceptable way of handling "integrated" projects.

A Chance from a Catastrophe

When Rudolf Wurzer started the new planning education, he had the real potential to create a kind of "Vienna School of Planning". As Klaus Kunzmann, who knew, or perhaps "experienced" him well, mentions in his essay, he destroyed this potential with his very difficult personality (to put it politely).

I myself, who worked intensively for him but never became close to him, was asked in 1976 to leave the institute in order "to get into practice" at the end of the year. I wanted to stay on, but after this message I started to contact all the people I knew in other organisations for potential jobs. I got a few offers but mainly in the field of local planning.

On August 1, 1976, the largest bridge over the Danube in Vienna, the so-called Reichsbrücke, collapsed, at 5 a.m. on a Sunday morning. It was and is one of the heaviest traffic spots in Vienna. It would have been an enormous disaster at a traffic peak, but at that time only one driver of a private car was drowned and one lonely public bus was left standing half in the water on the remnants of the bridge (the driver was saved by boat). That catastrophe completely changed my personal future.

After this catastrophe, of course the search for people to hold responsible began. As it later became clear from the research report, nobody living was responsible. It was a kind of design fault from 1937, when the bridge was built, and as consequence of this fault the developing erosion in one bridge pillar was not detectable during the usual inspections. But of course—a usual political reaction—people (not responsible) had to step down. And Rudolf Wurzer was suddenly offered a position in the new city government, politically heading the planning-related departments.

134   Gerhard Schimak

I was on vacation with my family in the countryside of Austria when I received a call to go to Vienna for a talk with Rudolf Wurzer. I went to Vienna for a day and Wurzer asked me—because "suddenly" I was the only person he could ask—to take over nearly all of his educational duties in the field of regional planning. And of course I should go on with a scientific career at the university. I accepted. Wurzer stayed in the city government from 1976 until 1983. The small joke at the end: When he returned after his political job ended, he told me to leave the university at the end of the year in order "to get into practice". When I reminded him that it was his advice to me to work on a scientific career, he simply answered mildly, "Yes, I said it, but that was seven years ago."

By that time, though still without tenure at the university, I had already established my position inside the university too strongly to consider a shift to practice. I was 43 years old; I had been married 14 years, and my wife Gertraud and I had three great children. I had worked at the university for more than 15 years, quite successfully, and in the seven years of Wurzer's absence with at least 20, sometimes up to 28, teaching hours per week. Crazy, but my reality. So I didn't accept his "advice" to get another job because I knew I had a good chance for tenure in the near future, despite his opposition.

But I decided—and there was something of my father's correctness in my mind—not to use my existing contacts. I asked for a separate evaluation of my past work, the first such case in our university. The dean had to create a new independent commission and to ask full professors to write evaluations of my work. They all were very positive. So I got my tenure—and Rudolf Wurzer's revenge came soon. He took away all my lectures, seminars and student projects on the planning course. I was only allowed to teach (mostly urban planning) on the architecture course. I tried to keep my knowledge and my contacts up-to-date. Even that ran into difficulties because Wurzer blocked many of my applications to go to conferences. Several times I had to ask for some private vacation days in order to go (secretly) to such conferences, without any financial support from my university.

Since I see planning in principle as part of everyone's life and spatial planning as an aspect or special form of planning which every human being does in one or the other way, that very personal experience strengthened my belief in incremental approaches in planning. How can you plan the future of a city or an area, when even in your own life one disaster or even unexpected event (two more happened to me later) could change the world around you totally and no prognosis could have given some assurance about a possible future? My personal experience: no certainty in planning my life, but the need to fight for my own future.

Internationalisation

At the end of 1989—still banned from planning education—I got a call from a friend, who was one of the directors of a small company, the EXPO-Vienna AG, which was established to plan and prepare a World Exhibition in the year 1995 as a joint project between Vienna and Budapest.

When the project began, Budapest was still the capital of a Communist country, with slowly emerging political changes. It was clear to all participants in Austria and Hungary that such a project, involving millions of visitors travelling between the exhibition sites in the two capitals, could not be managed by the usual lengthy and thorough border controls at the Iron Curtain. So it was an implicit background intention to "open" the border between the Communist East and the West.[5]

History went faster. In September 1989 the Hungarian government decided not to control any more at their border, if people from Communist countries leaving Hungary had permission (from their home country) to get to a Western country. This decision immediately led to an enormous stream of refugees, mostly East Germans, who vacationed in Hungary to get through Austria to West Germany. And that was the real starting date for the rapid collapse of the Communist world in Europe.

With the open borders, the joint EXPO project went on. I took unpaid leave from my university and, in early 1990, joined this World Exhibition Company as deputy head of the planning department. This project ended in 1991, with another small catastrophe for me. Initiated by a right-wing party in Vienna, with the argument that Vienna would be overrun by foreigners and criminals, a public vote in Vienna rejected the project. It had to be cancelled (Schimak, 1993b). The Budapest partners tried to handle the project by themselves but gave up six months later. For me it was a really traumatic shock, because I had totally fallen in love with the international spirit and atmosphere of the project.

So on October 1, 1991, I returned, frustrated by the loss of this chance, to my former job at the university—on the first day when Rudolf Wurzer went into retirement—doing my duties as a teacher, now including the planning students, and thinking about how I could get an international dimension into my work in educating planners. The first chance came sooner than expected.

One day in 1992 I was called by our secretary, who asked me—accidentally, as the only available person—to meet some people from the Faculty of Architecture from the Brno University of Technology. They were guests of our university and wanted to talk with our institute. In came a group of people from Brno, a large Czech town not far from Vienna, but for more than 40 years in a distant world separated by the Iron Curtain. The group was headed by the dean of external affairs from the Faculty of Architecture of Technical University (TU) Brno, Mojmir Kyselka.

Their basic question was how to run a university in a capitalist society. Beside this essentially unanswerable question, we discussed what we and they were doing. It soon became clear that Mojmir Kyselka and some of his colleagues were mainly interested in urban and regional planning. So, finally we talked about cooperating in some way. There was a proposal to look at our common Czech-Austrian border area as a region heavily influenced by 40 years of the Iron Curtain. We agreed to plan a three-day excursion with our and their respective students, into a segment of this cross-border area. This was, unexpectedly, the chance to bring an international dimension into the education of our planning students.

Planning at the Former Iron Curtain

That first excursion led to a joint student project (part of the programme of study) about cross-border spatial planning, with students and teachers from both universities, and the following year to a similar project with TU Praha (Prague) and the University of Budejovice. I was really not aware of the emotional issues we naively ran into by implementing these cross-border regional planning study-projects. Looking back, these were in fact real adventures in planning.

136 Gerhard Schimak

Of course, borders in Europe were created to a high degree by wars between ruling aristocratic clans, sometimes more peacefully by marriages (or even marriage contracts), and by using and then eventually losing countries as a pledge to other rulers for participating in war coalitions. The rise of nationalism (a child of romanticism of the nineteenth century, but still a present issue) gave a new dimension to the drawing of borders and finally led to two world wars.

With this knowledge we started a project on cross-border planning with our students from Vienna TU and students from TU Brno. It was located along parts of the border between Austria and southern Moravia in the Czech Republic, an area which formerly had a mixed Czech and German-speaking population. Until a few years before, the border, as part of the Iron Curtain, was marked in the East with barbed wire, watchtowers and kilometre-wide safety areas, in which even small villages were destroyed, and with a few heavily controlled border stations.

Crossing the Border in Your Mind

At the beginning we—from our side a colleague from our Institute of Landscape Planning, Hannes Schaffer, and me—started with excursions and small workshops on both sides. Very soon we got into heavy problems with incompatible statistics and maps. But immediately history was also there.

We heard stories about how badly the Czech population was treated and even expropriated by Nazi Germans after their occupation of the Sudeten area in 1938. And we heard also of the expulsion of the German-speaking population after the end of the Second World War. We saw the monuments or even observation towers, erected at the border by the people who had been displaced and who met there every year in order to look at their former villages and small towns just a few kilometres down from the hill. Until the fall of the Iron Curtain they were not allowed to get a Czech visa (because their birthplace in the Czech Republic was mentioned in their passports). We also met a mayor from a small Austrian border village—he was driven out with his parents in 1945—who told our Austrian and Czech students that despite the new open border, he would never in his lifetime set foot in the Czech Republic.

How to handle all this in a student project? Luckily there were two important preconditions. First we were dealing with students who knew and had heard about the "border emotions", but they had nearly no personal and emotional prejudices in that regard: the next generation. Second, from the teachers' side (from TU Brno particularly Mojmir Kyselka, and in later projects from TU Praha particularly Karel Maier), we were united in the conviction that this history should never happen again, and our work with students in the field of cross-border regional planning is part of avoiding repetition of the horrible past of nationalism: an emotional and fascinating goal for regional planning.

But a situation that you do not know how to deal with is, in my experience, not simply a challenge to one's knowledge, but a unique and fantastic chance to go into the unknown— crossing the borders in one's mind. We began every day with a discussion about how to go on, based on the experiences from the previous day. This was an incremental approach, which enabled us to try everything imaginable in the content and methods of the project.

There were also other main experiences for me after our first cross-border projects.

The Clash of East–West Planning Cultures

The first experience was a surprising and, for me, unexpected clash of planning cultures. We ended our project with different proposed scenarios for future development of the cross-border planning area. For us, this was a very interesting and stimulating end of the project, providing alternatives which could be presented to authorities or the public for further discussion—a next step which could not be easily simulated in a student project. I realised very soon that our Czech partners were not happy about this result. After long discussions it became clear that they could not go back to their faculty with five different options for a plan. According to their planning education in the Communist planning culture, a planner had to propose the "best", and "only", proposal for the future of the region. That was expected from him as a professional. A planner who proposed options would show that he did not know what is "right" or the "best" and therefore would not be professional enough. We agreed that our Brno teachers and students would take the five options and integrate them into one "best" planning proposal. That was done and led to an internal discussion at the TU Brno with a great result: In the future, two options were possible.

In Communist times, I had already had quite a few interesting contacts with universities and planning institutions, mainly in Poland, Hungary and Yugoslavia. And from these contacts I knew that "planners" saw their profession as a kind of "art for art's sake". They tried to plan in the best possible way according to their professional knowledge, but they usually had nothing to do with implementation and, of course, cynically little interest in it. For that "they" were responsible. "They" was the synonym for the ruling Communists. That was the reality of "planning" in Communist societies. The planner did the perfect plan. "They" decided and the planner did not have to get "dirty fingers".

In later projects this was no longer a problem. But this experience raised my awareness that the planning culture I was educated in is not the world. In discussions with planners from other countries (even from the so-called democratic West), you have to check carefully how they see planning (rather easily comparable) and especially their role as a planner (astonishingly different).

Planners and Creativity

Another experience in this first cross-border planning project with students would follow me through the rest of my life as teacher. As an educated architect moving increasingly into the field of spatial planning, I grew up with the impression—or better prejudice—that architects are the more creative, and planners are the more or less fact-oriented number crunchers.

The problem of incompatible plans and statistics, not to mention the different national planning laws on each side of the border, was in fact a chance to try a totally different approach to planning. So number crunching was out, and we could try to stimulate our students in different ways, to create a vision or scenarios of better futures with open borders in this economically rather dead area along the former Iron Curtain.[6]

For me—with my prejudices—it was a real and unexpected surprise that our number-crunching planning students exploded into creativity. It was like letting them loose into freedom from (in their usual education) predisposed knowledge expectations. They were simply great in their ideas and proposals and also in their presentations as part of the developing

138 Gerhard Schimak

project process. For me that experience, repeated in many later projects, made me aware of the hidden resources of creativity in our planning students. It also changed my view on the goals of planning education. I now believe it is very important not only to teach knowledge, but to include the opportunity for students to stimulate and develop their creative potentials.

Years followed when I could constantly progress the internationalisation of our programme of study, with yearly student projects in cooperation with universities in the US, Germany, Israel, the Czech Republic and Kosovo (the last of the cooperative student projects that I could personally take part in). Increasingly we also got research contracts, some inside Austria but some in cooperation with universities and other planning institutions from Germany, Italy and nearly all of the former Communist countries of Europe. These activities of international student and research projects are still going on very successfully,[7] but I personally had to disengage with most of them because another totally unexpected change occurred in my life.

Planning a University

The year 1998 held a big surprise for me. I was elected as deputy and vice rector of our university. That new situation totally changed my personal and academic life for nearly 13 years until my retirement in 2011. My duties (described at the beginning with the broad term of "resources") changed over my nearly 13 years in that position. They included mainly the university infrastructure, the university budget, issues of internal organisation and the creation (for the first time in the history of the university) of a strategic university development plan.

What I learned very quickly—I was constantly dealing with our economic advisers—was how much my knowledge of strategies, methods and instruments of spatial planning had its roots in—or was heavily influenced by—the much older and much longer developed knowledge about economic planning on the macro and micro levels. Of course this is a fact well known to people who are interested in the development of planning theories. But for me it was a surprise how close the knowledge of methods, tools and strategies of planning to run a company is to the knowledge of how to plan the development of a region or a town. This was another milestone on my way to seeing "planning" principally as a very general task to try to shape the future of a country, a region, a city, a company or other institution, and of course of one's own life.

The Institutional Integration

It became one of my first tasks as vice rector for resources to start a kind of reorganisation programme for the small institutes which still persisted across most of the university (the "Duodez-principalities"). Only two of the eight faculties had already done this internally. In quite a few cases, with closely related research fields, mergers were not very difficult. But it was much more difficult in the case of planning, where each specialisation had its own chair and institute. We had "chairs" for local planning, for urban and regional research, for law, for sociology, for traffic policy, for urban design, for regional planning, for landscape planning and for public finance and infrastructure policies. Facing such diversity, the discussions about who could merge with whom became more and more senseless.

One evening I had a discussion with a few colleagues about the merger issue. At that very moment, with frustrated people around me, it became clear that in order to cut this Gordian

Educating Planners **139**

knot, we had not only to think about merging former institutes but about a totally new (at least for our university) internal structure for such a new entity.

I remembered, from my time at the EXPO-Vienna AG, meetings with the huge international civil engineering firm of Ove-Arup. This very successful company explained their fascinating internal grid organisation.[8] This is a structure well-known to advisers in the organisational scene. My proposal to move in such an organisational direction was well received but with some scepticism about realisation. For that I found a congenial partner in the "chair" professor for local planning, Heiner Hierzegger, somebody who knew from his daily work about the problems of integrating special knowledge into planning projects. On another occasion we had talked about organisational grid systems, and I knew he liked them. After discussing my proposal with him, he immediately took it into his own hands and finally convinced most of his "chair" colleagues to accept it. Some of the chairs, especially those teaching mainly in architecture who did not want to integrate into an organisational "planning" structure, merged with other architectural institutes. But at least "regional planning", my personal scientific background, was cut out from the former Institute of Urban Design and Spatial Planning (the main part stayed with the architects) and could be merged into the new organisational entity.

So the "Department of Spatial Planning" was created with (at that time) seven full professors and some 50 scientific staff. The department has an internal statute (unique in our university) with a rather democratic and slightly complicated structure. The grid structure meant that the original institutes stayed as so-called subject centres (Fachbereiche), but also research areas (Forschungsgruppen) can be and were created with elected heads, who have to draw their scientific staff mainly from the subject centres for specific scientific tasks.

To institutionalise that with all its consequences on staff management is still an ongoing but, from my point of view, interesting and slowly developing process. I know that structures do not solve problems, but they can strongly support or hinder possible developments.

The Experience

Basically I am a practitioner. Highly interested in theoretical disputations, but always using my experiences from practice as a kind of filter for looking critically at theoretical approaches, for checking their potential of usability in practice or for better understanding the realities of practice. I now realise how much my appreciation of what is really important in my professional life and my present knowledge of planning and educating future planners comes from reading, contacts and practical experience, and how little comes from my original university education.

I was heavily influenced by reading books, often not directly related to planning topics. For instance, John Steinbeck's *Grapes of Wrath* (Steinbeck, 1948), which I read in my early youth, stimulated my awareness of social questions and injustices.

I have also had a long and continuing interest in history because I soon became aware that one cannot understand the present without knowing the past. The past did not just show up in our cross-border projects; it was everywhere: in the reasons why people identify with their region and town, in existing spatial structures, or in how and why present spatial laws and organisational structures for planning were developed.[9] This interest led me to more general history-related literature like Karl Popper's *The Open Society and Its Enemies* (Popper, 1975) or an Austrian historian's book *Warum Europa?* (*Why Europe?*) (Mitterauer, 2003), which gives a

140 Gerhard Schimak

fascinating description of the medieval roots and preconditions of the very specific development of Europe's society.

Another aspect of interest was, and remains, education issues. I am still grateful that Klaus Kunzmann, when we both worked at the same institute at the TU Vienna, suggested to me reading *Summerhill* by A. S. Neill (Neill, 1969), a book which at that time was wrongly labelled under the subtitle of "anti-authoritarian education". That was not really the aim of Summerhill, a school running on principles of teaching which were totally different from the education I received. The book did not deal with university education, but it made me aware of how important it is to trust in the very personal strengths of each individual pupil. The role of teachers is to create the conditions for freedom to develop their, sometimes hidden, potentials at their own pace. This book, and later inspirations, gave my wife Gertraud and me the strength to educate our three children "differently" from contemporary dominant educational principles. My wife Gertraud, who began as a teacher, later became founder and head of the Rudolf-Ekstein-Centre in the city of Vienna, an institution to support and promote the integration of children who have special needs for support in their emotional and social development. She finally practiced privately as a psychotherapist and became a congenial partner for me in all questions of education.

Later in my life I became more and more interested in another, highly neglected, but planning-related field of evolutionary epistemology, a science mainly influenced or shaped by Nobel Prize–winner Konrad Lorenz. His book *Die Rückseite des Spiegels* (*The Backside of the Mirror*) (Lorenz, 1973) and related literature strengthened my existing doubts about the value of predictions in planning, because the inbuilt ability of our brain to make predictions is a necessary function for survival on a very short-time basis. This capability gives us a certain degree of secure feelings, but it is also misleading in leading us to believe in or at least heavily overestimate the ability of middle or long-term predictions to provide certainty for planning a secure future. Predictions can be useful tools to understand possible consequences of ongoing processes, but they are not the future. The consequence is my deep conviction as a planner that we cannot know the future, but we can try to shape it.

After these important influences on my way of thinking, I want to mention at least three key issues, which followed me throughout my life as a planner and educator.

How Much Planning Education

The creation of the programme of a study of planning at my university in Vienna was based on the experience that the knowledge needed could not be provided by additional lectures in the architecture course. It led finally to a very broadly established field of research and teaching within our "school of planning".

But the main issue was not just about lecturing and teaching. It is a deeply educational issue: not only to learn and grasp the necessary knowledge, but also to develop strategic thinking, to raise awareness of the interdependencies of specific knowledge, to deal with complex issues in a systematic way. All that can only be taught to a certain degree. It is a process of forming thinking, which has to be stimulated in the brains of the students—and of course cannot end at graduation. Such an education needs considerable time within a planning programme of studies. Therefore I am deeply convinced that to educate a planner—and well understood it's an education of generalists (an old discussion, see also Faludi, 1978)—needs a full bachelor's and master's programme.

Living Democracy

Born during the Second World War and growing up in its aftermath, I soon became very interested in politics and began to read every available newspaper. Politics were everywhere. The horrible movies about the Nazi concentration camps, which were shown in all Austrian schools, were important in my anti-fascist education. There were lengthy discussions in our family with relatives and friends, some of them former Nazi party members (in the range from disappointed "believers" in Hitler to a neighbour who became a party member in order to save— successfully—his Jewish wife), about their experiences during the war and the Nazi times.

But living in Vienna, 60km from the Iron Curtain, the issue of Communist societies also became more and more relevant to me. I had the chance to visit relatives in Czechoslovakia and Hungary and later in East Berlin. That meant getting much—quite openly provided between relatives—first-hand information about the reality in Communist countries. During my student years and especially after discussions with heavily trained Communists (at a Communist "World Youth Festival", organised by the Eastern Bloc in Vienna in 1959), I became aware that I needed much more theoretical background and even took private courses and joined discussion groups to learn and understand more about political and social theories.

It became and, still is, evident to me what luck—very different from the life of my parents— I have had living nearly my whole life in a democratic society. This was and is also a crucial issue in my work in spatial planning. I know that the Communist system was in many aspects a heavily "planning" society. And the Nazis also placed an emphasis (even building up a specific organisational structure for that) on spatial planning. They did spatial planning with very similar instruments to those we all use now. But they had to a high degree (the Nazis even more than the Communists) totally different goals—different from those of a democratic society—and were using planning instruments in a way which is unacceptable for a democratic approach to planning.

I know that a democratic approach cannot simply be "taught". In some theoretical aspects yes, but it needs a democratic environment free from fear, in which "teaching" is happening. It is especially important for the education of planners, who have to live and deal with political and society-oriented issues.

I spent my early years of studying and working in a university with a very authoritarian structure. I then worked (based on a new university law) from 1975 until 2002 in a very democratically organised university. And I learned there—simply in daily university life—much about democracy, its potentials and its limits. And I am still proud, that I was in 1998—together with my colleagues in the so-called rectorate (executive board)—elected as deputy rector by a democratic vote from a university assembly consisting of 400 elected members. This was— until now—the last real democratic election of this executive body in our university.

I then lived and worked with a new law from 2002 onwards, which made the universities much more independent, but also a kind of company with the usual non-democratic authoritarian top-down structure. My colleagues and I tried to keep up at least some of the former democratic structures, but we soon had to recognise the increasing decline of engagement in university issues by members of the university who see no real chance of influencing top-down decisions.

In my opinion it is very important for the planning education in my university that the Department of Spatial Planning created in 2005 still has a very democratic internal structure,

142 Gerhard Schimak

seen by some outsiders as being the "last island of democracy" in our university. This democratic structure is totally based on the free will of the department members, not guaranteed or supported by the university organisation. A very fragile structure, but necessary, because how can you educate students for planning with democratic values in a non-democratic, authoritarian environment?

Enabling Creativity

From the beginning of my practice years in planning, there was a (for me) slowly emerging and widening gap between problem definition and developing planning proposals. I know now that it is just the—in the planning community often neglected—issue of "creativity" which can provide the bridge between knowledge and the possibility of another future. Planning is not simply about solving present problems or giving answers to predictions. It's about shaping a desirable and possible future.

I see spatial planning at its core as a creative task, based like all creativity on knowledge of the past and the present, but also on the hopes, visions and dreams of the people affected. And we have to accept that finally it is not the planner, it is the people who are planning. And it is the task of planning educators to create an environment free of fear where students can develop their feeling of responsibility for the common good of society, but also become aware of the creative potentials of their own personality. Only persons who were allowed to detect their own creativity in an encouraging learning situation know how to stimulate creativity-enabling processes in others.

The noble task of teaching planning is not only to provide the necessary knowledge of the profession, but to cultivate among our students the awareness that a "plan" is not simply the result of professional work and that a planner can and should not only advise people, but should try to encourage their internal creativity; to stimulate them to develop their own visions; and finally simply to help the affected and concerned people to shape their own dreams of a better future.

Notes

1 Andreas Faludi had just left the institute, and it was there that I met and befriended Klaus Kunzmann when he joined the staff.
2 A similar process of recognition happened in Germany (see Kunzmann, 2017).
3 He knew the Austrian chancellor, Josef Klaus, quite well, as well as other ministers. Josef Klaus, before becoming chancellor, was governor of the province of Salzburg when, in 1956, the Salzburg parliament voted for the first Austrian Provincial Law on Spatial Planning, a milestone in the development of the legal basis for spatial planning in Austria.
4 At that time, the standard five-year programmes of study were usually divided into a two-year first part and a three-year second part. The first part did not end with an official degree, so the second part could not be called "postgraduate". The first planning course included only a "second part" and could be entered by students who had finished a first part from a defined range of other studies. A first part was added to the programme of planning study in 1973, in the beginning again as "studium irregulare".
5 Such an intention may sound naive. But all official World Exhibitions have to be based on an international treaty, and the Hungarian government was—signing this contract—totally aware of the consequences of opening the Iron Curtain.

6 That vision of open borders became reality some 15 years later, when the Czech Republic joined the Schengen treaty inside the European Union.
7 In this regard I have especially to mention my former students and now colleagues Thomas Dillinger, Petra Hirschler, Nina Svanda, Hartmut Dumke and Beatrix Haselsberger, working at the department.
8 A grid organisation consists of (according to the term grid) "vertical" knowledge areas with the specialists in this field, and "horizontal" project-oriented areas, which draw experts from the knowledge areas according to the needs of the project.
9 My doctoral thesis dealt with the historical development and status of regional planning in Austria (Schimak, 1984).

References

Dillinger, T. (2012). Planerinnen und Planer ausbilden—Über die Anfänge des Studiums Raumplanung und Raumordnung an der TU Wien [Educating Planners—About the Start of the Study of Spatial Planning at the Vienna University of Technology]. In Fakultät für Architektur und Raumplanung, Technische Universität Wien (Ed.), *Stadt: Gestalten: Festschrift für Klaus Semsroth* (pp. 205–209). Wien-New York: Springer.

Faludi, A. (1978). *Essays on Planning and Education.* Oxford: Pergamon Press.

Kunzmann, K. R. (2017). Places Matter: Creativity, Culture and Planning. In B. Haselsberger (Ed.), *Encounters in Planning Thought: 16 Autobiographical Essays from Key Thinkers in Spatial Planning* (pp. 202–221). New York: Routledge.

Lindblom, C. E. (1959). The Science of "Muddling Through". *Public Administration Review*, 19, pp. 79–99.

Lorenz, K. (1973). *Die Rückseite des Spiegels: Versuch einer Naturgeschichte menschlichen Erkennens* [Behind the Mirror: A Search for a Natural History of Human Knowledge]. München-Zürich: Piper.

Mitterauer, M. (2003). *Warum Europa? Mittelalterliche Grundlagen eines Sonderweges* [Why Europe? The Medieval Origins of Its Special Path]. München: Beck.

Neill, A. S. (1969). *Theorie und Praxis der antiautoritären Erziehung: Das Beispiel Summerhill* [Summerhill: A Radical Approach to Child Rearing] (H. Schroeder, trans.). Reinbek: Rowolth.

Popper, K. (1975). *Die offene Gesellschaft und ihre Feinde* [The Open Society and Its Enemies] 2 vols. (P. K. Feyerabend, trans.). München: UTB Francke.

Schimak, G. (1980). Der Ingenieurkonsulent für Raumplanung und Raumordnung [The "Consulting Engineer" for Spatial Planning]. *Berichte zur Raumforschung und Raumplanung*, 24 (5), pp. 33–35.

Schimak, G. (1984). *Der Einsatz des Planungsinstrumentariums rechtswirksamer überörtlicher Entwicklungsprogramme in den österreichischen Bundesländern* [The Use of the Planning Instrument of Legally Binding Regional Development Programmes in the Austrian Federal States] 2 vol. (unpublished doctoral dissertation). University of Technology Vienna.

Schimak, G. (1993a). Die Entwicklung der Studienrichtung Raumplanung und Raumordnung [The Development of the Study Programme of Spatial Planning]. In D. Bökemann (Ed.), *Studienrichtung Raumplanung* (pp. 40–41). Wien: Fakultät für Architektur und Raumplanung, Technische Universität.

Schimak, G. (1993b). Weltausstellung 1995 Wien—Budapest. Ursache und Konsequenzen der Absage Wiens [World Exhibition 1995 Vienna—Budapest. Cause and Consequences of the Cancellation by Vienna]. In H. Häußermann & W. Siebel (Eds.), *Festivalisierung der Stadtpolitik, Stadtentwicklung durch große Projekte* (pp. 108–133). Opladen: Leviathan-Sonderheft.

Steinbeck, J. (1948). *Früchte des Zorns* [Grapes of Wrath] (K. Lambrecht, trans.). Konstanz/Stuttgart: Diana.

Wurzer, R. (Ed.). (1970). *Strukturanalyse des Österreichischen Bundesgebietes (1970)* [Structure Analysis of the Austrian Federal Territory]. Wien: Österreichische Gesellschaft für Raumforschung und Raumplanung.

Wurzer, R. (Ed.). (1994). *Raumplanerausbildung in Europa, 20 Jahre—Raumplanung im Aufbruch*. [Education of Planners in Europe, 20 Years Advancement of Spatial Planning]. Informationen zur Raumplanung, 1. Wien: Institut zur Erforschung von Methoden und Auswirkungen der Raumplanung der Ludwig Boltzmann-Gesellschaft. Technische Universität.

Terminology Glossary

Faculty: In the context of the Austrian university system, a faculty is the administrative part of a university headed by a dean and dealing with a specific scientific field. It includes the whole scientific (including professors) and administrative staff, the dean's office, smaller internal units like institutes and departments and laboratories needed for research and teaching.

Rectorate: Is the group of persons heading the whole university and consists of the rector, a deputy rector and several vice rectors.

10

FROM INFORMING POLICY TO COLLABORATING RATIONALLY

Judith E. Innes

My intellectual journey has been grounded in a desire to improve the quality of public decisions. As child in Boston I observed major planning blunders and as staff to a congressman I witnessed uninformed decision making. My first idea was to develop better data, but later I realized that information would have to be socially constructed in dialogue for users to be motivated to act on it. In the third phase I learned how power in society can distort information and groupthink can blind us to underlying realities. This idea led me to Habermas, who proposed a dialectical process among diverse voices to challenge assumptions and drill down to robust understandings. The latter offered a critical lens on the collaborative policy dialogues I was observing and allowed David Booher and me to develop normative theory for how collaboration can be rational, though in a different sense from the positivist version of the term. We found that facilitators' best practices largely mirrored the conditions Habermas laid out for communicative rationality, and that when they did so, long-term improvements occurred in practices and institutions for decision making.

In the late 1990s complexity science transformed my thinking, so that today I see everything through that lens. The world is a complex adaptive system where interventions have unpredictable results and where planners have to learn new ways of understanding. In a world in constant motion, evidence is not enough. Collaborative planning must become central to effective public decisions.

I never expected to have a career, much less be a professor. Gender barriers were high, but without a career plan I took advantage of opportunities as they came. My best work has been collaborative, as colleagues stimulated and sharpened my thinking. Amazingly I have arrived where I hoped from the beginning—to a new model for planning and policy-making.

Early Influences

What Would Be My Role in Life? Mixed Messages from My Family

As a child I assumed I would be a wife and mother. My mother had quit her life as a dancing star when she married my father. My father expected to protect me until he handed me over to my husband. I had to help around the house, while my brothers' only job was taking out the garbage. On the flip side my parents sent me to the finest private school for girls in the region, where I got a first-rate education from women with advanced degrees. My brilliant father, who was leader of the Massachusetts Senate, talked to me about policy, lawmaking, and philosophy. He admired two women he worked with—one a senator and the other the secretary of state. Though my mother's IQ was identical to his, he regarded her as a beautiful, funny airhead, while she cultivated the image. She taught me to cook, shop, and dress, and she told me I should never challenge a man by showing that I know something he does not. She took no interest in my studies. Such mixed messages were confusing then and troublesome when I began my career.

Values Rooted in Family Culture

My father came from a line of influential political leaders committed to public service and the pursuit of ideas. My great grandfather was publisher to transcendentalists such as Emerson and Thoreau and active in the abolitionist[1] movement. My grandfather, a powerful political figure, assisted governors and presidents, while leading civic initiatives. He started the first night law school so the poor could become lawyers. My father was a lawyer and legislator who eventually became leader of the state senate, where he devoted much of his time to crafting and passing innovative legislation, including the state's first fair housing and fair employment laws. This family identity impressed upon me that I had much to live up to, and that it is possible to make a real difference.

Unitarianism taught the values of tolerance, justice, and equity, and a search for truth and meaning. It was up to each individual and his/her conscience to do the right thing. This heritage partially accounts for my choice of planning as a field to pursue these values. My family culture also drew on Scottish philosophy and epistemological inquiry.

Three Planning Blunders in Boston

We lived in central Boston, in the district my father represented. Our house backed onto an Esplanade beside the Charles River, where we walked and played. When I was seven I got my first lesson in bad planning and politics. Although the Esplanade had been built with a donation that stipulated it would never be used for a road, the legislature proposed to do exactly that. Both the donor and my father opposed the idea, and my father argued that the road could be built over the nearby railroad tracks. My father would not back down so politicians used parliamentary tricks to narrowly push the road proposal through. By 1951, Storrow Drive had replaced the Esplanade. Fourteen years later the Massachusetts Turnpike was built over the tracks.

Boston in the 1950s was in decline, with population and commerce moving to the suburbs. Ostensibly to improve the economy, a governor and legislature pushed through the Central Artery project, a partially elevated expressway through Boston's North End. My father fought it as a lawyer for the leather and wool industries, which would be destroyed. He proposed undergrounding the artery but lost the battle. The new highway quickly became clogged; the industries expired; and a tight knit Italian neighborhood was divided. Fifty years later the Big Dig, at the time the most expensive public works project in the US, finally undergrounded the artery.

In the fifties we used to drive past a vast area of rubble-filled blocks in the heart of the city, which disturbed and puzzled me. Boston was in the midst of an urban renewal program that was to become infamous. The city had torn down an Italian/Jewish neighborhood on the grounds that it was blighted, with an underlying intention to expand downtown. Herbert Gans, who lived there as a participant observer before the demolition, wrote his famous *Urban Villagers* book describing a tightly knit community where residents' identities were intimately bound up with their homes and neighborhood (Gans, 1962). The book, along with articles documenting the grief of displaced residents, was a major factor in discrediting urban renewal in the US.

Challenges of Being a Woman

In the 1950s and '60s, it was not easy to be a woman if one did not follow a traditional path. Gender discrimination was central in my life until the late 1980s. As high school graduation approached, my father expected me to go to cooking or secretarial school. My school, however, expected me to go to Radcliffe[2] and, as a Harvard alumnus, my father relented. I entered college at 17, majoring in English because I liked novels. Assuming I could not go to graduate school, I pursued an active social life, getting mediocre grades. In my all-female preparatory school I felt free to speak up and excel in my classes, but at Harvard men dominated, and my mother was correct that being smart was bad for a woman's social life. Men ran all the organizations, many of which excluded women. I was especially disappointed when Harvard's humor magazine, the *Lampoon,* would not even consider an article written by a woman, as I wanted to be a humor writer.

On graduation in 1963, I applied for editing jobs in publishing houses but they turned me down expressly because I was a woman, while hiring my male classmates. Luckily a friend was moving out of her job as assistant to Dr. John Gordon, a renowned Harvard professor of public health, and she passed the position to me. Work for him continued my education in practical ways. As an epidemiologist, he taught me that one could use statistics to devise strategies for social problems by documenting whom they affect and under what circumstances. From him I learned how to prepare journal articles. My second job was also serendipitous, as Dr. Gordon recommended me to head the publications office at the Department of Nutrition and Food Science at MIT. It was a trial by fire for a 22-year-old to take over an office staffed by women old enough to be her mother and to edit faculty papers.

1964: A Turning Point

The year I married, 1964, was a turning point for American society as well as for me. The predictable world of my youth gave way to a world dominated baby boomers, who flouted convention, joined mass protests, and lived in communes. After the assassination of President Kennedy (JFK) in late 1963, his successor Lyndon Baines Johnson (LBJ) started the War on Poverty and the Great Society program, targeting deteriorating inner cities. His signature achievement was the passage of the Civil Rights Act, designed to protect "negroes" from discrimination in restaurants, schools, and workplaces, incidentally including civil rights equality for women. This law did not produce immediate change, but it emboldened leaders to demand their rights in sit-ins and protests. The Free Speech Movement at Berkeley asserted students'

148 Judith E. Innes

right to protest on campus. Recreational drug use emerged among middle-class youth, as did the counterculture of the hippie generation. The US secretly began an escalating war in Vietnam, and by 1967 antiwar protests took over campuses. JFK's brother was assassinated during his campaign for president, and not long afterwards beloved civil rights leader Martin Luther King was gunned down. Nothing would ever be the same.

As a married working woman I watched the turmoil from a safe distance, wondering what it might mean. I knew nothing of the new civil rights for women. Sexism was not in my vocabulary and, much as I railed against discrimination, it seemed to be the natural order of things. The nascent women's movement seemed extreme and impractical. At least half of my college class had married within a year of graduation. Women were on the cusp of change, caught between the old and the new with no preparation, guidelines, or role models. We had to invent ourselves as we went along, forced into careers for which we were not prepared.

When my husband, Richard de Neufville, completed his MIT PhD in 1965, we headed to Washington, where he was a White House fellow assigned to Defense Secretary Robert McNamara. I became legislative assistant for a congressman, and it was in that role that I discovered the intellectual project that has motivated me. The congressman was a moderate of few opinions and a safe district. When he had a significant vote, he asked us to get information for him, and we invited civil servants, lobbyists, and scholars to talk with us. Library of Congress staff even wrote us a book when they could not find what we needed. But after we gave the congressman our recommendations, he called his buddies to decide how to vote. The data that so many had created to inform public decisions did not inform him, even when he wanted it to. I concluded the problem was neither the politicians nor the data, but the system of producing and using it.

Planning Education at MIT: Searching for Keys to Informing Policy

When we returned to Cambridge, where Richard began as an MIT professor, he told me he would pay for my graduate school. It took me only 30 seconds to say yes, though I had never considered the possibility. It took me a bit longer to decide on a field. Harvard Law School would admit only three women, and one of them would not be me. Neither MIT nor Harvard admitted women to their business schools. Eventually I decided on city planning because a) it could admit someone from English literature; b) there were two planning programs nearby; c) my father told me (wrongly) the field did not discriminate against women; and d) I thought I could explore my interest in information use in public policy. I went to MIT's Department of Urban Studies and Planning (DUSP) because Harvard had closed their applications.

For the first time since high school, I applied myself and got top grades. It was all fascinating, except for land-use planning and design. Wonderful as Kevin Lynch was as a professor, I could not tell the difference between a good design and a poor one. My interest was in ideas—Lee Rainwater and Herb Gans taught the concept of inequality, and Lloyd Rodwin reflected on the nature and purpose of planning. Then in a watershed moment Jack Howard, the professor who had advised the city to replace the Esplanade with a highway and tear down Gans's urban village, told us with tears in his eyes that his generation of planners had failed. We should go out and do better. I went home, threw out my notes, and resolved to find a new model for planning.

My preliminary goal for my PhD was to develop a rational model for social policy. I took a dozen quantitative methods courses, from modeling to systems analysis to economics and statistics, so I could become an expert. After Nathan Glazer suggested that social indicators could influence policy, I decided to design an indicator. After I prepared my dissertation proposal, committee member Martin Rein told me the first chapter on history should be the dissertation. He was right, but it was Hayward Alker who turned the idea into a rigorous research design. In a grubby diner near campus he wrote my hypothesis on a napkin: "If an indicator is influential, it is also scientifically sound." This I would test by comparing two indicators: the unemployment rate and the standard budget, a yardstick of income adequacy. I would do in-depth interviewing, examine documents, and tell the story of each.[3] It was a model of research that I have used ever since, comparing cases in terms of theory about what makes for success.

The research confirmed my original intuition: Useful and used information require a whole system. The so-called rational model was wrong in positing that "experts" and policymakers have separate tasks and that the expert role is only to provide data and analysis. Decision makers would not use or act on indicators unless they understood their meaning and trusted their accuracy. Intensive dialogue among stakeholders, decision makers, and experts was prerequisite to design of an influential indicator. In the course of their discussions, a policy was forged. Moreover, institutional arrangements for producing accurate, unbiased numbers over time would be needed, including regular reporting of the indicators' movements, along with requirements that policymakers respond. These contentions have not been contradicted since I published the findings in a book (de Neufville, 1975; Innes, 1990). The insights were foundational for my later work.[4]

At MIT I had no mentor, but I did take full advantage of access to Harvard and MIT faculty. Hayward Alker introduced me to network theory; Lisa Peattie taught me fieldwork; and Sam Bowles radicalized my thinking. Daniel Patrick Moynihan, a practitioner/scholar who later became a US senator, read my dissertation and told me it was good. When I had to remove Rein from my committee, Moynihan advised me to ask Daniel Bell to replace him. Bell also liked the dissertation and offered to pass it to his editor at Basic Books. Bell and Moynihan set me on an academic path. Only after talking with them did I imagine that my dissertation could be a book.

After my oral examination, the committee filed out past me without a word. My chair told me he was disappointed that I did not impress his colleagues more. When I asked if I had passed, he said yes. Neither he nor anyone else offered suggestions about what I might do next. An academic route did not occur to me because I had never had a woman professor. There was only one woman on the entire Harvard faculty, and at MIT even Lisa Peattie was only a lecturer. I went home and cried for a long time.

What ended my despair was a telephone call from Michael Teitz, chair of the Department of City and Regional Planning (DCRP) at the University of California Berkeley (UCB) asking to interview me. He had called MIT looking for women with a PhD in planning because he had decided DCRP needed its first woman on the tenure track. Three women went for interviews. I lost to Janice Perlman, but Teitz offered me a lectureship for spring 1974, when my husband was due for a sabbatical at UCB.

We spent the winter of 1973–4 in London, while Richard was at University College (UCL). I worked nonstop writing my book while he took care of shopping and the nanny for our two-year-old. We were fortunate to have the resources to pay for her. With new teaching

150 Judith E. Innes

responsibilities looming, I wrote the book in three months. I was to teach a course in comparative land-use policy and heard that Peter Hall had just written a book on the topic. When I contacted him, he suggested meeting at the Royal Geographic Society. It turned out he was on his way to UCB, so he also had questions for me. He kindly brought me paper and pens from his office, as the oil crisis had made both rare commodities in London.

Starting an Academic Career: Developing Ideas and Research

Back at home in Cambridge, Massachusetts, still with no idea what next, I met a woman at a cocktail party who, after a brief conversation, told me I should take her position at Tufts University. Once again, thank goodness, a job had come looking for me. The department head had been one of my professors at MIT, and he quickly hired me. This experimental program, started by Hermann Field, wartime prisoner, novelist, and visionary, was titled "Urban Social and Environmental Policy"—essentially about sustainability, though we did not have the term. I spent a year with stimulating colleagues and new ideas about the value of bringing diverse citizens together (Krimsky & de Neufville, 1978).

In 1976 another tenure-track position opened at DCRP, and I decided to go on the job market. MIT had no interest in hiring me, nor did Harvard. Berkeley, Princeton, and University of Southern California made offers. While I knew that as a woman I benefitted from affirmative action,[5] I did not for a moment think I did not deserve the offers. I was qualified; I had written a book; and I was good at interviews. Princeton was my choice because it was nearest to home, but my meeting with the vice president was abruptly cancelled when a member of the advisory committee blackballed me because I planned research that would not include an economist. It was then I recognized the academic hegemony of economists and their insistence on their rationalist worldview. I took the Berkeley job, hopeful that my husband would get the tenured position in civil engineering for which he was highly qualified. When that fell through, our marriage, which was already troubled, came apart. It was sad and a struggle to share responsibility for our son across country in the ensuing years.

A starting position in a research university is always challenging, as one has to design courses on topics of current interest; build teaching skills for lectures, seminars, and studios; do administrative work; and find time and money for research and writing. Everything had a steep learning curve, and I worked every free minute. Merit reviews every three years involved multiple levels of evaluation, with publications the key to positive results. Looking back I realize that my activities were structured by these expectations. I wrote mainly peer-reviewed journal articles over the years, as book chapters did not count and books would take too long. Merit increases brought money, and since my salary was small this was important.

My next book was a disappointment, but the process taught me much about the publishing business. In 1977, I had organized an interdisciplinary symposium at the Lincoln Institute of Land Policy to help develop theory for land use. I edited the papers and wrote chapters for *The Land Use Policy Debate in the U.S.* (de Neufville, 1981). Plenum, a small publishing house, accepted the manuscript, but the editor sat on it till I flew to New York to tell him I needed it for my tenure case. The personal touch worked as he pulled it from the bottom of the pile. Plenum did little to publicize the book, however, and then went out of business. I had hoped it would start a debate that would elevate land-use planning from the rule of thumb approach to a conceptual level, addressing underlying values and allowing reasoned discussion from multiple perspectives. The book was little reviewed and disappeared from view. It did however help me to get tenure because several leading planning academics read it and wrote supportive letters.

By the early '70s the Nixon administration had dismantled Great Society programs, replacing them with block grants to states and cities, which were more project than policy oriented, making my focus on urban social policy irrelevant. I taught social indicators briefly, but the fad waned, along with social policy as a planning subfield. The National Environmental Protection Act (1970) turned the attention of many students away from cities to the natural environment.

My first theoretical paper was inspired by talks with systems scientist Sir Geoffrey Vickers, a visiting scholar at the Institute of Urban and Regional Development (IURD) at UCB, in 1977. His idea of appreciative systems—the activity of attaching meaning to communication—was the basis of my article "Validating Policy Indicators" (de Neufville, 1978), which contends that validity depends on context, and is tested with the aid of theory, but ultimately must make sense to those who are part of the system. This became a fundamental idea for me.

With little research funding, my strategy was to build intellectual capital through teaching, so I designed a popular course on the history and theory of land and environment in American thought and practice. Then, building on a compelling literature in organizational behavior, I developed a second course on implementation of plans and policies.

Two devastating setbacks changed my trajectory. A new department chair arrived straight from directing San Francisco's planning department. He told me I could not teach these courses, saying implementation was about zoning, not organizational behavior, and that talk of land policy was inappropriate in planning. He seemed to believe we already know what to do and that planning education was merely about developing the skills to do it. I had to develop new courses, and later I could not reinstate the old courses, as other faculty had taken them on. Then I launched a historical study of urban renewal, but when my graduate assistant published the research as his own, I ended my brief career as an urban historian. As a result I ended up with only methodology and planning theory teaching and no content specialty.

After these events I turned to more thinking and theorizing, with an article confronting the orthodoxy of the "rational," technical approach. Karen Christensen and I challenged the bureaucratic ethic that actions should be optimal (de Neufville & Christensen, 1980). We pointed out that with multiple goals, optimizing did not make sense and that embedding those "optimal" choices in bureaucratic rules was not adaptive. We were proud of the article, but colleagues either ignored or actively disliked it. Thirty years later, adaptiveness became a watchword in planning, and optimizing virtually vanished from the vocabulary. I learned that if an article is ahead of its time, its ideas will not be heard.

In "Planning Theory and Practice: Bridging the Gap" (de Neufville, 1983), I began an effort to move planning theory away from elaborating the rational model and toward broad, practice-relevant inquiry. At the time planning theory mainly involved essays by social scientists offering theories and dilemmas about the economy, the state and society, and decision-making procedures, but it did not address planning as a professional activity. My article contended that planning was a paradigm in crisis, in that theory did not mesh with practice but led to cognitive dissonance and alienation of practitioners. I proposed an agenda for planning theorists: confront the dilemmas; ground theorizing in research on practice; use holistic, interpretive methods; and create new imagery of what planning is and what planners do. While I do not know whether the article was influential or simply prescient, this was exactly what a new generation of planning theorists did in the ensuing years.

152 Judith E. Innes

In 1981 I came up for tenure. It was an anxious time as some colleagues objected to my theoretical leanings. Others, I was told, simply could not accept that a woman merited tenure. No doubt my mother's voice in my head had prevented me from asserting myself. The vote gave me a bare majority—not enough in many departments for a case to go forward—but at the university level it sailed through.

Pushing Further into Theoretical Territory

By the 1980s phenomenology and the social construction of reality had supplanted positivism and the rational model for me. A novel opportunity came my way, to see how a social construction process can work in an organization and change minds, practices, and policies. The US State Department wanted to include social needs in the *Country Reports on Human Rights*[6] and asked me to develop the indicators. When a Republican administration came in the following year, it proposed to abolish the reports altogether. Civil servants in the department hired me to evaluate the impact of the reports in the hope of protecting them. I discovered that, although the data in the reports had little direct influence on Congress, it had major impact on the diplomats who gathered the data. The horrific abuses they discovered changed their priorities and understandings, and they concluded that tolerating such abuses was morally distasteful and counterproductive. The reporting process also legitimized and empowered human rights groups to become influential in national debates (de Neufville, 1986).

Then I turned to environmental impact assessments and found, similarly, that those who put together the reports became internal advocates for the environment and that environmental advocacy groups became more politically powerful (Innes, 1988a).[7] I laid out the theory in a *JAPA* essay, which argues that data requirements 1) increase expertise and data resources in agencies and political processes; 2) empower some viewpoints relative to others; and 3) change the terms of planning debates by shaping agendas and norms of discourse and by influencing which values become taken-for-granted bases for decisions (Innes, 1988b, p. 275).

My interests in the social construction of reality, urban history, and literature converged in an article on the role of myths in the definition of policy problems (de Neufville & Barton, 1987). At the time scholars gave little attention to metaphors or narratives, much less myths, in policy processes. The continuing hegemony of the rational model discounted such "subjective" and unquantifiable elements. We examined why hard data so often failed to persuade policymakers. They ignored economists' evidence that allowing tax deductions for home mortgage payments was a wasteful and regressive way to provide housing assistance. Our research showed that the ideal of homeownership was so deeply embedded in American history and politics that it had taken on a mythological quality. Homeownership was presumed essential to an independent and responsible citizenry, but no one tested this assumption. As a myth associated with the founding of the country, it was sacred, and it touched shared beliefs and emotions. Myths and stories, we concluded, may be necessary to motivate public action, but they also conceal realities and contradictions and legitimize policies that benefit the powerful. Planners, we said, should not ignore these but become adept at using alternative narratives to frame issues.

The article, "Knowledge and Action: Making the Link" (de Neufville, 1987), built on all these ideas to argue that a phenomenological view of knowledge should replace the positivist one for planners. It allows a focus on specific situations where planning takes place, forces

From Informing to Collaborating **153**

attention to the meanings of problems to the actors, and thus offers a better link of knowledge to action. I began to realize that the titles of my articles and books had typically assumed a world in process, undergoing social construction.

Institution Building in the 1980s

New challenges presented themselves as the planning academy unfolded as a newly self-aware field. In the 1980s my main focus was institution building. The Association of Collegiate Schools of Planning (ACSP), which began as an appendage to the practitioner organization, the American Planning Association (APA), decided to hold its conference separately and to start its own journal. Though I was skeptical, I joined the effort to build a professional organization for the planning academy. I was associate editor for the *Journal of Planning Education and Research* (*JPER*) and an ACSP board member in the formative years. I was principal organizer of the annual conference in San Francisco in 1983 and put together a program featuring John Friedmann, Jack Dyckman, Richard Bolan, and other academic stars for 300 attendees. Today the conference is far more complex, serving many professional purposes for a thousand or more participants, but those early conferences were exhilarating.

At the time APA was conducting its own assessments of the schools, angering academics. After intense battles, the American Institute of Certified Planners (AICP) and ACSP agreed to create a joint Planning Accreditation Board (PAB). As members of PAB, Gene Grigsby and I led a successful rebellion against APA's attempts to control PAB.

In 1990 I chaired a commission on the PhD, to investigate how well US doctoral programs were serving the academy. We assembled an all-star group of faculty, each of whom conducted research on topics such as job placement, mismatches in supply and demand, and time-to-degree. The report (Innes, 1993) resulted in new initiatives, including an annual workshop to assist PhD students in preparing dissertations. Shortly afterwards, the Association of European Schools of Planning (AESOP) began research on the PhD in Europe and invited me to Venice to share ideas.

The University of California[8] has a strong tradition of faculty governance in which I participated, serving on faculty senate committees. The experience taught me how the university works, and it built my networks across campus. I joined the Association of Academic Women, an organization designed to help women succeed, and took over as president for a time. We invented ourselves as we went along, with few senior women faculty as role models.

Building Skills and Intellectual Networks

The best thing I did for my academic career was to join a women's writing group, where six of us met biweekly to listen to one of us read our work aloud and to react. We learned "reader-based writing" instead of writer-based, following Dunlap's model (2007). Our writing improved dramatically. Over a decade three of us got tenure, one was promoted to full professor, and another managed to write the book she had been stuck on for years. As I write today I still imagine Kathy Roper, German historian, as my audience and realize she will not know what I am talking about unless I write in a clear, jargon-free way.

A second valuable activity was a five-day teaching workshop. I am not a natural teacher, and when I started, I overprepared and lectured to students, whose attention I did not always keep.

154 Judith E. Innes

The workshop allowed us to react to others' teaching and see our own mistakes in the process. It taught me to offer the important points in the first five minutes of class and to recognize that attention spans are seldom more than 20 minutes. I made even my largest classes interactive, engaging students in exercises and joint learning. I learned to be spontaneous and enjoy teaching in a way that fit my abilities.

IURD was a place to meet, build international networks, and be exposed to new ideas. There were lectures, dinners, and discussion groups for people from across the campus, along with an impressive procession of visiting scholars. Andreas Faludi came one year, as did Alessandro Balducci, Enrico Gualini, and many others. Patsy Healey visited in 1983, and she and I quickly hit it off. On a long hike in Point Reyes National Seashore, we discovered the many ways our thinking intersected. I encouraged her to come to an ACSP conference, and she invited me to a British/Italian planning theory conference in Turin, which she was organizing with Luigi Mazza. We started a regular correspondence, sharing our thinking on many topics.

After my setbacks I had lost some intellectual energy, but the 1986 Turin conference revived my thinking and pointed me in new directions. Judith Allen impressed us all by using Habermas's idea of communicative action to show how citizen rhetoric and dramaturgical action changed city policy (Allen, 1993). The conference confirmed the importance of Habermas's inclusive perspective for professions like planning that work holistically on places in the midst of economists, scientists, and engineers who reduce the world to variables. Mindful of how social constructions can colonize the lifeworld, conceal contradictions, and reify existing power relationships, I turned to the Frankfurt School of Critical Theory, which offered a way out of this pernicious circularity by questioning assumptions and using dialectical processes.[9] Habermas's concept of communicative rationality offered guidelines for dialogue and suggested that group deliberation could be rational. These ideas offered a path to an alternate way of planning.

A New Trajectory: Consensus Building and Collaboration

A sabbatical in 1988–9 at the Lincoln Institute of Land Policy in Cambridge, Massachusetts, sent me on a new line of inquiry. It began with a comparative study of the implementation of growth management legislation in three states. US planners had latched onto growth management as their contribution to environmental protection, and Vermont, New Jersey, and Florida had set up different types of legislation. Vermont's was a regulatory approach relying on court challenges for enforcement. Florida's was a bureaucratic model, where towns submitted plans to a state agency for approval. New Jersey's was a multitiered collaborative process engaging lawmakers, stakeholders, and citizens in preparing a consensus-based state land-use plan. I found that courts in Vermont were unwilling to decide disputes, sending them to mediation, and bureaucrats in Florida ended up negotiating with local governments. In all cases, dialogue and negotiation over the meaning of growth management was essential (Innes, 1992) to implementation of the laws.

On my return I learned that California was working on its own growth management legislation using a cutting edge consensus-building process, while the National Estuary Program was doing the same with the management of San Francisco Bay. These projects offered me the opportunity to inquire into how people use information in decisions and into how dialogue and negotiation work.

The work on data requirements had led me to a kindred spirit, Judith Gruber in the UCB Department of Political Science, who was to become a professional collaborator and close friend. We examined 13 consensus-building cases, including the Growth Management Consensus Project (GMCP), a stakeholder-based effort sponsored by the state legislature, the San Francisco Estuary Project (SFEP), and two habitat restoration projects (Innes et al., 1994). Observing the skilled process management of the GMCP by the Center for Collaborative Policy (CCP),[10] I realized how deliberation could be powerful for controversial planning decisions. During the research I interviewed planner and future collaborator, David Booher, co-chair of the GMCP, working at the time as a lobbyist for business and developers. This project was foundational for me. Judy and I found that participants built shared political, social, and intellectual capital, which kept them at the table and endured regardless of whether agreements were reached.

The William and Flora Hewlett Foundation was central to the growth of consensus-building knowledge and practice in the US. Its Conflict Resolution Program was started by Roger Heyns, chancellor of UCB during the turmoil of the 1960s with its heavy-handed crackdowns by Governor Reagan. On Heyns's retirement he became president of the foundation, where his priority was to find new ways of making peace. The program funded centers for conflict resolution across the country, supported state conflict resolution offices, and funded conferences bringing practitioners and experts together. Hewlett helped launch CCP, which David Booher later joined as senior advisor. CCP worked for state, regional, and local agencies, helping them to develop plans, policies, and programs on controversial issues through stakeholder-based consensus-building processes.

A New Planning Theory Paradigm Emerges

The first joint ACSP/AESOP conference in Oxford in 1991 was a pivotal moment in planning thought. At a plenary session a dramatic debate took place among David Harvey, Andreas Faludi, and junior planning scholars. While Faludi was defending his brand of "procedural planning theory," others were bringing in new insights from practice, and Harvey was challenging the entire enterprise. What I saw was a community of planning scholars forming. The observation led to my most controversial paper, "Planning Theory's Emerging Paradigm: Communicative Action and Interactive Practice" (Innes, 1995). My argument was that the rational theorists, who derived their inspiration from Popper and wrote essays about how planning ought to be, were being supplanted by communicative theorists who looked to Habermas and Foucault and got their insights from in-depth studies of practice. At the second joint ACSP/AESOP conference in Toronto in 1996, John Bryson facilitated a session with John Forester, Patsy Healey, and myself, asking whether a new paradigm existed. In the audience the older generation said mostly, "No, nothing is ever new"; the intermediate generation said, "Yes, let's explore it"; and the younger generation said, "Why are we even talking about this? Let's get on with it."[11]

The clamor following publication of the article was a surprise. I walked into a panel at the next ACSP conference to hear Charlie Hoch defending me—from what I had no idea. It turned out that political economists had taken offense at what I had written. The panel was designed as a debate,[12] where critics contended Habermas was naïve about power and challenged the idea that communication could be powerful. The biggest lightning rod was my claim that communicative theory could emerge as the dominant paradigm in planning theory. Several further "debates" took place at later Oxford Planning Theory conferences, and critics published numerous articles about what was wrong with communicative planning theory (CPT). Later some communicative theorists publically apologized for my claim or suggested I did not really mean it. I did mean it, however, and my prediction was correct. CPT conference talks and articles proliferated, illuminating a rich array of practices where communication made a difference. By 1998 even critics began to note the "hegemony" of CPT (Tewdwr-Jones & Allmendinger, 1998), though other lines of thought continued. By 2001, a distinguished scholar from outside planning theory (Hopkins, 2001, p. 400) declared that CPT had "reached the status of the claimed paradigm shift."

The reaction of political economists was puzzling because my article focused on the supplanting of the rational procedural paradigm. I did not mention them, as I saw their work as urban theory and untouched by communicative theorists. I was happy, however, that the article generated debate and called attention to the ideas of creative researchers and theorists who inspired a new generation of planning scholars. The paradigm paper was to be my most cited article for many years. Criticisms of the article and the CPT community continued, with communicative planning theorists occasionally playing defense, but mostly just getting on with their work. Many of the claims were just plain wrong, particularly the oft-repeated contention that these theorists ignored power. While they did not share the Marxist idea of a powerful capitalist state that disempowered planners, they developed nuanced understandings of many types of power in planning, including the ability to shape agendas and convene forums, and they demonstrated how communication power works.[13] Critics largely ignored the idea of communicative action, conflating it with collaboration, which they then attacked, often by criticizing Habermas. They doubted collaboration worked as reported, ignoring the theorists' field research and the rich accounts of practice they cited. The saddest part of all this has been the missed opportunity for constructive interchange and mutual learning.

Directing IURD: New Challenges and New Projects

Meanwhile, another surprising opportunity came my way. Peter Hall, who had been director of IURD since Mel Webber retired, returned to England to take up a post at UCL. The advisory committee, headed by a former chancellor noted for his support of women, recommended me as interim director. I was dubious, as I had no experience in fundraising, but he insisted I would do a good job. My assumption was that I would keep the seat warm for the male faculty member who was the heir apparent, but I decided to accept because it would be great to have a secretary for six months to organize my files. I got the nod for director in 1994 and everything changed. It meant challenging responsibilities to build IURD's research and community outreach programs, support graduate students, contribute to urban policy, and create a vital venue for interdisciplinary dialogue. I was respected by colleagues and worked with university leadership. Never again was my gender a problem. My networks across campus became assets. I had release time from teaching, so I could not only manage IURD but also conduct field research.

The funding picture was improving, and I raised millions in grants. Under the Clinton administration the Department of Housing and Urban Development revived after years of neglect, and IURD got major grants for multidisciplinary community partnership work. Major federal granting agencies stopped insisting on "scientific" proposals with hypotheses and quantitative evidence, so I was able to get grants to explore cutting-edge experiments in collaborative water policy-making in California. We evaluated the San Francisco Estuary Project, following up on the networks and political and intellectual capital that participants had built (Innes & Connick, 1999). We observed the Sacramento Water Forum, a six-year stakeholder-based dialogue to prepare a plan for protecting the river while developing new water supplies. The Water Forum, facilitated by CCP, was to become the gold standard for David Booher and myself, both in how it was managed and in the extensiveness of its outcomes (Connick & Innes, 2003; Connick, 2006). It was from this case, more than any other, that we were to build our theory of collaborative rationality.

I continued to explore cases that seemed to be successful. There are so many ways to fail and so few to succeed that positivist-style comparison of successes and failure cannot isolate variables that make the difference. I sought stories to deepen our understandings of how success happens and to allow unanticipated findings to emerge. Getting such research published was a challenge, especially in the *Journal of the American Planning Association* (*JAPA*), whose editors sought "rigor." I persisted in the face of criticism from reviewers who did not trust qualitative information. Our articles were ultimately accepted, typically after two—three years of back and forth.

A New Partnership and New Theory

David Booher and I by 1996 had begun seeing each other in a relationship that built on our shared interest in consensus building. I discussed my findings with him, and he helped me make sense of them. As a voracious reader of theoretical literature, he called my attention to ideas that illuminated what we were seeing. He had moved from lobbying to consensus building, spending time building CCP. He had intended to be a professor of political science, but after his master's, his plans were upended by the Vietnam War and a tour of duty in the US Air Force. When he came back, he got a master's in planning so he could go directly into practice. We shared and developed ideas, often focusing on the tension of theory and practice.

In 1997 we attended an MIT conference that featured some of the great thinkers of complexity science. The ideas were challenging, but we began to see glimmers of how they could revolutionize our thinking about planning processes.[14] Most compelling was the idea that complex systems could be self-organizing and adaptive, both unpredictable and patterned. Complexity thinking called the linear model into question and undermined the assumption that we can intervene in a machine-like world and produce the outcomes we intend. Our challenge was to find a role for planners and planning in such a world.

In our first joint paper (Innes & Booher, 1999a), we were inspired by a Peter Gabriel song about role-playing games: "If looks could kill, they probably will." In these games players take on fantasy roles, go on quests, and meet dangers. The analogy allowed us to see consensus building as a way of trying out possibilities and testing consequences through participants' imagining of future situations. Like game players, they made use of whatever tools, ideas, or practices they could find to solve a problem. The process was not one of argument or debate, as Habermas contended, but a cooperative, creative exercise.

Our second article, today our most cited, was grounded in complexity theory (Innes & Booher, 1999b). At the time the Hewlett Foundation, among others, was calling for evaluation

158 Judith E. Innes

of consensus building. Conventional evaluation—where the purpose is to see if a program achieved its goals—is not appropriate because consensus building does not begin with shared goals, and it has unanticipated benefits such as learning, networks, and political and social capital (Innes et al.,1994). In the article we lay out a framework for evaluation, applying criteria that draw on a combination of complexity theory, communicative rationality, and the practices of successful facilitators. A good process would be self-organizing, engaging diverse players who learn from one another, experiment with ideas, challenge assumptions, and use high-quality information, seeking consensus only after significant effort to satisfy all interests. Desirable outcomes would include high-quality agreements, social and political capital, learning, new networks, and agreed-on knowledge. Second- and third-order outcomes would include changes in practices and flexible, networked organizations, which improve overall system performance. We used the framework to assess California water planning and management (Connick & Innes, 2003). Ambruster (2008) used it in her comparison of expert-run state water planning in 1998 with the consensus-building approach of the 2005 plan. We fielded inquiries from academics and practitioners across the country as they applied the framework to governance theory, public management practice, transportation, and sustainability, as well as many environmental tasks.

Expanding Collaboration Theory

In the 1990s we assessed CALFED, at the time the most complex collaborative environmental planning process in the nation. It was a "build as you go", self-organizing system for California water policy and management that federal and state officials set up informally, without legislation or oversight. This research produced several articles, including one on the value of informal action to get things done when problems are wicked and too complex and shifting for top-down decision making (Innes et al., 2007). Another, drawing on complexity theory, demonstrated that the approach makes for resilience in complex governance systems (Booher & Innes, 2010). CALFED's messy but successful process ultimately inspired our theory of "collaborative rationality" (Innes & Booher, 2010), which lays out the conditions for collaboration to produce "rational" results in the real world.

As the new century arrived we expanded our theory of collaborative dialogue beyond planning into governance, with a chapter in Maarten Hajer's *Deliberative Policy Analysis* (Innes & Booher, 2003). We developed the acronym DIAD for the conditions that would make for rational collaboration, including diversity of interests, interdependence among them, and authentic dialogue, where participants speak sincerely and comprehensibly, legitimately represent an interest, and are supported by accurate, trusted information. As the diagram below shows (Figure 10.1), we contend that such processes result in first-stage consequences such as joint learning, reciprocity, and creativity, and second-stage system adaptations such as shared meanings and innovation.

In a later oft-cited article (Innes & Booher, 2004), we applied the ideas to critique obligatory methods of public participation like public hearings and comment as worse than useless because they encourage extreme rhetoric and divisiveness and do not result in learning. We proposed a dialogical approach, inclusive of diverse views to ensure mutual learning and build trust.

Our evaluation of the James Irvine Foundation's Collaborative Regional Initiatives (CRI) program allowed me to link complexity thinking to governance. The foundation supported

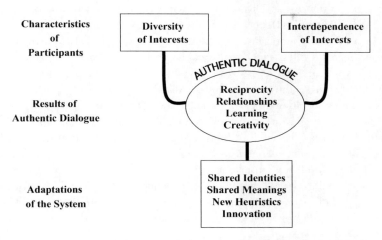

FIGURE 10.1 DIAD Diagram: Bringing together diverse and interdependent interests can result in authentic dialogue (DIAD), which in turn can produce desirable and collaboratively rational outcomes

Source: Author.

civic entrepreneurs, who collaborated to help achieve regional sustainability and fill gaps in what government was willing or able to do. In four in-depth case studies we[15] identified specific accomplishments like new institutions and practices and intangible outcomes like learning and networks. We found keys to success were related to CRI's theories of change, network design, development of information, and adaptiveness (Innes & Rongerude, 2005). Later we developed theory about how civic networks can contribute to sustainability in complex regional systems (Innes & Rongerude, 2013).

Judy Gruber and I found an opportunity to study the supposedly collaborative Metropolitan Transportation Commission (MTC) in the San Francisco Bay Area.[16] Our hypothesis was that the more collaborative their work, the more likely decisions would focus on regional welfare rather than parochial concerns. This did seem to be the case, but MTC's director shut down collaborative work shortly after we started. We did not have enough data to test our hypothesis, so to get value from the project we looked for puzzles. What did not make intuitive sense? We noticed that participants shared the view that compact development was good and that transportation had a role to play, but there was ill will among them anyway. We posited that differing planning styles—technical, political, advocacy, and collaborative—were behind the unpleasantness. It was to take three years of back and forth with *JAPA* reviewers and editors, who wanted us to *prove* our theory, though we had used our research to *develop* the theory. We persisted, and the paper ended up getting the *JAPA* Best Article award that year (Innes & Gruber, 2005). Editors are cautious, and a new approach has a high bar to meet. A paper challenging the status quo or reframing big questions is, nonetheless, more likely to be an important contribution than one that adds data to an existing frame. An author should persist if he/she believes in his/her work.

160 Judith E. Innes

Articulating Collaborative Rationality

In 2004 I resigned as director of IURD, and in 2005 David and I started work on our book, *Planning with Complexity* (Innes & Booher, 2010). It was time to pull our ideas together and flesh out our theory of collaborative rationality. It was time for me to fully articulate the model of planning I had been seeking since MIT. The book would be for future students, colleagues, and reflective practitioners. It would describe the cases that had influenced our thinking, but not been published. It would provide an in-depth understanding of collaborative processes that was not available in handbooks. As senior faculty with plenty of publications, I no longer had to focus on three-year merit increases. It was slow going with a full teaching load, travels to an ailing mother on the East Coast, and the usual departmental responsibilities, but we finished the manuscript in 2009.

The book put the point to my academic career. My primary project had been accomplished, and others would have to take it forward. The crash of 2008 and the ensuing Great Recession had taken a heavy toll on the university, which was cutting back drastically. Everyone got pay cuts; students engaged in massive protests over tuition increases; staff were let go; and IURD became a shell of its former self. Morale was low and the sense of community elusive. It was time to move on.

In 2011 I retired from UCB, with a plan to promote the ideas from our book in as many places as I could, continue writing, get into better physical shape, and develop my neglected right brain by doing watercolors. Finally I had enough distance from the unending criticisms of our work to write an article that would offer a way to embrace the differences and build a more constructive discourse for the field (Innes & Booher, 2015).

Parting Thoughts for Planners and Educators

My biggest concern about planning is that too many educators fixate on solutions rather than assessing options. Planning culture involves creating visions and marketing rather than testing them. Even when the visions are implemented, they fall short and have unintended consequences. In a complex system, this is unsurprising, but even a little research may uncover the impracticality of a concept. Unfortunately the planning profession too often sticks to ideas that do not work, despite the evidence. Some beliefs have a sacred quality and cannot be questioned.

Planners are not entitled to impose their personal or professional beliefs on the world. Garden cities, the interstate highway system, urban renewal, and high-rise public housing have each been the mantra of their day, but none have worked as expected. Similarly the new urbanism, sustainable communities, and transit villages will not be panaceas. These fads will be replaced by others. Instead of assuming the mantle of expert, planners' real contribution can be to develop informed and collaboratively rational proposals by creating dialogues among knowledgeable and diverse stakeholders. Planners should work with many kinds of people, respect their ideas, and understand that what emerges is likely to offer a more robust and nuanced strategy than what they have in their professional toolkits.

Notes

1 Abolitionists worked for immediate emancipation of slaves.
2 Radcliffe was the college for women, who actually took all classes at Harvard. There were separate admissions and men outnumbered women 4 to 1.

From Informing to Collaborating **161**

3　I could find little guidance for my methodology, so I made it up as I went along, relying most heavily on *The Conduct of Inquiry* by Abraham Kaplan (1964) to ensure that my evidence would be persuasive and to understand measurement itself.

4　Eventually I summed up my ideas on information in a *JAPA* article (Innes, 1998).

5　This was the program that is now the norm in public universities in the US, requiring open public searches for faculty positions coupled with special efforts to recruit women and underrepresented minorities.

6　These annual State Department reports to Congress offer data on human rights abuses in every country, in accord with the Universal Declaration of Human Rights.

7　In 1988, with my son off to college, I decided to go back to my maiden name.

8　UCB is part of a 10-campus UC system.

9　Our PhD student, John Forester, turned me on to Bernstein's *Restructuring of Political and Social Theory* (1976) as an introduction to the Frankfurt School.

10　It was then called the Center for Public Dispute Resolution. It is located at California State University Sacramento.

11　Fischer and Forester (1993) and Mandelbaum et al. (1996) were two collections that reflected the communicative turn.

12　The papers were published in volume 17 of *Planning Theory* (1997).

13　See the work of Throgmorton, Sandercock, Forester, Hoch, and Bryson, and Crosby, as well as our "Network Power" (Booher & Innes, 2002).

14　I found the most accessible starting places to be Waldrop (1992), Kelly (1994), Kauffman (1995), Axelrod and Cohen (1999), and Capra (2002).

15　The team included professors AnnaLee Saxenian, Karen Christensen, Judith Innes, and Karen Chapple, along with DCRP graduate students Jane Rongerude, Gerardo Sandoval, and Enrique Silva, along with several others.

16　This agency produced a regional transportation plan and allocated funding to projects.

References

Allen, J. (1993). Smoke over the Winter Palace: The Politics of Resistance and London's Community Areas. *Occasional Papers*. London: University of Westminster Press.

Ambruster, A. (2008). *Collaborative vs. Technocratic Policy Making: California's Statewide Water Plan*. Sacramento, CA: Center for Collaborative Policy, California State University Sacramento. Retrieved at http://www.csus.edu/ccp/publications.html

Axelrod, R., & Cohen, M. D. (1999). *Harnessing Complexity: Organizational Implications of a Scientific Frontier*. New York, NY: Free Press.

Bernstein, R. J. (1976). *The Restructuring of Social and Political Theory*. Philadelphia, PA: University of Pennsylvania Press.

Booher, D. E., & Innes, J. E. (2002). Network power in collaborative planning. *Journal of Planning Education and Research*, vol. 21, 221–236.

Booher, D. E., & Innes, J. E. (2010). Governance for resilience: CALFED as a complex adaptive network for resource management. *Ecology and Society* 15(3), 35.

Capra, F. (2002). *The Hidden Connections: A Science for Sustainable Living*. New York, NY: Anchor Books.

Connick, S. (2006). *The Sacramento Area Water Forum*. Berkeley, CA: Institute of Urban and Regional Development, University of California Berkeley.

Connick, S., & Innes, J. E. (2003). Outcomes of collaborative water policy making: Applying complexity thinking to evaluation. *Journal of Environmental Planning and Management,* vol. 46, 177–197.

de Neufville, J. E. (1975). *Social Indicators and Public Policy: Interactive Processes of Design and Application*. Amsterdam: Elsevier Scientific Publishing Company.

de Neufville, J. E. (1978). Validating policy indicators. *Policy Sciences,* vol. 10, 171–188.

162 Judith E. Innes

de Neufville, J. E. (1983). Planning theory and practice: Bridging the gap. *Journal of Planning Education and Research*, vol. 3, 35–45.

de Neufville, J. E. (1986). Human Rights reporting as a policy tool: An examination of the state department country reports. *Human Rights Quarterly*, vol. 8, 681–699.

de Neufville, J. E. (1987). Knowledge and action: Making the link. *Journal of Planning Education and Research*, vol. 6, 86–92.

de Neufville, J. E., & Christensen, K. (1980). Is optimizing really best? Symposium on optimizing, implementing and evaluating public policy. *Policy Studies Journal* Special issue No 3, 1053–1060.

de Neufville, J. I. (1981). *The Land Use Policy Debate in the United States*. New York City, NY: Plenum Publishing Corporation.

de Neufville, J. I., & Barton, S. (1987). Myths and the definition of policy problems: An exploration of homeownership and public-private partnerships. *Policy Sciences*, vol. 20, 181–206.

Dunlap, L. (2007). *Undoing the Silence: Six Tools for Social Change Writing*. Oakland, CA: New Village Press.

Fischer, F., & Forester, J. (Eds.). (1993). *The Argumentative Turn in Policy Analysis and Planning*. London: Duke University Press/UCL Press Limited.

Gans, H. (1962). *The Urban Villagers: Group and Class in the Life of Italian-Americans*. New York, NY: Free Press of Glencoe.

Hopkins, L. D. (2001). Planning as science: Engaging disagreement. *Journal of Planning Education and Research*, 399–406.

Innes, J. E. (1988a). Effects of data requirements on planning: Case studies of environmental impact assessment and community development block grants. *Computers, Environment and Urban Systems*, 12(2), 77–88.

Innes, J. E. (1988b). The power of data requirements. *Journal of the American Planning Association*, vol. 54, 275–278.

Innes, J. E. (1990). *Knowledge and Public Policy: The Search for Meaningful Indicators*. New Brunswick, NJ: Transaction Books.

Innes, J. E. (1992). Group processes and the social construction of growth management: Florida, Vermont and New Jersey. *Journal of the American Planning Association*, vol. 58, 440–453.

Innes, J. E. (1993). Report of the commission on the doctorate in planning: Executive summary. *Journal of Planning Education and Research (JPER)*, vol. 12, 168–171.

Innes, J. E. (1995). Planning theory's emerging paradigm: Communicative action and interactive practice. *Journal of Planning Education and Research*, vol. 14, 183–189.

Innes, J. E. (1998). Information in communicative planning. *Journal of the American Planning Association*, vol. 64, 52–63.

Innes, J. E., & Booher, D. E. (1999a). Consensus building and complex adaptive systems: A framework for evaluating collaborative planning. *Journal of the American Planning Association*, vol. 65, 412–423.

Innes, J. E., & Booher, D. E. (1999b). Consensus building as role playing and bricolage: Toward a theory of collaborative planning. *Journal of the American Planning Association*, vol. 65, 9–26.

Innes, J. E., & Booher, D. E. (2003). Collaborative Policy Making: Governance through Dialogue. In M. Hajer & H. Wagenaar (Eds.), *Deliberative Policy Analysis: Governance in the Network Society* (pp. 33–59). Cambridge: Cambridge University Press.

Innes, J. E., & Booher, D. E. (2004). Reframing public participation: Strategies for the 21st century. *Planning Theory & Practice*, vol. 5, 419–436.

Innes, J. E., & Booher, D. E. (2010). *Planning with Complexity: An Introduction to Collaborative Rationality for Public Policy*. London: Routledge.

Innes, J. E., & Booher, D. E. (2015). A turning point for planning theory?: Overcoming dividing discourses. *Planning Theory*, vol. 14, 195–213.

Innes, J. E., & Connick, S. (1999). San Francisco Estuary Project. In L. Susskind, S. McKearnan & J. Thomas Larmer (Eds.), *The Consensus Building Handbook: A Comprehensive Guide to Reaching Agreement* (pp. 801–827). Thousand Oaks, CA: Sage Publications.

Innes, J. E., Connick, S., Kaplan, L., & Booher, D. (2006). *Collaborative Governance in the CALFED Program: Adaptive Policy Making for California Water*. Berkeley, CA: Institute of Urban and Regional Development, University of California Berkeley.

Innes, J. E., Connick, S., & Booher, D. E. (2007). Informality as a planning strategy. *Journal of the American Planning Association*, 73, 195–210.

Innes, J. E., & Gruber, J. (2005). Planning styles in conflict: The metropolitan planning commission. *Journal of The American Planning Association*, 177–188.

Innes, J., Gruber, J., Neuman, M. and Thompson, R. (1994). Coordinating Growth and Environmental Management through Consensus Building. *Policy Research Program Reports*. Oakland, CA: University of California. Vol. 1 retrieved at: https://escholarship.org/uc/item/308983c0?query=Coordinating%20Growth%20and%20Environmental%20Management#page-3 and Vol. 2 retrieved at: https://escholarship.org/uc/item/6tg1s896?query=Coordinating%20Growth%20and%20Environmental%20Management

Innes, J. E., & Rongerude, J. (2005). *Collaborative Regional Initiatives: Civic Entrepreneurs Work to Fill the Governance Gap*. San Francisco, CA: James Irvine Foundation. Retrieved at: http://www.irvine.org/publications/by_topic/civic.shtml

Innes, J. E., & Rongerude, J. (2013). Civic networks for sustainable regions: Innovative practices and emergent theories. *Planning Theory and Practice*, vol. 14, 75–100.

Kaplan, A. (1964). *The Conduct of Inquiry*. San Francisco, CA: Chandler Publishing.

Kauffman, S. (1995). *At Home in the Universe: The Search for the Laws of Complexity*. London: Viking.

Kelly, K. (1994). *Out of Control: The Rise of the Neobiological Civilization*. Reading, MA: Addison-Wesley.

Krimsky, S., & de Neufville, J. I. (1978). An experiment in environmental education for citizen advocates. *Journal of Alternative Higher Education*, vol. 2, 210–222.

Mandelbaum, S. J., Mazza, L., & Burchell, R. (Eds.). (1996). *Explorations in Planning Theory*. Rutgers, NJ: CUPR Press.

Tewdwr-Jones, M., & Allmendinger, P. (1998). Deconstructing communicative rationality: A critique of Habermasian collaborative planning. *Environment and Planning A*, vol. 30, 1975–1989.

Waldrop, M. M. (1992). *Complexity: The Emerging Science at the Edge of Chaos*. New York, NY: Simon and Schuster.

List of Abbreviations

ACSP: Association of Collegiate Schools of Planning
AESOP: Association of European Schools of Planning
AICP: American Institute of Certified Planners
APA: American Planning Association
CCP: Center for Collaborative Policy
CPT: Communicative Planning Theory
DCRP: Department of City and Regional Planning
GMCP: Growth Management Consensus Project
IURD: Institute of Urban and Regional Development
JFK: John Fitzgerald Kennedy, US President 1960–1963
LBJ: Lyndon Baines Johnson, US President 1963–1969
MIT: Massachusetts Institute of Technology
MTC: Metropolitan Transportation Commission, San Francisco Bay Area
PAB: Planning Accreditation Board
UC: University of California (10-campus system)
UCB: University of California Berkeley

Terminology Glossary

Baby boom: In the US the baby boom included the 76 million people born between 1946 and 1964. The group was so large that its demands and culture dominated society for decades.

164 Judith E. Innes

Faculty: University educators, including professors and lecturers.

High school/preparatory school: The last four years of education before entering university. A student graduates at approximately 18 years of age.

Master's degree: In planning, the accredited degree requires two years of study after undergraduate education is complete. The program is highly structured with course work required in subject matter areas, analysis, and research methodologies, and in planning history/theory.

Ph.D. programs: These are less structured than master's programs, but they typically involve another two to three years of course work including methodology, some examinations, and then two years of independent research and writing on a topic of the student's choice.

Staff: Support employees in the university.

Undergraduate education: The first four years of university after high school.

Urban renewal: A US program made possible by the Federal Housing Act of 1949, which gave cities subsidies to buy land, clear "slums," and either build public facilities or turn it over to private developers to revitalize city centers.

11

A RENEGADE ECONOMIST PREACHES GOOD LAND-USE PLANNING

Barrie Needham

> . . . there comes a stage in people's lives when they no longer have to justify their existence; when it is right and proper for them to spend their time reflecting on what they have been and what they have done and trying to make better sense of it.
>
> *(Williams, 2012, p. 243)*

Land-Use Is Important

The way in which land is used is important for people: where they live, in what kind of house, where they go to work, how they get there, where their children go to school and play, where and how their food is produced and so on. And the way in which one person uses land can affect how others use land. So land-use is a matter of shared concern. Systematic efforts by government bodies to influence how people use land so that land-use becomes better—in one way or another—we call land-use planning. It is sometimes called spatial planning, especially when applied at a scale larger than cities. But at all scales the "object" is how land in particular locations is used, so I prefer the concrete term "land-use planning". It is this activity which fascinates me and which has occupied me professionally for the last 50 years. The reason why I concentrate on this activity, although many other complementary activities are often placed under the term "spatial planning", is given later. I have tried to develop a coherent framework for talking about that activity systematically and for improving the practice, and I have paid particular attention to the way in which development processes are organised and managed. Initially I did this using economic theories. Now my approach is more humanistic, for I want to prevent planning thought and practice being taken over by economics.

The Formative Experiences

At Home

Growing up in post-war Britain formed me and shaped my thinking about land-use planning. There was a sobering austerity coupled with the determination to build a better world

166 Barrie Needham

and the conviction that that could be done only with much government involvement. That involvement included land-use planning, expressed in publications such as "Start Planning Britain Now: A Policy for Reconstruction" (Calder, 1941) and "Britain Must Rebuild" (Pick, 1941) and radical legislation, in particular the 1946 New Towns Act and the 1947 Town and Country Planning Act.

As a boy I was not aware of such political aspirations for a better Britain. But I was acutely aware that some people lived in much worse conditions than my family, for every day I took the bus from our "leafy suburb" to a primary school in a council housing estate.[1] Later, that awareness was sharpened by daily travel to secondary school, for that took me through the older suburbs and the centre of Manchester. The centre had been badly bombed, the reconstruction came very slowly, and in the summer the rosebay willow herb grew profusely on the bomb sites, almost the only colour in that dreary city centre. It was much later that I read Engels's *The Condition of the Working Class in England in 1844.* That describes the living conditions in and around Manchester, and some of the streets that Engels visited were still recognisable when I passed them in the mid-1950s: "dreadful slums". It was not just the contrast with my own living conditions that was so great, but also with the countryside just outside the Manchester conurbation. In 1932 there was a mass trespass of Kinder Scout, part of a huge, privately owned estate in the Peak District, by people from the cities protesting against this enormously unfair distribution of "living conditions". That protest contributed to the Access to the Countryside Act (1949) from which I was able to profit in my youth, with much pleasure.

At University

The first two years at university I studied "natural sciences", mainly physics and maths. I can recommend this as a formative experience. It requires rigour and precision in thinking, and it offers clearly defined concepts which must be handled logically. But I could not see myself working as a physicist, so I switched to economics, in which subject I graduated. Like physics, economics tries to build a coherent body of knowledge which is open to critical but respectful development. I have been looking for such a coherent body of knowledge about land-use planning ever since. How can you discuss the evolution in thinking about a certain topic without a conceptual framework for ordering your thoughts?

In My First Work

After graduating (1964) I took a job with a planning consultancy in London. Economics was only just being applied to planning, and the consultancy did not really know what I should do but gave me lots of room to explore. It was a very formative first few years, and it exposed me to the ways in which urban designers and architects look at land-use and the physical environment.

As part of my economics degree, I had studied applied economics, and it was applied economics at the micro-scale which so interested me. This is the study of how the economic context within which people act can be deliberately modified so as to change those actions in a desired direction. In my ignorance, I had expected to find that town planning also worked with such theories. I was sadly disappointed. True, there were shopping models, traffic models, theories about real estate economics and industrial location, loose economic ideas about housing markets and land markets. But only a few of those theories could be made sufficiently operational for practical use. And even in those cases, there was little evidence that the theory was true, in the sense of making predictions which were reliable. It was my job, as a fledgling economist in planning, to know about those theories and to apply them. The first task was to apply shopping models, and I was shocked to discover on how many untested assumptions they were based and how uncritically they were used.

In the Netherlands

In 1978 I went to the Netherlands as an economist working within the Department of Spatial Planning at the University of Nijmegen (now called the Radboud University).

In that country, the professional body of land-use planners is small and weak. People who work in one way or another in land-use planning do not see themselves as part of a professional group. Related to this, there is no public conception of "the planners". Spatial planning (*ruimtelijke ordening*) is not something done by planners but by state agencies. There is also widespread public agreement that land-use planning is good and useful. A huge amount of money is put into it (Buitelaar, 2007, Appendix B), and taxpayers do not complain about that. Many plans and development projects are contested, but not the underlying idea that strong public involvement is desirable. In the Netherlands I was freed from the cramping thought that land-use planning is about resolving competing demands on land.[2] Dutch people think much more positively about land-use planning: It is about creating places and spaces which could not be realised without public planning.

Another contrast with England is that in the Netherlands land-use planning as an academic discipline is seen as deriving from human geography, not from architecture or civil engineering. Geography is a social and behavioural science, not a design science, and rigorous theories are expected of it, especially theories about how people use space. Related to this is the requirement that a discipline which is recognised as a university study be able to justify itself academically. When I arrived in 1978 I was pleasantly surprised to find the claim that there was a science of land-use planning (*planologie*), defined as "a scientific and methodological reflection on spatial ordering and planning, forming—on the basis of empirical research—descriptive, exploratory and normative theories" (my translation, see Needham, 1988). It was an eye-opener after the a-theoretical arguments that I knew in 1960s and 1970s England.

Dutch practice too provided an intellectual challenge, for the development process there—most building took place privately on land provided by municipalities—was different to that in most other countries. The Dutch themselves took that practice for granted; they did not "problematise" it. I did (Needham, 1992).

I have followed no formal course or training in planning. My knowledge has come from these experiences and the associated reading. How I have selected and interpreted that knowledge has been influenced by some of my core values.

The Values Which I Bring to Bear

It is only slowly that I have become aware of the values which I apply to the activity of land-use planning. There are three sets. The first I have already mentioned: academic rigour. This involves building upon the work of others in open, rational, critical discussion. Actions should,

168 Barrie Needham

as far as possible, be based upon that knowledge. The second is distaste for the misuse of power. Land-use planning requires that government bodies exercise power over citizens. That is inevitable, but it should be done in a legitimate way, and public money should be used effectively and efficiently. The third is concern for those with little social and economic power. The powers which government bodies have for land-use planning should not be used to further the interests of the rich and powerful, but those of the "poor and lowly". It is for this reason that I have done a lot of research into the provision of land for social housing (de Kam & Needham, 2000; de Kam & Needham, 2002).

"Poor and lowly" is a term from the Christian tradition, in which I grew up and am still active. It influences greatly the values which I bring to land-use planning. That all men are created equal is a premise of the Old Testament[3] (see also what Paul said in Galatians 3:28). Mary was a "leveller": "He hath scattered the proud in the imagination of their hearts. He hath put down the mighty from their seats, and exalted them of low degree" (Luke 2:51–3). The privileged (which includes most planners and all planning academics) are reminded that "much is expected of those to whom much is given" (Luke 12:48). I find the concept of Christian stewardship inspiring, especially in its active form (e.g. the parable of the talents, Matthew 25:14–30). In an old German translation of Psalm 119, we find "Ich bin ein Gast auf Erden" (I am a guest on Earth), which still inspires environmentalists.

The Activity of Land-Use Planning

Land Is Important

The older planners from whom I learned such a lot were architects/urban designers/planners (they did not always make the distinction) who had contributed to the post-war reconstruction of Britain. They were, in the terms then in use, town and country planners. They made land-use plans—at that time, mainly for town centre redevelopment, slum clearance, big housing developments and the protection of the countryside—and programmes for getting them implemented. They did that because it was obvious to them that the way in which land was used was important for people's welfare and well-being. And they were not alone: Some form of land-use planning is practised in many countries.

If you are professionally involved with land-use, then you need to be able to describe it accurately. Engineers measure stresses and strains, doctors blood pressure and heartbeats. What should land-use planners measure? Population density; intensity of land-use in different functions; how land is actually used; land prices; household size and how that is changing; who owns which land; floor area ratio, floor space ratio, floor space index (all the same); building heights and road widths; housing densities per hectare; traffic movements between locations; and so on. All very down to earth (literally) but all important for daily living, and not only in a small, densely populated country like the Netherlands.

A Conceptual Framework for Land-Use Planning

For such an important activity, a robust conceptual framework is useful. Academic rigour demands such a framework, and the desire to systematically improve the activity requires it. A large part of my work has been trying to develop such a framework. I am not talking about a comprehensive theory, rather a coherent collection of partial theories, or a structured body of knowledge. Or, if you prefer, a paradigm. Because I know the planning systems in two countries well (England and Wales, and the Netherlands), and because I have done much cross-national research into planning systems (a lot together with academics in other countries, often using EU research grants—see e.g. Needham, 1999; Kragt et al., 2000), I have been able to develop a paradigm which, it seems to me, is applicable to many countries, and I set this out in Needham (2000b). This builds upon work done in the department at Nijmegen over the last 50 years (Needham, 2013). My book *Dutch Land-Use Planning* (2014) applies that paradigm in detail to the practice in one country.[4]

Planning and Land-Use Planning

The rise of theories about the general activity of planning was a powerful stimulus for thinking about the activity of land-use planning. This began—at least in England—in the 1970s. An invaluable and very influential contribution at that time was the book by Faludi entitled *Planning Theory* (Faludi, 1973). Some people received the idea of a general theory about planning gratefully and linked it to the existing discussions about the possibilities of societal planning in general; the "classics" were Hayek, 1944; Mannheim, 1940; Popper, 1945, 1957. Interest in this topic has grown enormously and has overflowed into, and mixed with, theories about policy and about management.[5] This has helped theories about *land-use* planning to be developed, precisely by exposing some of the taken-for-granted assumptions of the older planners regarding how people use land, how policy instruments work and how plans and policies produce effects or fail to do so.

Nevertheless, the relationship between the generic activity of planning and the specific activity of land-use planning has been too little explored. Faludi's work (1973) distinguished between procedural theory (about the generic process, theories *of* planning) and substantive theories (about the activities which were being planned, theories *in* planning). But without identifying those characteristics of land-use planning which distinguish it from other types of public planning, it is not possible to say which aspects of procedural theory, and which substantive theories, are most relevant for land-use planning, And, therefore, it is not possible to develop a theory of land-use planning specifically.

The Specifics of Land-Use Planning

The starting point for my attempts to develop such a theory is a particular and identifiable activity, namely spatial or land-use planning, which can be found in many societies. What makes land-use planning different from all other types of planning is—of course—that it is about land-use, the surface of the Earth and how people use that: about "place and territory". But so is geography. It is about constructing spaces: But that is what property developers do. It is about using land: But that is what we all do. It is about planning the development of a location: But that is what the managers of large private estates do or what a firm does when it builds and maintains a huge chemical complex. There is "something more" to spatial planning (Davoudi & Pendlebury, 2010): What is it? That has to be sought in a further specification of the types of activities which it includes.

The activity which is specific to land-use planning is that a state body takes actions to influence how its citizens use land—their own land and that of others. The purpose of this activity

170 Barrie Needham

is to create in a particular area (which can be big or small) a land-use which meets certain aims. It has the following characteristics:

- A government body (which we call the planning agency) wishes to see a certain area developed in a certain way (which can include conservation). It sets down this spatial wish in some form of document (a plan, a policy, etc.).
- In order to realise that wish, the planning agency has powers with which it can influence how people use land. These include powers under public law which can be imposed to restrict the exercise of property rights in land, such as planning permits and compulsory purchase, powers to give subsidies and impose levies, powers to undertake campaigns to influence thinking about places and powers to build infrastructure.

It follows from this that there are two things that differentiate a theory of land-use planning from theories of—for example—economic planning, or military planning: It is about how land is used, and it involves the exercise of public powers to influence how citizens use their land. It is this latter which gives rise to the oh-so-important issue of legitimacy in land-use planning.

I make no apology for focussing on land-use planning as a *government* activity, at a time when academics stress the importance of *governance*. I acknowledge fully the importance of the latter. However, most effective governance of changes in land-use requires a constructive contribution from state bodies, using powers which they alone are entitled to use, such as granting or withholding building permits or using compulsory purchase. There is no good governance without good government.

Improving Land-Use Planning

My conviction that land-use planning is important leads me to want to improve it. There are two aspects in particular which have occupied me: that it be effective and efficient, and that it be legitimate. Effectiveness and efficiency are the touchstones of any technology, including a social technology like land-use planning. The activity is carried out to achieve a particular effect. Is that being achieved? And could it be achieved more easily? A *social* technology should be evaluated against additional norms. Are the goals legitimate? Are the means legitimate? Do the ends justify the means? Who decides? Who gains and who loses? In the rest of this chapter I discuss these two aspects of land-use planning: its technology and its legitimacy.

How has my education in economics influenced this? It was as an economist that I started work. My first publication (Needham, 1967) was an economic analysis of how land on industrial estates was used;[6] the second (Needham, 1971) was on the limitations of economic analysis when applied to land-use planning. And so I have continued. Economic theory provides exceedingly useful tools for analysing the practice of land-use planning. But it is inherently limited, and therefore limited when applied to improving that practice.

Good land-use planning requires good education of land-use planners. In the Netherlands, land-use planning is acknowledged as being not only useful but also an essential contribution to many other types of public policy. I have worked for more than 30 years educating people to work in Dutch planning practice. Of the many graduates from our department in Nijmegen, one became a minister in the national government; one a secretary of state; two have been members of parliament; several have been mayors (*burgermeesters*) or on the municipal executive;

a lot have been members of a municipal council, especially in Nijmegen itself. We have tried to educate our students to do land-use planning well, critically and with engagement.

Effectiveness and Efficiency in Land-Use Planning

Land-Use Planning as a Technology

The idea that land-use planning is a technology will disturb some who emphasise the political and ideological sides of planning, but to me it is evident. The people working in planning departments are being paid to achieve results. What those results should be—the aims of the planning—is a political choice, as is the way in which that should be done. Public planning is necessarily a political activity: But if politicians decide that something should be done, it is an obligation to the citizen that serious attempts are made to achieve the chosen aims.

A technology is judged not only by its effects, but also by the efficiency with which they are achieved. It would be good to be able to say something about the latter, but it has received very little attention. I have supervised a little empirical work on this, enough to show that land-use planning often works exceedingly inefficiently, without any recognition that this is so (e.g. Buitelaar et al., 2006).

Knowledge about How People Use Land

Effective planning requires knowledge about how people decide to use land. As mentioned above, I was not impressed by the quality of the economic theories which I was supposed to use in my early working years. Partly in reaction to this, I wrote a book in 1977 (Needham, 1977) with the pretentious title *How Cities Work*. I still think that the aim was good, but it was much too generalist for a young academic. And I did not know at that time about the much better American books with a comparable aim (although not very suitable for the English situation), such as Chapin (1965). I also gave insufficient attention to the interaction between the various activities which were the subject of the separate theories: about, for example, how a change in the housing supply can lead to a change in the supply of labour.

Land-use planning should be integral and is sometimes large scale. It needs reliable theories about the interactions between different land-uses in a large area and over a long period. It was once again American planners who attempted to fill this gap, with large-scale urban models. An article written after many years' experience with such models—"A Requiem for Large-Scale Models" (Lee, 1973)—showed just how difficult it is to make comprehensive theories in planning which are reliable enough to be applied in practice. I am not convinced that, 40 years later, such comprehensive theories are more reliable. From this I draw the conclusion that land-use planning (and by extension, any societal planning) should be modest, flexible and incremental. In this I remain in agreement with Popper (1945), whose work influenced me so much in the early years.

Knowledge of the Development Process

In the Netherlands, government bodies—especially municipalities—often get directly involved in development processes, in close collaboration with landowners and commercial developers (see e.g. Needham, 2014). The practice of "active municipal land policy"—whereby the municipality acquires development land, services it and sells building plots to developers—is now well known to planners internationally (although it is less common than previously). This has focussed my attention on a particular set of *partial theories* about how people use land, namely theories about the process of land-use change—the development process.

Understanding this process is important not just for the Netherlands. There used to be a widespread misconception that the development process is neutral, that it translates what is demanded (changes in land and buildings) without influencing in any way what is built. In economic terms, supply (the development industry) precisely reflects demand and has no interest in interpreting it. This assumption is as naïve as saying that the motor car industry has no influence on the types and numbers of cars which are built. It was shaken by detailed studies of physical development at the local scale (Ambrose & Colenutt, 1975; Marriott, 1969) and more recently by studies which show how locational choices at the scale of the region, the nation and even the world are influenced by the development industry (*Regional Studies 48,* 2014).[7] The form of the built environment is influenced by the actors who create it: Who are they? What are their practices? How is the development process organised? What is the division of labour? How do those who supply the finance influence what is built? What is the influence of those who supply land? What role does and can public land-use planning play in this?

A lot of my research has been into such questions, and it has taken me into details which many land-use planners regard as esoteric: internal rates of return, discounting rates, the difference between the gross and the net initial return, residual values and so on. Other aspects on which I have focussed are more concrete. These include the effects of price changes on land-use demand (the price elasticity of demand—Needham, 2000a): how the supply of land and buildings reacts to changes in price (the price elasticity of supply); how land price influences building density; how land prices change in response to changes in the density of development. Without such knowledge, the land-use planner is an amateur up against real estate professionals.

The Institutional Turn

"Typical for an economist, such concerns", might be the dismissive reaction. But "the economic way of thinking" (to use the title of an influential book—Heyne et al., 2010)[8] can be much more flexible than assuming a one-dimensional "homo economicus" whose behaviour can be represented in quantitative models. The "old" institutional economics of Veblen and Commons went out of fashion because it was too descriptive and particular. The "new" institutional economics (associated in particular with the works of Coase, Williamson, Ostrom, North) tries to avoid those mistakes. After discovering those works in the 1990s, I applied them to planning (Needham, 2006) and to land markets (Needham et al., 2011).

Land-use planning has also taken an "institutional turn". This is the idea that people's actions are influenced by the practices, expectations, ideas and rules within which they act. It combines easily with institutional economics, and the combination makes it possible to construct more reliable socio-spatial theories. However, its importance for land-use planning is greater. The powers available for land-use planning are themselves institutions, some of the many which influence people's actions. This can be expressed as follows: On each plot of land there is a "regime of land laws", of which the planning rules are only a part (Geuting &

Needham, 2012). This view is much more fruitful than regarding planning measures as "interventions" in a "market" supposedly free from rules. It allows a better integration between socio-spatial theories and theories about how planning measures work (see below). I incorporated this institutional turn into my research into planning and development processes in Needham (2006).

Knowledge about How Land-Use Can Be Influenced

Much land-use planning consists of making land-use plans and policies and assuming that—somehow—they will affect what is built and how that is used. A good understanding of the connection between the plan and its effects is essential for effective planning, and has occupied me greatly.

At the very local scale, people build, or do not build. How does land-use planning affect that? One possible way is through the building (planning) permit. That has led me to research into the relationship between the content of the supposedly binding land-use plan (the Dutch *bestemmingsplan*) and the granting of a building permit—the connection was loose (Buitelaar et al., 2007); to research into how the content of the plan was shaped to take account of the realities of land ownership by developers (Needham et al., 2000); to research into how Dutch municipalities use their ownership of land in order to determine what may be built, by whom, when and where (see e.g. Needham, 2003); to many investigations into the relationships between land policy/land management and land-use planning (e.g. Needham, 2002). That public ambitions for how land should be used are realised in ways other than those prescribed by planning law (see e.g. Needham, 1989) does not mean that the land-use planning is bad (although it can jeopardise the legitimacy of such planning—see later). It does mean that planners should know about such mechanisms.

In more abstract terms, there is need for a more explicit "instrumentation theory" (my translation of the Dutch term *instrumententheorie*: see Bressers & Klok, 1987). This is the theory about the effects on a policy variable of taking a particular measure under particular circumstances. I tried to contribute to this theory with my PhD thesis, "Choosing the Right Policy Instruments" (Needham, 1982). A government body choosing an instrument to effect a particular land-use change can apply "instrumentation theory" appropriate to the situation. It is striking how rarely that is done systematically. Again I pose the question of effectiveness and efficiency (legitimacy comes later). And again "the institutional turn" is very useful, for it focusses attention on the institutional context within which people act, in this case, how they make land-use decisions. That context is much broader than the price mechanism, at which many economists stare blindly (see Needham & De Kam, 2004).

Knowledge about How Plans and Policies "Perform"

At a higher spatial scale, we must recognise that much planning policy is made by government bodies for implementation by *other* government bodies (usually those lower in the hierarchy). It is important to know how the policy will "perform", that is, how it will influence the planning measures taken by the "receiving" bodies. A plan which has not been implemented literally has not necessarily failed (Mastop & Faludi, 1997). Nevertheless, a plan which is deliberately made to perform well will be more effective (Mastop & Needham, 1997).

This recognition has led me to study Dutch land-use planning by the national government: Why does the national government think that it will have any effect on what is built? It is striking that most descriptions of Dutch planning written in English concentrate on that national level (e.g. Faludi, 1991; Mastop, 2001). One of the reasons is that the national government often makes foreign language translations of its own policy documents. However, it is my opinion that municipalities are far more important for influencing how land is used. This raises the question, therefore: "How does national planning perform at the local level and by what mechanisms?" The answers given for Dutch land-use planning (Needham, 2015) might be relevant for other countries too.

The Limitations Inherent to Land-Use Planning as a Technology

Every technology should take account of its inherent limitations. In this case, they concern the extent to which societal problems are affected by land-use, and the possibility of changing land-use purposefully.

The idea that society could be moulded by appropriate land-use planning was strong, albeit often implicit, 50 years ago. It was later caricatured in the Netherlands by describing it as the belief that society was "makeable" (*maakbaar*). Much earlier it was described as physical determinism—the idea that people's behaviour can be influenced by changing their physical surroundings—and strongly rejected (see e.g. Gans, 1968, pp. 33–43). However, land-use planning should not be too humble. The idea that social and economic problems in deprived neighbourhoods can be resolved by improving the physical fabric has been brought into doubt, as has the idea that traffic congestion can be solved by building more roads. But it has also been observed that people's local actions and their sense of safety and well-being are influenced by their physical surroundings. This has led, for example, to the successful planning of town centres: These have not been written off, as was predicted by some in the 1970s, but have become more popular.

Ideas about the possibility of changing land-use purposefully have also shifted, more in theory than in practice. There is an argument that society is so complex, heterogeneous and dynamic that predictions (e.g. about the effects of applying a measure) are impossible or too unreliable (see e.g. van Gunsteren & van Ruyven, 1995). That implies the end of planning and of most other public policy (and the end of long-term investment by private firms).

Another (theoretical) argument is about the extent to which it is possible by deliberate actions to change land-use. I arrived in the Netherlands in the middle of a lively and sometimes fierce debate[9] about Marxism (or, more neutrally, historical materialism). The Marxist argument was that land-use planning was an integral part of the capitalist system, and that how it was practised could be explained in that way. The practical conclusion was, from a Marxist analysis, that, it is not possible to say very much about how land-use planning *should* be carried out in a capitalist society, for capitalism determines the form and content of that planning.

Then there is the idea that it is impossible to change land-use by deliberate actions, other than marginally, for land-use is the result of international economic forces which have to be accepted. Or the result of fundamental human wishes—more money, more space, more ease, more welfare, etc.—which should not be resisted. Or the result of something mysterious called "the market", before which we should bow down in obedience. The idea that it is impossible to influence land-use developments means that land-use planning is misguided.

That we still have a lot of serious land-use planning implies that most people do not take those extreme views. I agree with them: Land-use planning is limited in what it can achieve, but it is not helpless and can be more than window dressing.

The Legitimacy of Land-Use Planning

It will be clear from the values that I set out at the beginning that land-use planning, as an activity of the state, should serve its citizens as individuals—in particular the most vulnerable citizens—and that the state should always be answerable to its citizens. Land-use planning should be legitimate, and it should be seen to be legitimate. Paradoxically, it is the situation in the Netherlands which made this clear to me. For there, the legitimacy of land-use planning is largely undisputed, and I see how lack of political attention for this sometimes enables public bodies to take actions which disregard the principles of good government, justified by the argument that the results will be "in the public interest". Dutch government bodies are sometimes arrogant, and there is an incipient corporatism in the relations between municipalities and property developers.

Land-Use Planning for Whom?

Land-use planning should be legitimised in terms not just of its effects "for society" (or worse, "for the economy"), but of its effects on identifiable (categories of) citizens. Restricting building in a beautiful landscape might not benefit those living there, but it should benefit others who enjoy it occasionally. If a new road is built for the economic development of an area, who in that area will benefit? One of the ethical principles underlying land-use planning is some form of utilitarianism: It can be justifiable to damage some for the benefit of others, if the net result would be a gain (Hoekveld & Needham, 2013). But then one wants to know who would gain and who lose? Should the losers be compensated? Are some sorts of losses unacceptable, even if compensated? All people are not equal, and some can use a gain, others can accept a loss, better than others.

When land-use planning started to be practised systematically (around the middle of the nineteenth century), it was primarily to improve living conditions for poorer people. That was also so when I started: slum clearance and housing redevelopment. At that time transport planning had to safeguard the mobility of those without cars or unable to drive. Now, distributional questions (who benefits? who pays?) are rarely raised, and land-use planning to redistribute living conditions more evenly is incidental. True, sustainability receives more attention, and sustainability can be regarded as a question of redistributing from the present to future generations. But in much planning nowadays, sustainability is about achieving economic growth with an easy conscience. Affordable or social housing sometimes receives attention, but not if the land could be put to more profitable use. The more recently introduced ideas of furthering social inclusion and parity of access (or territorial equity) might reinvigorate attention to distributional issues in land-use planning (see e.g. CEC, 2010).

Protecting the Citizen

For centuries there have been state (private or civil) laws about how people may use their land and buildings. These enable a citizen (legal person) to take action against another citizen (legal person) if the latter uses her land in ways which damage the former. Property rights are an example of this. While it is recognised that rich citizens often use them more effectively than poor citizens, the laws' potential for protecting all citizens must be safeguarded.

The laws created by the state for land-use planning are another way of regulating how people may use their land and buildings. But there is a big difference: If you breach those laws, it is the state which takes legal action against you, not a private legal person. Planning laws are public, or administrative, law (as are environmental laws, traffic laws, building regulations, etc.). And if the (little) citizen is in conflict with the (big) state, she needs extra protection.

The Principles of Responsible Government

Parliament, as the lawmaker, gives public bodies great powers over their citizens, so it is correct that those bodies are expected to, and can be obliged to, use those powers responsibly. In the Netherlands there is a legal doctrine called "the principles of responsible government" (*beginselen van het behoorlijk bestuur*—Needham, 2014, p. 302 et seq.), which is similar to the idea of "due process" in the United States, and to the grounds on which a citizen can apply for a "judicial review" in England.

Because the powers which public bodies have been given for land-use planning can affect the citizens greatly (and not just financially), the state has provided safeguards to protect the citizen against misuse of those powers. If "due process" is breached, the citizen may take legal action. Alexander (2002) discusses this under the name of "planning rights". This too is an issue which interests few land-use planners: They often regard such "rights" as getting in the way of good planning. In this respect, practice has hardly changed since I was first involved 50 years ago.

How Far Should Land-Use Planning Go?

This question too arises from my experience in the Netherlands, where land-use planning is very ambitious. Where the intensity of land-use is so high, there are lots of opportunities for land-use conflicts. The Dutch response is a plethora of rules and permits for regulating land-use. On the whole, the citizens support this as being necessary for achieving the environmental qualities which they want. However, both public law (such as for land-use, traffic, environmental protection) and private law can be used to resolve land-use conflicts. So the question should be asked: "The state has made private (civic) law to enable citizens to resolve their own conflicts: To what extent is state involvement under public law necessary in addition?" (see e.g. Hayek, 1989; Needham, 2006). Without an answer, the citizen can be stifled under overlapping rules.

Another set of questions can arise when land-use planning goes beyond measures taken to resolve conflicts over land. The planning agency can say: If we do no more than resolve such conflicts, then a suboptimal land-use will arise. We—the state agency—can steer the citizens in such a way that they create a better land-use, one which would not have been possible if we had just resolved conflicts. A plan for the redevelopment of a town centre is a clear example of this. The planning agency is saying in effect: This is what people want; we will help them to achieve it. This type of land-use planning too is very common in the Netherlands. But what if not everybody whose condition would be "improved" would be happy with the improvement? May the state try to impose what Davy (2007) calls "mandatory happiness"? What if the land-use planning measures would transgress the protection of property rights offered by private law? And what if the costs of such projects are so great that they exceed the improvement to those who benefit, whereby others also have to pay? Again, I consider that these questions should be asked more often.

How Far Should Land-Use Planning Discriminate?

I think that land-use planning should discriminate in favour of poorer people, if necessary at the expense of richer people. But it discriminates in another way too, which often seems to be arbitrary: It discriminates between people purely on the basis of where they live or own property.

The state gives people rights over land and buildings, but this is never absolute. So the state can restrict how I may use my property rights, with building ordinances, fire and safety regulations and environmental requirements. Such laws are usually socially accepted because they apply to everyone wherever they live. They belong to the many restrictions which are the cost of living close together. Land-use planning however is different. For when the state imposes *planning* restrictions on how I may use my land, the content of the restrictions varies according to the location; for example, in some locations housing is permitted but not industry. So the restrictions on the exercise of my property rights are not generic but locationally specific (Needham, 2009).

This poses difficult questions, which most planners recognise but do not want to tackle (Moroni, 2007). Citizens are being treated unequally. It is expected that actions by public bodies equally affect all people in the same category (*"égalité devant les charges publiques"* is the name of the legal doctrine). It is clear that land-use planning often does not, for the consequences of the plan vary according to the accidents of land ownership. Some of those consequences are financial: You become very rich, or you are prevented from becoming very rich. Others are material: Permission is given to build a shopping centre at the end of your street, with the attendant parking and traffic problems.

The financial aspects of this have been investigated and debated for decades but are still not resolved. In England the debate used the terms "compensation and development" and resulted in development rights being nationalised in 1947. This was an elegant—if largely ineffectual—action, but at least it recognised the inequalities brought about by much land-use planning. And the debates about it influenced my thinking greatly, for it invited the application of economic theories to land-use planning measures, something which was absent in the Netherlands when I went there in 1978. The Dutch have rules for compensating for some kinds of loss caused by land-use planning (see Needham, 2014, pp. 123–124). In the course of my 50 years in land-use planning, there has been little progress in tackling this question. Most planners do not want to recognise the problem. Or they search desperately for win–win situations. It is one more example of how many planners do not want to acknowledge the inevitably distributional effects of land-use planning.

The Importance of Law

It continues to surprise me how little attention is paid to law in most planning thought (Alterman, 2017; Needham, 2007). Outside the US, law is often regarded as difficult, or boring, best left to planning lawyers.

178 Barrie Needham

There are strong functional reasons why planning thought should incorporate a thorough knowledge of planning law. One is that law provides the planning agency with many of the powers with which plans can be realised: development control, compulsory purchase and so on. It was my interest in the effectiveness of land-use planning that generated my interest in planning law. Another is that *civil* law, including the laws on property rights, influences the way in which people exercise those rights, hence the form of the built environment without public planning, and hence also the effects of *public* planning laws on the built environment (Geuting & Needham, 2012). Planning gives scant attention to this. Yet another functional reason why law is important is that it imposes restrictions on the way the planning agency may make and realise plans: The planning agency can try to bypass some of these, but if it is checked, a lot of time and money have been wasted. As a corollary, knowledge of those laws can help to prevent planning agencies from choosing goals which are not feasible.

Those are reasons to do with the technology of land-use planning. I am glad that they have, in the last few years, become better recognised, with the academic association Planning Law and Property Rights.[10] There is also a more principled reason why planning thought should include knowledge of planning law. It is that law often embodies ethical principles (Hoekveld & Needham, 2013; Needham & Hoekveld, 2014), and these should be in the forefront of planning thought.

An Ethical Code for Planning Agencies

Attention for ethics in planning has certainly grown in my working life, but it has followed a path which is not fully logical. The American literature is almost entirely about how the individual planner should act ethically. I do not underestimate the importance of this. But the actor with the *formal* responsibility for taking planning measures is the planning agency, not the planner. The code of professional conduct of the English Royal Town Planning Institute does consider this. After listing the norms which the individual planner should observe, it adds: "Members . . . shall take all reasonable steps to ensure that all town planning matters in the organisation . . . are conducted in accordance with this Code, whoever undertakes such work." It is surprising that organisations such as hospitals, old people's homes, banks and research centres have ethical codes, but planning agencies do not. It is true that from their position as public agencies they are supposed to conform to the general principles of responsible government (see above). But it would be desirable if they were to supplement that with the ethical considerations specific to land-use planning, a "domain ethics" of planning (Hoekveld & Needham, 2013).

The Legitimacy of Economic Analysis

As an economist working in land-use planning, I was expected to justify that activity as a way of correcting for market imperfections. The argument was that all would be for the best in this best of all possible worlds if the market worked perfectly. So, if there are "market imperfections", land-use planning should try to compensate for them. This argument assumes that there is a perfect market and that this would produce the best results (maximum welfare). If this assumption were true, then removing those imperfections would lead to better results.[11] But the idea of a perfect market has to be rejected. An economy would not work, or only very partially, without laws (institutions) made and enforced by governments in order to facilitate transactions between citizens (Needham, 2006). The idea of the perfect market (a market without rules) creating an economic optimum is a phantasm: And therefore it cannot be used as a criterion of whether "government intervention" would produce something better or worse.[12] Moreover, market outcomes (including the prices which are often used uncritically in cost-benefit analysis [CBA]—see below) are strongly influenced by power relationships, and economics ignores those. So the supposed economic optimum depends on the power relationships.

This criticism of the idea of the perfect market does not mean that the idea of a market imperfection is never useful. Sometimes it is clear that external effects, or monopolies, or transaction costs, are preventing something from happening which most people would regard as desirable. Work in institutional economics has shown that some market imperfections can be removed by creating new property rights (restructuring markets: see Geuting & Needham, 2012), and that this might work better than government actions to replace markets (e.g. Coase, 1974; Webster & Lai, 2003).

There is another economic argument, namely that the proposed planning should always be evaluated in terms of its economic efficiency. There should be no land-use planning which does not improve this. In its most formalised version, the assumption is that all effects of land-use planning can be expressed in terms of economic utility, and that land-use planning should try to increase that. No plan should be approved where the costs are greater than the benefits, and that plan should be chosen where the ratio of benefits to cost is the highest. But again, who loses and who benefits?

Cost-benefit analysis was making its appearance in the 1960s, when I started work. It was clear that making such an analysis was a task for an economist. And so I was set to work. From the start I was critical, partly because of the course on welfare economics that I had followed as a student. (The lecturer was Amartya Sen. Later he was awarded the Nobel Prize for Economics, partly because of his work on the ethical aspects of economic theory.) I was aware of optimising concepts such as the Pareto-optimum, the Kaldor-Hicks criterion and so on. And from our textbook (Little, 1957) I had learned that they all required making interpersonal trade-offs: One person might be made better off and another worse off. How was one to draw up the balance, particularly if one person was richer than the other? Some form of utilitarianism is inevitable (see above), but it should never be subsumed into a technical exercise.

Another criticism of using land-use planning to increase economic efficiency is the implication that CBA can be used for a *comprehensive* evaluation of a plan or project. The reasoning behind the assumption that all effects can be combined in this way is usually tautological (Needham, 2006, pp. 67–68). The "economic way of thinking" may be flexible (see above), but it is inherently limited.

To Be Continued

The most important message that I would give to young planners (land-use planners!) is this: Remember that space, or land-use, is your stage of operation. Space matters to people: In it they "live and move and have their being".[13] It is important for their welfare, individually and collectively. The task of land-use planning is to try to change places and spaces so that better living conditions are created. People are not interested in abstract space, but in specific, concrete spaces. So get up from behind your desk and explore places. Thoroughly. Preferably on foot or

180 Barrie Needham

on a bike. See how places work, how people use them. In order to improve your understanding of this sometimes subtle relationship, read not only academic literature but also novels. In some of them, the places are as important as the people, and the places embed the actions.[14] They remind us how important places and spaces are for people. Use this as inspiration for making land-use planning better.

Notes

1 This is an estate of "affordable housing" built and managed by the municipality.
2 In a textbook which has been used for the education of UK planners for decades, it says: "Planning might usefully be defined as the process by which government resolves disputes about land uses" (Cullingworth & Nadin, 2002, p. 2).
3 One of the first Dutch textbooks on land-use planning had the subtitle "For Everyone a Place Under the Sun" (Berg, 1981). The term "a place under the sun" comes from Ecclesiastes.
4 An alternative paradigm is that put forward by Innes (1994).
5 Some university departments of spatial planning (my own included) are now in faculties of management.
6 As was one of my last, 46 years later (Needham et al., 2013).
7 http://www.tandfonline.com/toc/cres20/48/3#.U8ZlCaiLkyA
8 Heyne also wrote on the limitations to the economic way of thinking: http://www.acton.org/pub/religion-liberty/volume-8-number-4/limitations-economic-way-thinking
9 It had led to my institute being closed for several weeks.
10 http://www.plpr-association.org/
11 But note that, according to the "theory of the second best", if it is impossible to correct one imperfection, it might be better not to correct other imperfections (Lipsey & Lancaster, 1956). Further, account has to be taken of possible government imperfections, whereby planning—however well intentioned—might produce results worse than the imperfect market (e.g. Gordon & Richardson, 1991).
12 It is partly for this reason that Williamson (1999) says that, when considering a policy question, it is not sensible to compare the existing situation with the optimal situation, but with feasible alternative ways of pursuing the chosen policy goals. And see for a similar argument Coase (1960, p. 154).
13 To paraphrase the Anglican "Book of Common Prayer".
14 I mention just a few that have stuck in my mind: George Orwell's *Coming Up for Air* (1939), Michael Frayn's *Spies* (2002), the terrible *Wuthering Heights* by Emily Brontë (1847). Read also the Wessex novels of Thomas Hardy, and the Five Towns novels of Arnold Bennett, to see how people and places are (or were) integrated.

References

Alexander, E. (2002). Planning rights: Towards normative criteria for evaluating plans. *International Planning Studies*, 7/3, 191–212.
Alterman, R. (2017). Planners' Beacon, Compass and Scale: Linking Planning Theory, Implementation Analysis and Planning Law. In Haselsberger, B. (Ed.), *Encounters in planning thought: 16 autobiographical essays from key thinkers in spatial planning* (pp. 260–279). New York: Routledge.
Ambrose, P. J., & Colenutt, B. (1975). *The property machine*. Harmondsworth: Penguin.
Berg, G. J. van den. (1981). *Inleiding tot de planologie: voor ieder een plaats onder de zon*. Alphen aan den Rijn: Samsom.
Bressers, J. T. A., & Klok, P. J. (1987). Grondslagen voor een instrumententheorie. *Beleidswetenschap*, 1/1, 7–97.
Buitelaar, E. (2007). *The costs of land use decisions*. Oxford: Blackwell.

A Renegade Economist **181**

Buitelaar, E., Cobussen, T., & Needham, B. (2007). Sturen met bestemmingsplannen. *Stedenbouw en Ruimtelijke Ordening, 6,* 55–57.

Buitelaar, E., Mertens, H., Needham, B., & de Kam, G. (2006). *Sturend vermogen en woningbouw.* Utrecht: DGW/NETHUR partnership nr. 34.

Calder, R. (1941). *Start planning Britain now: A policy for reconstruction.* London: Kegan Paul.

CEC. (2010). *Platform against poverty and social exclusion. A European framework for social and territorial cohesion.* COM (2010)758 final, SEC (2010) 1564 final, 16 December 2010: Brussels.

Chapin, F. S. (1965). *Urban land use planning.* Urbana: University of Illinois Press.

Coase, R. H. (1960, 1988). The problem of social cost. In Coase, R. H. (Ed.), *The firm, the market, and the law* (pp. 95–156). Chicago: University of Chicago Press.

Coase, R. H. (1974, 1988). The lighthouse in economics. In Coase, R. H. (Ed.), *The firm, the market, and the law* (pp. 187–214). Chicago: University of Chicago Press.

Cullingworth, B., & Nadin, V. (2002). *Town and country planning in the UK.* London: Routledge.

Davoudi, S., & Pendlebury, J. (2010). The evolution of planning as an academic discipline. *Town Planning Review, 81,* 613–646.

Davy, B. (2007). Mandatory happiness? Land readjustment and property in Germany. In Yu-Hung, H., & Needham, B. (Eds.), *Analysing land readjustment* (pp. 37–55). Cambridge, MA: Lincoln Institute of Land Policy.

de Kam, G., & Needham, B. (2000). *Land for social housing.* Hilversum: Comité Européen de Cordination de l'Habitat Social.

de Kam, G., & Needham, B. (2002). Woningcorporaties op de grondmarkt. *Tijdschrift voor de volkshuisvesting, 3,* 35–40.

Faludi, A. (1973). *Planning theory.* Oxford: Pergamon Press.

Faludi, A. (Ed.). (1991). Fifty years of Dutch national physical planning. *Built Environment,* Special Issue, *17,* 1–77.

Gans, H. J. (1968). *People and plans: Essays on urban problems and solutions.* London: Cox & Wyman.

Geuting, E., & Needham, B. (2012). Exploring the effects of property rights using game simulation. In Hartmann, T., & Needham, B. (Eds.), *Planning by law and property rights reconsidered* (pp. 37–54). Farnham: Ashgate.

Gordon, P., & Richardson, R. H. W. (1991). *Anti-planning.* Paper presented at ACSP-AESOP Congress, Oxford.

Hayek, F. A. (1944). *The road to serfdom.* London: Routledge & Kegan Paul.

Hayek, F. A. (1989). Spontaneous (grown) order and organised (made) order. In Modlovsky, M. (Ed.), *Order—with or without design* (pp. 101–123). London: Centre for Research into Communist Economies.

Heyne, P., Boettke, P., & Prychito, D. (2010). *The economic way of thinking.* Upper Saddle River, NJ: Prentice Hall.

Hoekveld, G., & Needham, B. (2013). Planning practice between ethics and the power game: Making and applying an ethical code for planning agencies. *International Journal of Urban and Regional Research, 37,* 1638–1653.

Innes, J. E. (1994). Planning theory's emerging paradigm: Communicative action and interactive practice. *Journal of Planning Education and Research, 14,* 183–189.

Kragt, R., Needham, B., Tönnies, G., & Turowski, G. (2000). *Deutsch-Niederländisches Handbuch der Planungsbegriffe.* Hannover: Verlag der Akademie für Raumforschung und Landesplanung.

Lee, D. B. (1973). Requiem for large-scale models. *Journal of American Institute of Planners, 39,* 163–178.

Lipsey, R. G., & Lancaster, K. (1956). The general theory of the second best. *Review of Economic Studies, 24,* 11–32.

Little, I. M. D. (1957). *A critique of welfare economics.* Oxford: Clarendon Press.

Mannheim, K. (1940). *Man and society in an age of reconstruction.* London: Routledge.

Marriott, O. (1969). *The property boom.* London: Pan Books.

Mastop, J. M. (2001). Dutch national planning at the turning point. In Alterman, R. (Ed.), *National-level planning in democratic countries* (pp. 210–256). Liverpool: Liverpool University Press.

182 Barrie Needham

Mastop, J. M., & Faludi, A. (1997). Evaluation of strategic plans: The performance principle. *Environment and Planning B*, *24*, 815–832.

Mastop, J. M., & Needham, B. (1997). Performance studies in spatial planning: The state of the art. *Environment and Planning B*, *24*, 881–888.

Moroni, S. (2007). Planning, liberty, and the rule of law. *Planning Theory*, *6*, 146–163.

Needham, B. (1967). The density of industrial estates. *Journal of the Royal Town Planning Institute*, *53*, 455–456.

Needham, B. (1971). The cost-benefit fallacy. *Official Architecture and Planning*, *34*, 47–49.

Needham, B. (1977). *How cities work*. Oxford: Pergamon.

Needham, B. (1982). *Choosing the right policy instruments*. Aldershot: Gower.

Needham, B. (1988). Continuity and change in Dutch planning theory. *Netherlands Journal of Housing and Environmental Research*, *3*, 89–105.

Needham, B. (1989). Strategic planning and the shape of the Netherlands through foreign eyes: But do appearances deceive? *Built Environment*, *15*, 11–16.

Needham, B. (1992). A theory of land prices when land is supplied publicly: The case of the Netherlands. *Urban Studies*, *29*, 669–686.

Needham, B. (1999). *The EU compendium of spatial planning systems and policies, volume the Netherlands*. Luxembourg: Office for Official Publications of the European Communities.

Needham, B. (2000a). Land taxation, development charges and the effects on land use. *Journal of Property Research*, *17*, 241–257.

Needham, B. (2000b). Spatial planning as a design discipline: A paradigm for Western Europe. *Environment and Planning B: Planning and Design*, *27*, 437–453.

Needham, B. (2002). De grondmarkt, het grondbeleid en de Vijfde Nota ruimtelijke ordening. In Bolsius, E. (Ed.), *Academische Reflecties: de wetenschap aan het woord over de Vijfde Nota* (pp. 157–170). Den Haag: Ministerie Vrom.

Needham, B. (2003). One hundred years of public land leasing in the Netherlands. In Bourassa, S. C., & Hong, Y.-H. (Eds.), *Leasing public land: Policy debates and international experiences* (pp. 61–82). Cambridge, MA: Lincoln Institute of Land Policy.

Needham, B. (2006). *Planning, law, and economics*. London: Routledge.

Needham, B. (2007). Land use planning and the law. *Planning Theory*, *6*, 183–189.

Needham, B. (2009). Commentary on: Property rights protection and spatial planning in European countries. In Ingram, G. K., & Hong, Y.-H. (Eds.), *Property rights and land policies* (pp. 230–232). Cambridge, MA: Lincoln Institute of Land Policy.

Needham, B. (2013). *A significant contribution to knowledge*. Nijmegen: Department of Geography, Planning and Environment, Radboud University Nijmegen.

Needham, B. (2014). *Dutch land-use planning*. London: Ashgate Publishing.

Needham, B. (2015). The national spatial strategy for the Netherlands. In Knaap, G. J., Nedovic-Budic, Z., & Carbonell, A. (Eds.), *Planning for states and nation states in the U.S. and Europe* (pp. 297–332). Cambridge, MA: Lincoln Institute of Land Policy.

Needham, B., & de Kam, G. (2004). Understanding how land is exchanged: Co-ordination mechanisms and transaction costs. *Urban Studies*, *41*, 2061–2076.

Needham, B., & Hoekveld, G. (2014). The European Union as an ethical community and what this means for spatial planning. *European Planning Studies*, *22*, 1010–1026.

Needham, B., Louw, E., & Metzemakers, P. (2013). An economic theory for industrial land policy. *Land Use Policy*, *33*, 227–234.

Needham, B., Segeren, A., & Buitelaar, E. (2011). Institutions in theories of land markets: Illustrated by the Dutch market for agricultural land. *Urban Studies*, *48*, 161–176.

Needham, B., te Raa, P., Spit, T., & Zwanikken, T. (2000). Kwaliteit, winst en risico: de invloed van het Vinex-onderhandelingsmodel op de programmatische ontwikkeling van Vinex-locaties. In Tweede Kamer, vergaderjaar 1999-2000 (Ed.), *Notie van ruimte: op weg naar de Vijfde Nota ruimtelijke ordening* (pp. 177–311 in volume of appendices). Den Haag: Sdu Uitgevers.

Pick, F. (1941). *Britain must rebuild*. London: Kegan Paul.

Popper, K. (1945). *The open society and its enemies*. London: Routledge.

Popper, K. (1957). *The poverty of historicism*. London: Routledge & Kegan Paul.

van Gunsteren, H., & van Ruyven, E. (Eds.). (1995). *Bestuur in de ongekende samenleving*. Den Haag: Sdu Uitgevers.

Webster, C., & Lai, L. W. C. (2003). *Property rights, planning and markets*. Cheltenham: Edgar Elgar.

Williams, R. (2012). *Faith in the public square*. London: Bloomsbury.

Williamson, O. E. (1999). Public and private bureaucracies: A transaction costs economics perspective. *Journal of Law, Economics and Organization, 15*, 306–342.

Abbreviation

CBA: Cost-benefit analysis

Terminology Glossary

Compensation and betterment: Compensation refers to financial compensation for those with property which loses value because of spatial planning regulations; betterment to the increase in financial value of property caused by spatial planning regulations.

Compulsory purchase: This is a synonym for eminent domain, or expropriation.

Council housing estate: This is an estate of affordable housing built and managed by the municipality. (Note that I have already explained this in endnote 1.)

Municipality: This is the lowest spatial level of government in the Netherlands.

Secondary school: For pupils from the age of 11 to 18.

12

STRATEGIC PLANNING AS A CATALYST FOR TRANSFORMATIVE PRACTICES

Louis Albrechts

> . . . I consider it [change] fundamental, and because I believe that if one were convinced of the reality of change and if one made an effort to grasp it, everything would become simplified.
>
> *(Bergson, 1946/1992, p. 131)*

Moral and Intellectual Positioning

My personal mindset is very much influenced by the incredible "Golden Sixties". They brought me hope, despair, openness and a changing world view. Hope and a changing world view as I graduated in this period in three different subjects: social sciences (1965), study of developing countries (1966) and planning (1971). Social science provided me with tools for analysing and understanding structural issues in society. But it fell short in providing answers. My study in developing countries pushed me to go beyond Western realities and practices. Planning turned the focus of analysing for the sake of analysis towards analysing for the sake of providing answers. Despair came as my hometown was shaken by the shutdown of the traditional coal industry which had dominated its economy, its physical layout and its social tissue for more than 60 years. The reaction of the miners was fierce, and two of them were killed in a protest rally. In the aftermath of May '68, together with some students at the university, I chose the side of the miners. I became inspired by fascinating experiments in the former Yugoslavia,[1] where extensive group interactions in self-managed firms promoted greater communication and worker commitment. It made me focus on the way in which people are excluded or included and the way relationships between people are organised. I fully realised that this needed a focus on the structural problems in society. This urged me to construct a type of planning that provides a critical interpretation of the structural challenges and problems and that thinks creatively about possible answers and how to get there. With my PhD (1974) I constructed, as a first step in this direction, a voluntaristic planning model. Over the years, my thinking and acting evolved to a more radical type of strategic spatial planning (Albrechts, 2001, 2004, 2006a, 2013, 2015) with a clear focus on structural issues such as future (uncertainty, creativity, envisioning); diversity (race, class, age, religion); equity (unequal development); inclusivity (inclusion, exclusion); action (implementation, selectivity). Strategic implies for me that some decisions and actions are considered more important than others and that much of the process, which is inherently political in nature, lies in making tough decisions about what is most important for the purpose of producing fair, structural responses to problems, challenges, aspirations. I define strategic planning as a transformative and integrative public sector–led, but co-productive, socio-spatial process through which visions/frames of reference, justification for coherent actions and the means for implementation are produced that shape and frame what a place is and what it might become. Transformative change is about systemic change (deep change) in society that cannot be undone. For me it is based on equity and social justice. I view raising awareness of the structural problems and challenges our cities and regions are facing—building new ideas and processes, broadening the scope of the (im)possible, and an active engagement in arenas that matter—as the main purposes of strategic planning. It is not just a contingent response to wider forces but also an active force in enabling change, and it cannot be theorised as though its approaches and practices were neutral with respect to class, gender, age, race and ethnicity (Sandercock, 1998; Albrechts, 2002). Strategic planning must symbolise some good, some qualities and some virtues that the present lacks (diversity, sustainability, equity, spatial quality, inclusiveness). My experiences in practice taught me that the capacity of a strategic spatial planning system to deliver the desired outcomes is dependent not only on the legal-political system itself, but also on the conditions underlying it. These conditions—including political, societal, cultural and professional attitudes towards spatial planning (in terms of planning content and process) and the political will on the part of the institutions involved to set the process in motion (and, even more difficult, to keep it going)—affect the ability of planning systems to implement the chosen strategies. For me, strategic planning points to implementation. I see this as the pattern of visions, policy statements, plans/strategies, programs, actions (short-, medium-, and long-term), decisions and resource allocation that defines what a policy would be in practice, what it would accomplish (and for whom) and why it would do so from the points of view of various affected publics (see Bryson & Crosby, 1992, p. 296). My international involvement (AESOP, foreign PhD students, sabbaticals, visiting professorships, a research project in Ecuador, UN-Habitat) provoked in me a more radical type of planning and pushed me to focus even more on the ways in which people are excluded or included and the way relationships between people are organised. This took me to the concept of co-production (as a political strategy) and working with conflicts (Albrechts, 2013, 2015).

Setting the Scene

Genk: Uneven Development, Diversity, Neoliberalism, Uncertainty

Born in 1942, I grew up in Genk, a regional city in the north-east of Belgium in the province of Limburg, a province that lagged behind the rest of Belgium in both economic and cultural terms. Genk, historically an unimportant and small city, grew slowly to a population of 2,000 in around 1900. This peaceful village was the home of landscape painters and writers. In 1901, a large quantity of coal was found in a nearby village. Soon after, the "Black Gold" was also found in Genk. After World War I, the village started to attract a large number of both Belgian and foreign immigrant workers (initially Polish and Italian, later Turkish) and quickly became

186 Louis Albrechts

the biggest city in the province of Limburg after the capital city Hasselt, peaking with a population of 70,000. The mines left an imprint on the structure of the city and its soul. The city evolved around the headquarters of three different mining companies. Each of these developed a "company neighbourhood" with housing, cultural activities (including churches and cultural centres) and sports infrastructure. This de-concentrated development prevented the development of a real core for the city, which kept its rural appearance. As in many other company-towns, the mining companies exercised a tight control over the lives of their workers.

In 1966 one mine closed, and by the end of the 1980s the two remaining coal mines had also closed. In the early 1960s, the Belgian government was able to attract the Ford Motor Company, and a body and assembly factory was started. In its heyday the company employed—excluding suppliers and subcontractors—14,000 workers and produced almost 480,000 cars annually. Genk thus became the industrial centre of Limburg, offering over 45,000 jobs, making it economically the third most significant city in Flanders, with a population including about 85 different nationalities. The mix of Flemish and Mediterranean culture made Genk a true multicultural society.

On Wednesday, October 24th, 2012, the employees of the Ford factory were given the news that the factory was to be closed. The management of Ford Europe had decided to relocate most of its activities to a more modern factory in Valencia, Spain, where wages are much lower than in Belgium. The closure has been a savage blow to the economy of Limburg in general and Genk in particular.

By 2014, all the employees would have to find another job. This obviously directly affected the 4,264 employees but also means a great loss for over 5,000 indirect employees of the factory's suppliers and subcontractors. Altogether, approximately 10,000 people lost their jobs or saw their business severely cut back. Many of the 4,264 employees of Ford Genk are couples, whose families with children now see their situation drastically changed from a double income to no income family. The fact that my parents lost their economic base in the early days of the war, as had happened to my father's family during the First World War; our difficulties in having children; the (almost fatal) illness of our youngest daughter; my wife's (active) passion for art—all made me deeply aware of and sensitive to the impact of the political-economic context, to uncertainty and the need for creativity. This resulted in a lifelong concern for inequality.

From Local to Global

I went to kindergarten in a convent school and had my primary education in a friars' school which was located just across from our house. The transition to secondary education was an important one, not only because of the distance to be covered by bike, but mostly because it was a shift from a familiar, safe and caring environment towards the unknown. In secondary school, I came into contact with the sons of migrant workers. I spent six quiet but, all in all, not very exciting years there. Only four of my classmates went on to university. As I was the first of my family to enter university, I had no feedback at home about what to study or what career path to follow. My choice of the social sciences was thus more the result of elimination than a positive choice. The move to the university (1961) and to a university city opened up a fascinating new world for me by introducing me to completely new fields of study, cultural activities, political and social discussions, an intellectual

Strategic Planning as a Catalyst **187**

environment, activism and making new friends and by organising my own life away from home. I became active in clubs supporting workers in their struggle to fight the closure of the coal mines. This strongly influenced my choice of topic for my master's thesis, "Co-determination (*Mitbestimmung*) in the German Steel and Coal Industry". My later concern with citizen involvement (from participation to co-production) was definitely stimulated by this experience.

As many social sciences at the time were about analysis and explanation, I was looking for something more action oriented. I came into contact with the postgraduate programme urban and spatial planning, a two-year postgraduate program organised by an interfaculty institute.[2] We entered the first year with just four students. Although the content of the programme proved to be disappointing (lack of theoretical depth, lack of a critical attitude, no link between the different components of the programme, not the slightest introduction to the literature), the subject itself started to fascinate me. To compensate for this absence, I combined the programme with a degree in the study of developing countries, which forced me to think beyond Western realities and practices. I took the latter degree in 1966 and in the same year finished both the course work and practical work for the planning degree. After one year of obligatory military service I was asked to join the Institute for Urban and Spatial Planning at Leuven University as an assistant for campus planning. Although the topic of a then booming university was interesting, the job became too administrative, and I became more and more encapsulated in the university administration. Fortunately, I was able to go back to the institute, finish my master's thesis and start a PhD. The Institute for Urban and Spatial Planning was very much involved in practical work (regional plans, subregional plans, local land use plans, transport studies). The professor in charge of the institute and some of my colleagues had a leading role in these plans. I myself became involved in mobility studies. Unfortunately, as the professor in charge suffered from multiple sclerosis, he was rarely present at the institute, and we had to find out everything by ourselves. This was a hard but at the same time very rewarding period. The only opportunity to deepen my theoretical background was to search for (the rather scarce) opportunities for short stays abroad. I was fortunate to be able to spend some time in Greece, Austria and the UK. These study visits laid the foundation for my subsequent international involvement: corresponding member, German Academy for Research and Planning "Deutsche Akademie für Raumforschung und Landesplanung" (from 1982 onwards); member, Standing Committee of the International Working Party "Managing the Metropolis" (also 1982); co-opted member, Executive Committee Regional Science Association (UK) (1985–1992); president, Association of European Schools of Planning (1990–1992); initiator of the World Planning School Congresses and chair of the first (Shanghai, 2001) and second (Mexico City, 2006) World Planning Schools Congresses.

I finished my PhD, "Strategic Factors in Urban Planning as Applied to Parking", in 1974 and was appointed, first as a lecturer (1974) and some years later as full professor (1978), in the Department of Architecture, Urbanism and Planning at Leuven University. From 1977 to 2002, I was asked to take up several positions (member of the executive committee, vice president of the board, chair of the executive committee) at the Centre for Ecology and Forestry, a study centre which in its heyday employed more than 80 people. This opened my eyes to ecology and the more technical aspects of environmental issues. In 2001, I was invited to chair the planning commission of my hometown. In 2007, I became emeritus but still handled some of the projects I had been involved in: some projects of my own and more recently, the last phase

188 Louis Albrechts

of a big research project led by my successor and the editorship of *European Planning Studies* (the journal I founded with Phil Cooke in 1993).

Major Shifts in Thinking and Acting

My intellectual journey in the planning field is indebted to the education I went through, the prevailing planning system and political context in my home country, my international involvement, my encounters with theory and practice and my inquiry into the epistemology of my practice.

From Survey to Action

As a planning student, I was heavily indoctrinated with Patrick Geddes's famous aphorism, coined in the early twentieth century: "survey before plan". In the planning classes, survey-analysis–plan was propagated as the planner's grand rule of good practice. So in much teaching and practice work, the most persistent emphasis was on the survey method. The prevailing planning model in my country at that time produced static documents, which were used as a control tool for the actions of third parties and as (legal) frameworks for spatial development and the construction rights of landowners. In this way, planning claimed bureaucratic and political control and offered legal certainty for investors. An additional aim was to avoid clientelism and corruption within the permit policy. In these plans, conceptions of the future were based on linear derivations from the present and tended to create the impression that there was something logically and factually inevitable in both the sequence and the final configuration of predicted events. I soon realised that this approach resulted in plans that are closed systems constructed to solve specific classes of problems in the light of given goals which had been conceived outside the plan's own system. The whole rhetoric of planning as consisting of "administrative" work undertaken to regulate the implementation of given policies was not very appealing to me, and I became intrigued by the complex and surreal narrative of writers and their ability to shift back and forth between tales of parallel worlds. In my contact with utopias, I valued the dimension of the "radically new", the transformative, and the dimension of bringing something new into being. This undoubtedly laid the foundation for my later interest in envisioning, creativity, innovation and a contemporary utopian tradition (see Harvey, 2000).

As soon as I joined the Institute of Urban and Spatial Planning, a colleague and I started to look for a shift away from the dominant approach and its rhetoric. A study stay at the Athens Centre of Ekistics in the late 1960s and a four-week programme at the Salzburg Seminar in American Studies (Mel Webber, Arthur Naftalin, Jack Dyckman, Robert B. Mitchell) brought me into contact with a whole new literature and made me aware of the usefulness of theory. McLoughlin's book *Urban and Regional Planning* (1969) and Chadwick's *A Systems View of Planning* (1971) provided a first (although mechanistic) alternative to Geddes's scheme and an introduction to systems thinking. Systems, as sets of components together with the relations between the components and between their attributes, gave an obvious opening to a relational approach. The book *Perspectives of Planning* (1969), and more specifically the contribution by Hasan Ozbekhan, *Towards a General Theory of Planning,* became an eye-opener for me. Planning, as conceived by Ozbekhan, begins with a vision of what sort of future a community wants, and/or what sort of existing problems they want to remedy or avoid. Planning is then done not only to see what sort of actions would be suitable but also, and indeed primarily, to see what systemic and policy changes might be suitable or necessary. The new literature taught me that the future cannot be logically deduced from the past using forecasting techniques and that a community has (within limits) a responsibility for its own future.

As a reaction against the prevailing planning approaches, and inspired by a new literature, a voluntaristic/structure model was developed. The basis was laid in three PhDs[3] at the Institute for Urban and Spatial Planning at the University of Leuven—van Havre (1973), my own (1974) and Vermeersch (1976). The model was influenced by the work of Massé (1962, 1967), Berger (1964), de Jouvenel (1964), Jantsch (1967, 1970), Ozbekhan (1967, 1969) Ladrière (1969) and Perin (1970). This voluntaristic/structure planning model became (and still is) the official approach in Flanders. The model is based on a concept of rationality (extended rationality) and a concept of time (psychological notion of time). In this model, the future transcends mere feasibility and results from judgments and choices formed with references: first to the idea of what is desirable, then to that of betterment. Such futures might (and perhaps must) be imagined as differing radically from present reality; they must represent situations which are not mere temporal extensions of the here and now; they must be free of the weight of what we are able to simply predict. A particular future state becomes an act of choice that involves valuations, judgments and decisions, and as these decisions are carried out they lead to a gradual shift in a desirable direction. To avoid pure idealistic thinking, however, over the years the views of social critics such as David Harvey, John Friedmann, and Susan Fainstein have been integrated into the approach. The governing characteristic of this model is that it defines and, therefore, contains within itself the direction towards which it is guided. It is a process in which the outcome is invented or created as something new, rather than as a solution arrived at as a result of the manipulation of givens. A link can be drawn to Bergson's concepts of duration (*durée*) and virtuality. For Bergson, duration is the unified flow of time or becoming, so durée is becoming, and virtuality provides us with a way of seeing the future as bound up with the continual elaboration of the new, the openness of things (see Grosz, 1999, p. 28). In this sense, becoming is a movement of differentiation, divergence and self-surpassing or actualisation of virtualities in the light of the contingencies that befall them (see Grosz, 1999, pp. 27–28). This way of thinking provoked for me a shift in planning from an ontology of "being", which privileges outcome and end-state, towards an ontology of "becoming", in which actions, movement, relationships, conflicts, process and emergence are emphasised (see Chia, 1995, p. 601; Chia, 1999, p. 215). It became an argument for thinking in terms of the heterogeneous becoming of institutional transformation, the otherness of institutional outcomes and the immanent continuity of institutional traces.

My involvement in international conferences and my presidency of AESOP brought me initially into contact with ACSP and APSA (Asia) and later with ANPUR (Brazil) and ANZAPS (Australia and New Zealand). Intensive contact with their leadership made me aware of how much we could learn and benefit from each other. This made me think about a worldwide forum of planning schools. With the first World Planning Schools Congress in Shanghai (2001) this idea turned into reality. My chairmanship of the first and second World Planning Schools Congresses, my term as chair of the advisory board of the global Research Network on Human Settlements (UN-Habitat HS-Net), sabbaticals in Newcastle upon Tyne and Perth, a research programme in Guayaquil,[4] an extensive and active Erasmus network, and teaching in a programme with students mostly from Africa, Asia, Latin America and the former Eastern

190 Louis Albrechts

European countries pushed me to go beyond Western realities and practices and strengthened my sensitivity to the problems of the urban poor, the disadvantaged and unequal development.

Neoliberal Context

One of the first major projects (1982) I became involved in concerned unequal development. A major incentive for setting up this project was the experience I went through in a backward province, the closure of the major employer (the coal mines) in Genk. This project resulted in three books: *Regional Development* (1983), *Regional Inequality* (1984), both in Dutch, and my first edited book in English, *Regional Policy at the Crossroads* (1989). Drawing on David Harvey, Ed Soja, Alain Lipietz, Louis Althusser and Doreen Massey, I argued that neoliberal policies have allowed capital to restructure in ways that are socially and spatially uneven. According to neoliberal dogma, distributive injustice is a temporal problem that will eventually be ironed out as economic growth continues. But many practices demonstrate that the rollout of neoliberal policy privileges urban and regional competitiveness mainly through the subordination of social policy to economic policy and new, more elitist forms of partnerships and networks (see Jessop, 2000; Allmendinger & Haughton, 2009, p. 618). As neoliberalism assumes that socio-spatial problems have a market solution (see Peck & Tickel, 2002; Purcell, 2009), its aim was and continues to be to depoliticise the economy (Friedmann, 1992, p. 83) and subordinate everything to the economic realm and the sovereignty of the market (Mouffe, 2005, p. 92). Indeed, I witnessed neoliberal attempts to create competitive cities and regions by generating investments in major cities and urban regions (see also Olesen & Richardson, 2012, p. 1692). Such investment projects became a key component of the neoliberal shift from distributive policies, welfare considerations and direct service provision towards more market-oriented and market-dependent approaches aimed at pursuing economic promotion and competitive restructuring (see Swyngedouw, Moulaert & Rodriguez, 2002, p. 572). In many cities, urban revitalisation is presented as an opportunity to change economic hierarchies and functions within the urban region by creating new jobs and strengthening the city's position in the urban division of labour. Within (and constrained by) the framework of the market society, places and communities face the challenge of constructing (or rejecting) and implementing the discourses of cultural diversity, sustainability, equity and place quality and, subsequently, creatively transforming their own functioning and practice. This creative transformation refers to changes in governance relating to current and historical relations of dominance and oppression. My experiences in practice taught me that questions have to be raised about whether spatial planning practices are able to resist the hegemonic discourses of neoliberalism. As a result, I became aware that planning faces major ontological and epistemological challenges. These may imply the scope of planning, approaches, use of skills, its context, resources, knowledge base and/or involvement of a wider range of actors. An emerging democratic deficit as a central impact of neoliberal policies became a major concern. Class, gender, race and religion do matter in terms of whether citizens are included or excluded in the process (see Young, 1990).

Learning from Practice

I always valued a combination of academic work and work in professional practice—such as the Mechelen transport, the Flanders structure plan and others. These personal and practical

Strategic Planning as a Catalyst **191**

experiences combined with the critical literature I read—Harvey (1982), Friedmann (1987, 1992) and Krumholz and Forester (1990)—made me aware that taking a clear stand was important. Even more than the professional literature, two Latin American artists shook me up in this respect. The first, Oswaldo Guayasamín, I discovered while working on a five-year research programme with a local university in Ecuador, at an exhibition in Guayaquil. Guayasamín's images capture the political oppression, racism, poverty, Latin American lifestyle and class division. I came across the second artist, Diego Rivera, in Mexico City. Rivera revolutionalised modern mural painting and was the principal figure in launching the "Mexican Renaissance". By chance, I discovered his autobiography *My Art, My Life* (1991). For me it became a richly revealing document. It is Rivera's apologia: a self-portrait of a complex and controversial personality. It is one of the frankest confessions I have ever read. The breadth of his sympathies, his vitality and his love for life run through his prose as they do through his paintings. Both artists are extremely clear about where they stand politically.

In the same spirit, when the government invited me and a colleague to prepare a plan for Flanders—a region of six million in the north of Belgium—we wanted to make it clear what we stood for. Accordingly, we first wrote a policy document that explained our view on the definition of the problem of preparing such a plan, on the process we intended to follow and on its likely content. In this way, we made it clear from the outset that we were partisans of certain outcomes over others, such as the interests of weak groups and neglected functions and certain patterns of future socio-spatial development. The purpose of this document was to find out if we were in line with the minister's views. The minister accepted the document we produced and even turned it into his official policy document. Second, we urged the establishment of a substantial planning unit within the central administration; and third, we asked that two greatly contested legal regulations be repealed. All this was considered necessary to make a point to the public at large that the minister was completely serious about a new spatial policy, which had been promised for many years.

In this process I learned most by going out, almost on a daily basis,[5] to talk in public about what I was doing, to listen to the problems, concerns, ideas and doubts of very different groups. I realised that most people will not go on the "long march" of socio-spatial transformation unless, within reasonable periods of time, they see compelling evidence that the process will produce acceptable results. In our approach, therefore, I looked for short-term results to build the credibility needed to sustain efforts over the long haul and help to test visions against concrete conditions (see also Kotter, 1996). But I was very careful not to maximise short-term results at the expense of the longer-term future. After a five-year process, the plan was accepted by both the government and the parliament, and a new planning decree was passed. As a result planning was back on the political and social agenda; a new wind was blowing, and it created a new élan in the planning department. After years of decline, the number of urban inhabitants increased and the number of planning students tripled. Moreover, the new planning discourse had a clear impact on lower-level plans (provincial and local) and on sectoral plans; it initiated a considerable number of strategic projects, and the influential transport plan (1999–2001) for Flanders departed from the basic principles of the Flemish Strategic Spatial Plan. The plan won a European award and enabled some successful processes. But there was also a dark side to all this. The older planners who left the planning department were replaced by young and inexperienced planners. They were often too rigid and technocratic, and they regarded the plan as a "bible" rather than as a guide. After the elections, the socialist party—a very important actor in backing up this process—refused to claim the portfolio of planning.

192 Louis Albrechts

The government failed to realise a supply policy for housing, industrial estates and nature. As a result, from 1999 onwards[6] planning started to lose its drive and eventually disappeared from the political and social agenda. I now regret that my international involvement distracted me from daily practice in Flanders.

My experience in practice made me aware that the role of planners couldn't be reduced to that of mere facilitators, but that they had to play an active role (such as opening the spectrum of possibilities) in planning processes. This also implies that since planners are deeply and inextricably implicated in the real relations of power, their role in different processes must become the subject of critical investigation. Guayasamín and Rivera taught me that when painters, and in my case planners, cooperate subserviently with government regimes and dance to the tune of the prevailing political dogma of control and subjugation of parts of the population by conceiving and implementing one-sided policies, they are—as handmaidens to power—as guilty of and complicit in abuses as the governments for whom they work.

Digging into the Epistemology of My Practice

Inspired by Schön (1984), I felt the need to inquire into the epistemology of my practices. This allowed me to evaluate and make sense of what I had learned in practice relative to a wider theoretical context, and test the depth and comprehensiveness of these practices. Abstract conceptualisation and generalisation of the accumulated knowledge of learning-in-action helped me to see some of what can be learned from practice and to gear my theoretical reflections, my teaching and research to the actual realities of practice (see Schön, 1984; Forester, 1989; Hoch, 1994). So I learned that there is a need for a social basis to build upon; that skills (technical, social, empathic) remain very important; that planners need to be aware that they have a highly political role to play if they so choose. I also learned that broadening the scope of possibilities, the process of "discourse structuration" and its subsequent "institutionalisation" are perhaps more important than the plan itself (Albrechts, 1999a; Albrechts & Van den Broeck, 2004). In this way, at least in Flanders, a new discourse became institutionalised—embedded in norms, in ways of doing things, attitudes and practices—and provided a basis for some change in regional, provincial and local government arenas, sector departments and consultants.

My involvement in practice, supported by some literature (see Schön, 1984), prompted me to set up a research project (Albrechts, 1999b, 2002) to explore the widening gap between universities and practitioners, research and practice, systematised thought and practical action. This gap is related to the relationship between the kinds of knowledge honoured in academia and the kinds of skills, competence and attitudes valued in professional practice. Within a Delphi-based methodology I used distinguished academics and highly regarded practitioners—from different parts of the world—as a relevant category of analysis. A quick glance at the answers showed substantial differences of opinion between the two groups. Through their comments, many of the practitioners provided a specific window into their world, their own reality. They gave me approaches to consider and practical directions to explore, and they warned me against a tendency to presume knowledge of what citizens need and want. Their answers revealed careful judgments of constraints and opportunities and told me about the daily professional and political challenges of encouraging public involvement in their planning practice. Their answers showed me their struggle with the political system. Their theorising in practice suggested new possibilities and opportunities.

What I Have Learnt

If I look back, transformative practices, envisioning as a tool to broaden the scope of the possible, and power became key concepts in my thinking and acting.

Working in a Context of Power

As my experiences (Albrechts, 2003a, 2003b, 2006a) clearly demonstrate, each decision-making process is heavily influenced by the distribution of power both within society and in specific institutional contexts. Power is at the heart of every argument affecting planning. It is therefore necessary to take structural relations of power into account, as they include some and exclude others from involvement in decision processes. In my experience, one of the most important manifestations of legal and spiritual life is that whoever has true power is able to determine the meaning of concepts and words (see Schmitt, 1988). With regard to crucial political (and by extension planning) concepts, meaning therefore depends on who interprets, defines and uses them. Who concretely defines what spatial quality, equity, accountability, sustainability and legitimacy are in a specific process? I once initiated a research project to unravel the power relations in the structure plan for Flanders process and in Perth (Albrechts, 2003a, 2003b, 2006a). I interviewed political key actors—the leading ministers and influential members of their cabinet in office during the period that the structure plan for Flanders was prepared—to reconstruct what actually took place in the course of decision making and implementation, in the transition from plan to formal adoption of the plan, and in its actual implementation, as opposed to what planners normatively would like to see happen. While on sabbatical in Australia, I did the same for Western Australia (Albrechts, 2006a) and concluded that power relations must be built into the conceptual framework of planning and looked at in a given context, place, time and scale, with regard to specific issues and particular combinations of actors (see Healey, 1999). This research project helped me to discover the "whys and wherefores" of how political actors handle plans, projects and planning processes. The Flemish case illustrates that power is not an abstract analytical concept, but a concrete set of relations which are inextricably part of the existing social, cultural, economic and political reality. The case shows that spatial planning practice is also an active force in enabling changes (see Foucault, 1980; Healey, 1997b). As a planner, I tried to act as counterweight, mobiliser, builder of alliances and presenter of real political opportunities. I learned from action not only what works but also what matters.

Transformative Practices

The voluntaristic model and the political-economic context made me focus on structural problems (Albrechts, 2010, 2013, 2015; Albrechts & Balducci, 2013). This brought me to the concept of transformative practice needed to provide answers to the structural problems. The transformative agenda is a modern term for structural change that has been discussed by many in the past (Ozbekhan, 1969; Etzioni, 1971; Schön, 1971; Friedmann, 1987) in the context of planning theory. It differs from the established or traditional way of thinking, in which there is no choice and no awareness of other possibilities.

Transformative practices focus on the structural problems in society; they construct images/visions of preferred outcomes and how to implement them. Transformative practices

194 Louis Albrechts

simply refuse to accept that the current way of doing things is necessarily the best way. Transformative change is a process that evolves in many small ways to produce an emergent pattern, which, retrospectively, comes together and becomes evident in what history may then describe as "a transformative moment" (Chia, 1999, p. 212; Healey, 2005, p. 158). I see transformative practices as differing radically and structurally from the present reality. They focus on new concepts and new ways of thinking that change the way resources are (re)used, (re)distributed and (re)allocated, and the way that regulatory powers are exercised. I learned from practice that the spectrum for transformative practices cannot be so open that anything is possible. Conditions and structural constraints on "what is" and "what is not" possible are put in place by the past. These conditions (such as the neoliberal context) that—remaining unchanged—predetermine outcomes have to be questioned and challenged in the process. In order to imagine conditions and constraints differently, we need to deal with history and try to overcome it. This defines the boundaries of a fairly large space between openness and fixity. Dealing with the transformative demands that we think serially, associatively and holistically (quantum thinking in the terminology of Zohar, 1997, pp. 32–40). I subscribe to Zohar's three kinds of thinking: the brain's intellect, heart and spirit. With the intellect, we define directions and a logical series of actions for navigating towards them. The heart of the brain forms associative or parallel thinking that finds associations between things, events, people and structures, tapping experience and learning by trial and error. The third kind of thinking is the brain's spirit—intuitive, insightful, creative—with which we challenge our assumptions, break our habits, change our mental models and escape from old paradigmatic ways of thinking. It invents new categories of thought, creates new patterns and new language, unifies, integrates and sees the whole picture, and seeks out new paths when our rule-bound and habit-bound thinking can't cope.

A number of strong manifestos for structural change have been drawn up. They left an imprint on my thinking and acting: for reconsidering the absolute faith in economic growth (Mishan, 1967; Hamilton, 2004); for living interculturally (Sandercock, 1998, 2003; Landry, 2000); for reacting against existing and persistent inequalities (Harvey, 2000); and for creating a more sustainable society (Sachs & Esteva, 2003). I learned from experience that in order to (even partially) implement such manifestos or new policies, society needs to mobilise all necessary resources in such a way that these new ideas develop the power to "travel" and "translate" into an array of practice arenas (different tiers of government, private sector, civil society), transforming these arenas, rather than merely being absorbed by them. Indeed, until a change truly "sticks" by becoming institutionalised in the system at different levels,[7] social norms, shared values and, most of all, the (governance) culture of a locality, it is always subject to degradation as soon as the stimuli associated with a change effort are removed (Kotter, 1996, 2008). Only those ideas, images[8] and ways of thinking that accumulate sufficient power to become routinised may then "sediment" down into the cultural ground, which sustains ongoing processes and feeds into new processes (Albrechts, 1999a; Albrechts & Liévois, 2004; Healey, 2005, pp. 147–148). Until changes sink down deeply into the culture, new strategies remain fragile and subject to regression. Beliefs and expectations matter just as much as reality. Real transformation takes time and dedication and therefore risks losing momentum if there are no short-term objectives to meet or actions to celebrate.

Envisioning

I realised that the challenge for transformative practices is to find a systematic method that provides a critical interpretation of existing reality and that thinks creatively about possible futures and how to get there. Indeed, it is one thing to know where you want a place to go, but quite another thing to get the place to move in that direction. The kind of creativity I have in mind is a creativity which refuses to accept that the current way of doing things is the best way and which breaks free from concepts, structures and ideas that are only there through the process of institutional continuities (Albrechts, 2006a, 2006b).

The normative viewpoint developed in the voluntaristic planning model produces quite a different picture. It pushes me to reflect creatively and innovatively on the concepts and techniques I use and the logics I apply in tackling problems and challenges. It invents, or creates, new practices—in relation to the context, the social and cultural values to which a particular place/society is historically committed—as something new rather than as a solution arrived at as a result of existing trends. Envisioning reveals how things can be different, how things could truly be better, how people can become innovative, how we can unlock the natural creativity of the actors involved to improve our cities and regions, how we can legitimise these natural tendencies that are typically inhibited or suppressed by the daily demands of our governance systems. The construction of different futures, which lies at the very heart of transformative practices, requires creativity and original synthesis. To construct visions for the future, we need both the solidity of the analysis that seeks to discover a place that is and that might exist, and the creativity of the design of a place that would not otherwise be. This is also somehow in line with Habermas's knowing (understanding challenges and the available options) and steering capacity of the state to take appropriate action and deal with challenges (Habermas, 1996).

As a practitioner, I try to think afresh and, as it were, reinvent the place I am working in to secure a better future and improve its quality. Therefore, planning theory and practice must involve a creative effort to imagine futures that are structurally different, and to bring this creative imagination to bear on political decisions and the implementation of these decisions. Creativity as a process stimulates the ability to view problems, situations and challenges in new and different ways and to invent and develop original, imaginative futures in response to these problems, situations and challenges. "Ability" focuses more on "how" one thinks rather than on "what" one thinks. This presumes that specific skills are needed to make clear what the possible impact of strategies will be on the very specific environments and concerns of citizens.

When I go out to discuss a project I am working on, I always try to make the images relating to spatial quality, equity, fairness and sustainability highly specific and detailed. If these images are not accessible, if they cannot be understood, then no one will be able to act on them. Creativity is not limited to a particular stage of the planning process. Planners must link spatial quality, equity, fairness and sustainability to all phases in the process, to every single step, to all strategies, to all actions. They must make the culture of spatial quality, equity, fairness and sustainability an integral part of the big picture. As I had access to the council of ministers and the parliament when I was working on the Flanders plan, I always tried to stress these issues at these high levels and in the innermost circles of governance.[9] I learned that spatial quality, equity, fairness and sustainability are not "happy accidents", which implies that they have to be managed in an intentional and systematic fashion.

196 Louis Albrechts

What I Stand For

For most of my career I argued that to cope with problems and challenges spatial planning needs both a critical debate that questions the political and economic processes of which existing planning approaches are an integral part and a search for new ideas. It is to this debate and the search for new ideas (Albrechts, 2013, 2015; Albrechts et al. 2017) that I want to contribute.[10] Looking back I now regret that the fetish for international publications backed up by the universities and a publisher's market dominated by journals in English meant that I published very little in Dutch. This means that most of my publications are not accessible to the Flemish planning community. I would now be more balanced in this respect.

I realise that in a surprising number of countries planning systems have changed little from the model I responded to in the 1970s and even where the nature of plans has changed, the basic principles of the regulatory system tend to remain. This is cause for serious concern given the nature and scale of the problems and challenges which localities and indeed entire countries are facing all over the world: problems of poverty and diversity, persistent inequality, environmental issues, and the impact of the neoliberal context. Secchi and Viganò (2011) frame the current condition of cities all over the world as a new urban question that arises in connection with globalising markets and financial systems. I agree with their call for new infrastructures: new principles and theories that can act as guides for finding reliable solutions for complex problems related to growing social inequalities, the environmental crisis and the right to mobility. Against this call and the background of the challenges, statutory planning instruments (master plans, land-use plans) seem to be ineffective because they are designed for situations of relative stability and certainty and reasonable clarity about the problems to be addressed. All these traits are lacking in contemporary cities and their regions. As an academic and an occasional practitioner, I am committed to a type of planning that is able to play a role in these challenges and able to embed the transformative practices needed.[11] As a reaction to comprehensive master plans and land-use plans, I conceived strategic planning as an approach that is oriented to issues that really matter, that is adaptive to changing circumstances and that evolves with new information, new knowledge (scientific and local) and changing contextual conditions. As my practices clearly demonstrate, strategic spatial planning is not a monolithic block of axioms set in stone. It is not a single concept, procedure or tool. In fact, it is a set of concepts, procedures and tools that must be carefully tailored to the situation at hand if desirable outcomes are to be achieved. The context forms the setting of the planning process but also takes form and undergoes changes within the process. I never looked upon strategic spatial planning as the ultimate model, nor as a new ideology preaching a new world order, nor as a panacea for all challenges. Strategic planning is not meant as a substitute for but as a complement to other planning tools (statutory planning, urban design). For me it is a method for creating and steering a (range of) better future(s) for a place. Its focus on "becoming" produces quite a different picture than traditional planning.

Contours for a More Radical Strategic Spatial Planning

In my hometown, a former mining area with a considerable Turkish migrant population, I witness a changing and increasingly negative attitude towards diversity. As chair of the local planning commission, I deplore the lack of imagination in the plans, projects and strategies and the lack of structural responses to these challenges. Within this context, a basic purpose of a more radical strategic spatial planning (Albrechts, 2013, 2015) is to unravel and resist the influence of international neoliberal ideologies on planning theory and planning practices wherever they might be. Its aim is to provide direction without a fixed destination, movement without prediction, to tackle problems, raise awareness, meet challenges, broaden the scope of the possible (see Zizek, 1999, p. 199, about the art of the impossible; Hillier, 2007), encourage hopes and dreams, appeal to values (equity, social justice), provide a frame for decisions and challenge existing knowledge, conventional wisdom and practices. This also implies taking on board the wishes and aspirations of the disadvantaged and the urban poor. Strategic planning provides an arena (a space of deliberative opportunities in Forester's [2010] terms), an open dialogue in which a plurality of interests and demands, opinions, conflicts, different values and power relationships are addressed. The actors in these arenas reflect on who they are and what they want and in this way articulate their identities, their traditions, their values. As such, strategic spatial planning deals with values and meanings, and related judgments and choices formed with reference to the ideas of desirability (Ozbekhan, 1969), the good society (Friedmann, 1982) and betterment (see also Campbell & Marshall, 2006). The normative dimension inscribed in strategic spatial planning is of an ethical nature, as it always refers to values (equity, social justice) and specific practices (see also Healey, 2010, for the crucial normative foundation of strategic spatial planning). Without the normative, I fear that we risk adopting a pernicious relativism where anything goes (see Ogilvy, 2002). My ethical stance, taken on substantive and procedural issues, depends on my particular context and my intellectual journey. My aim for transformative practices pushes me to enlarge the language of the debate and bring on board the social or human dimension, to open up strategic spatial planning for social innovation, and to look at strategic spatial planning as "a social project".

Acknowledgements

I benefited from comments by John Friedmann and three anonymous referees.

Notes

1 The breakup of Yugoslavia occurred as a result of a series of political upheavals and conflicts during the early 1990s.
2 I use the term urban planning, which is not exactly a translation of the Dutch term *stedenbouw* (German *Städtebau*) and spatial planning (*ruimtelijke ordening;* German *Raumordnung* or French *Aménagement du Territoire*). The institute (IISRO) Interfaculty Institute for Urban and Spatial Planning was founded in 1960 as the first planning institute at a university in Belgium. This happened under the impetus of geography professors involved in regional planning.
3 These PhDs were conceived on an individual basis by the three candidates. There was almost no intellectual support from the staff (faculty).
4 Amongst others the relationship between the global coffee network and spatial structures in the city of Guayaquil.
5 The almost complete lack of a communicative tradition and culture posed serious problems and was certainly a weak point in the process. I went out as much as possible to listen, to speak and to debate at very different places and for very different groups. I learned that most people got their information from hearsay and that some pressure groups were distributing deliberately false information (some articles in newspapers accused us of being Communist and aiming to destroy villages and deport

198 Louis Albrechts

people to the cities as Ceausescu did in Romania). By meeting the public, we were able to give correct information on the impact the plan had for their city or municipality.

6 From 1999 to 2014 conservative ministers were in charge of spatial planning in Flanders.

7 I am fully aware that getting it institutionalised locally is not sufficient. In some cases, it's at the level of the nation, or as with climate change, even on a global scale. One can only do so much locally, and it's not really safe and secure until the whole of organised society is with the new paradigm or model. I am grateful to John Friedmann for this comment.

8 I conceived the image of the Flemish Diamond (Albrechts, 1998) as an international network. It was well picked up in international forums. I now deplore that I didn't spend enough energy to have it equally accepted and used at the local, regional and national levels.

9 I had a strange relationship with the minister of planning. For him I was fully in charge of the plan, fully responsible for its content. For him it was "his" plan. So he used me and I knew that. As he remained distant from the plan, it was me who had to explain and defend the plan to the Council of Ministers, the parliament and the media. These direct contacts proved to be very beneficial. It gave me the opportunity to explain the logic of the plan, its sense of reality, its background philosophy and its impact on certain parts of the country and on certain sectors (see Albrechts, 1999a).

10 Such as the output of the Strategic Planning to Strategic Projects research project: two books, one with Van den Broeck and Segers (2010) and one with Oosterlynck, Van den Broeck, Albrechts, Moulaert and Verhetsel (2011).

11 I fully realise that as a full-time academic I don't have to earn my living with my work in practice. But for me the purpose of planning is not just to realise a plan as such. If planners manage to broaden the scope of possibilities (process and content) and create a momentum in civil society, I consider a process to be successful.

References

Albrechts, L. (1974). *Strategische factoren in de ruimtelijke stedelijke planning*. Unpublished doctoral dissertation, Leuven: University of Leuven.

Albrechts, L. (Ed.). (1983). *Regionale Ontwikkeling (Regional Development)*. Leuven: Acco.

Albrechts, L. (1998). The Flemish Diamond: Precious Gem and Virgin Area. *European Planning Studies*, vol. 6, 411–424.

Albrechts, L. (1999a). Planners as Catalysts and Initiators of Change: The New Structure Plan for Flanders. *European Planning Studies, 7(5)*, 36–46.

Albrechts, L. (1999b). Planners and Change: How do Flemish Planners on the Shop Floor Cope with Change? *Sociedade e Territorio, 29*, 36–46.

Albrechts, L. (2001). In Pursuit of New Approaches to Strategic Spatial Planning. *International Planning Studies*, vol. 6(3), 293–310.

Albrechts, L. (2002). The Planning Community Reflects on Enhancing Public Involvement: Views from Academics and Reflective Practitioners. *Planning Theory and Practice*, vol. 3(3), 331–347.

Albrechts, L. (2003a). Power and Planning: Towards an Emancipatory Planning Approach. *Environment and Planning C*, vol. 21(6), 905–924.

Albrechts, L. (2003b). Planning versus Politics. *Planning Theory*, vol. 2(3), 249–268.

Albrechts, L. (2004). Strategic (Spatial) Planning Reexamined. *Environment and Planning B*, vol. 31, 743–758.

Albrechts, L. (2006a). Shifts in Strategic Spatial Planning? Some Evidence from Europe and Australia. *Environment and Planning A*, vol. 38(6), 1149–1170.

Albrechts, L. (2006b). How to Enhance Creativity, Diversity and Sustainability in Spatial Planning? Strategic Planning Revisited. *Asian Pacific Planning Review, 4(1)*, 1–27.

Albrechts, L. (2010). More of the Same is Not Enough! How Could Strategic Spatial Planning Be Instrumental in Dealing with the Challenges Ahead? *Environment and Planning B*, vol. 37(6), 1115–1127.

Albrechts, L. (2013). Reframing Strategic Spatial Planning by Using a Coproduction Perspective. *Planning Theory*, vol. 12(1), 46–63.

Albrechts, L. (2015). Ingredients for a More Radical Strategic Spatial Planning. *Environment and Planning B*, vol. 42(3), 510–525.

Albrechts, L., & Balducci, A. (2013). Practicing Strategic Planning: In Search of Critical Features to Explain the Strategic Character of Plans. *DisP, 49(3)*, 16–27.

Albrechts, L., Balducci, A., & Hillier, J. (Eds.). (2017). *Situated Practices of Strategic Planning: An International Perspective.* Abingdon/New York: Routledge.

Albrechts, L. & Liévois, G. (2004). The Flemish Diamond: Urban Network in the Making. *European Planning Studies*, vol. 12(3), 351–370.

Albrechts, L., Moulaert, F., Roberts, P., & Swyngedouw, E. (Eds.). (1989). *Regional Policy at the Crossroads: New Perspectives for Regional Planning and Development Policies for the 1990s.* London: Jessica Kingsley.

Albrechts, L., Swyngedouw, E., & Van der Wee, D. (1984). *Regionale Ongelijkheid (Regional inequality).* Leuven: Leuven University Press.

Albrechts, L. & Van den Broeck, J. (2004). From Discourse to Facts: The Case of the ROM Project in Ghent, Belgium. *Town Planning Review*, vol. 75(2), 127–150.

Allmendinger, P. & Haughton, G. (2009). Soft Spaces, Fuzzy Boundaries, and Metagovernance: The New Spatial Planning in the Thames Gateway. *Environment and Planning A*, vol. 41, 617–633.

Berger, G. (1964). *Phénoménologie du temps et prospective.* Paris: P.U.F.

Bergson, H. (1992). *The Creative Mind: An Introduction to Metaphysics.* Secaucus, NJ: Carol Publishing Group.

Bryson, J., & Crosby, B. (1992). *Leadership for the Common Good: Tackling Public Problems in a Shared power World.* San Francisco, CA: Jossey–Bass.

Campbell, H. & Marshall, R. (2006). Towards Justice in Planning: A Re-appraisal. *European Planning Studies*, vol. 14(2), 239–252.

Chadwick, G. (1971). *A Systems View of Planning: Towards a Theory of the Urban and Regional Planning Process.* Oxford: Pergamon Press.

Chia, R. (1995). From Modern to Postmodern Organizational Analysis. *Organization Studies*, vol. 16(4), 579–604.

Chia, R. (1999). A "Rhizomic" Model of Organizational Change and Transformation: Perspective from a Metaphysics of Change. *British Journal of Management*, vol. 10, 209–227.

De Jouvenel, B. (1964). *L'art de la conjecture.* Monaco: Du Rocher.

Etzioni, A. (1971). *The Active Society: A Theory of Societal and Political Processes.* London: Collier Mac Millan.

Forester, J. (1989). *Planning in the Face of Power.* Berkeley, CA: University of California Press.

Forester, J. (2010). Foreword. In M. Cerreta, G. Concilio, & V. Monno (Eds.), *Making Strategies in Spatial Planning* (pp. v–vii). Dordrecht: Springer.

Foucault, M. (1980). *The History of Sexuality.* New York, NY: Vintage.

Friedmann, J. (1982). *The Good Society.* Cambridge, MA: MIT Press.

Friedmann, J. (1987). *Planning in the Public Domain: From Knowledge to Action.* Princeton, NJ: Princeton University Press.

Friedmann, J. (1992). *Empowerment: The Politics of Alternative Development.* Oxford: Blackwell.

Grosz, E. (1999). Thinking the New: Of Futures Yet Unthought. In E. Grosz (Ed.), *Becomings: Explorations in Time, Memory, and Futures* (pp. 15–28). Ithaca, NY: Cornell University Press.

Habermas, J. (1996). Normative Content of Modernity. In W. Outherwaite (Ed.), *The Habermas Reader* (pp. 341–365). Cambridge: Polity.

Hamilton, C. (2004). *Growth Fetish.* London: Pluto Press.

Harvey, D. (1982). *The Limits to Capital.* Oxford: Oxford University Press.

Harvey, D. (2000). *Spaces of Hope.* Berkeley, CA: University of California Press.

Healey, P. (1997a). The Revival of Strategic Spatial Planning in Europe. In P. Healey, A. Khakee, A. Motte, & B. Needham (Eds.), *Making Strategic Spatial Plans* (pp. 3–19). London: UCL Press.

Healey, P. (1997b). *Collaborative Planning, Shaping Places in Fragmented Societies.* London: Macmillan.

Healey, P. (1999). Institutionalist Analysis, Communicative Planning, and Shaping Places. *Journal of Planning Education and Research, 19*, 111–121.

Healey, P. (2005). Network Complexity and the Imaginative Power of Strategic Spatial Planning. In L. Albrechts & S. Mandelbaum (Eds.), *The Network Society: A new context for Planning?* (pp. 146–160). New York, NY: Routledge.

Healey, P. (2010). *Making Better Places: The Planning Project for the Twenty-first Century.* Basingstoke, Hampshire: Palgrave Macmillan.

Hillier, J. (2007). *Stretching Beyond the Horizon: A Multiplanar Theory of Spatial Planning.* Aldershot, Hampshire: Ashgate.

Hoch, C. (1994). *What Planners Do: Power, Politics and Persuasion.* Chicago, IL: Planners Press.

Jantsch, E. (1967). *Technological Forecasting in Perspective.* Paris: OECD.

Jantsch, E. (1970). From Forecasting and Planning to Policy Sciences. *Policy Sciences*, vol. 1, 31–47.

Jessop, B. (2000). The Crisis of National Spatio-Temporal Fix and the Ecological Dominance of Globalizing. *International Journal of Urban and Regional Research*, vol. 24, 323–360.

Kotter, P. (1996). *Leading Change.* Boston: Harvard Business School Press.

Kotter, P. (2008). *A Sense of Urgency.* Boston: Harvard Business School Press.

Krumholz, N., & Forester, J. (1990). *Making Equity Planning Work.* Philadelphia, PA: Temple University Press.

Ladrière, J. (1969). Déterminisme et responsabilité: Le language de faction. *Questions Scientifiques*, *140*, vol. 140(1), 9–30.

Landry, Ch. (2000). *The Creative City: A Toolkit for Urban Innovators.* London: Earthscan.

Massé, P. (1962). L'esprit prospectif et l'application. *Revue Prospective*, *10*, 17–38.

Massé, P. (1967). Les attitudes envers l'avenir et leur influence sur le présent. *Etapes de la Prospective*, 335–344.

McLoughlin, J. B. (1969). *Urban and Regional Planning: A Systems Approach.* London: Faber and Faber.

Mishan, E. (1967). *The Costs of Economic Growth.* London: Staple Press.

Mouffe, Ch. (2005). *On the Political.* London and New York: Routledge.

Ogilvy, J. (2002). *Creating Better Futures.* Oxford: Oxford University Press.

Olesen, K & Richardson, T. (2012). Strategic Spatial Planning in Transition: Contested Rationalities and Spatial Logics in 21st Century Danish Spatial Planning. *European Planning Studies*, vol. 20(10), 1689–1706.

Oosterlynck, S., Van den Broeck, J., Albrechts, L., Moulaert, F., & Verhetsel, A. (Eds.). (2011). *Strategic Spatial Projects: Catalysts for Change.* London: Routledge RTPI Library Series.

Ozbekhan, H. (1967). *The Triumph of Technology: "Can" Implies "Ought".* System Development Corporation, SP2830.

Ozbekhan, H. (1969). Towards a General Theory of Planning. In E. Jantsch (Ed.), *Perspectives of Planning* (pp. 45–155). Paris: OECD.

Peck, J. & Tickel, A. (2002). Neoliberalizing Space. *Antipode*, *34*, vol. 34(3), 380–404.

Perin, C. (1970). *With Man in Mind: An Interdisciplinary Prospectus for Environmental Design.* Cambridge, MA: MIT Press Cambridge.

Purcell, M. (2009). Resisting Neoliberalization: Communicative Planning or Counter-hegemonic Movements? *Planning Theory*, vol. 8(2), 140–165.

Rivera, D. (with Gladys March) (1991). *My Art, My Life: An Autobiography.* New York, NY: Dover Publications (originally published in 1960 by The Citadel Press).

Sachs, W., & Esteva, G. (2003). *Des ruines du développement.* Paris: Le Serpent à Plumes.

Sandercock, L. (1998). *Towards Cosmopolis: Planning for Multicultural Cities.* Chichester: John Wiley & Sons.

Sandercock, L. (2003). *Cosmopolis II: Mongrel Cities in the 21st Century.* London: Continuum.

Schmitt, C. (1988). Völkerrechtliche Formen des modernen Imperialismus. In *Positionen und Begriffe* (pp. 162–180). Berlin: Duncker & Humbolt.

Schön, D. A. (1971). *Beyond the Stable State.* New York and London: Norton & Co.

Schön, D. A. (1984). *The Reflective Practitioner: How Professionals Think in Action.* Aldershot: Avebury.

Secchi, B., & Viganò, P. (2011). *La Ville poreuse, Un projet pour le Grand Paris et la métropole de l'après-Kyoto.* Genève: Edition Metis Presses.

Swyngedouw, E. et al. (2002). Neoliberal Urbanization in Europe: Large-Scale Urban Development Projects and the New Urban Policy. *Antipode*, vol. 34(3), 542–577.

Van den Broeck, J., Albrechts, L., & Segers, R. (2010). Strategische Ruimtelijke Projecten: maatschappelijk en ruimtelijk vernieuwend (Strategic Spatial Projects: Socially and spatially innovative). Brussels: Politeia.

Van Havre, D. (1973). *De waardering van de woonomgeving*. Unpublished doctoral dissertation, Leuven: University of Leuven.

Vermeersch, Ch. (1976). *Het niveau van de structuurplanning als integrale benadering in een dynamisch planproces*. Unpublished doctoral dissertation, Leuven: University of Leuven.

Young, I. (1990). *Justice and the Politics of Difference*. Princeton, NJ: Princeton University Press.

Zizek, S. (1999). *The Ticklish Subject*. London: Verso.

Zohar, D. (1997). *Rewiring the Corporate Brain: Using the New Science to Rethink How We Structure and Lead Organizations*. San Francisco, CA: Berret-Koehler.

List of Abbreviations

ACSP: The Association of Collegiate Schools of Planning
AESOP: Association of European Schools of Planning
ANPUR: Associação Nacional de Pós-graduação e pesquisa em planejamento Urbano e Regional; Brazilian Planning Association
ANZAPS: The Australia and New Zealand Association of Planning Schools
APSA: Asian Planning Schools Association
ARL: Deutsche Akademie für Raumforschung und Landesplanung

Terminology Glossary

Deutsche Akademie für Raumforschung und Landesplanung (ARL): Founded in 1946, the Academy for Spatial Research and Planning is a research institute for the spatial sciences performing service functions in both fundamental and applied areas of research. In terms of its organisational structure, the ARL is an interdisciplinary personal network with the task of bringing together competences within the spatial sciences.

Ekistics: Science of human settlements developed by Constantinos Doxiades.

European Planning Studies: Provides a forum for ideas and information about spatial development processes and policies in Europe. The journal publishes articles of a theoretical, empirical and policy-relevant nature and is particularly concerned with integrating knowledge of processes with practical policy proposals, implementation and evaluation.

Flemish Diamond: A network that takes the form of a set of physically separate urban areas. The three largest cities—Brussels, Antwerp, Ghent—and the regional city of Leuven together form the anchors of the diamond-shaped urban constellation. Almost four million people inhabit this area, making it one of the larger urban regions in Western Europe. Like the internationally better-known networks of the Randstad and the Rhine-Ruhr Area, but quite unlike the primate cities of London and Paris, the Flemish Diamond is an example of a polynucleated urban system.

Salzburg Seminar in American Studies: Provides a forum for future leaders from around the world to engage in intellectual dialogue on a variety of global themes.

UN-Habitat: The United Nations programme working towards a better urban future. Its mission is to promote socially and environmentally sustainable human settlement development and the achievement of adequate shelter for all.

13

PLACES MATTER

Creativity, Culture and Planning

Klaus R. Kunzmann

Throughout my life as an active planner, I have focussed my attention on places, their iden-tity, their history and people, and their political and economic environment. For me places are more important than planning theories, more important than *Zeitgeist* approaches to the development of cities and regions. Places reflect the cultures and values of those who live and work there, and they determine the actions of those who plan or guide their spatial develop-ment. Places are made and defended by people who speak a local language when they defend the spaces they love. Places are embedded in cultural traditions, in art and craft environments, which reflect the past but also show pathways into the future. I identify places by their images, both positive and negative. They may be images of historic monuments or iconic buildings, of waterfronts or spectacular hillside locations, of skylines and townscapes, of boulevards and parks or of war-demolished city centres, deserted ruins and even obsolete brownfields. Wher-ever I have lived and worked, whether on shorter or longer assignments—and my passion for planning took me to many places around the globe—I tried somehow to identify with them and address their challenges, as I perceived them. I have lived and worked in Augsburg, Munich, Stockholm, Paris, Vienna, Bangkok and Potsdam, and more recently in Taiwan and China, though most of my professional life I spent in the Ruhr, that old industrial region which is still struggling to find a new post-industrial identity after the demise of its coal mining and steel production. For shorter periods of time, I also lived and worked in other places in Asia, the Middle East, Africa and North and South America, before retiring to Potsdam, where I live in winter, and nearby Templin, where I live in summer, and where I enjoy life with my second wife, Wang Fang, a Chinese citizen from Beijing.

Augsburg: The Cradle of My Passion for Creativity and Culture

I was born in Karlsruhe, Germany, in 1942, during the Second World War, and my parents soon left the city for a few years and moved to Graz and Kremsbrücke, a mountain village deep in the Austrian Alps. After the war, I grew up in the Bavarian city of Augsburg, where my father, a chemical engineer who graduated from the University of Technology in Munich, had secured work as the editor of a scientific chemical journal. The city's rich history, which nurtured my passion for cities and places during my school years from 1952 to 1961, had for a short time been one of the world's first global cities, ruled by affluent merchants in the fifteenth century. The wealth of the Fugger and Welser families gradually eroded in the seventeenth century, when Spain, France and the Netherlands did not, or could not, repay the generous loans the families had extended to them. Centuries later, this Renaissance city turned to making textiles, machinery and even airplanes, but it gradually lost its former magnitude. Like so many other cities in Germany, Augsburg was heavily bombed during the Second World War, though physically the city recovered rapidly from the war.

The gymnasium I attended for nine years followed the rigorous rules for Bavarian curricula in the humanities. Besides studying Latin, English and French, languages that were not my favourite subjects in school, I never failed to enjoy the art classes. We had good teachers, among them one who spent an entire year teaching us about the holocaust and how democracy functions. Another curious facet of Augsburg stayed with me throughout my life. The gymnasium was the school from which Berthold Brecht, born in Augsburg in 1898, had graduated in 1917. He started his career as editor of the school's student newspaper, wrote theatre criticism, and published his first poems. For my whole professional and academic life, his critical and provocative writings encouraged me to never remain quiet but to spell out my observations and concerns. Aside from going to school, and supported by my liberal and culturally minded mother, I frequently visited the local opera and theatres, watched movies (James Dean, Ingmar Bergman and Italian productions), participated in editing the school's newspaper, and showed my art work in local exhibitions. For a while I also worked in a bookshop attached to an art gallery, and I travelled with my father to places of his dreams, to Venice and Paris. Occasionally, I had long discussions with the father of a friend, who as a member of the German parliament and treasurer of the city of Augsburg was very much involved in local politics. These discussions nurtured my interest in politics and governance.

Munich and Stockholm: Entering the Field of Planning

In 1961, after successfully passing the entrance examinations, the nearby School of Architecture at the University of Technology in Munich accepted me. Before taking up my studies there, however, I had to spend an obligatory three-month internship as a construction worker, to learn whatever I could about bricks and mortar and about working with foreign labour. After this brief interlude, I spent the next five years commuting 60km from Augsburg to Munich. The high rents for student accommodation in the Bavarian capital city were beyond my family's budget.

The School of Architecture in Munich was not generally thought of as an innovative, inspiring institution. I worked as a student assistant with the chair of history of the arts, Luitpold Dussler. During my studies I focussed on drawing classes and on projects in urban design and urban development, taught by Gerd Albers, the doyen of the German planning community. He was one of the first German students after the war, studying at the Illinois Institute of Technology in Chicago with Ludwig Mies, van der Rohe and Ludwig Hilberseimer. Albers's experience as city planner in Ulm, Trier and Darmstadt, and his continuous involvement as a jury member in city planning competitions in Germany, made him an immensely influential bridge-builder between the planning academy and planning practitioners, as well as between the German and the Anglo-American worlds.

Gerd Albers and his assistants, particularly Peter Breitling, later professor of urban design at TU Graz in Austria, were my mentors and idols, and they opened my mind to the achievements of planning beyond Germany's borders. From them I learnt about the evolution of planning thought, from its early beginnings to Ebenezer Howard and on to Patrick Abercrombie, Kevin Lynch and Jane Jacobs. Their writings made the planning field particularly attractive to me. Additional highlights during my studies were long art excursions to Italy, Venice, Florence, Siena and other Northern Italian towns, with the chair of history of the arts. Participating in these study tours, I could combine learning about art and architectural history with my passion for drawing picturesque townscapes.

Another long-lasting experience during my five-and-a-half years of architectural studies in Munich was the studio work in small teams. Here I enjoyed the cooperative spirit, the many evenings of arguing about this and that. We were spending long nights and weekends trying to find appropriate solutions for urban challenges and the right wording to justify urban design proposals. My final studio work and examination in urban planning was a concept plan for an ideal new town, a challenge that accompanied me for a long time thereafter.

University regulations at that time required students to spend academic holidays working on construction sites and in architectural studios. After a year of studying I travelled to Stockholm and knocked on Swedish architects' doors. Again I was lucky. Fred Forbat, a renowned German-Hungarian architect, who had to leave Germany in 1938, offered me a summer job in his influential town-planning studio in the city. This nurtured my interest in urban planning. From working in his firm, I learnt much about housing, human urban design and urban planning in Sweden, and even more about Scandinavian social values. And I learnt of the importance of the state holding a human hand over land when developing life spaces for citizens. Returning from Sweden, I focussed my studies almost exclusively on urban planning. Architecture became just a necessity to get a university degree. I returned to Stockholm several times during my university studies. Later, in 1964, I had a similar experience, when as a *nègre* (an intern) in an urban design office in Paris, doing work on social housing in the *banlieue* of the city. I explored Paris with my eyes, not as a tourist but as a *flaneur,* following in the footsteps of Walter Benjamin.

Professional literature, including planning literature, did not play a big role in my studies in Munich. To my shame, I have to confess that I never entered the university library during my studies. The books which I read at that time, upon recommendation of Gerd Albers, were written by Alexander Mitscherlich, *Die Unwirtlichkeit der Städte* (Mitscherlich, 1965), Werner Hegemann, *Das Steinerne Berlin* (Hegemann, 1930) and Hermann Mattern, *Gras darf nicht mehr wachsen* (Mattern, 1964). I do not know whether these books have ever been translated into English. Other books I read were German translations of Anglo-American classics by authors such as Ebenezer Howard or Jane Jacobs. Apart from these books, we mainly learnt from architectural magazines and the *Stadtbauwelt,* the only urban planning journal accessible to me at that time. Otherwise I just read novels, written by renowned German writers such as Arno Schmidt, Hans Henny Jahn, Walter Koeppen, Hermann Kesten and other literary icons of post-war Germany, hardly known in the Anglo-American world. I probably benefitted more from such literature than from architectural *Zeitgeist* journals. Later, when supervising studios at the university, I used to recommend students who were preparing to work in another country to read love stories or crime novels instead of statistics, in order to learn about places, about life, miseries, peoples' hopes and values—the subjects of planning.

At that time (the fateful year of 1968), Munich experienced the first beginnings of the German student revolution. The University of Technology in Munich was always much less politicised than departments of sociology or economics, of course. To be frank, I was much too occupied by my gradual withdrawal from architecture, and explorations in the field of urban planning, and by my internships in Sweden and Paris, to be interested in what I thought was just student politics. Moreover, my daily commuting between Munich and Augsburg did not leave much time for participating in revolutionary action. I had no interest in fighting with the Bavarian police force.

After graduation as a diplom-engineer in architecture in 1967, I worked as a project assistant to Gerd Albers, on an urban regeneration project for the city of Ulm. This project was one of the first such projects in Germany, promoting the value of traditional urban environments and opposing the demolition of historical city quarters which had survived the Allied war bombing. Parallel to such applied research work, I participated in a pilot postgraduate course on urban planning, offered by the School of Architecture at the university. One of the few teachers we admired on the course was Karl Ganser, who later in his professional career became the much-renowned manager of the IBA Emscher Park, an innovative regional strategy to reimagine the declining industrial region in North Rhine-Westphalia. In 1968 there was a memorable three-week field trip to the UK, led by Gerd Albers. We visited a number of English and Scottish new towns, as well as urban regeneration schemes in Glasgow and Liverpool. This confrontation with planning challenges and achievements in the British Isles triggered my subsequent interest in planning in the Anglo-American world.

Vienna: Widening My Scope of Planning

After finishing my studies in Munich I was lucky to land a job as lecturer in urban and regional planning at the *Technische Universität Wien* (Vienna University of Technology), where Rudolf Wurzer became my boss and PhD mentor. His chair had a long tradition. At this university Karl Mayreder, an influential Viennese city planner, taught urban planning at the turn of the nineteenth century. Karl Heinrich Brunner-Lehenstein, Mayreder's assistant, wrote an early volume on planning theory, *Baupolitik als Wissenschaft* (building policy as science), which today would be standard reading in planning theory classes, if translated into English (Brunner-Lehenstein, 1925). Brunner-Lehenstein left Austria in 1932 and emigrated to Latin America. After the Second World War he was for a short time chief planner of Vienna, but he did not leave any significant imprint.

Rudolf Wurzer was an influential mover between academia, politics and planning practice. From him, from the spirit of the tradition of the chair, and from being in Vienna, a place full of insights into the rich history of planning, I learnt much about planning culture in another country and widened my scope of planning. During four thorny years working under his authoritarian regime as chair of planning and later as rector of the Vienna University of Technology, I was confronted with all dimensions of planning, from urban design to national spatial planning. I learnt how important it is to bridge theory and practice at local, regional and national tiers of planning and decision making. Due to his controversial personality, his contributions to the field are either no longer appreciated in the scholarly planning world or have even been forgotten. His character did not allow him to establish an influential Viennese school of planning thought, which he could have easily done. And due to language barriers, the Anglo-American world was not on his radar. All this led to him and his extensive German writings being forgotten in Austria and beyond. Maybe one day, a text will be excavated. However, because of his egocentric passion for planning and his ambition to introduce spatial planning as a scientific discipline in its own right, the School of Architecture at Vienna University of Technology has become a stronghold of planning education in Austria and beyond. He laid the foundations.

Because of the prominence of the chair in Austria, many planning projects were carried out during my time at the university. One of the most ambitious projects, commissioned by the Austrian government, was to develop a national spatial plan for Austria. This work required much commitment and political manoeuvring by the ambitious chair holder and left him little time for students and academic work. This in turn gave my colleagues and me space to communicate with students and colleagues. One outcome of all this interaction with creative students was the development of a plan for full-time, five-year interdisciplinary spatial planning education in the engineering tradition, centred around studio work and fully independent from traditional disciplines, such as architecture, civil engineering or geography (Klotz & Kunzmann, 1970).

In Vienna I read Austrian literature written by Robert Musil, Hemito von Doderer and Josef Roth. Influential German language literature on urban design and development attracted my attention: Camillo Sitte, of course, and Otto Wagner and Adolf Loos. Besides the work of Karl Brunner-Lehenstein, the *Theorie der Raumplanung* (theory of spatial planning) of Dieter Bökemann deserves to be rediscovered. Unfortunately his inspiring volume on the important role of the public sector in planning (Bökemann, 1982) has never been translated into English, even in summary.

Vienna in the late '60s and early '70s was a very innovative environment in urban development. I really liked the creativity of the city with all the contradictions between tradition and modernity. The architectural students I had to co-supervise during my four years in Vienna were full of crazy ideas about urban life and the *Gestalt* (design) of life spaces. Their activities and controversial actions were a steady source of inspiration. During my years teaching urban design and urban planning at the School of Architecture, I mainly supervised the studio work of architectural students. Every academic year we selected a medium-sized town in Austria (such as Zwettl, Amstetten or Wiener Neustadt) and asked the architectural students to produce a comprehensive development concept for the town, based on extensive local empirical studies, local observations and communication with citizens and local decision makers. Professional, not academic, ambitions dominated urban planning education in Austria at that time. Given the parochial Austrian planning culture, the students were not encouraged to read English, French or Italian literature on planning. Looking over the local fence was limited to innovative urban development projects, which could be used as models for local challenges.

My own PhD dissertation on "Grundbesitzverhältnisse in historischen Stadtkernen Österreichs" (land ownership in historical city centres in Austria), which I wrote upon the strong "advice" of my *Doktorvater,* and finished during the last year of my stay in Vienna, was not really my favourite topic (Kunzmann, 1971). It had just been a piece of academic work to get the academic ordination and certificate. I would never have finished this piece of work if my next boss, the chief executive officer of a large consulting firm in Düsseldorf, Germany, had not insisted on the academic title, which is still so important in German-speaking society. When I informed him that I would love to come, though without the prestigious title, he told me that without the title I would not really be welcome and not of much value for the firm. This frank statement hurried my work along and later opened the door for my professorial assignment at the School of Planning at the University of Dortmund.

Bangkok: Struggling with Asian Planning Culture

I next lived and worked in Düsseldorf in Germany. There my assignment was to expand the consulting services of a globally active firm, which at that time was one of the biggest consulting firms in Germany. My task was to build up a new division of urban and regional planning within the firm. I spent a lot of time on acquisition work and writing project proposals for project contracts. However most of my time was not spent on an ambitious urban development project in Bangkok/Thailand, which had seduced me to accept the job in the private sector. The aim of the three-year project, which was co-financed by the German and Thai governments, was to find solutions for the notorious traffic problems of the capital city, a task which is of course beyond the capability of a single project and beyond the influence of planners. A large team of German traffic engineers, transportation and urban planners, as well as urban economists, working together with counterparts from the Thai Government, developed a comprehensive transportation master plan for the city. The strategic project, closely monitored by the World Bank, taught me how to cooperate with engineers and economists, to listen to their arguments, and to argue that non-technical "urban" dimensions of city development are equally important. In the context of this project I spent almost a year in Bangkok. I found that the kind of planning I had learnt in Germany and Austria did not really give appropriate answers for the challenges of accelerated urban development in a city like Bangkok. This made me aware that other places and planning cultures require tailor-made endogenous, practice-oriented solutions, not just the transfer of academic or professional recipes. Sustainable development was not yet a concern at that time, and the social dimensions of urban development were not a field stated in the government agreement. In contrast, the recommendations for separate bus lanes, for an elevated rapid transit and for additional highways, well justified by mobility arguments and economic benefits, were welcomed by the Thai government and the local road-building corporations. During a visit to Bangkok 40 years after the delivery of the final report to the Thai government, I saw that in one way or another many of the technical recommendations have been implemented. At least the traffic in Bangkok is not much worse than it was 40 years ago. Bangkok was the place which opened my eyes to the developing world and to later explorations in foreign planning cultures.

The Ruhr: My Laboratory of Lifelong Learning

In 1974, with my experience in fast-developing South East Asia in mind, the declining industrialised Ruhr in Germany became my next learning environment and laboratory for the following 32 years. When I applied for the position as professor and director of research at the school in Dortmund, I had not much hope for being selected. I had not much research experience and could not present an impressive publication list. At that time, papers published in internationally refereed journals were not yet a criterion for being appointed as a professor in planning in Germany. This academic tradition and the power of Anglo-American publishers had not yet conquered continental European academic environments, at least not in the field

208 Klaus R. Kunzmann

of urban and regional planning, which was considered to be a practice-oriented engineering discipline. To my own surprise, I was appointed as the then youngest professor of the University of Dortmund. Later I learnt that it was my brief consultancy experience which was decisive in my appointment, as well as the expectation that some of my professorial colleagues would benefit from this experience for personal consultancy contracts with city and regional governments. The school in Dortmund was founded in 1968 by Gerd Albers, as the first planning school in Germany fully independent from traditional faculties such as architecture or geography. Now, with more than 1,400 students, it is most probably one of the biggest planning schools in Europe. My formal assignment was to build up an interdisciplinary planning research institute. During my 32 years at the University of Dortmund my activities focussed on seven action fields:

- Establishing and profiling an interdisciplinary research institute;
- Promoting comprehensive planning education for German and international students;
- Responding to regional challenges in the Ruhr;
- Exploring the role of culture and creativity in planning;
- Looking beyond the Ruhr;
- Preparing for a European planning culture;
- AESOP: reaching out to the community of planners in Europe.

In my day-to-day work in Dortmund these seven fields of action were highly interconnected. They forced me to be flexible, communicative and creative.

Establishing and Profiling an Interdisciplinary Research Institute

During the first decade of my assignment in Dortmund my major task was to build up the *Institut für Raumplanung* (Institute of Spatial Planning), a joint centre of research, which was vaguely conceptualised by the founders of the school after the model of the former MIT-Harvard Joint Center of Urban Studies in Cambridge, USA. According to the founding documents, the research institute in Dortmund should be interdisciplinary and act as a catalyst to the then 15 or more chair holders, representing sectoral fields of spatial planning from urban design and urban planning to *Landesplanung und Raumordnung* (regional/spatial planning), from sociology to economics and law, from civil engineering and systems analysis to real estate management. However, despite this impressive range of subjects, interdisciplinary research did not take place at the school. Very soon I experienced the limits of interdisciplinary research in planning in a university system built on independent chairs, continuously competing for support staff, working space and resources. The institute was well equipped with technical staff, though only one position was assigned for a researcher. Hence, I had to rely on external research funding. This forced me to broaden my interests and react to external research programmes rather than pursue my own research interests. The school itself had no joint research agenda when I started my job. The chair holders could never agree on a joint interdisciplinary research focus, and I did not have the vigour to bring them together during my time as director of the institute. The chance to do interdisciplinary research was missed. Even when I left 32 years later, no common vision was guiding the school's research.

One other project, however, could be realised. Publishing a joint departmental publication series was another challenging task, which I accomplished with help of a classmate from Munich (Ursula von Petz). From 1975 onwards, more than 140 publications on a broad spectrum of research and student reports, of dissertations and habilitations as well as conference proceedings have been published. They have become known all over Germany, Austria and Switzerland as the *Blaue Reihe* (blue series) and contributed immensely to the marketing of the school within the German-speaking planning community.

Promoting Comprehensive Planning Education for German and International Students

My interest in planning education stemmed from Vienna and continued over more than a decade. I was convinced that planning should be an independent discipline. Rather than carrying out research, developing a consistent curriculum (avoiding the mere addition of space-related disciplines) in a heavily state-regulated environment of higher education kept the faculty and me busy. As a newcomer to the school I was soon thrown into the thorny chairmanship of the school's curriculum commission. Following democratic university regulations at that time, all decisions within the school were the outcome of long and tedious consensus-finding processes between three groups: tenured professors, junior staff (assistants to the chair holders) and students. After tedious debates until late in the evening and over weeks, we found a consensus for a model, which was essentially conceptualised by junior staff and which the discipline-minded chair holders did not really like. This new model of planning education turned out to be a success story thereafter. In essence, the four-and-a-half-year (nine semesters) engineering curriculum centred on student group work in one-year real-world projects, structured lectures and interdisciplinary examinations along theoretical and methodological dimensions of planning. The students received the title *Diplomingeneur Raumplanung* after passing all the interdisciplinary examinations and writing a 100- to 150-page dissertation on a self-selected subject of empirical research and innovative, proactive, action-oriented planning.

It has always been an enormous struggle to convince the responsible desk officers in the State Ministry of Science and Research, supervising all business in the public university, to accept the curriculum; to accept that master's and PhD dissertations could be written in other languages, such as English or French; and to accept that the graduates from the School of Planning will be accepted to work in the heavily regulated public sector as planners in local or state governments. The faculty had to cross swords with powerful architectural institutions, the schools of architecture, the association of German architects and the regional chamber of architects, who sensed that the intellectual domain (and the job market) of architects in the field of urban planning could be in danger. In Germany, this struggle is not yet over. With the renaissance of urbanism at the beginning of the twenty-first century, this conflict has rather resurged. It is still mainstream thinking among architects and architectural schools in the country, and much supported by popular media, that one house is architecture; two houses are urban design; three houses urban planning; and five houses regional planning. If cities are ugly or have traffic or social problems, planners are responsible; if they are beautiful and lively, the architects get the credit. My passion to defend spatial planning as an independent academic discipline kept me busy throughout my years at the university (Kunzmann, von Petz & Schmals, 1990; Kunzmann, 2004a). I assume my introduction to planning as a profession, written at that time,

210 Klaus R. Kunzmann

commissioned and published by the Bundesanstalt für Arbeit (Federal Labour Office) in Germany (Kunzmann, 1992) has been my most successful and most read publication. It triggered much interest in planning among German high school graduates.

For years I sat on federal German commissions on reform in higher education. As chairman of a newly formed independent commission for planning education, established by the standing Conference of Federal Ministers of Culture in Germany, I had to find agreement among the many representatives of planning-related institutions in Germany, on a curriculum which would regulate planning education across the country. Before universities in Germany got relative freedom to decide on curricula, ministries had to approve all curricula on the basis of framework curricula, valid for the whole nation. The final session of this Germany-wide reform commission, which I chaired, took place in a monastery on the Schwanberg in Bavaria, which I had chosen. Whenever in my academic life there was a reason to organise such a special event, I did not select a venue in a university classroom, a hotel facility or in a ministry. I rather searched for a place, an ambience, a secluded location, which had a certain genius loci and symbolic significance. Places matter. The Schwanberg, amidst Franconian vineyards, was such a place. There the Schwanberg model of planning education found approval after long and controversial debates (Kunzmann, 1995). More than a decade later, the Bologna agreement forced the school to adapt its innovative curriculum and to cut the curriculum into two segments, an undergraduate and a graduate segment. After long discussions I had convinced my colleagues to offer a four-year bachelor's degree in planning (to be accepted by the public sector as a full professional education) and to add a one-year master's degree to focus on a selected field of specialisation, rather than the usual three plus two-year structure offered in other German and Austrian planning schools.

One more thing I wish to mention in this context. Systematic lecturing of planning theory and practice was not my strength. Consequently, I focussed my activities in the school on the supervision of doctoral students, mainly from developing countries, and on international comparative studios. Studios had an almost religious status in the school. They were carried out over two academic semesters by a group of 15 students and supervised by two members of the staff with different disciplinary backgrounds. From regular student assessment, which I had introduced while acting dean of the school, we had learnt that the studios were the essence of planning education in Dortmund. In these studios the students learnt to explore local or regional conditions in a rather holistic way, to do empirical research; to identify the challenges; to organise their work in teams; to communicate, argue, and defend their positions; to moderate internal conflicts; and, finally, to present the results, recommendations for proactively dealing with the local or regional challenges to a professional outside world. I had supervised such comparative studios on international themes, which, as a matter of principle, were linked to planning challenges in the Ruhr or Germany. There we learnt from Rotterdam, Liverpool, Glasgow, Pittsburgh, Los Angeles and even from China. The deliberate view out of the window aimed exclusively at learning about planning back home.

Responding to Regional Challenges in the Ruhr

The concept for the interdisciplinary research institute suggested that applied research should be embedded in the region to target regional challenges of structural change and regional restructuring. The immense economic and social challenges of structural change, and the half-hearted political efforts to revitalise the polycentric region and its cities, were an immensely rich applied research laboratory. Three projects, carried out in the '80s and '90s, helped me to understand the region.

The first applied research project on the Ruhr was a study on the revitalisation of brownfields in the region. I had to overcome criticism from influential industrial landowners, who stubbornly argued that brownfields are not a problem in the region. Though, graciously, I did get support from a few cities to carry out the project. To be frank, my interest was not so much in the quantitative empirical study of how many former coal and steel production brownfields were still waiting for a post-industrial use. There were indeed many, making up around 30% of the Ruhr territory. My interest was rather in what to do with such areas. Upon whatever intervention, most probably by the influential industrial landlords, the report and the recommendations for alternative uses were never published. Another early research project on the Ruhr was a comparative study on the implications of economic and structural change on urban development in Liverpool, Cardiff and the Ruhr, financed by the Anglo-German Foundation for the Study of Industrial Society. The research partners in the UK were Brian McLoughlin and Jeremy Alden, who regrettably have passed away. As in many intercultural comparative projects, we spent much time explaining the local and regional planning cultures to the other team members. We learnt more about planning and decision making in our own region through explaining the mechanisms to other team members in another language. Regrettably, we did not make the last hundred metres to the desk of a publisher.

When it became clear that coal mining would gradually move from the centre of the Ruhr to the northern fringe, I applied for funds for another applied project that aimed to explore the spatial implications of coal mining in this agricultural region. This project on the impacts of coal mining on the fringe of the Ruhr soon made me the enemy of the powerful coal-mining corporation in the Ruhr.

In 1989, the International Building Exhibition Emscher Park (IBA), a special German format of promoting innovative urban and regional development initiated in the late '90s by the State Ministry of Urban Planning in Düsseldorf, became a much-applauded public sector effort to reimagine the Ruhr. During the second half of the IBA initiative, I was asked to join the scientific advisory council, though it was very much a decorative position without any significant influence. The advisory position, however, gave me the opportunity to access the initiative's rich information base and learn why and how good ideas in political planning and decision-making processes can be implemented or not. Over a 10-year period, the IBA was a magnet for visitors from all over the world. I spent many days showing colleagues around the IBA flagship projects in the region. I wrote about the IBA (Kunzmann, 2004d), though a book project never materialised, and presented the project on many occasions in the US, Australia, Japan and China. My suggestion to use the IBA as a good reason to establish an English master's in regional restructuring at our school did not find internal support.

More than once during my active time in the Ruhr, I used my imagination to explore possible futures for the region and the larger metropolitan region Rhein-Ruhr region. I wrote numerous chapters for books on imaginative and creative scenarios for possible futures in the Ruhr, assuming that the regional public would prefer to hear about optimistic futures rather than empirically based analytic reports on development trends in the region (Kunzmann, 2004b, 2013). Together with the lord mayor of Duisburg, I launched a scenario on a possible agency for a Rhein-Ruhr metropolis, which turned out to be politically extremely

212 Klaus R. Kunzmann

naive. Maybe one scenario, which I wrote for the popular journal *GEO* in 1989, found more readers (Kunzmann, 1989).

In retrospective I believe I should have summed up all my experience of more than 30 years living and working in the Ruhr and written a theory of regional restructuring in old industrial regions. All my commitments, interests and passions, my frequent travelling, and a lack of personal discipline stopped me from writing down the rich experience of living and working in the Ruhr for three decades. I regret this very much.

Exploring the Role of Culture and Creativity in Planning

When covering mainstream regional policies in the Ruhr, I realised that the role of culture for regional restructuring was not a prime concern for the pragmatic political class in the polycentric urban agglomeration. This observation caused me to write an essay for the much read German weekly *Die ZEIT* in 1988 (Kunzmann, 1988). It was my first effort to address the theme. Later, in 1988, when a regional agency that was sponsoring cultural projects in the state launched *Kultur 90*, I suggested exploring the importance of culture for the local economy. To my surprise they accepted my suggestion and asked me to explore this much-neglected and underrated segment of local economies. It was the beginning of many more studies and projects in the field of culture, creativity and urban development.

Together with colleagues in the region, I became involved in writing the first German report on the importance of cultural industries, for the Ministry of Economics of the state of North Rhine-Westphalia. My interest in this subject brought me to a two-year contract from the Ministry of Economics to develop a concept for a music industries park in my home city, Bochum. I had asked a member of my staff, who loved to play music instead of crunching numbers, to join the project and use it as an empirical base for a doctoral dissertation. After two years the doctoral candidate passed the examination, though our efforts to develop the park in Bochum failed. Places matter, so do people. While the local cultural department was enthusiastic about the project idea and supported us, the local economic development agency had no interest in the project. At that time Richard Florida had not yet written and marketed his books on the importance of the creative class. Two decades later, after Opel, the subsidiary of General Motors in Germany closed its local factory, the city made some efforts to establish cultural industries in the city. They came too late. We were too early.

During this time, the Anglo-German Foundation supported a project exploring the creative city paradigm in the context of a small conference in Glasgow. We invited British and German cities which we thought had a creative profile and launched a joint paper to promote the creative city paradigm (Landry et al., 2011), which later, together with the rising international interest in cultural industries and creative industries triggered by Charles Laundry and Richard Florida, became a worldwide fad, particularly in Japan, China and Taiwan.

Another inspiring event was a meeting on creative culture and urban development in 2002, to which I invited a small number of friends and colleagues, at the Villa Vigoni on the occasion of my sixtieth birthday. The German-Italian Centre for European Excellence and Cultural Exchange was a wonderful setting, on Lake Come opposite the Rockefeller Foundation in Bellagio, to discuss the theme in a relaxed and inspiring environment. Among many others, John Friedmann, Leonie Sandercock, Patsy Healey, Alessandro Balducci, Joao Cabral, Louis Albrechts, Andreas Faludi and Dieter Frick joined the event and contributed their creative thinking to our lively discussions, only cut off by delicious Italian food served in the secluded Italian villa.

All these projects and activities on culture, creativity and urban and regional development led to many German and a handful of English publications on the theme (Behr, Gnad & Kunzmann, 1989; Kunzmann, 2004d; Ebert, Kunzmann & Lange, 2012) and, much later, to the publication of a book on "Creative Cities in Practice" for a Chinese publisher in Chinese, together with Tang Yan, an ambitious colleague in Tsinghua University in Beijing (Tang & Kunzmann, 2013

Looking Beyond the Ruhr

Privileged by working in the comparatively generous German university system, during the long university holidays I frequently escaped for a few weeks. I participated in expert missions to developing regions in Africa, Latin America, the Middle East and Asia. An early project, which I will never forget, brought me to Venezuela in 1975. For a month I was stationed in Maracaibo, with a view of the oil fields in the lake, to work on a feasibility study on a new town for coal miners in the jungle facing the Columbian border. Today it sounds weird, but I had a helicopter to search for a suitable location for the proposed mining town in the jungle, which I had baptised Ciudad Guasare. Not surprisingly, my study was soon shelved. The coal city project has never been implemented. Other missions to other places from 1975 to 1990 were funded by German Development Aid or the United Nations Development Programme (UNDP). My particular interest in participating in such missions was to promote small and medium-sized towns (Jensen, Hennings & Kunzmann, 1978). This policy field was very much supported by the federal German government for some time, to demonstrate the benefits of balanced urban development in the respective country, and planning from below (Drewski, Kunzmann & Platz, 1989). Related projects brought me to the Yemen Arab Republic, Nepal and Malawi, where local German project teams tried to promote and implement the concept. During frequent visits to Nepal, I launched the UDLE (Urban Development through Local Efforts) project, which was one of my favourite endeavours during those years. Thereby local efforts meant local self-governing governments.

Whenever I had some time left from my planning business in Yemen and Nepal or else-where, I used my free weekends for extensive on-site sketching. I was rarely alone when drawing. Tourists with big cameras were an everyday phenomenon in Bhaktapur/Nepal, though a tourist with a sketchpad was still an exception and a curiosity. Hence I was almost inevitably surrounded by a swarm of children who carefully monitored my drawing skills. Since my early exploration in the arts during my high school years, I always liked to draw. It was my favourite medium to pin down and conserve emotional and factual impressions of places and buildings. In contrast to the many snapshots with the camera, I always remember the locations in Yemen or in Nepal that I drew. The local explorations with the drawing pad gave me the opportunity to work with my own eyes, but also with my ears and nose in order to explore life in the streets and squares, without reading thick sociological volumes. I could learn what kind of actions local citizens pursue; how they sell and buy; how they move, meet and communicate; how they enjoy a free minute. Sociologists call this empirical method participatory observation. For me, the local explorations with my pad and pencils were an important element of my professional stays abroad. In a very personal and emotional way they perfectly supplemented the many technical discussions in ministries and town halls, and the official documents on urban development in the countries I visited.

All these and other projects, which brought me to Brazil, Kenya, Jordan and Oman, made me a part of the global development industry. The related networks with German Development Aid institutions were an excellent frame and base for developing training courses in Dortmund for planners from Brazil and Taiwan, and later on a master's programme for planners from developing countries, which I had labelled SPRING (Spatial Planning for Regions in Developing Economies). This programme, conceptualised with colleagues from the school, was established in Dortmund in 1984 (Jensen & Kunzmann, 1982). It took me a while to find an appropriate partner in Africa, who was willing to "buy" the innovative concept of a two-year master's degree, where one year (theoretical and methodical base) was offered in Dortmund, while during the second year field studies (to come from knowledge to action, from theory to practice) would have to be carried out in Africa. In the end, an expatriate British planner, then head of the school in Kumasi and searching for funds, accepted the concept, and SPRING was started in 1985. Later, Bangkok, for a five-year period under the local management of Hans-Detlef Kammeier, and thereafter Manila, joined the programme. The contents of this English-language master's degree programme were exclusively targeted at developing countries. All lectures and seminars were oriented to development challenges in Africa and Asia. Dortmund and Germany just happened to be the venue of the programme. Planning experience and achievements in Germany were deliberately not taught. This rather blue-eyed concept followed an ideologically driven bottom-up philosophy, targeted to a kind of barefoot planner, who would then get a certificate from the African partner school, deliberately not from Dortmund!

For me this represented an explicit anti-colonial approach. However, I soon realised that the certificate was more important than the content and that the participants left Dortmund almost without any knowledge of the planning system and planning achievements in Germany and in the Ruhr. Today I am convinced that we made a mistake.

Later in the '90s another unusual overseas project was my involvement as a coaching partner to a Japanese architect-planner in a competition to find an appropriate use for the huge US American airbase in Okinawa, Japan. I had suggested using the airfield for the promotion of cultural and creative industries, though soon after, when the governor had to step down, political priorities changed. The US Army is still occupying the land. I liked the tropical island and returned there to celebrate my sixty-fifth birthday on the white beach together with young Japanese honeymooners.

Preparing for a European Community of Planning and Planners

Very early in my Dortmund years I had started to do some research on spatial planning in Europe. An unpublished study for the Federal Ministry of Interior in 1975, exploring the European dimension of spatial planning, was the beginning. This study opened the door to participating in the CEMAT in Torremolinos, where the Charta of Torremolinos, a milestone in the development of a European spatial planning agenda, was discussed. I made a memo-proposal to this charter (Kunzmann, 1978), which was well received. In the years thereafter, the Council of Europe asked me to draft a concept for European regional planning and present it in Strasbourg, to promote European cross-border spatial planning (Kunzmann, 1983).

While participating in a project for the EU White Book, together with a colleague from Britain, I co-authored (with Michael Wegener) a report on "Urbanisation in Europe". This report found many readers across Europe, though it was only published as a mimeographed research paper in Dortmund (Kunzmann & Wegener, 1991). For this report I sketched the image of Europe as a bunch of grapes (see Figure 13.1), which became quite famous thereafter, although it did not find the approval of the editors of the Europe 2000 report.

I imagined that a bunch of grapes represents the diversity of European regions much better than the "Blue Banana". My intention was to provide a symbol for a more balanced spatial development in Europe, for a Europe of city regions (Kunzmann, 1992, 1989, 1998, 2001, 2006, 2007). I wanted to contrast the empirical banana with a simple representation of my vision of a balanced Europe.

A highlight of my involvement in European planning discourse was my 1993 participation in two thematic *Carrefours Europeens* workshops with Jaques Delors, the then commissioner of the European Commission, at his office in Brussels. For two long days we sat around his table in Brussels, listening to what the 25 or so participants from all over Europe had to tell him. He wanted to learn from European researchers where the European territory was heading. Another memorable experience was my assignment to the scientific advisory council of DATAR (Délégation interministérielle à l'aménagement du territoire et à l'attractivité régionale) for a period of three years. This job, initiated by Jean-Louis Gigou the germanophilic director of DATAR, gave me many opportunities to learn about the concerns of French national territorial planning in a slowly converging Europe.

In the early '90s, after a long personal struggle, I decided not to accept the offer of the University of Technology in Vienna to take over the prestigious chair in urban and regional planning from Rudolf Wurzer. Instead I made the establishment of a new chair for spatial planning in Europe a condition for remaining in Dortmund. With some additional financial support from the European Commission this chair got the personal tag of a Jean Monnet Professor, a title which still keeps me linked to the network of European professors who are passionate promoters of the European project.

It has been my ambition to communicate to students in our school that Europe is a peace project, a challenge for planners at all tiers of planning and decision making, but also a job market for internationally minded planners (Kunzmann, 2004a). My aim was to widen their horizons and to offer them first insights into the mechanisms of European territorial policies

FIGURE 13.1 The European Grape

Source: Author's draft.

216 Klaus R. Kunzmann

for a later occupation in the public sector, not to become academic theorists on European spatial or territorial development. I was very much determined to maintain the visibility of Europe within the school. However, by the beginning of the twenty-first century I realised that Europe is less and less appealing to planning students, just as European spatial planning has lost momentum for European policymakers.

AESOP: Reaching Out to the Community of Planners in Europe

When attending the ACSP Conference in Austin/Texas in 1985, I met Patsy Healey. We were both impressed by the flourishing annual jamboree of members of planning schools in North America, presenting the results of their research and exchanging their experience in preparing planners for practice and research. And we both felt that European schools of planning needed a similar institution as a European forum of exchange (see Healey, 2017). Upon return from Austin we immediately explored possibilities for establishing a similar association in Europe, in a continent divided by languages, religion, culture and political traditions. I invented an acronym, AESOP (Association of European Schools of Planning), bridging planners to the popular Greek philosopher, slave and storyteller Aesop, whose name fits perfectly to the ambitions of planners: to plan for people, to communicate with people and to use narratives and storytelling in planning and decision-making processes, not just plans and evidence-based maps or quantitative studies. In February 1987, with the help of Patsy Healey, I invited a small group of academic planners to Dortmund to discuss whether it would make sense to establish a European association of planning schools. They are all shown in the famous AESOP picture on the terrace of Schloss Cappenberg (see Figure 13.2).

Places matter. Searching for a spiritual location with a genius loci to trigger off the ambiguous project, I selected Schloss Cappenberg, a small castle north of Dortmund, which was owned from 1824 to 1831 by Freiherr vom Stein, a Prussian statesman who promoted the abolition of serfdom in Germany and introduced reforms that paved the way for establishing a modern municipal system. During World War II the castle served as a place of safety to protect works of art from Allied bombing.

In Cappenberg we agreed to establish the association, and we agreed on the name. My own aims and expectations 28 years ago were ambitious: I expected that an association of planning schools in Europe could provide a transnational, a pan-European, academic community of scholarly exchange. By providing an exchange platform for joint and comparative research planning, I hoped that planning researchers could benefit from the network. At a time when the ERASMUS exchange programme in Europe was just about to start, I anticipated that the existence of a European network of planning schools could facilitate and promote the exchange of planning students; finding that the planning community in Germany was very much inward looking, I hoped that an international network could open the window to European-wide perspectives on the discipline in Dortmund and prepare the ground for a next generation of much more international planning educators; I expected that the initiative would strengthen the reputation and the status of the Dortmund planning school within the home university; finally, being a strong advocate of planning education as an independent academic discipline, I expected that a recognised international association would offer pan-European support for planning education as a discipline in its own right.

FIGURE 13.2 The founding fathers of AESOP on the terrace of Schloss Cappenberg near Dortmund, Germany

Source: Author's archive.

Most of these ambitions have been achieved, in fact more than that. The vitality of AESOP is represented by the many activities which the association has successfully carried out.

Today, 28 years after the Cappenberg meeting, AESOP is an established association, with 150 members in 50 countries. (Mironowicz, 2013). One of my own ambitious aims has not been reached. Planning as an independent discipline is still not fully recognised in Europe, and its rationale is vanishing. In recent years I have even changed my mind and favoured a more insurgent approach to planning education, by infiltrating planning into traditional programmes, such as architecture, economics, management and real estate development.

Exploring New Horizons of Life after the Ruhr

When retiring from the University of Dortmund in 2006, I hosted an international conference on the implications of China's economic growth for Europe, to escape from crocodile tears and to prepare the grounds for a life after the Ruhr. Friends and colleagues came to Dortmund, among others John Friedmann, Peter Hall, Dieter Frick and Ivan Turok. Though I was increasingly learning about urbanisation and urban development in China, I thought I should explore the consequences of what is going on in China for cities and regions in Europe. The publication, which contained many of the contributions to that event, was published shortly after (Kunzmann, Koll-Schretzenmayr & Schmid, 2008). The theme is still keeping me busy collecting and piling up books and papers, though I have learnt over the years that, despite being married to a Chinese woman, Wang Fang, whom I met in Dortmund in 1994, I will never be able to become a specialist on planning in China. After my retirement in Dortmund I moved to Potsdam in winter and to Templin, in rural Uckermark, in summer. I felt more than 30 years living and working in the Ruhr was sufficient. Though the quality of life in the Ruhr, totally underestimated by people living outside the region, was enormous, I wanted to live in a different, a slow, environment. Walkable Potsdam, a strange amalgamation of a small, reconstructed baroque residence town and a functional socialist city, became our new home. Being close to culturally thriving Berlin and to a country house on the lake in the nature reserve of the Uckermark, a gentrified rural region North of Berlin, were the criteria influencing our location decision. Enjoying the slowness of these two places, I continued to travel across Europe and China to talk about German achievements in urban and spatial planning and development or bridging international and national planning experiences. At least once a year we travel for a few weeks to China, to teach at various universities, combining work, tourism and family visits. China has indeed become an exciting modern laboratory of post-industrial city planning. I am trying hard to understand how planning is done in this rapidly urbanising country (Kunzmann, 2015). Though the more often I am in China, the more I communicate with students and colleagues at Chinese universities, and the more I read about the country, the less I feel I understand the country and its polity. Not speaking or reading a word of Chinese, it is almost impossible for me to comprehend the planning culture and the sociopolitical rationales of urbanisation policies in China. Though what I see with my eyes, and benefitting from experience and creative imagination, I can easily envision the immense social conflicts within this consumption-driven and politically suppressed society.

When not travelling, I enjoy being in the countryside, cooking, reading and writing on a broad range of planning themes for invited chapters in books and articles for journals. I am not writing about planning theories or developing new theories. This is not my competence; my writings are more essayistic observations than empirically based scientific papers, and I write mostly in English not in German, being aware that Germans do not like to read English papers written by German authors. My extensive, fragmented writing evolved from being engaged in places and inspired by places rather than from reading and responding to international discourses in planning literature. It results from project assignments, from applied research projects, or just from concerns with local or regional development. I always aimed to cover challenges which I felt should be addressed. I wished to target readers who were multipliers in institutions, which would have an impact on policies, not the academic readers of refereed international journals.

Coming to the end of this journey of over 50 years of involvement in planning, I would like uncover the principles which guided my professional and academic activities. Otherwise I could not have endured the immense burden of continuous job and family conflicts. Above all, as the title of my essay suggests, places matter. When identifying with a place, I used a broad range of means such as reading maps, novels and local histories; screening accessible media; talking to professionals in local and regional institutions, and to bus drivers, artists and shop owners. I used my eyes, my camera and my sketchbook for participatory observation. I found this more important than looking at statistics, which I have never trusted. Over the 50 years of my professional life, I have learnt that being unable to talk and understand a local language, not knowing the values and ambitions of the people who inhabit a place, is a serious constraint on efforts to plan and on turning concepts and plans into reality. I have found, too, that the ability to improvise is essential for a planner, and that imaginative visions for the future are useful narratives to select preferred options. I did and spoke out and wrote what I liked to do, not what others expected me to do. I avoided academic cocooning in academic circles and milieus. Looking ahead, being visionary, finding a balance between pragmatism and utopia in a city, a region was my self-defined mission. By relentlessly looking out of the regional churchyard to learn, not to copy, I committed myself to lifelong learning. Learning is a lifetime undertaking that calls for patience, modesty and the ability to listen, but even more for curiosity and passion. This is what makes planning both a challenging and a fascinating profession. I always felt privileged to be a planner. I have always been suspicious of fashionable and transient political and academic trends; I aimed to think holistically, while facing up to and targeting local reality, political, social, economic and aesthetic challenges. Above all, however, I have learnt from all the places where I have been: **Places matter.**

Acknowledgements

I benefitted much from comments by H. D. Kammeier; particularly, however, by Trixi Haselsberger and her patience; and from three anonymous referees, who tried to bring order to my draft.

References

References to my writings are a selection. I refer mainly to texts written in English, though to reach German readers most of my writings were in German.

Behr, V., Gnad, F., & Kunzmann, K. R. (Eds.). (1989). *Kultur—Wirtschaft—Stadtentwicklung.* Dortmund: Dortmunder Beiträge zur Raumplanung, Bd. 51.

Bökemann, D. (1982). *Theorie der Raumplanung.* München: Oldenbourg.

Brunner-Lehenstein, K.H. (1925). *Baupolitik als Wissenschaft.* Wien: Springer.

Drewski, N., Kunzmann, K. R., & Platz, H. (1989). *Promotion of Secondary Cities.* Eschborn: Schriftenreihe der Deutschen Gesellschaft für Technische Zusammenarbeit (GTZ), Bd. 213.

Ebert, R., Kunzmann, K. R., & Lange, B. (2012). *Kreativwirtschaftspolitik in Metropolen.* Detmold: Rohn Verlag.

Healey, P. (2017). Finding My Way: A Life of Inquiry into Planning, Urban Development Processes and Place Governance. In B. Haselsberger (Ed.), *Encounters in Planning Thought: 16 Autobiographical Essays from Key Thinkers in Spatial Planning* (pp. 107–125). New York: Routledge.

Hegemann, W. (1930/1988). *Das steinerne Berlin. Geschichte der größten Mietkasernenstadt der Welt* (Bauwelt-Fundamente, 3). Braunschweig: Vieweg.

Jensen, B., Hennings, G., & Kunzmann, K. R. (1978). *Dezentralisierung von Metropolen in Entwicklungsländern.* Dortmund: Dortmunder Beiträge zur Raumplanung, Bd. 10.

Klotz, A., & Kunzmann, K. R. (1970). Zur Ausbildung von Raumplanern—Vorschlag für Wiener Modell (mit Klotz, A.). In K. Klotz, K. R. Kunzmann & H. Reining (Eds.), *Planung—Raum—Ordnung* (pp. 101–113). Wien: Festschrift für Rudolf Wurzer.

Kunzmann, K. R. (1971). *Grundbesitzverhältnisse in historischen Stadtkernen und ihr Einfluss auf die Stadterneuerung.* Wien: Springer Verlag, Schriftenreihe der Österreichische Gesellschaft für Raumforschung und Raumplanung, Bd. 19.

Kunzmann, K. R. (1978). Anmerkungen zur Erstellung einer Charta der Europäischen Raum-ordnung. *Informationen zur Raumentwicklung, Bonn-Bad Godesberg, 11(12),* 939–948.

Kunzmann, K. R. (1982). The European Regional Planning Concept. *Ekistics, 49(294)*, 217–222.

Kunzmann, K. R. (1983). The European Regional Planning Concept. *Council of European, Regional Planning Study Series, 45*, 28–39.

Kunzmann, K. R. (1988). Mehr Kultur an die Ruhr. *Die ZEIT, 14, April 1988.*

Kunzmann, K. R. (1989). Ausflug ins Morgenland. *Geo-Sonderheft Ruhrgebiet, 3*, 32–38.

Kunzmann, K. R. (1992). *Einführung in das Studium der Raumplanung.* Nürnberg: Blätter zur Berufskunde der Bundesanstalt für Arbeit.

Kunzmann, K. R. (1995). Das Schwanberger Modell zur Ausbildung von Raumplanern. *Raumforschung und Raumordnung, 5(53)*, 369–374.

Kunzmann, K. R. (1998). Network Europe: A Europe of City Regions. In L. Bekemanns & E. Mira (Eds.), *Civitas Europa—Cities, Urban Systems and Cultural Regions between Diversity and Convergence* (pp. 119–131). Bruxelles: Peter Lang Verlag.

Kunzmann, K. R. (2001). *La "Banane bleue" est morte! Vive la "Grappe européenne"! Les Cahiers du Conseil. Numéro spécial "Espace Européen & Politique Française des Transports".* (Conseil général des ponts et chaussées. Ministère de l'Equipement des Transports et du Logement, Paris), *2*, 38–41.

Kunzmann, K. R. (2004a). Unconditional Surrender: The Gradual Demise of European Diversity in Planning. *PlanerIn, 4*, 5–7.

Kunzmann, K. R. (Ed.). (2004b). *Reflexionen über die Zukunft des Raumes.* Dortmund: Dortmunder Beiträge zur Raumplanung, Bd. 111.2.

Kunzmann, K. R. (2004c). Creative Brownfield Redevelopment: The Experience of the IBA Emscher Park Initiative in the Ruhr in Germany. In R. Greenstein & Y. Sungu-Eryilmaz (Eds.), *Recycling the City: The Use and Reuse of Urban Land. Lincoln Institute of Land Policy* (pp. 201–217). Cambridge: Lincoln Institute of Land Policy.

Kunzmann, K. R. (2004d). Culture, Creativity and Spatial Planning (Abercrombie Lecture). *Town Planning Review, 75(4)*, 383–404.

Kunzmann, K. R. (2006). The Europeanization of Spatial Planning. In N. Adams, J. Alden & N. Harris (Eds.), *Regional Development and Spatial Planning in an Enlarged European Union* (pp. 58–70). Aldershot: Ashgate.

Kunzmann, K.R. (2007) The ESDP: The New Territorial Agenda and the Periphery in Europe. In N. Farrugia (Ed.), *The ESDP and Spatial Development of Peripheral Regions.* Valetta: Malta University Publishers Limited.

Kunzmann, K. R. (2013). Ruhrgebietslied. In M. P. van Dijk, J. van der Meer, & J. van der Borg (Eds.), *From Urban Systems to Sustainable Competitive Metropolitan Regions: Essays in Honor of Leo van den Berg* (pp. 71–91). Rotterdam: Erasmus University.

Kunzmann, K. R. (2015). Urbanization in China: Learning from Europe? A European perspective. *International Journal of Urban Sciences, 19(2)*, 119–135.

Kunzmann, K. R., Koll-Schretzenmayr, M., & Schmid, W. (Eds.). (2008). *China and Europe: The Implications of the Rise of China for European Space.* London: Routledge.

Kunzmann, K. R., von Petz, U., & Schmals, K. M. (Eds.). (1990). *20 Jahre Raumplanung in Dortmund: Eine Disziplin institutionalisiert sich.* Dortmund: Dortmunder Beiträge zur Raumplanung, Bd. 50.

Kunzmann, K. R., & Wegener, M. (1991). *The Pattern of Urbanisation in Western Europe 1960–1990.* Report for the Directorate General XVI of the Commission of the European Communities as Part of the Study 'Urbanisation and the Function of Cities in the European Community', Schriften des Instituts für Raumplanung, 28.

Landry, Ch., Bianchini, F., Ebert, R., Gnad, F., & Kunzmann, K. R. (2011). The Creative City in Britain and Germany. In Ch. Reicher, K. Heider, S. Schlickewei, S. Schröter & J. Waldmüller (Eds.), *Kreativwirtschaft und Stadt: Konzepte und Handlungsansätze zur Stadtentwicklung* (pp. 137–160). Dortmund: Dortmunder Beiträge zur Raumplanung, Dortmund, Bd. 138 *(Reprint of a Study for the Anglo-German Foundation 1996).*

Matterm, H. (1964) *Gras darf nicht mehr wachsen (Bauwelt Fundamente, 13).* Berlin: Ullstein.

Mironowicz, I. (Ed.). (2013). *AESOP Yearbook: Silver Jubilee Edition.* Warsawa: AESOP & Wroclaw University of Technology.

Mitscherlich, A. (1965) *Die Unwirtlichkeit unserer Städte: Anstiftung zum Unfrieden.* Frankfurt: Suhrkamp.

Tang, Y., & Kunzmann, K. R. (Eds.). (2013). *Creative Cities in Practice: European and Asian Perspectives.* Beijing: Tsinghua University Press (in Chinese).

List of Abbreviations

AESOP: Association of European Schools of Planning

CEMAT: Conférence Européenne des Ministres de l'Aménagement du Territoire, the standing conference of ministers in Europe, responsible for spatial planning

DATAR: Délégation interministérielle à l'aménagement du territoire et à l'attractivité régionale (France), the think tank of the French government in the field of territorial/spatial planning, located in Paris

ERASMUS: Student exchange programme of the European Union, in existence since the late 1980s

EU: European Union

IBA: International Building Exhibition Emscher Park, a state policy initiative of the state of North Rhine-Westphalia for promoting structural change and urban regeneration in the Ruhr

SPRING: Spatial Planning of Regions in Growing Economies (An English language master's degree programme offered by the School of Planning of the Technical University of Dortmund)

UDLE: Urban Development through Local Efforts (A development policy of the government of Nepal)

UNDP: United Nations Development Programme

Terminology Glossary

Die ZEIT: The most prestigious weekly journal in Germany.

Landesplanung: Spatial planning at the state level in Germany.

Projects: Practice-oriented study projects (studios) for students at schools of planning in Germany.

Raumordnung: Spatial planning at the federal level in Germany.

Raumplanung: Spatial planning, a term used for urban, regional and federal planning in Germany.

14

CHALLENGING INSTITUTIONS THAT REPRODUCE PLANNING THOUGHT AND PRACTICE

Cliff Hague

Why Does Planning Promise So Much but Deliver So Little?

I became a planner out of a sense of idealism, a child of the era that sought to build a better world after the horrors of World War II. However, there is an enduring gap between what planning promises and what it delivers. The vision of equitable and sustainable development is inspirational. It is betrayed by realities. Over a billion people are living in slums. Despite the close association of statutory town planning with public health, almost half of city dwellers in Africa, Asia and Latin America still suffer from at least one disease caused by lack of safe water and sanitation (World Health Organisation/UNICEF Joint Monitoring Programme for Water Supply and Sanitation, 2005).

The cities of the rich countries also are riven by gross inequalities in living conditions and opportunities that translate into differentials in life expectancy. Boys born in Glasgow today can expect to live 7.5 years less than those born in a neighbouring suburban local authority (Scottish Government, 2014). The gap at neighbourhood level between poor areas and wealthier ones is even wider within the same conurbation.

Such outcomes cannot be reduced to the actions of urban planners. But they raise fundamental questions about what planning is for, and who it benefits. Planners have limited powers: but why do the institutions that planners have power to shape—planning schools and professional associations—not rage against the twenty-first-century urban condition? Where is the passion to "make cities and human settlements inclusive, safe, resilient and sustainable", as the UN Sustainable Development Goal 11 states?

I have tried to challenge and change institutions that reproduce planners' ideas, practices and interpretation of their professionalism. I was a founder of the Radical Institute Group and became president of the Royal Town Planning Institute; I was also president of the Commonwealth Association of Planners, which became a global voice advocating pro-poor and gender-aware planning. This essay uses my experiences to explore the opportunities and constraints encountered in "re-inventing planning".

Harpurhey: Pride in Class and Place

"Give me the child for his first seven years and I will give you the man". The Jesuit maxim has resonance. I was born in 1944 in a small, rented, terraced nineteenth-century house in Harpurhey, about two miles from Manchester's city centre. Our house was like millions of others in the industrial cities of England. It had two rooms upstairs and two downstairs, and a small paved backyard where there was a toilet and coal shed. The front door opened directly onto the street. I lived there with my parents and widowed grandmother.

Harpurhey became one of the most deprived neighbourhoods in England (Manchester City Council, 2014). In the early 1950s it had corner shops, cobbled streets, terraced houses, small workshops, two open-air markets, cinemas, churches, lots of pubs and a couple of parks. Not far away, gap sites created by World War II bombs remained undeveloped. There were winter smogs and everyday aromas from the dye works (acrid) and the biscuit factory (sweet). In 1951 there were 30 infant deaths per 1,000 live births in England and Wales, but 35 in Manchester (Taylor, 1962).

Alfred Street Elementary School was within walking distance from home. It was the school my mother (and my wife's mother) had attended before starting work at 14. My father had been at a similar school nearby, also leaving at 14 in 1930, a bad year for an unqualified lad to enter the labour market. In the 1930s only about 10% of children from elementary schools across England were selected to go on to secondary education. In areas like Harpurhey, the proportion would have been even lower. Nobody in my extended family had received a secondary education.

The 1944 Education Act made free secondary education a right. It was a building block of the post-war welfare state. An examination decided whether you were amongst the 25%–30% who went to a grammar school for your "11-plus" education or to a "secondary modern" or to a technical school. I was one of two boys from our Alfred Street class of 35–40 who passed for the local grammar school. "The grammar and secondary modern schools' intake largely reflected the class structure of society" (Sumner, 2010, p. 96).

This upbringing gave me a strong awareness of class. Pride and resentment bristled in working-class identity. The pride was strongly gendered. Women shopped, gossiped, served in shops and looked after the house. Men worked—the effete middle class sat in offices; the decadent rich lived off unearned income. Except for my schoolteachers, men were mostly figures in the shadows, invoked to threaten, or in the case of teachers to inflict, violence. The men around me were largely silent, except for occasional reminiscences about their experiences in the recent war. Class was intermingled with place. There was pride in coming from Manchester. I was deeply conscious of England's North/South divide, which again was linked to masculinity ("soft" southerners) and class.

Cambridge: Learning to Organise and Lead Institutions

I went to Magdalene College, Cambridge, in 1963, to study geography. Like grammar school, it was a difficult transition. Magdalene drew a very high proportion of its members from England's most famous private schools. Being there did nothing to smooth my class consciousness and sense of guilt at my own good fortune. Without the welfare state I could not have trod these cloistered courtyards of privilege.

Cambridge was leading geography's quantitative revolution. I was supervised by Peter Haggett and David Stoddart. Heterodoxy and open debate infused the teaching and defined my understanding of academic life as a critical and rigorous pursuit of knowledge and understanding. However, for me geography took second place to student politics. I became membership organiser, and then chairman, of Cambridge University Labour Club in 1965–66. Student politics were intense and bitter. The (mostly private school-educated) Marxist Left vied with those of us (mostly from state schools) whose affinity was with the Labour Party, which from 1964 to 1966 was in government for the first time since 1951, though with a tenuous majority.

My later attempts to change planning institutions drew on skills of organisation and leadership that I acquired through student politics. I learned how to mobilise support, write short polemics, negotiate, work a committee, manage what we would now call a database, create a new organisation (Cambridge University Fabian Society) and advocate for my beliefs without fear. I learned how to deal with the press: I had a weekly appointment with a reporter from the local evening newspaper.

As graduation loomed I had little idea of what I wanted to do. The university's Careers Service provided suggestions, including "town planning", about which I knew little. However, I had attended a Labour rally in October 1965, where the housing minister, Richard Crossman, gave an inspiring speech. His diaries record: "I had gone to Cambridge to address a regional Labour party demonstration in The Guildhall. A thousand people turned up. There was tremendous enthusiasm and a standing ovation" (Crossman, 1975, p. 345).

The idea of a great programme of public sector housebuilding appealed to me as a way of transforming working-class opportunity through the welfare state. Labour was re-elected, with a large majority, in March 1966. It produced a national plan and promised to set up regional councils and boards to carry through regional economic planning. These would assist areas with chronic unemployment and stop the drift of people and jobs to the West Midlands and London. That's what "town planning" sounded like, a field of public policy that, by strategic public investment, could deliver opportunities to working-class people.

The Careers Service arranged for me to meet the county planning officer of Norfolk. Major Maxwell was one of the generation who came into planning from wartime service, bringing all the confidence and style of a military commander. My recollection of our meeting is that he was brief and direct, saying something like, "Planning. Fine career. Don't go and do something damn stupid like teaching."

A Rude Awakening

Getting married straight after graduation, Irene and I needed to find income and a house. The easiest option was to return to Manchester. I could get a place and a bursary for the full-time postgraduate planning course at Manchester University; Irene could get a job as a primary school teacher; and her mother was able to speak to the local rent collector, who found us a house around the corner from where she lived. As Willmott and Young (1962) showed, this was a common means for working-class young couples to access housing. The house had been built in the 1820s and had a cellar with an earth floor, which had been a separate house.[1] There was an outside toilet but no bath. It was demolished in Manchester's slum clearance programme soon after we left in 1968.

My postgraduate planning course was a rude awakening and a culture shock. It strongly influenced my thinking about planning. Though Brian McLoughlin left soon after I began the course, George Chadwick was developing a "systems view of planning". Mike Batty, a young researcher and co-contributor to this volume, was a stimulating presence. I was familiar with systems theory, modelling and statistical methods from my undergraduate degree and was drawn to this approach to planning. I read the articles in the *Journal of the American Institute of Planners*. However, studio projects dominated the curriculum, and I found much of the teaching distinctly low-key and descriptive, not analytical or critical.

My outspokenness got me into trouble. At the newly created staff-student committee, I spoke like a union shop steward. Next morning, my "yearmaster" warned me that this had made me a "marked man" with the head of department. I also questioned why our studio projects expected us to conserve and enhance rich neighbourhoods, or make proposals for marinas, but did not address the housing conditions of the poor. At the end of my first year, in an interview with the head and a senior lecturer, I was told that I did not have "a proper professional attitude" so should not return for the second year. I replied that I was confident that I had passed everything and had the right to go into second year.

Gradually I came to realise that the issues went deeper than my own behaviour. They were central to the view of planning that underpinned our programme and to attempts to define planning as a profession. Conflicting views about the nature of planning had been presented to the Schuster Committee (1950). The committee defined two functions of planning: "1) the determination of policies—social, economic and strategic; 2) the preparation and carrying through of a plan for the use and development of land in conformity with these policies" (Schuster, 1950, para. 53). It said planning was a "team job" that was limited but not determined by the technical aspects of design. This had opened the door for social science graduates to enter the profession, which until then had been overwhelmingly made up of architects, surveyors and engineers.

The committee's stance was significantly at variance from that presented by the Town Planning Institute (TPI) and by its past president Thomas Sharp. The TPI argued that planning was a technical exercise, the core of which was the design of two-dimensional plans for the use of land. To enter the planning profession, a person needed to be able to prepare a plan "in the sense of something set out on a drawing board" (Schuster, 1950, para. 122). Sharp was forthright: "Planning is design: design is one man's responsibility (with, of course, the subordinate help of assistants)" (Schuster, 1950, para. 71). The idea seemed to me to be elitist and undemocratic. It masked the social, economic and political choices being made.

In 1965 Thomas Sharp and his followers had carried the day at an emergency general meeting of the TPI, rejecting proposals to broaden the base of the planning profession: an exclusionary professionalism. They set about reviewing education and membership policy to ensure that—contrary to what Schuster had argued—only those able to design a plan could be planners. The idea of "specialisms" within planning was anathema. These views remained contested, but in the Manchester University planning school there was no contest. Planning was design. It was not about public policy or regional economies, let alone about class politics.

I could not understand why graphical presentation seemed to matter much more than the content of what was being proposed when our studio projects were being assessed. Gradually I realised it was because this view of planning separated planning from any policy context and hence also from a political context. "Planning is design and design is one man's responsibility" applied not just at the site scale, but at urban and regional scales. The planning education curriculum developed by the TPI after 1965, and used for its professional examinations and accreditation of planning programmes, explicitly required that students practised design at all these scales. Thus courses were typically built around design-based studio projects that began with a site or village, and then looked at a rural area, then a town and finally a region. The scale changed but the core skill—the ability literally to draw the plan—and the technocratic message did not.

This pedagogy had come from architecture. Years later I discovered that Patrick Geddes (1915) in *Cities in Evolution*[2] had warned against planning education following the path taken by architecture education. Geddes argued that planners needed technical understanding but also a grasp of administration and regulation. Above all, planning education had to be steered by the study of "civics", that kaleidoscope of history, culture, psychology, sociology, ecology and more, which fired Geddes's thought and practice.

A further provocation in my planning education came with the realisation that staff were undertaking consultancy work in South Africa. Three out of a staff of about 10 were white South Africans, but other staff members were also involved. The Sharpeville massacre had taken place in 1960 when the South African police fired on a crowd of black protestors, killing 69. I was a member of Anti-Apartheid and had a poster of Nelson Mandela's Rivonia Trial speech on the wall of my undergraduate room. I was shocked that staff were designing racially segregated urban areas: that town planning, which I had naively assumed to be a progressive force, could be used for such purposes, and that such actions could be defended as "professional".

"The present can become an epoch in which the dreams of the past for an enlightened and just democracy are turned into a reality. The massing of voices protesting racial discrimination have roused this nation to the need to rectify racial and other social injustices." These inspiring words open Paul Davidoff's 1965 article on advocacy planning. They spoke of a fundamentally different view of planning than the one I was being taught. In my second year I did enough to get by in the studio work so I could do more reading. We had no access to European literature, and apart from *Town Planning Review* there was little from the UK. Compared to the *Journal of the American Institute of Planners,* the *Journal of the Town Planning Institute* was pedestrian. Thus my ideas were shaped by American authors, particularly Foley's (1960, 1963) dissection of the ideologies of British planning, and Melvin Webber's writings. Mitchell's (1961) characterisation of "wouldn't it be nice if . . ." plans, which paid scant regard to means of implementation, seemed to define what we had to produce in the studio. Fired with enthusiasm and a diploma in town planning, I went to put into practice these new ideas from across the Atlantic.

Slum Clearance in Glasgow

In May 1968, as students built barricades in Paris, Glasgow Corporation offered me a job as a planning assistant. I wanted to work in a big city, boost jobs, clear slums, and help build council houses and play areas for working-class kids. I was taken aback by conditions in Glasgow, particularly in the interwar slum clearance estates and in the worst tenement areas. A major storm in January 1968 had left a lot of roof damage. Gap sites abounded, and the east end of the city in particular was visibly impoverished. Sectarianism was very evident in the graffiti, the football, and the Labour Party, where I was soon asked, "Are you a Catholic or a Protestant?" Ideas I might have entertained of a political career were put on hold indefinitely.

My first assignment was on the future of Yorkhill, an inner-city area where the dock had recently become disused and transferred into council ownership. My report identified strengths, weaknesses and constraints in Yorkhill, reviewed "the metropolitan context" and set 11 goals against which to evaluate two main alternative options. Option A was to retain good housing but redevelop the worst for new residential uses. Option B, to address "the serious problems of the decline of Glasgow as a commercial centre", was redevelopment for a major exhibition centre. Analysis of "goal satisfaction" showed that there was little to choose between the two, and in either case "a thorough study of the economics of the scheme" would be needed. This "goals achievement" approach (Hill, 1968) was a novelty within Glasgow's Planning Department, though its inconclusive outcome did little to inspire interest amongst senior members of staff. A decade or so later, an exhibition centre was developed on the former dock.

Glasgow's Planning Department also employed two sociologists. By March 1969 the director was "anxious to draw up a programme of work for the sociology team".[3] I composed and submitted a response. It proposed "a thorough study into redevelopment". It referenced Gans (1962) and Fried (1963, 1967) on the social impacts of urban renewal in Boston, as methods that might be followed "to ascertain pre- and post-relocation attitudes to redevelopment" so that "we would have a scientific assessment of the social effectiveness of our policies".[4] It further argued that there should be analysis of "the economic consequences of Comprehensive Development Area (CDA) Planning—the effect on firms and shops and house values within a CDA, the post-clearance location of industrialists, etc."

I was called into the office of a senior planner. He handed me back my one-page note. In the top left-hand corner, the director of planning had written, "Can we try to cut down on this type of report?" [sic]. My attempt to change the institutional culture had failed: I was too junior, too cocky, and I had no influential allies. It was another five years before the clearance programme collapsed in the face of public opposition, management failures and financial unreality.

Why had I come to doubt the benefits of slum clearance? My day-to-day work made me aware of the blighting effect on houses and businesses of a 20-year development plan that declared 29 redevelopment areas. Explaining face-to-face to dumbfounded backstreet small businesses that we were going to compulsory purchase their premises was a salutary experience. Crucially, my reading of the American planning literature enabled me to interpret what was happening. This was the kind of "unitary planning" (Foley, 1964, p. 59) that had been the basis for the Manchester University programme, a "long-range locational-physical plan" built on a presumed consensus in which knowledge was irrelevant because design and political commitment could make it a "self-fulfilling prophesy". What Glasgow needed was Foley's adaptive approach, "policies and proposals" as courses of action "to influence metropolitan development", developed from a methodology that was "empirical-analytic-economic".

In what might have been an attempt at correction therapy, I was dispatched to meetings with engineers who were unabashed by the thought that their new urban expressways would thrust by the windows of first-floor tenements, or that there would be no pedestrian access across a four-lane highway being driven through a residential area. Similarly, the city architect in his huge office in the marble-staircased Glasgow City Chambers disdainfully explained to me that my design brief for low-rise, high-density housing on a site would not alter his decision to have six high-rise blocks contracted from a major construction company. The blocks and the expressway are there today. My dreams of planning providing the transformation of

228 Cliff Hague

working-class areas were being put into practice by professionals who seemed to care nothing for the lives of the people they were nominally serving.

I worked with Sean Damer, one half of Glasgow Planning Department's "sociology team", on a paper critically reviewing the Skeffington report (1969) on public participation in planning (Damer & Hague, 1971). We had observed at first hand Glasgow's faltering attempt at public participation, in the Govan CDA. Drawing on the pluralist American literature, e.g. Meyerson and Banfield (1955), Jacobs (1961), Arnstein (1969) and Webber (1968), and the advocacy planning movement, we challenged the dominant assumption in UK planning that a plan represented, in an unproblematic way, the public interest. We argued that "planning is involved in a power struggle: this power is not just to do with the zoning of land. It has also to do with the fact that certain uses of land can enhance or constrain people's life chances" (Damer & Hague, 1971, p. 225). We concluded that without "redistribution of power, participation in planning alone is meaningless" while declaring that "the days of tacit acceptance of autocratic decisions about the urban system are over" (pp. 229–230). As evidence we cited "the increasing tendency towards militant, and effective, tactics by citizens' action groups" (p. 231). I followed this paper with another that looked at public participation in the context of theories of participatory democracy (Hague & McCourt, 1974).

What Kind of Planning Education for What Kind of Planning?

Still in thrall to higher education as a progressive force, in 1969 I enquired about doing part-time teaching at the Department of Town and Country Planning at Edinburgh College of Art/Heriot-Watt University. I was offered and accepted a full-time post. "There has never been a time in which ideas on the subject changed so rapidly: the most progressive course of 1960 would have been sadly outdated by 1970," wrote Hall (1973, p. 68). What were the drivers of change? Reaction against comprehensive redevelopment was starting to appear, both in practice and in the UK literature on planning (e.g. Davies, 1972; Dennis, 1970, 1972). There was also the international student movement, with its calls for student involvement in programmes: The Students' Planning Association was active. Recruitment of staff, like myself, from social science backgrounds also changed the planning schools. The Education for Planning Association, chaired for a while by co-contributor Barrie Needham, provided an important network that brought together many young UK planning academics. In 1973, the Centre for Environmental Studies published a report on planning education. It argued that while there were many courses teaching physical and land use planning, courses were needed that emphasised social and economic problems, resources and means.

Within the department where I was teaching, achieving change was contentious. Early in 1973 senior undergraduates called an open meeting to demand change in their programme, and for staff to do research—not architectural consultancy. I chaired a small committee of staff and students to redesign the programme. We went for radical change, introducing semesters and reading weeks, giving assignments to all the proto-modules we designed so that students would have to write essays or undertake analytical projects in topics like economics. We introduced four options in the senior part of the course: Rural Resource Planning; Urban Social Problems and Policies; Urban Design; and Urban Management. Each student would have a personal mentor. The dominant role of the yearmaster, responsible for all the practical work and for student guidance and support—and so able to make or break a student's

Challenging Institutions **229**

career—would be abolished. In short, we created the kind of planning programme that is now familiar in the UK, though not universal. Over the next two years we lost four of our six architect planners from the staff, and we were soon under attack from those who controlled planning education in the UK.

As the new course leader redesigning the programme, I had two related aims. We would create an intellectually challenging programme, helping students to learn to think critically and analytically about planning, rather than just training them to be planners. Around this time, James Simmie described planning schools as "intellectual deserts" (Milne, 1975). The second aim was to create different kinds of planners, able to work in new ways and in different institutions; to be a resource for poor communities; and to change planning practice in local government. This was not as fanciful as it sounds, because the UK planning system itself was changing, with the introduction of the new, more strategic structure plans to replace the detailed and static development plans from the 1947 planning legislation.

The chair/head of department post was vacant from October 1973 to January 1975. It was a difficult time to recruit a planning professor. Local government reorganisation and a property boom meant that salaries were not competitive with practice, and few established planning academics had any research record. During this period we ran the department in an open and democratic way with extensive student involvement. Then Ian Melville arrived to fill the vacant post. Reportedly recommended by the (now) Royal TPI (RTPI) he had no research pedigree and refused to give lectures. He strongly adhered to the principles that had structured the planning programme at Manchester. Internal conflict with staff and students followed, and the university sent in two professors to investigate. Their report supported the right of the head of department to impose his own will, even if that meant overriding the views of the rest of the staff. My attempts at institutional change had been partially successful, but at a price. We had to do as we were told, or be closed down.

The Radical Institute Group

In 1971 the RTPI consulted members on alternative ways that it might develop. The consultation revealed little support for the "no change" option. There was some support for the option to become the "Institute of Planning" (i.e. broadening the scope from land use planning towards planning as a process as practised in corporate, social, economic and environmental planning). Another option favoured by some was to become the "Institute of Community Planning". However, the most popular option amongst those members responding to the consultation was the "Institute of Environmental Planning". This proposed broadening the institute's scope and membership beyond "town planning". Importantly, it promised that "the greatest freedom and flexibility would be given to educational institutions for innovation and to develop reputations for particular aspects" (RTPI, 1971, p. 26). However, the institute's council remained dominated by planners with qualifications in architecture, engineering or surveying, and less sympathetic to change. The chair of the education committee, who would have to lead any change in education policy, was an architect-planner in private practice. The "freedom and flexibility" that the democratic consultation process had endorsed were not implemented.

I was inspired by Alinsky's (1971) book that was written for "those who want to change the world from what it is to what they believe it should be". His maxim that you should make

230 Cliff Hague

your opponents live up to their own book of rules provoked subversive ideas. Professionalism was the core of the legitimacy of both the RTPI and those who ran planning education, professionalism as defined in a particular ideological way by those who controlled the RTPI. So, take control of the RTPI and define the professionalism of planners in a different way! Simple.

In 1975, together with a few friends, and with access to the columns of the recently created independent weekly *Planning* newspaper, we formed the Radical Institute Group, to stand a slate of candidates in the RTPI Council election. Our first manifesto declared "RIG wants a broader based institute", with an explicit reference to the "Institute of Community Planning" option. It also called on RTPI to sever all links with the South African Institute of Town and Regional Planners and with South African planning schools. It said the RTPI should also give evidence, as the Law Society had, to the Royal Commission on the Distribution of Income and Wealth, addressing topics such as company cars, inadequate public transport, second homes, inner cities and deprived estates. We also supported the principle of land nationalisation, the idea that ownership of land should be vested in the state, which could then grant leases to private individuals or companies to use land. Fortunes made by property developers by gaining planning permission were contentious in 1970s Britain, and there was a campaign for land nationalisation.

RIG attracted outrage and hostility. Building a network of supporters and finding people willing to take the risk of standing for election as an RIG candidate was somewhat hit and miss. There were no fax machines, let alone e-mail or social media. We relied on the (sometimes erratic) postal service to circulate drafts of manifestos and comments upon them. Much depended on mutual trust and loyalty. There was no formal leadership: While those frightened by RIG saw us as a tight cell receiving instructions from Moscow, the reality was quite the opposite! Cohesion came through those elected to RTPI Council, who met in caucus the night before the council, going through the council papers and agenda and deciding tactics for the next day's meeting—then going to a cheap Italian restaurant together.

By the time I was elected in 1979, RIG members made up about a third of RTPI Council, and a number of basic democratic reforms in RTPI governance had been achieved. Places on council were no longer reserved for Fellows (regardless of how few votes they polled); you no longer needed to be nominated by two Fellows to stand for election to council, and elections were by single transferable vote.

I was able to lead work on the RTPI Education Committee to carry through a major reform of education policy and accreditation requirements that, in essence, has endured from 1982 until now. To be accredited, courses would be required to have a "core" but also "specialised studies", with schools given explicit freedom about how they developed the latter. Accreditation boards would now consider research performance. Students should have direct experience of democratic decision making (RTPI, 1982). It took three years to get the changes approved because of almost unanimous opposition from the heads of planning schools. One powerful head argued that "as a profession we have no research tradition",[5] as if it was simply a fact of life, rather than the logical outcome of the planning education system that he had helped to entrench. With hindsight the system that we created looks commonplace, but it had to be voted through council in the face of resistance. This was a major success in changing a planning institution and influencing the socialisation of new planners.

In the early 1980s RIG led RTPI working groups that published reports on *Planning in a Multi-Racial Britain* and *Women in Planning,* as well as work on economic development.

Eventually, after shilly-shallying and a high-level visit, the RTPI agreed to break its ties with apartheid. We were also able to change the RTPI Code of Professional Conduct so that it required that members "shall not discriminate on the grounds of race, sex, sexual orientation, creed, religion, disability or age and shall seek to eliminate such discrimination by others and to promote equality of opportunity".

This amounted to significant institutional change in the RTPI. It would not have happened when it did without RIG: There were plenty of opponents on RTPI Council, but also, crucially, some friends and others who were open to persuasion. RIG demonstrated that it was possible to change significant aspects of a major professional planning institute through cooperative, practical action supported by a channel of communication to the wider membership. RIG's actions defined an alternative, radical professionalism that sought to equate the idea of a profession with being partisan for inclusion and equity. It challenged the orthodoxy that supporting the status quo was non-political.

Community-Based Planning and Its Limits

Soon after moving to Edinburgh, I was invited to become involved with the Craigmillar Festival Society, an innovative community organisation developed by a group of women in the city's largest and most deprived public housing estate. For over 10 years I attended meetings with local residents, helped them learn how to do surveys, and represented them at meetings with officials and councillors, in public inquiries and at the Examination in Public of the Lothian Region Structure Plan. We campaigned for housing modernisation and against road developments through the area and private housing on nearby fields. We managed to get a small industrial estate, but we were powerless to prevent job losses when local industries closed or relocated. My involvement was rooted in instinctive class solidarity and a guilty sense of responsibility to use my education and skills to benefit a working-class community. I was seeking an alternative way of doing planning compared to the practice I had been part of in Glasgow.

The Festival Society invented a term, "liaison government".[6] The idea was that the area should be managed by a cross-cutting partnership between local government and local residents. This gained some traction locally and nationally in the mid-1970s. Edinburgh's council ran a pilot project in Craigmillar, in which the planning department took an active part, though the housing department, landlord to the vast majority of residents, was notably distant. In 1976 we were able to scale up this approach through a successful bid for European anti-poverty funds to create a Comprehensive Plan for Action, the first such award made directly to a community group. However, despite all the energy and idealism, as cuts began to be made in UK public spending in 1976–77 (after the oil crises and International Monetary Fund intervention), political and officer support drained away, unemployment began to rise, and hard drugs and then AIDS began to feature amongst Craigmillar's problems. The innovative, community-based planning model could not deliver in the face of these structural changes.

I read David Harvey's *Social Justice and the City* when it came out in 1973. It challenged me to rethink my previous scepticism about the value of Marxist theory. Then there were two conferences organised by the Centre for Environmental Studies in early 1974 and 1975 at which Harvey and Manuel Castells were prominent speakers. I read Marxist-inspired critiques of the development of cities and regions (e.g. Habermas, 1971, 1974, 1976; Pickvance, 1976; Castells,

232 Cliff Hague

1977, 1978; Cockburn, 1977). There were also publications from *Community Action* magazine, and the Community Development Projects, an experimental initiative from the UK's Home Office (i.e. internal affairs ministry) with 12 local action teams backed by researchers working in deprived neighbourhoods and towns. The post-war settlement was unravelling as "stagflation" gripped post–oil crisis economies. Social democracy entered its long crisis.

The ideas of this period underpinned my book *The Development of Planning Thought* (Hague, 1984). After introducing Marxist theories of the economy, states and ideology and relating these to the history of planning in the UK, the second part tried to apply the theory to the development of Edinburgh. It concluded with a prescriptive chapter which linked to the alternative economic strategy of the UK Left in calling for "a planned alternative to market-led growth", with a national plan focused on tackling regional inequality and coordinating sectors through an interregional spatial dimension.

Actually Existing Socialism

Beginning in the early 1980s I made professional visits to Czechoslovakia. Berthold Hornung, deputy city architect of Prague, had escaped on 21 August 1968 when the Russian tanks crushed the Prague Spring. He arrived in Edinburgh. He had numerous Czechoslovakian contacts, and he helped me to visit them. These visits, together with the writings of Havel (1975), French and Hamilton (1979), Konrad and Szelényi (1979), Musil (1981) and Szelényi (1983), gave me a grasp of the operation and results of planning under what the authorities claimed to be "actually existing socialism".

I met many planners and spent days walking the streets of Prague, Bratislava, Brno (and Budapest and East Berlin as my own contacts grew). I absorbed the historic urban centres, the decaying nineteenth-century tenements where the least favoured lived, gems from the art nouveau and art deco periods, the neoclassicist buildings from the Stalin era, the shoddy-looking factories and the panel housing estates of the 1970s and 1980s as the regime belatedly tried, and failed, to buy consent and tackle under-urbanisation. I rode the cheap and crowded trams where every fourth person seemed to be in a uniform; I stayed in gloomy hotels and ate dumplings in restaurants with long menus but few items actually available. I inhaled the pollution and rode in Trabants that broke down; I saw the statues of heroes, the banners proclaiming peace and progress, and the bullet holes from the slaughter during 1939–45 and the uprisings of 1956.

I came to understand the technocratic nature of the planning practice in these places: Claims to scientific rationality provided a basis for depoliticised discourse and professional survival. I learned to speak carefully in public places and to be cautious about whom to trust. I began to understand irony and humour as survival strategies. I did not publish anything from these visits, for fear of creating problems for the people I was meeting. It was only after 1989 that I felt able to record some reactions (Hague, 1990; Hague & Prior, 1991).

Surviving

Back in my day job, the need for survival had again become acute. The university had long since relieved Ian Melville of his head of department role, but there was a new existential threat. The Thatcher government was keen to cut higher education. Planning was a soft target.

A 1983 review of planning programmes in polytechnics sought closures. Through its education committee, of which I was vice chair, the RTPI had managed to defer final decisions for a year by setting up its own review, in which I was centrally involved. However, by 1985 a working group on town and country planning had been established to make recommendations to all the funding bodies (i.e. for polytechnics and universities). The RTPI's stalling strategy had some success, since, as the UK economy began to recover from its depressed state, we were able to collect evidence to challenge the manpower planning assumptions that had been the pretext for substantial closures of planning courses.

However, closures were still proposed, including the planning programmes at Edinburgh College of Art/Heriot-Watt University. The recommendation to close us was a surprise and illogical. We had postgraduate (full-time and part-time) and undergraduate planning, and a postgraduate housing programme that was professionally accredited. In contrast, another Scottish planning school that only had an undergraduate programme was proposed to be the locus for a new postgraduate planning programme. I felt that my own profile and political stance were factors. At 41, with four young children, a wife looking after them and not in paid employment, and a widowed mother in Manchester to support, I faced being out of a job.

Our department and its programmes survived, after an anxious and draining process of lobbying that stretched over a year. However, combined with the return of the Thatcher government in the 1987 election, it was time for a personal reappraisal. I stood down from RTPI Council. RIG was finished. I was no longer active in Craigmillar, where the Festival Society itself was struggling as cuts bit once more. But I still had a job—back in Manchester for Christmas 1987, nobody I met amongst the extended family and neighbours was in full-time work.

To earn money and be able to communicate regularly and quickly with UK practitioners, I began to write a monthly "Diary" in *Planning*, the weekly newspaper. I had few illusions left about planning under capitalism or communism, just an enduring impractical belief in the idea itself. At this low point, I drew inspiration from the way my Czech friends used humour to survive. The diary was humorous and widely read across the profession. It combined personal anecdotes from family life (e.g. Nelson, the one-eyed goldfish) with professional commentary. It ran in one form or another for the best part of 20 years.

In 1990, my RIG colleague Robin Thompson had become RTPI president. What's more, the RTPI secretary-general—late in the evening and after several drinks—suggested to me that I should stand again for RTPI Council and aim to become president. Vanity whispered, "Why not?"

Globalisation and Rapid Urbanisation

Part of our departmental survival strategy had been the creation of a "developing countries" planning programme. In 1992 I found myself at the University of Engineering and Technology in Lahore, delivering a six-week teaching assignment. It was part of a three-year project to help develop a master's programme in planning, and it was linked to a slum-upgrading project in Faisalabad. I had an immersion into rapidly urbanising colonial/postcolonial settlements. I could see how planning had (re-)created English garden suburbs, at some remove from the old city's shoulder-hugging lanes and aromatic bazaars. I saw the cantonment, the colonies where the better off and the expats lived, and the open drains in the informal settlements.

234 Cliff Hague

I had read about rapid urbanisation for an Open University course that I had tutored. I was familiar with the seminal argument of Turner (1972, p. 526): "The basic problem of the slums is not how to eradicate them, but how to make them liveable." However, I had not fully grasped the way that planning operated in Pakistan and in many other rapidly urbanising countries. Out-of-date plans based on protracted surveys had a narrowly physical base and seriously underestimated rates of urbanisation. Implementation was shaped by clientist politics and corruption. The poor were criminalised for trying to find somewhere to live. In seeking to build their professionalism, planners here were aspiring to the exclusive, elitist and technocratic model of the pre-RIG RTPI.

In 1995 I was honoured to be invited to South Africa to give a keynote address to a retreat that was seeking to forge a new planning profession for the post-apartheid era. Paul Jenkins, who had worked in Mozambique and South Africa and was doing a part-time PhD with us, kindly took me round Cape Town and its townships before the conference began. Seeing the divided townscapes created by apartheid planning was still a shock. At breakfast before the conference began, I asked a white planner what he hoped to get out of the two-day event. His reply was "maintenance of professional standards". I edited my presentation to make it more forceful in its negation of past planning practice in South Africa. It was a unique two days that led to the formation of the South African Planning Institute.

As RTPI president, in 1996 I attended the UN's Habitat II summit in Istanbul. I was struck by the extent to which planning and planners were marginalised. The UN's Human Settlements work was mainly about housing. Governments across the rapidly urbanising world seemed to have given up on planning.

Also in my presidential year, I represented RTPI to the Commonwealth Association of Planners[7] (CAP). RTPI, the largest member, was dissatisfied with CAP's lack of activity. With support from the RTPI, I became president of CAP in 2000. I was determined to change CAP; it had to be connected to the UN's Habitat Agenda goals agreed in Istanbul—sustainable human settlements and adequate shelter for all. I created and wrote a newsletter, *CAP News*. In the first issue I set out my agenda:

> We need to change CAP for two reasons. First there is the global significance of urbanization; second is the need to support member organisations and the planners who belong to them . . . professional planners have an important role to play, but that they need to rethink the scope and nature of their practice. Rapid urbanization has rendered obsolete the techniques, policies and instruments of much traditional town planning. Planners have been slow to recognise the imperatives of poverty alleviation, community empowerment, and to create opportunities for women in development. Nor has planning practice been sufficiently involved in the knowledge economy and informed by research. CAP by itself cannot deliver a transformation, but it should be a focus for ideas, innovations and mutual learning.

Over the next decade we built up CAP, strengthening its links with Commonwealth organisations including a ministerial-level body, the Commonwealth Consultative Group on Human Settlements, and with UN-Habitat. I coined CAP's strapline, "No sustainable development without sustainable urbanisation, and no sustainable urbanisation without effective planning". CAP produced a guide on gender and planning (Hague with Malaza et al., 2009), work on food security (Caldwell & Lang, 2014) and a review of planning education provision (Hague, 2010). After the 2004 tsunami CAP helped initiate a post-disaster re-planning project involving the Sri Lankan and Australian planning institutes. CAP supported capacity-building events for planners from small island states in the Pacific and the Caribbean, as well as the formation of an African Planners' Association.

CAP developed the argument that it was necessary to "re-invent planning" and create a "New Urban Planning". We worked closely with senior figures in UN-Habitat to target the 2006 World Urban Forum (WUF) in Vancouver, and to try to mobilise the RTPI and the American Planning Association (APA) to use their resources and influence to advocate for a new kind of pro-poor planning. This was ambitious, but an advantageous set of circumstances meant we had to try. The WUF was in a Commonwealth country, and the Canadian Institute of Planners (CIP) had good access to the preparations. The WUF theme was "Sustainable Cities—Turning Ideas into Action" (in Barcelona in 2002 it had been "Urban Cultures"). It was now or never. Could the professional institutions be mobilised in common cause, a Global Planners' Network advocating to and for professional planners across the world practices that could work for, rather than against, the urban poor?

Through a series of global conference calls CAP, RTPI, APA and CIP, along with UN-Habitat and the European Council of Spatial Planners prepared a Global Planning Conference in Vancouver leading into the WUF, to get planners there. CAP got Commonwealth funding to take representatives of planning associations from more than 12 developing countries. We drafted and circulated a paper, "Re-inventing Planning" (Farmer et al., 2006), and produced a book, *Making Planning Work: A Guide to Approaches and Skills* (Hague et al., 2006) that was launched by the executive director of UN-Habitat. The final report of the WUF recorded that the forum

> . . . placed a strong emphasis on planning as a tool for urban development and environmental management, and as a means of preventing future slum growth. This view was accepted not just by government officials and urban planners themselves, but also by civil society groups that wanted planning to be more inclusive, transparent and ethical.

The UN-Habitat "Global Report on Human Settlements" for 2009 focused on planning sustainable cities. It said, "Urban planning is essential to crafting solutions to the pressing urban problems of the 21st century, yet the professional planning practices in place have not always been able to keep pace with the challenges faced by urban areas" (p. 185). Similarly, CAP was able to get formal endorsement of the importance of new approaches to planning from the Commonwealth Heads of Government Meeting (CHOGM), which recorded that "Heads recognised that rapid urbanisation was posing a significant challenge in many Commonwealth countries, and that new and inclusive approaches to urban planning and management were central to achieving the Millennium Development Goals" (CHOGM, 2009, para. 74). A report on the state of Commonwealth's cities (Hague & French, 2010) followed.

However, support from the major professional institutes was lukewarm. There was no grasp that a Global Planners' Network had to reach out beyond the Atlantic. To the leaders of RTPI, APA and CIP, re-inventing planning was a niche concern for rapidly urbanising countries. They did not engage with the proposition that pro-poor planning might be needed in the increasingly divided cities of rich countries. I stepped down from CAP in 2010.

Into Retirement

I had a heavy teaching and administrative load, as well as undertaking contract research to bring in the money the school needed to balance the loss of income as numbers on the undergraduate planning course declined. We could not be too selective about what contract research to take on, but some of the projects were particularly worthwhile. I was part of a team that produced a good practice guide on planning for diversity and equality (School of the Built Environment, Heriot-Watt University, 2005), and on international experience of participatory planning (School of the Built Environment, Heriot-Watt University, 2003). I also worked on a European Commission–funded INTERREG project in the North Sea Region, which led to a book (Hague & Jenkins, 2004). I was involved from the start in the ESPON programme (European Spatial Planning Observation Network), which works closely with the European Commission. Contract research brought me close to practice, provided funding for me to expand my international interest in planning and in equitable and community-based planning innovations. It also generated material that could be used in teaching. Contract research is a good model for planning schools.

I received no time allowance for my work with CAP, or for bringing in extra contract research. I felt under immense pressure, so when I could take my pension in 2004, I retired from the university and became a freelance researcher. Since 2004 I have worked on further INTERREG projects, mainly in the Baltic Sea Region, with small rural municipalities from peripheral regions. I have worked extensively on ESPON, including co-authoring all three synthesis reports of the 2013 programme, crafting sentences to balance the political priorities of the client with the evidence from research—a central challenge for all practising planners. Leaving the university gave me more time for research, and for CAP. I was able to write *Regional and Local Economic Development* (Hague et al., 2011), a global review of practices, in which we argued that bottom-up initiatives are vital where states are weak and markets will not deliver social inclusion and sustainable development. Ideas from the book and my INTERREG work underpin a more recent study of small towns in Scotland (Hague, 2013).

Looking Back and Looking Forwards

The recurrent theme in my career is a critical stance towards much of conventional planning practice, and attempts—through action, teaching and writing—to find alternative, more inclusive and equitable forms of planning. I have seen the management of conflict as central to the work of a planner, an insight that began with my own class consciousness. I have never accepted, nor rejected, the institutions that planners have built—in particular planning schools and professional bodies. I have sought to engage with them in a critical and practical manner. I argued, for example, that

> . . . urban planning as a profession is still often demarcated by a concern only with the location and distribution of land uses and the control of development, and is seen as almost exclusively based in the public sector . . . this marginalization of planning means that an integrated and practical approach to human settlements has also been marginalized.
>
> *(Hague et al., 2006, p. 83)*

I have been privileged to be paid to teach planners and to travel to many parts of the world. Seeing places is a valuable way of learning. The dynamism in planning today is in the Global South. What kind of planning capacity might develop there? Priorities are likely to include the knowledge and skills to reduce vulnerability to natural disasters, deliver participatory slum upgrading, create more environmentally friendly cities and cope with fierce conflicts over the development of land. The great strength of the planning idea is its holistic understanding of places. Most policymakers and other professions have narrower perspectives.

I see formidable challenges—climate change, urban growth (but in some places decline), migration, water shortages, food security, refugee tent cities, post-conflict resettlement and reconciliation, natural disasters and technological hazards. We need the best brains and highly committed people to engage with these as planners. For all the dark side of its Enlightenment underpinnings, planning should be about bringing hope and using science to create better futures for all. It won't be planning like my generation knew it. It won't be the kind of bureau-cratic/corporate business-led planning that has been the norm in the UK for a generation. It will though have some ancestry in the "liaison government" of 1970s' Craigmillar, and in the struggles and innovative pro-poor practices described in Hague et al. (2011). Go and invent it through your own thought and practice.

Notes

1 Such dwellings are described in F. Engels's *The Condition of the Working Class in England*—see e.g. p. 57 of the 1969 edition, St. Albans: Panther Books.
2 Chapter 13 is "Education for Town Planning, and the Need of Civics".
3 "Sociological research programme", Glasgow Planning Department Private Departmental Memorandum, SND/MH, 12 March 1969.
4 "Towards 'A Sociological Research Programme' " 2/CBH/MM, 19 March 1969, mimeo.
5 Professor Paul Brenikov, Newcastle University, in RTPI News, November 1977, p. 79.
6 For more details see Hague (1982), especially Figure 1, p. 234.
7 There are 53 Commonwealth countries, though not all have professional planning institutes—many are small states. Over 25 national institutes, such as RTPI, Canadian Institute of Planners, Kenyan Institute of Planners, etc., are members of CAP.

References

Alinsky, S. (1971). *Rules for Radicals*. New York, NY: Random House.
Arnstein, S. R. (1969). A Ladder of Citizen Participation. *Journal of the American Institute of Planners, 35,* 216–224. doi:10.1080/01944366908977225
Caldwell, W., & Lang, K. (2014). *Perspectives on Planning for Agriculture and Food Security in the Commonwealth*. Discussion Paper. Retrieved from Commonwealth Association of Planners website: http://www.commonwealth-planners.org/images/documents/food.pdf
Castells, M. (1977). *The Urban Question: A Marxist Approach*. London: Edward Arnold.
Castells, M. (1978). *City, Class and Power*. London: Macmillan.
CHOGM. (2009). *CHOGM Communique: Commonwealth Heads of Government Meeting, Republic of Trinidad and Tobago, 27–29 November 2009*. Retrieved from The Commonwealth website: http://thecommonwealth.org/sites/default/files/news-items/documents/TrinidadandTobagoCHOGM-Communique2009.pdf
Cockburn, C. (1977). *The Local State: Management of Cities and People*. London: Pluto Press.

Crossman, R. (1975). *The Diaries of a Cabinet Minister, Volume One, Minister of Housing 1964–66*. London: Hamish Hamilton and Jonathan Cape.

Damer, S., & Hague, C. (1971). Public Participation in Planning: A Review. *Town Planning Review, 42(3)*, 217–232.

Davidoff, P. (1965). Advocacy and Pluralism in Planning. *Journal of the American Institute of Planners, 31(4)*, 331–338. doi:10.1080/01944366508978187

Davies, J. G. (1972). *The Evangelistic Bureaucrat*. London: Tavistock.

Dennis, N. (1970). *People and Planning*. London: Faber and Faber.

Dennis, N. (1972). *Public Participation and Planners' Blight*. London: Faber and Faber.

Farmer, P., Frojmovic, M., Hague, C., Harridge, C., Narang, S., Shishido, R., & Vogelij, J. (2006). *Re-inventing Planning: A New Governance Paradigm for Managing Human Settlements*. Retrieved from the Global Planners' Network website: http://www.globalplannersnetwork.org/pdf/reinventingplanningenglish.pdf

Foley, D. L. (1960). British Town Planning: One Ideology or Three? *British Journal of Sociology, 11(3)*, 211–231. doi:10.2307/586747

Foley, D. L. (1963). *Controlling London's Growth: Planning the Great Wen 1940–60*. Berkley, CA: California University Press.

Foley, D. L. (1964). An approach to metropolitan spatial structure. In M. M. Webber, J. W. Dyckman, D. L. Foley, A. Z. Guttenberg, W. L. C. Wheaton, & C. B. Wurster (Eds.), *Explorations into Urban Structure* (pp. 21–78). Philadelphia, PA: University of Pennsylvania Press.

French, R. A., & Hamilton, F. E. I. (1979). *The Socialist City: Spatial Structure and Urban Policy*. Chichester: John Wiley.

Fried, M. (1963). Grieving for a lost home. In L. J. Duhl (Ed.), *The Urban Condition* (pp. 151–171). New York, NY: Basic Books.

Fried, M. (1967). Functions of the Working Class Community in Modern Urban Society: Implications for Forced Relocation. *Journal of the American Institute of Planners 33(2)*, 90–103. doi:10.1080/01944366708978003

Gans, H. J. (1962). *The Urban Villagers*. New York, NY: The Free Press.

Geddes, P. (1915). *Cities in Evolution*. London: Williams and Norgate.

Habermas, J. (1971). *Toward a Rational Society*. London: Heinemann.

Habermas, J. (1974). *Theory and Practice*. London: Heinemann.

Habermas, J. (1976). *Legitimation Crisis*. London: Heinemann.

Hague, C. (1982). Reflections on community planning. In C. Paris (Ed.), *Critical Readings in Planning Theory*, (pp. 227–244). Oxford: Pergamon Press.

Hague, C. (1984). *The Development of Planning Thought: A Critical Perspective*. London: Hutchinson.

Hague, C. (1990). Planning and Equity in Eastern Europe: Raking Through the Rubble. *The Planner, 76(12)*, 19–21.

Hague, C. (Ed.). (2010). *Planning Education across the Commonwealth*. London: Commonwealth Secretariat.

Hague, C. (2013). *Small Towns in a Small Country: Findings from the Built Environment Forum Scotland's Small Towns Initiative*. Retrieved from the Built Environment Forum Scotland website: http://www.befs.org.uk/uploads/resources/case-studies/13.09.03-Small-Towns-Report.pdf

Hague, C., & French, W. (2010). *Urban Challenges: Scoping the State of the Commonwealth's Cities*. London: ComHabitat.

Hague, C., Hague, E., & Breitbach, C. (2011). *Regional and Local Economic Development*. Basingstoke: Palgrave Macmillan.

Hague, C., & Jenkins, P. (Eds.). (2004). *Place Identity, Participation and Planning*. London: Routledge.

Hague, C. with Malaza, N., Todes, A., & Williamson, A. (2009). Gender in Planning and Urban Development. *Commonwealth Secretariat Discussion Paper 7*. London: Commonwealth Secretariat.

Hague, C., & McCourt, A. (1974). Comprehensive Planning, Public Participation and the Public Interest. *Urban Studies, 11(2)*, 143–155. doi:10.1080/00420987420080311

Hague, C., & Prior, A. (1991). Planning in Czechoslovakia: Retrospect and Prospects. *Planning Practice and Research, 6(2)*, 19–24. doi:10.1080/02697459108722809

Hague, C., Wakely, P., Crespin, J., & Jasko, C. (2006). *Making Planning Work: A Guide to Approaches and Skills*. Rugby: Practical Action.

Hall, P. (1973). Manpower and education. In P. Cowan (Ed.), *The Future of Planning* (pp. 44–68). London: Heinemann.

Havel, V. (1975). Letter to Dr.Gustáv Husák, General Secretary of the Czechoslovak Communist Party. In J. Vladislav (Ed.), (1989). *Václav Havel: Living in Truth* (pp. 3–35). London: Faber and Faber.

Hill, M. (1968). A Goals Achievement Matrix for Evaluating Alternative Plans. *Journal of the American Institute of Planners, 34*, 19–29. doi:10.1080/01944366808977215

Jacobs, J. (1961). *The Death and Life of Great American Cities*. London: Cape and Penguin.

Konrad, G., & Szelényi, I. (1979). *The Intellectuals on the Road to Class Power: A Sociological Study of the Role of the Intelligentsia in Socialism*. Brighton: The Harvester Press.

Manchester City Council. (2014). *Introduction to the Harpurhey/Lightbowne Local Plan*. Retrieved from the website of Manchester City Council http://www.manchester.gov.uk/info/500104/north_manchester_regeneration/2878/harpurhey_lightbowne

Meyerson, M., & Banfield, E. (1955). *Politics, Planning and the Public Interest*, New York, NY: The Free Press.

Milne, R. (1975, 21 March). Planning Course Standards Face Strong Criticism. *Times Higher Education Supplement*.

Mitchell, R. B. (1961). The New Frontier in Metropolitan Planning. *Journal of the American Institute of Planners, 28*, 169–175. doi:10.1080/01944366108978451

Musil, J. (1981). *Urbanisation in Socialist Countries*. London: Croom Helm.

Pickvance, C. G. (Ed.). (1976). *Urban Sociology: Critical Essays*. London: Tavistock.

RTPI Royal Town Planning Institute. (1971). *Town Planners and Their Future*. London: Royal Town Planning Institute.

RTPI Royal Town Planning Institute. (1982). *Guidelines for Planning Schools*. London: Royal Town Planning Institute.

School of the Built Environment, Heriot-Watt University. (2005). *Diversity and Equality in Planning: A Good Practice Guide*. London: Office of the Deputy Prime Minister.

School of the Built Environment, Heriot-Watt University, Department of Geography, DePaul University, Chicago, Studio Cascades, Spokane, & Christine Platt, Durban. (2003). *Participatory Planning for Sustainable Communities: International Experience in Mediation, Negotiation and Engagement in Making Plans*. London: Office of the Deputy Prime Minister.

Schuster, G. (chairman). (1950). *Report to the Minister of Town and Country Planning of the Committee on the Qualifications of Planners*. Cmd.8059. London: His Majesty's Stationary Office.

Scottish Government. (2014). *Wide Variation in Life Expectancy between Areas in Scotland*. Retrieved from the Scottish Government website: http://news.scotland.gov.uk/News/Wide-variation-in-life-expectancy-between-areas-in-Scotland-b89.aspx

Skeffington, A. (chairman). (1969). *Report of the Committee on Public Participation in Planning*. London: Her Majesty's Stationary Office.

Sumner, C. (2010). 1945–65: The Long Road to Circular 10/65. *Reflecting Education, 6*, 90–102.

Szelényi, I. (1983). *Urban Inequalities under State Socialism*. Oxford: Oxford University Press.

Taylor, W. (1962). Social statistics and social conditions of greater Manchester. In C. F. Carter (Ed.), *Manchester and Its Region: A Survey Prepared for the British Association* (pp. 171–186). Manchester: Manchester University Press.

Turner, J. F. C. (1972). Uncontrolled urban settlement: Problems and policies. In G. Breese (Ed.), *The City in Newly Developing Countries: Readings in Urbanism and Urbanization* (pp. 507–534). Englewood Cliffs, NJ: Prentice-Hall.

UN-Habitat. (2009). *Planning Sustainable Cities: Global Report on Human Settlements 2009*. Nairobi: United Nations Human Settlements Programme; and London: Earthscan.

Webber, M. (1968). Planning in an Environment of Change, Part 1: Beyond the Industrial Age. *Town Planning Review, 39(3)*, 181–195.

240 Cliff Hague

Webber, M. (1969). Planning in an Environment of Change, Part 2: Permissive Planning. *Town Planning Review, 39(4)*, 277–295.

Willmott, P., & Young, M. (1962). *Family and Kinship in East London.* Harmondsworth: Penguin.

World Health Organisation/UNICEF Joint Monitoring Programme for Water Supply and Sanitation. (2005). *Water for Life: Making It Happen.* Retrieved from the World Health Organisation website: http://www.who.int/water_sanitation_health/monitoring/jmp2005/en/index.html

List of Abbreviations

AIDS:	Acquired Immune Deficiency Syndrome
APA:	American Planning Association
CAP:	Commonwealth Association of Planners
CDA:	Comprehensive Development Area
CHOGM:	Commonwealth Heads of Government Meeting
CIP:	Canadian Institute of Planners
ESPON:	European Spatial Planning Observation Network (2002–2007), European Observatory Network for Territorial Cohesion and Development (2008–)
INTERREG:	European Territorial Cooperation
RIG:	Radical Institute Group
RTPI:	Royal Town Planning Institute
TPI:	Town Planning Institute
UN:	United Nations
UNICEF:	United Nations Children's Fund
WUF:	World Urban Forum

Terminology Glossary

Anti-Apartheid Movement: The Anti-Apartheid Movement was a British campaigning organisation that was formed in 1960 in opposition to South Africa's practices of *apartheid*. It called for a consumer boycott of South African goods, imposition of economic sanctions, and the expulsion of South Africa from the Commonwealth (which happened in 1961). It had wide support in the Labour Party and amongst trade unions, but it was not a party political body. It dissolved in 1994.

Comprehensive Development Area: Under the UK planning legislation dating from 1947, it was possible to designate Comprehensive Development Areas which, once approved, provided central government financial support for redevelopment. A lay-out plan had to be produced for the area. Once approved by central government, the local authority would acquire land and premises within the CDA by negotiation or by compulsory purchase (called "eminent domain" in North America). Land would be cleared and rebuilding undertaken by the local authority and/or private developers.

Council housing: Public sector housing built and managed by local authorities, with subsidised rents. From 1918 until 1979 council houses were built in considerable numbers in the UK.

Interwar slum clearance estates: A change in UK housing policy in the 1930s led to lower standards of design in council housing and the prioritisation of council house tenancies for people being moved from slums. While earlier council estates had a mix of artisans and even white-collar workers, the interwar slum clearance estates were populated almost exclusively with very poor households. Typically such areas lacked social facilities and were often stigmatised, and many have remained so.

Planning assistant: The professional entry-level post in local government in the UK.

Skeffington report: An official UK study published in 1969 that set out the principles for public participation in the planning system.

Specialisms (within planning programmes): The word "specialism" carried very contentious overtones in the professional politics of planning education in the UK from the 1950s to the late 1980s.

Examples of specialisms would be fields such as urban design or regional planning. However, the term implied a postgraduate route into planning, with people who had a first degree in architecture or geography, for example, largely refining and adapting the knowledge and skills they already had. In the struggle to build a separate and distinct planning profession, independent of the established professions such as architecture or engineering, there was seen to be a need to define knowledge and skills unique to town planning and central to the delivery of planning education. A professional planner would therefore be trained on an undergraduate planning programme, as a "generalist", able to design plans for the use of land at any spatial scale.

Staff: The academic staff—"faculty" in North America.

Yearmaster: Like the architecture programmes from which they had grown, planning programmes in the UK in the 1960s (and for long after, and still today in some countries) were organised so that each student cohort had a "yearmaster", who led their studio teaching for that academic year, organised any residential study visits, sorted out administrative matters affecting the teaching and provided mentoring if necessary. There were no "yearmistresses", though eventually "year tutor" began to be used.

15

A SCIENCE OF CITIES

Prologue to a Science of Planning

Michael Batty

Origins of an Idea

During my entire academic life, I have been concerned with building symbolic representations of cities in terms of their spatial structure and dynamics while simultaneously researching planning processes conceived of as problem-solving in which such tools might be made applicable. This has meant building "models" of the phenomena and implementing them using digital technologies. In this quest, I have learned that models are abstractions, simplifications; they do not pretend to describe or simulate a world in all the detail we can imagine, but they distil the essence of that world, leaving out much that others might consider significant.

Over many years, I have gradually concluded that *powerful theory* is necessary to any quest for understanding. All the models of cities that I have dealt with have theoretical roots in rather dramatic simplifications of the spatial structure of cities, drawing on urban economics, social physics, transportation behaviour and geo-demographics. These theories and their models are based on very distinct ways in which we might manipulate and explore urban futures, ways which are transparent and have a clear but limited logic. This means that such models can be critiqued rather sharply in contrast to looser, more descriptive theory that always admits ambiguity. But at the same time, these theories and models exist in a context of *unpredictability* that has become more obvious—at least to me—during my lifetime when the notion that we can predict the future in any but the most short-term and obvious ways has come under continued scrutiny. The assumed logic of model-building is first to predict the present or the past, and if this first test is passed your model is acceptable in some minimalist sense for future predictions. But as we know, the future is unpredictable. This is a dilemma that one learns to live with, but it has profound implications.

As part of my quest to build models that inform planning, I have spent a lot of time attempting to communicate specialist knowledge. This has primarily been through *visual media*—opening the "black box" to others who are not privileged in knowledge of its workings, as well as rapidly displaying the predictions that such models provide. It is all too easy to generate predictions that are hidden away and obscured by the model, but over the last 30 years, our new technologies have become explicitly more graphical, and this has been of enormous importance in enabling one to communicate and critique their essence. My own work, however, based on developing quantitative models, is somewhat different from a good deal of what is talked of in these essays. I tend to see the city system as being somewhat separate from the planning task. Of course they merge into one another; sometimes planning is part of the problem, and there is a great kaleidoscope of possibilities in this array. If I am critical of what has happened with the planning project in these last 50 years, it is that many planners and planning theorists have forgotten the city. My view is that they must rediscover the city, for at this juncture in time there are quite remarkable changes taking place due to new technologies and changing values that are destined to change our behaviours in cities in quite fundamental ways. From my early career, when I was exposed to the systems approach, to my recent work on complexity, this has had an important influence on how we build our models, generate new theory and apply it in planning. It is a task that will never be finished, and one purpose of this essay is to convince you of its importance.

Early Life, Defining Moments: Liverpool in the 1950s

As in most personal histories, a life is often preordained yet also determined by a succession of historical accidents. I was born in Liverpool in 1945, just before the end of World War II. In the summer of 1959 my parents took me and my brother on our usual seaside holiday to Grange-over-Sands, a seaside resort north of Blackpool, where we stayed for two weeks in a guest house, sampling the delights of a usual English summer. There they struck up a friendship with a couple from Oldham whose daughter, then 17, was in the process of applying to go to university, a pretty rare event amongst my parents' family and acquaintances. We visited these friends the following autumn, and in their conversation about what their respective children should do in life, they produced a 1959 prospectus from the University of Manchester for an undergraduate course called "Town and Country Planning". Their daughter had considered this as a possibility, but in the event, she went to art school. Town and country planning, it seemed, was not quite architecture and certainly not art, but nevertheless it was design tinged with a little social science, and my dad was quite attracted to this. I remember him quite vividly saying to me, "If you became a town planner, you would always have a job." In those days, the shadows of a world war still lingered; there were many bomb sites in Liverpool that no one seemed to care about; the mass housing programme to clear the slums of an industrial past was only just gearing up; and memories of the 1930s Great Depression were still deeply entrenched in the British psyche. Being a town planner did indeed seem like something worthwhile that would lead to a "good job".

The second accident that determined what I was to do relates to our educational system: back to 1950, when I first went to primary school. Some two years into the school, aged six or seven, we were streamed into classes A, B and C on the basis, I presume, of tests in reading, writing and arithmetic. There I stayed, being "tuned up" to pass exams until the "big one", which in the British education system was the so-called 11+. This was a national examination, administered locally, taken by all children aged 11+, and on the basis of the results about 20% were "sent" to a grammar school, the rest to a secondary modern school. Grammar schools were organised around a rich diet of academic subjects, while the other schools produced young adults destined for a world of work where thinking was not a prerogative and where the intention was to fill the gap until age 15, when you could go dig coal, keep the trains running or become a shop assistant. It was a dreadful way of schooling that was quickly abolished by the socialist Labour governments of the 1960s.

So in 1956, I went to a boys-only grammar school, Quarry Bank High, where after the first year we were streamed again by abilities into classes A, B and C. At the end of the third year, at age 14, the A stream was subdivided yet again into two groups, arts and sciences. In the arts stream you would follow the classics, languages and history, and in the science stream physics, biology and chemistry. Some subjects were common, like mathematics, but the stream you were in dictated what you could then do after age 15 or 16, always assuming you passed five subjects at the national ordinary level examinations stage. At that point you entered the sixth form, where you chose three subjects that you would study in depth for two years and which would dictate entirely what you could do at university. If you had been in the arts stream all this time, then there was no way you could study science or medicine because you simply had not taken the right examinations. Of course it cut both ways. Someone who had not followed the arts stream could not do history or geography or English or French at university, largely because by age 18 you were too far adrift of the syllabuses in any area to start a university course in that subject.

This streaming into arts and science was particularly pernicious. Surely, you may ask, there were children who were good at arts *and* science? Of course there were, but it was the schoolmasters (boys-only remember, not one female teacher in the school) who determined what you would do. I found myself in the arts stream largely because I scored slightly higher marks in subjects like history and geography than physics and biology. I suspect now that there were other constraints on how many boys could actually go into one stream or another and that the mechanism was partly a blunt instrument of resource organisation. But my going into arts then dictated what I might do subsequently, and of course at age 14, I didn't have a clue. By 16, however, I did have some ideas. I first thought I might like to be a geologist, and I remember a tearful session with my parents who were told that I needed to pass physics, maths and chemistry at advanced level to get into university to read geology. I then toyed with the idea of architecture, but again I had no physics or mathematics and no art either, and that route was barred. I was however a skilled draughtsman, quite good at art too, and from my "woodworking" skills, I was one of only one or two boys in the entire school selected to follow an ordinary level course in geometrical and engineering drawing. Not quite architecture but close, and this did indicate that my school was not entirely top-down in its dictation of what its pupils should do.

In 1961 when I entered the second year of the sixth form, the last year before I took the advanced level examinations designed for that tiny proportion of the age group that had survived the rigours of the system to consider university, we were interviewed by the headmaster about where we wanted to go and what we wished to do there. By that time, my dad had planted the seed of town and country planning in my head, and I duly told the headmaster that I wanted to be a town planner. He then asked me if I knew anything about town planning, and all I could say was that it was about drawing plans! He berated me and asked, "Have you not heard of Patrick Abercrombie?" Clearly he had and although he was a teacher of German, Liverpool was a small world, and Abercrombie, deceased by then but only recently, had been a Liverpool man. I had not heard of him, of course, but I remember the headmaster's words to this day ringing in my ears: "Go away, Boy, and read something about town planning and then come back and we will discuss it!" Duly chastened, I retreated to the Liverpool Central Reference Library and retrieved Abercrombie's (1935) little book *Town and Country Planning* and devoured it. It did indeed seem to mesh with my interests, and as the headmaster subsequently said, "Town planning is alright because at least it is sufficiently academic to be worthwhile and it also lets you indulge your drawing skills."

And so that is how I chose to become a town planner, or rather how the world determined that I should become one. In the last year of the sixth form, I flirted, given the fact that I was in yet another stream one year ahead of most boys in the age group, with staying on and trying the Oxbridge examinations, but my parents did not think this was a good idea. No one had ever been to Oxford or Cambridge from my family; no one knew where these places were; no one had ever been to a university; and my dad was keen that I should move on as fast as I could. In fact, I did also flirt with doing economics at the LSE and then land economy, which seemed a bit like planning, at the College of Estate Management in London University. In the event, I only applied to one university—Manchester—to do the four-year course in town and country planning. And that is about as preordained as one can get, as I will recount in my subsequent portrayal.

To complete the picture of my growing up in Liverpool, I must say something of that marvellous city and the grammar school I went to. To get a feel of those times, you can do no better than reading Volume 1 of Mark Lewisohn's (2013) wonderful book *The Beatles—All These Years,* in which he talks about how the group was formed and what Liverpool's inner suburbs were like. Lest you do not get the message, one of the group attended my grammar school, although five years older than myself, and if I might indulge myself a little further, I will show you a picture of what the world looked like in 1957 at that boys' grammar school in England (see Figure 15.1). I will come back to this at the very end of this essay, but despite the political incorrectness and strong regimentation of the education it offered, it was a wonderful school and I have much to thank it for. Philip Norman in his 1981 book *Shout!: The Beatles in Their Generation* said: "In later years, after it had produced two Labour cabinet ministers—(Lords) William Rodgers and Peter Shore—Quarry Bank came to be nicknamed 'the Eton of the Labour Party.' " In fact many years later, under the Blair government, (Lord) Peter Goldsmith, a boy some five years below me at Quarry Bank, became attorney general, also a Labour party appointee. Lest you think that going to the same school as a Beatle is somehow rather special, John Conway, the Princeton mathematician who invented the cellular automata called the "Game of Life", was in the same class as Paul McCartney at another Liverpool grammar school, the Liverpool Institute.[1] The 11+ examination that separated and divided did lead to some interesting juxtapositions in British society, as any list of prominent people clearly reveals.[2] But let me steer back to the main story, because in 1962, having taken my advanced level subjects in history, geography and economics, I "went up" to Manchester, where I was to spend seven happy years, reaching out for many things that had been not been possible because of the educational obstacle course that dominated my early years.

FIGURE 15.1 Quarry Bank High School, Liverpool, 1957

Source: Author's archive.

Machines, Models and Metaphors: Manchester in the 1960s

One of the nice things about writing a personal history if you come from Liverpool is that it is easy to write about your own experiences with the humour of that city in mind: Liverpudlians take everything tongue in cheek. The humour is ". . . fast, dry and so often containing a black, sad undertone that strikes a chord of understanding, but without arousing pity."[3] When I applied to the University of Manchester in 1961, I was called for an interview at the department which, with architecture, was located on the first two floors of the old dental school and was duly interviewed by the professor and the senior lecturer, Roy Kantorowich and George Chadwick (author of *A Systems View of Planning,* published 10 years later). It is amazing to think that two of the key people in the department could spend their time interviewing a prospective undergraduate. I shudder to think how little time we spend now in this role, but it worked. I was impressed, if not a little intimidated.

In fact, I did not realise that the university system was so small and paternalistic that this sort of interaction was possible. There was no publish or perish culture then, no grant writing and getting, no jet-setting internationalism in crowded airports, no running around telling the world that you are the biggest and the best, no rankings; it was simply different. My dad, who had just learned to drive, actually parked the car outside the department while I went in for my interview. Like the headmaster before, they asked me what I knew about town planning and what I had read, and I duly responded—because by then I had learned my lesson and was pretty familiar with the literature (there was not that much)—that I was reading Lewis Keeble's (1959) book *Town Planning at the Crossroads.* Kantorowich and Chadwick both grinned and I wondered why, little knowing that Keeble, something of a maverick, had been a lecturer at Manchester before moving to University College not long before. When they asked me where I would live—in what hall of residence—I professed complete ignorance and simply said I would have to ask my dad. I volunteered the fact that he was outside—only if you came from Liverpool would you say that—and so they asked him in. I wonder if it is the only interview ever conducted in the Town Planning School at Manchester where father and son were both interviewed by the head of department and his deputy! I like to think so. There was time for this in the old world, and I regret that those times have passed.

So up I went to Manchester in October 1962. In the same class, I met my future wife, and we have both stuck with town planning throughout our lives. As soon as I got there, I realised that planning stood astride two very different worlds: the worlds of explanation, which were the worlds of social and physical science, and the worlds of design. In fact planning subsumed both, and there was an inevitable, indeed essential, tension in everything we did: cities versus planning and vice versa. The course was a strange mix of subject areas and ideologies. Heavily dominated by studio work, learning in Atelier-style tradition, we were treated to subjects from many different perspectives. We learned statistics and rudimentary location theory, construction and highway engineering, civic (not yet called urban) design, basic economics, property and planning law: a great profusion of subjects that we all seemed to take in quite naturally. I believe that we successfully absorbed all this because we were young and optimistic—we were not trained in anything to speak of as we were undergraduates—not geographers, not architects, not economists, not anything—and also because the studio work that occupied much of our time—probably 80% of it—was so all embracing. In fact the studio started small scale in year one, at the level of street furniture, but veered to large scale by the end of the year and then in subsequent years blended everything from urban design to regional planning across the

248 Michael Batty

urban–rural continuum. This was the great strength of our degree. It was truly absorbing and offered an environment for continual debate, discussion and experimentation.

In my first and second years, I began to learn a little about how one might study cities systematically, largely through the works of the location theorists, through urban geography and the incipient domain of regional science, but it was not until the third year that the excitement began. In the United States this was the era of mathematical models, of computer applications, of transport planning and community renewal. Cities were literally exploding through the decline of their downtowns—through decentralisation, through sprawl—and they were pervaded by fiscal crises and racial segregation. We read the writings of Lowdon Wingo Jr., Mel Webber and many others who were writing about cities and their planning in an information age. The idea of systems was coming onto the agenda, and Brian McLoughlin and George Chadwick, lecturers in the department along with Lyn Davies and Frank Medhurst, promoted a systematic, almost scientific view of how one might understand cities and thence plan them.

My subsequent mentor, George Chadwick, ran the final year of the degree. Trained originally as an engineer, then landscape architect, he introduced us all to what some of us have taken to calling over the intervening years "the science of cities" and "the science of planning" (Batty, 2013). Location theory and urban models formed the science of cities, and design methods the science of planning. The writings of Britton Harris, Walter Isard, Peter Haggett and many others were infused with design theorists such as Christopher Alexander, all set against a background of cybernetics and general systems theory. John Friedmann (writing here too) with William Alonso (1964) provided an influential source of material, and their edited treatise *Regional Development and Planning* became mandatory reading, along with the May 1965 special issue of the *Journal of the American Institute of Planners* on urban development models (Harris, 1965).

There was much else happening in the world of planning. Cities were recognisably more complex than they were hitherto, and new metropolitan agencies were being set up in Britain to deal with their longer-term planning. The Greater London Council set up in 1964 was the doyen of places for planning, and at the end of our course, the majority of the 17 students in my year who graduated set off for London, to seek "fame or fortune on streets paved with gold". The south beckoned, as it has done for the last 100 years or longer, and by the mid-1960s, London was the place to be. The US West Coast, of course, was also another haven for hippies, flower power, sun, sand and surf, but the optimism of those post-war years really came to fruition in "swinging London". Below I show a photograph of our final year group taken in a pub in Ashford in 1966 (see Figure 15.2). We were extremely close, as spending 80% of one's time in open plan studio does let you get to know others. I will come back to this, but the *boy number 1* in this and the previous photo is me and the *girl number 2* is my wife. More of this at the very end of this essay, where the defining moments of these and later years will become clearer.

I stayed in Manchester after my degree, for the department offered me the chance to do research—I was the only PhD student in the department—and George Chadwick became my advisor. In terms of my research, I was torn between researching models of cities or models of planning and decided, of course, to do both. In the course of a PhD this is an overly ambitious task, but 1966 to 1969 were the years when I filled in and learned many things that I felt I should have learned earlier—largely mathematics and statistics, and some physics, but this was quite hard outside the traditional environment of disciplined learning and scrutiny that one

A Science of Cities 249

FIGURE 15.2 Manchester University's Town and Country Planning Class of '62 in a pub in Canterbury, Kent, April 1966

Source: Author's archive.

gets in the classroom and the laboratory. I also learned to program computers, starting with Atlas Autocode where programs were submitted on paper tape. If you made an error, you had to splice the tape, punch the segment again, and stick it back into the tape. I could tell you a lot about working with computers in those days, but I do not have time. Suffice it to say that it was Brian McLoughlin's group that helped me learn about gravity models, and this led to building my first urban models in 1967, which ultimately propelled me out of Manchester and to pastures new. My work on design methods continued but my path had been set in that I would pursue both, with the science of cities eventually taking over in my later years. The science of design, however, did not lay dormant, and I worked on both until I became embroiled in the complexity theory that has dominated my work during the last 25 years. More recently with the development of geodesign and my current liaison with Carl Steinitz (2012) in UCL, design ideas have come back onto my agenda.

My telling you all this that happened half a century ago should give you some sense of why I continue to do what I do. I left Manchester because my job was ending. I had also married in early 1969, and my wife gave up her job as a planner working on Telford New Town with the John Madin Design group to move back to Manchester, and by that summer neither of us would have jobs. But as my dad so presciently predicted, if you were a town planner there would always be jobs (then, of course, not necessarily now). So despite the call to practice, I took a job in the University of Reading to work on a large grant won by Peter

250 Michael Batty

Hall (involving the development of urban models) and where my colleague Dave Foot (who had worked on shopping models in Manchester and taught me my programming skills) had been appointed a lecturer. My wife also took a job as a lecturer in planning at Oxford College of Technology, soon to be renamed Oxford Polytechnic and now Oxford Brookes University, and that is where we met an entirely new group of young planners: Andreas Faludi through Glen McDougall, Basil Dimitriou and John Glasson to Patsy Healey, two of them also making an appearance in this book.

Let me dwell a little on the wider perspective of what was happening, both to me and to planning and our understanding of cities in those years. I have written a short account of this in the book edited by Wood and Jay (2002), where I talk about the development of the systems approach during the 1960s at Manchester. Somehow, what was happening to our approaches to cities and planning during my Manchester years fitted my interests particularly well. The model of cities we adopted was primarily economic, tinged with what was called then and now social physics, which saw the city as a system of interacting parts whose mechanisms appeared to function as classical physical systems: potential, gravitation and so on. The model of planning was that of the controller, a function of intervention that was based on the cybernetic metaphor of the steersman, with cities being kept in equilibrium through course correction based on negative feedback. These models were supposed to work in tandem and would reinforce the rights and correct the wrongs that the industrial city had produced during the previous 200 years. Of course it did not take long to figure out such models were deeply flawed. Cities were never in equilibrium, contrary to many appearances. They were continually changing, a kaleidoscope of variety. The systems planning that was being introduced was, as Jane Jacobs (1961) so presciently argued, as much a part of the problem as part of the solution. The notion that cities were complex systems, built from the bottom up rather than planned from the top down, was many years in the future, and by the end of the 1960s when I left for Reading, the dominant model was the one that was articulated in the two books of my Manchester mentors, Brian McLoughlin's (1969) *Urban and Regional Planning* and George Chadwick's (1971) *A Systems View of Planning*. As a student I came in reading Lewis Keeble's (1951) *Principles and Practice of Town and Country Planning* and went out clutching McLoughlin and Chadwick's optimistic statements of where the cutting edge of planning should be.

Cutting Academic Teeth: Reading in the 1970s

When I went to Reading University in 1969, Peter Hall, head of the Department of Geography, was fast becoming a living legend. His books *World Cities* (1968) and *London 2000* (1963) were widely acclaimed, and he was hard at work on his massive treatise *The Containment of Urban England* (1973), which is the most comprehensive treatment of the impact of the post-war British planning system ever to be written. Peter, of course, has a contribution in this volume, but illness prevented his attendance at the Vienna conference where these essays were first presented. He was able to present by Skype, but he passed away while we were editing our contributions. I have recorded my debt to him in a little more detail on my blog and in various obituaries I have written,[4] but I will simply say his influence on me and our field has been enormous, and it will continue to echo down the years.[5] In 1969, I became a research assistant on a project that Peter had been successful at winning on modelling and information requirements for urban planning, which was to be anchored in applications of spatial interaction models to the Reading region.

During those years, my own models of cities occupied one side of the planning coin and rational processes of design the other, and I largely spent my 10 years at Reading pursuing both in parallel. There was an intellectual tension between the two, for urban models were much more structured and technical in focus and required a reasonable amount of mathematical and computational skill to construct, while plan-making processes were largely conceptual, but I managed to juggle both. It was during those years that I met many people who had founded the field and were still active in it. A wonderful trip to the US in May 1970—starting with Britton Harris at Penn, moving to see John Kain and Jay Forrester at Harvard-MIT, thence to Ira Lowry at RAND in LA, William Goldner and Paul Wendt in Berkeley, and finally Stu Chapin and Shirley Weiss at Chapel Hill, University of North Carolina—was a superb introduction to the scene. Combined with our close association with Alan Wilson, Doreen Massey and the group at the Centre for Environmental Studies in London, the group at Land Use and Built Form Studies in Cambridge led by Lionel March and Marcial Echenique, and the group at Liverpool around Ian Masser, I acquired a close network of scholars, many of whom are still active today. The high points of my Reading years were the succession of visitors that Peter managed to bring to the campus to present their work. Because Peter lived in London, and Reading was only 40 miles away, with the airport in between, we received a succession of international visitors. It was there that I met such hallowed luminaries as Mel Webber, John Friedmann (writing here too), many of those who were central to the development of contemporary planning thought, and quantitative geographers such as Brian Berry, Leslie Curry, Waldo Tobler and Gunnar Olsson, all of whom were deep thinkers in the field. I wrote about some of these experiences in my article for Peter's eightieth birthday-festschrift volume (Batty, 2014).

At Reading I worked on urban models, extending them in two directions: first by exploring how they could be made operational using a variety of quantitative methods and second making them temporally dynamic. The research programme I had joined at Reading provided the momentum, and although it ended after three years, my work continued when I was appointed lecturer in 1972 and began a career in teaching. I pulled together the various articles and papers I had written into my first book *Urban Modelling: Algorithms, Calibrations, Predictions* (1976), which I considered to be a very natural step in what I was doing, and at the same time I took a year's leave of absence as a visiting assistant professor in transport planning at the University of Waterloo, where there was a very productive group of engineers building urban models. In the year I spent there, 1974–5, Lionel March, who was director of Land Use and Built Form Studies in Cambridge, also took a sojourn as professor of systems design, and we engaged in many joint projects. This was my first foray into living in North America, which I was to renew some 15 years later. The relatively harsh winter climate of southern Ontario equipped me and my wife rather well for returning to that part of the world when we moved to Buffalo, New York, in 1990.

What was happening to planning thought in those days was in fact a complete re-evaluation of the technocratic model. First the experience of actually building urban models, particularly in the US, was fraught with problems. Lee (1973) in his "Requiem for Large Scale Models" painted a devastatingly bleak picture of the experience, focussing particularly on the fact that besides the inability of the model-builders to second guess the resources needed to

252 Michael Batty

build such artefacts, the models themselves and their theoretical bases were highly limited. In short our knowledge of cities and the way their problems were articulated could not easily be embraced by the quantitative models that were eventually built: The models were not very good. The gap between theory and reality was bigger than anyone had ever expected. This was beautifully articulated by Rittel and Webber (1973) in their notion that problems in planning were wicked—if you began to tackle them they would "fight back" in Piet Hein's (1969) immortal phrase, and often the solutions designed to alleviate them would actually make these problems worse.[6]

The second perspective that forced planning into a very different mode came from the social sciences. Deep structural forces in society, embedded in the very philosophy of capitalism itself, suggested that the kind of planning that had been developed was merely window dressing, that planning was completely superficial and could do little to alleviate the deep problems of inequality in contemporary societies. This came to dominate discussion. Planning theory, which had been articulated best by people like Faludi (1973) (also writing here), appeared superficial in comparison to these more profound differences, and the notion that planning was part of the problem gained ground. The focus on urban models lost its appeal, and by the end of the 1970s, the movement had virtually gone underground. Beacons still burned in isolated pockets of academia, but there was general acknowledgement that the world of cities was considerably more complicated than anyone had ever anticipated and that our theories of how cities actually worked were woefully inadequate. What had seemed like salvation in the early 1960s was regarded as disaster some 20 years later.

Running a Department, Keeping Research Alive: Cardiff in the 1980s

In 1979 I moved to Cardiff as a professor. From then until 1990, I acted as a relatively senior academic, involved in many roles from head of department to dean. The University of Wales was then composed of semi-autonomous colleges, like the old University of London, and the college in Cardiff I joined was the (University of Wales) Institute of Science and Technology (UWIST), a tiny institution with some 1,900 students and 16 departments. There were two professors in each department, 32 in all, and these composed the core of the senate, which ran the place academically. Clearly if you are one of 32, there is a degree of scrutiny that does not exist in larger places. I tell you this because at Cardiff everyone knew everyone else, and you could not avoid knowing the principal (= vice chancellor/president). As a professor one tended, in this close environment, to acquire committee jobs especially if you were absent from the senate meeting, for the principal would always recognise this and when you returned you would have acquired another job.

Anyway, I was back in a planning school, and what a planning school it was. It was a battlefield from day one. The quality of the faculty was excellent, and there is little doubt that in my Cardiff years, I was amongst a group of people who had by the far the most trenchant views about planning and cities I have ever encountered. By the time I left it was a fairly quantitative planning school, but it also had some top-class social scientists and planning theorists. In 1979, there were three groups: the positivists, the social theorists and the rest who were planners, designers, pragmatists and practitioners. The positivists were daggers drawn with the social theorists, and I found myself in the middle. The crucial issue at Cardiff was the fact that these two warring factions each contained individuals who identified more with Wales than with town planning, were Welsh by birth and language, and had come back to Wales after their education in England. Town planning was a convenient department to belong to; there was no geography, no transport and no political science in the Welsh capital's colleges, and town planning thus became a convenient base. Essentially the positivists were mathematical statisticians while the social theorists were Marxists, and the battleground was the town planning curricula.

During the first five years I was there, I continued my work on urban models but with a focus more and more on spatial analysis, and I paralleled this with work on models of the design-decision-making process. I also decided to register for a PhD. You may remember from my Manchester years that I had in fact stayed there after my undergraduate degree to do a PhD, but I had never completed it. But by 1980, a PhD was becoming more important, and although most of the faculty did not have such a degree, there was strong momentum to complete one. In fact in a British university, because there is no course work, it is easy to register for such a degree as all one has to do is write the thesis. But there was no quick route to do this. Registration was for four years part time, and because I had quite a bit of unpublished material in the area of dynamic urban models, I was able to build on this, completing the PhD in 1984. The thesis, like all such theses in those days, was then deposited in the university library and the National Library of Wales. There it remained, unread I presume, until some three years ago when I chopped up the bound typescript, scanned it on our new office copier that turned it into a PDF in 15 minutes, and then put it on my blog and made it available for all to see![7]

Another important theme that ran through my early years at Cardiff involved the journal *Environment and Planning B*. For diverse reasons, including those to do with broadening the scope of the journal to embrace systematic physical planning, I decided to join editor Lionel March as co-editor in 1981. The problem that the journal faced then and for many years thereafter was its niche market, which was tiny and growing very little. Lionel had become rector of the Royal College of Art, and he was particularly preoccupied with affairs of state there, so I attempted to put the journal back on the road by broadening the scales that it dealt with but still focussing on methods and models of the design and planning processes, rather than of the city system that was more the focus of *Environment and Planning A*. It took a long time before the journal attracted enough unsolicited submissions for it to be truly self-sustaining, and thus my role in those early years was to run it as a combination of solicited special issues and unsolicited articles. This worked rather well, and in 1985 I became editor.

My research had always been about how we might translate systematic approaches to cities and planning into its practice, and this is what I began to put my efforts into at Cardiff. To this end, I was convinced that visualisation was the way forward and in the early 1980s, with the advent of the microcomputer and accessible computer graphics based on screen memories, I decided to reskill in computer graphics, in the belief that if we could add visual interfaces, primarily in the form of maps, to urban models, we could make these visual interfaces more immediate, more interactive. My focus on graphics led me to writing a more popular book, *Microcomputer Graphics: Art, Design and Creative Modelling,* which I published in 1987. Frankly the book did not do very well, as it was badly timed, but if you look at it now, you will see the focus on new methods of mathematical rendering, namely the use of fractals, which came to dominate my research in the late 1980s. Once I had mastered some of this, I was joined in the quest by Paul Longley, who was appointed to Cardiff as a lecturer in 1984 to support my research area. Our first paper was all about fractal rendering, but we soon switched to city structures themselves, exploring their cartography, their hierarchical

254 Michael Batty

structure, and simple physical models in analogy to diffusion processes that all began to fill in the big picture as to how cities were structured. Temporal dynamics came onto the agenda, and we soon became immersed in the wider science of systems which were built from the bottom up. The idea that cities essentially evolved and grew like biological systems was in direct contrast to the top-down systems approach that conceived of cities more like machines than organisms. So by the late 1980s, some 25 years or more after being exposed to and influenced by the systems approach, I was immersed in the complexity sciences, which has dominated my research ever since.

This concern for how cities looked and my focus on computer graphics also pushed me towards cartography and geographic information systems, which were all in the air in the late 1980s. And this of course dominated my next move, but before that I should say something about the institutional context in which all this was happening. I was thrust unwittingly into being the head of department. I had by now acquired a lot of jobs in the college, and I then acquired even more. In fact these were the years when we made some very good appointments in the quantitative area, as the focus changed somewhat to people skilled in transport and GIS joining the department. But despite all this, the place was killing me. Our work on fractals and cities was going very well, but I felt I was not suited to running a department, even if it was a little less fractious than when I first went there. I decided to seek new pastures. I had been courted many times by US universities, and when Stewart Fotheringham, a kindred spirit who had spent the year 1988–9 in Cardiff as a Leverhulme Research Fellow, joined the NSF (National Science Foundation) National Center for Geographic Information and Analysis (NCGIA) at SUNY–Buffalo, he laid the groundwork for my going there a year or so later as director. I responded positively to the offer from Buffalo, and in late 1990 we made the move. In fact, I was to be joining a department and centre which had many key people in geography who had made major contributions to fractals, so Buffalo was not just about GIS, but it did fill in many of the gaps that any self-respecting quantitative geographer needed to fill. Last but not least, we knew what living in the snow belt was all about from our experiences in Waterloo some 15 years before, and we felt we could cope.

Escaping to America, Learning GIS: Buffalo in the Early 1990s

Buffalo was a breath of fresh air—forget all your prejudices about the rust belt, the snow belt, New York, America and the war in Vietnam. We arrived some six weeks before the first Iraq war broke out, when the US economy was in the deepest recession for many years due to the end of the Cold War. Yet America was and is the land of opportunity, and the NCGIA at SUNY–Buffalo, which I was to direct, was as optimistic a setup as one might imagine. It was like a return to the 1960s, reinforced by the fact that the NCGIA was a consortium of three sites in very different parts of America—in California at Santa Barbara, in rural Maine at Orono, and in Buffalo, the archetypal rust belt city but a city lying in the shadow of Toronto, the heart of prosperous Anglo-Saxon Canada. I spent a happy five years there, returning to Britain frequently—for I did not burn my bridges—and my fractals work with Paul Longley continued.

In fact, Buffalo was the place where I learned a bit of Unix and C; where I began to explore cellular automata, complexity and artificial life; and where with Paul Longley, I put together our book *Fractal Cities: A Geometry of Form and Function,* which was published in 1994. This was the culmination of eight years of research. It is my most highly cited contribution, which is somewhat amazing because Academic Press, which published it, was absorbed by Harcourt in 1996, and although the 1,500 copies of the printed book sold out quickly, they did not reprint. As a consequence, we were given the rights in the late 1990s, and we scanned the book and put it on the Web at *www.fractalcities.org*. At the time of writing (10 October 2015) there have been 21,615 downloads of all or part of the book, and our citation count is some 1,370. In fact, although we did not realise this at the time, what we were doing was establishing quite a strong link between traditional theories of cities based on urban economics and social physics and the whole issue of what cities physically looked like in terms of the size and shape. Our book, we think, still points the way for others to elaborate. The potential of this line of inquiry was recently and surprisingly lauded by the eminent urban economist Jacques Thisse (2014) in a review of my more recent book *The New Science of Cities* (Batty, 2013), which builds on those ideas on fractals that we developed some 30 years or more ago.

There is one other feature of my years in Buffalo that I need to relate. My wife, who was also trained in town planning as I noted at the onset of this essay, has always understood what I have done, and she accepted our sojourns in foreign parts with good grace. In fact at the University of Waterloo from 1974 to 1975, she studied for an MSc in systems engineering, and her thesis was published as an article in *Environment and Planning B* (Batty, 1977). In Buffalo, she took a PhD in political science and again accomplished it with ease, writing an interesting thesis on public policy and Les Halles in Paris, but in the process also working with a colleague on "Gorbachev's Strategy of Political Centrism" during the "Glasnost" period (Batty & Danilovic, 1997). Our decision to return to the UK was prompted largely by domestic concerns, but the core grant from NSF for the NCGIA was ending. I briefly flirted with Berkeley, where Peter Hall's previous job had been repackaged into a form that blended transport with urban planning. In fact at Christmas in 1994, on the way back from Buffalo, I visited Peter at his house in west London to discuss Berkeley, and he told me that a centre for GIS was being discussed in UCL. That Christmas I was wheeled in to see the UCL provost and we discussed such a centre. He decided that if the costs looked right he would pursue it and would ask me if I would like to direct it. No promises but two months later he called me and offered me the job.

Building a Science of Cities: CASA at UCL from 1995 Onwards

At UCL I had a rather different mandate from Buffalo—to build a new research centre in spatial analysis and GIS with a strong focus on cities and human settlements. This was always to be a soft money outfit, so grant-getting was the order of the day. CASA stands for Centre for Advanced Spatial Analysis, a rather precocious term for what we do, but a great acronym, and I can say this with alacrity because I did not invent the term. There was literally nothing there when I arrived in August 1995, and I have told the story many times of how UCL had no record of me on my first day, no office, no nothing, but I had a salary: There was more than a little irony in the implication that because you were at UCL what more could you ever want.

Once I got there, I took the job seriously and applied for research grants. Of course in my first year, the unthinkable happened: I applied for three research grants—quite substantial ones—and lo and behold I was successful. At the end of my first year, in mid-1996, we made our first appointments: some four research assistants (postdocs in US parlance) and two PhD students, together with our administrator, Sarah Sheppard, and myself. We were up and running. I must refrain from telling you the detail of those times, for UCL in those years was a roller coaster ride, and there are a thousand stories about winning the war and losing the peace. But the research programme that we began is more to the point in this essay. My focus on theories of cities in terms of the models that I had been building was clear enough, and a major force in our programme, but it is impossible to build a centre around urban modelling *per se,* so really four strands developed in those early years: GIS and spatial analysis; visualisation of cityscapes and 3D; the emergence of cyberspace and the information or virtual city; and urban simulation using new bottom-up type methods such as agent-based and cellular automata, which lie at the heart of complexity theory.

In those years, we went hell for leather for new forms of visualisation and new kinds of simulation, developing many of our ideas through our PhD students: David O'Sullivan, now at Berkeley; Paul Torrens, now at New York University; Naru Shiode, now at King's College; and Muki Haklay, still at UCL. Martin Dodge, one of our first research assistants, and Andy Hudson-Smith, our graphics and visualisation whizz-kid, were also part of that group. They are all professors now, and I am proud to have been associated with this brilliant cohort of graduate students, who have gone on to do great things in fashioning a science of cities. David O'Sullivan's path-breaking book *Spatial Simulation* (2013), Paul Torrens's (2004) book *Geo-Simulation,* Muki Haklay's edited collection (2010) *Interacting with Geospatial Technologies,* and Martin Dodge's two major books, *Mapping Cyberspace* (2000) and *Atlas of Cyberspace* (2002) reflected those remarkable times in the early days of CASA. We have had spin-offs from CASA too. Mark Thurstain-Goodwin, who ran our town centres project, founded GeoFutures (www.geofutures.com). Intelligent Space, run by Jake Desyllas, was another spin-off in pedestrian modelling eventually acquired by Atkins, and even Open Street Map is a kind of CASA spin-off in that its founder, Steve Coast, was our part-time systems administrator running our Unix systems. Latterly a new company focussed on urban modelling, called Prospective Labs, involving myself and Alan Wilson, has been spun-off to apply our urban simulation work.

In 2000 I convinced the provost to hire Paul Longley, my erstwhile colleague at Cardiff, to come to UCL, where he became deputy director of CASA. He built up our PhD programme from its early roots and also put the geo-demographics area on a good footing. In 2003, we published an edited collection of CASA's work, *Advanced Spatial Analysis: The CASA Book of GIS,* which paraded our wares in that everyone who wrote in the book was a member or ex-member of CASA, as a postdoc or PhD or faculty. In those years, I personally began to put together my thoughts on complexity, and in 2005, I published my fourth book, *Cities and Complexity: Understanding Cities with Cellular Automata, Agent-Based Models, and Fractals,* which drew together many of these thoughts and set the direction for our more recent research.

The Next 50 Years: When Worlds Collide

Fifty years has passed since I first entered the planning school in the University of Manchester, and although my first thoughts about town planning were both radically different and remarkably resonant with the ideas I now hold, I think we understand cities a little better than the rudimentary knowledge we had half a century ago. I am encouraged too by the fact that at long last there does seem to be a sustained effort underway to ground our knowledge in more systematic ways of seeking generalisations about cities in terms of their physical form. At the same time, we are recognising that what I and others have called here "A Science of Cities" is one of many such sciences, many perspectives, many paradigms that both compete and complement one another in providing a more substantial base for thinking about cities than we have ever had before (Batty, 2013).

In all of this, I must return to the role of planning thought and theory. Planning has changed in the way it has been articulated as theory, and once again complexity theory holds the key to my own interpretations. I see this as a switch from thinking of cities and their planning as top-down to bottom-up activity, and this is quite consistent with planning's current focus on communicative dialogues, which tend to see the planning system as blending with community concerns through a process of negotiation. On this path, planning has also indulged itself with notions about how the large-scale structural issues that dominate our society determine local action and how the political economy of the city and the state influence what we are able to do, defining the problems that we feel able to tackle and often the way we might tackle them. Complexity theory, to me, has much to say about these matters, and of late planning theorists writing in this volume have embraced this perspective too (Healey, 2006; Innes & Booher, 2010).

My current thoughts about the next 50 years relate to the way information technologies are permeating the city and modern life. Computers will eventually enter every facet of life, and whatever can be computable will be so. This notion of the universal machine has always seemed mysterious to me, but each additional wave of new IT always takes us by surprise. It is obvious in hindsight that once we had the right kinds of sensors linked to computers, data from every place where sensors could be located would be streamed in real time, generating what is currently called "big data". The notion that we can get city data in real time is also shortening the time horizons over which we think about the future in cities. The challenge here is to make sense of how these information technologies are changing our world and to anticipate such change.

So, to finish on some personal recollections. Twenty-three years after I first went to the grammar school shown in the first photograph at the beginning of this essay, the boy identified as *number 1* (me) took the girl identified as *number 2* (my wife) to visit the girl identified as *number 3* (Linda) in the second photograph, who was then living in New York City near the Rockefeller Center. Linda had moved to the US in 1968 after meeting an American who carried her case across Piccadilly Circus and who was doing a master's in international relations at the LSE. They went to Wharton, where I met them on my first trip to America in 1970, but they had long ago split up, and Linda was by then running a prosperous real estate company in Manhattan. We were on our way to Toronto, where I was editing a book with Bruce Hutchinson from my Waterloo days. In the late evening of 8 December 1980, about the time we left Linda's apartment, the boy identified as *number 4* in the 1957 school photograph was shot dead at point blank range outside the Dakota Building in Central Park West, a mile or so away. For a day or so the world wobbled on its axis, and the coincidence of being in Manhattan when this happened and being at school with him has lived with me forever. To conclude I can do no better than point you to some lines from his song "Imagine," which became the most popular song of the twentieth century. If you go to this Web link you can find the song and indeed the music: http://www.oldielyrics.com/lyrics/john_lennon/imagine.html. It is full of the hope not only for ourselves but in particular for its messages about how we confront the planning project and a science of cities that I and others have tried to echo through these pages. Enjoy!

258 Michael Batty

Notes

1 http://www.nytimes.com/1993/10/12/science/scientist-at-work-john-h-conway-at-home-in-the-elusive-world-of-mathematics.html
2 http://en.wikipedia.org/wiki/Calderstones_School
3 *The Hitchhikers Guide to the Galaxy*, http://h2g2.com/edited_entry/A280892
4 http://epb.sagepub.com/content/41/5/761.short
5 http://www.spatialcomplexity.info/archives/2163
6 As Piet Hein (1969) said: "Problems worthy of attack, prove their worth by fighting back."
7 http://www.spatialcomplexity.info/archives/747; the thesis has been tweeted (not read) seven times!

References

Abercrombie, P. (1935). *Town and Country Planning*. London: Hutchinson University Library.

Batty, M. (1976). *Urban Modelling*. Cambridge: Cambridge University Press.

Batty, M. (1987). *Microcomputer Graphics*. London: Chapman and Hall.

Batty, M. (2005). *Cities and Complexity*. Cambridge, MA: The MIT Press.

Batty, M. (2013). *The New Science of Cities*. Cambridge, MA: The MIT Press.

Batty, M. (2014). Great Planning Disasters. In M. Tewdwr-Jones, N. Phelps & R. Freestone (Eds.), *The Planning Imagination: Peter Hall and the Study of Urban and Regional Planning* (pp. 28–39). London: Routledge.

Batty, M., & Longley, P. A. (1994). *Fractal Cities*. San Diego, CA: Academic Press. www.fractalcities.org.

Batty, S. E. (1977). Game-theoretic Approaches to Urban Planning and Design. *Environment and Planning B*, *4*, 211–239.

Batty, S. E., & Danilovic, V. (1997). Gorbachev's Strategy of Political Centrism: A Game-Theoretical Interpretation. *Journal of Theoretical Politics*, *9*, 89–106.

Benenson, I., & Torrens, P. M. (2004). *GeoSimulation*. Chichester: John Wiley.

Chadwick, G. F. (1971). *A Systems View of Planning*. Oxford: Pergamon Press.

Dodge, M., & Kitchin, R. (2000). *Mapping Cyberspace*. London: Routledge.

Dodge, M., & Kitchin, R. (2002). *Atlas of Cyberspace*. London: Addison-Wesley.

Faludi, A. (1973). *Planning Theory*. Oxford: Pergamon Press.

Friedman, J., & Alonso, W. (Eds.). (1964). *Regional Development and Planning*. Cambridge, MA: The MIT Press.

Haklay, M. (Ed.). (2010). *Interacting with Geospatial Technologies*. Chichester: John Wiley.

Hall, P. (1963). *London 2000*. London: Faber and Faber.

Hall, P. (1968). *World Cities*. London: Weidenfeld and Nicholson.

Hall, P., Gracey, H., Drewett, R., & Thomas, R. (1973). *The Containment of Urban England*. London: Allen and Unwin.

Harris, B. (Ed.). (1965). Urban Development Models: New Tools for Planning. *Journal of the American Institute of Planners*, *31*, 90–171.

Healey, P. (2006). *Urban Complexity and Spatial Strategies*. London: Routledge.

Hein, P. (1969). *Grooks 1*. New York, NY: Doubleday.

Innes, J. E., & Booher, D. (2010). *Planning with Complexity*. New York, NY: Routledge.

Jacobs, J. (1961). *The Death and Life of the Great American City*. New York, NY: Random House.

Keeble, L. (1951). *Principles and Practice of Town and Country Planning*. London: Estates Gazette.

Keeble, L. (1959). *Town Planning at the Crossroads*. London: Estates Gazette.

Lee, D. B. (1973). Requiem for Large Scale Models. *Journal of the American Institute of Planners*, *39*, 163–178.

Lewisohn, M. (2013). *The Beatles—All These Years*. London: Little Brown.

Longley, P. A., & Batty, M. (Eds.). (2003). *Advanced Spatial Analysis*. Redlands, CA: ESRI Press.

McLoughlin, J. B. (1969). *Urban and Regional Planning*. London: Faber and Faber.

Norman, P. (1981). *Shout!: The Beatles in Their Generation*. London: Touchstone Books.

O'Sullivan, D., & Perry, G. (2013). *Spatial Simulation*. Chichester: John Wiley.

Rittel, H. W. J., & Webber, M. M. (1973). Dilemmas in a General Theory of Planning. *Policy Sciences*, *4*, 155–169.

Steinitz, C. (2012). *A Framework for Geodesign*. Redlands, CA: ESRI Press.

Thisse, J. F. (2014). The New Science of Cities by Michael Batty: The Opinion of an Economist. *Journal of Economic Literature*, *52*, 805–819.

Wood, C., & Jay, S. (2002). *Reflections of 50 Years of the Manchester School of Planning and Landscape, 1952–2002*. Manchester: University of Manchester.

List of Abbreviations

CASA:	Centre for Advanced Spatial Analysis
GIS:	Geographic Information Systems
LSE:	London School of Economics
NCGIA:	National Center for Geographic Information and Analysis
NSF:	National Science Foundation
RAND:	Research and National Development (Corporation)
SUNY–Buffalo:	State University of New York (at Buffalo)
UCL:	University College London
UWIST:	University of Wales Institute of Science and Technology (Now University of Cardiff)

Terminology Glossary

Advanced Level Examination: A British examination taken at age 17–18, which determines which higher education institution a pupil will qualify for.

Atlas Autocode: An early computer language that was succeeded by Algol, Pascal and later object-oriented languages.

11+: A British examination which was held nationally for schoolchildren aged 11–12 to sort them into schools designed to emphasise intellectual or practical abilities.

Faculty: A colloquial term used to collectively characterise academic staff in a British university including research assistants, research fellows, lecturers, senior lecturers, readers and professors, in contrast to its formal usage in a US university where faculty are teaching members of the academic staff.

Geodesign: A structured process of physical landscape, urban design and/or regional planning informed by geographic information systems (GIS) technologies.

Grammar School: British schools for pupils passing the 11+, who were judged intellectually more able. The system was in place across the UK until 1964.

Ordinary Level Examination: A British examination taken at age 15–16 that determined whether or not a pupil will progress to study three subjects in their last two years of high school (now replaced by GCSEs [Certificate of Secondary Education]).

Principal, Provost, Rector: All terms for the equivalent of vice chancellor in a British university (equivalent to president and provost all rolled into one position in an American university).

Secondary Modern School: British schools for pupils not passing the 11+, who were judged intellectually less able.

16

PLANNERS' BEACON, COMPASS AND SCALE

Linking Planning Theory, Implementation Analysis and Planning Law

Rachelle Alterman

The invitation to contribute to this volume has given each of us, "The Chosen 16", the rare opportunity to reflect rigorously on the evolution of our own thinking as part of broader global trends. Our thoughts will not remain as reminiscences recounted to a group of respectful students visiting elderly scholars at the fireside. For me, this opportunity comes many years before I plan to retire.

My personal and academic worlds are hybrids of continents and cultures spanning both sides of the Atlantic. My childhood years were spent in Israel, my family and academic home today. From the age of 12 to 24 I lived in Canada, first with my parents (diplomat father) and later with my husband. I have spent several interspersed years in US planning and law schools. European culture and planning education are also very familiar to me. During my childhood in Israel I was immersed in European languages, culture and cuisine brought by my parents' friends—Jewish refugees from Europe. I am deeply involved in European planning education and research collaboration.

Much of my scholarly endeavour has aimed at creating a bridge between planning thought in North America and Europe, and lately also between the advanced economies and developing countries. The Israel of my childhood was a poor, developing country. Many of my parents' friends were newly arrived survivors of the Holocaust or Jewish refugees from Arab countries. They were penniless and were housed at first in tent camps. Luckily, my parents were among the small number of young people who decided to emigrate from Poland on time, pre–World War II. I did not experience deprivation directly, except for food rationing. But these memories have helped me understand some of the challenges facing developing countries.

What have I learned from the exercise of delving inwards? I now realise that three seemingly unconnected themes have been intertwined in my work: *planning theory, implementation analysis* and *planning law.* I picture them as the *beacon*, the *compass* and the *scale*. Planning theory is the beacon because it provides planners with the normative-ethical light, with a sense of public mission. Implementation analysis is the compass because it offers realistic directions that planners should take in order to achieve their missions. Planning law is the scale—the proverbial symbol of justice. It helps planners to balance contending goals and interests. However, what is considered appropriate or just also differs from country to country. So I have adopted the powerful perspective of *cross-national comparison* to provide an additional sense of scale. The connections among these ingredients are the backbone of this chapter. Interspersed are chronological accounts of my roles as a student, planning educator, builder of new academic institutions, and a researcher with a resolve to transfer knowledge across continents and disciplines.

Throughout this journey, being a female student and academic was a pervasive fact, so I shall begin with that story.

A Female Planning Student in Canada

In 1968 I was the only woman among 12 students in my class in the Department of City Planning at the University of Manitoba. Although the department was not new, the only previous female student had enrolled a year earlier. In the large Engineering Faculty, where my husband was a student, there was only one female student—the first since World War II. The Faculty of Law had only two female students. Female students were not allowed to wear trousers, even in Winnipeg's −30°C weather! Here is another story: I may have missed being Bill Clinton's classmate in Cambridge, UK! Were it not for the males-only rule of the Rhodes Scholarship at the time, I would probably have been nominated as the Manitoba Rhodes Scholar in the same year as Bill Clinton. A male friend of mine won the award, with the second-highest grades.

Canada at the time was very gender-unequal. The national TV and newspapers had no female reporters beyond fashion and home. During my undergraduate studies, I was the only married woman in the entire College of Social Science. It's not that I married unusually early (20 was common then), but that female students rarely continued their studies after marriage. Whenever my name would be called out, the "Mrs" would reverberate throughout the halls. The title Mrs had always agitated me. Why should women have to carry their marital status in public, while men's remains as their private domain? The Feminist Movement's Ms was a linguistic invention with deep implications.

My husband and I may have been different because Israel at the time had better gender-equality norms than the USA or Canada. In my childhood, I had many more professional female role models than as a teenager in Canada. When Betty Friedan's seminal book *The Feminine Mystique* reached Winnipeg in 1969, my husband and I read it together. It helped us understand the rationale for what we were practising instinctively.

Despite the gender challenges, being a student in Manitoba provided excellent grounding for my love of planning.

The Beacon: Planning Theory

I first realised that planning theory was my beacon in July 1969, during a working visit to subarctic Churchill in northern Manitoba. This was the "summer" in that desolate town. I flew there from Winnipeg as part of my student job as a planner with the Manitoba branch of the Canadian federal government's Public Works Department. I was then a graduate student in the City Planning Department at the University of Manitoba.

My task was to propose urban planning policy for the town's future, after the army base was phased out. Churchill's population was composed of army personnel and their families, civilians employed in government or commercial services, and an isolated tribe of Northern Indians (as they were called then). Having studied sociology in my BA honours degree, I recognised that the tribe was in a state of severe social and health breakdown. My written report to the federal government went well beyond the official mandate and added unconventional recommendations to help improve the state of the Indians within the town's fabric.

Baffled by the dilemmas embedded in my first real-life planning task, I decided to devote my master's thesis to making sense of them. I looked to the then-nascent field of planning theory to be my beacon. Unlike "regular" theories, which search for explanations for external phenomena, planning theory is mostly inward-looking (as explained in Friedmann, 2017). My journey across cultures and continents may have stimulated and influenced my view of planning theory and education.

Studying Planning Theory during the Field's Early Years

Even back in 1968–70, when I took my Master in City Planning degree in Manitoba, planning theory offered me powerful lenses for analysing the gap between the ostensibly technical task I had been assigned in Churchill and the complex conflicts I discovered even in such a small town. The analysis culminated in my first academic paper, "The Ubiquity of Values in Planning" (Alterman & Page, 1973). We argued that the value conflicts that played out in Churchill were embedded in four dimensions: the planner's own culture, language, knowledge and personality; the planning profession's inherent conflicts between the "scientific method" and "ideology and ethics"; the employers' values; and the interests and worldviews of the various "client" groups. Value conflicts occurred within each of these dimensions and across them. If this model seems somewhat naïve today, it's because planning theory has made much headway.

My thesis advisor and co-author was Father Dr John Page—a Jesuit priest and rector of the Jesuit College at the University of Manitoba. Unfortunately, he did not publish much and passed away in midlife, but he taught me the importance of recognising the deep philosophical grounding of planning thought. Dr Page, who had earned his PhD from the University of Pennsylvania's path-breaking planning school, introduced an up-to-date planning theory course to the planning programme at the University of Manitoba. His own teachers and colleagues at Penn included Britton Harris, Martin Meyerson, Paul Davidoff, Tom Reiner, Ann Strong, Seymour Mandelbaum and other giants in American planning thought. Meyerson and Banfield's 1955 book, *Politics, Planning and the Public Interest,* which was already a classic, opened my eyes to the role of politics in defining the elusive "public interest".

Almost all the authors we read in OUR planning theory class and those I read for my thesis were Americans. A few years after I graduated from planning school, a young European scholar—Andreas Faludi (a colleague in this volume)—assembled the writings of the leading American authors in his *Reader in Planning Theory* (1973). He thus played a major role in framing planning theory and facilitating its journey across the Atlantic.

Over the years, I have come to know most of the American theorists personally and benefitted from their advice. Interestingly, Canadian planning education at the time was not greatly influenced by British scholarship, despite the Commonwealth affiliation. Nor did World War II resonate much in our readings, unlike the accounts of the European authors in this volume.

One day in 1968, Paul Davidoff visited Dr Page and our planning theory class. He had a "Davidoff for Congress" pin on his jacket. He spoke with the passion of a secular missionary, telling us that if planners wish to influence, they should not shun politics (he was not elected). We had all read Davidoff's 1965 paper "Advocacy and Pluralism in Planning"—a paper that reflected his legal training. That paper is still the most-read in American schools (Klosterman, 2011) and also a classic outside the USA. In later years, when I met Davidoff at conferences in the USA, I told him he may have been the subliminal role model in my decision to study law, but he died in midlife before I had made much headway in my quest to link planning theory and law.

Back in Israel—A Woman in the Academy

Despite attractive offers in Canada and the USA, in 1970 my husband and I decided to return to Israel. I felt that as a planner I could have greater impact in a small country undergoing rapid change. I registered for a PhD in planning at the Technion—Israel's oldest university (established pre-State in 1924), with high international prestige and very high expectations of its faculty and students. The Faculty of Architecture and Town Planning was as old as the Technion.

Upon our return to Israel, we realised that gender equality, though better than in Canada or the USA at the time, still had far to go. While the proportion of female students in architecture was higher than in the USA and Canada, the percentage of female faculty members was very low in the entire university. When I was about to graduate with my PhD in 1976 and expressed interest in academia, one of the full professors—all male architects—said to me bluntly: "We don't need any women here." Without the backing of my mentor, Morris Hill, who was an all-through humanist, I would have had little chance of getting an academic position.

In 1972 a small group of female graduate students and young academics, led by an American doctoral student from Haifa University, founded the first feminist group in Israel. The group pioneered institutional and legal changes that became models for other cities and the nation. I was responsible for the newsletters and media. Being known as a feminist was not always pleasant, but both my academic advisor and my husband shared the egalitarian norms. In 1973, Shulamit Aloni—Israel's clearest voice for gender equality and a Member of the Knesset, the Israeli Parliament—decided to form her own party. With no organization or resources, she turned to our small feminist group to assemble the required signatures for forming a new party. We approached passersby on city streets, and despite some derisive comments, managed to get the necessary number of signatures. The RATZ Party (later MEREZ) was formed. The elections were delayed because of the terrible October 1973 war. In the 1974 elections RATZ spearheaded the issue of the occupied areas and became Israel's major peace party. Before the 1988 elections, Aloni asked me to join her slate for the Knesset. I agreed at first, following Davidoff's steps, but soon realized that planning education and research, not party politics, were my calling.

Many years later, in 1994, after I became the first female full professor ever appointed in the Faculty of Architecture and Town Planning, I resumed feminist activity, this time as the advisor to the Technion president on the status of women. I served in this post for a full decade. The Technion became a national model for path-breaking policies for gender equality in Israeli academia, and other universities followed our model. I asked a Technion female statistician to develop a model to test whether there were signs of possible discrimination towards female faculty in the length of time for promotion from rank to tank. Guess what . . . ?

264 Rachelle Alterman

Things are very different at the Technion today. Recruiting more female faculty has become a declared objective. There are dedicated scholarships for female faculty members to go for postdocs abroad—a requirement in Israeli universities.

Teaching and Researching Planning Theory and Public Participation

The Graduate Program in Urban and Regional Planning was a programme under construction. It was established in 1969 by Morris Hill. He too was a Penn graduate and, by coincidence, Dr Page's classmate. Hill, known best for his Goals Achievement Matrix (Hill, 1968), ensured that planning theory would be a core course.

The Technion's planning programme was Israel's first. As in most other countries at the time, Israeli architects or civil engineers considered their professions as encompassing urban planning. During the programme's formative years, students lacked role models of what planners could do as planning practitioners. I saw that my mission in the planning theory course was even more crucial than in countries where the profession was well established, and I sought a way of measuring the evolution of the students' conceptions of planners' roles. I then came across Howe and Kaufman's (1979; Howe, 1980) questionnaires about American planners' roles and ethics, scaled from "technically oriented" to "politically oriented". I adjusted the scenarios in the questionnaires to the Israeli context and applied them every year. In the 1980s, the Israeli class average leaned to the "technical" side. But over the years, the average moved more to the "political" side, reflecting the deep-seated changes that occurred both in Israeli society and in planners' roles as change agents.

Wishing to stimulate change in the norms of governance prevalent in Israel back then, I developed Israel's first course in public participation. My aim was to couple the "beacon" view that sees participation as an ethical call, and the "compass" perspective that seeks effective change. To accompany the course, I developed a conceptual framework for designing alternative modes of public participation, with an eye to implementation in a variety of contexts (Alterman, 1982). Colleagues and I wrote Israel's first *Guide to Public Participation in Planning* (Alterman, Churchman & Law Yone, 1981). This guide became popular among planners and NGOs. Gradually, we helped to create participation norms in government agencies. On the research front, Morris Hill, a graduate student and I analysed the degree to which public participation actually impacts the decisions of planning bodies. We chose to analyse the UK because the official rules about public participation had already been institutionalised there. We discovered influence, but to a modest degree (Alterman, Harris & Hill, 1984).

I would like to share my thoughts about language of publication—a burden often felt by academics who don't happen to live in one of the few English-speaking countries. My university, like many elite universities around the globe, bases its hiring and promotion criteria on international academic publications. Early on I decided that if I wanted to be relevant to local decision makers and the general public, I should be willing to do "extracurricular" work and publish in Hebrew as well. Many of the 60 books, papers and reports published in Hebrew have indeed had direct impacts—a nice reward for the difficulties of being an academic in a tiny country with its own unique language.

In 1981–2 I took my first sabbatical year and, with my husband and our two kids, went to the University of North Carolina in Chapel Hill. Ed Kaiser, Raymond Burby and David

Godschalk were my eminent seniors. I co-taught planning theory and what may have been the first course on comparative land-use planning.

Planning versus Policy Analysis

By that time, I was acquainted with the British legacy of planning education and practice. I was concerned about the strong trend whereby many American planning schools—unlike their European counterparts—were emulating the fast-growing field of public policy studies. My concern was that planning would lose its anchor in land, thus leaving a vacuum. The professions from which planning broke away would step back in, thereby rolling back essential achievements of planning research and practice.

So I sought out Professor Duncan MacRae, an eminent scholar from Chapel Hill's Public Policy School. Our introspection of our respective fields produced the paper "Planning and Policy Analysis: Converging or Diverging Trends?" (Alterman & MacRae, 1983). I am told that the Planning Accreditation Board, which assesses planning schools in the USA, found this analysis useful. Perhaps we contributed something to planning education in the USA by curtailing the trend of becoming too "footloose" and generic and abandoning its unique spatial understanding.

Communicative Planning and Language

A decade later, my students and I were inspired by the remarkable turns in planning theory towards communicative, deliberative and collaborative planning (Innes, 1995; Healey, 1997; Forester, 1999). I was especially tantalised by the attention given to the use of language in planning communication. Tamy Stav and I employed concepts derived from linguistics to analyse, quantitatively, the language of selected American and UK plans. We assessed the degree to which the words and syntax conveyed public openness. In another study, we developed scales to evaluate the language of Israeli government plans when addressing the land issues of the Arab or Druze citizens of the State of Israel (excluding the occupied areas). The findings about this highly contested issue showed a trend of rising fairness over time in the government argumentation (Alterman & Stav, 2001). A colleague and I are currently studying modes of communication in legally mandated public hearings in Israel, the UK and the Netherlands. Seemingly minute variations make a great difference in practice.

Planning Theory and Situations of Crisis

Sometimes, research topics just come our way. I had never intended to study the role of planning theory in times of crisis. In 1990, a once-in-an-academic's-lifetime challenge came my way. I received a phone call from a national planning administration official who said: "You teach planning theory, don't you? Do you know what approach we may use to handle the unprecedented crisis on our hands?" Israel was experiencing a totally unanticipated wave of immigrants from the collapsing Soviet Union—penniless, of all ages and health conditions. The expectation was that the existing population of 4.7 million was to absorb 1.5 to 2 million new immigrants within three years, starting immediately. I had no idea how to respond. None of the planning theories I had been teaching had any answers.

Nevertheless, I agreed to serve on several Israeli national and professional decision bodies which were quickly established. The Israel of 1990 was no longer the developing country of the '50s. Government bodies were looking for strategies that could avoid mass housing shortages and social upheaval. In a small country, I was able to be a participant-observer in major decision bodies, but I needed time and distance to digest what I experienced.

In 1992–3, while on sabbatical at the University of Wisconsin, Madison, I sat back to analyse the large box of government reports which I had taken along. I also searched the literature in planning, public policy and corporate management for theories to guide decisions in similar crisis situations. The literature on disasters was unsuited to what I called a "positive crisis". About to give up, I came across Karen Christensen's modest paper (1985). She offered insight into how charismatic political leaders can reframe a crisis situation into a less imposing problem and channel other decisions around it. This shed light on how the crisis in Israel was indeed managed to a reasonable degree. My analysis was first published as an article (Alterman, 1995) and later as a book, *Planning in the Face of Crisis* (Alterman, 2002).

Although my research focus today is more in the direction of planning law and land policy (discussed later), my interest in planning theory has not subsided. While pursuing international comparative research, I have had opportunities to observe planning education in more parts of the world. Planning theory as we know it is by no means a universal component of planning education. A paper on the transferability of planning theory is still on my "to write" list.

The Evolution of Planning Education and the Profession

Perhaps because I chose to live in a country where planning education was not yet well established, I became keenly aware of the difficulties facing planning education and the profession in various parts of the world.

The Hybrid Model of Planning Education

Planning is a relatively new profession, one that Donald Schon (1983, p. 23) classified as among the "minor professions". Planning first became recognised as independent from architecture in Britain in the 1930s and initially made its way only among English-speaking countries. In many countries, planning has not yet established its independent educational and professional turf. Other professionals carry out planning work. Their identity varies across the world, reflecting very different traditions (Alterman, 1992).

Looking back at my education in Manitoba, I realise that the planning degree already had a relatively long history, having been accredited in 1952, among the first four schools in Canada.[1] The planning profession too was already well established through the Town Planning Institute of Canada, founded in 1919, only five years after its globally pioneering parent—the British (today Royal) Town Planning Institute.

The planning education I received at Manitoba was a hybrid between the older physical planning, design-oriented model and the newer social science model that had already been adopted by leading American planning schools. The European authors in this volume also note their experiences with this transition. This hybrid model later enabled me to help in phasing in planning education in Israel. I was also able to understand different modes of planning education in other parts of the world, where the social science model is not yet dominant.

The transition mode in Manitoba also applied to student admission. Unlike leading planning schools in the USA, in Manitoba the first student with a social science degree was admitted only in 1967, the year before I enrolled. In my class I was the only student with such a background. In order to enter the MCP programme, candidates like me were required to complete an additional year beyond their BA degree (pre-master's BA honours). But once admitted, a student with background such as mine received excellent training in physical planning too.

The Uphill Battle to Establish Planning Education and the Profession in Israel

The establishment of planning education in Israel turned out to be a much rougher ride than I had expected. As a PhD student-teacher and later a young academic I became involved in an intense professional "turf war", which is not over to this day.

The nascent planning programme at the Technion, established in 1969, was (and still is) located in the Faculty of Architecture and Town Planning. However, the term "town planning", as the school had been named since its foundation in 1924, was not intended to mean more than urban design. The faculty members—all architects—never intended to offer a planning degree.

The story of how planning was introduced into the Technion after all is almost incredible. In 1968 the faculty members in Architecture had a severe internal ideological dispute between two contending views of architectural concepts. The university imposed an external dean. At this fortuitous time, Morris Hill, who had just arrived from the USA, approached the new dean with the idea of introducing US-style planning education. The Technion's leadership saw this as an opportunity to introduce a group of "unaffiliated" faculty members to help quell the feud. I arrived as a PhD student in 1970, at the same time as three newly recruited faculty members in planning—all with PhDs from US planning schools.

Since then, the small Graduate Program in Urban and Regional Planning has flourished academically. Gradually, colleagues in architecture have come to recognize planning as a field and to cooperate in interdisciplinary teaching and research. However, the Israeli professional architects' association is no less adamant today that the "real" planners are architects. They express their opposition in the legal arena, the workplace and the media.

I was convinced early on that as a planning educator I had a duty to help create the planning profession beyond the university. I could not tolerate the disparity between the high-grade professional education we were offering and the hurdles the graduates were encountering in exercising their profession. So I became active in the nascent Israel Planners' Association, served as its deputy head, and spoke up for planning in many public and professional forums. In retrospect, I realise that I was risking my chances of tenure; all the senior faculty were still architects.

In 1995, while providing pro bono advice to the Knesset regarding a proposed amendment to the planning law, I succeeded in "sneaking in" a modest but landmark change regarding membership of the various public planning committees. Where the law had previously called for "architect or engineer", now anyone with an "urban and regional planning education" would also be eligible. For the first time in the long history of planning legislation in Israel (dating to pre-State years), the term "urban and regional planner" finally appeared in the legislation. However, these changes pertain to public service positions, often unpaid.

268 Rachelle Alterman

Since then, the architects have successfully blocked all attempts at further legislative progress. For example, in 2012 they resisted my proposal to update the antiquated legal title "chief municipal engineer" to "planner" to reflect the fact that the role is mostly urban planning. Opposing the mere change in language, they argued that some future legislation might go further and open up this position to non-architect planners.

Despite the hurdles, our graduates' excellence and commitment have won them wide recognition and demand in the marketplace. Today they hold key planning positions in government, private and NGO sectors—all but those positions still closed to them by law. The Israel Planners' Association too has come of age.

I assume that the rather bumpy road travelled in the formation of the Israeli planning profession is not unique globally.

Milestones in the Globalisation of Planning Education and Research

Fully matured academic fields have a global community of peers. The planning academy is not yet there, but it is making significant progress. I was fortunate to be able to witness first hand the major milestones in the gradual, and still ongoing, internationalisation of the planning academy. This has meant a lot to me in my own research and teaching.

In the autumn of 1981 in Washington DC, ACSP, the Association of Collegiate Schools of Planning (USA), launched its first conference held independently of the American Planning Association. I was probably the only non–North American present. ACSP was the first large-scale continental association of planning schools in the world. At that time, planning academia was still very much nationally based, and to some extent it still is. However, to a modest extent, ACSP was already somewhat transnational from the start because it enabled overseas schools to become "corresponding members". I registered the Technion as the first corresponding school. The conference proved to be a major milestone not only in the evolution of planning academia in the USA but also internationally.

In 1987, a group of leading European academics in planning (several of whom are also participants in this book) founded AESOP, the Association of European Schools of Planning. Klaus Kunzmann, AESOP's first president, recounts how he and Patsy Healey—the association's founding mother—came to the idea of forming a European continental association to parallel ACSP.[2] However, the idea of forming AESOP was much more than a second continental association emulating ACSP. I regard it as the most significant milestone in the formation of a global planning academy.

Unlike ACSP, AESOP constituted the first large multicultural and multilingual forum where planning academics would be able to exchange knowledge. English was the common language. To me, this event marked the real maturation of our field and its release from the national umbilical cords that held it back from becoming a globally relevant field of knowledge. I travelled from Israel to attend the inaugural ceremony in Amsterdam.

Over the years I observed how planning academics from different countries, who at first had little common ground, gradually began to share knowledge. I witnessed how the level of academic exchange rose year by year, levelling out initial disparities, especially between academics from the British Isles and those from the Continent. A vibrant intellectual community was emerging.

I gradually became "addicted" to the AESOP conference, and I have never missed a single one (including joint ACSP-AESOP and global meetings). AESOP's openness offered me the opportunity to initiate the Planning and Law Track, later to become the International Academic Association on Planning, Law and Property Rights, whose story I shall recount later.

I was surprised and deeply honoured when, during its twenty-fifth annual conference in Ankara, AESOP decided to make me an honorary member. I became the fifth and the only non-European thus honoured, joining Klaus Kunzmann, Louis Albrechts and Patsy Healey—the association's first three presidents—as well as Andreas Faludi, one of the founding fathers. They are all represented in this book.

In the early 1990s, when I was still one of the few academics involved in both ACSP and AESOP, I wrote a paper intended to strengthen the bridge across the Atlantic, titled "A Transatlantic View of Planning Education and Professional Practice" (Alterman, 1992). There, I analysed the different modes of planning in the USA and the UK and compared these to the still-emerging planning education in the various parts of continental Europe. Using this paper as a benchmark, one can assess the great progress made in spreading planning education and professionalism in all parts of Europe, including Eastern Europe. This progress is largely a result of AESOP's wise and inclusive efforts.

Following AESOP, more continent-based planning associations have been established. But the most important next landmark was the establishment of the Global Planning Education Association Network. I was present at the inauguration of GPEAN in 2001, during the first World Planning Conference held in Shanghai. Planning had achieved another major milestone.

However, planning education and the planning profession are as yet far from global. There is much work still to be done to introduce or enhance planning education and the profession in many parts of the world, including the countries which need planning the most.

The Compass: Implementation Analysis

Planning theory is largely introspective; it searches for the guiding light from within planning thought. To make planning effective anywhere in the world, norms and ethics are not enough. Planners also need to learn more about how to navigate in the real world of public decision making. Planners should understand the real-life contexts of public decision making. Implementation analysis is the compass, the instrument that planners should use to steer their ship through the rough waters between planning goals and the shores of reality. The compass helps not just to keep to the desired direction, but also to change direction when necessary.

My PhD research was devoted to learning what happens within the "black box" of the implementation process. I aimed at the mundane trajectory that characterises the life of most plans: delays, poor inter-agency coordination, declining political commitment, resurgence of unresolved conflicts, etc. My special interest was in legally anchored ("statutory") land-use plans and instruments. In US and Canadian legal terminology this would include comprehensive plans, zoning regulations, subdivision controls, planned unit development and the like (Alterman, 2005). I chose to focus on these because they were—and still are—the regulatory planning instruments routinely employed in most countries, though with important variations.

I'd like to share a bit about the bumpy path of PhD research—especially across oceans. My advisor, Morris Hill, was not convinced that the topic was worthy of research because I could not find any previous work of this genre. One day in 1972 I discovered Daniel Mandelker's

270 Rachelle Alterman

book *The Zoning Dilemma* (1970). It was a recent arrival in our university library, located thousands of miles from the author's Washington University in St. Louis. To me, finding this book was discovering a treasure. Mandelker analysed not only the law of zoning, as other books had done, but also gave a quantitative measure of deviation from the comprehensive zoning through rezoning, exceptions or variances. So here was a renowned American planning law scholar who thought that empirical research about implementation in planning was worth doing! In need of conviction, I wrote him a letter. Mandelker replied quickly, by "snail mail" standards. His encouragement was the confirmation I needed to go ahead. I met Dan in person a few years later. By then, I was studying law. He has been a major help and inspiration in my academic career.

Finding a theoretical grounding for my PhD research on implementation was not easy. Most of the literature in planning, political science or law at the time adopted a self-deluding view, assuming that if decisions were made "correctly", then implementation would follow. So I developed a rudimentary theoretical framework of my own. It sought to connect the approval of plans to the legal and administrative decisions that follow over time—those that are consistent with the approved plan (down to building permits), and those that entail amendments or variances and exceptions. Using statistical analysis, I tried to identify explanatory variables that may help planners understand how and why plans gradually derail. To this day, those who cite the papers that emanated from this research (Alterman & Hill, 1978; Alterman, 1979; Alterman, 1980; Alterman, 1981a) often note that there is a need for more empirical research about implementation.

But soon after I finished my dissertation in 1976, I learned that while I was struggling to develop my rudimentary theoretical framework, Pressman and Wildavsky (1973) had already published their brilliant book, *Implementation* (with humorous subtitles). With no Internet, I missed the opportunity of benefitting from their tantalising conceptual model. They demonstrated schematically that the probability that a law or policy would be fully implemented is very low because it declines quickly with each clearance decision required along the way. Although some have criticised the Pressman and Wildavsky model for being overly pessimistic, I find their argument a compelling "wake-up call", especially for urban planners who deal with "wicked problems" (Rittel & Webber, 1973) and multi-sector issues requiring a plethora of "clearances".

Pressman and Wildavsky's book triggered a rich variety of theoretical frameworks and contesting debates—such as between the "top-down" and "bottom-up" approaches to implementation analysis. However, these studies referred to public policy in general and rarely focused on the challenges of urban and regional planning. When I learned that Patsy Healey and colleagues in the UK shared my idea that planning theory and implementation analysis complement each other, I travelled to meet her at Oxford Polytechnic. In the 1980s I wrote several conceptual papers about implementation analysis tailored for planning (Alterman, 1982, 1983; Alterman, Carmon & Hill, 1984).

I later used implementation analysis as my compass for evaluating large-scale planning policies: Israel's statutory planning system (Alexander, Alterman & Law-Yone, 1983), the ambitious Project Renewal (Alterman, 1987, 1991), and the strategies for the "Israel 2020" long-range planning project. Although research by policy scientists and planners about implementation theory has diminished, some of the underlying concepts have migrated to "new institutionalism" (Verma, 2002) and "complexity theory" (Innes & Booher, 2010).

The Scale—Part I: Planning Law

The third image guiding my work is a scale. This image conjures up planners' need to find a balance between conflicting goals. In my research and teaching, I have focused on two perspectives that offer planners a scale: first, planning law, which seeks fairness; and second, cross-national analysis with its capacity to provide a comparative sense of proportionality, of scale. I will first focus on my research in planning law and then on comparative analysis.

The Interrelationship between Planning and Law

During my PhD research I became aware that in order to understand the implementation process for a statutory plan, I needed to learn about issues such as the legal powers of the various bodies; the interrelationships between planning law, administrative law, municipal law, taxation law and constitutional law; the implications of ambiguity in the wording of plans or the legislation itself; the limits to discretion; and the important role of court decisions. Rather than viewing the law as an outsider, I decided to harness the knowledge of law to enlighten my research and empower my students and the planning profession.

Gaining a law degree turned out to be the most difficult of my academic challenges. The problem was the timing. I registered for the law degree right after completing my PhD, just when I was starting an academic career. Because of the heavy teaching loads assigned to new faculty at the time, I had to spread my studies over more years. During this period, we had our first child and then the second, but with a time-sharing husband, children were never a deterrent.

When I finally graduated in 1984, I was sure that the journey was well worth it. Since then, a major part of my academic work has been directed towards bridging the rift between planning and law. Understanding the workings of the legal system is no less important for planners and their citizen-clients than understanding, say, transportation systems or housing markets.

The Policy Impacts of Planning Law Research

Planning law is an endless field for research, thirsty for much more theoretical as well as empirical scholarly endeavours. Over the years, I have studied many aspects of planning and related laws. My experience is that planning law research can have an impact if it addresses issues of public concern and does not remain on the abstract, doctrinaire level. Of course, such research has to be independent, not commissioned. My own planning law publications—alone or with my graduate students and postdocs—have been cited scores of times by the Israel Supreme Court and lower courts and have influenced legislation on key topics. Here are four among many examples.

After publishing two papers in international law journals without any local effect, I decided to publish in Israeli law journals in Hebrew. My first paper addressed my concern that local statutory plans were much too detailed, thus inevitably leading to many amendments. I argued that even without legislative change—which would have been unlikely then—planning bodies are authorised to approve flexible types of plans (Alterman, 1981b, Hebrew; see also Alterman, 1980). The Israeli Supreme Court adopted my view almost immediately, but practice has been slow to change. Only in 2013 did the Knesset amend the planning law in this spirit.

272 Rachelle Alterman

A second example is a 1985 paper, where I criticised a Supreme Court decision on expropriation law (eminent domain) delivered several years earlier (Alterman, 1985; Hebrew). There, the court interpreted the legislation as permitting compensation for only 60% of property value, as had been the practice. But in 2001, the Supreme Court dramatically reversed its approach, a rather rare occurrence in jurisprudence. The decision was based largely on my argument.

A third example is a paper which I wrote especially to "save" Israel's exemplary land readjustment law from a pending court decision that might have emptied out its usefulness (Alterman & Hevroni, 2006; Hebrew). Land readjustment is a planners' dream-world instrument, available only in a few countries around the globe (Alterman, 2007a). This instrument can shift and resize the locations of private land parcels and at the same time change zoning rules and gain land for public infrastructure. Fairness among all landowners is built into the instrument. The court cited our paper and adopted the essence of our argument. Land readjustment retained its potency and continues to be widely used for development and redevelopment.

A final example pertains to Israel's exacerbating housing-affordability crisis. On this issue, in 2011 Israeli cities witnessed the largest Occupy Wall Street type of protests in the world, relative to population size. Colleagues and I published two books in Hebrew about regulatory instruments for affordable housing in several countries and their applicability to Israel. The books became part of the intensive public debate among NGOs, the media and Knesset deliberations.

The Scale—Part II: Cross-National Comparative Research

During the initial years following my legal studies, my research was naturally focused on my home country. Most legal research is indeed domestic. But I soon discovered that if I wanted to evaluate my country's planning laws, I needed some external perspective. In other words, I needed a sense of scale which cannot be gained just from looking inwards, within one's national "silo".

Why Comparative Research?

Some legal fields are guided by international norms or philosophical doctrines. This is not the case with planning laws. To determine what a "good" law is and what the range of feasible alternatives may be, cross-national comparative analysis can be very helpful. To untrained eyes, planning laws in different countries may seem similar to each other. In fact, my research has shown that seemingly small variations entail major differences in planning policy and practice. This holds even for neighbouring countries with similar sociocultural and physical characteristics (Alterman, 2010, 2011a). Where planning laws are concerned, the devils are indeed in the details—but so are the angels! The capacity to learn systematically from other countries' laws is a valuable policy resource.

However, conducting cross-national analysis of laws and practices is not an easy task. Comparative research in planning law was especially difficult because there was hardly any comparative research published, nor networks of planning law scholars anywhere in the world. Before the Internet, access to legislation and court decisions was difficult, and even today most countries publish their planning laws and court decisions only in their domestic language. So, for every topic in planning law or practice, I had to search for a local planning or property law academic to help me understand the intricacies of the system. In my journeys I met leading planning law or land-regulation scholars in various countries and collaborated with some in research. To save others from the need to do these kinds of arduous academic searches, I decided to establish a global academic platform for planning and law—a story to which I devote a separate section below.

As I became better acquainted with an expanding set of planning law "systems", I learned that there is no planning law system which has a high degree of satisfaction domestically. However, through a comparative prism, countries can learn from each other about alternative ways of approaching planning laws.

Examples of Comparative Research

Exposure to other countries' modes and approaches—each very different from the others—has helped me to provide answers to questions that had no absolute answers of right or wrong, extreme or moderate, or even just or unjust. I will give a few examples from among the many planning law conundrums that I have researched or am currently researching alone or with my doctoral students.

The first example is the question of whether it is legally appropriate to require private landholders to contribute to public services (in land, construction or money) when they seek permission to develop. This is what Americans may call *exactions* or *developer agreements*, the British call *planning gain* or *planning obligations*, the French call *participation* and the Australians in New South Wales call *contributions* and *voluntary planning agreements*. Initially, my interest was triggered by the Israeli law that allowed for hefty quasi-compulsory land dedication (Alterman,1990a). Planners saw this as a fair and necessary means of obtaining land for public services; but lawyers regarded this practice as "government robbery".

I faced a dilemma. Which side should I take? So I sought to learn about this issue in several other countries. I discovered that although this issue takes somewhat different forms and degrees in other countries, the debates surrounding it are very similar. This topic became the theme of my first comparative book titled *Private Supply of Public Services* (Alterman, 1988a). I assembled and wrote the book while on my second sabbatical year—this time at New York University—where I enjoyed the collegiality and advice of the eminent Alan Altshuler. The book encompassed the USA, England, France and Israel. Especially fascinating to me was an audacious form of American exactions called "linkage fees"—then an evolving practice—so I followed with additional field research and critical analysis (Alterman, 1988b). The transferability of American practices to the UK was another challenge (Alterman, 1990b). The issue of developer obligations continues to fascinate me because it highlights the tensions between public and private goals and interests. A PhD student and I are completing a legal-empirical comparative study of developer agreements in the UK, New South Wales (Australia) and Israel.

Farmland preservation was another topic where I felt the need for a comparative scale. Israel has very strict legal protection of farmland, defined in an extreme way to encompass almost any undeveloped land in the country. In effect, all development proposals must receive clearance from a national-level body. I had done empirical research in Israel to look at the relevant body's decisions, and I didn't know whether these were unreasonably strict for a country with a steep growth curve or just right for open space protection. This riddle led to an (award-winning) paper that compared farmland protection laws and policies in six countries

(Alterman, 1997). The comparative scale unlocked the answer: Israeli law was ostensibly the strictest, but the Netherlands achieved the best protection.

In the 1990s I was part of the "Israel 2020" team, which sought to provide a knowledge base for long-range planning for a country with high density, a high growth rate and many external challenges. I wanted to rethink our somewhat antiquated planning law.

Once again, I felt the need for a comparative scale. We assembled a group of leading scholars, mostly in planning law, whom I had met in previous years. This led to the book *National-Level Planning in Democratic Countries* (Alterman, Ed., 2002) based on a rigorous 10-country comparative scheme. The conclusions were counterintuitive. They showed that external factors such as population density, legal regime or economic wealth cannot "explain" why some countries adopt one approach or another to planning law. In fact, nations sometimes choose to take about-turns from time to time. There are many "degrees of freedom" in designing planning laws, and these can be subject to ideology or debate.

The final example: The relationship between planning regulations and land values has bedevilled legislators and planners ever since the first national planning law in the world was enacted, in 1909 in Britain. Planning laws and the rules prescribed through them are major determinants of land values and are inevitably intertwined with issues of distributive justice. Should planning laws entitle landholders to claim compensation for planning regulations that diminish property values, or do landowners have a social duty to bear the brunt? And what about the reverse issue, the "windfalls"? There have been several theoretical and normative treatises on this subject, but I wanted to learn how different countries approach this issue in their laws and practices. As surprising as it may seem, no one had previously done systematic comparative research on this intrinsically universal issue.

I set out to write *Takings International* (Alterman, 2010), which addresses the decline side of property values due to planning controls. This turned out to be the largest-scale systematically comparative research on planning law ever published, encompassing 14 jurisdictions—40% of all OECD countries. The findings showed that the laws in place actually covered a very broad spectrum—from no compensation rights at all, to generous compensation rights. Once again, the findings were counterintuitive. One cannot guess a country's rules based on any intuitive factors such as legal regime, density, culture, economy or political ideology. For example, when the political-ideological debate raging in the USA about "property rights" is positioned along the comparative scale, both sides are seen to fall close to the middle rather than at the extremes (Alterman, 2011b). The book's findings have already influenced legislative changes in both the Netherlands and Israel—countries with extreme compensation rights. On the "windfalls" (or betterment-capture) side, my research shows that contrary to the enthusiasm of theoreticians, most countries today have chosen not to adopt an overt windfall-sharing rule, preferring indirect modes [Alterman 2012].

I have touched on only a few of the topics addressed in my ongoing comparative research. Each topic has produced some unanticipated findings and has opened up new horizons for theoretical development and further research.

Establishing the International Academic Association on Planning, Law and Property Rights—PLPR

After many years of having to seek out like-minded researchers in other countries, I decided to establish the world's first international academic platform with a mission to bring together planning researchers interested in law, and legal researchers interested in planning. New academics would have a much easier time finding partners for research than I did; cross-disciplinary research would be stimulated; and comparative research would get a boost. I knew I would have to build this up gradually. So at first I approached the two major associations of planning academics—ACSP and AESOP—with the idea of establishing a conference track on this topic. AESOP proved to be more receptive to the idea. Patsy Healey helped me to promote the idea by teaming me up with Willem Salet of Amsterdam and Benjamin Davy of Dortmund, and the AESOP Planning and Law Track was born. Since 1999 I have served as its co-chair (with other local partners) . The Planning and Law Track later became AESOP's pioneering "thematic group".

After several years, I felt that the thematic group within AESOP had matured enough to be able to evolve into an independent academic association which could bring together academics not only from planning schools, but also from law schools and real estate schools. In 2006, PLPR was launched in an inaugural conference held in the Hague (hosted by the Dutch government), and in the University of Amsterdam (hosted by Willem Salet and Leonie Janssen- Jansen). I became PLPR's founding president. Today, PLPR is a vibrant platform for research collaboration and co-publication. The association's annual conferences, held in a different country every year, draw academics from many parts of the world, and many early career researchers.

Sharing Knowledge with Developing Countries

After many years of studying the advanced-economy countries, I feel obligated to share more of my knowledge for the benefit of the Global South and countries in transition. After all, there are only a few dozen advanced-economy countries. The rest of humanity deserves much more attention from planning scholars. The problem is that the laws, regulations and policies born in developed countries are usually not suitable, at times even harmful, for the developing world (Alterman, 2013). Perhaps some of the recollections of my childhood in Israel, when it was a developing country, have helped me to cross the deep divide that separates the advanced from the developing countries.

My first try at knowledge transfer to a developing country was to Israel's neighbours—the Palestinian Authority (Alterman, 2007b). In 2011 the OECD invited me to a team to assess Poland's urban policy. Focusing on Poland's still-rudimentary planning laws and housing policies, I recommended transition strategies. In recent years, I have been volunteering time to UN-Habitat in Nairobi, to think about land-based financing for public services, new conceptions of planning law and how to minimize corruption.

Lately, I have also been asked to share my knowledge with the Chinese national and municipal governments on topics of comparative planning law, public land policy, housing regulation, land expropriation and illegal construction. The Chinese context differs markedly from most developing countries. Chinese decision makers convey an insatiable thirst to learn from advanced economies. Some of my publications are being translated into Chinese.

Epilogue

I feel exceedingly privileged to be a professional planner, educator and scholar. No other profession seeks to understand the complex interrelationships between societies, cultures, economies, politics, administrations and the physical world all at the same time—not just in abstract theory or philosophy, but literally "on the ground". No other profession charges its practitioners with a mission to improve people's lives in so many aspects at once. No other profession offers its practitioners a "broadband" spectrum of roles, positions, levels and locations from which to choose, and opportunities to evolve and change during the course of one's career. And think about it: The planning profession is also the best background to enjoying one's tourist vacations! Like medical doctors, we are interested in every part of the body of cities and regions, are not deterred by areas of decline, and are eager to think of solutions. In a world where the majority of humanity lives in cities—the hubs of economies, cultures and political decisions—we have the profession of the future.

My own journey in planning education and research is by no means over. There is need for so much more research in planning and planning law!

Notes

1   http://umanitoba.ca/faculties/architecture/programs/cityplanning/about.html
2   See Klaus Kunzmann, "Giving Birth to AESOP" in the "History" tab of the official AESOP site: http://www.aesop-planning.eu/en_GB/what-is-planning

References

Alexander, E., Alterman, R., & Law-Yone, H. (1983). *Evaluating plan implementation: The national planning system in Israel.* Progress in planning monograph series, 20. Oxford: Pergamon Press.
Alterman, R. (1979). Whatever happened to our land use plan: A method for analyzing transformations in planned land uses. *Socio-Economic Planning Sciences, 13*, 275-283.
Alterman, R. (1980). Decision making in urban plan implementation: Does the dog wag the tail or the tail wag the dog? *Urban Law and Policy, 3*, 41–58.
Alterman, R. (1981a). A method of monitoring land use plan implementation: Case study of an Israeli statutory plan. In H. Voogd (Ed.), *Strategic planning in a dynamic society* (pp. 205–224). Delft: Delftsche Uitgevers Maatschappij.
Alterman, R. (1981b). The planning and building law and local plans: Rigid regulations or a flexible framework. *Mishpatim (Laws), (Law Journal of the Faculty of Law, Hebrew University, Jerusalem), 11*, 197–220.
Alterman, R. (1982). Implementation analysis in urban and regional planning: Toward a research agenda. In P. Healey, G. McDougall & M. Thomas (Eds.), *Planning theory: Prospects for the 1980s* (pp. 225–245). Oxford: Pergamon Press.
Alterman, R. (1983). Implementation analysis: The contours of an emerging debate (Review essay). *Journal of Planning Education and Research, 2*, 63–65.
Alterman, R. (1985). Exactions of land for public services: Toward a re-evaluation. *Mishpatim (Laws), (Law Journal of the Faculty of Law, Hebrew University, Jerusalem), 16*, 179–245 (Hebrew).
Alterman, R. (1987–8). Opening up the "Black Box" in evaluating neighborhood programs: The implementation process in Israel's project renewal. *Policy Studies Journal, 16*, 347–361.
Alterman, R. (Ed.). (1988a). *Private supply of public services: Evaluation of real estate exactions, linkage and alternative land policies.* New York, NY: New York University Press.
Alterman, R. (1988b). Evaluating linkage and beyond: Letting the windfall recapture genie out of the exactions bottle. *Washington University Journal of Urban and Contemporary Law, 32*, 3–49.
Alterman, R. (1990a). Developer obligations for public services in Israel: Law and social policy in a comparative perspective. *Journal of Land Use and Environmental Law, 5*, 649–684.
Alterman, R. (1990b). Developer obligations for public services, American style: Lessons for British planners. In P. Healey & R. Nebarro (Eds.), *Land and property development processes in a changing context* (pp. 162–174). Farnham: Gower.

Alterman, R. (1991). Planning and implementation of Israel's "project renewal": A retrospective view. In R. Alterman & G. Cars (Eds.), *Neighborhood regeneration: An international evaluation* (pp. 147–169). London: Mansell.

Alterman, R. (1992). A transatlantic view of planning education and professional practice. *Journal of Planning Education and Research, 12*, 102–117.

Alterman, R. (1995). Can planning help in time of crisis? Public-policy responses to Israel's recent wave of mass immigration. *Journal of the American Planning Association, 61*, 156–177.

Alterman, R. (1997). The challenge of farmland preservation: Lessons from a six-country comparison. *Journal of the American Planning Association, 63(2)*, 220–243.

Alterman, R. (Ed.). (2001). *National-level planning in democratic countries: An international comparison of city and regional policy-making.* Liverpool: Liverpool University Press.

Alterman, R. 2002. *Planning in the Face of Crisis: Housing, Land-Use, and Mass Immigration in Israel.* London: Routledge.

Alterman, R. (2005). A view from the outside: The role of cross-national learning in land-use law reform in the United States. In D. R. Mandelker (Ed.), *Planning reform in the new century* (pp. 309–320). Chicago: Planners' Press.

Alterman, R. (2007a). Much more than land assembly: Land readjustment for the supply of public services. In B. Needham & Y. Hung Hong (Eds.), *International experiences in land readjustment* (pp. 57–86). Cambridge, MA: Lincoln Institute for Land Policy.

Alterman, R. (2007b). Land and housing strategies for immigrant absorption: What the Palestinians can learn from the Israeli experience. In R. Brynen (Ed.), *Palestinian refugees: Challenges of repatriation and development* (pp. 163–217). London & New York: IB Tauris.

Alterman, R. (2010). *Takings international: A comparative perspective on land use regulations and compensation rights.* Chicago: American Bar Association Publications.

Alterman, R. (2011a). Comparative research at the frontier of panning law: The case of compensation rights for land use regulations. *International Journal of Law in the Built Environment, 3*, 100–112.

Alterman, R. (2011b). The US regulatory takings debate through international lenses. *The Urban Lawyer, 42–3*, 331–355.

Alterman, R. (2012). Land use regulations and property values: The "windfalls capture" idea revisited. In G Knaap & N. Brooks (Eds.), *The [Oxford] handbook of urban economics and planning* (pp. 755–786). Oxford: Oxford University Press.

Alterman, R. (2013). Planning laws, development controls, and social equity: Lessons for developing countries. *World Bank Legal Review, 5*, 350–392.

Alterman, R., Carmon, N., & Hill, M. (1984). Integrated evaluation: A synthesis of approaches to the evaluation of broad-aim social programs. *Socio-Economic Planning Sciences, 18*, 381–389.

Alterman, R. Churchman, A., & Law-Yone, H. (1981). *Guide to public participation in planning.* (Hebrew, Eng. abstract). Center for Urban and Regional Studies, Technion. Second (1987) and third (1996) editions published by Michlol–Technion's textbook publishers.

Alterman, R., Harris, D., & Hill, M. (1984). The impact of public participation on planning: The case of the Derbyshire structure plan. *Town Planning Review, 55*, 177–196.

Alterman, R., & Hevroni, H. (2006). Land readjustment as a tool for obtaining land for public needs: A cross-national review. *Real Property Law (Mekarkein), 5(1)*, 3–34. (Hebrew).

Alterman, R., & Hill, M. (1978). Implementation of urban land use plans. *Journal of the American Institute of Planners, 44(3)*, 274–285.

Alterman, R., & MacRae, D. Jr. (1983). Planning and policy analysis: Converging or diverging trends? *Journal of the American Planning Association, 49*, 200–213.

Alterman, R., & Page, J. (1973). The ubiquity of values and the planning process. *Plan (Canada), 13(1)*, 12–26.

Alterman, R., & Stav, T. (2001). *Conflict and consensus through language: Trends of change toward the Arab sector in Israel as expressed in urban and regional plans.* Tel Aviv: The Tami Steinmetz Center for Peace Studies, Tel Aviv University (Hebrew).

278 Rachelle Alterman

Christensen, K. (1985). Coping with uncertainty in planning. *Journal of the American Planning Association*, *51(Winter)*, 63–73.

Faludi, A. (Ed.). (1973). *A reader in planning theory*. Oxford: Pergamon Press.

Forester, J. (1999). *The deliberative practitioner: Encouraging participatory planning processes*. Cambridge, MA: MIT Press.

Friedmann, J. (2017). Planning as a Vocation: The Journey So Far. In B. Haselsberger (Ed.), *Encounters in planning thought: 16 autobiographical essays from key thinkers in spatial planning* (pp. 15–34). New York: Routledge.

Healey, P. (1997). *Collaborative planning: Shaping places in fragmented societies*. London: McMillan.

Hill, M. (1968). Goals achievement matrix for evaluating alternative plans. *Journal of the American Institute of Planning*, *34*, 19–29.

Howe, E. (1980). Role choices of urban planners. *Journal of the American Planning Association*, *46*, 398–409.

Howe, E., & Kaufman, J. (1979). The Ethics of Contemporary American Planners. *Journal of the American Planning Association*, *45*, 243–255.

Innes, J. E. (1995). Planning theory's emerging paradigm: Communicative action and interactive practice. *Journal of Planning Education and Research*, *14*, 183–189.

Innes, J. E., & Booher, D. E. (2010). *Planning with complexity: An introduction to collaborative rationality for public policy*. London: Routledge.

Klosterman, R. E. (2011). Planning theory education: A thirty-year review. *Journal of Planning Education and Research*, 31, 319–331.

Mandelker, D. R. (1970). *The zoning dilemma: A legal strategy for urban change*. Indianapolis, IN: Bobbs Merrill.

Pressman, J., & Wildavsky, A. (1973). *Implementation*. Berkeley, CA: Berkeley University Press.

Rittel, H. W. J., & Webber, M. M. (1973). Dilemmas in a general theory of planning. *Policy Sciences*, *4*, 155–169.

Schon, D. A. (1983). *The Reflective Practitioner—How Professionals Think in Action*. New York: Basic Books.

Verma, N. (Ed.). (2002). *Institutions and planning*. Boston, MA: Elsevier.

Terminology Glossary

Note: The following definitions are my own. My designation of the countries where these terms apply (as distinct from other countries) is roughly based on my comparative research.

Comprehensive plan: In US professional planning terminology, a comprehensive plan refers to a planning document for an entire city or region, which is less site-specific than zoning regulations and also contains broader policies. In some states, preparation of a comprehensive plan to guide zoning decisions is mandatory. In other states, local governments may argue that the "plan" is submerged within the zoning regulations and need not exist as a separate document. In most US states, the law does not require strict compliance with the comprehensive plan, and its role is advisory rather than binding.

Expropriation of land: Denotes the legal taking of land by an authorised body for a legally approved purpose. This term is used outside the USA and British-influenced countries. In the USA the equivalent term is eminent domain, and in British-influenced countries is it compulsory purchase.

Planned unit development: A term used in American planning law to denote a specific set of rules about land development or conservation that apply in specific sites or projects and replace the zoning regulations.

Planning system: In professional planning terminology in many countries (excluding the USA and Canada), planning system broadly refers to the hierarchy of formal institutions and their main powers as established by national (or subnational) planning legislation.

Statutory plan: A generic term used in most countries—outside the USA and Canada—to denote the types of land-use plans that are mandated or enabled by national (or subnational) legislation ("statutory" or regulatory). Such plans usually set the policies and regulations about permitted use of land

and permitted amount and type of development (construction), and they are usually accompanied by a map. The legislation may provide for several types of statutory plans, often in a hierarchical relationship according to level of government or geographic span. Statutory plans may be strictly binding or allow for a range of discretion, and they may be very detailed or general. In many countries, detailed plans at the local level are the legal basis for issuing development permits.

Zoning: In the USA and Canada this is a key term denoting regulations enacted by local governments, usually as bylaws, whereby land is divided into zones according to a set of categories, each specifying the type of use permitted (for example, residential, commercial, industrial). The rules may also specify the types and quantities of development (construction) permitted. In most states and provinces, enactment of zoning regulations is mandatory, and decisions about development permits and the like must be consistent with these regulations. Zoning is usually accompanied by a map. The categories and subcategories of zoning are often very detailed and pertain to specific sites. Outside the USA and Canada, the function of regulating land-use is usually achieved through detailed statutory plans (see definition).

17

ON THE EVOLUTION OF
A CRITICAL PRAGMATISM

John Forester

My "bias for practice" has led me to ask how planners can work in politically realistic and ethically progressive ways. That bias presumes that we can learn from planning and related practices that have effectively engaged power and conflict, bureaucratic challenges, racial and gender exclusions, and more.[1] So I have watched, worked with, and interviewed fascinating and creative planning practitioners, less because they seemed either just typical or magical exceptions than because I wondered how we might learn from practice about better planning. Here I reconstruct the intellectual path I've called a "critical pragmatism" to try to encourage more responsive, expert, and creative planning practices.

The year after I finished my dissertation, I hoped to publish its central, "critical theory"—inspired argument as an article (Forester, 1981). I sent a friend a draft for comments. By the passage mercilessly criticizing Charles Lindblom's incrementalism, my friend wrote, no less unsparingly, "How dead does the horse have to be, before we can stop beating it?"

I learned slowly from his candor and impatience: Unbridled criticism becomes less valuable, trustworthy, and generative the less it informs constructive analysis to do better. "Critical" talk can be cheap, even self-righteous, particularly when questions of "What to do now, in the face of power?" go unanswered.

Planning Theory's Dirty Little Secret

In the late 1970s, students of planning faced a curious problem: Ambitious social theories omitted social actors; attractive political theories ignored political action. The twentieth-century's ethical challenge—the "good Nazi's" moral excuse, "I was just doing my job"—raised a pressing theoretical and practical problem: If judging others from afar was suspect, not judging raised just as many ethical problems.

Years later, still perplexed that planning theorists so often evaded this challenge of assessing what planners might really do in diverse planning contexts, I wrote polemically about "planning theory's dirty little secret." That secret: *No matter how much we theorize* planning systems, promising ideas, or threatening ideologies, *somebody still has to do the work.* So theories of state power or neoliberalism, for example, without accounts of astute practical resistance, risk being not "critical" but rhetorically self-indulgent and evasive. Because racial, gendered, and class "domination" are political, historically contingent—not ontological or unchangeable—any "critical" theory must illuminate *how to resist such injustice or violence,* or its appeals to rights or justice will be just wishful thinking. No critical theory can stay silent about action, ethical choice, and political judgment, without becoming more facile complaint than practical critique. If we are to work toward social and economic justice and not just talk about it, somebody, politically, practically, and ethically *has to do the work.* So, planning theories that fail to illuminate that work—planning theories keeping their dirty little secrets—risk irrelevance and even complicity with systems of injustice.

But what was I to do instead? Metaphors mattered: Planning seemed more like "organizing or disorganizing attention" than technical "problem-solving." Yet endlessly "critical" articles discovered breathlessly that economic inequality and racial and gendered segregation were all "political," all stunningly about "power." Was this news? Maybe Berkeley had jaded me, but most writing about the politics of planning seemed to end just where it should have begun. Of course politics and power shape planning! But that's not the conclusion, that's the challenge. What now is to be done, and *how?*

Born into a Viennese Jewish refugee family, I grew up in San Francisco as a high school and college student in the 1960s. Both my family's escape from fascism and the civil rights and feminist movements shaped my left-liberal politics, but my aptitude for math and science (and low English scores) led me to study engineering at UC Berkeley. I would get bachelor of science and master's degrees in mechanical engineering (1970, 1971), even though from my sophomore year onwards I was deeply involved in community work and campus organizing. Hardly attracted to the engineering of the defense industry, my family's experience, '60s sensibility, and community work fed my curiosity when I discovered, the year after my master's degree, that Berkeley had a vibrant city planning graduate program.

In Berkeley I had found no shortage of self-assured technocrats here or equally self-righteous ideologues there, and I was always unsure about the ground between the two (who sometimes, of course, were identical). I had studied enough engineering to appreciate the deep appeal of systems, the alluring elegance of mathematical solutions, the heady power of mastering techniques to get answers that worked. But what if my equations didn't do much justice to the social and political world?

I was surrounded, too, by sectarian groups, red and green, left and environmental, gendered and not, and more. I felt the depth and passion of sectarian conflicts: I saw how many activists had found the one right way, "the" explanation for inequality, commodification, racial or gender domination, or injustice (Walzer, 1980). Berkeley overflowed with solutions and systems, slogans and sectarians—all with potential appeal, none obviously having the last word, the true path to Truth or Justice. Little wonder that decades later I would respond to rediscoveries of "Justice!" with déjà vu and frustration: "Yes, of course, but how?"

These temptations of facile theorizing remain today. Whenever theories of "the system" displace analyses of resistance, we risk having less political or ethical critique than technocracy. Both political orthodoxy and technocratic fervor can threaten what we need instead: a context-sensitive and critical (i.e. power sensitive) pragmatism, one engaging both complex settings of action and the ambiguities of good work, and thus the demands of justice, compassion, kindness, and beauty (Forester, 2012a, 2012b).

282 John Forester

Berkeley's student movements espoused sweeping ideas of political change, but without much clarity about how to achieve such ends. Along with the rhetoric of ideals—Save the earth! Smash the state! End racism! End patriarchy!—and the rigors of technocratic thinking, whether as systems analysis, cost-benefit analysis, or optimization and so forth, always came nagging questions, "But beginning where, with what prestructured data set or with what popular base or truly committed set of partners?"

For three years, as an undergraduate engineering student, I'd worked at UC Berkeley's Community Projects Office supporting "service-learning" projects in poor communities in San Francisco's East Bay. With one eye on community needs and one on differential equations, I quickly came to doubt self-serving rhetoric and progressive pieties on several sides. Listening to the devout left, I was less sure that capitalism's demise, pulling history forward, lay just around the corner. But I wondered equally about the promises of rigorous but no less righteous technologists for whom technical mastery reigned supreme.

Looking back, I think that Paulo Freire saved me, for in *The Pedagogy of the Oppressed* (Freire, 1970) he interwove four often competing concerns: (i) the face-to-face, interpersonal realities of community work; (ii) the political-economic structures through which the rich got richer and the poor stayed poor; (iii) the broad Judeo-Christian tradition I felt an affinity with, notwithstanding my family's expulsion from Vienna for being Jewish; and (iv) crucially, the pragmatic Socratic philosophy of asking generative, evocative, even revelatory questions. Because Freire so provocatively challenged top-down, technocratic "banking education" with a dialogically interactive, co-generated "problem posing education," his eye-opening book had circulated widely in applied fields far beyond Hanna Pitkin's political theory seminar in which I read it. Little did I realize that the underlying concepts making sense of Freire's critical, dialogic work as a Brazilian adult educator would be developed ambitiously—and more usefully than I could have imagined—by a young German philosopher who had provocatively broken away from both an economistic and an overly idealized Marxism, Jurgen Habermas (1970, 1979).

I came to appropriate and extend Habermas's work along the lines and inspiration of Freire's pragmatic, questioning, educative, world-shaping humanism and pragmatism, with the help of Steven Lukes's cogent *Power: A Radical View* (Lukes, 1974). Luckily, I'd read John Austin and Stanley Cavell in Pitkin's course, so the idea of a Freirean "pragmatics" of speech seemed simple enough: Yes, we actually *do* things (promising, insulting, demanding, offering, asking, objecting, proposing, betraying, and so on) in acts with words that we hold each other responsible for ("Did you say . . . ?" "But you said . . ." and so on). Today, theorists call this "performativity." As Henk Wagenaar and Gabriel van den Brink recently helped me to see, my pragmatic debt to Freire remains central to the "critical theory" of planning practice I came to develop. Although it will astonish critics who misunderstood my appropriation of Habermas's work, imaginary ideals of speech had precisely *no role here:* The power of agenda-setting, selective attention, and the politics of misinformation did.

I suffered through, but survived, my dissertation, then taught part-time in 1977–8 at the University of California, Santa Cruz, and I was lucky to get a job at Cornell University's Department of City and Regional Planning, beginning July 1978. Reading Habermas, first with fellow students Dudley Burton, Jan Dekema, and Chip Downs, and then in a Freirean and Wittgensteinian way with Hanna Pitkin, Martin Krieger, and Jack Dyckman, opened up vast new ways, I thought, to study planning practice. Now I might explore planning

Evolution of a Critical Pragmatism **283**

practices less through espoused intentions or ideals, and more through deeds, performances, and actions—their micro-politics. Facing years of "publish or perish" pressures at Cornell, I was learning constantly, too, about strategies of academic writing, as I tried to develop this micro-political approach to planning (Forester, 2014).

Vulnerabilities of Power, Possibilities, and Practice Studies

Early on at Cornell, I was lucky to meet an extraordinary organizer, wit, and raconteur, lecturer at Columbia University and doctoral student at Cornell, Rob Burlage. Rob saw politics as always involving pragmatic, local, and interdependent relationships, not just visionary ends. Rob's influence, I believe, led me to the phrasing, and framing, of "planning *in the face of* power," planning *engaged with* inherited inequalities and institutional obstacles (Gitlin, 1987). "In the face of" suggests a "political phenomenology" (Dallmayr, 1976), and that phrase echoed feminist work exploring "relational" thinking, as in Carol Gilligan's influential *In a Different Voice* (Gilligan, 1982). But how could I develop this in critical studies of planning? John Page solved that problem for me.

A Canadian who'd worked in China, Page helped me see how to extend the critical theories I had been reading so they could illuminate complex planning contexts. Theorizing about intentions or outcomes (the nature of justice, oppression, empowerment) was commonplace, but it always seemed like one hand clapping, begging pragmatic questions: "OK, we see justice or empowerment in theory—but how do we get there? Does the theory imply anything practically?"

Page taught me—with a simple comment in the hallway during Cornell's 1979 Planners' Network Conference—how to better integrate theory and grounded practice. He'd said tersely, frustrated with speakers who'd just used far too much "critical" jargon, "You know, we'd do much better in this field if we'd *just* finish the sentence that begins, 'WHEN I am planning, . . .'"

We can all point to comments that changed our lives, but usually they come, for better or worse, from loved ones. Page's comment changed my life though, for he showed me how to interpret *and extend* difficult writings about situatedness and power and claims-making now by resolving the drama posed by, "When I am planning, ..." Page was asking analysts and theorists not simply to be observers, extending "When *they* are planning, . . ."—but to think more deeply, even more personally and politically, about agency—and about temporality ("When"), and about planning as a living project ("are planning")! He asked not about planning in the abstract but about planning as a lived, felt, contingent struggle. So, when I am planning transportation in Chicago, . . . or when I am doing economic development in Johannesburg, . . . or when I do environmental planning in Seoul, . . . what then do [relevant theories suggest that] I have to worry about, to work with, *in my context*? What issues of power, timing, beneficiaries, coalitions, conflict, strategy . . . can be shared across contexts? I have tried to develop and honor Page's and Burlage's gifts ever since, no less than Freire's and, more analytically, Habermas's and Lukes's.

Obviously, whatever I can do as a planner depends upon context, but depends *upon what more specifically*? Planning theorists must ask, "How do (concepts like) power, respect, negotiation, exchange help us to assess just what can and cannot be possible in differing contexts?" I explored this contingent sense of planning relationally: Planners interacted with others,

284 John Forester

sometimes facing opposing or strategic behaviors, other times wondering with allies, "What do we do now?" Such a context-situated, relational sense of power leads to practical questions not only of what *I can* do, *but also* of how the abilities of Others I am related to might be *limited, vulnerable,* contingent (Gaventa, 1980)!

This simple thought—that we're interrelated, often interdependent, but always contingently so—implies we're always negotiators, like it or not, not only when we haggle at a market, where we know not to "believe" a seller's opening demand, where we know we need to probe, to learn, to test the waters to see what the Other might accommodate. During Berkeley protests, I remembered my naive surprise when an administration official once said informally, "Just because we rejected those student demands, that didn't mean we didn't want to talk to see what else could be done." One lesson: Don't confuse what antagonists say formally, for public consumption, or to save face, or to stake out a claim, with what they might nevertheless really be able to do. The students *had* wanted to talk, even about the "non-negotiable" demands. This means not that life is gamesmanship or poker, but that political actors always need to be wary of being too literal, tying our own hands, presuming, "They'll never . . . ." It's useful to remember that even the apparently "powerful" may be more needy, vulnerable, and internally conflicted, and so be practically more "willing" to do far more, than they *publicly* admit. Presuming that *little* is possible, we quit too early, and we end up with just the little we expected, or less (Forester, 2009).

How could this inform day-to-day planning? In the early '80s, practice studies became popular. Medical sociologists studied how doctors and nurses actually practiced—not just their intentions!—as they interacted with patients. Michael Lipsky (1980) famously explored the discretionary practices of "street level bureaucrats." So Howell Baum, Charles Hoch, and I convened a breakfast caucus for years at ACSP meetings, for faculty studying planning practice, and we learned from each other's insights.

Planning in the Face of Conflict, in Cleveland, in Morally Entangled Contexts

Struggling with teaching and writing, I published in both applied and theoretical journals between 1978 and 1985. The more applied essays fed *Planning in the Face of Power* (1989); the more theoretical, years later, went into *Critical Theory, Public Policy, and Planning Practice* (1993). After that early writing, I spent my first sabbatical at MIT in 1985–6. From Larry Susskind's turn from citizen participation to public dispute resolution, I learned quickly that whatever negotiations looked like from the outside, their creative insides could be fascinating, surprising, crucially producing gains that *none of the negotiating stakeholders initially even thought possible* (to say nothing of still less informed academic observers!). That insight suggested important lessons for planning theory, moving beyond "social learning" to examine grounded practices of planners often acting as intermediaries "in between" multiple stakeholders. From Norman Krumholz and Don Schön I was surprised to learn that what practitioners did practically was often far richer than their espoused theories suggested.

Evaluating the MIT introductory planning course (Forester, 1989, chapter 10), I saw that what Don Schön did with groups, even in the classroom, went far beyond his social-psychological theories of reflection in action and organizational learning. That foreshadowed my later argument: Planners need to be not only "reflective practitioners" but deliberative practitioners too—interacting deliberatively with others, shaping reputations, solidarity, expectations, and shared commitments as well as reflective judgments—for we were always political, interacting with others (Forester, 1999).

Similarly, after Norman Krumholz invited me to collaborate on writing *Making Equity Planning Work,* I realized that Norm's actual work far exceeded in richness, insight, creativity, and political savvy his own powerful but narrow definition of equity planning as "providing choices for those who had few" (Krumholz & Forester, 1990). This was a brilliant, left-leaning reframing that inverted the motto of market advocates, 'free to choose'—as Milton and Rose Friedman's bestseller was eventually titled (Friedman & Friedman, 1979). Nevertheless, Norman's progressive rationale for government intervention, providing "more choices to those with few," hid behind its elegant formulation an astonishing richness of political experience. Here was skill, insight, and capacity that his work under three mayors demonstrated practically—richness that our book began to portray and that students still find illuminating through detailed cases.

These three lessons, from Susskind, Schön, and Krumholz, all pointed in a similar direction, one that John Austin had hinted at when he wrote "fact is richer than diction": The political world is always more complex than our theories of it, certainly more complex than anyone's quick summaries suggest, whether those come from politicians, planners, or faculty. So our analyses always need to probe not just the vulnerabilities of the powerful but also our or anyone's *presumptions* of power.

My earlier essay had explored the politics of listening as a "hermeneutic praxis," an interpretive practice always anticipating that what we mean and care about reaches far beyond words, "what we say." But my early sense of how, through speech acts, we performed agenda-setting and more—shaping attention selectively when we made claims to or upon others—had overly narrowed my own sense of the encompassing, institutionally rich staging of planners or organizers, bureaucrats or community activists. My concern with the micro-politics of planning threatened to become too "micro," despite the apparent success, wild misreadings and all, of *Planning in the Face of Power* (1989).

Collaborating with Krumholz on his story of ten years' work as Cleveland's planning director taught me about much more than the politics of information. So did a small Cornell grant for "Innovations in Undergraduate Education." This grant led me to an entirely new research approach, and to a depth of analysis I had barely imagined, thanks to Martha Nussbaum's writings about literature and ethics (Nussbaum, 1986, 1990; Forester, 1999).

From the Politics of Information to the Richness of Practice Stories

I had proposed simply to bring the practice of our urban studies graduates to the students now taking the same class these graduates had taken years before. I wanted to say to my undergraduate students, "Here's the current work of students who were sitting in your seats ten years ago; here's what they're doing now!"

What I'd intended seemed clear, but implementation was tough. How was I to pull this off? How would we learn from those graduates? What could surveys really tell us? We spent a year making false starts: My student assistants identified graduates working in diverse fields, but we stumbled as we tried to learn and convey what work they were really doing.

286 John Forester

Then I got lucky when Linda Chu showed up in my office. She was a master's student in planning with a background in journalism and experience in interviewing and writing. Linda soon interviewed a graduate, Maxine, who worked for a New York City transportation agency trying to connect the LaGuardia and John F. Kennedy airports by subway.

After recording the interview and writing it up, Linda brought me her description of Maxine's work. Her three-and-a-half page essay was clear, but something seemed to me to be missing.

I reached up to my bookshelves and handed Linda Studs Terkel's famous bestseller *Working* (1974). I thanked her for her first draft, and then I asked her to try an experiment, to do what Terkel had done: "Let's try something new. Could you take your recorded interview, transcribe it, and then edit it so that you have Maxine's story—just as she told it to you on the telephone to answer your questions—but with your questions edited out so that the remaining text will read as the story of her work in her own words?" (Forester, 2012b). Little did I know that what Linda did then would change the next ten years of my writing, my research method, and my ability to learn about the politics, ethics, anthropology and sociology of planning.

Linda returned a week later with a new text of nine pages or so, and what she gave me was Maxine's story, in Maxine's words, with just a bit of editing to drop sentence fragments and to help a reader follow along. I took this "first-person voice practice story," this "profile" of Maxine, to my next undergraduate class meeting, and I explained just what Linda had done: "Maxine took this class several years ago, and here's her story of what she's doing now, in her own words." So I asked my students to join me in this experiment—to read and evaluate Maxine's story for the following class meeting to see if it might be useful—but just as an "extra," if time allowed. I had already assigned readings for that next class.

We met again the next Tuesday, and I had few expectations. As I've recounted in the *Deliberative Practitioner* and in an essay on the discourse analysis that practitioners must do in their own practice (Forester, 1999, 2012b), half of my students had not read Maxine's "practice story" at all. But half of them *had* read it—apparently with eyes and minds widening—and when I asked what they thought, my world changed forever.

"The Most Practical Thing I've Read in This Program in Three Years"

Marjorie spoke first, simply but deeply, "Now I know what to tell my mother when she asks me what planners do!" I listened, and I wondered how in the world could this interview, with Linda's editing, have given Marjorie the confidence to answer this question that haunts our interdisciplinary field?

But then came Sean's even more striking observation, probably not influenced by his sitting next to Marjorie: "This is the most practical thing I've read in this program in three years!"

I didn't know whether to laugh or to cry. Something in Linda's and Terkel's strategy of *preserving the first-person voice* had really connected with these students, had really *shown* them part of planning as well as *told them "about"* planning. They seemed relieved to find not jargon but the power of ordinary language. They seemed refreshed: not academic abstraction but vivid images, vivid context. They seemed instructed, too, substantively ("the most practical thing," Sean had said).

I felt like laughing because of the sheer surprise at how strongly this "simple" reading had moved my students, how ready they were to talk about details, not vague generalities. I'd

Evolution of a Critical Pragmatism **287**

found a way of producing new teaching materials, it seemed, that might contribute to students' understanding, engagement, and analysis as many other readings had not. But I felt like crying too, for I had no idea *why* the students had responded to this material as they had. I was clueless before a wonderful discovery—so what now?

Six weeks later, serving on the Cornell University Press Editorial Board, I saw a reference, in a footnote, to an essay of Martha Nussbaum's, "Finely Aware and Richly Responsible" (I would later discover what that meant), followed by the striking subtitle: "Literature and the Moral Imagination." As my *Deliberative Practitioner* argues, Nussbaum's essay brilliantly explains why and how Marjorie and Sean responded as they did to Linda's presentation of Maxine's interview. Here, after all, in Maxine's practice story was a vivid but ordinary language account of the felt complexity of her job, the various demands and goals and obligations she wrestled with, the various political and bureaucratic and community players who made transportation planning so really, so realistically, messy—what Nussbaum referred to as a story's power to convey the "moral entanglement" of its characters. It was not Linda's word choice—or some academic's word choice—but Maxine's direct expression of how she felt and how she thought about her everyday work and its prospects: here frustrated, there hopeful, here uncertain, there learning, and much, much more (Forester, 1999).

Studying Practice in a New Way: Assessing Profiles of Practitioners

Marjorie and Sean, Linda and Maxine taught me how much ordinary academic writing obscured, as faculty wrote more for journal editors than for curious readers. For years now, my students' close readings of detailed practice stories have taught me about teaching methods and materials alike—but also about a powerful strategy of doing interview-based, theoretically informed research (Forester, 2006, 2012b). In 25 years of teaching since that time, such practitioners' accounts remain the teaching materials that my students embrace most eagerly (with all due respect to my colleagues' writing) (Forester, 2013a).

Nussbaum showed me how, analytically, to explore the contested and political qualities of these "profiles" of diverse planners. Here were practitioners' "practice stories" narrated in their own words, *describing not their opinions* generally about their work but giving *accounts in detail, in messy cases, of both objective complexities and subjective responses,* for better and worse, to the challenges and opportunities they faced.

So the lead essay of my *Deliberative Practitioner,* portraying this turn of research, represented my contribution to the *Argumentative Turn in Policy Analysis and Planning,* which I co-edited with Frank Fischer (Fischer & Forester, 1993; Forester, 1999). That earlier book was more popular in political science, surprisingly, as a move toward a "post-positivist" policy analysis, than it was in planning. We argued that we should understand policy analysis in practice less as "solving problems" or "solving equations" or producing technical "answers"—a technocratic view—than as shaping agendas or discourses, ways of framing policy problems and opportunities, narrative ways of understanding policy options and implications. Giandomenico Majone had explored this approach before Fischer and I did, but our book extended his argument (Majone, 1989). If policy *analyses* were complex, selective, multidimensional stories, then were not policy *analysts* equally complex storytellers, teachers, agenda setters, agents of political and moral imagination? This suggestion resonated strongly with the most compelling definition

288 John Forester

of planning I knew: that we could understand—as my Berkeley friend and colleague Stephen Blum had quoted Jurgen Moltmann—planning as "the organization of hope"—not in intention alone but in deed, in performance.

Learning about Value (Not Values):
Normatively, Not Prescriptively

Nussbaum argued that literature—complex stories—could teach us not just about events but about identity, not just about relationships and interactions, but about value and significance too. From stories we could learn not just who espoused what values—that's the trivial part—but more profoundly about *value:* not just about consequences but about what's consequential, significant in our lives, what we might honor or shun, find better or worse. I found that argument intriguing and compelling, provocative but perplexing. Surely we did "learn about value" and not just "facts" in ordinary life, but how did we do that? How in the world did planners and policy analysts actually "learn about value"? No planning analyst had explored this.

The point was not that planners should (or should not) espouse or celebrate or recommend any *values in the abstract* (Do Justice! Create Beauty! Be Efficient!), because, of course, since the world is complex, planners have to make *value-laden choices in specific cases* about what to attend to and what to neglect all the time. Those choices inescapably reflect biases and values, preferences and interests. We're normative beings, whether we are loudmouths about what we value or not.

But similarly, as we listen to others, we seem to learn about *how things matter,* about what's more or less significant, as we come to see events, resources, or even particular people as more or less salient or significant, consequential, in shifting contexts. Reading Thomas Sugrue's masterful history of postwar Detroit, for example, helps us to appreciate (to evaluate, to get the significance of) issues of race and employment and housing in urban areas—even if Sugrue never explicitly espoused abstract values of social justice (he did not need to, for he detailed the injustice) (Sugrue, 1996). So we may *learn about value* in many ways, as we listen and pay attention carefully to the world around us, without ever being lectured at *about* values! But I wondered, then, how planners at work *learned normatively* from complex stories, as Nussbaum suggested they must. Could I look and see?

By the early '90s, I had observed planners at work by sitting in periodically as a "fly on the wall" at city planning staff meetings in a local city hall. Nussbaum's essays had persuaded me that on the job, in everyday work with others, planners had to tell and to listen carefully to stories all the time (cf. Throgmorton, 1996; Sandercock, 1998; Hoch, 2011). Planners and their colleagues told these everyday stories not for entertainment but to get work done. "What happened at the meeting last night?" produced not a dry list of facts but a grounded story representing multiple practical judgments about what the questioner at work needed or wanted to know. In a negotiation too, of course, "How much can you do for me?" evokes typically not a simple factual response but a carefully selective answer, a practical story, of what one negotiator or party might do, or refuse to do, for another.

But how did anyone *learn about value* from these stories? If we believe planning to be deeply normative and value-laden, even as we seem to presume that we learn about "*the facts of a case*" all the time, how in the world could it be that we (or planners!) can also *learn about* value?

I wanted to see how this worked. So as I sat in a planners' staff meeting one morning, as I listened to that morning's conversation about current projects, I made two lists. The "facts" would go on the left, and I would list claims of "value" on the right. As the staff talked, I listed facts easily: who was involved, what they'd said, what they did and when, what deadlines loomed and which passed, what politicians wanted and when they wanted it, community suspicions, fears and demands, and on and on. But I had nothing under the "value" heading. Something was wrong: Nussbaum was all wrong or I was, or both, it seemed.

But then, staring at that blank right-hand column and the very detailed "fact" column on the left, I had a small "Aha!" All of a sudden, I realized clearly that my column of "facts" reflected not just any facts, but certain, particular facts: facts that the staff judged—determined, supposed, appreciated, considered on the basis of their practical experience, their competence, their training, and their readings of the situations at hand—*to matter,* to be important, to be "of value," "at stake," not just to be vaguely relevant to the cases at hand. As Max Weber taught long ago, value and fact were deeply conjoined, not separate, and the facts at hand were those about which the staff were *saying, practically now—but implicitly, not explicitly*—"We need to heed these facts; we need to honor and *pay* attention and respond to *these* facts." How to put this "learning about value" best, I wondered? *These* facts were valuable: "*the facts that mattered!*"

So, with Nussbaum's help, I could see that the stories that planners tell enact not only political agenda-setting and power in practice, but they work to constitute, frame, select, articulate, and set out the moral and normative character of the world so that others may recognize and grasp it. We learn about value, then, as we learn about how the facts matter: what roles they play in diverse projects and practices, institutions and forms of life shaped by what others do.

But Nussbaum had more in mind than post–positivism or rejecting a value-free (a worthless?) social science. After all, the question of her subtitle, "Literature and the Moral Imagination" was essentially *"How can we learn about ethics*—not rules, not commandments, but obligation, kindness, betrayal, responsibility, care, fairness, dignity and indignity, and so on—*from novels?"* Reading her essay in the context of the planning classroom, I saw that she was also answering my question, "How could planning students learn about better and worse planning, good moves and bad moves, sensitive and callous responses, tact and tactlessness—and very much more about better and worse ways of acting practically—from thoughtful and experienced planners' own stories?"

A New Pedagogy Building upon Practice Stories

Fortunately, a few years later I began to collaborate with a Cornell assistant professor in adult education, Scott Peters. Scott had heard about these profiles of practitioners from his students. A trained historian, he quickly realized that these practice stories portrayed details of professionals' work in a far more nuanced way than most academic studies.

Scott and his research assistants soon produced profiles of university "extension agents" seeking to transfer knowledge from the university to off-campus communities. In an early profile Scott's group came upon a quote that echoed for years. Talking about her work with poor women—often immigrants, often beset by intersecting issues of race, class, education, culture, and poverty—to plan more nutritious meals, a nutrition educator pointed to these essential complexities by saying of a particular young woman, "It's not about the rice!" Cooking the rice, after all, was the easy part.

Here Scott and his colleagues had found a way to evoke—through this practitioner's own words in her detailed profile—so much more than her technical job description had even

290 John Forester

begun to acknowledge. Soon after that, Scott and I obtained a small grant for teaching support. That let us hire then-doctoral student Margo Hittleman to help us develop a "Profiles of Practitioners" website. A decade later that website still helps our students develop profiles of practitioners of their choice as term paper projects in our Cornell classes (http://courses2.cit.cornell.edu/fit117/).

Another small grant from the Fund for Research in Dispute Resolution (FRDR) had helped me too. After my MIT sabbatical, I'd signed up at the Tompkins County Community Dispute Resolution Center, for training as a community dispute mediator. I mediated local disputes often enough to keep my certification: a barking dog here, a landlord/tenant case there, a small commercial dispute, and so on. So then with a small FRDR grant, I hired master's student David Stitzel to help me write about the ethics and politics of mediation. We drafted a score-able teaching simulation exploring new territory: How could a planner, employed by local government, possibly work as a successful, non-neutral mediator too (Forester & Stitzel, 1989)?

In around 1990 I reported our results at a FRDR research meeting in Atlanta, where I met and interviewed MIT-trained, professional mediator Susan Podziba. Susan had co-mediated a striking process enabling the City of Chelsea, MA, to rewrite their city charter in a bottom-up, participatory process—under the watchful eyes of state officials and no end of lawyers (Podziba, 2012). I hadn't profiled any mediators, but as I sat with Susan and kept exploring "How did you deal with . . . ?" questions, I began to see the striking difference it made to ask not "What did you think about X?" questions, but instead, "How did you handle [or deal with, or respond to] X?" instead.

The result was so revealing in its detail, complexity, and richness for exploring public policy dispute resolution that it led me to a new research focus. Before a year's sabbatical at the Technion in Israel, I had concentrated on profiling our Cornell planning graduates with the wonderful help of research assistant extraordinaire Brian Kreiswirth (Forester & Kreiswirth, 1993). After the sabbatical, always interested in issues of public participation and its inherent conflicts between stakeholders, I began to focus on lessons we might learn by profiling thoughtful and experienced mediators of public disputes.

On that sabbatical in Israel in 1993–4, I was lucky to team up with Raphäel Fischler, a postdoc from the University of California, Berkeley, and Deborah Shmueli, planning professor at the University of Haifa, and we interviewed roughly 50 architect-planners. Even though I had worked in the same building as Cornell's architecture faculty, I spoke to more architects during that year in Israel than I ever had at home. After several years of editing and getting approvals for publication from a selection of our interviewees, we then went through 20 publisher rejections—too much Israel for an American planning audience, too much planning for an Israeli audience—before we found public history series editor Michael Frisch at SUNY Press. He was well worth waiting for: Frisch wrote such an insightful recommendation letter to SUNY's editor in chief that it should have been published itself. Our collection of Israeli community builders' profiles was finally published seven years after the sabbatical (Forester, Fischler & Shmueli, 2001).

Practice Stories of Handling Long-Standing Public Disputes and Conflicts

Returning to Cornell in 1994, I began to work more closely with profiles of mediators—work that I could publish only after I lost too many years first to family turbulence, then to service

Evolution of a Critical Pragmatism **291**

as department chair, then to a marital separation leading to divorce. So after writing all too sporadically in the mid- and late 1990s, a sabbatical year at MIT in 2002–3 let me turn fresh attention to essays exploring mediators' practices, only published years later as *Dealing with Differences: Dramas of Mediating Public Disputes* (Forester, 2009).

Working with the first-person voice profiles of mediators detailing their actions, surprises, adaptations, learning, process design, and more, I found myself closer than ever to situations of what some have called "agonistic" conflict: conflicts of both interests and values, conflicts that were not going away—not going anywhere near erasure or invisibility—but yet lending themselves to provisional, temporary, practical resolutions or accommodations allowing affected parties to live together without doing violence to each other (cf. Gualini, 2015).

I see in retrospect that I was both anticipating and responding to more theoretical accounts of urban conflicts and even more particularly to *the forms of democratic response* pragmatically possible in such conflicts. Some planning theorists, following Chantal Mouffe and Ernesto LaClau, worry that "consensus building" implies erasing, denying, or presumptuously "solving" and so ending deep conflicts over identity, territory, and more (cf. Mouffe, 2005; Purcell, 2008). They are half-right, but not right enough, as if driving by looking only in the rearview mirror. Along with deep conflicts, questions of "What can and should we do now?" also persist. Because theory is not everything, and criticism implies alternatives, pragmatic imperatives also resist erasure. We can certainly acknowledge, recognize, and celebrate the deep and abiding conflicts present in democratic societies. We should certainly be deeply suspicious of any claims to consensus that would ever promise to erase or dismiss or wholly transcend or deny the depths, for example, of identity conflicts or of long-held commitments to territory or sanctity (of nature or religious beliefs). But that's the *easy* part—saying in effect at a great academic distance, "Vive La Difference!"—recognizing that deep conflicts in part shape who we are, that deep differences of identity and commitment and hope and vision will persist.

The more difficult questions, however, arise just because Mouffe and LaClau bring us to the real *inevitability of having to face and actually live with* such conflicts. So how, we need to know—and should be *curious enough* to ask, following Mouffe and LaClau's work—can democratic actors, for better or worse, contingently and practically, politically and ethically, handle such ongoing conflicts without killing each other and with some coherent sense of "doing well (rather than disastrously) democratically?" These are questions that activists, organizers, and planners in real time and space cannot avoid: They face persistent conflicts and must make political and ethical choices every day about how to respond pragmatically.

Neither agonists nor planning theorists can avoid these questions either: Given the inevitability of conflict, deeply held differences of identities and commitments, how can we imagine, enact, and evaluate better or worse ways of confronting, and not just rhetorically celebrating, the persistence, inevitability, and non-erasure of such agonistic conflict? If we listen closely, we might hear the ghost of John Page: "Could we please finish the sentence that begins, '*When I am resisting* neo-liberalism . . .' or '*When I am resisting* the pressures of globalization . . .' " So here too, the challenges of exposing planning theory's dirty little secret remain: In the face of neoliberal pressures, how might planners, activists, negotiators—practical people in various capacities—actually, in diverse settings, really respond? We need to explore real cases and learn from practice.

Much of my work since 2002, in lectures and essays, in *Dealing with Differences* (Forester, 2009), in the practitioner profiles in *Planning in the Face of Conflict* (Forester, 2013a) and in work on conflict, improvisation, and governance with David Laws (Laws & Forester, 2015), speaks both practically and theoretically to these questions of democratic conflict and agonism. This work moves beyond my earlier work in *The Deliberative Practitioner,* not because mediated negotiations are not deliberative—they are—but because these profiles of facilitative leaders so vividly inform public policy and civic governance disputes, with their rich complexities and entanglements, as they raise analytic and theoretical questions that students of planning practices must face. This work also speaks more powerfully, pedagogically, than any work I have done before. I believe students who are hungry for a rich sense of practice situations continually embrace these practitioner profiles in part because the practice contexts they present remain free of being laundered by academic social scientists or planning theorists.

But these books go far beyond pedagogy. This work grounds and extends earlier work on "learning" in planning. It shows more clearly how, in settings of contentiousness and conflict, third-party sponsors or even municipal planners might design processes of convening, joint fact-finding, inventing, improvising creatively, and decision making. Drawing from these practitioner profiles, this work raises practical administrative questions—and shows possibilities—of process design as never before: for mediators make agreements no more than midwives make babies!

Here we see third-party resolution of conflicts not by creating harmony or erasure of difference but by *enabling* differing parties to meet and listen to one another, to debunk presumptions, to recognize new issues, to invent and propose new options, to recognize one another and craft accommodations that they as lived participants actually want now, if not forever after. In these cases we see complex questions of considered judgment arise, vital questions of how democratic actors can learn about value as well as learn about others, as stakeholders work through conflicts to create new environments, new spaces and places, and new relationships.

If planners, or planning theorists, care about "participation," they have to face what it expresses: conflict. But if we care about conflict, we have to assess and draw upon diverse ways of responding to, if never fully resolving, passionately engaged conflicts of interests, values, even identities. That's why I was fascinated by mediators' practices.

Invited to a conference in Melbourne, Australia, in 2004, a host's comment helped me vastly improve this work. My keynote lecture had presented Lisa Beutler's striking mediation of a contentious land-use case (Forester, 2009, chapter 7; 2013a, chapter 4). That afternoon one of my hosts told me, "So, in my panel session, I tried to do what you talked about in your lecture: I gave the enviros 5 minutes, then the developers 5 minutes, then I let them each rebut the other . . . ." I was bewildered, thrown. I thought, "Oh my God, no, no, NO: *that's* not *mediating,* that's another animal altogether; that's *moderating* a debate!"

I had not talked about moderating debates at all. What had happened here? As I thought about it, I learned several things. First, I suspected that many other people who were also unfamiliar with mediation assimilated it but reduced it to what they *did* know about, the "neutral" procedural role of a moderator. No wonder that mediators' creative, deeply evocative, questioning work—"Can you make a proposal, given what you've heard *them* say?" and so on—often seemed unappreciated, lost to view and analysis altogether!

But my host had very usefully identified a distinct process of great significance in public policy disputes: He saw that *debates* had to be managed fairly—even if he did not see that mediators were *far less interested in moderating debates than in encouraging negotiators to be more probing, inventive, and productive.* Just as a substantial literature distinguishes "debate" from "negotiation" (e.g., Raiffa, 1983; Susskind, McKearnan & Thomas-Larmer, 1999), so do third-party tasks of moderating differ enormously and very practically from those of mediating.

I realized, too, that both mediating and moderating differed practically from another commonly used "third-party" term, "facilitating." But what was the difference? Here Austin echoed: We could learn by paying close attention to "what we said when" (Austin, 1961; Cavell, 1969). We speak of "facilitators" typically helping a group have a conversation, a discussion, perhaps a dialogue in which participants could all speak and listen, consider new perspectives, enrich what they had to work with—but not moderating contentious debate, and not necessarily mediating, midwifing working agreements about what to do.

Now I could see, then, that complex planning processes might, arguably, need *somehow* to embrace all three of these "processes"—dialogue, debate, and negotiation—and therefore practical planners might need to learn the distinctively practical skills of *facilitating* a dialogic conversation, *moderating* an argumentative debate, and *mediating* a practical, action-oriented negotiation (Forester, 2009).

After Melbourne, I collaborated with David Laws of the University of Amsterdam during my 2008–9 sabbatical. Together we explored practices of diverse community planners, consultants, and intermediaries between stakeholders facing challenges of conflict, improvisation, and governance (Laws & Forester, 2015). What I later came to call the "triple helix" of managing processes of "dialogue, debate, and negotiation" seemed to surface problems and reveal opportunities of practice in a deeply context-sensitive way.

Moving Toward a View of Practical, Context-Responsive Improvisation in Planning

I was spiraling back but moving forward at the same. My first sabbatical year's research in Cambridge taught me how planners often played roles "in between" multiple and conflicting parties. As many social network actors do, planners were intermediating whether they liked it or not. In most cases, of course, they were not mediators. But caring about participation and emergent conflicts, many planners had a great deal to learn from mediators—from how mediators listened, from how mediators leveraged expertise, from how mediators encouraged invention and the crafting of actionable agreements (Forester, 2013a).

Acting "in between" multiple and conflicting parties, intermediating planners needed dialogic skills to assess and frame problems; they had use the best available technical arguments, debated as they might be; they had also to worry about "what to do now," about negotiating practical agreements—to widen this street, to protect or redesign that park, to draft this new regulation. Here we might see, I thought, fundamentally practical constituents of context-responsive planning practice in complex settings with shifting environments, where few rules dictate what to do.

In 2012 it was time to test this hunch. I had been editing a book on the post-Katrina Cornell-ACORN planning partnership that Ken Reardon had led (Reardon & Forester, 2016). A third enthusiastic reviewer for Temple University Press asked for more explanation: "Could Forester write more about how the project team improvised, given the chaos of post-Katrina New Orleans?"

As I thought about this, I wondered if the triple helix scheme—of managing dialogue, leveraging and employing expertise, and negotiating what to do practically—could provide a

294 John Forester

good, even if not linear, account of how the participatory action research project linking Cornell and ACORN had worked. Our team had talked to the residents to begin to learn what they wanted, hoped for, and thought they could do next. Our team leveraged technical expertise to do stunning GIS and physical inventory analysis of damaged properties to inform what residents could and could not afford to rebuild. Our team had also, with Reardon's wisdom, early on forged a partnership with ACORN, without whose political muscle or negotiating power the land-use analysis could never have had a hearing by city and state politicians and officials (Reardon & Forester, 2016). Intrigued, I thought the tripartite scheme might really have legs—but only in action research?

So, invited to lecture at SUNY Buffalo the following spring, I raised the stakes. Could this triple helix of dialogue, technical argument, and negotiation make sense not just of the New Orleans project, but also of work as *different* as Norman Krumholz's in Cleveland's City Hall (no action research there?) and Ric Richardson's striking land-use mediation in Albuquerque (Krumholz & Forester, 1990; Forester, 2013b)? The SUNY audience was encouraging, but I had surprised myself. In their very different contexts, Reardon, Krumholz, and Richardson had all woven together elements of this three-part framework.

After further presentations at Dublin's 2013 AESOP meeting and in a 2014 formal lecture at the University of Michigan, I realized that my Melbourne host's "instructive mistake" had led me to an analytically fruitful, practically powerful, and politically astute account of how planners could act creatively and improvise in complex and contentious cases. Creative planning surely requires learning from and then moving in new, practical contexts of action: learning about what needs to be solved; learning from the best available science and expertise about what's technically possible; and learning with others about what can be done. Put most simply, without (i) dialogic understanding, we risk solving the wrong problems. Without (ii) expert debate, we risk tilting at windmills and attempting the technically impossible. Without (iii) pragmatically probing creatively crafted, jointly acceptable moves, we might settle for insight but fail to act. These are the challenges of exploring practically value, fact, and action, each historical, social, and political. Without attention to these challenges, public deliberation will fail; mediated negotiations will fail; many planning projects, I suspect, will fail.

But the inescapability of these challenges—of diagnosis and dialogue, expertise and debate, negotiation and action—does not so much "explain" creatively improvised planning as much as, I believe, it provides a framework or infrastructure for practically situated and responsive action. The theoretical and practical issues here integrate many themes in my earlier work on the micro-politics of planning. Improvising well in planning presumes a wise ability to listen beyond words, an ability to decipher or learn deliberatively about value. Improvising well requires assessing power and possibility, the move to free ourselves from self-limiting cynicism and the presumption that needless suffering cannot give way to better lives for many. Improvising well to respond justly as multiple, plural, and conflicting stakeholders find themselves interconnected and interdependent will require planners to integrate dialogue, expertise, and negotiation (Forester, 2009; 2013a).

Note

1 This raises both empirical and theoretical challenges. Consider a simple example. If we wanted to understand the possibilities of superb cooking, we wouldn't study how people cook on average; we wouldn't focus on most common or shared characteristics. We might consider instead what some basic

budget might allow and then search for those who've been creative, imaginative, innovative, and well-regarded cooks within that basic budget. The systematic study of what's ethically possible but not yet actual remains seriously understudied in planning, having little to do with idealism and much to do with practicality, ethics, and politics.

Author's note

Thanks to Kathy Quick and Laura Saija for their comments on earlier drafts.

References

Austin, J. (1961). A Plea for Excuses. In J. Austin (Ed.), *Philosophical Papers* (pp. 122–152). New York, NY: Oxford University Press.

Cavell, S. (1969). *Must We Mean What We Say?* New York: Scribner's.

Dallmayr, F. (1976). Beyond Dogma and Despair: Toward a Critical Theory of Politics. *The American Political Science Review, Vol. 70, No. 1*, 64–79.

Fischer, F., & Forester, J. (1993). *The Argumentative Turn in Policy Analysis and Planning*. Durham, NC: Duke University Press.

Forester, J. (1981). Questioning and Organizing Attention: Toward a Critical Theory of Planning. *Administration and Society, Vol. 13, No. 2*, 161–205.

Forester, J. (1989). *Planning in the Face of Power*. Berkeley, CA: University of California Press.

Forester, J. (1993). *Critical Theory, Public Policy, and Planning Practice*. Albany, NY: SUNY Press.

Forester, J. (1999). *The Deliberative Practitioner*. Cambridge, MA: MIT Press.

Forester, J. (2006). Exploring Urban Practice in a Democratizing Society: Opportunities, Techniques, and Challenges. *Development South Africa. Vol. 23, No. 5 (December)*, 569–586.

Forester, J. (2009). *Dealing with Differences: Dramas of Mediating Public Disputes*. New York, NY: Oxford University Press.

Forester, J. (2012a). From Good Intentions to a Critical Pragmatism. In R. Weber and R. Crane (Eds.), *Handbook of Urban Planning* (pp. 285–305), New York, NY: Oxford University Press.

Forester, J. (2012b). Learning to Improve Practice: Lessons from Practice Stories and Practitioners' Own Discourse Analyses (Or Why Only the Loons Show Up). *Planning Theory and Practice, Vol. 13, No. 1*, 11–26.

Forester, J. (2012c). On the Theory and Practice of Critical Pragmatism: Deliberative Practice and Creative Negotiations. *Planning Theory, Spring, Vol. 12, No. 1*, 5–22.

Forester, J. (2013a). *Planning in the Face of Conflict: Surprising Possibilities of Facilitative Leadership*. Chicago, IL: American Planning Association Press.

Forester, J. (2013b). Creativity in the Face of Urban Design Conflict: A Profile of Ric Richardson. *Planning Theory and Practice, Vol. 14, No. 2*, 251–276.

Forester, J. (2014). Notes on the Craft of Academic Writing. In Elisabete Silva, P. Healey, N. Harris, and P. Van den Broek (Eds.), *The Routledge Handbook on Planning Research Methods* (pp. 40–54). New York, NY: Routledge.

Forester, J., Fischler, R., & Shmueli, D. (Eds.). (2001). *The Community Builders: Profiles of Israeli Planners and Designers*. Albany, NY: SUNY Press.

Forester, J., & Kreiswirth, B. (1993). *Profiles of Planners in Housing and Community Development, in Land Use and the Environment, in Historic Preservation, in Participatory Action Research, and Women in Planning* (Typescript). Ithaca, NY: City and Regional Planning Department, Cornell University.

Forester, J., & Stitzel, D. (1989). Beyond Neutrality: The Possibilities of Activist Mediation in Public Sector Conflicts. *Negotiation Journal, Vol. 3, No. 3*, 251–264.

Freire, P. (1970). *Pedagogy of the Oppressed*. New York, NY: Continuum Books.

Friedman, M., & Friedman, R. (1979). *Free to Choose*. New York, NY: Harcourt Brace and Co.

Gaventa, J. (1980). *Power and Powerlessness*. Urbana, IL: University of Illinois Press.

Gilligan, C. (1982). *In a Different Voice*. Cambridge, MA: Harvard University Press.

Gitlin, T. (1987). *The Sixties*. New York, NY: Bantam Books.

Gualini, E. (2015). *Planning and Conflict*. New York, NY: Routledge.

Habermas, J. (1970). *Toward a Rational Society*. Boston, MA: Beacon Press.

Habermas, J. (1979). *Communication and the Evolution of Society*. Boston, MA: Beacon Press.

Hoch, C. (2011). *What Planners Do*. Chicago, IL: American Planning Association Press.

Krumholz, N., & Forester, J. (1990). *Making Equity Planning Work: Leadership in the Public Sector*. Philadelphia, PA: Temple University Press.

Laws, D., & Forester, J. (2015). *Conflict, Improvisation, Governance*. New York, NY: Routledge.

Lipsky, M. (1980). *Street Level Bureaucracy*. New York, NY: Russell Sage.

Lukes, S. (1974). *Power: A Radical View*. London: Macmillan.

Majone, G. (1989). *Evidence, Argument and Persuasion in the Policy Process*. New Haven, CT: Yale University Press.

Mouffe, C. (2005). *On the Political*. New York, NY: Routledge.

Nussbaum, M. (1986). *The Fragility of Goodness*. Cambridge, MA: Cambridge University Press.

Nussbaum, M. (1990). Finely Aware and Richly Responsible: Literature and the Moral Imagination. In M. Nussbaum (Ed.), *Love's Knowledge* (pp. 148–167). New York, NY: Oxford University Press.

Podziba, S. (2012). *Civic Fusion: Mediating Polarized Civic Disputes*. Chicago, IL: American Bar Association.

Purcell, M. (2008). *Recapturing Democracy: Neoliberalism and the Struggle for Alternative Urban Futures*. New York, NY: Routledge.

Raiffa, H. (1983). *The Art and Science of Negotiation*. Cambridge, MA: Harvard University Press.

Reardon, K., & Forester, J. (Eds.). (2016). *Rebuilding Community After Katrina: Lessons from the New Orleans Planning Initiative*. Philadelphia, PA: Temple University Press (forthcoming).

Sandercock, L. (1998). *Making the Invisible Visible: A Multicultural History of Planning*. Berkeley, CA: University of California Press.

Sugrue, T. (1996). *The Origins of the Urban Crisis: Race and Inequality in Post War Detroit*. Princeton, NJ: Princeton University Press.

Susskind, L., McKearnan, S., & Thomas-Larmer, J. (1999). *The Consensus Building Handbook*. Thousand Oaks, CA: Sage.

Terkel, S. (1974). *Working: People Talk about What They Do All Day and How They Feel about What They Do*. New York, NY: New Press.

Throgmorton, J. (1996). *Planning as Persuasive Storytelling*. Chicago, IL: University of Chicago Press.

Walzer, M. (1980). A Day in the Life of a Socialist Citizen. In M. Walzer (Ed.), *Radical Principles* (pp. 128–139). New York, NY: Basic Books.

18

PRAGMATISM AND PLAN-MAKING

Charles Hoch

Overview

Do we need a theory to justify or explain how people make plans for places? I think not. Each person learns how to make plans growing up. This plan-making ability is part of the legacy of human evolutionary adaptation and cultural learning. Imagining the consequences of future action enables humans to consider what to do before doing it. Most human behavior follows contours of cultural tradition and social experience that people acquire at home, school, and work. These habits provide psychological fuel for the multitude of social routines people follow. Planning emerges as uncertain and unexpected events disrupt this continuity. People use imaginative conjecture to compare and assess potential responses. People plan.

Planning for communities, institutions, and organizations taps this tacit plan-making skill. The complex and complicated histories of how people plan places in and for diverse societies defy easy summary. Peter Hall's masterful book *Cities in Civilization* offers an excellent account of place-making (1998) (see Hall, 2017). John Friedmann provides a majestic overview of the currents of intellectual debate that informed the planning imagination in *Planning in the Public Domain* (1987) (see Friedmann, 2017). The entrepreneurs, master builders, engineers, generals, statesmen, accountants, financiers, speculators, swindlers, and clever makers of factories, skyscrapers, subways, campaigns, nations, loans, deals, and so much more used plans to tame and control natural forces and the uncertainty posed by their competitors. The successful adaptation of rational blueprints, strategies, regulations, and conventions yielded enormous gains in technical and economic growth and innovation.

The early spatial planning reformers for the most part recognized the efficacy of modern industrial expansion but hoped to tame the practices that produced the nasty side effects. For the first half of the twentieth century in the United States, the UK, and Europe the reformers made plans as professional consultants, activists, and government bureaucrats. Their plans produced mixed results. The Great Depression, sandwiched between two world wars, shifted attention to national policy. Government planning helped guide the economic and military conduct of war and reconstruction in its aftermath. As the demand for planning increased, so did the number of university schools and departments educating professional planners. For instance, in the US the number of planning schools and departments offering graduate degrees in urban planning increased from 4 in 1945 to 66 in 1975 (Krueckeberg, 1984). The proliferation of these schools created the audience for theory. Spatial planning emerged as an academic discipline that faculty developed and taught. Confident scholars envisioned ideas and skills that would not simply tame spatial problems but domesticate them within a rational urban system. The ambitious efforts to envision a unified systems order inspired the proliferation of critical planning theory ideas, including my own pragmatist variety (Hillier & Healey, 2008).

I left home to study as a true believer with strong doctrinal commitments. The complexity of the world and the intellectual rigor of graduate study taught me how to stop pursuing rational justification for judgment beyond the bounds of critical inquiry and practical solidarity. Rationality as conceived and practiced in modern institutions generates problems that go well beyond Max Weber's "iron cage" metaphor. The social, economic, and environmental problems that now accompany global urbanization emerge from the success of rational development. Pointing out the dark side of the rationality deployed by engineers, bureaucrats, technicians, designers, and economic analysts does not tell us what to do instead. I was attracted to the critical edge of pragmatist planning advice in part as it recognized that people can always make plans that draw upon the tacit plan-making skill each uses every day to negotiate uncertainty. Theorists need not solve the riddles of rationality before considering how to improve plan-making for places. The insights of pragmatist philosophy provide distinctions that spatial planners might use to shed light in the shadows to help people construct practical paths of reform.

The pragmatist approach I adopted envisions a liberal conception of deliberation as the best way (to date) for people to resist and reform problems of social and spatial complexity that accompany modern urban place-making. Since many plans shape what happens for any place, purposeful coordination will prove difficult as the powerful seek to avoid or undermine democratic collaboration. Meaningful collective action requires leadership, organizing, resources, trust, and more to turn plans into reality. Pragmatist spatial planning draws public attention to the promise of cosmopolitan places that support and nurture individual flourishing.

Pragmatist planning theory focuses on the concepts people can use to make plans together, testing how well these ideas improve practical judgment about complex problems often in unfavorable institutional settings. Those touched by the plan need be the ones who validate the consequences that ensue from its adoption. Planning offers advice that works as people take it. There are no shortcuts. Efforts to hand off the persuasive work of planning to institutional rules and government mandates will not work. Creating improved places requires that people learn to do the democratic civic work of governance that avoids the pitfalls of cynical statecraft, the seduction of corruption, the stupidity of simplistic maxims, and the many avoidable errors and temptations that accompany politics without attention to the multitude of plans in play.

A pragmatist planning theory helps people comprehend the limits of what plans do. It inspires people to study what and how plans contribute to commitment, choice, and action for places. But the pragmatist approach recognizes that plans do not make things happen. Plans offer advice and counsel, but only people and their institutions act. For the pragmatist, figuring out how to modify and amend the liberal moral framework for collaborative deliberation takes place as people touched by the consequences reconsider technical, political, and social relationships for each situation. For the pragmatist, democracy enhances the conceptual quality of the plan as people learn what it means and how it works, but also the authority and legitimacy of social dialog, consent, and compromise that cement intention, commitment, and action together. Professional spatial planning encourages a comprehensive outlook assessing the relevance and merit of future consequences for the many plans at play, even as coordination, reconciliation, and integration remain provisional and incomplete. Planning scholars still have much to learn about how people make plans together for places all over the globe and how we learn critically from one another. This explains the pragmatist focus on the kind of practice planners do. It also means that theory works more like a flashlight than the sun.

Intellectual Autobiography

I grew up the youngest in a conservative Catholic family. I enjoyed the security and insularity afforded by my father's successful career as an electrical engineer selling infrared siting systems in the aerospace industry. The household moved from Minneapolis to Fort Worth and then on to Dallas and back to Fort Worth before ending up in San Diego where, after 12 years of parochial school education, I started college study in a Diocesan seminary affiliated with the University of San Diego. Pursuing a double major in philosophy and psychology while living the regimen of early mass, daily meditation, and early lights out with a small community of other young idealistic men proved incredibly fulfilling. I discovered the power and discipline of intellectual inquiry together with others whose solidarity and friendship helped me understand the kind of person I was and might become. The doctrinal details that loomed so important at the time were merely vehicles used to cast the ideas we were learning into critical debates, theatrical performances, and practical pastoral work. I spent one semester teaching first graders and then another teaching inner-city middle school teens and spent my fourth year teaching philosophy to high school seniors. My frequent failures in each of these encouraged me to adopt what I later learned to call a participatory pedagogical approach. The meaning of concepts, arguments, and narratives required attention to the experience and context familiar to the student audience. This meant I had to adapt and adjust to meet their purposes and needs—something that proved neither easy nor natural to do. But I learned that I could do it and improve with practice.

A clever and fervent member of a small cohort, I was selected to attend theology studies at the North American College in Rome in 1970. This catapulted me into a challenging intellectual arena that clearly framed for me the institutional leadership role I was supposed to learn to play. Surrounded by brilliant students, selected from all across North America, I encountered a wider spectrum of intellectual views about Church doctrine, but more exciting was the range of opinion and argument about morality, politics, and social change. When asked to take an oath against modernism I was consciously awakened to the socialization I had taken for granted and embraced with innocent enthusiasm. My commitment to learning and inquiry began to trump my allegiance to the Church. Historical study and increasing familiarity with the details of the hierarchical culture and organization sapped my faith. I read and studied an amalgam of philosophy, social theory, and history that accelerated my exit even as it increased the burden of grief I felt at losing the community and solidarity of friends and colleagues.

Bereft and broke, I returned to San Diego after one year and agreed to work as education coordinator for a huge parish. A taciturn Irish pastor had turned parishioners against a convent of renegade Sacred Heart nuns. The practical demands of collaborating with parents

300 Charles Hoch

(mainly mothers), the amazingly dedicated (and maligned) nuns, and a host of volunteers nurtured a nascent feminist sensibility toward community-building in the shadow of the local patriarchy. The ironic handoff of religious education to empowered women finalized my complete loss of faith in Christianity and God. I looked for a secular escape hatch.

I returned to graduate school at San Diego State, studying clinical psychology. Conducting experiments and assessing the merits of different therapies did not keep my interest. I discovered urban planning in a fateful scan of the San Diego State College catalog! The urban form and cosmopolitan style I discovered living in Rome was not, I learned, a cultural accident, but the product of purposeful plans. I met with Jim Clapp, then director of the small master's degree in urban planning at San Diego State. Three hours of conversation and Lewis Mumford's *The City in History* (1961) and I was hooked. I entered the Master of City Planning Department with the 1973 cohort of planning students. I learned the craft of land planning with a policy and administration focus, taking entry-level internship planning jobs for the regional San Diego Comprehensive Planning Organization (CPO now SANDAG) and the newly formed San Diego Regional Coast Commission. The California environmental movement had established an innovative legal beachhead, and I was one of the grunts scurrying on shore to plan for nature. I did environmental planning, identifying open space areas, researching municipal regulatory practices, calculating and mapping noise impact contours, estimating beach access using punch card computer simulations, and staffing assorted meetings of local public officials and planners discussing environmental policy.

My philosophical training led me through some of the epistemic debates of contemporary continental philosophy. I read Kant and Hegel as a prelude to Marx, but I never completely abandoned the Aristotle gleaned from Aquinas. I took seriously the philosophical efforts to resolve and settle the split between science and belief; skepticism and commitment; fact and value. I brought to these readings my psychological outlook and the sensitivity to practical consequence acquired teaching children, organizing events, and collaborating with many different people to accomplish modest goals. Learning to make plans for places proved a useful transition. An experienced county planner and occasional mentor posed a question in 1974 that still informs my theoretical work. Do professionals make good plans or do they make plans to do good? The abstract philosophical tension between right and good seemed to me something planning should resolve, and yet practice treated the two as distinct. I was struck at the time that elected officials and various civic stakeholders make sophisticated political judgments about specific environmental policies and programs, and yet they display superficial ideological planning judgments about the same issues.

I applied for doctoral study at UCLA and was admitted in the fall of 1975. I got to learn from John Friedmann, who had just published his ambitious book *Retracking America* (1973). He critiqued the sort of rational planning he acquired studying planning at the University of Chicago and proposed social learning as the way to reconcile the crisis of valuing and knowing. Friedmann framed his work in relation to the theoretical ideas of Karl Mannheim about social planning, proposing trans-active planning to remedy the tension between values and knowledge.[1] He envisioned a synthesis that would scaffold social action.

Friedmann used social psychological insights to argue that people would need to engage in small group learning to develop understanding to bridge the value thought divide as they conceived plans for the future. He did not detail how such learning might work nor at the time appreciate how the institutional articulation of such learning would require a more complex set of changes than his proposals could anticipate. He later criticized his work for failing to deal with questions of social and political power (Friedmann, 1987), laying out a more detailed proposal for how social change might happen from the household scale up. I wanted to learn how planning as social learning might work in the context of the complex social and psychological conditions that shape what people believe and do.

As a doctoral student at UCLA, I explored the historical roots of the Progressive political movement in the early twentieth-century United States, paying attention to theoretical arguments about social change and the role of city planning. I entered the world of Marxist scholarship, plowing through all three volumes of *Capital* and the *Grundrisse* and the rapidly expanding extension of these ideas to urbanism and place, most notably the early work by David Harvey, Manuel Castells, and Henri Lefebvre. The conceptual analysis of political economy provided compelling critiques of social inequality and injustice that fuel and accompany US urbanization. But they offered little useful advice for practical planning (other than heroic resistance).

I also studied the work of critical theorists of the Frankfurt School where I discovered the Habermas of *Knowledge and Human Interests* (1971) and *Theory and Practice* (1973). Professor Allen Heskin and I obtained grant support to explore the pragmatist philosophical roots of the Progressive movement in the US. How did these ideas contribute to debates about the meaning and purpose of planning for public good? We hoped to debunk the limits of pragmatism as a rationale for public planning. Instead I discovered pragmatism and its pervasive influence as a contested set of ideas about the importance of practical judgment and learning as a guide for public policy reform. Pragmatism promised to offer more useful and practical understanding for the kind of social learning Friedmann proposed and in my mind a more useful resource for grasping planning than critical theory (Bernstein, 1971). Could pragmatist planning theory comprehend systemic exploitation and still conceive alternatives to reduce suffering and replace socially repressive norms and practices tied to social class, racism, and cultural exclusion? How could these encompassing questions about social injustice find meaning in making plans for places (Hoch, 2007a)?[22]

My dissertation work focused on social theory and policy, paying close attention to Marxist scholarship on urbanism to inform a detailed historical study of municipal incorporation and annexation in a large portion of Los Angeles County (Hoch, 1981). I did indeed document 1) how local government contributed to increasing socioeconomic and fiscal inequality within the metropolitan region and 2) how comprehensive plans for balanced municipal communities were displaced by the efforts of social and corporate elites to protect private land using municipal land use control, while obtaining fiscal subsidies from others for local services. I learned how powerful landowners made plans for places, obtaining municipal authority to legitimize and support their claims. The formation of uneven and unequal suburban municipalities in Los Angeles County could succeed because the ensuing governments contracted with the county government for urban service and infrastructure provision. Ironically, the creation of diverse suburban locales that Tiebout famously characterized as competitors for discerning migrants in a suburban market was actually a tool for hierarchical sorting along class lines. Comprehensive spatial plans for suburban places, which had combined the interests of a socially diverse community, were ignored. I wanted to figure out how spatial planning might work. I set out to reconcile the demands of the critical political economy with pragmatist contextual learning tied to practical democratic learning.

302 Charles Hoch

My intellectual mentor was Peter Marris, who came to UCLA soon after I arrived. He helped me through the dissertation, but mostly he taught me how to grasp the social and psychological meaning of uncertainty and the challenge for spatial planning (Marris, 1987, 1996). I learned from him how to pay attention to the uneven distribution of uncertainty across dimensions of privilege, status, position, and class. He introduced me to Berger and Luckman (1966) and how philosophical, psychological, and social theory could help us comprehend how people form attachments to place and how change can generate loss and ensuing grief. Several conceptual insights from Marris influenced my work. First, the meaning of plans combines emotional attachment and conceptual comprehension. We learn these meanings within specific cultural and personal relationships developed to anticipate and cope with uncertainty. Second, the uneven social distribution of uncertainty based on class or status not only burdens the working classes and socially marginal groups with ignorance, but it encourages them to feel morally responsible for this condition. Richard Sennett's work (1970, 2008, 2012) has proven especially helpful in understanding how people assimilate social conditions in personal terms that ironically undermine their capacity to recognize and resist exploitation. Third, efforts to foster forms of social reciprocity to remedy social inequalities must include attention to the details of the places people inhabit and their individual experiences.

I entered a competitive academic job market in 1978 with an almost completed dissertation and accepted an offer to teach in the Community and Regional Planning Department at Iowa State University. I taught land use, housing, and planning theory to earnest students from small towns across Iowa. Dissertation done, I turned my attention back to theory and read an essay by John Forester in the bulletin of the American Collegiate Schools of Planning (1980)—an essay that was printed without his permission. Forester was deeply influenced by pragmatist ideas exploring how the kind of democratic deliberation that Friedmann espoused might work in the context of ongoing power relationships. Forester (*Planning in the Face of Power*, 1989) used observation and interviews to describe how professionals might conduct deliberations in practical contexts. For instance, his study of mediation develops a robust form of professional action that helps bind together differences in moral outlook and conceptual understanding. His subtle and layered examples move us past the rigid stereotype of professional integrity as "Speaking truth to power!" (Wildavsky, 1974).

Forester, Howell Baum, and I met for breakfast in 1980, to discuss how we might study the practice of planning using distinct yet related approaches. Baum hosted early morning informal meetings at the annual ACSP conferences, inviting participants to discuss the study of planning practice. This eventually traveled onto the official ACSP program, in what later became the planning theory track. I absorbed the ideas of both, and we became close colleagues and friends. Meetings at the annual ACSP conference became an institutional anchor for the development of planning theory discourse. Thomas Harper and Stan Stein (2006) joined the pragmatist conversation in 1983, bringing philosophical discipline to the discourse. Seymour Mandelbaum (2000), the eloquent historian and theorist, entered the fray as well, holding us in thrall at his terrifying brilliance. (When do you expect to stop practicing planning and start doing it?) Many others contributed, and the conversations moved beyond the confines of theory to other intellectual and professional domains.

The early 1980s proved especially challenging to the planning profession in the United States, as the Reagan administration targeted federally supported planning institutions and programs for major cuts and elimination. I had taken an assistant professor position at the

University of Illinois at Chicago, hired as part of an effort to turn an urban sciences program into a planning school under the leadership of George Hemmens—a transportation planner from the Department of City & Regional Planning at the University of North Carolina who had embraced critical theory and hopes for a revival of the legacy of the Chicago Planning School at the public university. We collaborated on several projects. One involved a study of informal helping in three working-class Chicago neighborhoods hard hit by the loss of industrial jobs. We discovered that asking people about relationships with family, friends, and neighbors was crucial in learning about informal help. I focused on how the social meaning of these relationships—especially the quality of reciprocity—shapes how and what help people gave and received (Hoch & Hemmens, 1987).

Homelessness had become the focus of public attention, as destitute poor people unable to rent a place to live slept at train stations, under viaducts, and in parks. I joined the local homeless coalition and work on a citywide study of single-room occupancy hotels—buildings that house Chicago's single working poor. I quickly abandoned my stereotypes about hotel living, as interviews revealed how these high-density buildings provided an affordable urban community for the working poor. I met social historian Bob Slayton, a research analyst at the Chicago Urban League, and we teamed up to write a book about Chicago's homeless that redeemed the moral integrity of the old homeless.

My thinking about the homeless problems was a synthesis of pragmatist insights modified with critical insights from Michel Foucault and Richard Sennett (Hoch, 1986). The diverse assortment of residential hotels that accompanied the emergence of industrial cities in the US had provided a complex stratified residential infrastructure for the workers who traveled across the country building dams, harvesting crops, milling lumber, and wrangling cattle. The concentration of these hotels on skid row and tenderloin districts fostered urbane communities that made a place for even the most destitute to find refuge, social contact, and opportunities for employment. The working poor obtained both privacy and community, which many used to achieve social standing and autonomy.

As the manufacturing economy in Chicago dramatically restructured and contracted during the late 1970s and '80s, unemployment increased. As unprecedented numbers of people became homeless, reporters and liberal activists blamed job loss. They contrasted the new deserving homeless against their immoral skid row predecessors. Instead of telling a story of community lost they told a story about social need. The social service professionals planning for the homeless imposed the kind of judgments that Foucault had so cleverly analyzed and warned against. Ironically, the poor did not identify themselves as homeless. They offered more complex accounts of their struggles for autonomy and respect in the face of difficulty and failure. Our book tried to reframe the problem from serving needs to fostering community (Hoch & Slayton, 1989).

Preserving and building supportive residential housing became an important part of my professional life after this study. I worked with advocates, affordable housing developers, and social service providers lobbying local and state government to amend building regulations that outlawed residential type hotels and shift the focus away from shelters as solutions for homelessness. After a dozen years of study and advocacy I was invited to join the board of Lakefront SRO in 1998. In that capacity I provided counsel and support for the preservation and construction of thousands of affordable dwellings for very low-income, vulnerable people. These buildings provide privacy and community, enabling residents to obtain security and autonomy. Many of their needs persist, but they no longer define their identity or future.

The '80s were not kind to professional urban planners in the United States. The Reagan administration cut federal funding for local comprehensive planning and the system of regional planning agencies that had helped monitor and regulate the federal grants economy. Planning employment took a nose dive in the 1980s. The rise of conservative think tanks promoting neoliberal ideology mocked the idea that professional planners working as public employees could serve the public interest. The already tough job of local planning got harder. In 1986 I was asked by the president of the APA, Dan Lauber, to study the threat to planners generated by the conservative turn in government. I conducted a national survey for APA, investigating the relationship between political conflict and professional planners (Hoch & Cibulskis, 1987; Hoch, 1988). The best predictor of job-threatening conflict was holding a planning director position for a local government agency (municipality or county). Differences in style, method, or belief made little difference. In the US, professionals with some authority risked losing their job by offering advice that challenged private interests. I set out to learn in more detail how professional planners did planning work in response to these institutional challenges.

In 1988 Forester hosted a workshop of eight scholars (including Howell Baum, Linda Dalton, Patsy Healey, Norm Krumholz, Judith Allen, and Sy Adler) to discuss the manuscript he had prepared with Krumholz, the former planning director of Cleveland. After receiving our feedback on what became *Making Equity Planning Work* (Krumholz & Forester, 1990), Forester challenged the group to study a planning practitioner for a day. Linda Dalton responded by updating the review of research on planning practice (Dalton, 1989); Patsy Healey studied a colleague for a day and published her findings (Healey, 1992); and I spent two years observing and interviewing 39 planners, publishing the findings as *What Planners Do* in 1994. In that book I use pragmatist ideas to guide the research and argument.

As I conceived *What Planners Do*, I was trying to put the pragmatic ideas I was learning to practical use as guides for how and what I studied. Ironically, a book written out of theoretical conviction was treated more as a storybook about the practice of planning than a sustained argument about the theoretical meaning of planning practice. I began to recognize the limits of planning and plan-making as I considered the complex ways that professionals described and conducted their work as planners. The social, psychological, political, and cultural dimensions that inform and accompany the practical judgments professionals make include more than any pragmatic conception of planning could grasp and interpret. The limits included more than the ideological and institutional beliefs and norms of neoliberalism that were gaining momentum and intellectual respect.

Personally and practically, I struggled to find ways to practice spatial planning and to find ways to improve institutional relationships between the profession and academia. I was convinced on both theoretical and practical grounds that both would benefit from closer and more engaged contact. However, the merger and the ensuing separation of the ACSP from APA and AICP had left a deep residue of suspicion and mutual recrimination. The practitioners insisted upon training linked to professional experience, and the academics critical inquiry tied to university scholarship. These differences were to diminish over time. In retrospect, the separation was a good one for the academics who took practical steps to build a strong association that hosted an annual conference, develop a journal, and develop a national accrediting body with the eventual support of APA. I ran for the ACSP governing board in the early 1990s and decided to use my committee work to build some bridges. I created sessions at the annual conference of both APA and ACSP that invited practitioners from the AICP leadership to contribute in planning joint sessions. We focused on ideas and issues that were of joint interest.

I met Frank So, who was the director of the Chicago office for APA, as I studied how professional planners coped with political conflict (Hoch & Cibulskis, 1987; Hoch, 1988). It was in an ACSP meeting with Jay Chatterjee and So that I discussed the prospects for developing a textbook series for planning that would be published by APA Planners Press. I had proposed a revision of the *Green Book* that would tap the considerable resources of the planning faculty represented in ACSP. Frank mentioned that the publishers of the 1988 edition, *Principles and Practice of Urban Planning,* might consider publishing a new edition. I was hoping that APA would consider sponsoring a more expansive and theoretically informed text. But the decision to maintain ties with ICMA proved too strong to break. I did manage to convince Frank to allow me and co-editor Linda Dalton to put out a request for chapter proposals, in effect soliciting and reviewing chapter ideas from many of the best planning scholars. Thirty scholars eventually teamed up to collaborate in writing the text (Hoch, Dalton & So 2000). We continued the Green Book tradition that stretched back to the original 1941 edition prepared by Ladislaus Segoe and six practitioners. Only this edition adopted a distinctly pragmatic approach linking research and policy knowledge with practical problems (1941). The interdisciplinary approach earned the scorn of Israel Stollman, the former executive director who had engineered the ASPO-AIP merger in 1978.

Professional Development and Pragmatist Ideas

As a graduate student at UCLA in the late 1970s, I supported myself working as the director for a small urban studies program sponsored by Antioch College. Antioch embraced experiential education and a complex evaluation system that focused on learning outcomes rather than grades. I learned how to describe and evaluate experiential activity in relation to different concepts. Additionally, as a teaching assistant for Alan Heskin I helped coordinate the internship seminar for several large cohorts of UCLA master's students. We used group discussions, interviews, presentations, and various forms of active social learning to encourage student reflection and integration of concepts tied to their professional experience. The ideas we discussed with each other about practice had relevance for my own work as teacher and scholar. I developed a professional development seminar at the University of Illinois at Chicago (UIC) in 1982 and taught it for 25 years. Critical reflection on practical problems and stories focused attention on how to learn from experience that integrated attention to specific public problems combining political, professional, and personal beliefs (Hoch, 1984a).

I was not alone in carving a theoretical path informed by pragmatist ideas. Many planning analysts studying urban planning inspired by a pragmatist outlook conducted empirical work on planning practice. The debates that led to pragmatism's focus on how power, politics, and the public interest shape urban plans fueled these studies (Hoch, 1984b). How can professionals and other civic actors (aka stakeholders) who look to the future anticipate and build democratic intelligence in routine deliberations and even foster compassion in the face of conflict and tragic suffering (Forester, 1989, 1999, 2009)? What sort of institutional changes enhance the quality of democratic participation as they improve the efficacy of plans (Van Herzle, 2004;

306 Charles Hoch

Healey, 2010; Innes & Booher, 2010)? How do we make plans serving a public interest without distorting the plurality of interests that accompany the spatial complexity of the places people inhabit (Susskind & Cruikshank, 1987; Margerum, 2002; Goldstein & Butler, 2010)? How do we meet the demands of efficiency even as we reframe these to include new technologies, new modes of participation, and increasing sensitivity to demands for environmental sustainability (Throgmorton, 1996; Van Eetern & Roe, 2000; Umemeoto & Suryanata, 2005)? In research like this analysts look to the consequences of current conventions—usually focusing on very specific cases using detailed narratives and arguments. In these accounts, it sometimes helps to discuss what theory means for practice, but mostly the arguments and evidence draw attention to practical changes about what to stop doing and what to try, testing the efficacy of different types of democratic participation combining issues of social trust and legitimacy with concerns about cognitive competence and functional adaptability. The scholarship by Judith Innes played a prominent role.

Innes was busy doing research on planning practice at Berkeley in the early 1990s, exploring and testing different forms of collaborative planning for local community development and large regional water projects. In 1995, she published an article that claimed paradigm status for the awkwardly named communicative action theory. A few years later Patsy Healey published her book on collaborative planning (1997). These published works became the center of an amazingly fruitful theoretical debate about the politics of practice, inviting professionals and other practitioners into the conversation. The leftist political economists reacted most negatively. I got involved by accident. I posted a long e-mail response to a question about pragmatist planning theory to Niraj Verma's (Verma, 1996) planning theory LISTSERV. This attracted detailed criticism from Marsh Feldman, contrasting the idealistic relativism of pragmatism against the solid verity of critical realism. I turned the exchange into a paper for ACSP at the same session where Judith introduced her conception of *bricolage* (Innes & Booher, 1999). The e-mail debate found its way into the pages of Luigi Mazza's *Planning Theory Newsletter* (Hoch, 1997). Patsy Healey valiantly edited the polemical exchange. Different versions of the argument continue to emerge even to this day, as critics cast pragmatism as a kind of liberal utilitarianism or phenomenological idealism. I responded to another volley of criticism in an essay on "Pragmatic Communicative Planning" a decade later (Hoch, 2007a). Patsy Healey offers a cogent synthesis of both pragmatism (2009) and communicative action theory in the edited book recently published by Sanyal, Vale, and Rosen (Healey, 2012b).

Teaching and Learning Pragmatist Planning

I have spent most of my time teaching rather than doing professional planning. I taught the planning theory lecture class for 30 years. I also taught plan-making studio and workshop courses. In the lecture classes I work hard to communicate unfamiliar theoretical ideas to students. In the workshop classes I work mainly as advisor and coach. Few students find my pragmatist ideas attractive as theory, but they reconsider as I coach them about the meaning of problem framing, analysis, composing options, negotiating agreements, assigning responsibility, persuading skeptics, meeting deadlines, describing future effects, attributing causes, and making recommendations. Learning how pragmatist attention to problem setting, framing, context, purpose, and meaning can work to improve the practical grasp of what to do in the midst of a messy and complex situation proves more persuasive than intellectual argument. I do not impose a pragmatist doctrine but encourage students to use and assess the theory they use: the rationalist insisting that the findings of the analysis will convince the clients to change their ways; the designer whose beautiful rendering must not be sullied with ugly compromises; the advocate exposing the injustice for all to see; or the urbanist uncovering the contradictions of spatial policy. As the students work together as a group they may use the pragmatist framework to negotiate the doctrinal, personal, and methodological differences they have. This sort of learning was of course a version of the collaborative planning that my colleagues were studying, interpreting, and promoting. I wanted to learn even more about how pragmatist ideas might improve how students, professionals, and others make spatial plans.

After completing a three-year stint as director of our department, I turned my attention to research by cognitive scientists, neuroscientists, social psychologists, linguists, behavioral economists, and others studying how humans make plans for the future. I had a rudimentary knowledge of cognitive psychology, but I thought that many of the new findings had relevance not only for how individual planners make judgments for places, but that these ideas may improve how we study and understand plans and planning within diverse social and institutional settings. The cognitive research provided evidence for the pragmatist belief that people plan as they think rather than the other way round.

If people everywhere learn to plan as they develop from infant to adult, then we need not ground planning using theoretical justification. The debates about rationality, power, and the like reflect specific historical, cultural, and technical differences tied to familiar conventions that most of us learn growing up. The pragmatist approach treats the legacy of evolution as sufficient evidence for the adaptive powers of human inquiry and action. Adopting a pragmatic outlook means not having to make philosophical excuses for considering options before you decide. Humans acquired that cognitive capacity as a legacy from millions of years of evolutionary practice and thousands of years of civilized effort. Instead of casting theory as a conceptual foundation for planning practice, pragmatists imagine theory as a different kind of intellectual practice. In the spatial planning world, pragmatists avoid prescriptions tied to methodological rigor and certainty—making plans that fulfill rational expectations about correspondence. Is this the right plan? The pragmatists focus instead on the relevance of knowledge for the situation at hand, attending to the meaning and impact of future consequences. What difference will this plan make for our purposes now and later?

After the millennium I conducted a reconnaissance of spatial plan evaluation literature, deploying pragmatic distinctions to bind together different disciplinary viewpoints. In a *Planning Theory* article (Hoch, 2002) I review and describe how different kinds of practical plan assessment offer insight for plan-making without relying on strong claims about rationality. Professional planners make judgments that fall well short of rational optimization, yet still yield useful and meaningful results. Exploring how such judgment works led me to research by social psychologists, cognitive scientists, philosophers, neuroscientists, linguists, behavioral economists, and decision scientists.

Thirty-five years ago planning theorists contrasted synoptic, incremental, and various mixed theories about rational planning. But the cognitive research overwhelmingly sidelines the relevance of rationality as a prerequisite for practical judgments that include plan-making. The rational tools and methods matter, but not as theoretical foundations. The cognitive research provided evidence for the pragmatic conception of plan-making. I explored what this insight means for spatial planning theory in an essay (Hoch, 2007b) that integrated intention (Innes, 1995) and representation (Hopkins, 2001). When framed pragmatically, the two disparate approaches offer complementary insight available for practical plan-making. The convergence happens not by seeking convergence in disciplinary vocabulary and principles, but by focusing on consequences for use. The separations between analysis and synthesis are not epistemic, but practical. But what about the distinction between facts and values? As we make plans how do we attend to the desires and interests that motivate and inspire the purposes we imagine achieving? If rationality does not support professional planning advice, how do professionals cope with the complex interplay of emotional attachments that accompany spatial planning?

Research on emotions and practical judgment diminishes the strong distinction between descriptive and normative judgment. The prevalence of unconscious intuitive evaluation means that human cognition relies crucially on emotions to make sense of each other and the world. In modern society people acquire and nurture rational judgment that can critically review emotional influence (e.g., bias). But this intellectual and moral accomplishment offers only limited practical reach as we make spatial plans for communities of people. How do planning theorists conceive planning judgment that takes into account the unconscious emotional and social relationships shaping perception, attention, assessment, intention, and commitment? As I studied the importance of emotions for planning judgment, I focused on the split between objectivity and subjectivity that complements the conceptual divide between facts and values, analysis and interpretation. I used fieldwork interviews collected 20 years earlier to provide case examples of professional planners making judgments that offer useful and meaningful advice that escapes conventional classification as objective or subjective. A pragmatic approach to planning helps analysts and professionals understand how feeling works as part of the conceptual architecture for plan-making, combining causal attribution and moral interpretation (Hoch, 2006a).

But how do the many different people making plans for their city coordinate their many expectations? As professional planners make plans with and for other people, they hope to persuade people to consider options for the future. Doing this deliberately and democratically proves especially challenging. I explored this challenge in an essay that reviews Seymour Mandelbaum's argument that we imagine ourselves members of a liberal society composed of open moral communities (Hoch, 2006b). We can and do reconcile multiple memberships as we negotiate our differences in everyday life. While Seymour would avoid the pragmatist label, we both share a sympathy for pluralistic liberalism and appreciation for the exercise of practical virtue. The critical irony of a communitarian liberalism can promote the kind of civic respect needed to bridge the many communities we each inhabit. Democratic security and order rely on practical forms of egalitarian reciprocity that cut across and diminish uncertainty that reproduces privilege and exploitation. I use the political theory of James Bowman to argue that spatial plans provide important resources for coordinating the complex interdependent interactions that make these cosmopolitan communities possible.

Ironically, as I was imagining a pragmatist approach to complex interdependence, I was also studying efforts to mandate affordable housing plans in Chicago's wealthy suburbs (2007c). I conducted interviews with local elected officials and planners and found that making a plan need not involve offering meaningful advice. Most local housing plans met a legal standard but failed to offer any credible policies or steps to provide affordable housing. I argue that this was not the failure of planning. A few suburban municipalities did make plans to inform local public expectations and debate about affordable housing provision. Criticizing professional plan-making for failing to remedy important social inequalities, political corruption, or systemic bias too easily overlooks the important practical contributions that plan-making does provide (2007a). Adopting a comprehensive approach to local plan-making does not preclude political compromise, but it can shift attention to include practical tradeoffs that cope with interdependence and vulnerability otherwise excluded from consideration. A pragmatic approach provides a vocabulary for planning practitioners as they try to conceive future improvements for places shaped by complex forces beyond local control. Even in the midst of powerful political resistance, plan-making can show how practical egalitarian improvements can work. How might practitioners make these plans?

This question had animated my teaching, but now became part of curriculum discussions among my colleagues in the UIC planning department, as well as members of the Planning Accreditation Board (PAB) that I had joined in 2004. The rapid and successful growth of university planning schools in the US inspired the formation of the PAB by joint agreement of the American Planning Association and the American Collegiate Schools of Planning. Taking steps to assure university administrators that the planning discipline was theoretically informed and methodologically rigorous meant documenting in detail the academic quality of each member school. Pressure from practitioners to assess the professional relevance of the schools and complaints by planning school chairs about the onerous collection of compliance data fueled reconsideration of the review. I chaired the PAB curriculum criteria revision committee in 2005, which began a move from a focus on content to an emphasis on goals and outcomes. The focus on shared goals and outcomes shifted attention from the varieties of disciplinary expertise faculty bring to the curriculum to settle on planning and plan-making. At the same time similar discussions happened in my own department at UIC, as the 18 faculty considered shifting the focus of the core curriculum from applied social science (economics, statistics, and plan methods) to include a plan-making sequence (plan methods, plan-making lecture, plan-making workshop) for the first year. I had long argued for this shift among my peers, but a confluence of organizational changes and a willingness to collaborate resulted in approval of this change (Vidyarthi, Smith, Kawamura, Winkle & Zhang, 2012). It was not theoretical argument that persuaded my colleagues to change, but collaborative practical deliberation about purposes and outcomes. We could reach agreement on curriculum, pedagogical strategies, expected outcomes, and evaluation frameworks if we avoided disciplinary differences. We found room for convergence, developing practical judgments about how to teach together that were holistic, inclusive, and practical.

This experience proved useful for conversations about planning education for European schools of planning. Walter Schönwandt (2008), a colleague and friend, had studied practical problem-solving at the Institute for the Foundation of Planning at the University of Stuttgart in Germany since 1993. He introduced me to Bernd Scholl, the director of the Institute for Spatial and Landscape Development at the Swiss Federal Institute of Technology (ETH Zurich). Bernd invited me to join a small group of planning practitioners and educators to develop a program of higher education in spatial planning that reflected a deep commitment to practical plan-making with a distinct pragmatist flavor. We developed our ideas over three summer meetings hosted by Bernd at ETH in Zurich. Raphäel Fischler and I wrote the manifesto as part of a larger collection of positions and reflections for a practice-focused professional planning education (Hoch & Fischler, 2012).

The Future? Learn More and Better How to Make Good Plans

I have taught a class on planning theory at least once, and often twice, every year since 1979. When I started teaching as an assistant professor I tried valiantly to reproduce the current debates. My lectures would cleverly compile and condense the conceptual prerequisites drawn from philosophy, social, and political theory and were peppered with case examples. I learned that students studying to become professional planners want to learn what to do to plan and how to make plans. They had already concluded that making plans was important. That is why most applied and showed up ready to learn. I eventually adopted a pragmatist pedagogy that focused on using concepts introduced by notable practitioners who populate the history of spatial planning. My students still read ideas generated and promoted by most of the scholars at the ETH meeting, but they select and compare just a few of these ideas to demonstrate their learning. I do not expect them to write theory like we do, but to use a couple of our ideas to compare how planners and/or plans offer advice about what to do now to prepare for the future of a place. This approach treats the wonderful and diverse ideas of planning theory less as contestants for the true conceptual foundation of practice and more as diverse conceptual resources for comprehending the inherent complexity of spatial planning and plan-making. I do not try and distill the diversity of planning theory ideas but sample these and then focus on helping students use some of these to craft their own understanding of plan-making.

A few years ago I was asked to offer an overview of planning theory for the *Town Planning Review* (2011). As I prepared I studied some of the survey research on planners conducted by the American Planning Association and discovered that while four out of five professional planners learned about planning theory in school, very few reported using it on the job. My colleague Richard Klosterman (2010) had just tallied the content of planning theory classes in graduate schools across North America for the fourth time in 30 years. His survey revealed greater diversity of content than in the three previous decades. Professors of planning do not teach a theory for planning, but theories about planning. I make an argument that we should leave aside the quest for a theoretical foundation for practice and satisfy our hopes for convergence by focusing on how people use planning ideas as they make plans and do planning (Hoch, 2011).

As I study and learn how professionals and local stakeholders make plans for places in India (Vidyarthi, Hoch & Basmajian, 2013) and China (Wang & Hoch, 2013), the democratic dimensions of professional planning judgment prove surprisingly resilient. We have much to learn about the conceptual meaning of plan-making in different cultural and institutional settings. As planning ideas travel (Healey, 2012a) they change shape in ways that pragmatist theory can help interpret and revise.

The American Planning Association conducted a national opinion survey about community planning in the United States in June 2012. They found that four in five respondents supported collective purposeful planning for the future of their communities (APA, 2012). The survey did not mention the word government (or governance). Suspicion of government runs strong in the US, even as reliance on government policy and practice has never been so extensive. The APA leadership understood this and had the survey consultants cleverly frame the interview to focus on community at the local level. The important news is that most people in the US already understand the meaning and importance of planning as a useful tool for collective improvement. This finding does not square with the stereotype of widespread selfish

Pragmatism and Plan-Making **311**

individualism. The shift from government to governance in our theoretical debates reflects not only shifts in political theory and rhetorical innovation but taps the popular suspicion of the administrative state with the longing for community.

The good news is that we do not need to convince people about the usefulness of planning. Each person already does some planning. We do need to convince people why they should plan together for common problems tied to the place they inhabit. This proves to be a very difficult task because the complex causal relationships shaping the place require that we integrate scientific study with practical judgment. Sometimes we can use the materials and concepts on hand to consider facts and expectations and compose a plan that all agree to support. Other times we need to draw upon expertise to grasp the complex causes in play and describe the relevant facts that are neither obvious nor visible. In those, increasingly commonplace, situations professional planning expertise can provide crucial understanding of causal interactions and some of the salient risks while attending to diverse expectations and concerns (Hoch 2009). Taking a long-term comprehensive outlook as we make, compare, and assess plans for imagined future changes for a place remains relevant. I study planners doing just this in my fieldwork, and the more others do this, the more we will learn about how to cope democratically with the complex problems that the places we build create.

Notes

1 This separation was most famously formalized by the work of Immanuel Kant, whose monumental philosophical work shaped the contours of modern philosophical debate and the ensuing elaboration of social theory through the twentieth century.
2 Habermas describes his first visit with the pragmatist philosopher Richard Bernstein in 1972. He reports that Bernstein started helping him move away from a "naturalized Kantian pragmatism" to "the right kind of detranscendentalized Hegelian pragmatism, with an Aristotelian touch . . ." (Habermas, 2004, p. 29). See Hoch (2007a) for more about this version of Habermas.

References

American Planning Association. (2012). *Planning in America: Perceptions and Priorities.* Chicago: APA.
Berger, P. and Luckman, T. (1966). *The Social Construction of Reality: A Treatise in the Sociology of Knowledge.* New York: Anchor.
Bernstein, R. (1971). *Praxis and Action.* Philadelphia: University of Pennsylvania Press.
Dalton, L. (1989). Emerging knowledge about planning practice. *Journal of Planning Education and Research*, *9*, 29–44.
Dewey, J. (1927/1991). *The Public and Its Problems.* Athens, OH: Swallow Press/Ohio University Press.
Forester, J. (1980). What Are Planners Up Against? Planning in the Face of Power. *Bulletin of the Association of Collegiate Schools of Planning*, Summer 1980. [Published without permission].
Forester, J. (1999). *The Deliberative Practitioner: Encouraging Participatory Planning Practices.* Cambridge, MA: MIT Press.
Forester, J. (1989). *Planning in the Face of Power.* Berkeley: University of California Press.
Forester, J. (2009). *Dealing with Differences: Dramas of Mediating Public Disputes.* Oxford: Oxford University Press.
Friedmann, J. (1973). *Re-tracking America: A Theory of Transactive Planning.* New York: Anchor.
Friedmann, J. (1987). *Planning in the Public Domain.* Princeton, NJ: Princeton University Press.
Friedmann, J. (2017). Planning as a Vocation: The Journey So Far. In B. Haselsberger (Ed.), *Encounters in Planning Thought: 16 Autobiographical Essays from Key Thinkers in Spatial Planning* (pp. 15–34). New York: Routledge.

312 Charles Hoch

Goldstein, B. E. and Butler, W. (2010). Expanding the scope and impact of collaborative planning. *Journal of the American Planning Association, 76*, 238–249.

Habermas, J. (1971). *Knowledge and Human Interests*. Boston: Beacon Press.

Habermas, J. (1973). *Theory and Practice*. Boston: Beacon Press.

Habermas, J. (2004). The moral and the ethical: A reconsideration of the issue of the priority of right over the good. In S. Benhabib and N. Fraser (Eds.), *Pragmatism, Critique and Judgment: Essays for Richard J. Bernstein* (pp. 29–44). Cambridge, MA: MIT Press.

Hall, P. (1998). *Cities in Civilization*. New York: Pantheon.

Hall, P. (2017). Visions of Contemporary Planning: Stories and Journeys in Britain and America. In B. Haselsberger (Ed.), *Encounters in Planning Thought: 16 Autobiographical Essays from Key Thinkers in Spatial Planning* (pp. 51–70). New York: Routledge.

Harper, T. and Stein, S. (2006). *Dialogical Planning in a Fragmented Society*. New Brunswick, NJ: CUPR Press.

Harvey, D. (1973). *Social Justice in the City*. Baltimore: Johns Hopkins University Press.

Healey, P. (1992). A planners day: Knowledge and action in communicative practice. *Journal of the American Planning Association, 58*, 9–20.

Healey, P. (1997). *Collaborative Planning: Shaping Places in Fragmented Societies*. London: Macmillan.

Healey, P. (2009). The pragmatic tradition in planning thought. *Journal of Planning Education and Research, 28*, 277–292.

Healey, P. (2010). *Making Better Places: The Planning Project in the 21st Century*. New York: Routledge.

Healey, P. (2012a). The idea of "communicative" planning: Practices, concepts and rhetorics. In L. Vale, B. Sanyal, and C.D. Rosen (Eds.), *Planning Ideas That Matter: Territoriality, Governance & Reflective Practice* (pp. 333–357). Cambridge: MIT Press.

Healey, P. (2012b). The universal and the contingent: Some reflections on the transnational flow of planning ideas and practices. *Planning Theory, 11*, 188–207.

Hillier, J. and Healey, P. (Eds.). (2008). *Critical Essays in Planning Theory Three Volumes*. Aldershot: Ashgate.

Hoch, C. (1981). *City Limits: Class Segregation and Suburban Governmental Boundary Conflicts in Los Angeles County: 1940 to 1970*. PhD Dissertation, University of California at Los Angeles.

Hoch, C. (1984a). Doing good and being right: The pragmatic connection in planning theory. *Journal of the American Planning Association, 50*, 335–345.

Hoch, C. (1984b). Pragmatism, power and planning. *Journal of Planning Education and Research, 4*, 86–95.

Hoch, C. (1986). Homeless in the United States. *Housing Studies, 1*, 228–240.

Hoch, C. (1988). Conflict at large: A national survey of planners and political conflict. *Journal of Planning Education and Research, 7*, 25–34.

Hoch, C. (1994). *What Planners Do*. Chicago: Planners Press.

Hoch, C. (1997). Planning theorists taking the interpretive turn need not travel on the political economy highway. *Planning Theory Newsletter, 17*, 13–39.

Hoch, C. (2002). Evaluating plans pragmatically. *Planning Theory, 1*, 53–76.

Hoch, C. (2006a). Emotions and planning. *Planning Theory and Practice, 7*, 367–382.

Hoch, C. (2006b). Planning to keep the doors open for moral communities. *Planning Theory, 5*, 127–145.

Hoch, C. (2007a). Pragmatic communicative action theory. *Journal of Planning Education and Research, 26*, 272–283.

Hoch, C. (2007b). Making plans: Representation and intention. *Planning Theory, 6*, 16–35.

Hoch, C. (2007c). How plan mandates work: Affordable housing in Illinois. *Journal of the American Planning Association, 73*, 86–99.

Hoch, C. (2009). Planning craft: How do planners compose plans? *Planning Theory, 9*, 219–241.

Hoch, C. (2011). The planning research agenda: Planning theory for practice. *Town Planning Review, 82*, vii–xv.

Hoch, C., & Cibulskis, A. (1987). Planning threatened: A preliminary report of planners and political conflict. *Journal of Planning Education and Research, 6*, 99–107.

Hoch, C., & Fischler, R. (2012). Mission, goals and features of spatial planning. In B. Scholl (Ed.), *Higher Education in Spatial Planning*. Zurich: Swiss Federal Institute of Technology.

Hoch, C., & Hemmens, G. (1987). Linking formal and informal care: Conflict along the continuum of care. *Social Service Review, 61(September)*, 432–446.

Hoch, C., & Slatyon, B. (1989). *New Homeless & Old: Community and the Skid Row Hotel*. Philadelphia: Temple University Press.

Hoch, C., So, F., & Dalton, L. (Eds.). (2000). *The Practice of Local Government Planning*. Washington, DC: International City Managers Association.

Hopkins, L. (2001). *Urban Development: The Logic of Making Plans*. Washington, DC: Island Press.

Innes, J. E. (1995). Planning theory's emerging paradigm: Communicative action and interactive practice. *Journal of Planning Education and Research, 14*, 183–189.

Innes, J. E. and Booher, D. (1999). Consensus building as role playing and bricolage: Toward a theory of collaborative planning. *Journal of the American Planning Association, 65*, 9–26.

Innes, J. E. and Booher, D. (2010). *Planning with Complexity: An Introduction to Collaborative Rationality for Public Policy*. London: Routledge.

Klosterman, R. (2010). Planning theory education: A thirty year review. *Journal of Planning Education and Research, 31*, 319–331.

Krueckeberg, D. (1984). Planning and the new depression in the social sciences. *Journal of Planning Education and Research, 3*, 78–86.

Krumholz, N. and Forester, J. (1990). *Making Equity Plans Work: Leadership in the Public Sector*. Philadelphia: Temple University Press.

Mandelbaum, S. (2000). *Open Moral Communities*. Cambridge: MIT Press.

Margerum, R. (2002). Collaborative planning: Building consensus and building a distinct model of practice. *Journal of Planning Education and Research, 21*, 237–253.

Marris, P. (1987). *Meaning and Action: Community Planning and Conceptions of Change*. London: Routledge and Kegan Paul.

Marris, P. (1996). *The Politics of Uncertainty, Attachment in Private and Public Life*. New York: Routledge.

Mumford, L. (1961). *The City in History: Its Origins, Its Transformations and Its Prospects*. New York: Harcourt Brace & World.

Schönwandt, W. L. (2008). *Planning in Crisis? Theoretical Orientations for Architecture and Planning*. Aldershot: Ashgate.

Segoe, L. (1941). *Local Planning Administration*. Chicago: Institute for Training in Municipal Administration.

Sennett, R. (1970). *The Uses of Disorder: Personal Identity and City Life*. New Haven, CT: Yale University Press.

Sennett, R. (2008). *The Craftsman*. New Haven, CT: Yale University Press.

Sennett, R. (2012). *Together: The Rituals, Pleasures & Politics of Cooperation*. New Haven: Yale.

Susskind, L. and Cruikshank, J. (1987). *Breaking the Impasse: Consensual Approaches to Resolving Public Disputes*. New York: Basic Books.

Throgmorton, J. (1996). *Planning as Persuasive Story-telling*. Chicago: University of Chicago Press.

Umemeoto, K. and Suryanata, K. (2005). Technology, culture, and environmental uncertainty: Considering social contracts and adaptive management. *Journal of Planning Education and Research, 25*, 264–273.

Van Eetern, M. and Roe, E. (2000). When fiction conveys truth and authority: The Netherlands Green Heart planning controversy. *Journal of the American Planning Association, 66*, 58–67.

Van Herzle, A. (2004). Local knowledge in action: Valuing nonprofessional reasoning in the planning process. *Journal of Planning Education and Research, 24*, 197–212.

Verma, N. (1996). Pragmatic rationality and planning theory. *Journal of Planning Education and Research, 16*, 5–14.

Vidyarthi, S., Hoch, C. and Basmajian, C. (2013). Making sense of India's spatial plan-making practice: Enduring approach or emergent variations? *Planning Theory & Practice, 14*, 57–74.

Vidyarthi, S., Smith, J., Kawamura, K., Winkle, C. and Zhang, T. (2012). Teaching practical plan making in the core. *Town Planning Review, 83*, 625–646.

Wang, L. and Hoch, C. (2013). Pragmatic rational planning: Comparing Shanghai and Chicago. *Planning Theory, 12*, 369–390.

Wildavsky, A. (1974). *Speaking Truth to Power: The Art and Craft of Policy Analysis*. New York: Macmillan.

List of Abbreviations

AICP: American Institute of Certified Planners, a membership organization for professional planners in the US established after the ASPO-AIP merger in 1978.

AIP: American Institute of Certified Planners, the membership organization for professional planners in the US between 1917 and 1978.

ACSP: American Collegiate Schools of Planning, the organization of university-based planning schools and departments for the United States.

APA: American Planning Association, the membership organization for professional and all other urban planning officials in the US established in 1978.

ASPO: American Society of Planning Officials, a membership organization for elected or appointed planning officials between 1934 and 1978.

ICMA: International City Managers Association, the professional membership organization for city managers in the US.

PAB: Planning Accreditation Board, a nonprofit organization sponsored jointly by ACSP and APA to evaluate the quality of professional planning education by university-based schools and departments.

UIC: University of Illinois at Chicago

Terminology Glossary

Skid Row: An inner-city neighborhood with many low-rent hotels catering to single, low-income men.

PART 3
Epilogue

19

BACK TO THE FUTURE

A Personal Portrayal in the Interface of Past Planning and Planning Futures

Beatrix Haselsberger

In this book, 16 distinguished spatial planners with an average age of 75 (in February 2016), have unpacked the secrets of how and why they built their ideas over the last five to six decades. As a collection, these autobiographical essays provide an incredibly rich knowledge base which can be used to better understand how planning ideas have evolved and developed in some selected places throughout the world. However, our world is constantly changing, and spatial planning is not a static concept. Today's planning academics and planning practitioners have to work in a different context than that of the authors of these essays. Thus, the emerging question is: What lessons can be learnt from past experiences to enhance the future of spatial planning? There is no immediate answer to this question. However, through producing an intergenerational dialogue between the older generation of spatial planners and the next generation of spatial planners, a meaningful answer can begin to emerge.

This epilogue is written from the perspective of an early-to-mid-career academic spatial planner based in Austria. It addresses a broad audience, including current and future planning students, planning professionals as well as non-professionals who are eager to learn more about the fascinating world of spatial planning. In this epilogue, I seek to wrap up this book, partly by recapping, partly by counterbalancing the autobiographical essays of the older planners and partly by scrutinising some of the latest trends and circumstances in the field. From my own experience, I can see that addressing the interface between past planning and planning futures, or, in other words, between youthful vigour and mature wisdom, is an awkward endeavour. On the one hand, young planning academics and young practitioners face a continual dilemma of trying to step into the shoes of established spatial planners while also finding exciting new ideas to help spatial planning evolve in a different time and context. On the other hand, today's established spatial planners need to recognise the limitations of past and current planning approaches and must make their wisdom and experiences accessible for the next generation of spatial planners to carry it into the future. As a starting point in shaping contributions to the debate, it is readily accepted that today's young planning scholars need the assistance and advice of established researchers and academics in the field in preparing for their future role. Even more importantly, as many effects of planning actions are only visible in the long term,

318 Beatrix Haselsberger

there is a need to marry the impetuosity of youth with the wisdom of experience to produce genuine insight, learning and wise action.

Therefore in this epilogue I briefly discuss what I have learnt about spatial planning and about my future role as a spatial planner in the frame of this ambitious book. All of the arguments made in the next few pages build on my own background as well as my personal experiences and communication with the older authors who have contributed to this book over the last four years. Most of the points in my epilogue have not been written down in the essays, which unpack the records and thoughts of long, personal academic journeys. It is not the aim of this epilogue, as it is not the aim of the autobiographical essays in this book, to offer a merely scientific contribution that risks ending up in the archives of the academic ivory tower. On the contrary, I endeavour to paint a personal picture about spatial planning. In order to appeal to a wide spectrum of people who are destined to handle the future of spatial planning, I considered it necessary to remain "elementary" without being a stickler for details, to a certain extent. Staying elementary made me aware that some of the problems with which spatial planning is confronted today are elementary.

What is this epilogue all about? I first and foremost seek to create a meaning of the added value of spatial planning by summarising what I have learnt in discussions with the contributing authors. At the same time I draw from that a couple of problems that are, in my opinion, hindering spatial planning nowadays. I conclude this epilogue with some messages, which I have extracted for my future life as a spatial planner and which I hope are also stimulating others, who strive for enhancing the liveability and sustainability for the places we live in.

I am setting the scene for this epilogue with a personal, but in my view fundamental, experience. Whenever somebody asks me about my profession, I proudly say that I am a *Raumplanerin* (literal English translation: spatial planner). For me this is a fact. I hold a diploma (bachelor and master's) as well as a PhD in spatial planning. What I often tend to forget is that before I entered university, I had no idea what spatial planning was or even that it existed. How could I? Though it can be argued that as long ago as the eighteenth century, scientifically based knowledge about society was considered relevant to helping to improve the living conditions of the people, it was not until the mid-twentieth century that scientifically based spatial planning knowledge emerged and universities started to formalise and develop spatial planning programmes. From that time, the first handful of scholars were trained in spatial planning. In Austria, for example, those study programmes started in October 1970 (comparable to a today's three-year master's programme). So it should not come as a surprise to me that whenever I tell people that I am a spatial planner, they immediately ask: What is spatial planning?

This is a simple question, which every spatial planner (both academics and practitioners) should be able to answer without hesitating. But this is not the case. One of the underlying problems might be, as the contributions in this book demonstrate, that spatial planning encompasses different peoples, different planning cultures, different institutional and political embeddings, different fields of specialisation, etc. Therefore over the years many different definitions—or rather lengthy explanations—of what spatial planning is, have emerged. It seems to me that some of these explanations are personal attempts at self-manifestation resulting from the academic rat race, where the main objective is to leave a mark on the map. As a matter of fact, there are now upcoming voices in academia arguing that the effort to define spatial planning is futile. I absolutely disagree with this argument. It is true that spatial planning has manifold context-specific meanings stemming from its many roots and planning cultures and that it cannot be defined as a static concept for all times and places. But as I have learnt from the book authors, we are all planners who share a certain understanding of the substantive and procedural core principles, objectives and values of spatial planning, such as in regard to sustainability, liveability, spatial quality, equity, inclusivity, social justice, etc. It is this "substance of spatial planning", which, in my view, ties the many different context-specific takes on "what spatial planning is" together.

In my opinion it is high time that we, the current and future generations of planners, start to play in concert and work together on a shared and widely accepted explanation and definition of spatial planning. This definition should focus on the substance of spatial planning. Currently, spatial planning is so ill-defined and, to some extent, contentious that it appears to me that many spatial planners are not able to clearly explain the added value of spatial planning. All this makes me fear that in the long run spatial planning might not survive without a proper definition which clearly distinguishes it from other disciplines, such as architecture, geography or political science. Many of the book's contributors are slowly getting sick and tired of explaining and justifying themselves and their discipline on a regular basis. Some are even questioning whether they have failed in establishing a proper platform for spatial planning. The fact that several distinguished planners, who spent a significant portion of their lives in the field, have these questions is a disturbing but at the same time challenging signal for an early-to-mid-career planner like me. Considering that spatial planners all around the globe contribute to shaping, creating and making regions and cities and in doing so influence the living conditions of the people residing in these places, I do not even want to think about what our today's cities and regions would look like if there were no spatial planning and if spatial planning were done by non-planners. Though it is true that spatial planners make mistakes, as can be seen by looking at past planning disasters (some of them are mentioned by the authors in this book), I think that through learning from past planning experiences there is a chance to avoid making the same mistakes again in the future. In my view, such a learning process can only be fruitful if we have a clear picture of the real substance of spatial planning in mind. I therefore seek to share with you my personal explanation of what spatial planning is. I also provide a short personal definition, which sets out the essential attributes of spatial planning in a simple way, so that it can also be understood by the general public and finally contribute to the strengthening of spatial planning as a discipline. At this point I should highlight that the explanation and definition provided below summarise what I have learnt about spatial planning from all of these 16 distinguished planners who contributed to this book over the last couple of years. This is my personal view, which does not claim to be something absolute. I offer it here for the purpose of furthering the discussion about the future of spatial planning.

Explanation

Spatial planning is a professional activity and at the same time an academic discipline which, from the post–World War II period onwards, became embedded within the social sciences. For me, it has a social commitment to ensure the liveability of the built environment (including all its social, economic and political aspects)—with social justice as a guiding principle—and to secure sustainability of the natural environment. Spatial planning has at least four distinctive qualities, which in combination and interrelationship make up the unique characteristics of this field. First, spatial planning's substantive "material" objects of enquiry are both urban and rural spaces and their sustainable treatment at various scales of observation (from the neighbourhood level to the supranational scale). Second, spatial planning addresses the interface between knowledge and action in a recursive way. It reconsiders and evaluates actions in light of changing circumstances and consequently adjusts knowledge. Third, spatial planning is a context-dependent social endeavour where country specific geopolitical, sociocultural, economic, environmental, legal, administrative, local, regional, and national contexts and frameworks provide the rules of the game and so define the context-specific objectives of spatial planning. In accordance with these frames, endogenously shaped responses to specific planning situations emerge. Fourth, spatial planning should look at space in a holistic way and should produce integrative space-relevant knowledge by envisaging the interdependencies and consequences of conflicting interests.

Definition

Spatial planning is the scientific study of environmentally sustainable development, organisation and functioning of anthropogenic spaces in order to secure sociocultural needs.

Several of this book's authors made me aware that spatial planning is a relatively young scientific study, which is not yet fully established around the globe, when compared to traditional disciplines such as history, philosophy or medicine. Like many other new disciplines, spatial planning has also begun by taking a multidisciplinary approach. A multidisciplinary approach involves bringing a number of disciplines together, with each one working independently and primarily within their own frame of references and methods whilst being open and taking into account lessons from other disciplines. Even today spatial planning seems to have fluid boundaries with other disciplines, which enriches it from many directions. However, the field concerned, as I recognise it, is not a collection of different disciplines (e.g. architecture, geography, engineering, political sciences) which coexist and retain their disciplinary boundaries. Spatial planning has succeeded in becoming interdisciplinary, with varying levels of success depending on the country under consideration. An interdisciplinary approach weaves together forms of knowledge enriched by a broader perspective and produces new integrative knowledge through crossovers which goes with the need of a certain autonomy of the field. The authors in this book, who were at the forefront when spatial planning started its success story, are exemplars of how it was and is possible to occupy the space between disciplines and build new integrative knowledge. All of the autobiographical essays in this book provide a means to understand how spatial planning built its academic presence in the social sciences and how, step by step, it became a distinctive academic discipline in many parts of the world.

Spatial planning is derived from many different disciplinary perspectives and from many different places, as the 16 contributions in this book show. Because of these many roots, it turned out to be an impossible endeavour for the four senior members of the editorial advisory board to write a joint introductory chapter for this book. The objective of this chapter would have been to establish a broad overall picture of how the (planning) worlds around all the authors looked as they grew up and developed their ideas. I learnt from this unsuccessful writing attempt, and the many emotional discussions accompanying it, that there are huge differences in the way in which spatial planning is perceived and practiced in the different countries around the world. Even within supranational entities, like the EU or US, many different takes on what spatial planning is or should be can be detected. Moreover every country globally has its own country- and context-specific expression, which cannot be translated easily into any other language. For example, the meanings of the terms *Raumplanung, Raumordnung, Stadt- und Regionalplanung* (Austria, Germany, Switzerland), *Urbanistica, Pianificazione del territorio* (Italy), *Urbanisme et Aménagement du Territoire* (France, Belgium, Luxembourg), *Town and Country Planning, Urban and Regional Planning* (UK), or *Ruimtelijke Ordening* (the Netherlands) have all evolved in their own particular legal, socio-economic, political and cultural contexts. Strictly speaking, the terms are not internationally transferable to other countries, except in the most general sense.

The contributions in this book provide a means to understand that planning cultures and approaches naturally and traditionally vary from place to place, from context to context, and over time as well; they are all different from each other in a variety of ways. This contextual genesis of location-specific planning cultures and approaches made me aware that there cannot and should not be one single universal Anglo-American "big theory" or general valid global solution to spatial planning challenges. The emerging question then is whether this diversity is a problem. The answer is: No. On the contrary, as I started to understand in the frame of this book project, the strength of spatial planning lies precisely in its wide range, which provides us with an incredibly rich knowledge base for tackling future challenges in our continuously changing world.

As the net of professional contacts is ever-expanding, and planning ideas circulate through the Internet, I consider it important that we keep in mind that this does not mean that planning ideas must necessarily converge between countries or globally. They should not converge. If they did, it could be seen as a first brick in the wall of undermining social-cultural needs as well as the respective *genius loci*. Nonetheless there is great value in learning from planning ideas, both from other places and from other times. They provide us with a refreshing new perspective from seeing things in our own parochial churchyard, which enables us to critically question things we might have taken for granted so far. The difficulty in this enterprise however is not carving out planning concepts and ideas from one context and imposing them on a different one. Such attempts lead, unavoidably, to unpleasant consequences and interdependencies. Rather, we need to deconstruct and study planning concepts and ideas, in order to learn which responses to local, regional and national specific challenges can be carefully and sensibly transferred to another setting in a different time, context and situation. This also implies that we must refrain from pretending that we are experts in a different planning culture and approach from our own. A very difficult claim in a time when many young planners are seduced or forced to work in a different context than the one in which they were educated. But we need to keep in mind, as the essays in this book reveal to some extent, that every problem we solve creates new, unsolved problems. Moreover, the less we know about the country from which we "borrow" our solutions, and similarly the less we know about the country and the people for which we are planning, the more awkward the emerging problems will become.

The older authors of this book also made me aware that starting from the post–World War II period, spatial planning has been social science based. While before that time spatial planners focused merely on physical planning issues, after World War II a social commitment to plan the life space for and with the people in a sustainable way grew. I gathered from that two important lessons. First, spatial planning is neither a purely theoretical nor a purely practical endeavour. Similar to all serious disciplines, it is a combination of both theory and practice. On the one hand, it is planning practice which provides planning academics with a clinical gaze for perceiving spatial challenges "on the ground", including any relevant spatial relationships. On the other hand, planning theory should seek to illuminate planning practice by providing planning practitioners with a solid knowledge base for doing a good planning job as well as securing an excellent education based on scientific perceptions and disciplinary self-reflection. I feel that action without generated knowledge will not be successful because it tends to be short-sighted and error-prone. As I have mentioned before, spatial planning is not an arbitrary collection of several disciplinary perspectives in which every highly specialised expert involved (e.g. transportation planners, landscape planners, planning jurists, planning sociologists, planning economists and so forth) believes that his/her field is the most important one. Such a fight for pole position indicates that the experts involved in the spatial planning process are not in a position to see the wood for the trees and consequently are not able to look at the interdependencies between the different sub-areas of spatial planning. This could happen to generalist spatial planners as well, but if they feel responsible for working on the synthesis of the bigger picture, they might to some extent be successful in reducing some of the negative consequences for which the people "on the ground" would have to pay the bill in the end.

What became clearer to me in the frame of the many discussions with the authors writing in this book is that spatial planning cannot be understood only in bits and pieces. As indicated before spatial planners need to be generalists who, with the help of the knowledge provided from highly specialised experts, are able to see and understand the bigger picture. I learnt that only if we keep the big picture in mind can we adapt and respond properly to changing environmental and societal conditions. Our diverse world is constantly changing, so as to me it would be foolish to believe that we can stick to the mechanistic assumption of a simple cause and effect scenario. Have we not learnt anything from planning's colossal mistakes of the past?

From my own experience I know that the world of planning academia has become a battlefield with its own rules and that it is not always easy to get my voice heard. But, possibly it has been always this way. Luckily, in the frame of this book project, I managed to figure out for myself what I can do in order to not be trapped into short-lived mainstream thinking and how to break free from the oppressive chains of predefined system rules. I also realised that although it appears that spatial planners do not have much power to intervene in political power processes, they are not powerless.

To help me to remember the lessons learnt in my everyday life as a spatial planner, I created a list which describes some of the main characteristics that academics and practitioners alike, in my view, need to have for doing good spatial planning. I am aware that this list reads in some parts like a guide for "how to live a fulfilled life". But this does not mean that the points made are not specifically relevant for spatial planners. In my opinion, spatial planners should attach even more importance to them than the average person because they have the social responsibility to raise awareness and to be critical, sometimes even uncomfortable, guardians ensuring the environmentally sustainable development, organisation and functioning of our anthropogenic spaces in order to secure sociocultural needs.

The following list builds on what I have learnt from the older generation of contributors to this book. This list is my personal interpretation, which of course is also influenced by my specific context, of what has motivated and driven the book's authors when they were the newcomers to the field. As the world has significantly changed since the time this generation entered the field, I have carved out only those messages which also appear vital in today's context. Though the following list is a personal roadmap, I recommend it to everybody who wants to become a good spatial planner.

- *Be passionate and believe in your own way of thinking and acting!* One has to love the profession one has chosen. Otherwise the daily challenges of the professional life are an immense burden and a source of continuous job and family conflicts. If spatial planners become puppets of mainstream thinking or are doing their job just for the sake of money, they will never achieve satisfaction, nor will they be convincing or trusted.
- *Speak-out! No academic cocooning!* Spatial planners who wish to bridge theory and practice sometimes work in rough political and business environments. It is easy to cocoon ourselves in academic circles and milieus, but if planning academics wish to contribute to a better life in places, cities and regions, they must gather experience from within planning practice. They must speak out as well as engage with conflicts. In the long run, speaking out about what one feels, observes and anticipates will always be rewarded in one way or another.
- *Listen to people; reading international English journals is not a universal remedy!* Spatial planners are planning with people and therefore should always seek to have a discussion with them. Real mutual understanding requires easy communication. Spatial planners must communicate with citizens, stakeholders, politicians, real estate managers or lawmakers in their own local languages.
- *Look outside your own parochial churchyard to learn, not to copy!* Also spatial planners need to realise the necessity for lifelong learning and the must of exchanging planning ideas. Any experience from elsewhere is worth studying, whether it is positive or negative. But one has to be aware of both the contexts and the limits of comparisons and transferability.
- *Think holistically, while addressing tangible issues!* Spatial planners need to be generalists. With the help of empirical, quantitative knowledge as well as qualitative and tacit knowledge, they must look at the interdependencies of different approaches when facing and targeting concrete local, regional or urban tasks.
- *Plan the utopia, though remain rooted in your region!* Spatial planners should never give up developing ideas and scenarios for a better future. They must look ahead and explore pathways into the future, while reflecting on the past. Spatial planning is about finding a balance between pragmatism and utopia in a place, city or region.

All the distinguished planners in this book have made different, but remarkable, contributions to and for spatial planning. From what they have achieved collectively in recent history, we cannot assume that the success story of establishing spatial planning as a distinctive discipline will automatically continue in this direction. What worries me the most are the tremendous external pressures which squeeze our thinking and acting into more and more rigid containers. For example, our performance as academics is increasingly evaluated based on international university ranking indicators. Therefore, planning academics around the globe seek to increase their number of publications, and I even get the impression that nowadays more is written than read. In my view this "publish or perish" culture has resulted in many planning academics publishing just for the sake of publishing, and as a consequence they are trapped in an endless cycle of self-referential theorising. Further, I also recognise that in our time of globalisation, trends spread, virus-like, across the globe to the extent that they have also penetrated spatial planning through the growing "need" to win more and more research money from private investors or companies for doing applied "money-led" research. Similarly, the work of planning practitioners and consultants is often affected by neoliberal market dynamics. In order to survive on the private market, they have started to use their knowledge to help, for example, private development companies to push their interests through. The need to provide community services often takes a back seat. All this makes me feel that we seem to have less and less time to think about questions and answers and as a consequence sometimes forget about the real purpose of spatial planning.

The most important lesson I learnt from the authors in this book is that it is not true that if we want to keep our jobs or if we want to make a planning career we have to subordinate ourselves to these dynamics. We must not blindly follow short-lived mainstream trends or take for granted every short-sighted idea from policymakers. We, as professionals, are part of society and have the obligation to seek out sustainable solutions. Not just for us, but for the communities we are part of. We need to feel this responsibility and speak out to the best of our knowledge. Throughout their lives, the authors in this book have questioned mainstream thinking and external pressures. With the help of their individual autobiographical accounts, we get a good glimpse of what it implies to become a good spatial planner and how to create a future that everyone would like to live in. Together we can make a difference; let's face it.

Vienna (Austria), February 2016

INDEX

1984 (Orwell) 54

Abercrombie, Patrick 52–3, 86, 204, 245
Access to the Countryside Act 166
ACORN 293–4
active municipal land policy 171–2
advanced level examinations 244
Advanced Spatial Analysis: The CASA Book of GIS (Longley and Batty) 256
"Advocacy and Pluralism in Planning" (Davidoff) 263
AESOP *see* Association of European Schools of Planning (AESOP)
AFL–CIO Labor Council 35
African Planners' Association 235
Albers, Gerd 203–4, 205
Albrechts, Louis 99, 119, 184–97, 212, 269; *see also* strategic spatial planning (Albrechts)
Alden, Jeremy 211
Alessandri, Jorge 23
Alessandria, Italy, land use plan for 71–2; *see also* ancient future (Mazza)
Alexander, Christopher 248
Alexander, E. 176
Alinsky, S. 229–30
Alker, Hayward 149
Allen, Judith 154
Aloni, Shulamit 263
Alonso, William 22, 248
Alterman, Rachelle 260–76; *see also* planning theory; implementation analysis; planning law
alternative dispute resolution 96
Althusser, Louis 190

Amalgamated Society of Locomotive Engineers and Firemen (ASLEF) 62
Ambruster, A. 158
American Collegiate Planning Schools (ACSP) 114
American Collegiate Schools of Planning 302, 309
American Institute of Carried Planners 47
American Institute of Certified Planners (AICP) 153
American Institute of Planners 37
American Planning Association (APA) 47, 153, 235, 309, 310
Amin, Ash 117
Amoore, Derrick 52
ancient future (Mazza) 71–86; conclusions 85–6; ideology and experience 77–8; introduction 71; overview 71–2; participation and manipulation 75–7; planning lecture 78–81; planning theory 85–6; practice and theory 72; space and citizenship 81–2; spatial planning, technical knowledge/politics in 72–5; urban space, poetics of 82–5
Andersson, Åke 65
Anglo-German Foundation for the Study of Industrial Society 211
Animal Farm (Orwell) 54
Anti-Apartheid Movement 226
anti-authoritarian education 140
appreciative systems 151
Arendt, Hanna 16
argumentative turn 96
Argumentative Turn in Policy Analysis and Planning (Fischer & Forester) 287

326 Index

Arnstein, S. R. 228
Association of Academic Women 153
Association of Collegiate Schools of Planning
  (ACSP) 6, 153, 268
Association of European Schools of Planning
  (AESOP) 6, 102, 153; Alterman and 268–9;
  drafting of agreements for 85; Healey and 85,
  114, 118; Kunzmann and 216–17; Planning
  and Law Track 275
Athens Centre of Ekistics 188
Atlas Autocode 249
Atlas of Cyberspace (Dodge) 256
Atwood, G. E. 9
Austin, John 282, 285
autobiographical essays: ancient future (Mazza)
  71–86; collaborative planning (Innes) 145–60;
  contemporary planning, visions of (Hall)
  51–68; critical pragmatism (Forester) 280–94;
  educating planners (Schimak) 126–42;
  land-use planning (Needham) 165–80; as
  method of inquiry 8–12; planning, inquiry
  into (Healey) 107–21; planning, places and
  (Kunzmann) 202–19; planning, science of
  (Batty) 242–57; planning, utopian/realistic
  to transformative (Marcuse) 35–49; planning
  as vocation (Friedman) 15–31; planning
  processes/institutions, understanding and
  improving (Faludi) 88–102; planning theory,
  implementation analysis, planning law
  (Alterman) 260–76; planning thought/practice,
  re-inventing (Hague) 222–37; pragmatist
  planning theory (Hoch) 297–311; strategic
  spatial planning (Albrechts) 184–97; *see also
  individual essays*
autobiography: defined 9; as method of inquiry
  10–12; origins of 10; representational power
  of 11

baby boomers 147
Balducci, Alessandro 154, 212
Balzan Foundation Prize 67–8
Banfield, Edward C. 92, 94–5, 228
Banham, Peter 59, 60
Barker, Paul 60, 64
Barrett, S. 98, 116
Basic Books 149
Batty, Michael 5, 225, 242–57; *see also* planning,
  science of (Batty)
Baum, Howell 284, 302
Baupolitik als Wissenschaft (building policy as
  science) (Brunner-Lehenstein) 205
Beatles-All These Years, The (Lewisohn) 245
Beck, H. C. 51
Bell, Daniel 149
Benjamin, Walter 204
Benneworth, Paul 5

Berger, G. 189
Berger, P. 302
Berry, Brian 66, 251
betterment 44, 84
big data 257
Big Dig 146
Birkbeck College 57
Blum, Stephen 288
Bökemann, D. 97, 206
Bolan, R. S. 92, 153
Booher, David 145, 155, 157
Bookchin, Murray 30
Booth, Charles 56, 66
Borkenau, Franz 53
Bowles, Sam 149
Bowman, James 308
Bradley, Tom 37
brain: intellect thinking 194; spirit thinking 194
Brecht, Berthold 203
Breheny, Mike 114
Breitling, Peter 204
bricolage 306
"Britain Must Rebuild" (Pick) 166
British Council 90
Broady, Maurice 90, 91, 92
Bronfenbrenner, Martin 26
Brotchie, John 64
Brown, George 58
Brown, Pat 59
Brunner-Lehenstein, Karl Heinrich 205
Brussels 99–100
Bryson, John 155
Buber, Martin 19
Buchanan, Colin 86
Buchanan, James 63
Buchanan Report 72, 78
building planning theory 91–5
Bundesanstalt für Arbeit (Federal Labour Office) 210
Burby, Raymond 264
Burlage, Rob 283
Burnham, James 53
Burton, Dudley 282
Business Cycles (Schumpeter) 63, 64

Cabral, Joao 212
Caesar, Gus 55
Callaghan, Jim 62
Cambridge University Labour Club 224
Cameron, Stuart 117
Canadian Institute of Planners (CIP) 235
Capitalism, Socialism and Democracy (Schumpeter) 53
CASA *see* Centre for Advanced Spatial Analysis
  (CASA)
Castells, Manuel 38, 64–5, 231, 301
Cavell, Stanley 282
Center for Collaborative Policy (CCP) 155

Index **327**

Central Europe 101
Central Places in Southern Germany (Christaller) 55
Centre for Advanced Spatial Analysis (CASA) 255–6
Centre for Ecology and Forestry 187
Centre for Environmental Studies 58, 59, 95, 113, 231, 251
Cerdà, Ildefons 86
Chadwick, George 60, 93, 225, 247, 248, 250
chair institutes 133
Chamber of Architects 132
Channel Tunnel Rail Link 67
Chapin, F. S. 171
Chapin, Stu 251
Chatterjee, Jay 305
Chicago Housing Authority 92
Chinese Book of Changes (I Ching) 17
"Choosing the Right Policy Instruments" (Needham) 173
Christaller, Walter 55
Christensen, Karen 151, 266
Chu, Linda 286
Cities and Complexity: Understanding Cities with Cellular Automata, Agent-Based Models, and Fractals (Batty) 256
Cities in Civilization (Hall) 65, 297
Cities in Evolution (Geddes) 226
Cities of Tomorrow (Hall) 65
city council 37, 47
City in History, The (Mumford) 300
citizenship, space and 81–2
civil law 178
Civil Rights Act 147
Clapp, Jim 300
Clark, Colin 66
clientelism 188
Coast, Steve 256
"Co-determination (Mitbestimmung) in the German Steel and Coal Industry" (Albrechts) 187
Collaborative Planning (Healey) 115, 117–18
collaborative planning (Innes) 145–60; academic career, start of 150–2; Boston blunders 146–7; collaborative rationality 160; consensus building and 154–5, 157–8; expanding theory of 158–9; family influences 145–6; family values 146; gender discrimination 147; institution building 153; intellectual networks and 153–4; IURD director challenges/projects 156–7; MIT planning education 148–50; overview of 145; "Planning Theory's Emerging Paradigm" 155–6; theoretical leanings and 152–3; turning point 147–8
collaborative rationality 96, 158
College of Estate Management 245
Commonwealth Association of Planners (CAP) 222, 234–5

Commonwealth Consultative Group on Human Settlements 234
Commonwealth Heads of Government Meeting (CHOGM) 235
communicative action concept 19
communicative planning 96–7; language and 265
communicative planning theory (CPT) 156
communicative turn 98
Community Action (magazine) 232
community-based planning, limits of 231–2
community boards 39–40
community land trusts (CLTs) 46–7
company neighbourhoods 186
comparative research 261, 272–5; examples of 273–4; knowledge sharing and 275; need for 272–3; PLPR and 274–5
compensation 177; and development 177
complexity science 157–8
complexity theory 270
Comprehensive Development Area (CDA) Planning 227
comprehensive plans 269
compulsory purchase 76, 170, 178
Comte, Auguste 29
Condition of the Working Class in England in 1844, The (Engels) 166
Conference on Planning Theory 85
Containment of Urban England, The (Hall, Thomas, Gracey & Drewett) 60, 250
contemporary planning, visions of (Hall) 51–68; Berkeley, California move 63–5; childhood memories 51–2; England return 65–8; geography at Cambridge 54–6; *Great Planning Disasters* 61–3; intellectual influences 52–4; "Nonplan: An Experiment in Freedom" 58–61; planning in Scandinavia 56–8; teenage years 52–4
contributions 273
conventional evaluation 158
Conway, John 245
co-production concept 185
corruption 188
cost-benefit analysis 179
Council for National Academic Awards (CNAA) 114
Council for the Preservation of Rural England 53
council housing estate 166
Council of Ministers (EU) 99
Country Reports on Human Rights (US State Department) 152
Craigmillar Festival Society 231
"Creative Cities in Practice" (Tang & Kunzmann) 213
crisis situations, planning theory and 265–6
critical pragmatism (Forester) 280–94; information politics 285–6; overview of 280; planning, context-responsive improvisation

328 Index

in 293–4; planning in Cleveland 284–5; planning theory's dirty little secret 280–3; power, possibilities, and practice, vulnerabilities of 283–4; practice studies, pedagogy building upon 289–90; practitioner profiles, assessing 287–8; public disputes/conflicts, handling 290–3; value, normative learning about 288–9
Critical Theory, Public Policy, and Planning Practice (Forester) 284
Crosland, Tony 58, 62, 66
cross-border projects 136–7
Crossman, Richard 224
cross-national comparative research 261, 272–5; examples of 273–4; knowledge sharing and 275; need for 272–3; PLPR and 274–5
Culture of Cities, The (Mumford) 54
Curry, Leslie 251
cybernetics 248

Dalton, Linda 304
Damer, Sean 228
Danube channel 128
Daoist beliefs 17
Darkness at Noon (Koestler) 53
Das Steinerne Berlin (Hegemann) 204
DATAR (Délégation interministérielle à l'aménagement du territoire et à l'attractivité régionale) 215
Davidoff, Paul 37, 92, 226, 262, 263
Davies, Lyn 248
Davies, Richard Llewelyn 58, 59
Davoudi, Simin 116
Davy, B. 177, 275
Dealing with Differences: Dramas of Mediating Public Disputes (Forester) 291
Death and Life of Great American Cities, The (Jacobs) 61
decision-centered planning 90, 95–7
Decision-Centred View of Environmental Planning, A (Faludi) 94, 97
decision-making environment 92
de-concentrated development 186
De Jouvenel, B. 189
Dekema, Jan 282
Délégation interministérielle à l'aménagement du territoire et à l'attractivité régionale (DATAR) 215
Delft University of Technology 95
Deliberative Policy Analysis (Innes & Booher) 158
Deliberative Practitioner (Forester) 286, 287
Delors, Jaques 215–16
de Magalhaes, Claudio 117
de Neufville, Richard 148
densification 84
Department of City and Regional Planning (DCRP), University of California Berkeley 149

Department of Urban Studies and Planning (DUSP), MIT 148
Der Isolierte Staat (von Thünen) 55
de Ruijter, Peter 98
Desyllas, Jake 256
developer agreements 273
Development of Planning Thought, The (Hague) 232
Development Projects Observed (Hirschmann) 111
Dewey, John 17, 30, 109
dialogue: defined 19; radical practice and 19–20
Diamond, Derek 110
Die Räumliche Ordnung der Wirtschaft (Lösch) 55
Die Rückseite des Spiegels (The Backside of the Mirror) (Lorenz) 140
Die Unwirtlichkeit der Städte (Mitscherlich) 204
Die ZEIT (weekly journal) 212
Dilemmas of Planning Practice (Thomas & Healey) 119
Dimitriou, Basil 250
discourse structuration 192
Doak, Joe 114
Dodge, Martin 256
domain ethics of planning 178
Douglas, Mary 109
Downs, Chip 282
Drewett, Roy 60
Dror, Y. 92
Dryzek, John 118
due process 176
Dunlap, L. 153
duration (durée) concept 189
Durkheim, Emile 29
Dussler, Luitpold 203
Dutch Land-Use Planning (Needham) 169
Dyckman, Jack 153, 282
Dyckman, John 91

East Thames Corridor 67
Echenique, Marcial 251
Economic and Social Science Research Council (ESRC) 114, 116
educating planners (Schimak) 126–42; amount needed 140; building up a country 128–9; creativity and 137–8, 142; cross-border planning project 136; democracy and 141–2; east-west planning cultures and 137; experience and 139–40; internationalisation 134–5; Iron Curtain, planning at 135–6; overview of 126–7; planning school, start of 131–3; political dimension of planning 130–1; post Austrian State Treaty 127–8; practice to theory 130; practice years 129–30; Reichsbrücke bridge collapse 133–4; scientific challenge 131; Second World War and 127; study of planning 129; university planning 138–9
Education Act, 1944 223

ekistics 188
Eliot, George 66
Elson, Martin 113
Empowerment: The Politics of an Alternative Development (Friedmann) 28–9
English Tripos 54–5
enterprise zones 62
environmental impact assessments 152
Environment and Planning A (journal) 253
Environment and Planning B (journal) 253, 255
ESRC *see* Economic and Social Science Research Council (ESRC)
ethics in planning 178
Euclidean view of space 100
Euro–federalist 99, 100
European Commission 99
European Community 91
European Grape 215
European Planning Studies (Albrechts and Cooke) 188
European Spatial Development Perspective (ESDP) 100
European Spatial Planning Observation Network (ESPON) 236
European Union (EU) 27, 91; Council of Ministers of 99; planning challenges in 98–101
exactions 273
EXPO-Vienna AG 134

Fabian Society 57–8, 62, 66
facilitating 293
faculty 137, 153, 156, 160, 253, 256
Faculty of Architecture and Town Planning 263
Faculty of Architecture of Technical University (TU) 135
Fainstein, Susan 189
falsifiability 97
Faludi, Andreas 88–102, 111, 112, 114, 118, 154, 155, 212, 250, 252, 262; *see also* planning processes/institutions, understanding and improving (Faludi)
Federal Institute for Research on Building, Urban Affairs and Spatial Development 99
Federal Office for Building and Regional Planning 99
Feldman, Marsh 306
Feminine Mystique, The (Friedan) 261
Feuerstein, Günther 129
Field, Hermann 150
finding my way (Healey essay) *see* planning, inquiry into (Healey)
Fischer, Frank 118, 287
Fischler, Raphäel 290, 309
Florence, P. Sargant 55
Florida, Richard 212
Flyvbjerg, B. 11
Foley, D. L. 226

Foot, Dave 250
Forbat, Fred 204
Forester, John 19, 114, 118, 119, 155, 191, 280–94, 302; *see also* critical pragmatism (Forester)
Forrester, Jay 251
Foster, Christopher 58
Fotheringham, Stewart 254
Foucault, Michael 29, 303
Fractal Cities: A Geometry of Form and Function (Longley and Batty) 254–5
Frankfurt School of Critical Theory 154
Freedom Summer 36
Free Speech Movement 147–8
Frei, Eduardo 23–4
Freire, Paulo 282
French, R. A. 232
Frick, Dieter 212, 217
Fried, M. 227
Friedan, Betty 261
Friedman, Milton 21, 26, 285
Friedman, Rose 285
Friedmann, John 5, 15–31, 153, 189, 191, 212, 217, 248, 251, 297, 300; decision-making environment and 92; Euclidean absolute view of space and 100; Faludi and 94–5, 96; "The Good Society" course of 38; *see also* planning as vocation (Friedman)
Friend, John 93, 95, 96
Frisch, Michael 290
Fudge, C. 98
Fulbright grant 40, 90
Fund for Research in Dispute Resolution (FRDR) 290
Future of Socialism, The (Crosland) 66

Gans, Herbert 37, 147, 148, 227
Ganser, Karl 205
Geddes, Patrick 86, 188, 226
gender discrimination 147
gender equality, planning theory and 263–4
generalists 93
general systems theory 248
Genk, Belgium 185–6
geodesign 249
GeoFutures 256
Geographical Distribution of the Industrial Population 52
"Geography of the Fifth Kondratieff Cycle, The" (Hall) 64
GeoSimulation (Torrens) 256
German Development Aid 213, 214
Gestalt (design) 206
Gigou, Jean-Louis 215
Gilligan, Carol 283
Glasgow, slum clearance in 226–8
Glasson, John 250

330 Index

Glazer, Nathan 149
Glittering Coffin, The (Potter) 56
globalisation of planning education 268–9
Global Planning Education Association Network (GPEAN) 269
goals achievement approach 227
Goals Achievement Matrix 264
goal satisfaction analysis 227
Goddard, John 58
Godschalk, David 264–5
Goldner, William 251
Goldsmith, Peter 245
Good Society, The (Friedmann) 19, 20
"Gorbachev's Strategy of Political Centrism" (Batty & Danilovic) 255
Gordon, John 147
Gracey, Harry 60
Graham, Stephen 117
grammar school 53, 56, 245, 257
Grapes of Wrath (Steinbeck) 139
Gras darf nicht mehr wachsen (Mattern) 204
"Great British Parkway Drive In, The" (Hall) 59
Greater London Council (GLC) 110, 248
Greater London Plan 53
Great Planning Disasters (Hall) 63
Great Society program 147
Grigsby, Gene 153
Growth Management Consensus Project (GMCP) 155
Gruber, Judith 155, 159
"Grundbesitzverhältnisse in historischen Stadtkernen Österreichs" (land ownership in historical city centres in Austria) (Kunzmann) 206
Gualini, Enrico 154
Guayana Development Corporation (CVG) 22
Guayasamín, Oswaldo 191
Guide to Public Participation in Planning (Alterman, Churchman & Law Yone) 264

Habermas, Jürgen 19, 145, 154, 195, 282
Haggett, Peter 224, 248
Hague, Cliff 222–37; *see also* planning thought/practice, re-inventing (Hague)
Hajer, Maarten 98, 118, 158
Haklay, Muki 256
Hall, Peter 51–68, 92, 93, 94, 110, 150, 156, 217, 249–50, 297; *see also* contemporary planning, visions of (Hall)
Hamilton, F. E. I. 232
Hancock, Tom 58
Harper, Thomas 302
Harris, Britton 248, 251, 262
Harvey, David 38, 94, 115, 155, 189, 190, 191, 231, 301
Haselsberger, Beatrix 8

Havel, V. 232
Hayden, Dolores 30
Hayek, Friedrich 21, 26
Healey, Patsy 5, 107–21, 154, 155, 212, 250, 269, 270, 304, 306; AESOP and 216, 268; Alterman and 275; Conference on Planning Theory and 85; Euclidean absolute view of space and 100; *Planning Theory* and 94; *see also* planning, inquiry into (Healey)
heart of the brain thinking 194
Hegemann, Werner 204
Hein, Piet 252
Hemmens, George 303
Heseltine, Michael 62
Heskin, Allen 301, 305
Heyns, Roger 155
Hickling, Allen 96
Hierzegger, Heiner 139
High Speed One 67
Hilberseimer, Ludwig 203
Hill, Morris 263, 267, 269
Hillier, Jean 120
Himmelblau, Coop 129
Hinden, Rita 57
Hirschmann, Albert 111
historic break 21, 25–7
Hittleman, Margo 290
Hoch, Charles 155, 284, 297–311; *see also* pragmatist planning theory (Hoch)
Holden, Charles 51
Holland, Randstad 67
Home Policy Committee on Transport 62
Hooper, Alan 114
Hornung, Berthold 232
Hoskins, W. G. 57
Howard, Ebenezer 86, 204
How Cities Work (Needham) 171
Howe, E. 264
Howe, Geoffrey 62
Hudson-Smith, Andy 256
Hungarian Revolution 89
Hutchinson, Bruce 257
hybrid model of planning education 266–7

Illich, Ivan 30
Implementation (Pressman and Wildavsky) 270
implementation analysis 269–70; as compass 260
In a Different Voice (Gilligan) 283
Industries of London, The (Hall) 55–6
Innes, Judith E. 5, 19, 94, 96–7, 114, 118, 145–60, 306; *see also* collaborative planning (Innes)
Institute for Operational Research (IOR School) 90, 96–7, 98
Institute for Spatial and Landscape Development 309
Institute for the Foundation of Planning 309

Institute for Urban and Spatial Planning at Leuven University 187, 189
Institute of British Geographers 63
Institute of Science and Technology (UWIST) 252
Institute of Urban and Regional Development (IURD) 151, 156–7
Institute of Urban Design and Spatial Planning 132
institutionalisation 192
instrumentation theory 173
intellectual development phases of planning 90–1
Intelligent Space 256
Interacting with Geospatial Technologies (Haklay) 256
intergovernmental EU 100
international academic association on planning, law and property rights 274–5
International Building Exhibition Emscher Park (IBA) 205, 211
International Conference on Planning Theory 114–15
international work international experience 40–1
interwar slum clearance estates 226–8
Investment Property Databank (IPD) 116
Iron Curtain 89, 127, 134, 137; planning at 135–6
Isard, Walter 22, 248
"Israel 2020" 270, 274

Jackson, Alan 52
Jacobs, Jane 61, 204, 228, 250
Jahn, Hans Henny 204
James, William 120
James Irvine Foundation's Collaborative Regional Initiatives (CRI) 158–9
Jantsch, E. 189
Jay, S. 250
Jenkins, Paul 234
Jessop, Neil 93
Jobs, Steve 63
Johnson, Lyndon 37
Joint Center for Urban Studies 22
Journal of Planning Education and Research (JPER) 153
Journal of the American Institute of Planners 92, 93, 225, 226, 248
Journal of the American Planning Association (JAPA) 157
Journal of the Town Planning Institute 226
judicial review 176

Kain, John 251
Kaiser, Ed 264
Kantorowich, Roy 247
Kaufman, J. 264
Keeble, Lewis 247, 250
Kennedy, John F. 37
Kesten, Hermann 204
Keynes, Milton 54, 58, 59

King, Martin Luther 148
Kitchen, Ted 119
Klosterman, Richard 310
Knight, Julie 5
"Knowledge and Action: Making the Link" (de Neufville) 152
Knowledge and Human Interests (Habermas) 301
Koeppen, Walter 204
Koestler, Arthur 53
Kondratieff, Nikolai 63, 64
Kondratieff waves 66–7
Konrad, G. 232
Kreiswirth, Brian 290
Krieger, Martin 282
Kropotkin, Peter 30
Krumholz, N. 191, 284, 285, 294
Kuhn, Thomas 98, 99
Kultur 90 212
Kunzmann, Klaus R. 99, 114, 133, 140, 202–19, 268, 269; *see also* planning, places and (Kunzmann)

LaClau, Ernesto 291
Ladrière, J. 189
land decision units 97
Landesplanung und Raumordnung (regional/spatial planning) 208
Land Use and Built Form Studies 251
land-use planning (Needham) 165–80; characteristics 170; citizen protection and 175–6; conceptual framework 168–9; defined 165; discriminatory limits of 177; economic analysis, legitimacy of 178–9; ethical codes for 178; first work experiences 166–7; future of 179–80; home experiences 165–6; importance 165; improving 170–1; influences to 173; institutional economics 172–3; knowledge of development process 171–2; knowledge of use by people 171; land importance 168; law and, importance of 177–8; legitimacy of 175; limitations of, as technology 174–5; limits of 176–7; Netherlands experiences 167; performance of 173–4; planning and 169; responsible government and 176; science of 167; specifics of 169–70; as technology 171; university experiences 166; values applied 167–8
Land Use Planning and the Mediation of Urban Change (Healey et al.) 114
land-use plans 130
Land Use Policy Debate in the U.S., The (de Neufville) 150
Lauber, Dan 304
Laundry, Charles 212
Laws, David 292, 293
LDDC (London Docklands Development Corporation) 62

332 Index

learning by doing 71
Leavis, Frank Raymond 54–5
Lee, D. B. 251–2
Lefebvre, Henri 82–3, 301
Leontief, Wassily 20–1
Lewisohn, Mark 245
liaison government 231
Lincoln Institute of Land Policy 150, 154
Lindblom, Charles 62–3, 131, 280
linkage fees 273
Lipietz, Alain 190
Lipsky, Michael 284
LISTSERV 306
Liverpool Central Reference Library 245
local authorities (UK municipalities) 109–10
Local Government and Strategic Choice: An Operational Research Approach to the Process of Public Planning (Friend & Jessop) 96
location theory 248
London Docklands Development Corporation (LDDC) 62
London School of Economics (LSE) 60, 110
London Transport Museum 51
London 2000 (Hall) 57, 65, 250
London Voices (Hall) 68
Longley, Paul 253, 254, 256
Look Back in Anger (Osborne) 56
Loos, Adolf 206
Lorenz, Konrad 140
Los Angeles: The Architecture of Four Ecologies (Banham) 59
Lösch, August 55
Lowry, Ira 251
Luckman, T. 302
Ludwig, Mies van der Rohe 203
Lukes, Steven 282
Lynch, Kevin 148, 204

Mackenzie, W. J. M. 111
Macmillan, Harold 92
MacRae, Duncan 265
Madanipour, Ali 117
Majone, Giandomenico 287
Making Better Places (Healey) 120
Making Equity Planning Work (Krumholz & Forester) 285, 304
Making of Modern London, The (Weightman) 52
Making of the English Landscape, The (Hoskins) 57
Making Planning Work: A Guide to Approaches and Skills (Hague et al.) 235
Managerial Revolution (Burnham) 53
Manchester Guardian (newspaper) 55
mandatory happiness 177
Mandelbaum, Seymour 262, 302, 308
Mandelker, Daniel 269–70
Mannheim, Karl 15–16, 94, 300

Mapping Cyberspace (Dodge) 256
March, Lionel 251
Marcuse, Peter 35–49; *see also* planning, utopian/ realistic to transformative (Marcuse)
Margolis, Julius 21
market imperfections 178–9
market outcomes 179
Markusen, Ann 64
Marris, Peter 302
Marshall, Alfred 55, 73
Marshall Aid 89
Marvin, Simon 117
Massé, P. 189
Masser, Ian 251
Massey, Doreen 113, 115, 190, 251
Master in City Planning degree 262
mathematical models 248
Mattern, Hermann 204
Mayreder, Karl 205
Mazza, Luigi 71–86, 114, 154, 306; *see also* ancient future (Mazza)
McCartney, Paul 245
McDougall, Glen 94, 114, 250
McLoughlin, Brian 60, 93, 113, 211, 225, 248, 249, 250
McNamara, Paul 114
McNamara, Robert 148
Medhurst, Frank 248
Melville, Ian 229, 232
Member of the Royal Town Planning Institute (MRTPI) 93
Mensch, Gerhard 63
"Mexican Renaissance" 191
Meyerson, Martin 92, 228, 262
Microcomputer Graphics: Art, Design and Creative Modelling (Batty) 253
Middlemarch (Eliot) 66
Middle of the Night, The (Young and Hall) 66
milieu, defined 97
military-industrial complex 101
Mill, J. S. 29
Mills, C. W. 10
Milton Keynes Master Plan 59
Mitchell, Bill 65
Mitchell, R. B. 226
Mitscherlich, Alexander 204
Moltmann, Jurgen 288
Monnet, Jean 20
Montague-Barlow, Anderson 52
Mouffe, Chantal 291
Moynihan, Daniel Patrick 149
Mumford, Lewis 54, 300
municipality 172
Murdoch, Donald 53
Murdoch, Jonathan 117
Musil, J. 232

Index **333**

Musil, Robert 206
mutual learning 18
My Art, My Life (Rivera) 191
My Early Beliefs (Keynes) 54
Myrdal, Gunnar 21

Nabarro, Rupert 116
National Center for Geographic Information and
 Analysis (NCGIA) 254
National Environmental Protection Act 151
National Estuary Program 154
National Land Utilisation Survey 54
National-Level Planning in Democratic Countries
 (Alterman) 274
National Science Foundation (NSF) 254
National Union of Railwaymen (NUR) 62
near neighbourhood 101
Needham, Barrie 165–80, 228; *see also* land-use
 planning (Needham)
Neill, A. S. 140
neoliberalism 190
neo-liberal revolution 26
Netherlands Institute for Housing and Planning 98
new institutionalism 270
New Science of Cities, The (Batty) 255
New Society 59, 60, 64
New Towns Act 166
"Nonplan: An Experiment in Freedom" (Banham,
 Barker, Hall & Price) 58–61, 65
Norman, Philip 245
NUR (National Union of Railwaymen) 62
Nussbaum, Martha 285, 287–8, 289

objective knowledge 18
Observer (newspaper) 55
Occupy Wall Street 20, 272
Offe, Claus 115
Olson, Mancur 63
Olsson, Gunnar 251
omgeving, defined 97
Open Society and Its Enemies, The (Popper) 131, 139
Open Street Map 256
operational decisions 97
ordinary level examinations 244
Orwell, George 53–4
Osborn, Frederic 54
Osborne, John 56
O'Sullivan, David 256
Outsider, The (Wilson) 56
Ove-Arup 139
Owen, Robert 30
Oxford College of Technology 91, 92
Oxford Planning Theory conferences 156
Oxford Polytechnic (Oxpoly) 112–15
Ozbekhan, Hasan 188, 189
Ozkul, Basak Demires 68

Page, John 262, 283
Pahl, Ray 92
parent professions 93
Park Chung-Hee 25
participation 273
participatory budgeting 47
"Patterns of Cities to Come, The" (Hall) 59
Peattie, Lisa 149
Pedagogy of the Oppressed, The (Freire) 282
Pendlebury, John 117
Penguin Press 92, 93
perfect market 179
performance of plans 98
performativity 282
Pergamon Press 92, 93, 96
Perin, C. 189
Perlman, Janice 149
Perloff, Harvey 25, 37
Perspectives of Planning (Ozbekhan) 188
Peters, Scott 289–90
phenomenological view of knowledge 152–3
phronesis 11
physical functionalism 82
Pick, Frank 51
picture journalism 52
Picture Post 52
Pitkin, Hanna 282
place governance 107–8
planned unit development 269
Planners for Equal Opportunity 37
"Planners' use of theory in practice" (Healey) 113
planning: challenges, in Europe 98–101; as
 city-building 30–1; communicative 96–7;
 community-based, limits of 231–2; context-
 responsive improvisation in 293–4; decision-
 centered 90, 95–7; domain ethics of 178;
 epistemology for 17–18; ethics in 178;
 gender equality in 263–4; ideas, defined 4;
 intellectual development phases of 90–1; at
 Iron Curtain 135–6; metaphysics for 16–17;
 moral foundation for 18–19; as political
 practice 23–5; politics, social change and
 41–4; practical suggestions 44–5; professional
 ethics in 47–8; regional development
 21–3; restrictions 177; rights 176; Schuster
 Committee functions of 225; science of
 248; second-generation approach to 97;
 strategic 185; theory, building 91–5; thoughts
 3–7; TPI stance on 225–6; transactive 19;
 transformative 30, 45–8; urban 44; world
 cities and 27–8
planning, inquiry into (Healey) 107–21; AESOP
 involvement 118; career reflection 120–1;
 Collaborative Planning 117–18; conceptual
 exploration 115; conceptual perspectives 117;
 Dilemmas of Planning Practice 119; early life,

334 Index

childhood to planning doctorate 108–10; life rebalancing 119–20; Newcastle, academia at 115–19; Oxford Polytechnic (Oxpoly), academic life at 112–15; PhD experience 110–12; place governance planning 107–8; planning education at Oxpoly 112; research profile development 113–14; RTPI involvement 118; transnational encounters 114–15; urban land/property development processes 116; urban partnerships, ethnographies of 116–17
planning, places and (Kunzmann) 202–19; AESOP 216–17; Augsburg and 202–3; Bangkok and Asian planning culture 207; culture/creativity roles 212–13; European regional planning 214–16; expert missions to developing regions 213–14; interdisciplinary research institute, Dortmund 208–9; life after Ruhr 217–19; Munich School of Architecture and 203–5; overview of 202; planning education for German/International students 209–10; regional challenges in Ruhr 210–12; Ruhr in Germany 207–8; Vienna University of Technology and 205–7
planning, science of (Batty) 242–57; CASA at UCL 255–6; Institute of Science and Technology, Cardiff 252–4; Liverpool personal history 243–6; NCGIA at SUNY-Buffalo, New York 254–5; overview of 242–3; personal recollections 256–7; Reading University 250–2; University of Manchester 247–50
planning, utopian/realistic to transformative (Marcuse) 35–49; background 35–6; career in planning 36–40; examples of 45–8; final thoughts 48–9; international work 40–1; politics, social change and 41–4; prosaic practical suggestions 44–5
Planning Accreditation Board (PAB) 153, 309
Planning and Law Track (AESOP) 275
"Planning and Policy Analysis: Converging or Diverging Trends?" (Alterman & MacRae) 265
planning assistant 226
planning as vocation (Friedman) 15–31; apprenticeship years 20–1; epistemology for 17–18; historical perspective 25–7; intellectual/moral foundations 15–16; metaphysics for 16–17; moral foundation for 18–19; origins of planning and 29–30; political practice, planning as 23–5; poverty and 28–9; radical practice, philosophy of 19–20; reflections 30–1; regional development planning 21–3; world cities 27–8
planning challenges in Europe 98–101
planning doctrine 98
planning education, profession and 266–9; globalisation of 268–9; hybrid model of 266–7; in Israel 267–8
planning gain 273

planning ideas, defined 4
Planning in a Multi-Racial Britain (RIG) 230
Planning in the Face of Conflict (Forester) 291
Planning in the Face of Crisis (Alterman) 266
Planning in the Face of Power (Forester) 284, 285
Planning in the Public Domain (Friedmann) 30, 102, 297
planning law 178, 271–2; planning/law interrelationship 271; policy impacts of, research 271–2; as scale 260–1
Planning Law and Property Rights (PLPR) 178, 274–5
planning obligations 273
planning processes/institutions, understanding and improving (Faludi) 88–102; building planning theory phase 91–5; decision-centered planning phase 95–7; intellectual development phases 90–1; introduction 88; overview 88–90; planning challenges in Europe phase 98–101; planning doctrines shape minds phase 98; retrospect/prospect 101–2
planning restrictions 177
planning rights 176
planning school, start of 131–3
planning system, Israel's 270
planning theory 261–6; as beacon 260; communicative, language and 265; crisis situations and 265–6; dirty little secret of 280–3; gender equality and 263–4; vs. policy analysis 265; studying, during early years 262–3; teaching/researching, public participation and 264–5
Planning Theory (Faludi) 92, 93, 94–5, 102, 169
planning theory, implementation analysis, planning law (Alterman) 260–76; cross-national comparative research 272–5; female planning student in Canada 261; implementation analysis 269–70; overview of 260–1; planning education, profession and 266–9; planning law 271–2; planning theory 261–6
Planning Theory and Practice 120
"Planning Theory and Practice: Bridging the Gap" (de Neufville) 151
planning theory building phase: 91–95
Planning Theory in Practice 85
planning theory "mark 2" 97
Planning Theory Newsletter 85, 306, 307
Planning Theory: Prospects for the 1980s (Healey, McDougall & Thomas) 94
"Planning Theory's Emerging Paradigm: Communicative Action and Interactive Practice" (Innes) 155
Planning Thought Award 5–6
planning thought/practice, re-inventing (Hague) 222–37; Cambridge and organisation/leadership 223–4; community-based planning,

limits of 231–2; contract research and 236; departmental survival and 232–3; future of 236–7; Glasgow slum clearance 226–8; globalisation, rapid urbanisation and 233–5; Harpurhey and awareness of class and place 223; overview of 222; planning education types 228–9; postgraduate planning course 224–6; Radical Institute Group 229–31; socialism and 232

planning thoughts 3–7

Planning with Complexity (Innes & Booher) 160

planology 95, 97

Plenum 150

PLPR *see* Planning Law and Property Rights (PLPR)

Podziba, Susan 290

policy analysis 30; *vs.* planning theory 265

Politecnico di Torino 114

politically oriented 264

Politics, Planning and the Public Interest (Meyerson and Banfield) 262

Polycentric Metropolis, The (Hall & Pain) 67

Popper, Karl 18, 90, 131, 139, 171

Potter, Dennis 56

poverty, planning and rethinking 28–9

power, possibilities, and practice, vulnerabilities of 283–4

Power: A Radical View (Lukes) 282

powerful theory 242

practice studies, pedagogy building upon 289–90

practitioner profiles, assessing 287–8

"Pragmatic Communicative Planning" (Hoch) 306

pragmatist planning theory (Hoch) 297–311; described 298–9; future of 310–11; intellectual autobiography 299–305; overview of 297–9; professional development and 305–6; teaching and learning 306–9

Prebisch, Raúl 20

preparatory school 147

Pressman, J. 270

Price, Cedric 60

principal-agent theory 100

Principles and Practices of Town and Country Planning (Keeble) 94, 250

Private Supply of Public Services (Alterman) 273

procedural planning theory 94, 155, 169; critics of 97

professional development, pragmatist planning theory and 305–6

"Professional Ethics and Beyond" (Marcuse) 37

professional ethics in planning 47–8

Progress in Planning (Healey & Underwood) 113

Project Renewal 270

property rights 274

Prospective Labs 256

Proudhon, Pierre-Joseph 30

public disputes/conflicts, handling 290–3

public planning 43

qualifying association 93

quantum thinking 194

Radical Institute Group 222, 229–31

radical practice philosophy 19–20

radical strategic spatial planning 196–7; structural issues 184–5

Rainer, Thomas A. 92

Rainwater, Lee 148

Raison, Tim 60

Ranis, Gustav 26

rationality concept 189

rational model 149

reader-based writing 153

Reader in Planning Theory, A (Faludi) 92, 93, 94, 262

Reades, Jonathan 68

Reagan, Ronald 21

Reardon, Ken 293

rectorate 141

reflective practitioner 71

Regent Street Polytechnic 109

Regional and Local Economic Development (Hague et al.) 236

Regional Development (Albrechts) 190

Regional Development and Planning (Friedmann and Alonso) 248

Regional Development Policy: A Case Study of Venezuela (Friedmann) 23

Regional Inequality (Albrechts) 190

Regional Policy at the Crossroads (Albrechts) 190

Regional Policy: Readings in Theory and Applications (Friedmann & Alonso) 22–3

Regional Studies 92

Rehfeld, A. 100

Reichsbrücke 133

Rein, Martin 149

Reiner, Tom 262

"Re-inventing Planning" (Farmer et al.) 235

relational view of space 100

rent control 47

"Requiem for Large-Scale Models, A" (Lee) 171, 251–2

Research Network on Human Settlements (UN-Habitat HS-Net) 189

Retracking America (Friedmann) 18, 19, 24, 94, 95, 300

right to the city idea 84–5

Rittel, H. J. W. 97, 252

Rivera, Diego 191

Road to Serfdom, The (Hayek) 21

Robins, Kevin 117

336 Index

Robinson, Ira M. 91
Robinson, Jennifer 28
Rodgers, Bill 58, 66
Rodgers, William 245
Rodwin, Lloyd 22, 148
Roper, Kathy 153
Roth, Josef 206
Roth, Joseph 128
Royal Commission on the Distribution of
Income and Wealth 230
Royal Geographic Society 150
Royal Town Planning Institute (RTPI) 61, 91,
93, 112, 114; code of professional conduct of
178; Hague and 222, 229–31, 234; *Planning
Education Guidelines* 118; "Women in
Planning" subgroup 118
RTPI *see* Royal Town Planning Institute (RTPI)
Rudolf-Ekstein-Centre, Vienna 140

Sabel, C. F. 100
Saija, Laura 5, 7
Sailing to Byzantium (Yeats) 68
Salet, Willem 275
Salzburg Seminar in American Studies 188
Sandercock, Leonie 25, 212
San Diego Comprehensive Planning
Organization 300
San Diego Regional Coast Commission 300
San Francisco Estuary Project (SFEP) 155
Sanyal, Bishwapriya 27
Schaffer, Hannes 136
Scharpf, Fritz 96
Schimak, Gerhard 126–42; *see also* educating
planners (Schimak)
Schloss Cappenberg 216–17
Schmidt, Arno 204
Scholl, Bernd 309
Schön, D. A. 192, 266, 284
Schönwandt, Walter 309
School for Advanced Urban Studies (SAUS) 113
School of Architecture, Planning and Landscape 119
School of Architecture at the University of
Technology 203
Schuman, Robert 20
Schumpeter, Joseph 53, 58, 61, 63–4
Schuster Committee 225
Schwanzer, Karl 129
science of cities 248
Science of "Muddling Through", The
(Lindblom) 131
science of planning 248
scientific knowledge 18
scientific knowledge of society 18
scientific revolutions 99, 101
Scott Committee inquiry on rural land-use 54
Secchi, B. 196

secondary modern schools 223, 244
secondary school 166
second-generation approach to planning 97
Semi-Detached London (Jackson) 52
Sennett, Richard 302, 303
Sharp, Thomas 225
Shiode, Naru 256
Shmueli, Deborah 290
Shore, Peter 62, 245
Shout!: The Beatles in Their Generation (Norman) 245
Simmie, James 229
Simon, Saint 29
Singer, Hans 26
Sissons, Michael 65
Sitte, Camillo 206
Skeffington report 228
skid row 303
Slayton, Bob 303
Smith, Adam 29
Smith, Neil 39
So, Frank 305
social functionalism 82–3
socialism 232
Socialist Commentary 57
Social Justice and the City (Harvey) 38, 94, 231
social learning 18, 30
social mobilization 30
social reform 30
Sociological Imagination, The (Mills) 10
Soja, Ed 190
South African Planning Institute 234
South East Regional Economic Planning Council 58
Southern Electric System 52
spatial governance 75, 85
spatial planning 85; ancient future of 86;
definition 320–4; early-to-mid-career 5;
English language and 6–7; explanation 319–20;
in Netherlands 167; past and future 317–19;
retired/soon-to-be retired elders in 5; roadmap
323; as study programme at Vienna University
of Technology 132; technical knowledge/
politics in 72–5; term use of 75; *see also*
autobiographical essays
Spatial Planning for Regions in Developing
Economies (SPRING) 214
Spatial Simulation (O'Sullivan) 256
specialisms 225
spot zoning 96
SPRING (Spatial Planning for Regions in
Developing Economies) 214
Stadtbauwelt (urban planning journal) 204
Stalemate in Technology (Mensch) 63
Stamp, Lionel Dudley 54
Stanley, Albert 51
"Start Planning Britain Now: A Policy for
Reconstruction" (Calder) 166

Index **337**

statutory plans 270, 271
Stav, Tamy 265
Steigenga, Willem 97
Stein, Stan 302
Steinbeck, John 139
Steinitz, Carl 249
Stitzel, David 290
Stoddart, David 224
Stolorow, R. D. 9
strategic choice approach 96–7
"Strategic Factors in Urban Planning as Applied
    to Parking" (Albrects) 187
strategic planning, defined 185
strategic spatial planning (Albrechts) 184–97;
    critical debate/new ideas and 196; envisioning
    as tool 195; epistemology of practice 192;
    Genk, Belgium, growing up in 185–6;
    learning from practice 190–2; neoliberal
    policies and 190; overview of 184–5; power
    context, working in 193; radical 184–5,
    196–7; systems thinking and 188–90;
    transformative practices 193–4; university
    education 186–8
Strong, Ann 262
studio work 204
studium irregulare 132
subdivision controls 269
substantive planning theories 169
Sugrue, Thomas 288
Summerhill (Neill) 140
SUNY Press 290
survey-analysis-plan 131, 188
Susskind, Larry 284
Swiss Federal Institute of Technology (ETH
    Zurich) 309
systems theory 225
systems view of planning 225
Systems View of Planning, A (Chadwick) 93,
    188, 250
Szelényi, I. 232

Takings International (Alterman) 274
Tang Yan 213
target-oriented incrementalist 131
Tawney, R. H. 66
Tawney Society 66
technically oriented 264
Technische Universität Wien (Vienna University of
    Technology) 205
Teitz, Michael 149
Terkel, Studs 286
territorial-administrative complex 101
territorial view of space 100
TGV Atlantique (train) 67
Thames Gateway 67
Thatcher, Margaret 21

Theorie der Raumplanung (theory of spatial
    planning) (Bökemann) 206
Theory and Practice (Habermas) 301
Third Reich 90
Thisse, Jacques 255
Thomas, Huw 118–19
Thomas, Michael 94, 114
Thomas, Ray 60
Thompson, Robin 233
Thornley, Jennifer 94
Throgmorton, James 118
Thurstain-Goodwin, Mark 256
time concept 189
Times, The 59
Tinbergen, Jan 20
Tobler, Waldo 251
Törnqvist, Gunnar 65
Torrens, Paul 256
Totalitarian Enemy, The (Borkenau) 53
Towards a General Theory of Planning (Ozbekhan) 188
Tower, The (Yeats) 68
Town and Country Planning (Abercrombie) 245
"Town and Country Planning" (undergraduate
    course) 243
Town and Country Planning Act 166
Town and Country Planning Association
    (TCPA) 60
Town Planners in Search of a Role (Underwood) 113
Town Planning at the Crossroads (Keeble) 247
Town Planning Institute (TPI) 91, 93, 225–6
Town Planning Review 66, 226, 310
TPI *see* Town Planning Institute (TPI)
Traffic in Towns (Ministry of Transport) 72, 78
transactive planning 19
"Transatlantic View of Planning Education and
    Professional Practice, A" (Alterman) 269
transformative change, defined 185
transformative planning 30, 45–8; for structural
    problems 193–4
"Transport, Maker and Breaker of Cities" (Clark) 66
triple helix of managing processes 293
Tugwell, Rexford 21
Turok, Ivan 217
Tyne and Wear Development Corporation
    (TWDC) 116

"Ubiquity of Values in Planning, The" (Alterman &
    Page) 262
UDLE (Urban Development through Local
    Efforts) project 213
unachievable restless search concept 115
Underwood, Jacky 113
unfunded mandates 26
UN-Habitat HS-Net 189
UN Habitat II 234, 235
unitarianism 146

338 Index

United Nations Development Programme (UNDP) 213
United States of Europe 99
University of Dortmund 207–8; Institut für Raumplanung (Institute of Spatial Planning) 208–9
University of Manitoba 262
Upton, Robert 120
Urban and Regional Planning (Hall) 61
Urban and Regional Planning: A Systems Approach (McLoughlin) 93, 188, 250
Urban Complexity and Strategic Spatial Planning (Healey) 119
Urban Development through Local Efforts (UDLE) project 213
"Urbanisation in Europe" (Kunzmann and Wegner) 215
urban land and property development processes 116
Urban Modelling: Algorithms, Calibrations, Predictions (Batty) 251
urban models 248
urban partnerships, ethnographies of 116–17
urban planning 44
Urban Question, The (Castells) 38
urban renewal 147, 151, 160
Urban Social and Environmental Policy 150
urban space, poetics of 82–5
Urban Villagers (Gans) 147
Usher, David 116

Vaizey, John 57–8
"Validating Policy Indicators" (de Neufville) 151
value, normative learning about 288–9
van den Brink, Gabriel 282
van der Valk, Arnold 98
van Havre, D. 189
Verma, Niraj 306
Vermeersch, Ch. 189
Vickers, Geoffrey 151
Vienna Symposium: discussion formats used 6; objective of 6
Vienna University of Technology 6; Institute of Urban Design and Spatial Planning 126; Kunzmann and 205–6; Wurzer and 131–2
Viganò, P. 196
virtuality concept 189
voluntaristic planning model 184, 189; normative viewpoint in 195
voluntary agricultural camp 90
voluntary planning agreements 273
vom Stein, Freiherr 216
von Doderer, Hemito 206
von Thünen, Johann Heinrich 55

Wagenaar, Henk 282
Wagner, Otto 206

Walker, Herbert 52
Wang Fang 218
War on Poverty 147
Warum Europa? (Why Europe?) (Mitterauer) 139–40
Webb, Beatrice 66
Webb, Sidney 66
Webber, Mel 59, 156, 226, 228, 248, 251
Webber, M. M. 97, 252
Weber, Alfred 55
Weber, Max 17, 29, 289, 298
Weekend Telegraph 58
Weightman, Gavin 52
Weiss, Shirley 251
Wendt, Paul 251
What Planners Do (Hoch) 304
Wildavsky, A. 270
William and Flora Hewlett Foundation 155
Williams, Dick 102
Williams, Shirley 58, 66
Willmott, P. 224
Wilson, Alan 58, 251, 256
Wilson, Colin 56
Wilson, Harold 58
windfalls 274
windfall-sharing rule 274
Wingo, Lowdon, Jr. 248
Wise, Michael 55
Women in Planning (RIG) 230
Wood, C. 250
Working (Terkel) 286
World Cities (Hall) 250
world cities, planning and 27–8
World Cities, The (Hall) 67
World Planning Schools Congress in Shanghai 189
World Urban Forum (WUF) 235
Wozniak, Steve 63
writer-based writing 153
Wurzer, Rudolf 129, 131, 133–4, 205, 215

Xiaoping, Deng 27

yang force 17
yearmaster 225, 228–9
Yeats, W. B. 68
yin force 17
Young, M. 66, 67, 224

Zeitgeist approaches to development 202, 204
Zeitlin, J. 100
Zohar, D. 194
zoning 96, 269
Zoning Dilemma, The (Mandelker) 270
Zweig, Stefan 128